TOUCH!

MW00810553

MICHAEL
HAVERKAMP

SYNESTHETIC DESIGN

HANDBOOK
FOR A
MULTISENSORY
APPROACH

BIRKHÄUSER
BASEL

CONTENTS

CONTENTS

CONTENTS

FOREWORD

It is long known that the optimal design of products requires the comprehensive consideration of various senses. Only an approach in this manner can thoroughly meet customer expectation. To date, however, product characteristics were often designed for each individual sensory channel on a separate basis. Customer requirements were accordingly split into different, detached categories. Systematic approaches transcending the borders of individual senses were seldom employed. This would include, for example, the alignment of visual shapes with respect to the noise behavior of a device. As another example, the choice of tactile properties has to be made with direct reference to function, handling, visual and auditory appearance, temperature, and even to smell and taste. Within the field of perceptual psychology, it has been customary for decades now to analyze perceived sensory features independently for each sense and to interpret them as effects of separate features of the physical or chemical stimuli. This methodological restriction was eased and successively dispensed with towards the end of the twentieth century, however, as scientific discussions began refocusing on connections between the sensory channels, thus hailing the renaissance of synesthetic research. Indeed, for the first time, modern medical research techniques even facilitated the verification of specific phenomena on a physiological level.

The results of contemporary neuroscientific research have spawned psychological as well as philosophical discussions and have stimulated the creation of concepts for fine arts and music, indicating the increased preference for cross-sensory approaches. Nonetheless, the quest to identify and analyze connections between the senses does have a previous history, and it even encompasses the field of design. Various proponents of the Bauhaus school of thought have already dealt with the subject of connections between visual and auditory features. Especially Paul Klee and Wassily Kandinsky argued with respect to correlations in painting and music. During later decades, however, and in spite of the fulfillment of functional requirements, the design of industrial products was mainly focused on the visual form.

One important, historical reason for the limitation of the methodological approach was the unavailability of a systematic sound design in the past. Owing to the fact that all sounds of industrial products were predetermined by the parameters of the existing technology and dependent upon the physical conditions of operation, there was nearly no margin for optimizations at that time. For the last few decades, however, the creative space for optimizing sound design has been significantly expanded. Thus, artificial sounds are applied and utilized as signals for the feedback of technical functions and for the improvement of handling comfort. In the near future, active noise control and waveform-synthesis will even enable the elimination of noise caused by technical processes in daily routines. Those unpleasant sounds can then arbitrarily be substituted by synthetic or natural sounds. The continuous change from mechanically determined noise to electronic sounds – which can be creatively designed – makes it necessary to search for optimal connections between the senses and to develop systematic approaches. The connection of auditory and visual features for the data output of technical systems opens up a new, very attractive field of applied arts, and these applications can be extended to include further senses. Additionally, tactile perception plays an important role in the performance of complex tasks within the realm of human-machine communication. Furthermore, the influence of the odor of materials on the assessment of the customer is increasingly being recognized. Indeed, visual, tactile, and auditory features as well are all of considerable importance in the design of foods.

Thus, the time is ripe for assessing the new approaches and contemporary research in perceptual science and for examining conclusions for their possible pertinence with respect to systematic, multisensory design. In addition to the diverse, partially very specific findings of synesthetic research, all common perceptual mechanisms significant to connections between the senses are of notable importance as well. A conscious multisensory design must orient itself with respect to such processes of perception.

Up until now, a fundamental work systematically examining all strategies of cross-sensory connection occurring within the human perceptual system has not been published. Therefore, it is the principle goal of this book to provide a framework which includes and addresses each and every possibility of connecting sensory features. By virtue of this framework, it is intended to generate the basis for further detailed studies. Furthermore, with respect to specific practical applications, this comprehensive analysis aims at identifying and optimizing possible strategies, chosen from an extensive range of available tools. Above and beyond developing a systematic framework, this book intends to provide insight into the creative potential which can easily be cultivated. To achieve this goal, it is necessary to enlarge the horizon and to expand consciousness with respect to the cross-sensory interplay in everyday life. Therefore, this book also includes examples from topics such as music, fine arts, and motion pictures, in as much as they are appropriate to demonstrating elementary facts and capable of developing innovative forms of design. Just as in the case of Johannes Itten, whose Bauhaus lectures were based on the connection of "intuition and method" and on the "competence of subjective experience and objective recognition," this book will similarly follow a two-pronged approach.

Although there are already existing examples of successful multisensory design, these are seldom the result of systematic concepts. Therefore, through the utilization of various examples of specific aspects of cross-sensory connections, it shall be demonstrated that the consequent application of elaborated concepts is advantageous to the creative definition and design of products.

At this point in time, internal structures of established industrial sectors frequently hinder the targeted implementation of cross-sensory development processes. In particular, the strict separation of product optimization for each sensory channel into diverse departments with in-parallel activities often prevents the implementation of interdisciplinary concepts. Innovative, integrative approaches, moreover, mandate restructuring the division of labor with respect to the designing process.

This book presents concepts which have successfully been applied, although primarily as isolated approaches. Those concepts are now placed into an overall context based on findings regarding the function of the perceptual system. Thereby, it encompasses diverse possibilities such as mapping via elementary object features, including temporal or spatial correlations, as well as synesthetic metaphors and their application for perception examinations by virtue of the semantic differential.

On the other hand, the analysis examines approaches and design aids which have not yet been applied or which are adopted from other fields. Among others, the use of motion curves for describing the functional meaning of sound is discussed as well as the application of elementary perceptual shapes for the derivation of basic modules of design. While the discussed methods of design are not only relevant for product design, but also for various applications such as motion pictures, musical performances, video games, and the broad spectrum of multimedia events, these fields are considered as well. Furthermore, although often disregarded during the product design, the senses of smell and taste are discussed with respect to cross-sensory connections.

The main intention of this book is to advocate and inspire a consequent approach to multisensory design which offers – while emanating from perceptual processes – systematic concepts of product design.

The selection of objects and acoustic examples depicted in this book does not constitute an assessment of their value with respect to the design concepts presented. In each case, the examples were exclusively chosen to specifically illustrate the respective characteristics and accompanying circumstances. Accordingly, the interpretations of design characteristics discussed in this work do not necessarily coincide with the intentions of the designer, for they are aimed at addressing the awareness of the neutral observer.

At this point, I wish to thank the following persons and institutions for their assistance:

FORD Werke GmbH, Cologne for providing photographs and illustrations. HEAD acoustics GmbH, Herzogenrath and Dr. Klaus Genuit for sound examples and illustrations. For photographs and graphics, I particularly thank Adriano Abbado, Johannes Deutsch, Dr. Alexandra Dittmar, Patricia Duffy, Gerald von Foris, Eckhard Freuwört, Michal Levy, Natalia Sidler, Marcia Smilack, Carol Steen, and Matthias Waldeck. I am appreciative of the assistance of Katja Beisch with respect to the recording of the piece by Georg Philipp Telemann and by Bruno Leicht for information regarding color in jazz.

Additionally, I am grateful for the discussions and the impulses provided by Richard Cytowic (Washington D.C.), Prof. Hugo Fastl (Technical University, Munich), Prof. Brigitte Schulte-Fortkamp (Technical University, Berlin), Prof. Ute Jekosch and Dr. Ercan Altinsoy (Technical University, Dresden), Prof. Jens Blauert (Ruhr University, Bochum), Prof. Hinderk Emrich and Dr. Markus Zedler (Medical College, Hanover), Prof. Armin Kohlrausch (Eindhoven University of Technology), Prof. Bernhard Rothbucher (Salzburg University of Applied Sciences), Cretien van Campen (Utrecht), Dr. Sérgio Roclaw Basbaum (Pontifícia Universidade Católica de São Paulo), Dr. Jörg Jewanski (Münster), Dr. Reinhard Weber (University of Oldenburg), Dr. Markus Bodden (Essen), and Dr. Guenther Theile (Institute for Radio Technology, Munich).

I especially wish to thank Dr. Michael Dudley (Adverbismax.de) for his dedicated translation from German into English. Last, but not least, I thank my family for their great patience and support.

TASK AND FUNDAMENTALS

WHAT IS SYNESTHETIC PRODUCT DESIGN?

In the broad field of contemporary industrial design, the optimum customization of products is of ever-increasing importance. Design aspects play a crucial role in earning customers' acceptance and developing a brand identity. To achieve these goals, it is essential to align all perceivable features of a product as precisely as possible with customer expectations. Traditionally, the design of industrial products focused merely upon the visual appearance of objects. In the course of the last few decades, however, acoustic features have gained considerable attention. Indeed, the concept of sound design is increasingly being advanced and cultivated by systematic, sophisticated processes which are based upon established psychophysical approaches. A coordination of the desired product attributes between the different senses (modalities) does not occur, or it is based upon inadequate methodical standards. Perceptual psychology, however, acknowledges the close connection of diverse modalities and its significance in the comprehensive recognition and identification of objects. This includes the recognition of single shapes and patterns, usually summarized by the German term *Gestalt* with reference to the country where perceptual Gestalt psychology was first established. Figure 1.1 illustrates a typical operator's environment which requires the close interaction of various modalities.

FIGURE 1.1
The performance of complex operational tasks, such as steering a modern automobile, involves the coordination of virtually all human sensory channels. This goal can only be reached if the environment of the driver is closely aligned with his or her sensory capabilities. Thereby, an additional emotional benefit can be achieved as well.

In this context, the term *design* does not refer exclusively to the perceivable appearance of products and their aesthetic quality. In fact, it encompasses the entire product conception, including the technology, the choice of materials, and construction. For the customer, handling and functionality are just as essential as the feedback of those properties during usage of the product. Particularly important are the type and the quality with which the function is presented to the customer via various sensory channels (modalities). As an example, a vacuum cleaner has a variety of features: the visual appearance indicates a large or small volumetric capacity, high or low mobility, sufficient or insufficient hose flexibility, satisfactory or deficient accessibility of switches, among many other possible aspects. Turning on a switch might provide a sense of robustness, or just as well might act unpredictably and reveal a deficient performance. A typical sound is generated during operation of the vacuum cleaner. The sound can express suction power and cleaning efficiency. On the other hand, it could indicate a weak drive or a leaky hose. During its operation, an unexpected odor could conceivably indicate a risk of overheating, a potential safety risk.

Naturally, an effective design for all senses must offer exactly the functionality that the customer desires. That includes durability and ease of handling and maintenance. Legal requirements must be met as well, such as with respect to safety and environmental sustainability. Indeed, the actual shaping of the attractions to be perceived by the customer has to center on fulfilling these basic requirements. Thereby, it does not suffice that the device may be easily operated or utilized. Such an advantage must be effectively communicated to the user, for he has to ultimately perceive it. This information pertaining to the expected function(s) has to be conveyed via all participating sensory channels. Furthermore, the communication must contain positive messages that motivate the customer to claim: "That's exactly the product I need – it's easy to handle, it looks and feels good, it sounds nice, and I feel good about it."

**IT IS THE AIM OF SYNESTHETIC DESIGN
TO COORDINATE ALL SENSATIONS
STIMULATED BY AN OBJECT IN A MANNER
THAT RESULTS IN A PLEASANT,
HARMONIOUS OVERALL APPEARANCE WHILE
COINCIDING WITH THE PARTICULAR
FUNCTION(S) DESIRED.**

The term *synesthesia* has been derived from the Greek words *syn* (together) and *aisthesis* (sensation). However, it does not refer to the common situation involving the simultaneous arrival of sensory data by virtue of various modalities. To the contrary, synesthesia in its original definition refers to a specific manner of perception by which the stimulation of sensations in a certain sensory channel results in sensations further felt in one or more other sensory channels. In this manner, the perception of sound can additionally stimulate a sensation of visual shape and color. Such peculiarity of cross-sensory connection is a special phenomenon which is, in its pronounced form, found among relatively few human subjects. Nonetheless, it is an intensely investigated matter within the field of synesthetic research. In order to distinguish this specific phenomenon from other ways of cross-sensory connection within the human perceptual system, it shall hereinafter be referred to as *genuine synesthesia*, with reference to Richard Cytowic (2002). Its various phenomena and their possible relevance for product design will be discussed in Chapter 2.5.

In contrast to the specific, individual perceptual phenomena of genuine synesthesia, the term *synesthetics* shall herein denote the conscious design of objects with respect to connections between the modalities. This formulation was proposed by Christian Filk in the context of multisensory media aesthetics (Filk 2004). Accordingly, the term *synesthetic design* is derived from *synesthetics*. Thus, it emphasizes approaches towards the systematic design of cross-sensory relations. Contrary to the concept of *multisensory* design which deals with various senses, it does not necessarily focus explicitly upon possibilities of systematic cross-sensory connections. The term *synesthetic design* was also used by Giovanni Anceschi and Dina Riccò, who conducted studies of design of cross-sensory correlations at the Politecnico di Milano (Riccò 1999, Anceschi 2000). Their concept, however, is not based upon a precise separation of all possible forms of cross-sensory connections. Instead, both refer to Maurice Merleau-Ponty's theory of perception, which does not strictly distinguish between the specific phenomena of genuine synesthesia and common cross-modal correlations. Indeed, he concluded that "synesthetic perception is (...) the rule" (Merleau-Ponty 1945). A precise classification of the various mechanisms of cross-sensory connection within the perceptual system, however, represents a major step towards understanding the variety of perceptual approaches and towards systematic concepts for design. Therefore, this book follows that very approach. It postulates a separation of genuine synesthesia from common phenomena of cross-sensory perception.

All subjects are capable of establishing connections between the senses. Recent results of research on multisensory integration confirm that not only a single perceptual mechanism is applied, but a variety of strategies is involved in this task (see e.g., Spence 2007). Synesthetic design must thus be primary based upon those common processes. Synesthetics as methodology of multisensory design, however, encompasses all possible strategies of perceptual connections between the modalities.

SYNESTHETIC DESIGN HAS THE GOAL OF ACHIEVING THE OPTIMAL FIGURATION OF OBJECTS BASED UPON THE SYSTEMATIC CONNECTIONS BETWEEN THE MODALITIES.

Often, the conventional process of product design already encompasses various senses, as depicted by the illustration on the left-hand side of figure 1.2. Sight, hearing, and the sense of touch are in the foreground of most industrial products. The smell of materials, however, is given less priority, with the exception of food design, where taste naturally plays a major role. Each modality contains various features, which are indicated by the vertical bars in figure 1.2. For example, the visual features include, among many other characteristics, shape, color (hue), size, visual surface texture, and spatial orientation.

CONVENTIONAL DESIGN PROCESS SYNESTHETIC DESIGN

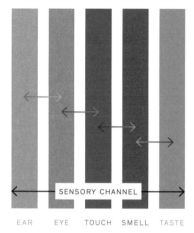
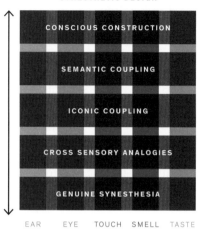

EAR EYE TOUCH SMELL TASTE

EAR EYE TOUCH SMELL TASTE

FIGURE 1.2
The conventional process of design (left-hand side) is primarily based on
the separate optimization of product features within the modalities.
If undertaken at all, research with respect to cross-sensory correlations is
limited to the latter phases of development. Synesthetic design
(right-hand side) is primarily focused on possible strategies of connection,
for which appropriate product features are subsequently selected.

In every sensory modality, the conventional process of design requires the definition of features and quality parameters that allow the assessment of a product's usability and customer value. Accordingly, the optimization transpires
within the modalities. The connection of features between the senses, on the
other hand, occurs only during the development phase. Historically, a consequent, systematic approach to optimizing correlations between the senses was
not undertaken. Instead, primarily intuitive methods were utilized.

The methods of synesthetic design proposed herein, however, are based
on knowledge of perceptual processes which enable connections between the
senses. These processes are classified into the five main strategies displayed on
the right-hand side of figure 1.2. The principle strategies encompass a variety of
specific mechanisms. The initial step of the designing process includes selection of those strategies which enable connecting modalities with respect to the
intended product. It is in the course of a second step rather than at this stage
that the selection of those product features deemed appropriate with respect
to the chosen strategies is made. A detailed explanation of those strategies follows in chapters 2.1 to 2.6. Subsequently, case studies will be presented and
specific applications will be described. Emphasis will be placed on the integration of the various strategies into a comprehensive design.

In contrast to the traditional approach of product design, with its primary focus on visual features, the future task of the designer will include intentionally influencing all senses (Riccò 2003; 2008). This especially applies with
reference to the pervasive presence of digital media in today's daily life – "digital

perception" as demanded by contemporary "infosensation" (Basbaum 2009). Thus, it is necessary to derive rules for utilizing mechanisms of cross-sensory interaction from the findings of perceptual science.

A sensible approach is to consider the process of perception as a process of communication. The product attracts the customer's attention with the appeal of a speaker and thus transfers information as well as emotions. An appropriate model of communication will be presented in Chapter 1.3.4. It corresponds to the definition advanced by Heinz Habermann: "Designers are responsible for harmonizing conceptions, thoughts, and ideas in a manner that easily can be understood by the recipient" (Habermann 2003, translated from German). Additionally, this information must be coded in such a way that it can be perceived and decoded by the customer. This definition, however, does not explicitly refer to multisensory perception. For synesthetic design, the following must be added:

AN OPTIMUM DESIGN FOR ALL SENSES REQUIRES THE COMMUNICATION OF PRODUCT FEATURES VIA AS MANY SENSORY CHANNELS AS POSSIBLE. THE CAPABILITIES OF EACH MODALITY HAVE TO BE ASSESSED DURING THE DESIGN PROCESS.

The coding of data most relevant for the customer has to be aligned between the senses in order to convey information in a comprehensible manner. In comparison to the other modalities, the connection of auditory and visual perception is particularly pronounced. Therefore, it is prudent to optimize the alignment of the auditory perception and the visual appearance of products with one another. Thereby, several very diverse questions need to be answered, such as: "Which indicator sound harmonizes ideally with visual features of the indicator switch lever?," "Which color scale best represents the timbre of engine noise?," or "How is the result of a noise assessment influenced by the brightness of the environment?"

To date, a systematic methodology for cross-sensory alignment pertaining to the visual and auditory modality has not been developed. Within the fine arts, music, and literature, however, the search for connections has a long history. That was often characterized by a conscious allocation of the attributes, whereas the involuntary, spontaneous sensation was taken into account less frequently. The often observed, common acceptance of such artistic approaches, nevertheless, indicates the broad prevalence of identical or at least similar concepts of perception. Therefore, the analysis of pictures and sculptures that attempt to visualize auditory sensations can yield material valuable to the development of comprehensive design concepts. The optimal measures for the alignment of visual design and product sounds, for example, can be derived from approaches examining the transformation of musical structure into color and visual shapes, such as those provided by *color music* [Farblichtmusik] or *musical graphics*. Additionally, literary works may provide clues for the verbal description of auditory perception. For the optimization of the complex appearance of an automobile, the overall sound as well as the noise behavior of all individual components must be considered. With respect to the integration of the driver into the human-machine system, it is necessary to optimize the sound quality and indeed the intelligibility of meaningful signals to enable a precise, functional feedback to the driver by virtue of the operational noise. By way of contrast, noise events without any informational content or useless or distracting noises should be minimized or eliminated.

An example shall demonstrate the importance of the appropriate alignment of modalities in relation to the expected function of a particular object. In this case, as depicted in figure 1.3, a conscious disagreement was created. It is a work of art shaped and colored like a fire extinguisher, yet, unlike a real fire extinguisher, has a crocheted surface finish. The visual appearance of a useful product, however, must be – as a whole and in its details – consistent with the customer's expectation within all modalities. Within the field of fine arts, a desired alienation effect can be created by fabrication of objects from materials which are obviously not feasible to fulfill a given function. Thus a perceptual conflict is stimulated. It demonstrates the high degree with which the expectation of functional capability is coupled to perceived multisensory features. In the case of a fire extinguisher, the surface of the pressure tank shall appear smooth and hard, thus implying and indicating the safe storage of the extinguishing agent. To be suggestive of this feature, nothing is less suitable than a filigree textile surface. A crocheted hose is similarly inappropriate. Even though it suggests or provides high flexibility, it is incapable of fulfilling the need for impermeability.

FIGURE 1.3
An example of the perceptual effect of the misalignment of visual appearance, tactile expectation, and function. In this case, appearance seems plausible, but the wool as a surface material is not suggestive of the expected function. Patricia Waller, Fire Extinguisher, crocheted object, 2001. © 2011, ProLitteris, Zurich.

Coming back to the search for appropriate cross-sensory alignment, the visual analogy to music is one of the important classical themes of discussions pertaining to connections between the senses (Phillips 1997, Brougher 2005). Practical applications such as the visual support of musical performance and the scoring of movies can be derived from those approaches. In the majority of modern-day concerts, across all genres, the accompaniment with colored light and video sequences plays an essential role. Classical music is only partly an exception, for example during concertante performances, whereas opera and ballet are characterized by visual aspects. For approximately three decades, the music video has been offering additional possibilities of audio-visual figuration. Even during the early stages in the development of a cinematic imagery, it was considered desirable to accompany the visual aspects with sound and music. During the first decades of cinema, it was not possible to store sound directly on film footage. Methods of optical or digital storage were invented later. The term "silent movie," however, is misleading, as sound and music was added to practically every movie performance. A few exceptions of soundless cinema can be found, namely in the case of artistic movies, where the absence of sound is explicitly required. This often follows the idea to provide a visual substitute for acoustic aspects. In this case, the term "visual music" is a popular description (Brougher 2005).

Nonetheless, it can be important to construct and cultivate acoustical signals in a manner that stimulates specific visual or tactile associations in the listener. This is essential in the case of broadcast advertising. Additional applications may include auditory guidance systems for the blind, or in situations when one has restricted sight; such as in emergencies with heavy smoke emissions. The central task of cinematic sound design is the search for specific sounds and music which most accurately support the screenplay.

Analogy to musical composition is also used by Giovanni Anceschi and Dina Riccò for description of cross-sensory cumulation of perceptual data. They employ the term "sensory register" to describe a modality which provides a base for the multisensory "orchestration" of the design process (Anceschi 2000). With respect to multisensory design, the quest for the "musicality of form" is of special interest, and it is the subject of broad discussion within the field of fine arts (Schawelka 1993).

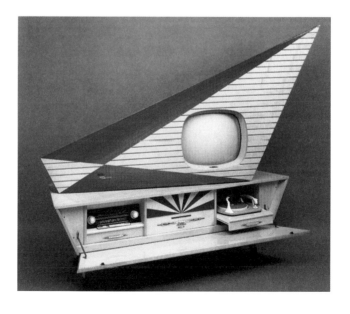

FIGURE 1.4
A Komet television and concert cabinet [Konzertmöbel]
by Cuba Imperial, 1954.

Concrete applications for the connection of music and form arise during the design of audio-visual devices. Figure 1.4 provides an example of such techniques in the 1950s. The Komet mixed-media system shown here includes a television set. The expressive visual appearance gives reason to presume that it is orientated according to specific cultural preferences, such as the musical taste of a customer focused on modernity and the future. Nonetheless, the increased specialization of the aspects of a product tends to relegate it to being a niche product without broad customer appeal. The reader might like to surmise what the most appropriate music would be given the design: folk, baroque, contemporary orchestra, psychedelic rock, or jazz?

A problem central to the search for connections between music and paintings arises in the combination of temporal, *dynamic* events with *static* properties – like form and color – of stationary objects. Accordingly, within the field of automotive design, great efforts are undertaken to reflect the dynamic driving properties of a vehicle by virtue of its static visual appearance. Thus, during a first peek into the car dealer's showroom, the customer can imagine the dynamic behavior of the product. *Kinetic design* is based on this approach. Figure 1.5 provides an example of the representation of dynamic features within a static painting by the Italian futurist Luigi Russolo. Vivid forms are derived from the abstraction of an animated event. Similar shapes are suitable to demonstrate dynamic properties of various kinds of products.

The dynamic forms shown here apply to vehicles of futuristic science-fiction movies as well as to real, modern-day sports cars. It bears noting, however, that at the time the image was painted, 1912 to 1913, automobiles were far more similar to nineteenth-century coaches than to modern race cars or jet airplanes. Obviously, the interpretation of such structures as dynamic is supported by a time-independent, commonly understood canon of comparable forms.

The question of a fundamental set of basic visual forms for synesthetic design will be discussed in chapter 3.3.

In contrast to visual and auditory features, so far, the smell and taste of objects have rarely been considered in the design of industrial products. Only when customer assessment degrades is immediate action taken. A displeasing odor can significantly affect the decision to buy a particular product. Materials used for packaging or tableware can degrade the natural taste of food. An optimized and comprehensive product design can only be achieved if the senses of smell and taste are also and in equal measure factored into systematic development processes. This point shall be emphasized throughout this book.

FIGURE 1.5
**Abstraction of a dynamic process into a
static image. Luigi Russolo,
Dynamism of an Automobile, 1912/13.**

1.2
PRODUCT DEVELOPMENT AS THE DESIGN FOR ALL SENSES

1.2.1
HUMAN-MACHINE COMMUNICATION

By operating complex technical systems, people become components of the systems themselves. They thus have to master a variety of diverse tasks. Simultaneously, the technical systems deliver information which has to be processed. This occurs primarily by virtue of different sensory channels. The information must be deciphered and its value understood. Furthermore, the ensuing actions of the user have to be disclosed to the technical system via operating elements. This results in a modification of the function of the total system, and this must be, in turn, acknowledged and interpreted by people.

In this regard, an automobile is a particularly illustrative example, owing to the functional diversity and variability of the entire system. Drivers and passengers alike even constitute spatial components of this system which envelops and transports them.

Indeed, the steering of the vehicle is in itself a highly complex process (fig. 1.6). The course of the road not only has to be visually followed, it must simultaneously be translated into information pertaining to the momentary position and the movement of the vehicle along the given path. In correcting the direction of movement by steering, results have to immediately be analyzed and assessed with respect to possible deviations from the desired course, and should an imminent danger of collision arise, appropriate actions must be taken with expedience. Additionally, it is necessary to recognize and identify objects on the street and along the roadside. Vehicles in motion have to be distinguished from those which are parked. The comprehension of the significance of symbols such as street signs and warning signals is required. The driver must be capable of judging the velocity and direction of vehicles moving ahead and of those approaching as well. Without a doubt, the recognition and the assessment of the complete situation take place in the course of a complex interaction involving diverse modalities. In addition to the visual awareness of the direction of movement, all changes in movement must be recognized even by virtue of the equilibrioception, namely the sense of balance, and via bodily receptors, for acceleration and deceleration involve forces that act upon and influence people. Dynamic forces result in the movement of the body with

22

1.2
PRODUCT
DEVELOPMENT
AS THE
DESIGN FOR
ALL SENSES
↓
1.2.1
HUMAN-MACHINE
COMMUNICATION

respect to the vehicle itself. Accordingly, the angle of view is modified, and this must be promptly corrected within the visual system in order to avoid a reduction of the awareness of the vehicle and of the environment.

1.2
PRODUCT
DEVELOPMENT
AS THE
DESIGN FOR
ALL SENSES
↓
1.2.1
HUMAN-MACHINE
COMMUNICATION

23

FIGURE 1.6
Driving an automobile demands the complex combination of the
simultaneous reception of information and the execution of operational tasks
such as steering, engaging the clutch, and shifting gears.

The properties of the pavement are audible from the noise of the wheels over the road, and can be similarly felt through vibrations. Additionally, further noises such as those caused by screeching tires or the activation of electronic stability programs (ESP) may be heard, indicating possible extreme situations.

The list of data which must be simultaneously recognized during the driving of an automobile can indeed be arbitrarily expanded, if the analysis explicitly encompasses not only the steering, but the sum of all processes as well.

Even carrying out the operational tasks requires a variety of individual actions which are supported by cognitive processes. In the case of steering, an expected deviation from the course must be translated from the muscles of the hands and arms into turning movements. Undoubtedly, changes in the position of the steering wheel are visually recognized – more important, however, is the feedback from the position of the hands and arms and from the forces sensed there by virtue of the receptors located in the musculature as well as in the tendons. The overwhelming majority of the sensory information is promptly employed to assure the motor coordination, and does not lead to conscious perception. Without this sensory function, however, it would be thoroughly impossible to execute any kind of deliberate movement. For its part, the technical system must be capable of contributing to the coordination, indeed, doing so while delivering the reactive forces which can be detected by receptors in the extremities. Earlier experiments conducted with power-assisted steering (PAS) demonstrated the necessity of receiving every single counterforce proportional to the steering process via the steering wheel. Should even one of these counterforces not be received, it is impossible to handle the vehicle with great precision. Only then is the driver able to "feel" whether the steering is appropriate for continued movement straight ahead or for a movement along a more or less serpentine road. A further requirement for the exact handling of the steering wheel is the accurate transmission of force from the hands onto the steering wheel. Therefore, the ideal steering wheel must be designed in a "handy" manner, and it has to be operated with appropriate grip force. Tactile receptors located in the skin along the palms of the hands and in the fingers deliver this information.

This observation of the multifaceted cognitive processes involved in steering, which is – following appropriate instruction – actually regarded as a simple task, illustrates the complexity of integrating people into demanding technical systems.

24

1.2
PRODUCT
DEVELOPMENT
AS THE
DESIGN FOR
ALL SENSES
↓
1.2.1
HUMAN-MACHINE
COMMUNICATION

FIGURE 1.7
The center console offers a variety of operating elements.
They serve to control the movement and the safety of the vehicle (gear selector,
parking brake, switch for the hazard lights, electronic
stability program (ESP), and acoustic parking assistance), they provide the driver
with information (infotainment system), they allow for climate control
(air conditioning, air ducts, control for heated seats, window defogger),
they contribute to maintaining the cleanliness of the car (ashtray, waste receptacle),
and to guaranteeing a certain degree of comfort (drink holder).
All operating elements must be capable of being easily reached with the hands
and must be meaningfully arranged.

IN THE COMMUNICATION
TRANSPIRING BETWEEN PERSONS
AND TECHNICAL DEVICES,
THE RECEPTION OF DATA VIA VARIOUS
MODALITIES IS NOT THE
EXCEPTION, BUT THE RULE ITSELF.

Figure 1.7 displays the variety of elements necessary for the operation and for the data output in the center console area – and even this represents only a small portion of the elements relevant to the driving of an automobile.

Already in the 1970s, it was recognized that the operator of a technical system is himself part of closed loops which function analog to pure technical systems while corresponding to methods of control engineering (cybernetics). Undoubtedly, the validity of these findings has its limitations, and these will be discussed below. This is, nevertheless, an initial approach to understanding the operation of technical systems and thus to getting an idea of the overall role of multisensory perception. The system as a whole is regarded as a Human-Machine System. Thereby, the interaction between the technical system and people is of particular importance – in terms of informatics, it is referred to as the Human-Machine Interface (HMI). Via this interface, information is transmitted to the human perceptual system and operational tasks are carried out. Generally, operational tasks require mechanical impact, such as movements or the application of forces. By virtue of voice command systems, steering instructions may be acoustically transmitted as well.

1.2
PRODUCT
DEVELOPMENT
AS THE
DESIGN FOR
ALL SENSES
↓
1.2.1
HUMAN-MACHINE
COMMUNICATION

25

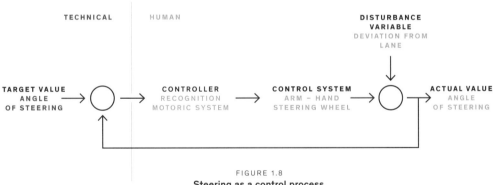

FIGURE 1.8
Steering as a control process.
The loop shown includes the driver and the steering wheel.
Discrepancies between the target value and actual value are recognized.
Via the motor system, the deviations are minimized by
alternating the angle of steering. The deviation of the vehicle from
the lane mandates, as a disturbance variable, the constant
adaptation with respect to the system.

In a closed loop, corresponding to figure 1.8, the actual value of a parameter is determined – in this case, it is the momentary position of the steering wheel, namely the angle of steering. The recognition of the vehicle's direction of movement delivers information as to whether an alteration of the steering wheel is necessary. Accordingly, it results in achieving the target angle of steering.

The discrepancies between the target and actual values are thus recognized by the controller – the human in this example – and appropriately compensated for. In this case, it is a motor command addressed to the musculature of the hands and arms, informing them to turn the steering so that the discrepancies between the target and actual values are minimized. The *Hand-Arm System* and the steering wheel constitute the *controlled system*. Changes in the course of the road, however, function as disturbance values and thereby cause discrepancies between target and actual values, thus necessitating the reinitiation of the control process.

Clearly, a more exact analysis of the operational procedure demonstrates that the description of the human-machine system via closed loops is not without its deficiencies, for perception is not limited to the transmission and processing of the information momentarily received by the sensory organs.

EVERY PERCEPTUAL PROCESS IS SUPPORTED BY STORED PATTERNS WHICH ARE ESTABLISHED IN THE COURSE OF LEARNING PROCESSES AND SERVE AS A SUPPLEMENTATION OF THE FRAGMENTARY OR INCOMPLETE INFORMATION RECEIVED VIA THE SENSORY MODALITIES.

Thus, in early childhood one must learn to identify objects and to classify them in the proper context. It is also necessary to learn to deduce short-term prognoses for the future from the perception of time-dependent processes. In this manner, and only in this manner, the safe steering of a vehicle can follow, for one must be capable of "predicting" the course of the road and the movement of one's own vehicle as well as that of others. The supplementing of perception with learned responses will be more closely addressed in section 1.3.4.

Moreover, the execution of movements is dependent upon learned patterns. In the observation of infants and small children, it is obvious that every intended movement requires intensive practice. Thereby, patterns which support the execution of movement are laid out and arranged within the motor centers of the brain. Even when the patterns are arranged in such a fashion that the movement process is, in principle, properly carried out, a further optimizing is necessary to minimize the energy utilized and to determine the most efficient, most effective solution.

Without a motor pattern, it is impossible to steer an automobile. Indeed, all of the pertinent movement processes have to be painstakingly learned. The learning process is hardly concluded with the earning of a driver's license, as the statistical frequency of auto accidents with respect to age demonstrates. With increasing experience, the pattern of movement and the ability to predict the course of observed processes improve. Driving along familiar roads thus requires the expenditure of less effort during the perceptual and motor processes as does driving along unfamiliar roads.

A MODEL OF INTERACTION BETWEEN PEOPLE AND TECHNICAL SYSTEMS MANDATES THE CONSIDERATION OF ALL LEARNED MECHANISMS WHICH SUPPORT THE OPERATIONAL PROCESS.

26

1.2
PRODUCT
DEVELOPMENT
AS THE
DESIGN FOR
ALL SENSES
↓
1.2.1
HUMAN-MACHINE
COMMUNICATION

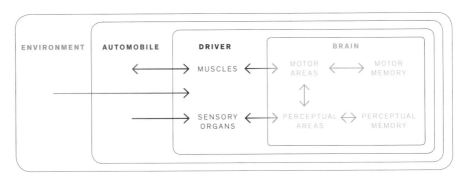

FIGURE 1.9
Informational processing during the driving
of an automobile.

1.2
PRODUCT
DEVELOPMENT
AS THE
DESIGN FOR
ALL SENSES
↓
1.2.1
HUMAN-MACHINE
COMMUNICATION
↓
1.2.2
FUNCTIONAL
DESIGN

27

Figure 1.9 depicts an expanded model – even this schema represents an over-simplification.

Stimuli emanating from the environment – such as the street, viewed through the windshield – and from the technical system – such as engine noise – are received by the sensory organs. The incomplete information is supplemented by memory contents. This enables the driver to estimate possible changes in the external conditions, such as the course of the road or the behavior of the automobile. These data serve to regulate the handling and are transmitted by the motor areas of the brain to the muscles. The motor areas are in turn supported by the motor memory. It provides instructions as to the nature of movements, which can be understood as stored "programs" of motion sequences. Sensory cells in muscles and tendons provide the perceptual system with information, as feedback, pertaining to the momentary motional activity, thus facilitating the implementation of corrective actions. Informational transmissions from the motor system to the perceptual system, furthermore, result in the enhanced visual awareness of the movements of one's own body, as compared with those of extrinsic objects (see section 2.1.3).

1.2.2

FUNCTIONAL DESIGN

In the definition of tasks for the designing of products, the pivotal objective is the conceptualization and realization of objects of utility, such as everyday articles that meet the consumer's expectations. The consumer must be placed in the position enabling him to understand and utilize the object as desired. This is a self-evident prerequisite for product development. First, the situation is clear: a chair must be suitable for sitting, a lamp for illuminating, an airplane for flying. The ultimate success of a product, however, depends upon the qualities of application it offers. Owing to the fact that, generally speaking, various manufacturers are capable of offering products for a certain purpose, it is particularly important that a given product offers additional advantages which exceed the bounds of the expected, pure utility. Undoubtedly, a simple log can serve as a seat, but it yields no comfort, and the physical sense of well-being is thus diminished within a short amount of time.

Furthermore, it is not very easy to move a log, and it is impossible to adjust its height so that it may accommodate the needs of a certain user. A poorly constructed airplane can similarly decrease the well-being of its passengers, giving rise to numerous negative consequences. Among them are: imprecise flight characteristics, loud noises, strong reverberations, unfavorable air conditioning, sudden oscillations of air pressure, uncomfortable and narrow seats, adverse lighting conditions, unpleasant odors, meals leaving a bad taste – due to the fact that the place for their preparation in the galley is too small and confined. Perhaps the flight passenger would not even have the possibility of improving his comfort, such as by adjusting the back of a seat or positioning a reading lamp. In addition to the obvious fulfillment of the basic function, the content of the information, communicated by the product to the user via his sensory organs, and the ability of the user to influence the product at will by virtue of his actions are of critical importance.

**AN OPTIMAL DESIGN MUST –
IN SUPPLEMENTING THE BASIC FUNCTION –
TRANSMIT A FEELING OF WELL-BEING
AND A HIGH STANDARD OF LIVING.
THIS OCCURS THROUGH ALL SENSORY
MODALITIES PARTICIPATING IN THE UTILIZATION
OF THE GIVEN PRODUCT.**

1.2
PRODUCT
DEVELOPMENT
AS THE
DESIGN FOR
ALL SENSES
↓
1.2.2
FUNCTIONAL
DESIGN

As a general rule, only a multisensory optimization is capable of conveying the expected high degree of quality. Simultaneously, the product must offer the desired possibilities of active influence. The pure functionality of the product encompasses primarily the fact that the technical system properly interprets the actions of the operator, thus enabling the desired processes to be initiated. Though this is obvious, it does not in and of itself lead to an optimal ease of handling. To achieve that goal, it is necessary that the operating elements provide the user with reliable information as to the execution of the functions. Even this occurs via sensory channels. Thereby, one must distinguish between information regarding the proper operation of the control elements and data pertaining to the exact reaction of the technical system itself.

**IN MANY CASES, THERE IS A CLEAR
SEPARATION OF THE OPERATING ELEMENT
FROM THE CONTROLLED AGGREGATE.**

Thus, a room light is normally controlled by a switch which is independently installed, separate from the light itself (fig. 1.10). When touched, the switch must feel solid and be capable of executing a clear, finite movement between two distinctly still positions. Additionally, a fleeting mechanical impulse or a clicking sound can serve to indicate and verify the arrival of the switch in the desired position. The most important indicator of the proper execution of the switching process itself is naturally the light which is turned on or off. Should the switch and the lamp be located in separate rooms, a customary situation in the case of bathrooms, the switch might be equipped with a supplementary signal such as an integrated glow lamp. It is important to note, however, that this signal pertains to the function of the switch and not to the function of the lamp being turned on or off.

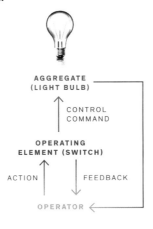

AGGREGATE
(LIGHT BULB)

CONTROL
COMMAND

OPERATING
ELEMENT (SWITCH)

ACTION   FEEDBACK

OPERATOR

FIGURE 1.10
Separation of operating element and aggregate using the example of a light and its switch.

1.2
PRODUCT
DEVELOPMENT
AS THE
DESIGN FOR
ALL SENSES
↓
1.2.2
FUNCTIONAL
DESIGN

———

29

In the case of desk lamps or nightstand lamps, light and switch often constitute a unit. Accordingly, the feedback from the operating element (switch) and from the aggregate (light) merge to comprise a unit as well. It this case, however, it can be irritating and lead to a sense of uncertainty if the switch moves unsystematically during its operation, such as backwards or to the side, or if it generates sounds which might lead one to believe that the product is defective. Indeed, the impression of the required functionality can arise only when the operating element and the aggregate exhibit the desired, *clear* reaction.

Nevertheless, there are serious efforts being undertaken to harmonize operating elements and technical systems with one another. An example may be found in the development of *touch screens* for computer and mobile phone systems. The tactile feedback during the operation remains a critical factor and can be problematic, for example, in the absence of a clear pressure point for the desired touching and thus switching.

As an example, the TRIO GmbH offers table lamps which may be switched on, adjusted according to various levels of brightness, or switched off simply by touching the foot of the lamp and thus activating electronic sensors (fig. 1.11). An additional merging is conceivable when the base (foot) and switch are integrated into the luminary, for example, in the form of a sphere which can be touched in order to activate the switching – although the danger of burning must be eliminated. In this case, the feedback from the aggregate and the switching element would be ideally coupled with one another, as schematically indicated in figure 1.12. This connection offers the advantage of avoiding the processing of doubled and thus redundant information by the perceptual system.

A further example is provided by the DOT-it LED light manufactured by OSRAM GmbH (fig. 1.12). This is a light in the form of a push button. To switch it on or off, one must push the middle portion containing the light diodes. The tactile responses of the switching process and the visual feedback of the function thus merge to form a single unit.

FIGURE 1.11
Table lamp with touch sensor.
In order to switch it on or off, one must simply touch the foot of the lamp.
TRIO GmbH, Arnsberg, Germany.

FIGURE 1.12
Light designed as a switch, OSRAM DOT-it.

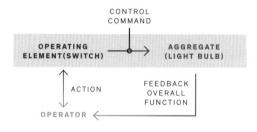

FIGURE 1.13
The coupling of operating elements
and the aggregate.

30

1.2
PRODUCT
DEVELOPMENT
AS THE
DESIGN FOR
ALL SENSES
↓
1.2.2
FUNCTIONAL
DESIGN

As already mentioned, the feedback pertaining to the functioning of the operating element may ensue acoustically, indicating the locking of mechanical components. ● ● An appropriate signal can be electronically generated, such as in the case of keypad tones for cell phones. Conversely, the operation can also be initiated via an external acoustic signal.

Thus, there are systems which react to the clapping of hands or to spoken words. Thereby, the direction of communications towards the operating element for the acoustic signal is reversed. Accordingly, functional feedback via sounds is initially limited, but it is subsequently possible by virtue of a chronologically subordinated operating signal. Similarly, a motion detector may permit a lamp to be switched on or off. This may offer aspects of comfort as well. The user does not achieve the considerable degree of precision, however, afforded by the precisely defined, tactile pressure point of a mechanical switch. Furthermore, the risk of a faulty circuit is increased. Thus, the designing of such systems requires careful attention, particularly with regard to relevant safety aspects in the process of switching.

1.2
PRODUCT
DEVELOPMENT
AS THE
DESIGN FOR
ALL SENSES
↓
1.2.2
FUNCTIONAL
DESIGN

31

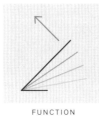   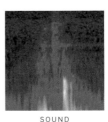

FUNCTION   VISUAL APPEARANCE   SYMBOL   SOUND

FIGURE 1.14
The switch of an electric parking brake (EPB).
The obvious visual design of the operating element must correspond
to the clear function of the parking brake, along with an
understandable symbol and a clear operating sound which doesn't
disintegrate into audible individual noises.

An unambiguous design must allocate individual, specifically defined objects with great precision to a certain function. These need to be clearly illustrated in the perceptual realm as well. In chapter 1.3.4, the *perceptual objects* projected into the consciousness will be addressed in greater detail. Figure 1.14 illustrates the demands placed upon the electric parking brake of an automobile. The design of the switch with a clearly defined *object character* correlates to the initiated, clearly defined, and manifest technical function. The object character of the allocated visual signal must similarly correspond to the operational sound. Analogous constellations pertain to nearly all operating elements of an automobile. The exact allocation of function, operation, and perception is known as *mapping*. Parameters suitable for multisensory mapping are presented in chapter 2.2.

In order to start a car engine, key switches were traditionally used; moving the switch to the right side activates the engine, moving the switch to the left side deactivates it. Considering the rather cumbersome act of turning the ignition key, a push button provides a more comfortable alternative for the driver (fig. 1.15). Because starting and stopping the engine are initiated by the same operational process – in both cases the switch works as a kind of *toggle* – precise feedback to the driver is necessary in order to inform him or her as to exactly which process is being carried out. For that purpose, the engine must be very audible, or the driver must receive reliable information via distinct optical, tactile, or acoustic signals.

FIGURE 1.15
Button for starting and stopping the engine.

1.2
PRODUCT
DEVELOPMENT
AS THE
DESIGN FOR
ALL SENSES
↓
1.2.2
FUNCTIONAL
DESIGN

The activation and the deactivation of a technical system comprise very simple forms of operation and may thus be utilized as an initial approach to the problematic as a whole. More complex forms of operation, however, require an appropriately adapted system of feedback with respect to the operating elements and the aggregates carrying out the desired tasks. As an example, figure 1.16 illustrates the operation of a manual parking brake (hand brake) via all participating senses. The proper functioning of the operating elements is transmitted to the driver by virtue of various sensory channels. In the case of common (traditional) design of parking brakes, the indicated five senses are involved. The information is transmitted as follows:

1.	APPLIED PULL FORCE SENSED THROUGH THE MUSCLE RECEPTORS (PROPRIOCEPTION); GRIP FORCE THROUGH TACTILE PRECEPTORS OF THE HAND
2.	MOVEMENT OF THE HAND-ARM SYSTEM
3.	THE VISIBLE POSITION OF THE LEVER
4.	THE AUDIBLE MOVEMENT OF THE LEVER MECHANISM (RATCHET)
5.	THE TACTILE VIBRATION OF THE LEVER DURING THE ENGAGEMENT OF THE RATCHET

**AS A GENERAL RULE, THE FEELING
OF SAFETY INCREASES IN DIRECT
PROPORTION TO THE NUMBER OF SENSORY
MODALITIES CLEARLY VERIFYING THE
DESIRED FUNCTION.**

Precisely at this point, the communication as to the certainty of the function is of critical importance to the driver.

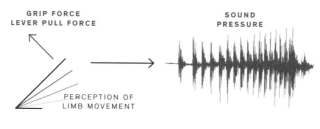

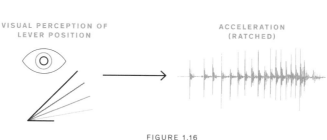

1.2
PRODUCT
DEVELOPMENT
AS THE
DESIGN FOR
ALL SENSES
↓
1.2.2
FUNCTIONAL
DESIGN

FIGURE 1.16
**Multisensory feedback during the operation
of a manual parking brake (hand brake).**

In the development of a design which concentrates on presenting the functional aspects of an object, solutions were sought at the beginning of the twentieth century which exclusively encompassed elements having a direct relationship to the possibilities of utilization. Figure 1.17 shows the design of a table lamp adhering to this principle. The foot of the lamp serves solely the aims of firmly positioning the lamp and receiving the switch and the cable, the swivel arm allows the positioning of the head of the lamp and, in turn, the head of the lamp enables the light to be radiated in the desired direction, while simultaneously avoiding lateral blinding.

FIGURE 1.17
**A table lamp adhering to the concept of a purely functional design,
as developed and taught in the late Bauhaus phase in Dessau. Marianne Brandt,
Kandem Bedside Table Lamp, designed for Körting & Mathiesen, 1928.**

Such a design forgoes decorative elements and very clearly indicates the technical possibilities to the user. In this example, the color is really the only visual characteristic not having a direct reference to the function. In keeping with a strictly functional design, the color was sparingly applied, as in the case of other historical and contemporary items of the AEG and *Braun* brands.

Functionalism was regarded as a method instead of a style. It focused on the logical and rational solution of practical problems (Fiell 2005a). The roots of this school of thought stretch back into the late nineteenth century, as functionalist approaches were first applied in the field of architecture. It is no accident that the guiding principle of functionalism – "Form follows Function" – was conceived by an architect, namely Louis Sullivan. The Bauhaus doctrine, which gives a significant role to multisensory aspects of designing, is indeed based upon the aforementioned principle. In the first half of the twentieth century, functional design was characterized by the utilization of steel and glass. Technical installations were not hidden. Instead, they emerged with an aesthetic quality. This is also reflected in the architecture, being particularly evident in the intentional emergence of ventilation pipes and supporting framework elements, for example, at the Centre Pompidou (Centre national d'art et de culture Georges Pompidou) in Paris and at the University Hospital in Aachen.

Functionalist design consequently avoids the use of any kind of decoration or ornament. Consistent with this principle, the German association of architects, artists, and builders, the Deutscher Werkbund, organized an exhibition in 1924 with the title *Form ohne Ornament* (Form without Ornament). The language of forms developed in this context accommodated the demands to utilize standardized components in industrial manufacturing and the need for generally understandable elements – for the distribution of large quantities.

34

1.2
PRODUCT
DEVELOPMENT
AS THE
DESIGN FOR
ALL SENSES
↓
1.2.2
FUNCTIONAL
DESIGN

IN THE MANUFACTURING OF TECHNICAL PRODUCTS, A FUNCTIONAL DESIGN IS PARTICULARLY INTERESTING, OWING TO THE FACT THAT IT ORIGINATES WITHIN THE TECHNOLOGY ITSELF AND THUS ACCEPTS THAT TECHNICAL COMPONENTS PLAY A MAJOR ROLE IN THE OVERALL APPEARANCE OF THE PRODUCT.

However, until functionalism's appearance in the 20th century, furnishing objects of daily use with ornaments and embellishments was regarded as an aesthetic obligation. Figure 1.18 shows a wall lamp in Art Nouveau style. The characteristic, organic forms are quite sparingly employed. Figure 1.19 reveals, on the other hand, why a comprehensive ornamentation was rejected by the functionalistic designers. In contrast to the functional design preferred today, characterized by clear structures, the overloading of objects with ornaments and non-functional attributes tends to diminish the appreciation for such objects. As a result of the lavish ornamentation and the use of a sea shell, one can barely recognize the fact that the baroque object shown here is a drinking vessel. Indeed, the decorative elements tend to impede the utilization of the drinking vessel in the ordinary course of a dinner at the table. This is, however, not an error. Instead, it affirmatively indicates the superordinated function which is devoid of all ergonomic objectives. Moreover, it is an object intended to impress the guests dining with the sovereign by virtue of its opulence and use of expensive materials, while testifying to his power to engage the best craftsmen. The object is aimed at demonstrating a noble societal presence and is thus not reduced to its simple use value. In this regard, one may speak of *functionality in the expanded sense*. Often, a lavishly luxurious ornamentation was employed to articulate financial power and political influence. Decorations using costly materials thus served to symbolize the demands of the respective owners, namely as members of a certain social class. Even due to this reason, the functionalism of the early twentieth century sought to design "democratic products" whose aesthetic appeal was not limited to a particular target group. This was achieved by refraining from any kind of symbolism. At the same time, however, it verified the evidence that symbolic elements decisively influence the overall perception and social function of products. Given that this concerns all sensory modalities, chapter 2.4 investigates the utilization and significance of the major symbolic design elements.

1.2
PRODUCT
DEVELOPMENT
AS THE
DESIGN FOR
ALL SENSES
↓
1.2.2
FUNCTIONAL
DESIGN

3 5

FIGURE 1.18
Design of a wall lamp in Art Nouveau style.
Inspired by botanical structures, the ornamentation appears as an

outgrowth of functional form. Brussels, late 19th century.

FIGURE 1.19
The drinking vessel in the form of a basilisk illustrates
the problematic of escalating ornamentation. Manufactured by
Elias Geyer prior to 1610, Grünes Gewölbe, Dresden.

THE SOCIAL FUNCTION OF A PRODUCT IS, NOTWITHSTANDING ITS PURE FUNCTION, AN ADDITIONAL VALUE OF GREAT IMPORTANCE, EVEN IN THE CASE OF ORDINARY ARTICLES OF DAILY USE.

This is, in the case of automobiles, just as obvious as it is when applied to most other products. A vehicle is not simply used to get from "A to B," it reveals to those in the driver's circle – friends, neighbors, and even enemies – his or her social status, just at it serves as a form of self-affirmation.

A cell phone's ring tone is another example of the social function of product perception. In order to signal an incoming call, while simultaneously differentiating it from other cell phones in the immediate vicinity, very simple tones would actually suffice. It is evident, however, that the user of a mobile phone also wishes to use the – inevitably publicly audible – ring tone as a status symbol. Thus, information about the customer's mood, tastes, feelings, and social standing are also transmitted. In this commercial area, there is a marked trend towards individuality, thus fueling the continued expansion of the repertory of ring tones used.

THE OPTIMIZATION OF ELEMENTS TO ACCOMMODATE FUNCTIONALITY IN THE EXPANDED SENSE IS, IN ADDITION TO THE OPTIMIZATION OF THE UTILITY VALUE, AN INTEGRAL COMPONENT OF MULTISENSORY DESIGN.

36

1.2
PRODUCT
DEVELOPMENT
AS THE
DESIGN FOR
ALL SENSES
↓
1.2.2
FUNCTIONAL
DESIGN

The aforementioned examples illustrate why, since at least 1960s Pop Art and postmodernism, ornament and decoration are again seen as important design components. The desire for individual representation extends well beyond pure functionality, and it wants to be fulfilled – or it wishes to display ironic reflection.

RELIABLE OR DEFECTIVE

All perceivable elements of design need figuration in a manner that is capable to express reliability and lack of any degradations of quality. The related challenges shall be briefly exemplified in case of audition.

An essential aspect of sound design concerns the associative implications connected to auditory perception. Just as the timbre of words and the intonation of speech transmit additional information – connotations or undertones – whose substance often extends beyond the statement itself, most sounds transmit additional information via associative and symbolic references. Besides the optimization of psychoacoustic parameters, it is of decisive importance to analyze these references with respect to the desired overall appearance of the product and to subject them to systematic optimizations. Thus, perceived features which suggest possible defects or safety concerns are particularly critical. A defect is indicated, among other possibilities, when an auditory perceptual object does not show the desired degree of clarity and indivisibility (section 1.3.4). If the rattling of individual, mechanical components or of a spring is heard after a car door is closed, or when the closing sound otherwise segregates into different, chronologically separate processes, it does not necessarily give the customer the impression of a system of reliable, optimized components.

Furthermore, if the acoustic behavior of components related to safety demonstrates unexpected variations or even chaotic processes, a feeling of uncertainty results. This could negatively impact upon the decision to purchase the product – if it even comes to such a decision – or it could result in unnecessary and extensive servicing claims due to customer dissatisfaction. Certainly, crunching sounds heard while turning a steering wheel do not comfort the driver. That also applies to a seat which does not come to rest and lock with a "click".

1.2
PRODUCT
DEVELOPMENT
AS THE
DESIGN FOR
ALL SENSES
↓
1.2.2
FUNCTIONAL
DESIGN

3 7

PARTICULARLY DURING THE EXECUTION
OF AN ACTIVITY WITH A HIGH RISK POTENTIAL,
THE TECHNICAL SYSTEM MUST TRANSMIT A
FEELING OF SAFETY AND RELIABLE OPERABILITY.

Secondary sounds can also contribute to the impression of a non-robust design. Such sounds occur as a result of sonic or oscillatory influences upon passively moved components. A typical example is the rhythmic shifting of parts of the interior trim against each other due to vehicular vibrations. Loud or unpleasant noises can thus arise in the form of squeaks and rattles (S&R), which then supplement the normal sound disturbances and ultimately lend the impression of a deficient fixation of the construction components. Owing to the fact that the sound damping of an automobile with regard to secondary sounds excited inside the passenger compartment is ineffective, these noises have a great potential for attracting attention.

DURING PRODUCT DEVELOPMENT,
IT IS THUS NECESSARY TO ASCERTAIN
WHICH SENSORY STIMULI AND PERCEPTUAL
CHARACTERISTICS BEST TRANSMIT
THIS INFORMATION AND WHICH PERCEPTIONS
SHOULD BE AVOIDED, WHERE POSSIBLE.

In some cases, it is not very clear whether a sound is desired with respect to a certain function. Automobile manufacturers look to avoid squealing brakes as much as possible. Neither manufacturers nor customers regard even the typical squeaking of high-performance brakes for sports cars, for example, as a positive characteristic. On the other hand, squealing brakes are among the more prominent noises mixed into films in the post-production phase, owing to the fact that they are indicative of dynamic stops in scenes involving automobiles.

The functional design must give the user an immediate impression of the possibilities made available to him by the technical product. This not only applies to the overall impression reflected by the purpose of a product. It is just as applicable to the operating elements. An *intuitive design* has to be instantaneously plausible to the user, allowing the product to be properly and effectively utilized without complicated thinking processes and without a detailed reading of the operating instructions. The interpretation of responses as feedback from the system should follow with similar ease and clarity.

FIGURE 1.20
Functional mapping of the gear selection positions
and the necessary directions of hand movement depicted upon
gear switch lever knobs of historical tractors.

38

1.2
PRODUCT
DEVELOPMENT
AS THE
DESIGN FOR
ALL SENSES
↓
1.2.2
FUNCTIONAL
DESIGN

As shown in figure 1.20, a simplified schema of functional mapping can be found on knobs for gear selection of vehicles. Within the scope of this application, a linear graph and the numbering of gears demonstrate the direction of required hand movement and the appropriate order of switch positions.

Today, even more attention is paid to intuitive operability. With respect to the variety of operational elements and signal sources in the course of complex technical systems, this is a basic requirement for controlling all operational conditions. Intuitive design is accordingly not merely a component of the overall aesthetic conception; moreover, the demands imposed by safety considerations and by ergonomics mandate the development of optimal solutions. An exact multisensory coordination of the elements of design improves the perceptibility and the interpretation of the function. In chapters 2.2 to 2.4, strategies of multisensory perception are discussed with respect to building the foundation for a sensible intuitive design.

Although functionality is a requirement for the operability of technical systems, it is not the intention of this book to favor a design based upon pure functionality over all other possibilities. Nor is it meaningful to highlight ideologically inspired concepts such as that of the "Good Forms" of the 1950s. Thus, this book does *not* exclusively demand that which Max Bill once defined as the expression of an object of daily use conceived in the sense of pure functionalism: "It was manufactured on the basis of an optimal economy of handling and structured on the basis of the economy of the resources employed." (Erni 1983, 5) Moreover, the entire spectrum of creative possibilities, including decoration and ornamentation as well as associative and otherwise significant elements, must remain intact. The function in and of itself is, nevertheless, a central theme which the designer must always confront, thoroughly independent of the ultimately chosen solution in individual cases.

1.2
PRODUCT
DEVELOPMENT
AS THE
DESIGN FOR
ALL SENSES
↓
1.2.2
FUNCTIONAL
DESIGN

39

ERGONOMIC DESIGN

Ergonomics represent a sector of applied science which examines the laws and parameters of the work of humans. The practical goal of ergonomics is to create appropriate conditions for the execution of operational tasks. Etymologically, the term is a juxtaposition of the Greek words *ergon* (work) and *nomos* (law or regulation).

ERGONOMIC DESIGN SERVES THE OPTIMAL ACCOMMODATION OF OPERATING ELEMENTS AND ALL OTHER TECHNICAL COMPONENTS OF THE HUMAN-MACHINE INTERFACE WITH RESPECT TO THE ABILITIES OF THE PERSONS INVOLVED.

Among the primary goals are the light and purposeful usability of technical devices, the minimizing of the energy required, and the avoidance of malfunctions on both sides of the human-machine interface. Accordingly, in the development of a steering system for an automobile, for example, the precision of steering is of utmost importance. The strength of the arms and hands must be exactly transmitted to the operating element, without resulting in exhaustion within a short amount of time. In this case, the ergonomic design can encompass accommodating the steering wheel with respect to the form of the hands and fingers. The distance and the inclination of the steering wheel with regard to the body must allow the comfortable positioning of the hands and the bending of the arms. This is achieved by an optimal adjusting of the seat position via the adjustment mechanisms of the seat and by the appropriate accommodation of the steering wheel position. This accordingly compensates for individual differences in body size. Additionally, the pedals can be outfitted with adjustment mechanisms. The optimal designing of the seat provides for a nearly fatigue-proof posture and reduces back pains as well as long-term damage to the vertebral column (e. g., Lumbar

Syndrome). It is particularly important with respect to drivers of buses or trucks and to operators of construction machines, for they would otherwise risk occupational injuries due to unbalanced postures and vehicular vibrations (Haverkamp 1990).

FIGURE 1.21
**The ergonomic design of a steam iron.
Braun SI 6575, FreeStyle, 1995–2005.**

Figure 1.21 illustrates the popular ergonomic design of a steam iron: the form minimizes the risk of injury and the water tank shields the hand from the underside. The handle is ergonomically accommodated with respect to the palm of the hand and enables ironing with horizontal movements as well as the filling and the positioning of the device, following usage or during a pause, in the vertical plane. During its usage, the form grants an optimal view of the foremost point.

 Besides optimization of handling capabilities, ergonomic design is also essential to transfer the needed perceptual information. Thus, the functional feedback is enabled by the identification and the optimization of transfer paths of stimuli. For example, an ergonomic hand lever provides forces, movement, vibration, temperature, and other sensations with a quality that enables the user to gain feedback from his activities.

 For both fields of application, the major problem in ergonomic design is the variability of the bodily capabilities and the body dimensions of the users. The deciding parameters must thus be individually determined in advance, or capable of being set by the user. In this respect, one relies upon statistical data pertaining to the measuring of bodies and body parts – particularly of the extremities; this is known as *biometric data*. Automobile seats must be appropriately adjustable, allowing the vast majority of customers to enjoy an ergonomically optimal seat position while facilitating the reaching of all operating elements and granting a sufficient view of all control elements and naturally of the road situation. Percentile data play a significant role in this regard. For example, the information of the 95th percentile, pertaining to the length of the underarm in the population as a whole, says that 95 percent of adults have this respective length or a shorter length. The fifth percentile reflects, accordingly,

40

1.2
PRODUCT
DEVELOPMENT
AS THE
DESIGN FOR
ALL SENSES
↓
1.2.2
FUNCTIONAL
DESIGN

a value which merely 5 percent of the entire population fall short of. If the driver's position is designed to achieve an optimal accommodation of the seat position for values between the 5th and the 95th percentile, it would accommodate 90 percent of the adult population. In this case, the arithmetic average of all biometric values is not used. Instead, the *central* or *median value* is utilized. This value is exceeded by 50 percent of the targeted group of potentially interested persons, whereas the other 50 percent fall short of it.

ERGONOMIC DESIGN NEEDS MULTISENSORY OPTIMIZATION IN BOTH DIRECTIONS: FIRSTLY, TO TRANSFER PERCEPTUAL INFORMATION AS A FUNCTIONAL FEEDBACK OF THE INTENDED TECHNICAL OPERATION. SECONDLY, TO COUPLE APPROPRIATE BODILY ACTUATORS (MUSCLES, SKIN AREAS) TO THE OPERATING ELEMENTS TO OPTIMIZE HANDLING CAPABILITY. AS MENTIONED BEFORE, THIS ACTIVITY IS CONTROLLED BY THE PROCESSING OF MULTISENSORY DATA.

1.2
PRODUCT
DEVELOPMENT
AS THE
DESIGN FOR
ALL SENSES
↓
1.2.2
FUNCTIONAL
DESIGN

41

Biometric date must be collected specifically for the potential client base. Thus in the Japanese market different values with respect to body measurement are used with respect to Europe or North America. It is also necessary to ascertain whether children and adolescents are to be considered in the respective product portfolio, such as for seat design for children in automobiles.

Ergonomic design is, as an essential element in the functionality of a device or of an object of daily use, a basic prerequisite for optimizing the conditions of use. In the course of this approach, the paths taken by the stimuli originating from the product along their way to the sensory organs will be identified, and possibilities of active influence will be examined as well. A requirement of the multisensory designing is thus the precise knowledge of the boundaries or marginal conditions within which the handling of the product takes place.

1.2.3
PRODUCT PLACEMENT AND BRAND IDENTITY

In order to offer and sell products in a sensible manner, a manufacturer must resolve two basic problems: first, the product must be developed and presented in such a manner as to convince the customer that buying the very product is necessary, thus expanding his own possibility of action and resulting in experiencing the added values of emotionality and life quality. It is important that this requirement is fulfilled not only for individuals, but also for large numbers of customers as well, allowing for and justifying the fabrication of the object within the realm of mass production. Considering the increased saturation of the market with products developed for the mainstream taste, it is increasingly difficult for the producer to distinguish himself from competitors and to accordingly achieve the desired degree of turnover with respect to the profit margin.

The second fundamental problem is faced by manufacturers with extensive product ranges, who must develop a product portfolio so that products are distinguishable from one another, making them available to customers so that products of different price and quality are understood and accepted. Accordingly, automobile manufacturers tend to offer motor vehicles in different segments of the market, ranging from small and mini cars of the A and B segments, vehicles in the middle-class categories (C and CD classes), to more luxury models (D, E, or S classes). Additionally, vehicles for commercial use – such as small buses and delivery trucks – as well as special vehicles such as convertibles or combinations of small transporters and sport utility vehicles (SUVs) are manufactured. Every model of the production range must not only fulfill the expectations of the customer, it must also demonstrate a corporate philosophy distinct from competing manufacturers. Additionally, the development of the product must accurately meet customer expectations and, at the same time, correspond to the entire range of products. This calls for a holistic design with a systematic optimization of the product characteristics in all sensory modalities.

42

1.2
PRODUCT
DEVELOPMENT
AS THE
DESIGN FOR
ALL SENSES
↓
1.2.3
PRODUCT
PLACEMENT
AND BRAND
IDENTITY

THE DEVELOPMENT CONCENTRATES ON TWO AREAS:

1.
THE MANUFACTURER'S IMAGE, BRAND IDENTITY AS REPRESENTED BY THE MULTISENSORY CHARACTERISTICS OF THE BRAND – BRAND IMAGE AS PART OF THE CORPORATE IMAGE.

2.
THE MULTISENSORY APPEARANCE OF THE PRODUCT WITHIN THE MANUFACTURER'S PRODUCT RANGE.

1.2
PRODUCT
DEVELOPMENT
AS THE
DESIGN FOR
ALL SENSES
↓
1.2.3
PRODUCT
PLACEMENT
AND BRAND
IDENTITY

43

Both aspects mutually influence each other: a strong brand supports the ability of the product to be sold; successful products strengthen the power of the brand.

The design of the *corporate identity* is concerned with the uniform appearance of companies, brands, and products as a means of distinguishing them from their respective competitors. It encompasses the uniform development of packaging, offices, factories, as well as letterheads for correspondence, Internet presence, and commercial advertising via radio, television, and the print media. Furthermore, it is aimed at persuading employees to conduct themselves in a manner consistent with corporate objectives and to help portray the company in a positive light, particularly with respect to public relations, for example by virtue of volunteer work outside of the company. Given increasing globalization of markets, a design must be effective and comprehensible internationally.

FIGURE 1.22
Functional design of a "radiogram" with phonograph and amplifier.
This radio/phono combo unit is a direct descendant of the legendary SK4,
"Snow White's Coffin," created by Dieter Rams and Hans Gugelot.
Braun Phonosuper SK5, 1955–64.

The German company AEG was one of the first firms to seek an overall design (Gesamtdesign) for all areas of the business. To this end, in the early 1900s architect and designer Peter Behrens began drafting plans to harmonize the appearance of company facilities, interior design (such as clocks), advertising, and the logo, consequently and comprehensively complementing the design of the product itself. An example of the systematic development of a corporate identity in more recent times is provided by the company Braun. Already in 1956, a uniform style based on the geometric simplicity, utility, and functionality of the product, while also including packaging, logo, and advertising, was advanced under the leadership of the designer Fritz Eichler. The functional, unadorned design corresponded to the expectations placed upon design in Germany's postwar era (fig. 1.22). The final overall concept received an award for corporate design during the Hanover Exhibition in 1983. Among the characteristics of this style are the remarkable aesthetic clarity resulting from the logical arrangement of all elements and the search for harmonious uniformity (Fiell 2005a).

In representing the image of a company, the trade mark, namely the signet or the logo, plays a pivotal role. Ideally, the key components combine to yield a practical symbol with high brand recognition, which in turn unifies the overall approach, specific to the particular firm, with the contemporary appearance of the product. In this manner, parallel to the appearance of the product itself, the brand image is supported by in-house symbolism. The brand logo denotes products, documents, selling points, and advertising as integral components of the brand activities. It identifies and characterizes the product appearance with all attributes as a conclusive part of the brand identity, and it impresses the seal of a consistent philosophy and a common strategy. Therefore, a considerable degree of importance is attached to the particular coherence and unequivocal message of the logo. For several years now, there have been efforts at developing the logo not only visually, but also in a multisensory fashion.

44

1.2
PRODUCT
DEVELOPMENT
AS THE
DESIGN FOR
ALL SENSES
↓
1.2.3
PRODUCT
PLACEMENT
AND BRAND
IDENTITY

IN TIMES IN WHICH TELEVISION IMAGES
AREN'T ALWAYS CONSCIOUSLY FOLLOWED BY
CONSUMERS, IT IS IMPORTANT THAT
A BRAND IS DISTINCTLY IDENTIFIED EVEN WHEN
A COMMERCIAL IS ONLY RECOGNIZED
ON AN AUDITORY LEVEL.

The traditionally more important visual identity of a brand is also often reinforced acoustically. For the purpose of enhancing brand identification, additional sounds, melodies, or even melodic fragments are utilized as acoustic signals. This facilitates the more succinct development of the logo in advertising via audio-visual media such as television, movies, and radio. By communicating through more than one sensory channel, the symbolism gains meaning and is endowed with emotional content. It thus becomes possible to use purely auditory logos (sound logos), such as on radio where logically no visual information is transmitted.

A painstaking, systematic designing of auditory brand symbols is the objective of *audio branding*. The perception of such identifying marks immediately communicates the value of the brand and produces positive feelings among customers, animating them to purchase the products. The painting by Roy Lichtenstein displayed in figure 1.23 illustrates the effect of auditory signals preferred in audio branding – less strikingly perhaps, but nonetheless comparable. The ironic expression of the picture comes from the intentionally exaggerated simplification of the context. Due to the great significance of acoustic logos, in recent times efforts are being made to provide sound design with a theoretical foundation (Bronner 2009a, Haverkamp 2009a).

With the merger of successful brands into the larger business groupings of multinationals, the question is how does this affect a brand identity. In such cases a great deal of attention is generally paid to maintaining the image of successful brands separate, and customers are often kept unaware of the business relationship among individual brands. Yet as long as the brands continue to present themselves as a distinct entity and meet customer expectations, going to such lengths is unnecessary.

Logos often lead a life of their own. The customer perception of a logo and how it relates to the quality of products often diverges from the actual evaluation of the product itself. This can have positive results. For example when a well-established logo needs to overcome a short-term problem of public acceptance, such as the introduction of innovative product designs customers need to grow accustomed to. Once a customer relates a positive experience of an *established* brand with the logo, the marketable value increases, even though some products offered do not correspond to this evaluation. Thus, a well-chosen corporate design can help to improve the constancy of positive customer evaluations.

The power of symbolism, nevertheless, also has its disadvantages. If the manufacturer intends to alter his brand image in a particular direction, it is conceivable that the expression or statement well-established among customers actually blocks the intended new orientation. In this case, substantial, consequent marketing efforts are necessary to affect an alteration of the customer perception of the logo. Indeed, in unpromising situations, the logo must be replaced by a entirely new, completely different emblem. Figure 1.24 illustrates how the appearance of a product that is widely regarded as prestigious can correlate to the established, traditional development of the corporate sign. In the depicted example of a high-performance special edition car, the color of the vehicle was intentionally chosen as a complementary color of the corporate logo, allowing the new brand attributes to be expressed on the basis of a longstanding company tradition. In simple terms, a complementary color can be understood as a contrasting hue which distinguishes itself to the maximum extent possible from the basic color. From 2006 to 2007, the marketing strategy of Ford was built on the contrast of orange to the blue logo. Accordingly, the accompanying slogan was: "Feel the difference." Chapter 2.4 addresses the multisensory design and development of brand symbolism in detail.

In order to match new products with customer preferences, the perceptual phenomena and mechanisms which function identically, or at least in a similar fashion, among as many people as possible must be precisely known. Indeed, the multisensory design must be based first and foremost on these mechanisms. Given that the perception of objects is always socially and culturally

1.2
PRODUCT
DEVELOPMENT
AS THE
DESIGN FOR
ALL SENSES
↓
1.2.3
PRODUCT
PLACEMENT
AND BRAND
IDENTITY

45

46

1.2
PRODUCT
DEVELOPMENT
AS THE
DESIGN FOR
ALL SENSES
↓
1.2.3
PRODUCT
PLACEMENT
AND BRAND
IDENTITY

FIGURE 1.23
The basic idea of audio branding. The product sound reaches
the ear of the customer and influences his or her mood in the desired fashion.
This working mechanism conveyed by the artist, using the example
of a melody penetrating the room, is adroitly ironized. Furthermore, the comic
style emphasizes the pithy, bold nature of the situation.
Roy Lichtenstein, The Sound of Music, 1975. © 2011, ProLitteris, Zurich.

influenced, there are strong regional divergences in the perception of products. For example, according to the particular cultural circle, colors can have different meanings. This will be further examined in chapter 2.4. Even acoustic tones and noises can be perceived and interpreted differently from one country to another.

1.2
PRODUCT
DEVELOPMENT
AS THE
DESIGN FOR
ALL SENSES
↓
1.2.3
PRODUCT
PLACEMENT
AND BRAND
IDENTITY

FIGURE 1.24
Successfully introducing new products requires a conscious, consequent approach to brand symbolism, which can even be articulated in the color scheme. For the Ford Focus ST (2006), the color Electric Orange was intentionally chosen as the complementary color of the corporate logo. By presenting the photo on the left as the color negative, the Ford Blue – characteristic of the company logo – makes its mark.

THE ESSENTIAL FACTORS NECESSARY FOR PRODUCT PERCEPTION MUST BE DIVIDED INTO THOSE HAVING A BASIC, GENERAL MEANING AMONG PEOPLE AS A WHOLE AND THOSE WHICH REQUIRE THE CONSIDERATION OF REGIONAL, CULTURAL, AND SOCIAL DIFFERENCES.

This applies, in particular, to the increasingly topical question as to the conditions which should be fulfilled in order to assure the global marketing of products in a promising, prosperous manner. The principal goal of this book is to distinguish the relevant mechanisms of multisensory perception from one another, thus facilitating the choice of appropriate product characteristics made by designers and developers for different customer groups. In this context, it is also the duty of product development to avoid risks which may arise due to errors or miscalculations involving cultural influences. A car design which enjoys great success in the United States, for example, might be rejected by Europeans – or vice versa. The impact of colors is just as culturally influenced as the perception of sounds related to the functioning of the product. Compared to Europeans, Asian customers tend to prefer clearer, lighter motor sounds. Such fundamental differences must be recognized prior to the product definition or in the early stages of development in order to reduce the risk of error when introducing a product into the market. Thus, the context of perception must be given a great deal of attention. It should also be noted that the customer expectations for a particular product have often been cultivated since his early childhood, for example, through the situation depicted in figure 1.25. The perception and the evaluation of objects often exhibit an "historical" component whose substantiation may be found in the life history of the individual. The phenomena of the dependency pertaining to context will be discussed in section 2.3.5.

In contrast to the intention to meet mainstream tastes as much as possible, it is often desired to draw the customer's attention to the brand by virtue of particularly impressive special models. In times of an omnipresent sensory overload by mass media, it is particularly challenging to arouse customer interest in things outside their typical perspectives. Manufacturers are thus eager to offer products capable of arousing these interests of potential new customers. Among them are the concept cars presented at trade shows that, though not yet in production, demonstrate the school of thought of the designers. Such models, namely vehicles having the primary duty of arousing attention, do not necessarily correspond to the expectations and needs of the majority of potential customers. Indeed, these concept cars might even stand in contrast to them. Some family fathers would definitely be interested in having a sporty two-seater, but such a vehicle would not necessarily respond to the function immediately desired. This contradiction, nevertheless, helps to increase the degree of attention with respect to those products, and this result is indeed desired by the manufacturer. In this regard, the pertinent phenomena such as *perceptual conflicts* and *cognitive dissonances* will be examined in Chapter 3.1.

48

1.2
PRODUCT
DEVELOPMENT
AS THE
DESIGN FOR
ALL SENSES
↓
1.2.3
PRODUCT
PLACEMENT
AND BRAND
IDENTITY

FIGURE 1.25
**Customer expectations for a product such as an automobile
are often already formed in childhood.**

Even products that meet the particular interests of a relatively small group of customers can be of value to the brand image. In this case, one speaks of *niche products*. By offering such a product, the manufacturer has the possibility of discovering a "free room" or "white space" among customer desires previously ignored by manufacturers, which allows the attentive provider the chance to gain a lucrative edge over the competition.

With respect to special customer wishes, it is thus necessary to take individual differences in perception seriously and to integrate them into the development process. Research related to synesthesia during the past fifteen years has unearthed a variety of interesting aspects pertaining to multisensory perception. These are thus included in this book and analyzed with regard to their significance to design in all sensory modalities.

**IT IS IMPORTANT TO UNDERSTAND
THAT PERCEPTUAL PROCESSES DO NOT PROCEED
IN THE IDENTICAL MANNER FOR
ALL PEOPLE – INDIVIDUAL DIFFERENCES
THUS CREATE BOTH PROBLEMS
AND OPPORTUNITIES IN THE DESIGN
AND DEVELOPMENT OF INDUSTRIAL PRODUCTS.**

1.2
PRODUCT
DEVELOPMENT
AS THE
DESIGN FOR
ALL SENSES
↓
1.2.3
PRODUCT
PLACEMENT
AND BRAND
IDENTITY

49

Just as technical products must offer the desired function, it is also evident that the smell and taste of foodstuffs can be systematically designed to correspond to customer expectations. No one eats something voluntarily that does not taste or smell good. Additionally, foodstuffs must have a good appearance, for the optic conveys, via associations, essential information as to whether a product is more or less fresh or even spoiled – and as to how it evidently tastes. Furthermore, in the last decades, it was discovered that tactile characteristics such as the sensations on the tongue or when chewing as well as the ensuing sounds are of nearly equal significance. A potato chip might taste good even though the bag was opened two days prior. The eating of such chips is not, however, generally seen as pleasant, as they feel rather slack and elastic; one misses the crispy, crunchy sound. Hence, when "crispiness" is one of the central product attributes, producers give a great deal of attention to the auditory characteristics of foodstuffs; indeed, in this case, efforts are even made to emphasize this in naming their product. Chips being consumed shall sound "crunchy" and "crispy" – and even the traditional German sausage known as *Knackwurst* ("crackling sausage") carries the archetypical sound in its name. Such onomatopoeia will be discussed in Chapter 2.3.2.

In contrast to the domain of foodstuffs, in the development of technical products, smell and taste are nowadays not regarded as to be of principal importance. This contradicts the fact that the overall impression which a product makes on the customer is also determined by smell. A car interior can smell distinctly *new* or *old*: in the first case, the effluvium of newly produced materials plays a role; in the second case, the smell of old materials creates a musty atmosphere. In each case, the overall impression can be negative. Efforts are thus made to design the smell of new vehicles in a way that does not negatively impact upon the decision to buy, while also assuring that the driver and his or her passengers do not suffer any limitations in their enjoyment of the vehicle. The smell is often regarded as a disturbance variable. Nevertheless, manufacturers are steadily becoming aware of the fact that a pleasant smell can help to promote a technical product as well as its use.

In marketing, fragrance is already being used as a means of positively influencing the consumer with regard to the product (Knoblich 2003). To date, available studies show that the smell of materials – at least when they reach the customer – must be afforded equal attention as that given to the other senses during product development.

IN ORDER TO ESTABLISH A
PRODUCT SUCCESSFULLY WITHIN A GIVEN
MARKET, IT IS ESSENTIAL
TO SYSTEMATICALLY OPTIMIZE THE
PRODUCT CHARACTERISTICS PERCEIVED
BY THE CUSTOMER. MOREOVER,
CATEGORICALLY ALL SENSORY MODALITIES
MUST BE CONSIDERED, FOR THE
MULTISENSORY IMAGE OF PRODUCTS
IN THE PERCEPTUAL SYSTEM REPRESENTS
THE DECISIVE BASIS FOR THE
EVALUATION BY THE CUSTOMER AND HIS
DECISION TO MAKE A PURCHASE.

In this context, even taste is important. During sales events, food is often offered in the form of snacks and beverages. In this case, the decisive question concerns ascertaining the flavors which most appropriately correspond to the product and to the desired corporate identity. Chips, currywurst, and Coca-Cola would hardly fit the presentation of a luxury limousine; the same possibly applies to offering caviar canapés for the purpose of promoting the sales of sturdy utility vehicles.

1.2.4
THE SIGNIFICANCE OF MULTISENSORY ENVIRONMENTS

1.2
PRODUCT
DEVELOPMENT
AS THE
DESIGN FOR
ALL SENSES
↓
1.2.3
PRODUCT
PLACEMENT
AND BRAND
IDENTITY
↓
1.2.4
THE
SIGNIFICANCE
OF MULTI-
SENSORY
ENVIRONMENTS

In the conception of products, the entire environment in which the perception of the product characteristics transpires must be taken into account. Thus, the customer does not perceive the automobile in an isolated manner, but in the realm of the given driving conditions, in the parking space in front of his house, in a commercial ad along a deserted highway, or in a specially designed showroom.

The significance of the context for the perception of the product characteristics through different senses will be observed in section 2.3.5. The product must be designed and developed with particular regard to the environment of use expected by the customer. In many cases, however, it is desirable to align the environment with the product, such as in the design of showrooms and exhibition stands. In advertising, the message of the product is characterized by the presented ambience, often by virtue of special situations. The context of the perception can affect the environments of actual usage as well as those of wishful thinking and fantasy, as figure 1.26 illustrates.

1.2
PRODUCT
DEVELOPMENT
AS THE
DESIGN FOR
ALL SENSES
↓
1.2.4
THE
SIGNIFICANCE
OF MULTI-
SENSORY
ENVIRONMENTS

51

FIGURE 1.26
A product must constantly be depicted in the environment
in which the customer is expecting it.

THE CONTEXT OF PERCEPTION DETERMINES WHAT ENTERS INTO THE CONSCIOUSNESS AND INFLUENCES THE ATTENTION SPAN AND THE QUALITY OF JUDGMENT.

Frequently, the environment is more or less completely determined by the technical system itself. As a general rule, the driver of a motor vehicle is thoroughly enveloped by the system which he steers. Only the windows allow him to view the external environment of the product which appears to move around him while driving. Complex technical systems often offer more possibilities than a person can simultaneously handle. Thus, the perception and interpretation of signals is reduced to a few singular events. Externally, a variety of symbols like traffic signs, traffic lights, and the signals of other automobiles must be recognized, in addition to iconic features like local characteristics and topographic attributes. Simultaneously, the multifaceted responses of the technical system have to be evaluated, among them are indicator lights and symbols, measurements of velocity and rotational speed, the fuel gauge, engine temperature, data pertaining to the air conditioning, and signals from components of the infotainment system such as traffic, weather, and navigational data. Conversation with passengers and the consideration of the wishes of children also in the car demand the driver's attention.

OF UTMOST IMPORTANCE IS MAINTAINING A DELICATE BALANCE OF THE SIGNALS GOING TO THE SENSES, SO THAT ONLY THE ESSENTIAL INFORMATION IS PROCESSED AT ANY GIVEN MOMENT.

Everything else, on the other hand, should blend into a pleasant background that does not demand attention but simply creates an enjoyable *atmosphere (ambience)*. The perception of the atmosphere is essential to the development of objects and environments. This includes the comprehensive judging and evaluation of a situation, even prior to the details being recognized by the perceptual system. If one enters into a living or conference room, it is often immediately clear if emotional tension is "in the air" or a relaxed, friendly atmosphere exists. Indeed, even before details are known – such as discussion points, conflicts, or general states of mind of those involved – one is capable of making a preliminary emotional assessment. Thereby, it is interesting that the first impression often contains a useful evaluation of the situation. This does not occur by virtue of logical thinking, but through the utilization of intuitive models within the perceptual system, and these can subsequently be comprehended and corrected on a conscious basis. The *somatic-marker* theory, discussed in chapter 3.5, is of particular interest. Every environment leads to a perception of the atmosphere. The perception of natural environments and of near-natural landscapes such as parks and gardens is often particularly intense. Life increasingly takes place, however, in artificial environments. As a result, buildings, residential spaces, shopping malls, offices, sports facilities, and other environments must be designed in such a manner that allows them to host pleasant living and working arrangements in which positive feelings accompany the inhabitants.

A characteristic feature of the perception of atmospheres is the great speed with which judgments can be made. Furthermore, the results of the intuitive processes involved tend to indicate a high emotional potential. It is thus clear that the designing of products requires especially painstaking efforts with respect to the desired atmosphere.

The first impression has a lasting influence on a purchasing decision. Even before the details can be studied, the overall judgment is conclusively reached. Particular aspects of the product will only then be considered, moreover, if positive feelings are at play from the very outset.

52

1.2
PRODUCT
DEVELOPMENT
AS THE
DESIGN FOR
ALL SENSES
↓
1.2.4
THE
SIGNIFICANCE
OF MULTI-
SENSORY
ENVIRONMENTS

FIGURE 1.27
Every working environment has its own multisensory characteristics.
Kitchens are an especially demanding challenge for designers,
given that ergonomic expedience, safety, and life quality must be equally optimized.
Additional design criteria result from the "landscape analogy."
Kitchen B3, Bulthaup GmbH, Bodenkirchen.

1.2
PRODUCT
DEVELOPMENT
AS THE
DESIGN FOR
ALL SENSES
↓
1.2.4
THE
SIGNIFICANCE
OF MULTI-
SENSORY
ENVIRONMENTS

53

Especially in cases in which the product surrounds or envelops the person making use of it, the positive atmosphere is the basis of relaxed use and safe handling. Atmosphere is a characteristic of quality which is significantly based on the participation of different senses.

The term *atmosphere* is discussed extensively by Gernot Böhme (Böhme 1995). According to his interpretation of synesthetics, a correlation of the sensory modalities to a certain atmosphere occurs to a great deal by virtue of the allocation of individual perceptual contents (Böhme 2002). This is an associative nexus of the type described in chapter 2.3 of this book.

The fact that landscapes can be evaluated in an intensively atmospheric manner has led to a transfer of the necessary characteristic, visual attributes into other modalities. Thus, Murray Schafer coined the term *soundscape* as an analogy to *landscape* (Schafer 1977). It encompasses the division of an auditory environment into components which are of primary significance and those which convey atmosphere. This transpires on the basis of perceptual processes which effectuate the differentiation of individual objects in the foreground from a relatively diffuse background. The awareness of the spatial distribution of perceived objects within the visual, acoustic, and tactile sense plays a very special role in this regard (see section 2.2.5).

FIGURE 1.28
Colors and forms serve to convey taste and also smell.
The shop window of a confectionery store in Brussels.

The landscape analogy can be applied to any environment. It leads to concepts which permit a working environment to be sensibly structured, particularly with respect to the operation of complex human-machine configurations. In the distribution of kitchen furnishings in Germany, the term *Kochlandschaft* ("cooking landscape") has become an established expression. Accordingly, the appropriate kitchen products are presented within the realm of a *Küchenland* ("kitchen land"). Figure 1.27 illustrates an example of the spatial positioning of kitchen furnishings. Spatially structured lighting systems create a *lightscape*, and efforts are made to offer the customer an eventful *emotionscape*. For spatially distributed and structured acoustic radiation, special soundscape compositions, specially designed and mixed, are used as ambient sounds to produce the desired atmosphere.

The multisensory character of the atmosphere is particularly evident when colors and forms make reference to other senses. In such a manner, even the perception of smell and taste can be intensified. The color of foodstuffs and their packaging are thus conceived with regard to smell and taste, for the consumer "eats with his eyes." Figure 1.28 depicts the shop window of a confectionery store. Characteristically "sweet" colors such as pink, purple, and silver are employed. Analogous to the attributes of confectionery products, round forms and soft materials from which the packaging as well as adorning ribbons and artificial blossoms can be created, are considered important. Those analogies of form and color will be discussed in greater detail in chapter 2.2. Even associative elements with nostalgic value, such as the silverware, support the presentation of the product (refer to chapter 2.3). In the example of the shop window, given the fact that the window pane prevents potential customers from obtaining a whiff of the aromas, the visual analogy has a certain transcending power and is thus of particular significance.

FIGURE 1.29
Multimedia events require the constant coordination of the stimuli with respect to the participating sensory modalities. Even the stage lighting plays more than one role. It follows not only the goal of the optimal illumination of the actors and musicians, but also pursues the objective of conveying emotional contents. As opposed to the perception of colors and movement, concrete forms fade into the background.

1.2
PRODUCT
DEVELOPMENT
AS THE
DESIGN FOR
ALL SENSES
↓
1.2.4
THE
SIGNIFICANCE
OF MULTI-
SENSORY
ENVIRONMENTS

Even the design of cultural events with concerts, theater, movies, visual arts, and/or dance increasingly takes place within multimedia landscapes. Traditional possibilities of stage shows exist in the gesticulation and mimic of the musicians as well as in colorful costumes and dance. It is now taken for granted that concerts for pop and jazz music are accompanied by colorful, animated illumination, often with video clips. In contrast to the search for an objective correlation between the senses triggered by music, light, and movement intensively pursued up until the mid-twentieth century, today the main focus is on free, creative design. Figure 1.29 illustrates an example among many others. The trend described is demonstrated by various films with multimedia, artistic pretensions, such as the film *Trip* by Frank Otto and Bernt Köhler-Adams (Otto 2007).

In developing multisensory approaches, it is noteworthy that the same set of design tools can be used in different fields. Therefore, beyond the boundaries of product design, this book provides material and concepts suitable for all applications which require configuration for more than only one sensory modality.

FUNDAMENTALS OF PERCEPTION

The decision of a customer favoring a certain product is undoubtedly influenced by such factors as expectations, social demands, previous knowledge, and basic emotional attitudes. Primarily, however, his or her decision is determined by the immediate perception of the product. Therefore, in order to understand the multisensory mapping of physical objects in the perceptual system, some of the essential characteristics of the reception of stimuli and the processing via different sensory channels shall be described. This inevitably necessitates the continuation of an interdisciplinary approach. For that reason, reference shall be made to pertinent studies, for their implications and conclusions shed much light upon the matter. Findings in brain research, for example, document the participation of various sensory modalities in perceptual processes (see e. g. Luria 1973).

PERCEIVING AND IMAGING AN OBJECT IN A CONSCIOUS STATE IS THE BASIS OF HUMAN COGNITIVE ACTIVITY. AS A MULTISENSORY PROCESS, THIS NEVER OCCURS WITH THE PARTICIPATION OF ONLY ONE MODALITY.

In order to assess sensory function, it is necessary to have knowledge of the physical and chemical dimensions describing and relating to all stimuli which influence the sensory apparatus. The most important dimensions will be explained in the framework of succinct excursuses.

The term *perception* encompasses all phenomena manifested in the consciousness as a result of the stimulation of the sensory organs. The professional literature often applies the distinction recommended by Helmholtz, namely between *perception* as acquiring awareness of objects and *sensations* as the consequence of specific sensory stimulation (Helmholtz 1863, 7). The distinction is significant to the discussion of perceptual objects in section 1.3.4. In order to describe sensations as elements which give rise to complex models of the perceived, these must be designated as perceptual *characteristics* or *qualities*. Among them are colors, brightness levels, and forms in figure 1.30.

In order to orient and move themselves within their environment, humans require a variety of information, which is made available by virtue of different sensory channels. This does not only apply to the external environment, but to conditions and activities of one's own body as well. The central nervous system, with its brain, spinal cord, and the related neural network in the form of nerve fibers, can be regarded as the core of the entire human system, the very basis of all sensory information, and the realm in which all activities are planned and controlled. In this respect, even body perception is a part of the external world of the perceptual system. In the consciousness, however, it must be distinctly separated from the world outside of one's own body. Otherwise, an interaction between one's own body and the external environment would not be possible.

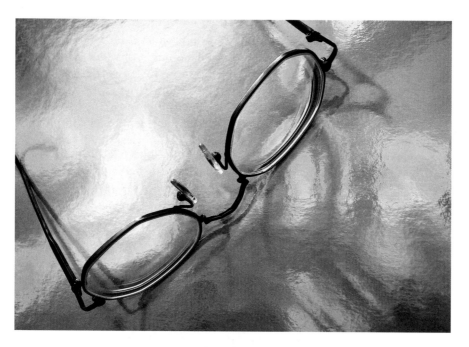

FIGURE 1.30
Vision enables the recognition of objects. Colors and forms are thus
among the more important subjective perceptual qualities.

The first step in the process of perception consists of the sensory organs receiving the physical and chemical stimuli. This includes the transformation of the stimuli into data formats which can then be processed by the neural system. Furthermore, the information received by every sensory organ will be converted into electrical impulses which are then sent through the nerve fibers to the various centers for further processing. For the purpose of differentiating it from the conscious awareness of object properties and body states, the term *perception* applies exclusively to the pure information processing of the stimuli. In accordance with the views of psychophysics, the terms *sense* and *sensory channel* refer to an instance or a processing step coupled to a specific sensory organ. The senses are commonly divided into five areas: *sight*, *hearing*, *touch*, *smell*, and *taste*. However, many more forms of sensory cells actually do exist. Moreover, various authors describe additional instances of shape perception and the connection of diverse sensory data as further senses – for example, as Gestalt experience. In this respect, Gestalt experience refers to the form-constructing capability of the human senses and encompasses the visual recognition of shapes and complete forms, as opposed to a collection of mere contours and lines. As a result of these extended definitions, one arrives at nine or even twelve separate senses (Schneider 1995, see also Van Campen 2008). These tend to correspond to philosophical approaches, such as those postulated in anthroposophy – and even the colloquially cited *sixth sense* is indicative of this orientation. Such approaches, however, are inherently inconsistent with the clear, physiologically motivated basis of a multisensory theory. Therefore, they shall receive no further consideration in the course of this book. Instead, it has to be noted that all sensory organs are connected to specific neuronal structures and both sensory organ and neuronal pathway define a sensory channel.

As verified in the course of daily experience, the respective sensory organs respond to stimuli only in a certain manner, which means that their behavior is *stimulus-specific*. Potentially disturbing influences, such as the appearance of bright structures due to the impact of pressure on the eyes, are isolated or "blinded out" as much as possible. Corresponding to the specific behavior of the respective sensory organs, one finds, in each case, an individual processing mechanism within the central nervous system and different locations of signal processing throughout the brain. One speaks of the *modal processing* of stimuli. Similarly, the perceptions effectuated by different sensory stimuli in the consciousness can clearly be distinguished from one another. This occurs by virtue of different subjective perceptual qualities, the *Qualia*. Problems associated with assessing the *Qualia* are discussed in section 1.3.6.

In correlation to the function of each sensory organ and the stimuli to which it responds, various senses (modalities) can be identified and distinguished from one another:

VISUAL **SEEING**

AUDITORY **HEARING**

OLFACTORIC **SMELLING**

GUSTATORY **TASTING**

VESTIBULAR **SENSE OF BALANCE AND BODY MOVEMENT**

TACTILE **TOUCHING**

THERMORECEPTIVE **FEELING TEMPERATURE**

PROPRIOCEPTIVE **POSITIONING AND MOVEMENT OF THE EXTREMITIES**

INTROCEPTIVE **BODY CONDITION AND ORGAN ACTIVITY**

NOCICEPTIVE **FEELING PAIN**

The human set of sensory cells includes receptors for electromagnetic waves (vision), mechanoreceptors for mechanical quantities (touch, proprioception), receptors for mechanical waves (audition), and chemoreceptors (smell, taste). Seeing and hearing are commonly regarded as *higher senses*, for they process a variety of complex data and deliver precise information, particularly pertaining to the environment outside of the body. No direct physical contact to the object of perception is necessary. All other senses, by contrast, either require a direct contact between the body and the object or the substance, or provide feedback about physical states. The organs for smelling and tasting mutually complement one another and even exhibit, as chemoreceptors, functional analogies. Given the fact that they deliver less detailed information than ears and eyes, they are described as *lower senses*. They carry out, nevertheless, significant functions in the choice of foodstuffs and thus in the avoidance of situations and substances dangerous to the body. Furthermore, they directly influence the intuitive assessment of objects and atmospheres. Not without reason, the assessment according to aesthetic criteria is referred to as *taste*.

The sense of balance, also known as the *equilibrioception*, ascertains the position as well as the movement of the head, and delivers in combination with the muscle receptors essential data regarding the orientation and movement of the entire body. In and of itself, however, the sense of balance effectuates a conscious perception only in exceptional situations, such as in the case of vertigo, and this dizziness is, as a rule, indicative of a disturbance in the control of body balance.

The tactile perception delivers information covering the structure of surfaces, the *texture*. This function is carried out by sensory organs of the skin which respond to the influence of forces. Therefore, it is necessary to employ the appropriate area of the skin for touching, allowing the object to be texturally or structurally analyzed. Thus, even without simultaneously seeing, a rather precise spatial depiction of objects is possible. The tactile comprehension of objects necessitates, nevertheless, the active process of touching (fig. 1.31). The combination of both – the active grasping and the passive perception – is also described as *haptics*.

FIGURE 1.31
The sense of touch facilitates the control of fine motor movements.
During the adjustment of the side-view mirror, mechanoreceptors
deliver information as to the operation of the control lever.
Simultaneously, the eyes monitor the result; e.g., by means of the visual
perspective via the side-view mirror.

Haptic perception even enables, in addition to the tactile receiving of information, an analysis of the temperature. Via receptors in the muscles and tendons, the heaviness and hardness of objects may be ascertained as well.

Perception of the body *introception*, literally the perception of internal stimuli, is relatively unspecific. It determines, nevertheless, the overall feeling with respect to well-being or complaints regarding pains or perceived health deficiencies. Moreover, the involved sensory organs are sensitive to slow movements, as illustrated in the case of seasickness, and they react to oscillations and sounds in lower frequencies *(infrasonic)*.

In that which follows, the sensory functions of seeing and hearing as well as the sense of taste shall be more closely examined. The point of departure is the physiological function of the sensory organs as well as the transmission of neuronal signals to higher centers of processing in the brain. Among the detailed literature in the field of sensory physiology are renowned standard works which merit particular attention (Campenhausen 1993, Lindsay 1977, Goldstein 2009). The observations in this book are limited to the analysis of parameters, which are essential to the connections between the modalities, as undertaken by the sensory organs:

CHARACTERISTICS OF THE COMPLETE APPEARANCE OF THE OBJECT, PARTICULARLY OF SPECTRAL QUALITIES
TIME RESPONSE AS A CHRONOLOGICAL ALTERATION OF THE OBJECT PROPERTIES
ROOM AS GEOMETRY, SPATIAL DIVISION, AND MOVEMENT OF OBJECTS

The characteristics of spatial perception shall only be peripherally addressed, in order to remain within the bounds of this book.

Not all stimuli for which a specific sensory organ is assigned lead to neuronal signals. Thus stimulation thresholds defining the minimum degree of influence necessary to stimulate a sensory organ are of particular relevance. Accordingly, in order to effectuate an event of auditory perception, for example, the sound pressure must exceed a minimal value. The borders between which the spectral characteristics can be perceived are also of importance. Taken together, they determine the frequency range a dynamic physical event has to exist within to result in a case of sensory perception. For example, the human eye can respond to electromagnetic waves only within a very limited frequency range. By comparison, infrared radiation and ultraviolet light can not be seen by the unassisted human eye. The range of acoustically or visually perceivable frequencies of various animals is significantly broader than humans. For spatial perception, the angle ranges in which objects may be recognized without movement are essential.

In addition to the stimulation thresholds, it is important which minimal differences of object characteristics are barely perceivable. Furthermore, in the realm of psychophysical experiments, *threshold differentials* – the *just noticeable differences* (JNDs) – were measured and are now available for the assessment of object qualities.

The stimuli received by the sensory organs are often too fragmentary or distorted (fig. 1.32). In addition, the physiological limitations of the signal processing also play a role. Table 1.1 gives an overview of the volume of data capable of being received by and processed in the individual modalities. The number of sensory cells in the visual area is the greatest, but numerous receptors are available in the respective areas for the senses of smell and taste as well. The amount of neurons designated to transfer the signals, on the other hand, is considerably less. Thus, the number of sensory cells in the eye is 100 times greater than that of the available nerve fibers. This "bottleneck" in the processing of sensory stimuli presumes in and of itself that the relay of the sensory cells enables the reduction of the data. For the further processing of the signals, up to and including the conscious perception, on the other

FIGURE 1.32
Continuously, perceptual processes deliver only fragmentary information
pertaining to the external world. Simple physical events can lead to
a distorted presentation of objects and persons, such as those displayed by
reflections of a body on the slightly moving surface of water.
Marcia Smilack, Man on Pier, 1994.

hand, considerably more neurons are indeed available, for the arriving information must be compared to stored data and patterns and transformed into a comprehensive, multisensory representation of the external environment and the body. The *channel capacity* of neuronal dataflow determines the speed of processing. Analogous to the digital processing of data in informational technology, it displays the amount of minimal units of information processed per second [bit/s]. The data is initially transmitted with great speed to the higher centers of processing. By comparison, the channel capacity of the conscious processing is notably less. The high number of neurons, however, indicates that many neuronal processes are involved in supporting the conscious processing, although they themselves do not enter into the foreground of the awareness.

THE ESSENTIAL DUTY OF THE HIGHER
CENTERS OF COGNITIVE PROCESSING IS THE
TRANSLATION OF A CONSIDERABLY
REDUCED VOLUME OF DATA INTO A DEPICTION
OF THE EXTERNAL WORLD, AND THIS
DEPICTION MUST APPEAR WITHIN
THE CONSCIOUSNESS AS A COMPLETE,
CONSISTENT REPRESENTATION WITHOUT
CONTRADICTION.

1.3
FUNDAMENTALS
OF PERCEPTION

61

MODALITY	RECEPTION OF STIMULI	CENTRAL NERVOUS SYSTEM		CONSCIOUSNESS	
	NUMBER OF RECEPTORS	NUMBER OF NEURONS	CHANNEL CAPACITY bit/s	NUMBER OF NEURONS	CHANNEL CAPACITY bit/s
EYES	2×10^8	2×10^6	5×10^7	10^{10}	$16 - 160$
EARS	3×10^4	2×10^4	4×10^7		
PRESSURE	5×10^5	10^4			
SMELL	10^7	2×10^3			
TASTE	10^7	2×10^3			
PAIN	3×10^6				
WARMTH	10^4	10^6			
COLDNESS	10^5				

TABLE 1.1
The reduction of information perceived within the perceptual process
(Habermann 2003, 258; primary source not mentioned).
The flow of information within the state of consciousness is considerably less than
the informational volume received and processed by the sensory organs.

THE SENSES OF DISTANCE: SEEING AND HEARING

SEEING

The human eye is sensitive to light stimuli. The sensory organ enables the visual recognition of objects as it evaluates the light reflected off of them. Figure 1.33 illustrates the general structure. The light reflected by an object (an arrow) reaches the lens via the transparent *cornea*. It penetrates the lens as well as the similarly transparent *vitreous body* which completely fills out the interior space of the eye, and it encounters the layer of photosensitive sensory cells of the *retina*. The light refraction – expressed in the *focal distance* – can be modified by the activity of the muscle fibers of the *ciliary muscle*, whose fibers encompass the lens in a radial manner. It is thus possible to influence the ray path, indeed, in such a manner that enables a sharp image of objects of differing distances to be projected onto the retina. The passage of the light through the convex lens, however, leads to an inversion of the ray path – the image appears laterally reversed and "stands on its head." The sensitivity of the eye is compensated for by the *iris*, a variable aperture in front of the lens. As a response to great brightness, the iris constricts, narrowing itself and accordingly allowing less light to pass through the pupil on its way to the retina.

The retina consists of a thick layer of sensory cells which serve either as *rods* for night vision or as *cones* for determining the color. Additionally, further neurons function in the initial processing of the signals and in their relay to the optic nerve. For the analysis of the spectral characteristics of the light, three different types of cones are available, appropriately responsive to short, medium, or long wavelengths and respectively described as S, M, and L cones. The activation of the S cone facilitates the perception of the color blue. The cones M and L enable, respectively, the perception of green and red. Indeed, the retina already serves as the initial step of the processing of images. Thereby, horizontal cells serve to delineate the edges of image elements.

The electric potentials (action potentials) arising as a result of the stimulation of the sensory cells are relayed via the optic nerve to the brain for further processing. In the bundling of all neurons in the optic nerve, their sequential arrangement corresponds to the position of the respective sensory cell along the retina. In the cross section of the optic nerve, a two-dimensionally depicted object is then projected into an area of intensified neuronal activity. The flat depiction of the object, as seen by the eye, remains for assessment along the visual cortex of the cerebrum.

The processing of the signals emanating from the retina throughout various steps, up to and including the cerebral cortex, can be described as the *visual pathway*, analogous to the auditory pathway with respect to acoustic

62

1.3
FUNDAMENTALS
OF PERCEPTION
↓
1.3.1
THE SENSES
OF DISTANCE:
SEEING
AND HEARING

processing. Schematically limited to the principal steps, figure 1.34 illustrates the course of neuronal connections. For the purpose of facilitating three-dimensional vision, the optic nerves of the right and the left eye are connected with one another in the *optic chiasm*, literally a junction of both optic nerves. Without being moved, each eye is capable of covering a certain range or *field of view*. The *visual field* of the face as a whole is thus composed of the fields of view of both eyes, and they overlap considerably in the central area. The neuron bundles, routed to the left and to the right after leaving the optic chiasm, contain information from both eyes. The variations in the data from both fields of view are assessed for the purpose of creating a spatial projection. Via the lateral geniculate nucleus of the thalamus, the images of both fields of view are projected into the primary visual cortex of the rear area of the cerebrum. This is allocated to both cerebral hemispheres, although in an inverse manner: on the right-hand side, the signals of the left eye are processed; on the left-hand side, the signals of the right eye are processed. Thus, the inner portion analyzes the data of merely one eye, whereas the outer portion assesses the signals of both eyes.

1.3
FUNDAMENTALS
OF PERCEPTION
↓
1.3.1
THE SENSES
OF DISTANCE:
SEEING
AND HEARING

63

THE EXTENSIVE DISTRIBUTION OF THE STIMULI ALONG THE RETINA, WHILE REMAINING INTACT IN THE OPTIC NERVE, IS PROJECTED AS A TWO-DIMENSIONAL, SPATIALLY DIVIDED IMAGE. THIS PROCESS, WHICH IS ESSENTIAL TO THE FUNCTIONING OF THE PERCEPTUAL SYSTEM, IS KNOWN AS RETINOTOPY – THE SPATIAL ORGANIZATION OF NEURONAL RESPONSES TO VISUAL STIMULI.

The retinotopic, neuronal picture which appears in this manner corresponds to both individual retinal images. This picture is distorted, however, for the area of the greatest resolution in the center, i. e. the *fovea*, occupies a broader area than that along the border of the picture. Although the area of the fovea adds up to 0.01 percent of the retina's area, the signals from the fovea activate 8 to 10 percent of the retinotopic map on the cortex. This expansion indicates the presence of a *cortical magnification factor* (Goldstein 2009, 82). The primary visual cortex was the first region of the brain which physiologists, towards the end of the nineteenth century, identified as an area of visual processing. For a long time, it was thought that this was the actual visual center in which the entire image processing takes place. With modern methods of measurement and with the spatial (topographical) classification of brain activities, the knowledge of the cerebral structure was considerably refined. At the present time, numerous separate areas dedicated to the visual processing of information are known. An analysis of the different parameters follows separately: areas for the exclusive processing of forms, colors, and movement. Interestingly, the areas of visual processing do not necessarily closely border on one another. Indeed, it involves a broadly distributed system which is pervaded by areas with other functions. In the visual cortex, after several steps of pre-processing, a further form

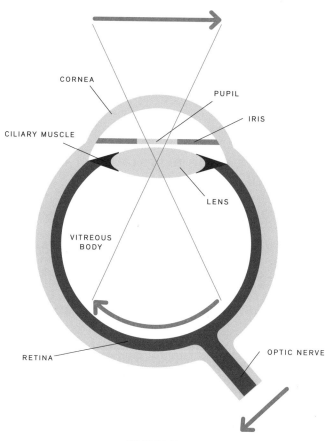

CORNEA

PUPIL

IRIS

CILIARY MUSCLE

LENS

VITREOUS
BODY

RETINA

OPTIC NERVE

64

1.3
FUNDAMENTALS
OF PERCEPTION
↓
1.3.1
THE SENSES
OF DISTANCE:
SEEING
AND HEARING

FIGURE 1.33
The structure of the eye.
Through the optical system consisting of the cornea, the lens, and the
vitreous body, light is directed towards the retina. In the retina,
the light energy is converted into neuronal signals, which in turn assess
the spectral composition. The location of each of the activated areas
along the retina is transformed into an appropriate position within the bundle
of nerve fibers comprising the optic nerve as well as along the
cerebral cortex.

1.3
FUNDAMENTALS
OF PERCEPTION
↓
1.3.1
THE SENSES
OF DISTANCE:
SEEING
AND HEARING

————————

65

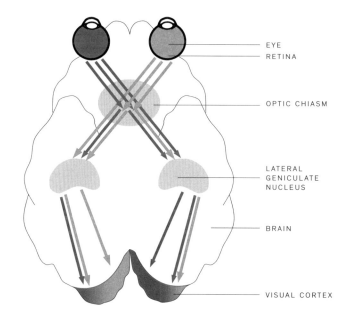

FIGURE 1.34
Visual pathway: conduction of the signals to the primary visual cortex
at the rear of the cerebrum. The interconnection of the paths
of the right eye and the left eye facilitate the viewing of a three-dimensional image.
Additionally, even the position of the stimuli along the retina is projected
into the appropriate position in the visual cortex.

of "edge detection" is carried out, this being for the purpose of transforming the comparatively rough retinal image into a sharp, clear perceptual picture. From this point on, one may, very generally speaking, identify two different primary directions of further processing, which each traverse the brain and flow towards the front. One processing stream flows "bottom-up," ventrally towards the temples, and serves to identify objects (the "what stream"). The other processing stream flows "top-down," dorsally through the region of the vertex, and serves to determine the position and movement of objects (the "where stream"). By some researchers, the "where stream" is interpreted as a "how stream," because it determines how an individual carries out an action (Goldstein 2009, 89). Both flow into the temple lobes, where the object identification and the spatial classification are concluded. The fact that the assessment of different parameters occurs simultaneously, as further explained in part 2, is of great importance to multisensory processing as a whole.

The processing of visual information in the brain exhibits different basic principles, and these are characteristic of the processing of other signals: the neurons are grouped into functional networks which respond to certain attributes of visual stimuli (Gegenfurtner 2000). The formation of functional units of neuronal processing is also referred to as *modularity*. The arrangement into groups within the cerebral cortex occurs, for example, as the neurons become superimposed with respect to one another, one being located above the other and each exhibiting mutually corresponding functions. The *specialization* of the neuron associations is also of considerable significance:

THE PROCESSING OF VISUAL INFORMATION
IS BASED ON SPECIAL UNITS,
WITH EACH UNIT BEING RESPONSIBLE FOR
ANALYZING ONLY CERTAIN ASPECTS
OF THE PERCEIVED STIMULI.
BEGINNING WITH THE EYE, THE COMPLEXITY
OF THE PROCESSED IMAGE ELEMENTS
INCREASES ALONG THE VISUAL PATHWAY.

66

1.3
FUNDAMENTALS
OF PERCEPTION
↓
1.3.1
THE SENSES
OF DISTANCE:
SEEING
AND HEARING

Figure 1.35 illustrates the scale of variations in color perception according to the respective wavelength. To the right of this depicted spectrum, namely towards greater wavelengths, or smaller frequencies, one would find the invisible range of thermal radiation (infrared, IR). The invisible radiation of shorter wavelengths beyond violet, on the other hand, is referred to as ultraviolet light (UV). In contrast to humans, many insects and birds have appropriate cognitive capabilities within these frequencies.

Given the fact that the iris allows the eye to adapt to different intensities of light, it is more difficult than for other senses to express the sensitivity of the eye in a numeric value. That is quite in contrast to the situation with the sense of hearing, as mentioned below. In measuring the energy absorbed by the respective cells, it is possible to obtain a value for the sensitivity of individual receptors, such as of the various cone forms. Thereby, it is presumed that the energy required to effectuate the action potentials in the sensory cells, for example, corresponds to the energy absorbed from the light which enters into the retina.

460 nm ———————————————— 530 nm ———————————————— 660 nm ————

FIGURE 1.35
The spectrum of light visible to the human eye.
The scale indicates the variations in color perception as caused
by the different wavelengths.

Figure 1.36 indicates the data of the frequency-independent sensitivity with regard to the three cone styles: s, m, and l (according to Campenhausen 1993). Each curve was standardized in the area of maximal sensitivity. Good examples of the theoretical characteristics of visual perception are also advanced by Rock (1984).

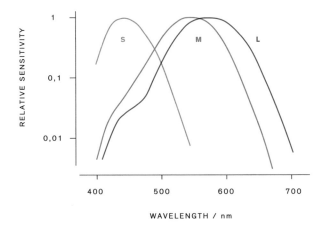

FIGURE 1.36
The relative sensitivity of the color receptors of the retina.
In the graph, the maximal sensitivity of each cone form corresponds to the value 1.
Seen in absolute terms, the sensibilities of the M and L cells are actually
almost identical, whereas the S cones are considerably less sensitive. The rods
necessary for night vision (scotopic vision), on the other hand, are even
more sensitive than the color receptors – their maximal sensitivity is in the
frequency range of the M and L cones.

1.3
FUNDAMENTALS
OF PERCEPTION
↓
1.3.1
THE SENSES
OF DISTANCE:
SEEING
AND HEARING

EXCURSUS: THE PHYSICAL NATURE OF LIGHT

Light is a form of electromagnetic radiation. This results from the interaction of electrical and magnetic fields with one another. Thereby, in the course of this interaction, the energy alternates periodically between the electrical and the magnetic portions. This effectuates an energy transport throughout the space which is defined as a *wave*. If one observes a fixed point within the space, the electrical and magnetic proportions constantly vary between minimal and maximal values. Should only one frequency – that is a single spectral line – be available, this occurs in accordance with a sine function (fig. 1.37). Such a periodic occurrence with reference to a particular point in the given space is referred to as *oscillation*. The cycle duration τ measured in seconds [s] is, thereby, the measurement of the velocity of change. In addition to the maximum values reached by the oscillating physical quantities – for example, the electrical or magnetic field intensity – the number of cycles completed per second is a characteristic quantity. This is known as frequency f, and it is indicated in Hertz [Hz].

as gas (air), liquid (water), and some solid bodies (glass), as well as in an absolute vacuum. The expansion of the energy within a given space transpires with the constant velocity c, the speed of light, which amounts to approximately 300,000 km per second [km/s]. If one observes the wave within a given space, at a given point in time, one notices a periodicity (fig. 1.38): The physical quantities exhibit maximal and minimal values, depending upon their distance. The process with respect to a specific frequency corresponds to, in turn, a sine function. The length of a period or cycle is determined by the speed of light and the frequency. It is also a characteristic quantity, namely the wavelength λ, indicated in meters [m].

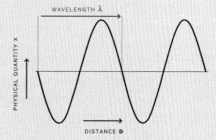

FIGURE 1.38
Two cycles of a sine function which describes the spatial variation of a physical wave quantity at a fixed point of time.

The speed of light c in its relationship to frequency f and wavelength λ:

$$1 \qquad c = f \cdot \lambda$$

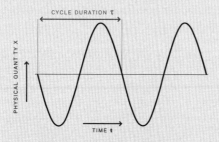

FIGURE 1.37
Two cycles of a sine function which indicate the temporal alteration of a physical wave quantity with respect to a fixed point in the given space.

As an electromagnetic wave, light is not bound with regard to any medium. It can propagate in various media or states, such

Visible light distinguishes itself from other forms of electromagnetic waves merely by virtue of its frequency: for radio waves and thermal radiation, lower frequencies are decisive, whereas x-rays and radio activity involve higher frequencies. The frequency of visible light is in the range of 390 to 790 THz (1 Tera-Hertz = 1 trillion oscillations per second). In the case of light, as compared to radio waves and sound, a specification as to wavelength instead of frequency is used. This encompasses the range from 380 to 780 nm (1 nm = one millionth of a millimeter). As indicated by figure 1.35, the wavelength 660 nm leads to the color perception *red*, whereas 530 nm and 460 nm result in the perception of the colors *green* and *blue*.

As a general rule, however, the light which encounters the eye usually does not consist of individual frequencies which correspond to pure, untainted colors during the perception. Indeed, there is mostly a mixture of different components. The spectrum of visible light is either composed of individual spectral lines, or it exhibits a continual progression which can be formed very differently. Figure 1.39 illustrates a comparable example of the composition of a spectrum consisting of individual spectral lines, as well as of a broadband frequency mixture from the auditory region. Subsequently, this latter observation will be expanded upon in the excursus examining the physical nature of sound.

The energy emitted by a source of light is physically measured as the total *radiant energy* of the object. In order to determine the visible portion of that energy, the *luminous energy*, the frequency-dependent sensitivity of the eye has to be considered. For that purpose, measured values are multiplied by a weighting function, which takes into account a simplified average sensitivity of the eye. Standardized weighting functions have been defined for both, the *photopic* (high energy which enables color sight) and the *scotopic* case (low energy which only enables black-white seeing, figure 1.40). The estimation of the visible light energy from the measured spectral power by application of the shown weighting functions is expressed as luminous flux, with the physical unit Lumen [lm].

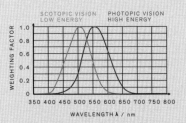

FIGURE 1.40
**Luminosity functions to consider
the sensitivity of the eye
for assessment of the energy
radiated by light sources.**

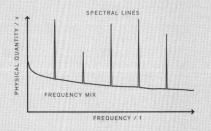

FIGURE 1.39
**The example of a spectrum which
is composed of diverse portions:
narrow-band spectral lines
and broad-band frequency mixture.**

In general, the impression of color can be described as a combination of hue, saturation, and brightness (lightness/luminance), thus defining the HSB (or HSL) *color space*.

Similar to the eye, the ear also serves the purposes of receiving and analyzing wave phenomena. Figure 1.41 depicts the general structure of the human ear. In this case, however, it involves mechanical waves which transport energy of movement via the oscillation of air molecules. These acoustic waves are diffracted around the head, the upper body, and the auricles, and effectuate an oscillation of the air columns in the auditory canal. Accordingly, acoustic energy reaches the *eardrum*, which is similarly brought to the point of oscillation or reverberation. The parts of the body which exert influence upon the acoustic wave up to the eardrum are referred to as the external, or outer ear. The eardrum is not a membrane which can freely reverberate. Instead, it is a cup-shaped, stiff structure with an elastic periphery. A network of collagen fibers serves to increase the stiffness. As a result, an optimal transfer of the oscillation energy is enabled from the eardrum to the closely associated auditory ossicles.

1.3
FUNDAMENTALS
OF PERCEPTION
↓
1.3.1
THE SENSES
OF DISTANCE:
SEEING
AND HEARING

7 1

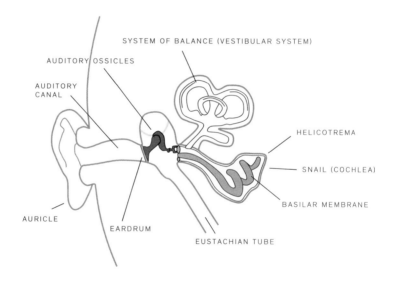

FIGURE 1.41
The structure of the ear and the balance system.
The reception of sound encompasses the transformation of acoustic
energy in mechanical, hydrodynamic, and, once again, mechanical energy.
Ultimately, in the basilar membrane, the energy is converted into
neuronal signals.

The auditory ossicles constitute the transmission path of the *middle ear (tym-panum)*, thus further transferring the oscillation energy to the *inner ear*. They are situated by virtue of elastic bands hanging within the tympanic cavity. The cavity contains air and is thus utilized to provide for pressure compensation behind the eardrum, being connected to the pharynx via the Eustachian tubes.

This particular arrangement is necessary, for the eardrum can sensitively respond to the acoustic waves entering into the acoustic canal only when the same air pressure exists on both sides. During the process of hearing, only the pressure fluctuation, which occurs as a result of the acoustic incident, shall lead to a perception, whereas the static air pressure, on the other hand, does not come into consideration. In the case of an insufficient compensation of pressure by the Eustachian tubes, as experienced in airline travel, with colds, or during diving expeditions, for example, the difference in pressure is initially often perceived as "pressure in the ears" and subsequently as pain. It is accompanied by, at any rate, an impairment of the sense of hearing.

The auditory ossicles are named according to their respective form: hammer, anvil, and stirrup. They function as a set of levers, scaled for the purpose of ultimately allowing the maximal amount of acoustic energy to be transferred to the inner ear. The inner ear analyzes the frequency of the sound. It contains a snail-like, meandering structure which is thus referred to as *cochlea* (snail). This, in turn, consists of canals filled with cerebrospinal fluid, liquid of the brain, in which the stimulation of acoustic waves hydrodynamically, literally as a liquid sound, is conveyed. The sensory cells are located in the basilar membrane, which pervades the cochlea as a narrow band.

The *sense organ for balance (vestibulum)*, which consists of three semi-circular, ring-like canals, is connected to the canal system of the inner ear as well. Movements of the head create movements of the fluid in the rings, which are registered by sensory cells and also assessed with respect to the direction of movement. Thereby, the direction and the inclination of the head as well as all changes of position due to movement can be determined.

FUNDAMEN-
TALS OF
PERCEPTION
THE SENSES
OF DISTANCE:
SEEING AND
HEARING

EXCURSUS:
THE PHYSICAL
NATURE
OF SOUND

Sound is a wave phenomenon that is based on the oscillation of particles in solid bodies, liquids, or gases. Thus, sound can not propagate within an absolute vacuum. The human ear is optimally suited for the perception of acoustic waves in the air. The basis for the expansion of sound in air is the movement of the air molecules about an inoperative state – oscillations. The molecules exert forces upon one another which, in turn, lead to a periodic oscillation of the air pressure around the climatically determined, static value. As a rule, acoustic waves come into being in the air as a result of their stimulation via oscillating mechanical structures (fig. 1.42).

acoustic field completely, as long as both values with respect to every point in the given space are known. The relationship between frequency and wavelength, as explained above in the excursus regarding the physical nature of light, applies here as well. The speed of sound is, however, in contrast to the speed of light, dependent upon the medium in which the expansion takes place. In the air, the speed of sound – with 20°C and a static air pressure of 760 torr – amounts to 343 meters per second [m/s]. Should the oscillation of the air particles be based upon a sine function, the sound process only contains a single frequency. The spatial distribution of the sound pressure also corresponds to – during a given point in time – a sine function, as indicated in figure 1.38. A mixture of different frequencies, however, results in an overlapping of sine functions. Figure 1.43 gives an appropriate example.

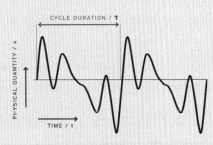

FIGURE 1.42
**Acoustic radiation of the side panel
of an automobile in a test set-up.
The yellow areas are indicative of the
areas of maximal sound intensity.
This depiction focuses on
the frequency range 250 to 4000 Hz.**

Should only one frequency be stimulated, the chronological course of the sound pressure at one location in the sound field thus corresponds to figure 1.37. The sound pressure effectuates, thereby, the movement of the air molecules, which also occurs periodically. The characteristic value for this movement is the momentary velocity of the particles – in acoustics, this is referred to as *sound particle velocity*. The time-dependent oscillation of sound pressure and particle velocity leads to the spatial expansion of energy, which is described as the acoustic wave. Sound pressure and particle velocity describe every combination of acoustic waves, meaning every

FIGURE 1.43
**Two cycles of a signal with several
frequency portions.
This spectrum corresponds to the
spectral lines of figure 1.39.**

As a general rule, sound field quantities are indicated in logarithmic form, i.e., as Sound Pressure Level (SPL); for the derivation, reference is made to section 2.2.3, equation 3. In order to comprehend the methods of the frequency analysis in the ear, figure 1.44 displays the cochlea in its "unrolled" form. It consists of three canals, from which the upper and lower canal are connected with one another via a small opening, the *helicotrema*. The basilar membrane serves as a wall of the middle canal. Via a membrane in the oval-shaped window, oscillations of the stirrup stimulate waves in the fluid of the upper canal *(scala vestibuli)*. These, in turn, propagate themselves, via the helicotrema and the lower canal *(scala tympani)* along their way to the round window, which is similarly sealed by a membrane.

The fluid waves create further waves along the basilar membrane, and these wander to the free end of the helicotrema. The basilar membrane is constituted in such a fashion that its breadth towards the helicotrema constantly expands, whereas the thickness decreases. In varying distance to the oval window, there are areas attuned to different frequencies. Should a wave, which is set forth by an audible sound, reach the end of the basilar membrane, a maximum deflection occurs in a certain position, as figure 1.44 suggests with respect to the frequencies 50, 200, and 1600 Hz. The position of maximal deflection corresponds to the frequency of the stimulating sound. The sensory cells in this area of the basilar membrane become activated in an intensive manner – they are, for their part, particularly sensitive to this frequency. The locations of maximal stimulation for high frequencies are found at the beginning, and for low frequencies at the end of the basilar membrane. Additionally, the sensory cells are involved in processes of feedback of neuronal activity, which maximize the sensitivity of the inner ear and improve the separation of the spectral portions.

74

1.3
FUNDAMENTALS
OF PERCEPTION
↓
1.3.1
THE SENSES
OF DISTANCE:
SEEING
AND HEARING

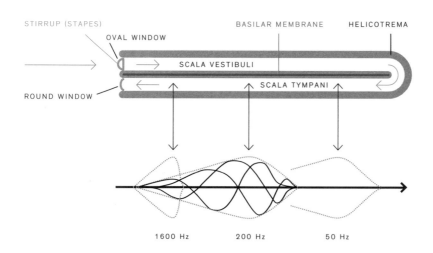

FIGURE 1.44
The structure of the inner ear: a schematic diagram
of the processing of the cochlea. The frequency analysis is based
on the projection of different frequencies onto different
areas of the basilar membrane. The spatial separation of the stimulating
frequencies is continued along the auditory pathway.

In assessing multisensory relationships, it is especially noteworthy that the spectral analysis of an acoustic incident follows the transformation of the frequency onto a position along the basilar membrane. The distribution of the frequency portions depending upon the location is continued in the auditory nerve, for it transmits the electrical signals of the sensory cells for auditory processing to the brain. The neurons of the auditory nerve correspond to the frequencies to be processed – their frequency behavior is demonstrated by characteristic *tuning curves* (Goldstein 2009, 274).

> ## AN IMAGE OF THE AUDITORY SPECTRUM IS PROCESSED AS A SPATIAL STRUCTURE OF STIMULATION. THIS IS IN CONTRAST TO THE PROJECTION OF THE RETINAL IMAGE ONTO THE VISUAL CORTEX, WHICH IS DEPENDENT UPON THE SPATIAL – AND NOT SPECTRAL – PROPERTIES OF STIMULI.

1.3
FUNDAMENTALS
OF PERCEPTION
↓
1.3.1
THE SENSES
OF DISTANCE:
SEEING
AND HEARING

75

In the case of multisensory connections, the particular proximity of spatial-visual and spectral-auditory attributes is conspicuous – for example, the preferred perceptual connection between visual height and auditory pitch (section 2.2.3). Notably, in German, auditory pitch is denoted as "tone height" [Tonhöhe]. At such a point, in considering the aforementioned type of depiction, a nexus could indeed exist between the visual cortex and the auditory cortex.

Taking a more detailed look, the basilar membrane consists of a component which carries the sensory cells and of a tectorial membrane, which is arranged above it. The sensory cells are equipped with fine hairs which touch the tectorial membrane. During the propagation of a wave, a relative movement takes place between both parts of the basilar membrane. This causes the movement of the fine sensory hairs, resulting in neuronal activity and accordingly leading to the transmission of the stimuli, via the auditory pathway, to higher levels of processing.

Figure 1.45 presents the auditory pathway in a simplified form. Along the cortex of each cerebral hemisphere, the auditory field – also known as *auditory cortex* – may be found. Via various ganglions *(nuclei, olives),* the auditory nerves are led from the inner ear (cochlea) to the auditory cortex. Thereby, the ganglions undertake a fundamental analysis of the acoustic signals. Already with the second ganglion, the superior olive, a relay of signal shares takes place between both ears, being necessary for the localization of acoustic sources.

The special distribution of spectral portions, as occurring along the basilar membrane, finds itself as a *tonotopy* in the realm of the auditory cortex. Lower frequencies are processed in the front and side areas, higher frequencies, on the other hand, in the middle and in the rear.

As figure 1.46 illustrates, auditory sensitivity is very frequency-dependent. ● In the infrasonic region below approximately 20 Hz, sounds are no longer audible via the sense of hearing – with large amplitudes, on the other hand, their vibration can certainly be felt by the mechanoreceptors of the body. With regard to high frequencies, the perceptual border diminishes with increasing age: small children can even be cognizant of 18 to 20 kHz. As humans become older, however, the capabilities decrease continually in this respect,

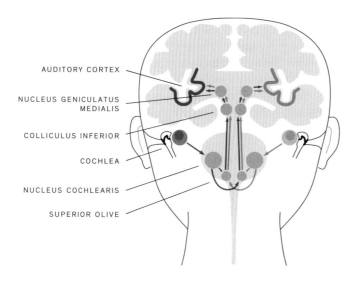

AUDITORY CORTEX

NUCLEUS GENICULATUS
MEDIALIS

COLLICULUS INFERIOR

COCHLEA

NUCLEUS COCHLEARIS

SUPERIOR OLIVE

FIGURE 1.45
The auditory pathway: neuronal processing paths for auditory perception.
With the transmission of the signal to the primary acoustic fields
(auditory cortex) on both sides, a contribution of the other side is taken into
consideration, in order to facilitate spatial hearing.

1.3
FUNDAMENTALS
OF PERCEPTION
↓
1.3.1
THE SENSES
OF DISTANCE:
SEEING
AND HEARING

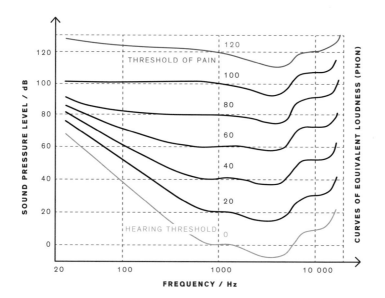

THRESHOLD OF PAIN

120

100

80

60

40

20

HEARING THRESHOLD   0

SOUND PRESSURE LEVEL / dB

CURVES OF EQUIVALENT LOUDNESS (PHON)

FREQUENCY / Hz

FIGURE 1.46
Sensitivity of the sense of hearing.
The curves represent the perceived volume (loudness) in comparison
to the physical sound level (vertical axis) and frequency.
Accordingly, for example, a tone of the frequency 100 Hz must be,
compared to a tone of 1000 Hz with a volume of 0 dB,
raised by 40 dB in order to be heard at all.

diminishing down to 10 kHz and even falling beneath that value. Corresponding to the frequency-dependent sensitivity, even tones with an equal sound pressure level can be perceived as if they were of different audio volumes, according to the particular frequency. The curve of equal audio volume – once known as *Phon* curves – indicate the amount by which a sinusoidal tone must be increased in order to generate the same perceptual strength in the realm of differing frequencies. In the present day, the term *loudness* is preferred as the perceptual quantity, owing to the fact that it considers the effects of interaction between different frequency portions. If the ear is irritated due to narrow-band noises, it decreases its sensitivity in the frequency range of this auditory stimulation. The frequency area with diminished sensitivity exceeds – particularly with regard to high frequencies – the frequency area of the stimulation. More quiet noises, which may be found in this area, are inaudible. This phenomenon is known as *masking*.

1.3
FUNDAMENTALS
OF PERCEPTION
↓
1.3.1
THE SENSES
OF DISTANCE:
SEEING
AND HEARING

77

Subsequent to the influence of loud sounds, a condition of reduced sensitivity exists in the involved frequency area. This impairment is only temporary, however, and depending upon the magnitude of the influence, the original hearing quality is normally restored after a few minutes or hours. Should loud noises be sustained for a long time, on the other hand, they can cause permanent damage to the sensory cells of the basilar membrane. In the damaged sensory cells of the frequency areas involved, the sensitivity can de impaired for life. Indeed, the ear itself hardly has the possibility of preventing acoustic damage – contrary to the eye, it can not close itself. Nonetheless, due to the unconscious tensing of the muscles encompassing the eardrum and stirrup, the acoustic energy entering into the middle ear can be filtered and thus be partly reduced.

At the beginning of every auditory evaluation, the measurement in a room of minimal sound reflection – for example, in an anechoic chamber in which the propagation of sound is not impeded by reflections (fig. 1.48) – is necessary. As the next step, the measurement data can be analyzed with respect to the psychoacoustic characteristics of the sense of hearing. It must be emphasized that the aforementioned psychoacoustic parameters relate to characteristics of individual sound events. They are, on the one hand, appropriate for describing the quality of noises and tones. On the other hand, they deliver no information as to the function of individual sound events in a larger context; for example, with respect to the perception of an individual tone as part of a melody or an accord. Furthermore, they yield no information pertaining to associative or symbolic contents, such as the recognition of the sound of a mosquito or of a technical warning signal. Psychoacoustic parameters are, nevertheless, also important figures with respect to the connection between the sensory modalities via cross-sensory analogies, for this contains correlations of individual characteristics and key parameters of the quality as perceived (section 2.2.3).

EXCURSUS: IMPORTANT PSYCHOACOUSTIC PARAMETERS

Psychoacoustic parameters enable estimation of parameters which describe the perceived quality of auditory perception. For the fundamentals of acoustic perception, see Roederer 1973 and Moore 2003; for spatial hearing, see Blauert 1997. The important psychoacoustic parameters of monaural hearing were particularly determined by Eberhard Zwicker and Hugo Fastl (Zwicker 1982 and 1999). Here is a selection:

LOUDNESS N [sone]: The loudness describes the subjectively perceived sound pressure originating from an acoustic stimulus. It is dependent upon the sound level and sound characteristics in the realm of frequency and time. Contrary to the sound level in [dB(A)], as prevalent in noise protection, however, the loudness is, even with the masking of individual signal portions, proportional to the strength of the perception. The sound level is derived from the measured sound pressure, although the frequency-dependent sensitivity of the sense of hearing is approximately depicted by virtue of multiplication with a weighting curve (A-curve). This proceeding is equivalent to the aforementioned calculation of the luminous flux of visible light. The loudness considers, nevertheless, masking effects in the frequency and time ranges. Furthermore, in the evaluation of complicated sounds, it provides values which, as a rule, more accurately correspond to the perception as the sound level (Zwicker 1982).

PITCH STRENGTH [%]: The pitch strength describes the pronounced nature of individual tones within the total sound. This is, nevertheless, a rather imprecise definition which, in many cases, does not accurately correspond to the perception. In the differentiation of individual spectral portions, the sense of hearing is extremely sensitive, allowing different musical instruments of an orchestra to be separately perceived with great ease. Contrary to this, the parameter pitch strength is appropriate for describing sounds with simple structures; for example, by the evaluation of broad-band emissions from industrial buildings which contain tonal components.

FLUCTUATION STRENGTH F [vacil]: The fluctuation strength describes the proportion of low frequency modulations in the frequency range below 20 Hz. These modulations are fluctuations of the intensity which may be perceived, in such low frequencies, as changes of temporal significance (amplitude modulation). Fluctuations in the frequency range – e. g., through an uneven speed of rotation – will not be detected by means of this parameter, although they would be very significant with respect to the perception of sounds containing tones.

SHARPNESS S [acum]: The sharpness describes the proportion of high frequencies within the spectrum as a whole. It is calculated by virtue of a complex algorithmic formula. Details may be found in the comprehensive research of Zwicker and Fastl (Zwicker 1999). Figure 1.47 illustrates the example of a tone with a fundamental frequency of 2 kHz and various combinations of overtones. If only the fundamental frequency is apparent, the tone is named a *pure tone*, which by addition of overtones is changed to a complex tone. Basic tone and overtones define the harmonics of a *complex tone*. As a result of various combinations of *harmonics*, diverse tone colors (timbres) and degrees of sharpness arise. Should only a relatively high overtone supplement the basic tone – as depicted in the third example – it does not necessarily blend with the basic tone; instead, it may be perceivable as a separate tone. In such a case, the perceptual situation is in essence significantly changed, now with two different sound objects, each having its own perceptual quality, meriting consideration.

ROUGHNESS R [asper]: The roughness describes the amount of fast modulations within the frequency range from 20 Hz up to 100 Hz. Contrary to the fluctuation of lower frequency, these amplitude modulations do not appear as changes of a temporal nature, but as a change of the tonal quality of a sound which is constantly perceived within the time domain.

This listing represents merely a selection of important parameters which describe the influences of the strength of the acoustic stimulus as well as of the temporal and spectral art of the auditory perception. These parameters already apply to hearing even with just one ear. Additionally, there are other parameters which pertain to spatial hearing – in such a case, the reception of the signal with both ears is required.

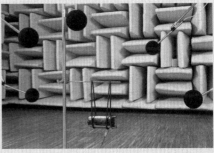

FIGURE 1.48
Sound measurement of a shaving razor in an anechoic chamber of Braun GmbH, Kronberg.

SOUND PRESSURE

FREQUENCY	2	4	6	8	10	KHz
FUNDAMENTAL FREQUENCY	↑	1.	2.	3.	4.	OVERTONE
	1.	2.	3.	4.	5.	HARMONIC

FIGURE 1.47
An example of the influence of overtones on timbre and sharpness of a tone. Here, the overtones exhibit the same amplitude as the fundamental tone.

1.3.2
PHYSICAL SENSES OF PROXIMITY

TOUCHING

Touching one's way through the environment delivers information pertaining to the objects of the immediate vicinity. For this purpose, the receptors of the skin are essential, in addition to the proprioceptive information provided with respect to the position and movement of the extremities. The latter aspect is referred to as *kinesthetic perception.* The primary receptors serve to assure the tactile perception arising by virtue of the contact between the body and the surfaces of the outer world, for they transmit mechanical stimuli such as pressure and vibration as well as temperature. Furthermore, the skin contains pain receptors. Although the tactile reception of stimuli is based on complex processes, it is, as a sense or proximity, less intensively researched than the senses of distance, such as seeing and hearing. This situational condition has nothing to do with a deficiency in complexity. Instead, it is more a question of the self-evident nature of this modality. The mechanical perceptual capability of the skin is based on the interaction of various receptor types, each having a high degree of sensibility with respect to mechanical stimuli: *Merkel's corpuscles, Krause's end bulbs,* hair follicle receptors, as well as *Vater's, Pacini's, and Ruffini's corpuscles.* These sensory cells are schematically illustrated in figure 1.49. The concentration of receptors can dramatically differ according to the respective area of the skin. Zones of greater concentrations are located on the fingers and hands as well as on the tip of the tongue.

Mechanical stimuli are processed separately from temperature stimuli and pain. The received stimuli patterns are projected onto the primary sensory field of the cerebral cortex, namely the somatosensory cortex. At that very point, a first detection of elementary patterns takes place. Particularly, even stimuli which occur during the active touching of objects are distinguished from those which arise merely through passive contact with the skin. Just as in the case of seeing and hearing, the stimuli encountered via bodily perception and touching are also projected as spatial (topographic) distribution along the cerebral cortex.

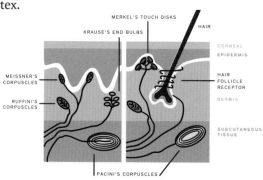

FIGURE 1.49
**The mechanoreceptors of the hairless (left) and the haired (right) skin
(according to Campenhausen, 1993).**

EXCURSUS: THE PHYSICS OF MECHANICAL QUANTITIES

The mechanical influence of objects upon one another is described by two forms of physical quantities: force quantities and movement quantities. *Forces* constitute the origin of the movement of matter – they are characterized by the direction of their influence and by their strength. For the influence of mechanical forces, it is necessary to have contact to the object being influenced by the forces. The physical unit of the force is the Newton [N]. If a force is not applied to a specific point, but extensively, the force is distributed across the contact surface. In this case, the force influence is sensibly referred to as *pressure*, namely as the force exerted per surface tension unit [N/m²]. Should a force result in a rotational movement, it is referred to as a *torsional moment (torque)*.

Movements are defined by the alteration of the position of an object within a given space. A typical characteristic of such is the momentary distance of the object with respect to a starting point or to a traversed path. In the case of periodic oscillations around an idle position, the term *deflection* is used. An alteration of the path per time unit is referred to as *velocity* [m/s or km/h as well]; in the course of molecular movement in the realm of the expansion of a sound, one speaks of *particle velocity* (note the excursus to the physical nature of sound above). During a ride in an automobile, a change in the velocity is perceivable as *acceleration* or *deceleration* in [m/s²], for force influences upon the body are involved.

Changes in the acceleration are perceivable as well; for example, during the increase of the fuel injection, during the application of the brakes, or the shifting of gears – but also during the movement across a pothole. The rate of change of the acceleration, specifically the derivative of acceleration with regard to time, is known as *jerk* [m/s³]. Thereby, it is important to note that each of the mentioned quantities describes an event of movement completely, inasmuch as they are known at the time of movement. Then, each passage of time may be calculated by converting the way, the velocity, the acceleration, and the jerk into one another. Each of these quantities contains the entire information characterizing the movement.

By means of force and acceleration quantities, the interaction of two objects with one another can be completely described.

A good presentation of the sensory depiction along the cerebral cortex is contained in Geschwind (1985). Figure 1.50 illustrates the perceptual thresholds of mechanical receptors as a function of the respective frequency. The frequency of maximum sensitivity is dependent upon the form of the receptor and may be found within the range of 50 to 200 Hz. The Pacinian corpuscles are, among the mechanical receptors, sensitive to the highest frequencies. Thus, it may be presumed that these are particularly important with respect to the perception of vibrations, for it is known that frequencies up to 1000 Hz may be perceived during exposure of vibration upon hands and arms (Griffin 1990).

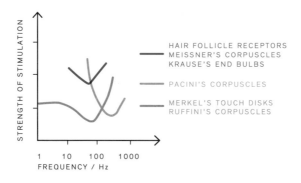

FIGURE 1.50
Sensitivity of the skin receptors, based on the level of stimulation in
table 1.2 (according to Campenhausen 1993). In this diagram, the strength of
stimuli needed to induce an equivalent sensation is plotted.
Therefore, minimum portions of the curves indicate maximum sensitivity.

82

1.3
FUNDAMENTALS
OF PERCEPTION
↓
1.3.2
PHYSICAL
SENSES OF
PROXIMITY

Meissner's and Krause's receptors may be found located in a minimal depth beneath the skin. In the frequency range of their greatest degree of sensitivity (10 to 100 Hz), they convey the perception of vibrations, which Campenhausen also refers to as *whirring* (Campenhausen 1993, 34) Hair follicle receptors react only to the movement of the small hairs, however, and not to constant displacements. This corresponds to the warning function of these sensory cells. Merkel's touch disks and Ruffini's corpuscles react, nevertheless, both to dynamic changes of pressure – such as those caused by vibrations – as well as static, temporally constant deformations of the skin.

Thus, the various receptor types react to different physical quantities and convey, correspondingly, different perceptual qualities, as reflected in table 1.2.

PERCEPTUAL QUALITY	RECEPTOR	PHYSICAL QUANTITY
PRESSURE	MERKEL'S TOUCH DISKS RUFFINI'S CORPUSCLES	PRESSURE AND STATIC DEFORMATION
TOUCHING	MEISSNER'S CORPUSCLES HAIR FOLLICLE RECEPTORS	VELOCITY
VIBRATION	VATER'S CORPUSCLES PACINI'S CORPUSCLES	ACCELERATION

TABLE 1.2
The functional realm of different mechanical receptors.

Generally speaking, tactile perceptions can be explained as the shifting of skin surfaces against one another. Thus, even quick movements of the hands, without them touching anything, can result in tactile perceptions.

As already suggested, one must distinguish between static and dynamic stimuli with respect to the stimulation of receptors. If one places his or her finger upon an object, fine particulars of the surface structure (texture) are even perceivable without movement. Small objects such as grains of sand can be localized in a relatively precise manner. The perception of static forces involved in touching constitutes, thus, an initial analysis of the surface and provides important evidence with respect to the recognition of objects. The stimulus increases in rather direct proportion to the finiteness of an elevation along the surface. Mechanisms of the *inhibition* within the nerve pathways, which transduce the stimulus to the brain, are responsible for this. They provide for a mutual inhibition of the transduction of stimuli in case of the simultaneous activation of various fibers of a nerve cord. Thus, the point of a needle – even when it does not cause any pain – will be perceived with greater intensity than the influence of similar pressure along a greater surface, for example, such as the flat end of a pencil. With the activation of the inhibition, the perceptual capability is not proportional to the pressure being applied. A further indication of the process of inhibition is the disproportional perception of very small forces. Touching the skin with a feather, for example, results in a "tickling" sensation of rather great intensity.

If the fingers are moved across an object, locally fixed, stationary irregularities of the surface can lead to a temporally alternating, dynamic change of the forces involved in touching. Thus, the static texture becomes transformed into a temporally alternating stimulation. This gives rise to the spectral characteristics of the stimuli: depending upon the relative velocity of the movement between the fingertips and the surface, various frequencies come into being, which in turn stimulate the various types of skin receptors in different manners. Accordingly, the gliding of the fingers along a surface with regular elevations with a distance of 1 mm to each other, with a velocity of movement of 10 cm per second, will result in a stimulation frequency of 100 Hz. As figure 1.50 indicates, the pressure-sensitive Merkel touch disks and the Ruffini corpuscles exhibit maximum sensitivity within this frequency. If the surface structure is irregular, a frequency mixture is stimulated. This corresponds to a noise process which generates a broad-band signal similar to a crackling sound. Should the velocity of the relative movement between the fingers and the object be increased, the frequencies of stimulation correspondingly shifts upward. In the aforementioned example, the frequency of 200 Hz is stimulated by virtue of a velocity of 20 cm per second. Additionally, the quality of perception is influenced by the frictional warmth arising from the gliding along the surface and stimulating the temperature receptors.

In the steering of a motor vehicle, even the tactile stimuli entering in to the feet and legs via the pedals are of importance. For the operation of the clutch, the brake, and the gas pedal, feedback pertaining to the operation and transmitted by virtue of the pedal force and pedal displacement is essential. Thereby, vibrations could result in disturbance variables, or they could convey data with respect to special operational conditions such as the employment of

1.3
FUNDAMENTALS
OF PERCEPTION
↓
1.3.2
PHYSICAL
SENSES OF
PROXIMITY

83

the anti-lock braking system (ABS). At 125 Hz, the perceptional threshold is at its lowest point. From that point, the threshold rises to both lower and higher frequencies. Perceptions of vibration and pedal force applied superpose each other, but subjective assessment of vibration is not influenced by pedal force in the range of 40 to 300 N (Zöller 2006).

PROPRIOCEPTIVE SENSIBILITY

The perception of the position, force, or movement of parts of the body is known as *proprioceptive sensibility* or *depth sensibility* – in contrast to the *superficial sensibility* in the skin. It pertains to the perception of one's own body.

The *Golgi organs* serve as sensory cells in joints, muscles spindles, and sinews. Without their reception of the stimulation, a motor action would generally not be possible. Proprioceptive sensibility incorporates the motor into regulatory circuits (control loops) and is thus the basis of purposeful movement processes and of optimized postures. The sensory information provided is constantly being evaluated, but it seldom enters into the consciousness in an explicit manner. The same applies to the internal bodily perception (introception) which delivers a somewhat specific feeling for the condition of the body and its organs. The available receptors in this respect, however, respond to vibrations and infrasound as well and accordingly influence the perception of noises and of the movement of the entire body.

Receptors for proprioceptive sensibility are capable of detecting static and dynamic forces. This is necessary, on the one hand, in order to recognize the position of the body and the extremities and of the forces applied, and to, on the other hand, gain and maintain awareness as to the processes of movement. In hearing and seeing, temporally constant portions, however, are blinded out. As described above, the static air pressure in the normal conditions involved in hearing is not perceived. Even the human eye does not react to the static electrical and magnetic fields available in the environment. Various bird species are, nevertheless, capable of using and evaluating the earth's magnetic field for the purpose of orientation.

84

1.3
FUNDAMENTALS
OF PERCEPTION
↓
1.3.2
PHYSICAL
SENSES OF
PROXIMITY

TEMPERATURE
AND PAIN

The sensory organs for temperatures consist of freely branched endings of neurons. They register the temperature of the skin and its changes. Pain can similarly be initiated via the stimulation of free nerve endings. There are findings, however, which speak for the existence of specific pain receptors.

Biologically, perception of heat and pain serve the same purpose, namely the avoidance of adverse or body-damaging environmental conditions. External temperatures which are considerably greater or less than the temperature of the body complicate its life-essential maintenance of constancy. Mechanical influences upon the body, as indicated by the sensation of pain, can be just as detrimental as a pathological change of bodily functions. Additionally, both senses support the mechanical senses of the skin during the investigation of objects: the characteristics of the thermal conduction of a material lead to a cooling or a warming of the skin in the area of the mechanical contact to its surface. Accordingly, the typical characteristics of an object may be found, leading to its identification. Thus, the reception of the temperature is associatively assigned in a direct manner, for example, with respect to a hot or cold cup of coffee or warm or colder air. Pain, on the other hand, is often immediately perceived as a stimulation, without being assigned or traced to its source – this is a *somatized* perception (Campenhausen 1993). The sense of temperature is also essential with respect to the perception of the atmosphere (ambience) of an environment. This is particularly so in the case of unusually extreme conditions (fig. 1.51).

1.3
FUNDAMENTALS
OF PERCEPTION
↓
1.3.2
PHYSICAL
SENSES OF
PROXIMITY

8 5

FIGURE 1.51
Temperature perception can also be conveyed in a visual fashion,
as indicated by this depiction of a frozen fruit bowl containing oranges.
ING-DiBa Icehouse, Cologne, 2006.

Given that the perception of the temperature is determined by the quantity of warmth received or given by the skin, the stimulation is not directly described by the outer temperature, but by the heat flux density; more specifically, by the warm energy which penetrates a certain area of the skin per time unit. Warmth emanating from an external source reaches the skin through the flow of air *(convection)* and via thermal radiation *(infrared light)*. Here, nevertheless, a role is also played by the body warmth which rises as a result of metabolic activities such as blood flow and muscular action. A portion of this warmth is dissipated along the surface of the skin, similarly via thermal radiation and convection as well. The evaporation of transpiration causes dissipation of thermal energy, via the thereby arising evaporation coldness. The temperature of the evaporation, however, is also determined by the movement, temperature, and humidity of the surrounding air. Due to the complexity of the thermal conditions within the skin, as outlined above, the temperature receptors do not react directly to the outer temperature – the perception of temperatures is, moreover, dependent upon the outer and inner context (fig. 1.52).

FIGURE 1.52
The perception of temperature is influenced by both
environmental and body conditions.

86

1.3
FUNDAMENTALS
OF PERCEPTION
↓
1.3.2
PHYSICAL
SENSES OF
PROXIMITY

Thus, one speaks of the temperature *as felt* and seeks to consider the influence of measurable outer conditions such as wind speed and humidity. Nevertheless, such an estimate remains incomplete, for physiological factors and the familiarization with respect to certain living conditions – for example, a hot or cold climate – significantly influence the perception of temperature. Additionally, the perception of temperature unleashes physiological reactions such as changes in the blood circulation within the skin or the reflex known as "goose pimples" – which in turn alter the temperature stimulation.

VIBRATIONS

In the range of high frequencies, the oscillations of mechanical bodies which are touched are primarily received by skin receptors, particularly by the Meissner and Pacini corpuscles (Griffin 1990). The greatest sensitivity of the fingertips exists in the range of 200 to 300 Hz and corresponds to the frequency behavior of the Pacini corpuscles. In the process of vibration, there is a direct relationship between the lowness of the frequency of stimulation and the level of active participation of the extremities, the head, and the inner organs. Thus, the relative movement of structures and the related forces can participate in the process of perception. Vibrations of the *hand-arm system* are also registered by receptors for proprioceptive sensibility. If the entire body is stimulated to *total body vibrations,* even receptors within the internal recesses of the body contribute to the perception of vibration *(introception).* Even with stimulation only in a certain direction, there are movements of body parts which encompass all spatial directions and rotary components (Haverkamp 1990). In the realm of lower frequencies of minimal Hertz, the sense of balance and the eyes contribute to the perception. The combination of very low frequencies beneath 1 Hz with great vibratory amplitude can cause *seasickness*. This phenomenon can appear as *carsickness* in automobiles as well, but it primarily affects the passengers and not the driver himself. Thereby, the sense of balance and bodily receptors are involved in the same measure. The greatest sensitivity with respect to total body vibrations in the vertical plane is experienced in the frequency range of 4 to 8 Hz while sitting. In this regard, the upper body exhibits considerable resonance. For lateral stimulation or those in the direction *forward-backward*, nonetheless, the greatest degree of sensitivity is found between 1 and 2 Hz. *Hand-arm* vibrations can be felt up to 1000 Hz, the greatest sensitivity, however, is registered at lower frequencies around 10 Hz.

1.3
FUNDAMENTALS
OF PERCEPTION
↓
1.3.2
PHYSICAL
SENSES OF
PROXIMITY
↓
1.3.3
CHEMICAL
SENSES

87

1.3.3
CHEMICAL SENSES

TASTING AND SMELLING

The sense of taste and the sense of smell are very closely related to one another. They are known as the *gustatory sense* and the *olfactory sense*. Figure 1.53 illustrates the context. The sense of smell supports the tasting of foods with the tongue (White 2007). Without the ability to perceive smells, it is not possible to distinguish between fine nuances of taste – and the identification of foodstuffs is thus made more difficult. One tends to associate the word fragrance with a pleasant scent. The fragrance of foodstuffs which supports the perception of taste is referred to as *aroma*.

FIGURE 1.53
Smell and taste maintain a rather intimate relationship to one another.
Accordingly, decorations consisting of aromatic and edible
elements are employed to enrich the multisensory living atmosphere.

THE SENSE OF TASTE IS, JUST LIKE THE
SENSE OF TOUCH AND THE TEMPERATURE SENSE,
A SENSE OF PROXIMITY. THE SENSORY
ORGANS FOR TASTING REACT ONLY TO OBJECTS WITH
WHICH THEY COME INTO IMMEDIATE CONTACT.

There are *chemoreceptors* arranged along the tongue and in the palatal area. On the tongue itself, the concentration of the sensory cells is particularly dense – they exist in wart-like structures, the *papillae*. Contrary to the olfactory organ, there are no sensory cells which directly respond to a singular tasting agent. There are, nevertheless, different forms of papillae *(filiform papillae, vallate papillae,* and *foliate papillae),* each having a different arrangement of sensory cells. The different types of sensory cells exhibit varying sensitivities with regard to the respective flavors.

Today, it is customary to divide taste into four primary categories, the *basic tastes* (Campenhausen 1993, 49; Goldstein 2009, 367):

SWEET	SOUR	BITTER	SALTY

These qualities of taste were in fact mentioned by Adolf Fick in 1864 (Fick 1864). They can be activated by the stimulation of the tongue with a weak electric current. Depending upon the frequency and the duration of the electrical stimulation, one of the four taste qualities is involved. The papillae sensitive to those four main qualities of taste are located in different areas of the tongue surface (fig. 1.54). As an additional taste, the quality advanced by the protein-rich nourishment, characterized by the Japanese word *umami* (e. g., induced by glutamate), is currently discussed, as well as a specific quality for the taste of fat. All other nuances of taste arise by virtue of the participation of the sense of smell. For the sheer savory aspect of meals, the visual attraction is of great significance – for "you eat with your eyes" (fig. 1.56). The perception of a tasty, appropriate preparation corresponding to the taste is essentially determined associatively by virtue of experience and sociocultural factors.

88

1.3
FUNDAMENTALS
OF PERCEPTION
↓
1.3.3
CHEMICAL
SENSES

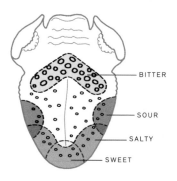

FIGURE 1.54
**Papillae and areas of specific
taste on the tongue.**

With respect to the sense of taste, two perceptual thresholds are of significance. In the case of minimal concentrations of tasting agents, a taste experience may occur without the taste quality being recognized. With a further increase, a threshold of recognition of the tasting agent will be reached. Then, with a concentration above this threshold, the actual identification may take place. A further complexity is the classification of the tasting agent and the activated perception, owing to the fact that the perceptual quality itself is dependent upon the concentration. Thus a saline solution even tastes sweet in a specific concentration (Campenhausen 1992, 52).

The receptors involved in receiving smells are located in the olfactory field *(epithelium)* in the upper region of the nasal cavity. The odorant molecules to be perceived enter initially into the nasal mucous membrane – at that point, they are dissolved and they stimulate, in turn, the sensory cells. In the nasal mucous membrane, there are approximately 350 different sensory cells, each being sensitive with respect to only one form of odorant molecule (Goldstein 2009, 360). Thereby, it involves cells of identical construction, but they contain different receptor substances. Each of these substances can bind a certain odorant molecule – this activates the neuronal stimulation. Just in order to form a large diversity with respect to receptor substances, 3 percent of the human genetic material is utilized. The specific signals for each form of stimulation are cumulated in the olfactory bulb. From this point on, every receptor type is connected to the olfactory center of the brain by virtue of a special neuronal path. Given that smells may be composed of combinations of different odorant molecules, the interaction of the receptors can lead to more than 100,000 distinctly different smells (Goldstein 2009, 360).

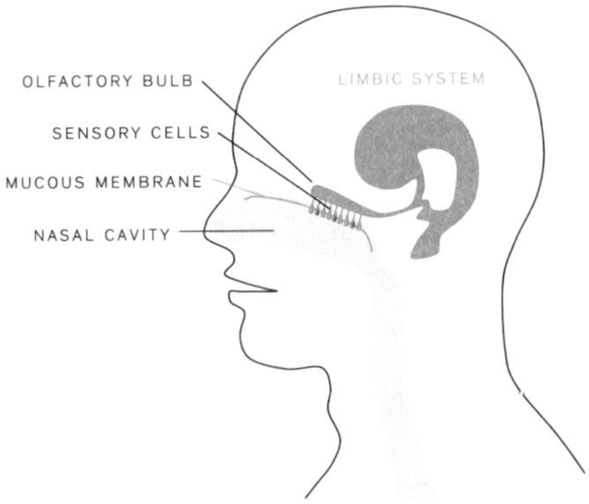

1.3
FUNDAMENTALS
OF PERCEPTION
↓
1.3.3
CHEMICAL
SENSES

89

FIGURE 1.55
The sensory cells for smell perception are closely
connected to the limbic system.

THE CONNECTION OF THE OLFACTORY
RECEPTORS TO THE CEREBRUM IS,
IN COMPARISON TO SEEING AND HEARING,
PARTICULARLY DIRECT AND AVOIDS
SOME INTERMEDIATE STEPS IN
THE PROCESSING OF THE SIGNALS.

Furthermore, as indicted by figure 1.55, the olfactory center is quite closely connected to the limbic system, as the center of emotion and memory.

Both aspects are essential to the recognition and the immediate influence of perceived smells, and thus are of specific importance for cross-sensory connection of olfactory stimuli.

FIGURE 1.56
The manner in which a meal is prepared, allowing it to appear attractive and giving it a fine taste, is strongly dependent upon culture and custom. On the left: fish freshly caught; on the right: fish prepared in the Spanish style.

An important function of the sense of smell consists of supporting the choice of appropriate foodstuffs (fig. 1.56). Simultaneously, it serves in a warning capacity and protects against impureness in the air being inhaled. However, not all detrimental elements can be perceived. Even the absence of oxygen in the air being inhaled is not noticed. In the technical application of elements detrimental to the health, this warning function can be addressed by virtue of mixing additional aromas *(odoring),* for example, in the case of natural gas, which is free of all smells in its original state. Typically, odoring substances including sulfur are added to make this dangerous gas perceivable. For some years, an artificial odor is available and increasingly applied to supersede sulfur (Gasodor® S-Free, developed by Symrise in 2001). Its smell was designed to be clearly perceivable, but exclusively utilizing environmentally friendly substances. Odor also plays an important, mostly subconscious role in sexual reproduction of animals as well as of humans. Pheromones are those substances which can affect the behavior of other people. It has been found that those chemical signals can cause *menstrual synchronicity* of women who live or work together (Goldstein 2009, 356).

Notwithstanding the smells which are interpreted within the realm of elementary warning functions, the evaluation of the perceived quality is not biologically determined. Indeed, the perception of smell is significantly influenced by associations of other sensory modalities. This is physiologically based on the fact that a major portion of the processing of stimuli occurs within the limbic system. Thus, it is possible, for example, that the smell of a meal which once caused nausea can once again lead to a sense of queasiness.

THE OLFACTORY SYSTEM
CAN EASILY BE CONDITIONED;
IN OTHER WORDS,
IT CAN BE BASED ON ASSOCIATIVE
CONNECTIONS
AND EVALUATIONS.

90

1.3
FUNDAMENTALS
OF PERCEPTION
↓
1.3.3
CHEMICAL
SENSES

The impressions which arise in this manner often remain intact for a lifetime. This being the case, the sense of smell is of critical importance to supporting a positive product image, for it is possible to establish a long-term associative evaluation with just a few perceptual events. In comparison to other modalities, a smell is particularly appropriate with respect to binding associations. Accordingly, a smell can invoke a picture of its source or of a complex atmosphere. That explains how the aroma of coffee can conjure up the view of a cup of coffee, the rattling of a coffee machine, or the ambience experienced while visiting a bistro. Fragrances are also easily capable of awakening "sweet memories."

Contrary to the rather well-anchored system of four qualities of taste, there is no generally recognized classification of smells. Although a person can distinguish among thousands of smells, no special terms are employed to describe the olfactory quality. The designation is purely associative by virtue of comparison to known sources of smells: "It smells like …" Of great importance, however, is the degree of positive or negative assessment (for example, *pleasant – unpleasant*), also known as the *hedonic* effect of odor. The system of six aroma classes described in table 1.3 was developed by J. E. Amoore and E. von Skramlik (cited in Campenhausen 1993).

1.3
FUNDAMENTALS
OF PERCEPTION
↓
1.3.3
CHEMICAL
SENSES

91

QUALITY: CLASS OF SCENT	STIMULUS: TYPICAL SMELL	EXAMPLE: "SMELLS LIKE …"
FLOWERY	GERANIOL	ROSES
ETHEREAL	BENZYL ACETATE	PEARS
MUSK-LIKE	MUSK	MUSKY
CAMPHOR-LIKE	CINEOL, CAMPHOR	EUCALYPTUS
FOUL	HYDROGEN SULFIDE	ROTTEN EGGS
PUNGENT	FORMIC OR ACETIC ACID	VINEGAR

TABLE 1.3
The classification of scents into six categories.

In chapter 2.3, a detailed scent circle with associative color assignments will be discussed.

Even when evaluating the sensitivity of the olfactory perception, one must distinguish between the perceptual threshold ("it smells like something") and the recognition threshold ("it smells like …"). Indeed, one one-thousandth of a milligram of vanilla per cubic meter of air, in other words, a concentration of 0.001 mg/m^3, suffices with regard to invoking an indefinite olfactory perception. In order to recognize the scent, however, the concentration must be approximately fifty times greater than at the perceptual threshold. The perceptual threshold strongly varies according to the substance. For butyric acid, it amounts to a concentration of 0.00016 mg/m^3; in the case of benzene, it is $1,000$ mg/m^3 (Mannebeck 1999).

EXCURSUS: THE NATURE OF CHEMICAL STIMULI

The sense of smell is based upon the perception of odorants existing in the atmosphere as particles or molecules. The olfactory perceptibility of odorants is determined by their ability to chemically influence the special receptor molecules in the sensory cells of the nasal mucous membrane. Aromatic substances are intentionally employed as *perfume* – this is a mixture of pleasant, odoriferous substances which can be maintained in a hard form or dissolved in solvent solutions. In the course of their evaporation in the atmosphere, these substances may be received by the nose. Another method consists of burning the basic substance in order to create a pleasant smell, commonly done employing resin or tree gum, frankincense or incense sticks. Important natural carriers of aromatic substances are vegetable oils, particularly the essential oils, which easily evaporate. A distinction is made between *natural, nature-identical,* and *synthetic* substances. An artificially manufactured substance is nature-identical, for example, if it exhibits exactly the same molecular structure as a natural substance.

Very minimal differences in the molecular structure can nevertheless be perceived. As an example, an artificial vanilla aroma shows a very similar molecular structure measured with respect to the natural substance, though with an inverted (mirrored) arrangement of molecules. Indeed, this difference can already be noted by many people. In contrast, molecules with different structures can cause similar sensations of odor (see example in Goldstein 2009, 359). Natural scents exist as a mixture composed of various substances, often more than a hundred different components (Luckner 2002, 269). However, the perception of a complex mixture of substances is generally based on the influence of a few *leading substances* (Hehn 2007).

Molecules and mixtures of substances which result in the perception of smells or tastes, and which are accordingly mixed with food articles, are described as *aroma stuffs* or *aromas*. Their chemical compounds belong particularly to the class of the *aromatic compounds, esters, terpenes, alkylpyrazines, aldehydes,* or *ketones*.

The human sense of smell is so sensitive that, up until the present day, no effective system of measurement is anywhere near being capable of being compared to this high degree of performance. A technical system would have to be capable of encompassing and identifying up to 200 aromatic components and their entire influence upon the perception. Owing to the fact that such a system has not yet been realized, humans are indispensable in the measurement of smells. An *olfactometer* is thus a device which mixes scent samples with air freed of all smells *(neutral air)* and presents them, along with defined dilutions, to a team of test subjects for evaluation (Mannebeck 1999).

PERCEPTUAL
OBJECTS

The goal of perception is to create a representation as complete as possible of the world surrounding the human subject. For this purpose, physical objects are to be recognized and classified in the overall framework of other objects – the *context*. The characteristics of the objects have to be identified and analyzed with respect to their significance. This also involves an evaluation as to whether a danger can emanate from the objects being perceived or as to whether they represent obstacles, whether they may be utilized for certain activities or even altered, whether they may be eaten … among many other aspects.

For the system engaged in the perception, however, it would hardly be sensible to evaluate all physical and chemical properties of each and every object. Indeed, this would lead to a flood of data occupying all capabilities of perception, processing, and evaluation – and that would ultimately prevent a decision involving direct activity being made in a short amount of time. Perception must process a variety of data with very great efficiency. This requires the reception of a very limited number of stimuli, on the one hand, while mandating a rapid analysis which is reduced to the most essential information. The basic concept which facilitates this procedure does not consist of depicting the reality as extensively as possible. Instead, it focuses on establishing simplified models of presenting the environment and objects by virtue of less complex characteristics which suffice to evaluate the objects perceived. These models appear in the consciousness as *perceptual objects, cognitive representations* which distinguish themselves from one another with clearly defined properties.

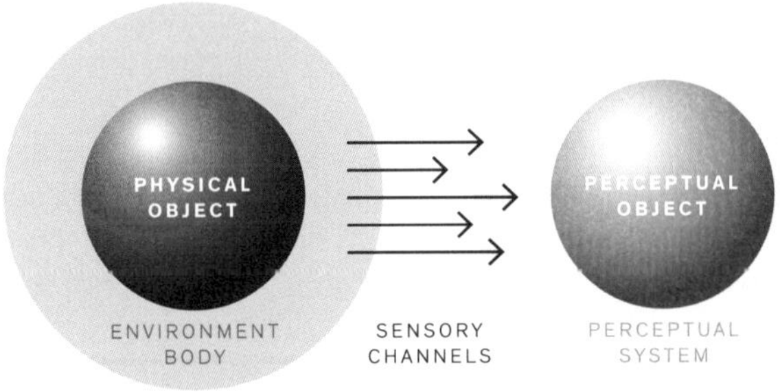

1.3
FUNDAMENTALS
OF PERCEPTION
↓
1.3.4
PERCEPTUAL
OBJECTS

93

FIGURE 1.57
A perceptual object, as a model of the physical or chemical properties,
corresponds to the stimuli received in the
environment or within the body by virtue of sensory organs.

PERCEPTUAL OBJECTS REPRESENT
THE PERCEIVED REALITY IN
THE CONSCIOUSNESS. THE CONCEPTION
OF OBJECTS IS ACCORDINGLY
THE CONCEPTION OF PERCEPTUAL OBJECTS.

Initially, as shown in figure 1.57, it appears that there is a direct relationship between a perceptual object and a physical object.

In the visual realm, the reduction down to the essential properties, for example, means that only a very limited frequency range will be perceived. Thus, we only see a small portion of the light that is being radiated or reflected. Additionally, the very large number of light spectra is transformed into a one-dimensional sensory quality: the color. Color is a model parameter created by the brain, and it does not exist in the physical environment – in contrast to our projected perception. The reduction of the spectral properties of the light down to this parameter is, however, sufficient for conveying the optical properties of objects and their surfaces. A complete identification of objects is first possible, nevertheless, after all essential properties are recognized.

GIVEN THAT THE OBJECTS OF THE ENVIRONMENT ARE CHARACTERIZED BY A VARIETY OF PHYSICAL AND CHEMICAL PROPERTIES, THE PERCEPTUAL OBJECTS ARE FUNDAMENTALLY OF A MULTISENSORY NATURE.

It follows, as a result, that perception reduced to a single sensory channel only exists in exceptional circumstances. In that case, it is possible for the generation of perceptual objects to take place within a single sensory modality. With respect to auditory stimuli, those perceptual objects have been analyzed in detail (Schaeffer 1976). Even when sensory stimuli are existent in only one modality, the system of perception endeavors to connect these to multisensory perceptual objects and to thus compensate for the missing modalities – with this obviously occurring on the basis of the paradigm that objects of the outer world constantly exhibit properties which involve various senses. Even the stimulation of only one modality with unknown stimuli directly leads to the construction of hypothetical, multisensory perceptual objects. This can be easily understood through a self-experiment; for example, by listening to unfamiliar sounds, electronic music, or soundscapes – or by looking at abstract art. Intuitive hypothesis are then shaped regarding the source of the sounds or the associative content of non-objective forms. The perceptual objects depicted on an ad hoc basis can exhibit, due to their hypothetical character, rather strange shapes. In the realm of auditory stimulation, they could resemble whirring and gyrating insects, or hard, heavy, and cold objects striking against one another.

In the course of a conference, a listener accordingly recommended allowing blind persons to make a purely auditory evaluation of sound situations. This approach ignores the fact, however, that even blind persons can generate multisensory perceptual objects within the sensory modalities available to them, particularly considering tactile properties. Persons who have gone blind, in comparison to those already born blind, have at their disposal developed visual areas within their brains and often speak of visual sensations, which accompany stimuli of other modalities (Wheeler 1920, Voss 1930, Collignon 2009, Sathian 2010). This supports the presumption of the hypothetical character of the generation of multisensory perceptual objects. The perceptual system

94

1.3
FUNDAMENTALS
OF PERCEPTION
↓
1.3.4
PERCEPTUAL
OBJECTS

endeavors to generate self-contained figures involving, where possible, all senses. This brings us to the central thesis of this book:

PERCEPTION IS FUNDAMENTALLY OF A MULTISENSORY NATURE.

However, this does not rule out the possibility of concentrating on only one sensory channel, for example in psychophysical experiments, and thus exploring the relationships between a stimulation and an isolated property of perception. The result, nevertheless, would constantly be the product of a conscious focusing which would generally have no significance with respect to the daily behavior of beings whose existence revolves around the manipulation of objects – and which thus has a multisensory orientation.

Perceptual objects, however, are not bound to fixed, substantial standards. They may also have a fleeting, instable nature, such as a cloud, a flame, a bolt of lightning, or a jet of water. They can arise, furthermore, by virtue of the absence of material – such as a hole – or be immaterial: the state, prestige, or the act of perception itself.

The omnipresent existence of perceptual hypotheses is also reflected in the development of imaginary pictures with respect to an invisible, unknown speaker – for example, while listening to a radio program. This can directly and properly evoke the picture of a speaking person. Facial features and the appearance of the speaker, however, can vary significantly in the imagination of different persons – and is suggestive of the great variance of the hypotheses themselves which in turn represent different perceptual experiences.

The daily, routine nature of multisensory objects may be found in the clothing we wear. The perception of one's own clothing occurs primarily via its inner surface, which is perceived by the tactile and thermal sensory cells of the skin. On the other hand, the clothing is visually evaluated externally – by others and by ourselves, particularly when we view ourselves in the mirror. Thereby, the sensory spheres of the outer and inner sides deliver very different data, and in spite of this, an interpretation of both being part of an object, namely of the clothing, occurs without contradiction (Zepter 1989).

1.3
FUNDAMENTALS
OF PERCEPTION
↓
1.3.4
PERCEPTUAL
OBJECTS

95

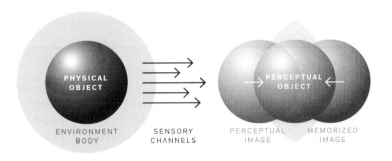

ENVIRONMENT   SENSORY   PERCEPTUAL   MEMORIZED
BODY   CHANNELS   IMAGE   IMAGE

FIGURE 1.58
A perceptual object consists of a correlation of currently perceived data and memory contents; for example, retained as image recalled from memory.

Perceptual objects, however, do not represent an exact depiction of physical structures, but are the results of an *estimation* of properties allowing a simplified model to be derived. As the basis of this estimation of the object properties, memory contents are employed as well. Increasing perceptual experience leads to an "internalization" of the perception through the increased significance of memorized images. In this regard, the word "image" refers to the depiction in an arbitrary, desired modality, not only in the visual realm. The momentarily perceived, multisensory perceptual image is a result of the correlation of the data, as directly recognized by the sensory organs, with stored images from memory, as illustrated by figure 1.58. Therefore, the process of perception is based not only upon the processing of current stimuli, but also upon the establishment of hypotheses derived from previously learned matters.

A comparison between the hypothesis and the current stimulation yields the third component of this process of perception, as proposed by the theory of perceptual hypotheses advanced by Jerome S. Bruner and Leo Postman, which is generally accepted in the present day (Bruner 1951; cited in Asanger 1999). This includes cross-sensory interactions. As an example, it has been demonstrated that the comparison process between a visually stimulated neural model, the expectation, and a current auditory input is implemented at very early levels of auditory processing (Widmann 2007). Accordingly, processes of memory are significantly involved in the process of perception. The *sensory memory* serves as a buffer or temporary storage during the reception of current data – stimuli may be stored here for the duration of a few tenths of a second (Lindsay 1977). Somewhat longer carrier storage times, up to several minutes, are made possible by the *short-term memory*. In the *long-term memory*, experiences and learned contents are stored for several years (Lindsay 1977). However, in the course of learning within their cross-linkage, even the neuronal structures between sensory organs and cortical fields adapt themselves to their respective tasks in such a fashion that one may speak of a *physiological memory* of the neuronal architecture of sensory processing. The ability of neuronal structures to adapt themselves to given tasks is described as *neuronal plasticity*.

In this manner, the perception can succeed in creating usable representations, even when based upon sketchy, fragmentary sensory information and the related, minimal volume of data. A projected image within the consciousness is, for example, considerably more exact and clear than the momentary retinal image. For this purpose, concealed areas of objects are reconstructed. The perceptual objects even contain an estimation of future changes; for example, the expected development of a process of movement. It is thus possible to view an event as a dangerous situation that is "on its way." The estimation of parameters can be understood as a process in which holes in the momentary perception are filled by memory contents, thus being supplemented by experience values. The model which is thus generated is that which we perceive as a picture of our environment. It corresponds to the actual, objective reality, however, merely with a limited probability.

The processing of the sensory input in the perceptual system, already on the neuronal level, is based upon decisions steered by probability. A neuron which is activated by sensory input answers with a sequence of electrical impulses

96

1.3
FUNDAMENTALS
OF PERCEPTION
↓
1.3.4
PERCEPTUAL
OBJECTS

(fig. 1.59). The frequency of occurrence of the impulses determines the further processing. This fundamental nature of neuronal processing determines processes on higher levels. The decision as to whether a stimulation leads to a conscious perception and as to the characteristics thereby felt may be traced back to statistical circumstances, instead of being based upon the simple, causal conveyance of information (Campenhausen 1993).

The creation of perceptual objects is founded upon decisions determined by probabilities in the neuronal network.

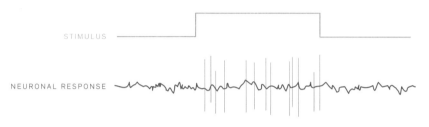

STIMULUS

NEURONAL RESPONSE

1.3
FUNDAMENTALS
OF PERCEPTION
↓
1.3.4
PERCEPTUAL
OBJECTS

97

FIGURE 1.59
Processing steered by probability along the neuronal level.
A stimulation is characterized by the frequency of occurrence of the
electrical pulses which it triggers in a nerve cell.
This example depicts the response of a cell which reacts to the stimulation.
Moreover, there are neurons which only spark when no stimulation
is present, as well as those whose reaction is restricted to special features
such as the employment or the ceasing of the influence.

Given that the relevance of perceptual objects is constantly monitored and updated, the perception can correlate well with the reality while not forfeiting its model character. In cases in which the sensory information does not suffice in order to properly judge a situation, erroneous reactions – popularly categorized as "human errors" – take place. Bringing about decisions is, however, the characteristic performance of systems steered by probability, even when there is an insufficiency of information. In the world of humans, as in the world of animals, an immediate action is often necessary, particularly in situations in which waiting to receive complete information could have fatal consequences. This applies, for example, to the flight in the face of natural enemies ("fight-or-flight response") or – quite similar – in crossing the street.

By some extremely quick reactions, however, the low probability of proper decisions is very clear. This is also justified by the minimized relevance of the perceptual object. Accordingly, in the testimony of witnesses pertaining to fleeting, sketchy observations, there are often great discrepancies. In describing an accident, for example, someone speaks of a blue car, while another saw a red car. In this case, the visual information was not sufficient, for it did not allow the color of the car to be recognized and stored in the memory. In the realm of the model construction determined by probability, an experience value was inserted for the color of the perceptual image. With a certain probability, the color is the right one, but not in another case. The ability of the perceptual system to base representations and decisions on simple, fragmentary data thus depends on *heuristic* approaches.

The cognitive development of perceptual objects encompasses the following areas of responsibility:

RECONSTRUCTION OF THE SKETCHY SIGNALS OF THE SENSORY ORGANS:
RECOGNITION OF PATTERNS

RECONSTRUCTION OF CONCEALED AREAS:
GESTALT FORMATION

CORRELATION OF PERCEIVED STIMULI TO OBJECTS:
GESTALT FORMATION

COMPENSATION OF FLUCTUATIONS OF THE ENVIRONMENTAL PARAMETERS:
ESTABLISHING CONSTANCY

DETERMINATION OF THE CONTEXT PARAMETERS,
SUCH AS SIZE, POSITION IN SPACE, RELATIVE MOVEMENT:
CONTEXT ANALYSIS

DETERMINATION AND RECONSTRUCTION OF THE MULTISENSORY PROPERTIES:
EVALUATION OF THE PERCEPTUAL EXPERIENCE

Perception is a dynamic process of the construction and verification of hypotheses in which the interpreting system organizes itself. In case of contradictions between data of the perception and data as a result of experiences *(imbalance)*, either the perceptual data are adjusted *(assimilation)* or the data of experience are modified *(accommodation)*. The high degree of efficiency of the perception is particularly evident in the rapid analysis of complex situations with known and unknown objects, as illustrated by figure 1.60. Only after extensive observation, however, is it possible to recognize details and to properly assess the objects with respect to one another.

98

1.3
FUNDAMENTALS
OF PERCEPTION
↓
1.3.4
PERCEPTUAL
OBJECTS

FIGURE 1.60
The unclear mixing of known and unknown objects in a daily situation –
in a typical children's room.

Accordingly, even the perception of products is a communicative process: the design "speaks to customers." The transmission of stimuli towards the construction of perceptual objects may thus be described on the basis of the model of communication depicted in figure 1.61.

**PERCEPTION IS A PROCESS
OF COMMUNICATION: STIMULI ARE PROCESSED
AND EVALUATED WITH RESPECT
TO THE INFORMATION SIGNIFICANT TO HUMANS.**

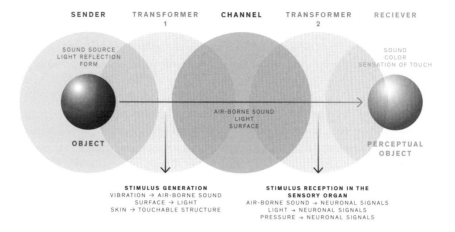

SOUND SOURCE
LIGHT REFLECTION
FORM

SOUND
COLOR
SENSATION OF TOUCH

AIR-BORNE SOUND
LIGHT
SURFACE

OBJECT

PERCEPTUAL
OBJECT

STIMULUS GENERATION
VIBRATION → AIR-BORNE SOUND
SURFACE → LIGHT
SKIN → TOUCHABLE STRUCTURE

**STIMULUS RECEPTION IN THE
SENSORY ORGAN**
AIR-BORNE SOUND → NEURONAL SIGNALS
LIGHT → NEURONAL SIGNALS
PRESSURE → NEURONAL SIGNALS

FIGURE 1.61
**Description of the transduction of stimuli for the
purpose of building perceptual objects,
utilizing a model of the theory of communications.**

1.3
FUNDAMENTALS
OF PERCEPTION
↓
1.3.4
PERCEPTUAL
OBJECTS

99

As a transmitter, a physical object communicates some of its characteristics properties, such as light reflection and form. These properties are converted into conveyable impulses via transformer 1, and they are in turn transmitted both as light and tactile, mechanical quantities to the sensory organs by virtue of a channel. The channel contains the media in which the transmission takes place – in the given example, these media are the surrounding air and the areas of the skin involved in touching. The sensory organs constitute transformer 2, and this carries out the implementation of the impulses into the data format of the perceptual system. As described above, perceptual objects are created there as models of the environment, and these appear in the consciousness as its representation. In figure 1.62, the paths of conveyance for sound, light, and tactile pressure stimuli are explicitly indicated.

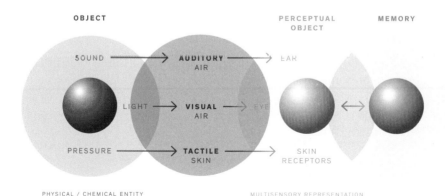

OBJECT

PERCEPTUAL
OBJECT

MEMORY

SOUND → AUDITORY
AIR
→ EAR

LIGHT → VISUAL
AIR
→ EYE

PRESSURE → TACTILE
SKIN
→ SKIN
RECEPTORS

PHYSICAL / CHEMICAL ENTITY

MULTISENSORY REPRESENTATION

FIGURE 1.62
**An application of the model of communication
from figure 1.61, in describing the construction of
multisensory perceptual objects.**

The properties of the perceptual object are stored in the memory and can support the perception of the underlying physical object in the future. In order to achieve the interaction of perception and memory contents necessary to construct perceptual objects, a common functional unit is required to serve as a surface upon which each of the two images is projected. This unit is evidently built in the realm of the primary sensory fields of the cerebral cortex. As indicated in Chapter 1.3.1, the sensory stimuli create patterns of a spatial nature, correlating to the retina in the case of a visual matter and, on the other hand, with spectral properties in the case of auditory matters. Such patterns are even formed during the construction of memory images. These images are not filed in the sense of pixel graphics, for that would be much too ineffective, considering the large volume of data to be stored. Nevertheless, it is likely that commands for the creation of these patterns are indeed stored within the cerebral cortex. Damasio refers to these commands as *dispositional representations* (Damasio 2006). Figure 1.63 illustrates this principle.

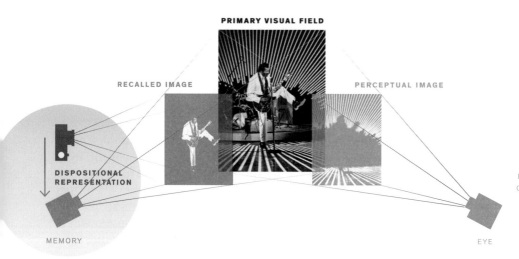

PRIMARY VISUAL FIELD

RECALLED IMAGE

PERCEPTUAL IMAGE

DISPOSITIONAL
REPRESENTATION

MEMORY

EYE

100

1.3
FUNDAMENTALS
OF PERCEPTION
↓
1.3.4
PERCEPTUAL
OBJECTS

FIGURE 1.63
**Projector model of the double function of the sensory fields
along the cerebral cortex as a screen for perceptual as well as memory images,
using the example of the processing of visual information.**

With the assistance of the commands mentioned, a memory image can be created. Its pattern presents, in simplified form, the pattern which was projected onto the cerebral cortex during the original act of perception. It also serves as a schema (concept) for the recognition of similar objects. This is the basis of the following assumption:

**THE PRIMARY SENSORY FIELDS
OF THE CEREBRAL CORTEX REPRESENT
THE LOCATION IN WHICH THE
MOMENTARY PERCEPTUAL IMAGES AND
THE MEMORIZED PATTERNS ARE COMPARED
WITH ONE ANOTHER, ACTUALIZED, AND
MADE MORE COMPLETE.**

The construction of sensible perceptual objects requires that the sensory stimuli of an object are summarized and clearly distinguished from those of other objects. One also speaks of processes of *integration* (consolidation) and *segregation* (separation). Integration encompasses the consolidation of similar structures to patterns. Such a *grouping* can refer to the affiliation to an identical object, or it can summarily aggregate a group of similar objects – both aspects contribute to the interpretation of the environment and increase the efficiency of the perception. Section 1.3.8 addresses the deductions of the laws of *Gestalt formation* of perceptual objects within the realm of *Gestalt psychology.*

1.3
FUNDAMENTALS
OF PERCEPTION
↓
1.3.4
PERCEPTUAL
OBJECTS

101

FIGURE 1.64
An example of the
grouping of visual information.

The performance capability of processes involving the integration of perceptual contents can be measured by virtue of the following illustrations. Initially, the silhouette illustrated in figure 1.64 demonstrates that it is possible to identify objects, even if the available information is reduced to a minimum. Form analogies serve as the basis of the recognition. From the outset, however, it is necessary to connect structures belonging together and to separate them, at the same time, from other structures. Thus, in accordance with the *analogy of forms,* both of the oval forms depicted in figure 1.64 are regarded as belonging together, while simultaneously being perceived as being separated from the lines. The lines connect with one another by virtue of the analogy relationship between rhythmic forms and a linear structure, which is perceived as being a unit. Via the principle of the construction of the *good form* [der guten Gestalt], discussed further below, the round forms as well as the lines are intuitively interpreted as consistent forms which (apparently) cut across one another without interruption. The individual, rounded form, below on the left side, however, can be allocated only after being identified as a bird in flight. This occurs via a *concrete association (iconic connection),* which correlates the herein illustrated form with a known living being – in this case, a bird – and thus initially establishing the relationship to the aforementioned round forms. In the overall nexus, the *context,* these are recognized as birds sitting on telegraph wires. The complete recognition of the entire situation, however, requires from the very outset a certain degree of visual experience with respect to telegraph wires, which – at least in Germany – is not so self-evident as it was some forty years ago.

FIGURE 1.65
The formation and the grouping of objects are also possible
when only sketchy information is available –
e. g., with an increasing degree of abstraction.

In chapters 2.2 and 2.3, the significance of analogy relationships and associations regarding the construction of multisensory perceptual objects will be discussed in greater detail.

Figure 1.65 demonstrates that a situation can be identified even after diverse adaptations or processing techniques are undertaken with respect to the image, although the number and structure of the image elements are increasingly reduced. In addition to the recognition of silhouettes, the interpretation of the spatial position of individual objects with respect to one another is particularly important. The latter is, for the purpose of orientation within a complex environment such as the city, or also within a forest, of a life-essential significance. In a real situation, the spatial perception assists in determining one's own position as well as the direction and the distance of objects in the vicinity. In the case of one-eyed *(monocular)* vision, the dimensional proportions of objects as well as their structures with respect to perspectives partially replace the spatially oriented vision, which is achieved with two eyes *(binocular)*. The diagonally running lines of the overhead wiring in the situation depicted span a sort of coordinate system which provides for spatial orderliness. That also applies to the walls of the railroad line to the left as well as to the line of houses in the background to the right. The capability of the perceptual system to properly identify even string-like patterns and film negatives is truly astounding. Nevertheless, it is indispensable in the course of daily life, for the orientation must be guaranteed at dawn and dusk, in the midst of diverse types of illumination, related to changing meteorological conditions, and with respect to the alteration of object surfaces – for example, as a result of ice, snow, or rain.

102

1.3
FUNDAMENTALS
OF PERCEPTION
↓
1.3.4
PERCEPTUAL
OBJECTS

PROCESSES OF PERCEPTUAL INTEGRATION
HAVE TO INITIALLY DETERMINE THE NUMBER AND
SPATIAL ALLOCATION OF THE OBJECTS.
SUBSEQUENTLY, IT IS NECESSARY TO
ASSOCIATIVELY IDENTIFY THE OBJECTS AND TO
DECODE POSSIBLE MEANINGS.

In the example indicated, an urban road environment has to be identified. For that purpose, known objects like houses, pavement, and cars need to be recognized by means of information stored in memory. Additionally, in this case, knowledge as to the significance of traffic signs and signal lights – and of their colors – is of great importance. In order to evaluate sounds related to that scene, the number of auditory objects which are independent of one another must similarly be determined. Their position within a given space can be estimated by virtue of spatial hearing. The sound objects also have to be identified and analyzed with respect to their meaning. As a rule, the result of the object recognition is the identification of the source; for example, of a person speaking. In this case, great importance is given to the contents of the language, which perhaps contain a warning with respect to traffic in the vicinity of a construction site. Following the successful grouping, the auditory perception contains individually, associatively, and semantically examined objects which are spatially allocated. Such an allocation is referred to as *soundscape*.

1.3
FUNDAMENTALS
OF PERCEPTION
↓
1.3.4
PERCEPTUAL
OBJECTS

103

FIGURE 1.66
The complexity of the operational elements demands
the careful coordination of visual, tactile, and auditory properties with
respect to grouping the objects to distinct perceptual objects.

Figure 1.66 illustrates an extracted portion of the complex environment surrounding the driver of an automobile, with various operational elements and indicating instruments as well as surfaces which are also designed with regard to the tactile perception. In order to achieve the optimal design, an exact analysis of the perceivable properties is necessary. After the information of each sensory channel has been evaluated, relationships between them have to be discovered, in order to establish the multisensory perceptual objects necessary to describing the outer world. This will be discussed further in part 2.

FOR MULTISENSORY DESIGNING, IT IS IMPORTANT TO ANALYZE THE PERCEPTION CAUSED BY AN OBJECT WITHIN EACH AND EVERY SENSORY MODALITY.

The first step must thus involve determining the number of individual perceptual objects. This is possible if one exactly comprehends the process of Gestalt formation as involving the integration, the grouping, and the segregation in individual cases. Moreover, it is sensible to first consider the intended object to be split into partial objects within each modality. The optimal number of the thus constructed partial objects can not generally be determined for all tasks of designing and building. On the other hand, however, the feedback pertaining to one function of such a partial object for each sensory channel is quite sensible. Thus, for example, only one sound shall be involved in the execution of the respective function. However, if a single operation is accompanied by multiple sounds, all being clearly distinguishable from one another, the impression of a non-robust or of an erroneous behavior of the system arises. Chapters 2.2 and 3.6 shall examine the disturbing effects which are based upon the unsuccessful accommodation of the number of perceptual objects – such as additionally disturbing signals, echoes, or effects of random behavior of construction parts.

104

1.3
FUNDAMENTALS
OF PERCEPTION
↓
1.3.4
PERCEPTUAL
OBJECTS

CONSTANCY

The determination of the identity of objects and living beings also belongs to the process of perception. An object must be capable of being recognized even if it is partially concealed or differently illuminated, if its position in the given space changes, if it is near or distant, or if it is moving. Persons can be differently dressed, can move themselves in a multifaceted manner, and can make use of various forms of gesturing or mimicry. Additionally, the voice can have a different timbre – it exhibits changes influenced by age, health condition, and psychological state. In order to classify the object properties independently of the boundary or marginal conditions of the perception, the data momentarily received by the sensory organs are accordingly modified by specific corrections. As a result, the best possible constancy of the perceptual contents, which comprises the features of perceptual objects, is achieved.

VISUAL FORM CONSTANCY ASSURES THAT AN OBJECT MAINTAINS ITS SHAPE, EVEN WHEN IT IS PARTIALLY CONCEALED, DIFFERENTLY ILLUMINATED, OR OBSERVED BY PERSONS HAVING DIFFERING ANGLES OF VIEWING AND VARYING DISTANCES.

The form constancy yields a constancy of the size of objects as well as of the surrounding space. Changing perspectives, positions, and movements accordingly do not lead to – in known situations – a change with respect to the perceived geometry of objects. Constancy of form and size also apply to the tactile and auditory sensory modalities. Constancy phenomena in the realm of hearing, for example, enable blind persons to orient themselves within rooms – astounding non-blind persons whose spatial hearing capability is considerably less developed.

THE AUDITORY ANALOGY TO COLOR CONSTANCY IS THE CONSTANCY OF THE TIMBRE.

The surface of an object is visually identified via an analysis of the light being reflected. For this purpose, the coloring of the light reflected by the surface area of the object must be known in order to avoid erroneous interpretations which may arise as a result of an apparently altered color of the surface area. By virtue of the analysis of all perceived colors in a given situation, however, the visual system is in many cases capable of identifying the coloring of the surrounding light – which lands upon the surfaces of the objects and is reflected by them – and it is also able to appropriately correct the perception. In this fashion, a subjective color constancy is created. A white surface area thus appears white, even when the surrounding light exhibits varying colors. Only after photographing a differently illuminated object, the differences become obvious: in spite of the different color of illumination, within the real ambience the vehicle presented in figure 1.67 is regarded as white. The color photograph reveals the color variance, if no white balance was carried out prior to the act of photographing. The perceived color now demonstrates great divergences, according to whether the illumination was made with daylight, a light bulb, or filtered light. Even the natural daylight itself can exhibit different colorations, such as the afterglow observed in the red evening sky.

1.3
FUNDAMENTALS
OF PERCEPTION
↓
1.3.4
PERCEPTUAL
OBJECTS

105

FIGURE 1.67
Color constancy in visual perception.
Despite the different colors of the illumination, the vehicle is
viewed as being white in reality. Only color photographs
reveal the color divergence.

Left: illumination with daylight.
Middle: illumination via a light bulb.
Right: illumination by virtue of daylight which
shines through a yellow curtain.

If a source of sound is moved around the head of a listener, it maintains its timbre. Even if it involves a person moving himself around the listener and speaking in a constant, steady tone, the acoustic nuances of the voice are not observed. On the other hand, if the signal is recorded with a microphone in the auditory passage, changes in the tone become obvious, being influenced by frequency-dependent acoustic diffractions around the head and in the vicinity of the auricles. The cause of these spectral changes may be traced to the fact that the functions of the outer ears in transmitting the sound – from the source to the eardrums – can differ, varying according to the direction of the incidence of the sound. The deformation of the acoustic spectrum thus contains information as to the direction. This property is important for directional hearing, and it is evaluated in order to ultimately localize the source of the sound. Thus the spatially determined spectral deformation of the sound is perceived as a spatial property, but *not* as a change of timbre.

Effects of the auditory constancy can also lead to the identification of a speaker, even though his voice is altered by virtue of a cold, through the telephone, or by his presence in surroundings characterized by echo-like reverberations.

ATTENTION

106

1.3
FUNDAMENTALS
OF PERCEPTION
↓
1.3.4
PERCEPTUAL
OBJECTS

With the assistance of the capabilities of directional hearing, it is possible to recognize certain sounds in the environment and to drown out others. This is even possible when sounds very similar to one another are involved. Thereby, the ability to grant attention to a certain discussion, although one finds him or herself in the middle of a crowd of people engaged in various, vivified conversations, is particularly impressive. This phenomenon is described as the *Cocktail Party Effect*. It demands merely the ability of the sense of hearing to distinguish among the various directions of the acoustic incidences. Even such effects are supported by multisensory connections that have been the subject of intensive research for a number of years (Spence 2004; Lukas 2009; 2010).

As parts 2 and 3 shall demonstrate, it is thoroughly possible to focus the consciousness upon a certain strategy with regard to multisensory contents. The example of auditory-visual classifications chosen in chapter 3.2, figure 3.16, illustrates that test subjects in perceptual experiments usually follow the prescribed definition of tasks on an intuitive basis. Three diagrams serve the purpose of allocating visual structures to acoustic signals. In each of the three cases, the test subjects seek to make a judgment in the realm of the prescribed categories. If, for example, only a choice of objects with iconic content is given, the classification also follows associatively.

Time and again, systematically erroneous interpretations accordingly arise. In his day, the Gestalt psychologist Köhler had already mentioned this particular aspect (Köhler 1929). In this manner, as a general rule, the very definition of tasks in psychoacoustic experiments forces the participants to direct their concentration to individual parameters. Thus, cognitive evaluations are systematically excluded and appear to exert no influence upon the perception. If an acoustic experiment – which is initially carried out while excluding other senses – should lead to a certain judgment, this can indeed exhibit divergences during the simultaneous presentation of the visual or of the tactile data, and this would also be a result of the fact that a portion of the attention is now being directed to the particular stimuli. Consequently, the experiment then illustrates a connection existing between the sensory modalities, but this connection can exclusively be influenced by the division of the attention. Accordingly, unintended influences by virtue of effects concerning the attention must be deliberately excluded from the realm of perceptual experiments.

THE METHODOLOGY EMPLOYED IN PERCEPTUAL EXPERIMENTS STEERS THE CONCENTRATION OF THE TEST PERSONS IN A CERTAIN DIRECTION. THUS, THE EXPERIMENTAL CONCEPT STEADILY INFLUENCES THE RESULT.

1.3
FUNDAMENTALS
OF PERCEPTION
↓
1.3.4
PERCEPTUAL
OBJECTS

107

Generally speaking, the simultaneous, conscious processing of stimuli via various sensory channels inevitably leads to the necessity of dividing the attention with respect to different modalities. Indeed, this very aspect can give rise to divergences in perception, as compared to cases in which the signals are processed only through a single sensory channel – an *intersensory bias* occurs (Spence 2008a). This being the case, music listeners often close their eyes in concerts, for it allows them to follow the course of the music more effectively. The reverse can be true in the case of a dynamic flow of images in a music video, for example, in which the pictures are intended to steer the attention of the listeners away from monotonous tunes.

VISUAL
AFTEREFFECTS

Aftereffects cause sensations after sensory stimulation expires. Those phenomena can change the temporal properties of perceptual objects or may result in additional, sometimes disturbing ones. Given that aftereffects often show a specific cross-sensory connection, the following presents a brief description.

If one observes a brightly illuminated spot or a narrow source of light for a long time, and then closes one's eyes, the illuminated area of the retina appears as a dark spot having a bright background. Thereby, colored light similarly leads to a colored afterimage which, nevertheless, exhibits the complementary color. A red source of light thus creates a green afterimage, yellow results in a violet afterimage, orange results in a blue afterimage – and vice versa. Should one, in the course of an experiment, mix light of the original color with the light of its complementary color – that means, as an *additive color mixture*, because the intensity of the stimulation is increased – a white light is the result. Indeed, owing to this daily experience, the complementary context of the color tones is known. On a color scale, complementary tones can be seen as those color pairs which exhibit, throughout all possible combinations, the greatest difference in the color tone. The observed aftereffect may also be understood as the temporary exhaustion of the sensory cells along the retina: receptors which are subjected to light of higher intensity, and/or to extended periods of exposure under such influence, require a number of seconds in order to regain the original degree of sensitivity.

Visual aftereffects are also related to movement. When observing the landscape from within a moving automobile, for example, an inverse effect occurs upon stopping: the stationary scenery may now appear to move forward. As a result, the final position of steadily moving objects which suddenly and surprisingly disappear is generally underestimated, meaning that they appear to be extrapolated, in comparison to the actual final position in the direction of movement. In this regard, one speaks of a *representational momentum (RM or RepMo)* – it can be evaluated by the perceptual system as an indication with respect to future developments. A positional aftereffect arises, on the other hand, when initially a resting object and subsequently a moving object are separately perceived, truly distinct from one another. The position of the resting object then appears to be shifted *against* the direction of movement *(displacement aftereffect, DAE)*.

AUDITORY
AFTEREFFECTS

Acoustic influences upon the ear already impact upon its sensitivity, at least temporarily. Following the influence of the sound levels which pose no threat of damage to the ear, the perceptual threshold is, nevertheless, increased in the short term. Accordingly, weak signals can be momentarily obscured. Such a post-masking can exist for up to approximately 200 ms subsequent to the deactivation of the masking sound (Zwicker 1999).

108

1.3
FUNDAMENTALS
OF PERCEPTION
↓
1.3.4
PERCEPTUAL
OBJECTS

Should a sound of a high level meet the ear for an extended period of time, an impairment of the auditory sensitivity can occur, and this could indeed be present for a relatively long period of time. After visiting a rock concert or a discotheque, for example, this effect can persist for several hours. The ability to hear ultimately normalizes itself, nevertheless, if the auditory sense has sufficient time in order to regenerate, while experiencing relatively minimal acoustic influences. The reversible shifting of the threshold of hearing is referred to as *temporary threshold shift* (TTS).

In the case of an extended influence during exposure to high sound levels, the hearing cells will be damaged on a long-term basis, for an irreparably permanent shifting of the hearing threshold takes place *(permanent threshold shift, PTS)*. This occurs as a result of the destruction of the sensory cells in the frequency ranges upon which the damaging sound exerts its influence. The resulting, irreversible hardness of hearing ultimately leads to a significant reduction of speech comprehension and accordingly diminishes the quality of life and the security of those persons affected – for example, in road traffic.

A known aftereffect in perceptual psychology is the influencing of dynamic parameters by sounds from previous auditory events. If a sound becomes increasingly muted, a second, subsequently perceived, constant sound yields the impression of an increasing sound level. This effect also applies in the reverse direction. Even the aforementioned *representational momentum* – the estimation of the further development of a movement – is present during the auditory perception of sources of sound which are being moved (Getzmann 2008).

TACTILE
AFTEREFFECTS

If an object is firmly grabbed by the hand, upon releasing the object and ending contact, a subsequent sensation can be felt for several seconds. The sensation arising in this manner corresponds to a virtual impression of the contact surface area. As the aftereffect is subsiding, the sensitivity of the affected sensory cells is reduced.

After touching a material with particularly good adhesive qualities, the after-sensation can feel somewhat "sticky" – giving rise to the impression that parts of the material stick to the fingers and, moreover, that these parts were removed from the surface of the object upon being released. Whereas such materials offer a particularly good grip contact and transmit this by virtue of the tactile perception, thus being ideal for utilization in the realm of operating elements, the release of the hand appears to result in an imprecise or an unpleasant sensation. In particular, the sensation felt upon releasing the material can be interpreted by the user as a deficiency in the robustness or solidity of the construction. Additionally, an intensive aftereffect following the conclusion of the hand contact can unintentionally grab the attention– occurring at a time in which the operational activity itself is already completed.

THE INFLUENCING OF VISUAL AND
AUDITORY AFTEREFFECTS

Visual and auditory aftereffects can mutually influence one another, at least when they are connected to perceptions of movement. Experiments conducted by Norimichi Kitagawa and Shigeru Ichihara accordingly indicate that a continual decrease in the size of a visual object, which is perceived as representing movement away from the observer, led test subjects to feel that a subsequently presented tone of a constant acoustic volume was increasing (Kitagawa 2002). A comparable, inverse aftereffect also occurred following the enlargement of the visual object – in this case, the tone was regarded as becoming softer. The influencing of visual aftereffects through alterations of an initially presented tone, however, has not been documented. In this case, there is a dominance of seeing, as compared to hearing. It has also been observed that high tones can increase the brightness of afterimages, whereas low tones cause them to loose their brightness (Zietz 1931; 1962). Aftereffects with respect to determining the position of static visual objects can also be caused by acoustic sources which are moving within the given space. Thus, it results in an apparent alteration of the visual position. This shifting, however, is not as considerable as it is in the case of the aforementioned positional aftereffect of a purely visual nature (Fischer 2006).

1.3
FUNDAMENTALS
OF PERCEPTION
↓
1.3.4
PERCEPTUAL
OBJECTS

109

SUBJECTIVE
OR OBJECTIVE?

A major problem within the scientific community always involved distinguishing the nomological reality surrounding people from the perceptual phenomena which it inspires. The greatest successes in research were thus regarded as being reached when it was possible to achieve this goal and to enable, at least within a limited area, a clear description of the reality. The problem of an *objective* description of the appearances has thus characterized the endeavors of science up until the present day. Even in technology, the description of the physical properties of a product, for example, initially received the primary focus, in contrast to the sensations which they cause among the customers.

If it concerns the marketable value of a product, on the other hand, the technical characteristics alone are incapable of providing meaningful criteria. Instead, the *subjective* significance to the customer is essential. In order to optimize the placing of a product in the marketplace, the phenomenology of the perceptual appearances is thus of critical importance. The same applies to the subjective impression of an artwork or the performance of music.

Even the development of psychophysics, particularly within the domain of psychoacoustics, was significantly influenced by a self-determined "compulsion of objectification." Objectivity described the independence of a finding from the perception of the individual. If the perception of the individual is itself the subject of the observation, however, at least a portion of the phenomena is only available to this individual who is sensing the perceptual qualities *(qualia)*. In the early days of natural scientific research involving perception, special subjective appearances such as the genuine synesthesia were appropriately included in the overall context, for example, by Hermann von Helmholtz (1910), Gustav Theodor Fechner (1860), the founder of psychophysics, Ernst Mach (1903), and others.

The further development, nonetheless, was increasingly marked by approaches limiting the observation to generally prevalent phenomena, which are verifiable to the maximum extent possible by virtue of physiological examinations – independent of the comments of the perceiving persons. This encompasses a paradigm which advances the principle of the similarity of the function of biologically comparable brain structures. This precept led to the increased reduction of the research down to the lowest levels of neuronal pathways, along which clearly determined, "firmly interconnected" properties are measurable. The strength of the auditory perception can, for example, be traced to the conveyance capabilities of the outer, middle, and inner ear, the spectral perception of structural circumstances of the *basilar membrane,* and fundamental neuronal properties (e. g., *tuning curves),* the localization of elementary interconnections of the left and right paths of hearing.

Owing to the approaches toward a comprehensive description of perception, for example, as sought by Fechner, inspired by a "doctrine of the relationship between body and soul ..." (Fechner 1867), a specialized discipline has been established, focusing its attention on physiologically fixed aspects,

110

1.3
FUNDAMENTALS
OF PERCEPTION
↓
1.3.5
SUBJECTIVE
OR OBJECTIVE

1.3
FUNDAMENTALS
OF PERCEPTION
↓
1.3.5
SUBJECTIVE
OR OBJECTIVE

111

FIGURE 1.68
Introspection: visual-synesthetic image
stimulated by the ringing bell of a clock on the wall.
According to Heinrich Hein (Anschütz 1927c).

while simultaneously excluding the realm of the sensory connections and the subjective perceptual qualities. In a certain sense, psychophysics have been transformed into "physio-physics," undoubtedly yielding, on the one hand, valuable findings as to the elementary processing of information by humans, but not yet satisfying the demand of a comprehensive description of perception. This development was supported by the mindset represented by *behaviorism,* which recognizes – in the psychological description – only phenomena which are measurable as quantities of stimulation external to the body, or descriptions of the behavior being triggered, as valid. *Introspections,* namely descriptions of internal conditions, images, feelings, etc., were thus, as phenomena of subjective nature, not taken into consideration in scientific circles (fig. 1.68).

ALL CIRCUMSTANCES OF DAILY LIFE
ARE CLOSELY RELATED TO INTRINSIC IMAGES,
CONCEPTIONS, AND ASSOCIATIONS.
THE INTROSPECTIVE ANALYSIS OF INTERNAL
IMAGES MUST THEREFORE BE AN
ELEMENTARY COMPONENT OF RESEARCH
IN THE REALM OF PERCEPTION.

For representatives of "classical" psychophysics, a genuine synesthetic connection of the sensory perceptions does not come into consideration, owing to the aforementioned reasons, for it contradicts the paradigm of the strict separation of the sensory perceptions. In this respect, Ernst Terhard regards the meaning of the term *acoustic color* [Klangfarbe] as being "naturally only metaphoric" (Terhard 1998, 372). Indeed, even a customer's decision is a result of individual perception. Thus, for several years now some scientists have criticized the limitation of perceptual research on strictly psychophysical approaches (e. g., Blauert 2009).

112

1.3
FUNDAMENTALS
OF PERCEPTION
↓
1.3.5
SUBJECTIVE
OR OBJECTIVE

A similar conflict between the view regarding objective measurable parameters of cognitive processes on the one hand and the consideration of the subjective content of perception on the other arises with the application of advanced technology pertaining to the analysis of brain activity. Brain imaging technologies based on various methods (MRI, EEG, PET, etc.) are capable of precisely showing locations of momentary neuronal activity and/or sequences of activation. Neuroscientists use this methodology in a meaningful manner to objectively evaluate the processes behind them and to understand cognitive strategies. The subjective content of perception, like the individual formation of perceptual objects, cannot be derived from a neuronal pattern. Hypotheses combining both the subjective and objective spheres are quite fragmentary; for example, it cannot be verified with absolute certainty whether the intensity of pain is correlated to the largeness of an activated brain area.

A holistic description of perception is only possible if the individual, subjective aspects are drawn into consideration and the initially not comprehensible phenomena are included.

QUALIA

The consciously experienced result of processes of perception, memory, and imagination is only accessible to those actually sensing these phenomena. Although the internal images arising can be described or sketched, they are constantly reserved for the perceiving subject. Nevertheless, for the perception and the evaluation of objects – and thus of products as well – these qualities are of considerable importance.

THE SUBJECTIVE QUALITIES OF
PERCEPTION – QUALIA – REPRESENT
THE INDIVIDUALLY EXPERIENCED
CONTENTS OF MENTAL CONDITIONS,
NAMELY THE QUALITATIVE
ASPECTS OF CONSCIOUSNESS.

1.3
FUNDAMENTALS
OF PERCEPTION
↓

1.3.5
SUBJECTIVE
OR OBJECTIVE
↓

1.3.6
QUALIA

113

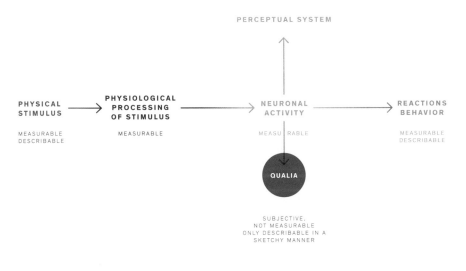

FIGURE 1.69
A schema explaining the perceptual
qualities – qualia.

For that which is experienced as a result of a particular stimulus, the description *perceptual event* is similarly employed – in contrast to the physical or chemical event causing the stimulation. The properties of a perceptual event as perceived determine its qualities, the qualia. Thus, as an example, changes within just a few properties can considerably influence the perceived quality of sound, as indicated by the example of thirty-eight small ventilators. ● In Japan, the term *kansei quality* is used with view on the perception of product features (Yanagisawa 2007).

A perceptual quality in the case of visual perception is, for example: "How does it feel seeing red?" This sensation is reserved for the respective individual. Accordingly, it is difficult for science to deal with such phenomena which defy an objective observation and are unable to be evaluated with respect to commonalities. As a result, the observation of subjective phenomena was excluded from psychological research. In the realm of *behaviorism,* only that which was regarded as scientifically verifiable was considered valid, being apparently objectifiable on the basis of observable, reproducible articulations of the behavior of test subjects. The analysis of human perception was thus reduced to the horizon of findings arising out of the behavioral research pertaining to animals. Behaviorism must therefore respond to the criticism that it pays the heavy price of excluding essential elements of daily life, even though its methods are exact. To the contrary, scientific thinking must primarily orient itself with respect to the phenomena, although they are of a subjective nature and thus virtually incapable of being assessed by a traditional methodology. Indeed, the retreat towards an established, although limited methodology is in this case certainly not future-oriented. Just within the past approximately twenty years, the preoccupation with the subjective qualities of perception has regained scientific acceptance.

REMARK: THE TERM QUALITY
IS HEREIN USED IN ITS
ORIGINAL MEANING, WHICH REFERS
TO "HOW SOMETHING IS."
TECHNICAL QUALITY MANAGEMENT,
HOWEVER, OFTEN INTERMIXES
IT WITH QUANTITATIVE ASPECTS;
E.G., THE GOODNESS OF PROPERTIES.

114

1.3
FUNDAMENTALS
OF PERCEPTION
↓
1.3.6
QUALIA

Figure 1.69 illustrates this context. Today, it is a recognized paradigm that every subjective appearance is completely correlated with a specific neuronal activity or is evoked by such. Quite to the contrary, in medieval *metaphysics,* one presumed a clear separation between the material – in this case being the body and its activities – and the human spirit. The physical or chemical stimuli influencing the sensory organs are measurable, similar to the physiological reactions and neuronal activities thus triggered. Accordingly, the reaction of a body can be objectively observed and exactly described. Only the subjectively experienced quality remains – at least for the present time – inaccessible with respect to an exact scientific analysis. In this regard, the recently initiated "objective pain research" is to be viewed skeptically. The methodology currently available is incapable of describing the subjective quality and the intensity of the pain. With regard to the neuronal activity related to the pain, however, it is a different matter – the correlation between subjective experiences and measurable brain activity is, nevertheless, not clear.

SOME EXAMPLES
PERTAINING
TO THE VIEWING OF COLORS
SHALL ILLUSTRATE
THE EPISTEMOLOGICAL
OBSCURITIES:

1.3
FUNDAMENTALS
OF PERCEPTION
↓
1.3.6
QUALIA

115

In contrast to people, some insects are capable of recognizing ultraviolet light. Assuming that these insects do have a color perception which is more or less comparable to that of humans – something that is in and of itself not verifiable – the prospect does give rise to one question in particular: Which color would correspond to the perception of ultraviolet light? Would it involve a color tone which is not known to us, one being unimaginable for us, or is the known color scale which ranges from violet to red, as perceived by our eyes, simply applied to another frequency area which thus encompasses the frequencies of the ultraviolet light?

It is similarly difficult to answer the question as to whether every person perceives the same color – or whether there could be differences in perception. Actually, the question is *not* concerned with whether every person can perceive the same frequencies, for example, which we designate as red, green, and blue, among others. It exclusively involves the sensation that is caused by a particular light impulse. Thus, in the realm of a thought experiment, one could presume that a light of the wavelength 460 nm, which we regard as *blue,* could be perceived by another person as green and even by a further person as red, as indicated in figure 1.70. It would accordingly be impossible to notice this fact externally, as long as every individual characterizes the sensation which is correlated to the stimulation as being *blue,* having learned to follow this convention already in his or her childhood. The scientific preoccupation with the subjective qualities undoubtedly contains some special problems – but this fact does indeed serve to increase its attractiveness.

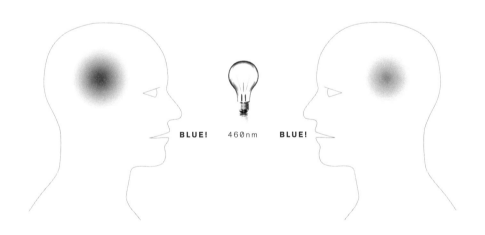

FIGURE 1.70
Qualia problem: from outside, it is not possible to
determine the individual perceptual qualities which are actually available.
Even linguistic articulations are of no further assistance,
for they are based upon the established conventions for describing objects.

The light bulb depicted here was deliberately not colored blue,
for colors do not exist in the physical world. A wavelength of 460 nm,
however, does give rise to a perceptual quality which –
according to conventions learned – can be described with the word "blue."

Subjective sensory qualities allow themselves to be verbally described only in an approximate manner. However, within the visual modality, there is the possibility of graphically presenting images of visual perception. Figure 1.71 provides an example of the visualization of a synesthetic image of perception stimulated by an olfactory impulse. Anyone who has ever attempted to draw his dream image on paper, or even with a computer drawing program, will confirm that the aforementioned example could only result in an approximate depiction. For the external observer of such graphics, it is also difficult to estimate the proportion of conceptual contributions and creative embellishments. As a matter of principle, a classification of graphic elements with respect to different strategies of multisensory connections is, however, theoretically possible (Haverkamp 2003b). In spite of the problems already mentioned, such visualizations are thus appropriate for supporting the discussion pertaining to demonstrating multisensory perceptual phenomena. Accordingly, this book shall make considerable use of such possibilities.

For a researcher interested in exact and generally applicable facts, it is not easy to accept the strongly individual distribution of subjective phenomena of the perception. In the meantime, however, psychological research confirms that which is already a permanent component of everyday life.

In a similar manner, the elements of dreams vary from person to person. Some dream of smells and even feel tactile sensations or hear sounds – for others, this is completely foreign. If one asks a randomly chosen group of people as to whether dreams are connected to colors, one encounters, generally speaking, three different groups of people: for some, colors in dreams are quite self-evident; others are just as certain that they see no colors in their dreams; whereas the third group claims not to know (!). Dream images without color are apparently accepted without further ado, and seeing in color does not appear to be an indispensable component of dreams. Evidently, sensory qualities even arise when only a small part of the object properties is evaluated.

The phenomenon of *blind sight* illustrates that certain steps of signal processing can continue to be active, even without a conscious perception. Amidst the dysfunction of primary cortical fields of visual processing, it is, parallel to the loss of the direct perception, no longer possible to see images of perception. In case of some persons suffering from this damage, however, it was possible for them to correctly point to the direction of light, although they claimed not to have seen it (Damasio 2006, 99).

In this context, it is important to realize that all perceived or memorized qualia are fundamentally sensory-specific – although the perceptual system is aimed at generating multisensory perceptual objects. Therefore, even the properties of memorized or conceived images can be clearly correlated to the respective sensory channels. As a general rule, the same applies to dreams. Furthermore, even in the case of reports of genuine synesthetic perception, consistent with chapter 2.5, the senses participating in the secondary sensation are always quite precisely indicated. Approaches in thinking which imply that synesthetic phenomena can be traced to a *mixture* of the senses or to *unclear* boundaries between the modalities are not supported by phenomenological findings. Moreover, the high specificity of such phenomena tends to speak for the participation of primary sensory fields of the cerebral cortex in the creation of subjective sensory qualities.

116

1.3
FUNDAMENTALS
OF PERCEPTION
↓
1.3.6
QUALIA

1.3
FUNDAMENTALS
OF PERCEPTION
↓
1.3.6
QUALIA

117

FIGURE 1.71
The smell of ammonium chloride and perfume.
A student's work from a class of Walter Behm in the 1920s
(Anschütz 1931).

A characteristic property of the qualia is the fact that they can constantly be spatially projected. Thus, the color of an object does not exist in the physical reality, for it is initially created in the perceptual system, namely in the brain. By virtue of the cognitive evaluation of the visual-spatial information, it is then possible to project the determined color tone back onto the place of the origin of the stimulus. As a result, this leads to an impression of an object being available in the given space, having a certain color tone – whose properties are directly recognizable – and being in and of itself spatially extended. As a further matter of fact, the spectral, temporal, and spatial properties of objects are initially analyzed on a separate basis. Thereby, a sensory quality is allocated to every property. This is the foundation of the synthesizing of a perceptual object. With the assistance of spatial information, this model of perception will then be projected back onto the location where the original stimulus presumably was generated. For this reason, it is at first not trivial to realize that we are, by virtue of perception, constantly confronted with perceptual objects as models of the reality, but not directly with the physical objects behind them.

QUALITIES OF PERCEPTION APPEAR CONSTANTLY IN A PROJECTED FORM.

118

1.3
FUNDAMENTALS
OF PERCEPTION
↓
1.3.6
QUALIA

If pain is stimulated in a finger, a perceptual process is released within the head. The projection back onto the finger serves the purpose of allowing one to consequently draw a conclusion from the situation, for example, removing the finger promptly from a hot stovetop. Generally speaking, the projection is so precise that it is not conspicuously evident in the course of the everyday routine – and the vase on the windowsill, for example, *is* simply blue. However, following the amputation of extremities, the projection becomes quite conspicuous, when the sensation of pain continues to be projected back onto the – now missing – extremity *(phantom limb pain)*. Even within artificial environments, it is clear that the projection arises as a "trick" of the perceptual system, and not simply as an inevitable implication of the physical properties of objects. Accordingly, in hearing a spatially confined source of sound, the location of the acoustic origin of the sound wave in most cases is identical with the auditory localized place – in consideration of the localization blur. Only following a stereophonic rendition, it becomes obvious that the perceived location usually diverges from the place of acoustic origin – the loudspeakers.

As a matter of principle, there is generally no difference between projections into the body and those toward the outer environment. During a stereophonic transmission – without considering the particular properties of the ears involved – and the subsequent listening via headphones, all acoustic events are projected into the head. Only in the course of an exactly aurally compensated transmission, the projection of the transmission actually corresponds to the places of the acoustic origin during the recording.

Principal differences of experience pertaining to perceptual phenomena also exist with respect to the intensity of the sensation or in the perceived *contact with reality.* This applies to dreams as well as to multisensory connections and particularly to genuine synesthesia. Here, a relationship with regard to the place of projection appears to exist: if synesthetic phenomena, like visual shapes induced by music, are projected towards the outer environment, they can be less clearly distinguished from those objects truly existing and situated there. Owing to the fact that the most divergent phenomena of perception can more or less be sensed as being real, a functionally overarching entity of the brain seems to exist which evaluates the contents of truth, i. e. the proximity of reality, of events which occur in consciousness. As a result, a dream can give rise to the impression of something dreamed *or* of a real process. Even conceptions can be confused with or mistaken for hallucinations (Siegel 1992). The boundaries apparently flow fluently into one another.

This touches on the question of whether sensory impressions – which are transmitted via the intermodal connection as described in part 2 – can be directly experienced. These could appear as an abstract idea or concept, or they can also suggest a real quality – such as in the case of an actual stimulation. Whether this gives rise to a qualitative difference, or simply a quantitative diversity along a "scale of the perceived proximity of reality," that is something that can not be answered on an ad hoc basis and must be reserved as the subject of future research.

1.3
FUNDAMENTALS
OF PERCEPTION
↓
1.3.6
QUALIA

119

GROUPING

As already indicated in Chapter 1.3.4, a primary duty of the perceptual system consists of correlating the stimuli received by the sensory organs to the respective perceptual objects, constructing a model of the objects of the world as precisely as possible. By virtue of the coordinated summarizing and separation of the properties of the object, a structured perception of the world arises, enabling purposeful actions and responses. However, even one's own body, which is also perceived by the sensory organs, belongs to the environment which envelops the perceiving subject. Therefore, in processing stimuli as sensory input, it is essential to separate the outer environment from one's own body. Figure 1.72 provides an example offered by Ernst Mach with respect to the perspective conveyed by one eye (Mach 1903). With this example, it is clear that the impression of the momentary perspective is initially not appropriate for navigating through the room. Perception must abstract from the relationship pertaining to the subject, and it must present the surrounding vicinity in an apparently objective manner, detached from the observer. In the depicted example, only the nose and the hands are directly recognizable as body parts. Arms and legs have to be attributed to the body, even though they are covered by clothing. An additional task is clearly distinguishing the body from the armchair in which it is resting. Additionally, the proportions must be intuitively corrected: hands and feet are in reality considerably larger than the nose, and the size of the room usually does not diminish with distance, even though this is suggested by the perspective. Additionally, the landscape in front of the window has considerably greater dimensions than the room, which in reality, in turn, is larger than the person sitting inside of it.

120

1.3
FUNDAMENTALS
OF PERCEPTION
↓
1.3.7
GROUPING

PERCEPTION MUST BE ABLE
TO ABSTRACT FROM LIMITED
SENSORY EXPERIENCE.
IN PERCEPTUAL SYSTEMS,
ERRORS ARE CORRECTED AND
GAPS ARE FILLED IN.

Perceptual processes achieve a comprehensive separation of one's own body from the environment immediately surrounding it. This is transformed into a coordinate system which appears as objective, being regarded as being free of subjective qualities. As an observer moves within a room, the image of the retina is moving as well, indeed, with all of the depicted elements of the given space. The observer senses, nevertheless, a movement of the body within the stationary room – which he also directly views as such. As a result of complex processing steps, a model of the reality is constructed, and this is in and of itself – at least in commonly experienced situations – coherent and characterized by clear structures and by simplicity. Accordingly, our image of the reality which surrounds us is considerably more coherent than that which is currently being conveyed to our perceptual system by our sensory organs.

1.3
FUNDAMENTALS
OF PERCEPTION
↓
1.3.7
GROUPING

121

Fig. 1.

FIGURE 1.72
The perspective of an eye which simultaneously contains
elements of the body and of the outer environment.
Drawing by Ernst Mach (Mach 1903).

122

1.3
FUNDAMENTALS
OF PERCEPTION
↓
1.3.7
GROUPING

FIGURE 1.73
An artistic retracing of the signal processing within
the visual system. Owing to the fact that the perceptual system is
designed to optimize the incomplete retinal image,
even the recognition of the depicted object is not difficult.
Claude Monet, Rouen Cathedral in the Evening, 1894.

By means of figure 1.73, this can easily be comprehended: out of the retinal image, and only as a result of the complex methods of the signal processing, a precise depiction arises which is indispensable to the recognition of objects and to orientation within the room. This is only possible by reason of the grouping of individual image points to larger, more sensible units. As already described, a process of grouping requires the consolidation *(integration)* of certain elements and simultaneously the separation *(segregation)* from other elements. Additionally, the recognized objects have to be completed. Already the recognition of both of the forms presented in figure 1.74 requires the comprehension of the structure by virtue of an analysis of the course of the lines and of supplements in the areas of the overlapping. The function of the parts can only be grasped in terms of the overall context. The context, however, can not be determined from analyzing elements whose connections to one another are unknown. Therefore, comprehension of the structure must be based on a recursive process which oscillates in a cyclical manner between the analysis of individual elements and of their hypothetical connection to one another. The paradox, according to which the entirety can not exist without reference to its elements, although it is just as impossible to sensibly correlate an individual element without reference to the entirety, may be resolved only in this manner. The perceived image is then the result of a process repeated in the aforementioned cyclical fashion, moving step by step towards a conclusive result.

1.3
FUNDAMENTALS
OF PERCEPTION
↓
1.3.7
GROUPING

123

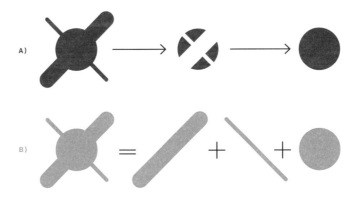

FIGURE 1.74
Grouping requires (A) the sensible consolidation (integration)
of individual elements as well as (B) the separation (segregation) of the
objects from one another.

While listening to music and sounds, similarly complex processes of grouping are taking place, without which the identification of acoustic sources and musical structures would not be possible. At the same time, tones can blend to form a chord and thus be bound within the frequency range as a figure *(simultaneous integration,* Bregman 1999). Tones which follow one another consecutively, on the other hand, can be bound to form a melody, a structure with a temporal context *(sequential integration).* Spatially hearing thereby allows the separation or the blending of events heard within the room. Even in the case of a sequence of individual tones quickly following one another, differences can be auditorily discerned when similarities of timbre or of frequency range of the fundamental tones exist between the individual tones. Figure 1.75 provides an example of the separation of melodies from the temporal structure of a composition. This particular piece is intended for a transverse flute without accompaniment. A flute allows only the respective individual tone to be played, whereas polyphonic tones are precluded due to physical limitations.

FIGURE 1.75
A composition for a solo flute which creates the
illusion of being played in two voices.
Georg Philipp Telemann, "7th Fantasia for Transverse
Flute without Bass," D major, allegro.
A) monodical theme; B) simulated passage in two
voices with the theme in the lower tones.

Although the solo flute can only yield an individual tone at any given time, collateral melodies can be perceived and distinguished from one another as independent auditory objects. ● Different tone pitches and timbres can facilitate this separation. Accordingly, the initial, distinct melody (a) can be discerned from the rapid sixteenth-note passage, thus (b) producing the illusion of a musical performance in two voices. The particular attraction of polyphonic music consists of the parallel existence of temporal and spectral groupings, which mutually influence one another, as well as of the alternating relationships between the foreground and the background.

124

1.3
FUNDAMENTALS
OF PERCEPTION
↓
1.3.7
GROUPING

GESTALT
PRINCIPLES

The introduction of the term *Gestalt quality* by Christian von Ehrenfels indicated in effect the origins of Gestalt psychology ("About Gestalt Qualities," Ehrenfels 1890). The term *gestalt* defines, thereby, mental formations which appear as independent units in the consciousness and which are clearly distinguishable from other objects. This also applies to the perceptual objects defined in Chapter 1.3.4. Gestalt quality is that which is yielded by the consolidation of all properties of such an object. Among the examples discussed by Ehrenfels are the room gestalt and the tone gestalt as already mentioned by Mach (1903) – that means, more specifically, the construction of a consistent spatial perception and the grouping for the purpose of forming auditory units. Proceeding on this assumption, it would be reasonable to define the multisensory gestalt quality of a perceptual object in the following manner:

1.3
FUNDAMENTALS
OF PERCEPTION
↓
1.3.8
GESTALT
PRINCIPLES

125

**MULTISENSORY GESTALT QUALITY
DESCRIBES THE CAPABILITY OF A PERCEPTUAL
OBJECT TO APPEAR AS A CONSISTENT
WHOLE AND TO THUS DISTINGUISH
ITSELF FROM OTHER MENTAL FORMATIONS.**

In times of the technical reproducibility of sensory stimuli – for example, via audio-visual media – the required consistency in the sense of freedom from contradiction is, of course, not self-evident. The playing back of the television sound via a stereo or surround-sound console does not necessarily result in the visual elements and the corresponding auditory events appearing together in the same location. Thereby, even movement will be seen, although the observer can sense neither acceleration nor vibration. Perceptions of the skin, the smell, and the taste are similarly excluded. Nevertheless, multisensory objects free of contradiction are perceived. The integration processes of the perceptual system required for this shall be discussed in chapter 3.1.

FIGURE 1.76
Even when they do exhibit different colors, similar objects
can be correlated to one another and consolidated. In the depicted example,
the balls serve to build a background from which the face and the
hands clearly distinguish themselves, although a large portion of the balls is,
in terms of the perspective, located in front of the child.

In the historical development, the analysis of gestalt qualities was initially limited to visual perception. Indeed, it corresponds to everyday life experiences that elementary groupings can arise with great self-evidence (fig. 1.76). Therefore, at the outset, gestalt psychology presumed a permanent set of regularities in the cognitive construction of gestalts which is anchored in the perceptual system. The well-known *gestalt laws* pertaining to the optical realm of experience were identified by the gestalt psychologists Max Wertheimer, Wolfgang Köhler, and Kurt Koffka, but they were only first compiled as a list and published by Wertheimer in 1923 (Fitzek 1996).

Figure 1.77 provides examples of these gestalt principles. A detailed description may be found in Metzger (1966) and Sternberg (2008). That work undertakes a distinction between the perception of gestalts and the perception of events.

The laws of *homogeneity* and *proximity* make reference to the grouping of individual visual elements. Figure 1.76 illustrates that similar objects can even be grouped when they exhibit different colors. The grouping of various light points into structures which are in and of themselves enclosed and which belong to one another is, for example, of acute interest in the development of automobile headlights operating by virtue of light-emitting diodes (LED).

126

1.3
FUNDAMENTALS
OF PERCEPTION
↓
1.3.8
GESTALT
PRINCIPLES

HOMOGENEITY/SIMILARITY:
SIMILAR STRUCTURES
ARE CONSOLIDATED

COMMON FATE
CONGRUENT BEHAVIOR LEADS
TO GROUPING

PROXIMITY
NEIGHBORING STRUCTURES
ARE CONSOLIDATED

GOOD GESTALT/PRÄGNANZ
FORMS ARE
PLAUSIBLY SUPPLEMENTED

FIGURE 1.77
Examples of important gestalt principles.
These are tendencies of the organization of perceptual objects
which are effective for all persons and which
serve the purpose of sensibly arranging perceptual objects.

THE PRINCIPLE OF COMMON FATE
IS PARTICULARLY IMPORTANT WITH RESPECT
TO THE TEMPORAL CLASSIFICATION
OF SENSORY IMPRESSIONS.

An object which visibly becomes smaller and smaller will be, for example, as a matter of preference, correlated to a tone which continuously diminishes in intensity.

Different laws of gestalt can also be applied to the auditory and to the tactile realms. Indeed, when touching objects contact is not necessarily made with the complete surfaces of the hand and the fingers. Nevertheless, in many cases, it is possible to correctly recognize the entire form of the object simply as a result of the touching sensation. On the basis of the principle of Prägnanz *(pithiness),* the section of a container onto which one places his or her hand will be expanded to a complete form.

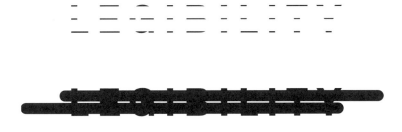

1.3
FUNDAMENTALS
OF PERCEPTION
↓
1.3.8
GESTALT
PRINCIPLES

127

9

FIGURE 1.78
The Prägnanz effect: demonstration of the
tendency of the perceptual system to connect fragments
as much as possible to shape a simple, "good form."
Above: the illustrated fragments can not easily
be filled in to form objects, below: the identification
of a concealed object simplifies the building
of gestalts through the continuation of disconnected lines.

An important application of the principle of Prägnanz is, accordingly, the reconstruction of partially concealed forms within the perceptual system. This is particularly possible when a distinct form can be identified as the cause of the concealment. Figure 1.78 provides an example of this effect. In the upper area, only the visible portions of four objects are depicted. Thus, it is relatively difficult to identify the objects. The recognition of the objects is facilitated, however, when the lack of individual components of the objects can be affiliated with the respective concealment by virtue of an easily comprehensible form, as indicated in the lower area of figure 1.78. This effect is characterized as the "picket fence effect," for it is indeed possible to recognize objects through a picket fence without further ado. This effect is similarly applicable to the auditory modality, when an acoustic signal is alienated by distracting noise. Particularly, periodically distracting signals, such as a recurring rustling sound, can be drowned out by the sense of hearing, owing to the fact that the distraction, as in the case of a picket fence, can be predicted and "fore*heard*" in advance, thus quite capable of being well analyzed by the mechanisms based on probability functioning within the perceptual system. Currently, the auditory processes of the recognition of gestalts are analyzed within the realm of an *auditory scene analysis* (Bregman 1990). ●

Due to the periodic nature of the movement of windshield wipers, it is, as a general rule, quite possible to ignore them and to thus avoid a disturbance of the viewing through the recurrently moving wiper blade. This has to be regarded during the construction of systems which steer the movement of the windshield wipers depending upon the number of raindrops falling upon the windshield. Movements which appear to be unsystematic can not easily be blinded out by the perceptual system, for they tend to arouse the attention of the driver, thus diminishing driving safety.

The multisensory gestalt formation is notably obvious in the case of identifying a scent. The scent is usually not recognized as the sum of individual properties, instead of that, it is directly associated with the image of a possible source. In most cases, the characterization of a scent includes a description of the source. Accordingly, one speaks of a lemon scent, a lavender fragrance, or the odor of benzine. This being the case, one may plausibly presume that a connection of the patterns of stimuli of scents with the attributes of other senses already takes place within the region of the cerebral cortex, which is directly attributed to the sense of smell – namely the olfactory cortex *(rhinencephalon)*. This particularly associative character of the sense of smell is physiologically supported by the direct connection between the sensory organ and the olfactory cortex as well as by virtue of its central location.

Even during the summarizing or consolidation of meaningful *(semantic)* elements with the purpose of forming reasonable units, the tendency to build uniform, complete gestalts free of contradiction can be observed. In this regard, during the interpretation of a language, a complete context is created by virtue of model building. If individual words contradict the meaning of the entire, complete sentence, a tendency towards resolving the contradiction exists. Thus, the human language-processing system aims at modifying the unclear or sketchy elements perceived in a linguistic context. As one listens to a song, conflicts of linguistic comprehension can arise, in particular, if the melody does not correspond to the accustomed intonation or accentuation *(prosody)*. Thus, there is the "mishearing" of words with the known, often curious re-interpretations of the text.

In this manner, the word "miracles" in a popular hit of the soul band Hot Chocolate with the text "I believe in miracles, since you came along, you sexy thing" erroneously understood, among others, as *knuckle,* as the name *Malcolm* or *Melcho*, as *milk bones, milk rolls, milkos, milk balls, mecos,* or *Myrtle* (Hacke 2004). One can characterize this as a *semantic building of gestalts,* which is often successful at identifying the meaning and making sense of it all, even in the case of the conveyance of sketchy information – and this can occasionally result in fun or humor by virtue of the confusion.

128

1.3
FUNDAMENTALS
OF PERCEPTION
↓
1.3.8
GESTALT
PRINCIPLES

FOREGROUND AND
BACKGROUND

1.3
FUNDAMENTALS
OF PERCEPTION
↓
1.3.9
FOREGROUND
AND
BACKGROUND

129

In real environments, considerably more sensory stimuli reach the perceptual system, as suggested by figure 1.73. Usually, stimuli of light make their way from the entire field of view to the retina. Thereby, the question arises as to the possibilities of sensible structuring and the efficiency of the concentration on the momentarily essential information. In addition to the grouping of similar forms in accordance with the aforementioned gestalt principles, the perceptual system must also provide for processes which extract the essential and which summarize less significant information. Such mechanisms could be described utilizing a schema consisting of a foreground and a background. In a landscape, mountains and vegetation as well as the sky and its clouds blend together to form merged structures, and in front of these structures, for example, paths and individual houses, distinguish themselves as points of orientation. In a sea of houses in the profile of a city, as observed from a distance, similar buildings – as indicated by figure 1.79 – form a homogenous background structure, from which special forms, such as individual multistory buildings, chimneys, or towers distinctly stand out. The distinct division into foreground and background structures is essential with respect to all modalities which characteristically have a spatial depiction of the sensory stimuli within the perceptual system. Similarly, figure and background relations decide as to the number of separated and individually analyzed perceptual objects in the auditory and tactile regions as well.

**IN THE DESIGNING OF PRODUCTS,
IT IS IMPORTANT TO EXACTLY DEFINE THE
FOREGROUND AND THE BACKGROUND
AND TO STEER THE PERCEPTION OF THE
USER IN THE DESIRED DIRECTION.**

Thus, an operating element which steers an important and possibly crucial function in terms of safety must clearly distinguish itself from the surrounding components. The erroneous operation of the system would be supported by unclear structures. Figure 1.80 illustrates this situation. In Case A, the red circle is clearly distinguishable from the background and is thus identifiable as a separate unit which comes to the foreground. In Case B, on the other hand, no clear distinction can be made as to whether the structure to the right or to the left constitutes the foreground or background. Depending upon the perspective of the observation, either of the structures can function as the foreground or background. The function simply "shifts" in the eye of the observer.

In the realm of a structured design, such "bistable" or "reversible figures" should be avoided to the greatest extent possible. Nevertheless, they serve to create a particular attraction which is popularly employed in visual arts. The graphic artist Maurits Cornelis Escher often worked with sequences of similar bistable figures. These can arbitrarily be attributed to the foreground or background. In the perspective of the observer, they accordingly appear to retreat or to "topple out" of the picture.

FIGURE 1.79
In a conglomerate of various houses, the majority
of individual objects blends to form a background structure.
In this view of a quarter of Istanbul, individual yellow
houses and sacred buildings move into the foreground.

A   B

130

1.3
FUNDAMENTALS
OF PERCEPTION
↓
1.3.9
FOREGROUND
AND
BACKGROUND

FIGURE 1.80
Forms as foreground and background.
In A, foreground and background are distinctly defined.
That is the goal of optimal, clear designing.
In B, both forms build a bistable figure. Either form can be
interpreted as foreground or as background.
This results in ambiguity, and this is to be avoided
as much as possible.

The painting of Cubist Juan Gris shown in figure 1.81 contains various bistable figures, such as the opening of a bottle, which can also represent the opening of the body of a guitar. Furthermore, spatial proximity and distance as well as open and concealed views are not defined. Thus seen, the guitar might be located on the table or even beneath it. The simultaneousness of different perspectives and conditions is typical of the dissecting Cubist analysis of the situation. Indeed, this increases the attraction of the picture – and it is comparable to listening to complex musical structures. Such a condition of ambiguity and complexity, however, does not lead to sensible structures in designing functional, multisensory objects and environments. Instead, the creation of a clear, unmistakable *hierarchy* is required.

Acoustic bistable figures can appear with equal voices in the realm of polyphonic music. The listener can consciously shift his attention to different

1.3
FUNDAMENTALS
OF PERCEPTION
↓
1.3.9
FOREGROUND
AND
BACKGROUND

131

FIGURE 1.81
Juan Gris, Guitar and Bottle, 1921 –
a work which plays which the relationships of the image elements
to the foreground and the background.

voices which accordingly move into the foreground. All other voices thus serve to build the accompanying or contrasting background. Comparable effects can be observed while listening to fugues by Johann Sebastian Bach – for example, in *The Art of the Fugue* or *The Musical Offering.* The effect is particularly clear when these works are played by an instrument with an equal loudness of the individual tones – as in the case of the harpsichord. In this case, the interpreting musician does not have the opportunity to dynamically accentuate individual parts and to thus clarify the ambiguous musical structure. Not by accident, the painting illustrated in figure 1.81 was occasionally quite explicitly associated with the music of Bach (Kahnweiler 1946). One may also compare it to the bistable figures in Giacomo Balla's painting *Forme Rumore* in figure 3.46.

GENERALLY SPEAKING,
ALL PERCEPTUAL PROCESSES INVOLVE THE
EXTRACTION OF PATTERNS.

PATTERNS ARE, AS OPPOSED TO
THE ENVIRONMENT, CLEARLY DEMARCATED,
SELF-CONTAINED PERCEPTUAL
STRUCTURES WHICH ARE DISTINCTLY
CHARACTERIZED BY VIRTUE OF THEIR
PROPERTIES (ATTRIBUTES).

Pattern recognition is one of the essential duties of the perceptual system. Indeed, it enables the interpretation of sensory stimuli and the deciphering of their meanings. An important basis of synesthetic design, therefore, consists of determining the patterns which are significant with respect to the connections between the sensory modalities and which are essential in contributing to the creation of multisensory perceptual objects.

1.3
FUNDAMENTALS
OF PERCEPTION
↓
1.3.9
FOREGROUND
AND
BACKGROUND

STRATEGIES OF PERCEPTION AND DESIGN

CONNECTION OF MODALITIES WITHIN THE PERCEPTUAL SYSTEM

OVERVIEW

2.1
CONNECTION
OF MODALITIES
WITHIN THE
PERCEPTUAL
SYSTEM
↓
2.1.1
OVERVIEW

———

135

In classifying the different strategies of the perceptual system with respect to their ability to connect data of the sensory modalities, it is advisable to review the five fundamental mechanisms mentioned in chapter 1.1. First, a comprehensive overview is presented here. Then, the implications on multisensory design will be extended with more detail throughout chapters 2.2 to 2.6. The fundamental strategies are depicted in figure 2.1 as circles. Utilizing the example of creating perceptual events in the visual modality via auditory stimuli, the parallelism of the strategies of connection is demonstrated. An auditory stimulus is received by the sense of hearing. This can result in perception or in the conception of visual phenomena. The participating processes can be spontaneous and stable (genuine) or spontaneous and context-dependent. It is even possible to consciously construct connections (see also Haverkamp 2009c).

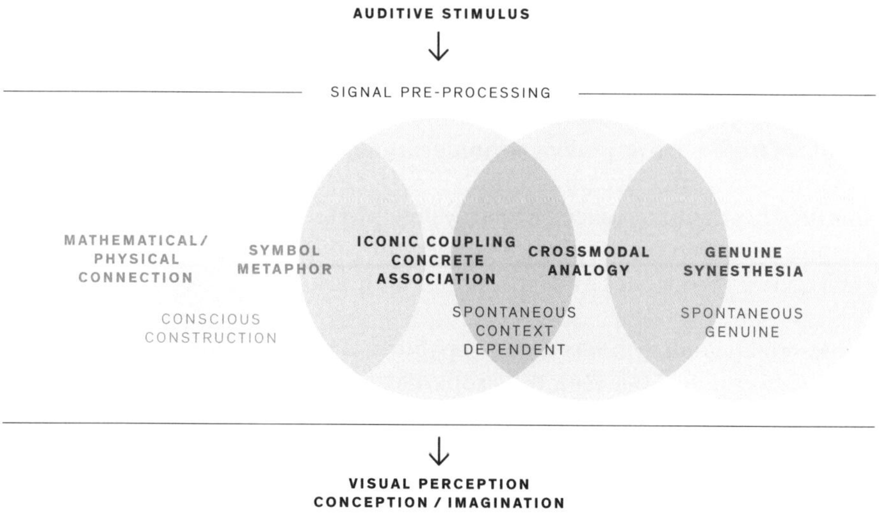

FIGURE 2.1
Schema of the strategies of cross-sensory connection
in the case of audio-visual connection.

The three circles in the middle play a decisive role in the perception and evaluation of objects or atmospheres, and they shall be described here as *intuitive strategies*.

FIGURE 2.2
Genuine synesthetic perception. Color perception of the tone pitch, combined with the associative conception of the piano keyboard as memorized. A drawing according to the description of a student of Wilhelm Voss, teacher of the visually impaired (Voss 1929).

Genuine synesthesia occurs only with respect to relatively few people. Thus, it is difficult for people to comprehend if they do not have similar perceptions on the basis of their own experience. Thus, people with genuine synesthetic phenomena must deal with the fact that no other individual can share their experiences. The related perceptual phenomena are based upon the appearance of individual attributes in the modalities which are not momentarily stimulated. In most cases, it involves abstract appearances which do not reveal a superordinated systematic of classification. Accordingly, an exclusively individual systematic exists, and this may be found by no other person with synesthetic perceptual phenomena. A tone heard, for example, can thus additionally give rise to the sensation of a color. Figure 2.2 provides an example of synesthetic color perception during the acoustic reception of piano tones – according to the description of a student in a school for the visually impaired. Further examples are presented by Rowedder (2009). In the case of persons who have gone blind, genuine synesthesia occurs considerably more often than in the case of persons without impairments of their visual capabilities. Following the intensity of synesthetic research in the initial phase leading into the 1930s, genuine synesthesia was generally ignored by the scientific community for a period of more than fifty years. Only very few authors dealt with this subject during that period of time, such as Ludwig Schrader (1969) and Lawrence E. Marks (1978). Not until some fifteen years ago, did a renaissance of the academic research in this field begin taking place, primarily precipitated by Richard Cytowic (1993). chapter 2.5 addresses the phenomenology of synesthetic perception as well as interpretive approaches and current research results.

Cross-modal analogy refers to the capability of each person to detect correlations (congruence) between the properties of objects above and beyond the boundaries of the senses. The thus summarized strategies of connection serve to connect, as does genuine synesthesia, individual properties such as color, roughness, volume, hardness, movement, and many other aspects. Figure 2.3 illustrates an approach to the visualization of the movement implied by a sound. ● The depiction chosen there can be traced back to Alexander Truslit (Truslit 1938), and this will be described in greater detail in sections 2.2.4 and 3.4.2. In contrast to genuine synesthesia, however, these connections are

10

136

2.1
CONNECTION
OF MODALITIES
WITHIN THE
PERCEPTUAL
SYSTEM
↓
2.1.1
OVERVIEW

systematic and quantifiable. Nevertheless, the allocations are not absolute, for there is a dependency with respect to the context. Therefore, as an example, the brightness of an object is not perceived as an absolute quantity. Instead, it is perceived in relation to other bright structures or to the brightness of the surrounding environment. Cross-modal analogies play a special role in the processing of unknown stimuli, for they enable, in the first place, the generation of new perceptual objects by virtue of the connection of individual properties. Due to its particular significance for product design, this perceptual strategy will be the first to receive a detailed description in this chapter.

2.1
CONNECTION
OF MODALITIES
WITHIN THE
PERCEPTUAL
SYSTEM
↓
2.1.1
OVERVIEW

137

FIGURE 2.3
The curve of movement of the sound of a windshield wiper.
Two cycles of movement are presented. Illustration by the author.

Concrete association or **iconic connection** describes the classification of perceived properties by virtue of the identification of multisensory objects. The form of the coupling functions thus only in the case of known objects. For example, the recognition of a known scent instinctively leads to a visualization of the source of the stimulation. Even sounds will be intuitively connected to its acoustic source. Visualizations of auditory events often exhibit structures which may be seen in the context of similar sounds. Figure 2.4 demonstrates this for the phenomenon "Bang." The visual appearance of an explosion delivers the structure with which the sound will be connected. Multisensory associations also build the necessary foundation of the onomatopoeia (chapter 2.3.2).

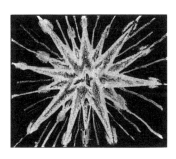

FIG. 2.4
Associative visualization of the sound event "Bang."
Student work from a class of Walter Behm
in the 1920s (Anschütz 1931).

Symbol and metaphor: In addition to the characteristics which enable the identification of multisensory sources of stimulation, objects can also be provided with superordinated meanings. These meanings manifest themselves as *symbolic* or linguistic *metaphoric* – they are often independent of the typical object properties. The siren of an ambulance makes reference to – parallel to the flashing lights – an emergency situation. This connection can only succeed, however, if the meaning of its attributes was already learned. This even applies to the processing of language. The effect of a comprehensible language along the level of symbols, therefore, fundamentally differs from the effect of incomprehensible sounds which exclusively make reference to associations. The associative recognition of a person as the source of spoken language *(causal listening)* is independent of the comprehension of the linguistic contents *(semantic listening)*. This will be detailed in chapter 2.4.

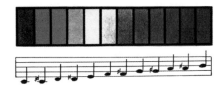

FIGURE 2.5
The transformation of a chromatic tone scale into a color scale for the Color Music of Alexander Wallace Rimington (1911).

Mathematical / physical connection distinguishes itself as a process based on conscious conceptions fundamentally from the other strategies. In contrast to the intuitive and involuntary processes of the other strategies, this encompasses the conversion of the parameters of different modalities into one another and the development of algorithms which provide for such a transformation. A well-known application is included within media players that provide computerized visualizations of music. Often, the comparability of physical quantities serves as the foundation. The most popular application is the attempt to computationally deduce tone frequencies and light frequencies from one another (chapters 2.6 and 3.4). Figure 2.5 illustrates the connection of spectral colors with respect to the tone pitch within an octave, whereas a color tone is allocated to every chromatic tone. Such concepts were utilized to visualize musical structures in the meaning of *Color Music* or to develop purely visual music. One may compare the clear systematic used here with the genuine synesthetic classification of figure 2.2.

—

The five strategies of connection contain, nonetheless, a variety of possibilities for connections between the sensory modalities, and these will be discussed further in subsequent chapters. In the scientific discussion pertaining to genuine synesthesia, the three "intuitive" strategies are often summarized and analyzed together. For this purpose, various terms were coined, among them *metaphoric synesthesia* (Marks 1990), *false audition colorée* as opposed to the *authentic* (Bos 1929), *strong* versus *weak synesthesia* (Martino 2001) or *Pseudo-Synesthesia* (Baron-Cohen 1997). This results in genuine synesthesia being regarded as a singular case of cross-modal connections and it

138

2.1
CONNECTION
OF MODALITIES
WITHIN THE
PERCEPTUAL
SYSTEM
↓
2.1.1
OVERVIEW

ignores, at the same time, the very significant fact that every person has a broad repertory of interconnecting sensory channels at their disposal, which may be systematically applied during perception. Without the differentiation of the various strategies as presented in this book, the discussion remains unspecific. Only a comprehensive analysis of the diverse forms of appearance of multisensory perception – being influenced by individual phenomena – can lead to more profound knowledge and can open up new possibilities for applications within the realm of design.

With respect to visual perception, it is known that the appearance of a product is defined by virtue of the perceived abstract properties as well as via associative and symbolic contents. Accordingly, even essential attributes of style are determined. Some styles consequently relinquish associative and symbolic content, such as the functionalism of modernity (Bauhaus, De Stijl, "Gutes Design" [Good Design] of the 1950s). Others are especially characterized by associative references or allusions, such as the attributes of Art Nouveau and classicism, post-modernity, as well as – by definition – all neo-styles. In the 1960s, schools of thought were formed which demanded adding symbolic elements to architecture, in order to achieve a "humane figuration," whereas the geometric abstraction of the modern and the relinquishing of ornamentation and symbolism – quite contrary to its intention – have been suspected of leading to the dehumanization of architecture and design (Fiell 2005a).

The goal of this book is to demonstrate that concrete associative and symbolic aspects, which have primarily been considered in the visual modality, are also of great significance in the other sensory channels. Together with the different, abstract properties of an object, the designer thus has a comprehensive repertory of elements for multisensory design at his or her disposal. This can and must be systematically utilized in the realm of a choice of appropriate strategies of interconnection. Accordingly, one can achieve optimal results in designing which directly appeal to the customers, facilitating the effective cooperation of all sensory channels. If this occurs in conformity with the desired functions of the product, a conclusive, holistic design is the ultimate result, thus providing a high degree of customer acceptance.

2.1
CONNECTION
OF MODALITIES
WITHIN THE
PERCEPTUAL
SYSTEM
↓
2.1.1
OVERVIEW

———

139

THE INTUITIVE STRATEGIES BASED ON CROSS-MODAL ANALOGY, ASSOCIATION, AND SYMBOLISM ARE SUITABLE FOR CREATING A DESIGN THAT PROVIDES CONNECTIONS BETWEEN THE SENSES, WHICH DIRECTLY APPEAR APPROPRIATE AND EASY TO INTERPRET.

In order to achieve the greatest possible acceptance among the customers and users of a product, an *intuitive design* must make use of these strategies of interconnection. As more closely discussed in chapters 2.3 and 2.4, it is a prerequisite, nevertheless, that associative and symbolic contents are known to the user. As an example, the illustrative sign *(icon)* for the motor, depicting certain operational conditions or technical malfunctions, must be familiar to the driver. If that is not the case, he or her might be unable to categorize possible problems or to effectively respond to the optical signals. The designer, on the other hand, having the benefit of comprehensive, detailed knowledge, has the problematic task of placing himself in the position of the customer. Indeed, the driver may find it considerably more difficult to decipher a technical symbol. In the worst case, this can mean that the symbol would be – as seen from a technical standpoint – thoroughly misinterpreted. This could naturally lead to a dangerous situation. The only method of minimizing the possible risks involves comprehensive customer research, allowing the signals and icons utilized to be more appropriately developed and adapted to correspond to the experience of the user.

Connections which are intentionally constructed on the basis of physical relations between the stimuli of different sensory channels are only understandable, as a matter of contrast, when they contain aspects of intuitive strategies. The motivation for the differentiation of the three intuitive strategies, cross-modal analogy, association, and symbolism, is derived from phenomenological observations as well as from the findings of brain research. Additional evidence may be found in the history of art and design.

EVIDENCE IN THE
PHENOMENOLOGY OF PERCEPTION

140

2.1
CONNECTION
OF MODALITIES
WITHIN THE
PERCEPTUAL
SYSTEM
↓
2.1.1
OVERVIEW

As the result of a perceptual process which manifests itself in the synthesis of multisensory perceptual objects, the perceiving subject is able to subsequently analyze specific steps of this process. In this manner, the properties of an object can be examined individually and independent of their respective functions. Even in perceptual experiments, test subjects can be compelled by the choice of experimental conditions to isolate certain object features from consideration. It is then possible to evaluate individual properties such as brightness, size, timbre, or roughness, independent of aspects of meaning. Conversely, objects with very different properties can be analyzed with respect to similar functions. Within the realm of auditory perception, Michel Chion appropriately distinguishes the act of listening to elementary acoustic properties *(reduced listening),* the determination of information regarding the sound source *(causal listening),* and the decoding of meaning *(semantic listening)* from one another (Chion 1994). These three forms of hearing correspond to the distinctions mentioned here with respect to the strategies of analogy, concrete association, and symbolism. The capability to consciously activate and deactivate certain mechanisms in the cross-modal connection provides an important possibility of the introspective recognition of perceptual processes. However, this can also cause erroneous interpretations of experimental results; for example, if processes which usually are combined in everyday life are separated from one another. Accordingly, the annoying or straining nature of a sound results intuitively in the consideration of its meaning and of the multisensory appearance of its source. In early experiments, on the other hand, the loudness was initially considered in an isolated manner, which led test subjects to regard the annoying, burdening nature exclusively as a function of the loudness.

Luria describes the special case of concrete associations as the basis of the unique talents of the mnemonist Solomon Shereshevsky (Luria 1968). In his consciousness, the associatively created images appeared quite pronouncedly and could be memorized in an unusually good manner. Memorized and conceptual images of such high intensity are also described as *eidetic* images. Additionally, Shereshevsky's visualizations were accompanied by genuine synesthetic, abstract perceptions of form which could clearly be distinguished from representational associations. In particular, unknown words and noises led to clear visual perceptions. Fundamentally, every noise created an immediate sensation of light and color as well as of touch and taste. In a similar manner, the image elements of figure 2.6 correspond to an overlapping of associative contents with synesthetic forms. ●

Similarly, the composer György Ligeti utilized concrete associations as the basis of his musical creativity. In this fashion, he configured his orchestral work *Lontano* (From a distance) with view on lyrics by John Keats ("Ode to a Nightingale"), a painting by Albrecht Altdorfer *(The Battle of Alexander)*, and the sequence of etchings *Carceri d'Invenzione* by Giovanni Battista Piranesi, showing fantastic images of ancient prisons.

2.1
CONNECTION
OF MODALITIES
WITHIN THE
PERCEPTUAL
SYSTEM
↓
2.1.1
OVERVIEW

141

11

FIGURE 2.6
This photograph by the synesthete Matthias Waldeck
illustrates visual impressions arising
while listening to brake noise – it shows associative
elements and synesthetic forms (stripes).

On the other hand, Ligeti also described experiences with genuine synesthesia, such as the sensation of color, form, and material texture, on the basis of auditory stimuli – and conversely, sounds which could be traced to the color, form, and consistency of materials. Additionally considered were synesthetic phenomena which were caused by abstract terms: "For example, the term *time* is nebulously white, slow and continually flowing from left to right, whereas it gives rise to a quiet, hhh-like sound." (Cited by Engelbrecht 1997)

EVIDENCE
IN BRAIN RESEARCH

The reception, processing, and storing of information arriving from the outer environment can be seen as a fundamental functional unit of the brain. In an approximate distinction, Luria mentions three steps of processing (Luria 1973). His concept is herein extended and regarded as the foundation of the scheme depicted in figure 2.7. It includes three fields. With the application of Luria's nomenclature, each field summarizes all areas related to the functionality described; e.g., the primary field contains all areas of single modality, as described before as the visual, auditory, somatosensory field, etc.

1.

A primary projection field which receives impulses from the sensory organs and transmits them to the body. The primary sensory fields of the cerebral cortex, onto which the arriving signals from the sensory organs are projected, as described in chapter 1.3, correspond to this. That is the location of the analysis of the sensory stimuli, following their disassembly into the smallest possible elements, and they are subsequently grouped to form functional patterns. The processing of individual stimulatory parameters creates the very foundation of cross-modal analogies. The interconnection of different modalities, however, does not directly follow in the primary field. For this purpose, multisensory zones are standing by to connect information from sensory-specific areas (Noesselt 2008). They may predominantly be found in the secondary field.

2.

A secondary field (for projection and association) in which the arriving information is processed and/or programs are activated. *Associative neurons* which synthesize patterns from the arriving stimuli may be found here. The thus facilitated fusion of individual parameters to complex perceptual pattern allows, in turn, the building of cross-modal analogies and the identification of objects. In this case, an interconnection is carried out beyond the sensory boundaries, and the strategy of concrete associations is accordingly realized.

3.

A tertiary field which consist of functionally overarching zones. With the participation of various areas of the cerebral cortex, the procedural handling of symbolic processes is made possible, particularly via the processing of language. This enables the deciphering of the *meaning* of multisensory perceptual objects.

142

2.1
CONNECTION
OF MODALITIES
WITHIN THE
PERCEPTUAL
SYSTEM
↓
2.1.1
OVERVIEW

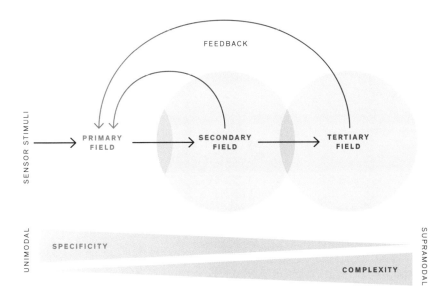

FEEDBACK

SENSOR STIMULI

UNIMODAL

SUPRAMODAL

PRIMARY
FIELD

SECONDARY
FIELD

TERTIARY
FIELD

SPECIFICITY

COMPLEXITY

2.1
CONNECTION
OF MODALITIES
WITHIN THE
PERCEPTUAL
SYSTEM
↓
2.1.1
OVERVIEW

143

FIGURE 2.7
The passing of sensory information takes place, extending from
the primary fields to higher levels of processing.
Similarly, data is returned, flowing (as feedback) from the higher
levels back to the primary fields. In the flow from the primary
to the tertiary field, the specialization decreases with
respect to a specific sensory channel (modal specificity) and with
regard to elementary steps of the processing.
Thus, complexity increases to the benefit of a superordinated
functionality which encompasses all sensory modalities.

From the primary to the tertiary field, so to speak, from "below" towards the region "above," the modal specificity, namely the specialization of the neurons with respect to certain sensory channels, steadily declines, whereas multisensory connections increase. Thereby, the primary areas are sensory-specific– *unimodal.* Luria describes the tertiary zones as *supramodal* (Luria 1973). The neurons of the primary field are significantly specialized with respect to certain properties of the sensory stimuli, such as color tones, the course of lines, or the direction of movement. The transduction of signals from "below" towards the regions "above" (bottom-up) is characterized by the increased distribution of duties among the left and right halves of the brain. In this manner, the regions for determining the meaning of language are allocated to, for most people, the left cerebral hemisphere, whereas the analysis of further auditory properties of speech, such as the intonation, transpires within the cerebral hemisphere located on the right-hand side.

According to recent scientific findings, an essential element of the multisensory processing consists of the *feedback* from processes in higher regions to the primary field. This is confirmed by research results within the realm of neuropsychology (e.g., Vroomen 2004, Molholm 2004, Noesselt 2008), and it is furthermore reflected in the phenomena of genuine synesthesia (chapter 2.5).

During childhood, the development of the brain occurs initially within the primary field, for the processes of identifying objects and of deciphering their significance can become more pronounced only subsequent to the preprocessing of the sensory stimuli. In the case of adults, in contrast, the *concepts* built in the tertiary field assume control over the entire system – the processing thus occurs *top-down* from the level "above" to the level "below." As a result of this, perception is increasingly influenced by preconceptions obtained over the course of life.

EVIDENCE
IN ART AND DESIGN

As already suggested, the different levels of the models depicted in figure 2.1 contain mechanisms which express themselves in artistic design with varying degrees of emphasis. Often, important stylistic properties may also be defined by confining the scope to certain strategies:

Mathematic/physical connections:
constructivism, color-light music, computer arts, media player

Symbolic level:
symbolism, allegory, surrealism, religious and political art

Concrete associations:
generally non-abstract art; especially Art Nouveau, Historicism, Neue Sachlichkeit, Realism, Pop Art, Fluxus – often mixed with analogies and symbolic elements

Cross-modal analogies:
abstract art, expressionism (fig. 2.8), Cubism, De Stijl, Bauhaus – all styles which are based on the utilization of simple, fundamental forms without iconic and symbolic references, such as the objective European style from the period of time prior to World War II up until and including today (fig. 2.9)

Genuine synesthesia:
musical graphics (often mixed with analogies and associative properties), musical images, synesthetic paintings of the *Farbe-Ton-Forschung* (Germany, 1920s to 1930s), color-tone research and more recent trends since the 1990s (see e.g., Berman 2008)

144

2.1
CONNECTION
OF MODALITIES
WITHIN THE
PERCEPTUAL
SYSTEM
↓
2.1.1
OVERVIEW

In the history of music, one can also find distinct directions which generate multisensory references via different strategies. As an example, *absolute music* is primarily dealing with abstract musical parameters such as key and modulation, with melody and its transformation, as well as with mathematical concepts (Dahlhaus 1994). Associations, symbolism, and poetic content, on the other hand, are excluded. The compositions created in this manner were often regarded as products of purely mental origin without emotional aspects. In the case of Johann Sebastian Bach's *Art of the Fugue*, for example, it was even assumed that this composition was solely intended for theoretical analysis and educational purposes, but not for general public performance (Kolneder 1977, 9). Figure 2.8 shows a visualization of music with clear, but also

2.1
CONNECTION
OF MODALITIES
WITHIN THE
PERCEPTUAL
SYSTEM
↓
2.1.1
OVERVIEW
───────
145

FIGURE 2.8
Baroque forms as associative elements as well as
analogies of the acoustic structure in the artistic visualization of music.
August Macke, Colorful Composition I (Homage to
Johann Sebastian Bach), 1912.

associative references to the musical forms of Bach's style. Further examples of music which were interpreted as theoretical constructions are the late string quartets of Ludwig van Beethoven as well as the atonal and twelve-tone works of Arnold Schönberg.

FIGURE 2.9
**Functional design on the basis of elementary forms –
with sparse color accents.
Electric typewriter Praxis 48, designed by Ettore Sottsass
and Hans von Klier for Olivetti, 1964.**

146

2.1
CONNECTION
OF MODALITIES
WITHIN THE
PERCEPTUAL
SYSTEM
↓
2.1.1
OVERVIEW

In contrast to this rather *abstract music,* however, music with associative, ono-matopoetic contents – such as in the symphonic creations of the nineteenth century – enjoys great popularity even today. This is particularly so when en-riched with additional significance, for example, as in the epic nature of the opera or in songs with a narrative substance. Thus, it is undoubtedly no acci-dent that contemporary pop music, transmitted by countless radio stations on a daily basis, almost exclusively consists of songs. On the other hand, in the opera or orchestral music of the nineteenth century, there was also a no-ticeable tendency towards symbolism. Particularly in the analysis of the opera music of Richard Wagner, it is evident that associative elements build the basis of creating musical symbols. This will treated in greater detail in section 2.4.5.

Cross-modal analogies and genuine synesthesia are based on the results of specific stimuli. This corresponds to the *sensations* according to the definition by Helmholtz (Helmholtz 1863). The iconic (associative) and symbolic connec-tions, on the other hand, are concerned with the actual *perceptions* in the sense of recognizing the factual elements and objects. Even though the terminol-ogy recommended by Helmholtz will not be utilized in this regard – this book generally speaks in terms of *perceptual qualities* rather than of *sensations* – the distinction involved is nevertheless a sensible demarcation of fundamentally different methods of processing sensory stimuli.

RULES OF
CONNECTION

The basis of the model depicted in figure 2.1 is the assumption that strategies of multisensory connection are initially independent of one another and that they thus function parallel to one another. It is known that the enormous achievement of the brain, with a high velocity of processing, and, simultaneously, a high degree of efficiency, can be traced to the principle of *parallel processing,* and this processing functions on all levels (Campenhausen 1993).

PARALLEL PROCESSING
IS ONE OF THE MOST SIGNIFICANT
FUNDAMENTAL PRINCIPLES OF
BRAIN FUNCTIONALITY.

In this manner, the signals flow from the sensory organs along parallel neuronal pathways which, due to their specific properties, begin carrying out analytic processes already during the course of the transduction of information. As a result of the neuronal linkage involved in these processes, spatial patterns are constructed in cortical areas, which are thus utilized for the creation of complex perceptual images.

A simultaneously organized division of labor may be found on every level of the neuronal architecture. These levels are indicated as follows – in the sequence moving from the smallest building blocks up to and including the superordinated, macroscopic functional units (Damasio 2006):

NEURONS
LOCAL CIRCUITS
SUBCORTICAL NUCLEI (E.G., INTERBRAIN AND HINDBRAIN)
CORTICAL REGIONS (E.G., THE PRIMARY SENSORY REGIONS OF THE CEREBRAL CORTEX)
SYSTEMS
SYSTEMS OF SYSTEMS

The brain achieves its performance capabilities, accordingly, not as a result of a few, highly complex procedures of informational processing. Instead, the source is actually quite complex, but highly flexible circuitry of an extremely high number of simple processes which take place simultaneous to one another.

For the purpose of effectuating an initial approach with respect to the different strategies of perceptual systems regarding the connection of information from different senses with one another, the following rules may be presumed:

1	DIFFERENT STRATEGIES OF MULTISENSORY CONNECTION ARE SIMULTANEOUSLY UTILIZED.
2	THE RESULTS OF THE CONNECTION ARE INITIALLY INDEPENDENT OF ONE ANOTHER AND CAN EVEN CONTRADICT ONE ANOTHER.
3	DIFFERENT STRATEGIES CAN ACHIEVE RESULTS WHICH ACTUALLY LEAD IN THE SAME DIRECTION.
4	IF DIFFERENT STRATEGIES SHOULD LEAD TO CONTRADICTORY RESULTS, THE PERCEPTUAL SYSTEM THUS ENDEAVORS TO HARMONIZE THEM. IF IT IS NOT SUCCESSFUL IN THIS REGARD, A *PERCEPTUAL CONFLICT* CAN ARISE AND BE CONSCIOUSLY FELT.
5	RESULTS OF THE CONNECTION CAN BE CONSCIOUSLY ACCEPTED, COMBINED, OR REJECTED.

Those rules may not be understood as laws which are fixed within the biological structure of the brain. Instead, they are a matter of processes which are successively established and optimized during the course of neuronal development.

In the course of gestalt formation, the perceptual system aims at integrating the results of the strategies of connection into a perceptual image free of contradictions. The processes involved are discussed in section 3.1.2.

A PARTICULARLY IMPORTANT AND INTERESTING PROPERTY OF MULTISENSORY PROCESSING IS THE FACT THAT STRATEGIES OF CONNECTION IN AND OF ITSELF CAN BE CONSCIOUSLY ANALYZED BY THE PERCEIVING SUBJECT. THUS, FURTHER MECHANISMS INVOLVED IN MULTISENSORY CONNECTION IN CONSCIOUSNESS CAN BE EXCLUDED.

148

2.1
CONNECTION
OF MODALITIES
WITHIN THE
PERCEPTUAL
SYSTEM
↓
2.1.2
RULES OF
CONNECTION

Accordingly, tests subjects in psychophysical experiments can thus be fixated on observing stimuli exclusively with respect to specific properties.

For example, the brightness of a lamp can be evaluated with regard to the brightness of the acoustic timbre of a sound. In the choice of appropriate experimental conditions, the result is thus independent of associative and symbolic aspects. Conversely, the experiment can indeed be exclusively focused upon aspects of the identification of the source or of the contents of the meaning.

Conditions of consciousness are not the result of the processing of a certain center within the brain. For a long time, such a center was sought, but never found.

CONSCIOUSNESS IS THE RESULT OF THE ENTIRE ACTIVITY OF THE BRAIN.

Details as to the creation of the conditions of consciousness, such as the perception of object properties or the personal "I" in one's own self, are still unclear. The example in which consciousness is analogous to a floodlight which is directed to different centers of the brain, facilitating the perception of the processes taking place and results arising in those centers, however, does appear to be appropriate. All other processes take place in the "non-illuminated" regions independent of the activities of the consciousness – they thus are located in the darkness of unconscious processing. An aid for the placing of "illuminated" regions is the *attention,* which leads to a selection of the arriving stimuli and which also determines which part of the perceived information shall enter into the consciousness. Evidently, the conscious steering of attention must be distinguished from unknown, to a certain extent undoubtedly biologically determined processes.

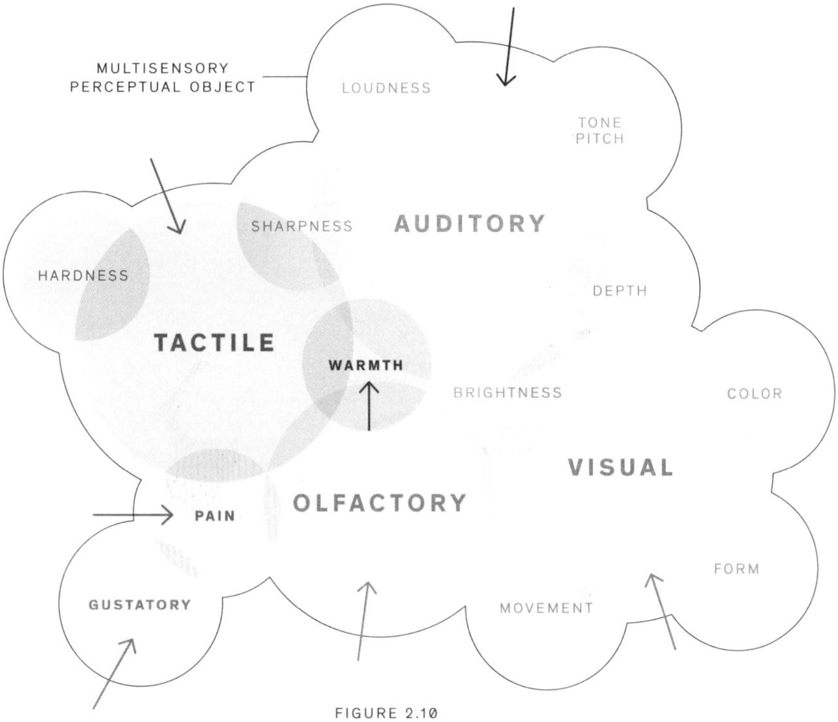

2.1
CONNECTION
OF MODALITIES
WITHIN THE
PERCEPTUAL
SYSTEM
↓
2.1.2
RULES OF
CONNECTION

———

149

FIGURE 2.10
A model of the multisensory perceptual object.
The sensory modalities involved are represented in the form of partial
quantities which are formed out of the perceived
properties (attributes). Some of the properties are
named as an example.

In building model-like descriptions of the connection between the senses, the question arises as to whether the perceptual objects are initially constructed in every participating modality, on a separate basis, prior to their amalgamation as multisensory perceptual objects, or whether individual properties such as color and tone pitch are directly and immediately interconnected. The perceptual experience indicates that, as a matter of principle, both methods are possible. On the one hand, isolated properties can be compared to one another in an experiment; on the other hand, purely auditory constructions such as elements of musical works can manifest themselves as perceptual objects of one isolated modality. Such "sound objects" are subsequently connected with corresponding visual constructions, such as constituent parts of a film scene. The apparent contradiction between the perceptual tendency to build multisensory representations and the existence of isolated "unimodal" perceptual objects is resolved when perceptual objects of individual sensory

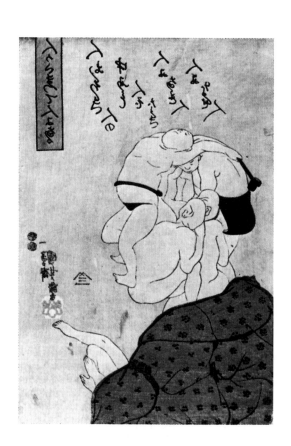

2.1
CONNECTION
OF MODALITIES
WITHIN THE
PERCEPTUAL
SYSTEM
↓
2.1.2
RULES OF
CONNECTION

FIGURE 2.11
Illustration of the holism involved in creating and designing.
Print by Kuniyoshi Ichiyusai, nineteenth century.

channels, in accordance with figure 2.10, can be seen as the partial quantity of multisensory perceptual objects, which in turn contain individual properties such as timbre, sharpness, granularity, hardness, and so forth. The decision as to which partial quantities of the whole shall consciously be perceived is precipitated by directing the attention – the "light beam" of the "floodlight." The multisensory perceptual object as well as the partial quantities which are allocated to the individual sensory modalities are the results of complicated perceptual processes. On the other hand, the individual property, such as color, brightness, or roughness, etc., can be attributed to a specific stimulation. A perceptual object is not a fixed cluster of perceived properties. Therefore, the herein used model of perceptual objects as cognitive representations of perception does imply dynamic features of those representations. While the receptors provide a continuous input of neuronal activity, perception and its representations are based on a continuous data stream. Although perceptual objects often provide the impression of constancy, they are in fact of a dynamic nature.

2.1
CONNECTION
OF MODALITIES
WITHIN THE
PERCEPTUAL
SYSTEM
↓
2.1.2
RULES OF
CONNECTION

The designing of complex products is, therefore, a very demanding matter, given the fact that the perceptual properties of the entire product can only be approximately assessed, in case that only the properties of the individual components are known. This applies both to the prediction of the perception of the product by the customer as well as to the functionality of the design.

THE HOLISM OF COMPLEX SYSTEMS EFFECTUATES THAT THE WHOLE, MORE OR LESS, PRESENTS SOMETHING DIFFERENT THAN THE PURE SUM OF THE COMPONENTS AND THEIR CONTRIBUTIONS.

Figure 2.11 illustrates the holistic principle utilizing a graphic depiction by the nineteenth-century Japanese artist Kuniyoshi Ichiyusai. The appearance of the head can not be explained with respect to the sum of the human bodies which comprise it. Here, many persons serve to build more than a group of persons.

SYSTEMS WHICH CAN BE COMPREHENDED RATHER PRECISELY AS THE SUM OF THE CONTRIBUTIONS OF THEIR ELEMENTS, SHOW REDUCTIONIST PROPERTIES.

On the one hand, an automobile comprises an enclosed, entire system which is, on the other hand, in and of itself a part of larger systems, such as the traffic system, the national economy, and the social structure of the respective society. Arthur Koestler coined the term *holon* for that which is simultaneously a whole and a part of a superordinated system (Wilber 1995). Holism effectuates an *added value* which does not stand alone among the accumulated values of the elements of design and which, therefore, may not easily de derived from them. In spite of an extensive catalog of demands for the components of a complex product, no preparatory work can completely substitute for the subsequent overall evaluation and the optimization taking place. This applies to automobiles, but it is also applicable to products of considerably less complexity. Generally speaking, the "holistic problem" can not even be thoroughly resolved by better planning, improved employee training, and more detailed surveys. As a matter of fact, this behavior of the system can be traced back to a theoretical, irrevocable property of the holon. Therefore, it is quite understandable that a completely manufactured product, despite its intensive, detailed development and the decades of experience of the developers, can often enough be accompanied by great surprises – indeed, in the case of the customers as well as of the designers and engineers who participated in its development. Nevertheless, one must realize that precisely this subtle holistic added value, being inherently difficult to estimate, can ultimately contribute greatly to the success of the product.

2.1.3
ELEMENTARY CONNECTIONS

152

2.1
CONNECTION
OF MODALITIES
WITHIN THE
PERCEPTUAL
SYSTEM
↓
2.1.2
RULES OF
CONNECTION
↓
2.1.3
ELEMENTARY
CONNECTIONS

Prior to undertaking a closer analysis of the strategies of connection which are of decisive significance with respect to building perceptual objects, it is advisable to first summarize the elementary mechanisms of connections required in the execution of basic body functions. In this regard, it primarily involves the exchange of information for the purpose of motor control. These connections of the sensory channels, however, do not normally appear as the result of individual stimuli in the consciousness. Thus, elementary connections were not involved in the model depicted in figure 2.1.

Some examples of elementary connections are:
→   The stimulation of the sense of balance leads to, by virtue of an interaction with proprioceptive data from the muscles and tendons, an optimizing of the body's posture and the processes of movement. Displacements of the retinal image are then optimally compensated for when caused by movements of the head. Thereby, the information pertaining to the movement of the vestibular system assists in a significant manner. If alternations of the retinal image are caused by movements of the body – for example, by the movement of one's own hand in front of the eyes – the proprioceptive information helps in correcting the perceptual image. This feature thus helps reading a book. However, if an object is moved without one's own participation, the compensation remains an exclusive function of the visual system. In such a case, a book being moved in front of the eyes is extraordinarily difficult to decipher (Campenhausen 1993).

Furthermore, without the sufficiently corrective functions within the perceptual system, objects being moved would not be recognizable as such, for they would instead appear as a sequence of overlapping images, thus causing a confusing, unclear maze of lines. Figure 2.12 is the result of the attempts of Futurist painters to retrace this effect by virtue of the perceptual path and to accordingly rescind the compensation with artistic means (see also section 2.2.4). Visual stimuli of an object being moved direct the movements of the eyes which follow the aforementioned object. Even within the course of this activity, a connection to the proprioceptive sensory cells of the eye musculature takes place. The same applies to the activity of the iris for the purpose of adapting the eye to the brightness of the surrounding environment.

→   During the execution of fine motor activities, the movements of the hand are steered by an interaction of visual, tactile, and proprioceptive information. Furthermore, in the case of manual writing, the tactile sensory stimuli serve to fixate the pen or pencil in the hand, whereas proprioceptive stimuli are essential with respect to regulating the position of the arm, the hand, and the fingers. If a cup filled with a fluid is carried from a light room into a darkened room, the contribution of visual information regarding the balancing of the object can be directly experienced.

→   Auditory stimuli lead to, by virtue of the process of directional hearing, intuitive movements of the head which accordingly serve to enhance the sharpness of the localization (Blauert 1997).

2.1
CONNECTION
OF MODALITIES
WITHIN THE
PERCEPTUAL
SYSTEM
↓
2.1.3
ELEMENTARY
CONNECTIONS

153

Although different regions of the brain contribute to the processing of multisensory information, many experiments concerned with elementary neuronal connections as conducted in recent years are concentrated on examining the region of the *superior colliculus.* This region may not be found in the cerebrum, the cortex along which the primary sensory fields are situated, for it is instead located in the middle brain (see the summary by Altinsoy 2006, 21).

Above and beyond that, there are also physical influences exerted upon different types of sensory cells. As a result of this, the mechanical vibrations which are caused by acoustic sources can also be sensed by the body. On the one hand, they are detected by the mechanoreceptors of the skin during contact. On the other hand, vibrations with a very low frequency do lead to infrasonic sounds which, although not longer capable of being heard by humans, nevertheless result in the stimulation of sensory cells within the abdominal region. The mostly deaf percussionist Evelyn Glennie vividly expresses her own personal approach to the perception and interpretation of music with the following words: "Hearing is a form of touching. (…) Something that is difficult to describe. Something that comes to you. You can sense it, as if you could reach out with your hand and touch the sound. You feel it, indeed, with your entire body." (Excerpt from the film *Touch the Sound,* Riedelsheimer 2005)

It is additionally known that a very high sound level can influence the balancing capability of the vestibular system, thus causing vertigo (Tullio 1929). This interaction is plausible, owing to the fact that a connection of the channel system of the inner ear and the vestibule physiologically exists (note fig. 1.41). The so-called *Tullio Phenomenon* appears, however, only in a disturbing form in the case of pathological alterations in the sense of hearing. A general

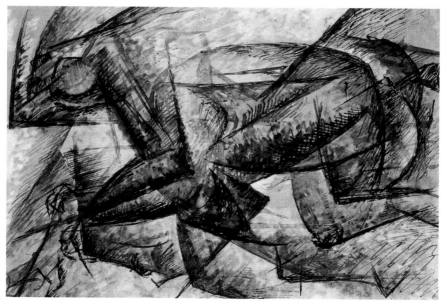

154

2.1
CONNECTION
OF MODALITIES
WITHIN THE
PERCEPTUAL
SYSTEM
↓
2.1.3
ELEMENTARY
CONNECTIONS

FIGURE 2.12
**Dinamismo di un ciclista (The Dynamism of a Cyclist)
Painting by Umberto Boccioni, 1913.**

consequence of this result was assumed pertaining to its influence upon the connection of the perception of music and movement (Truslit 1938), but could not yet be confirmed by medical research.

Furthermore, even the mode of operation or the sensibility of the sensory cells can be altered by stimuli for which the particular receptor is actually not designated. As a consequence, the Ruffinian corpuscles, for example, react more strongly to pressure stimuli if the skin is cold. Accordingly, cold objects which are resting on the skin can be perceived as heavier than they would in a warmer condition – a phenomenon which was already described by E.H. Weber in 1846 and appropriately characterized as *Weber'sche Täuschung (Weber's weight illusion,* Campenhausen 1993, 34).

As a general rule, vibrations which originate in the larynx during speaking or singing are not perceived, even though vibrations of the same amplitude are perceivable, if they are artificially created by a vibration exciter (shaker) located on the breast (Campenhausen 1993, 35).

2.1
CONNECTION
OF MODALITIES
WITHIN THE
PERCEPTUAL
SYSTEM
↓
2.1.3
ELEMENTARY
CONNECTIONS

155

FIGURE 2.13
Phosphenes as visible forms which are induced by the
electrical stimulation of the optic nerve.
Examples taken from the list evaluated by Eichmeier (1974).

An important property of the physiological construction of the sensory organs is the general tendency to avoid an undesired or a disturbing perception. In this sense, the eye has to be protected from forces which could influence the optic nerve and which could thus lead to a perception of illuminated figures. These appearances, alternately described as *phosphenes,* can be induced by slight pressure being applied by the finger to the side of the ocular bulb. They can also arise as a result of high pressure or accelerations, for example, as exerted upon the pilots of jet-propelled airplanes. Moreover, the properties of phosphenes also play a role in searching for fundamental forms of visual perception – as discussed in chapter 3.3. Figure 2.13 shows examples which became visible as a result of the electrical stimulation of the optic nerve (Eichmeier 1974). The avoidance of the reception of the stimulation by virtue of static, electrical, or magnetic fields is of greater importance, for these could significantly disturb the neuronal signal processing which would be quite susceptible. Therefore, for people, in contrast to some animals such as migratory birds, it is not essential to perceive the earth's magnetic field.

Some researchers assumed that feedback in the form of messages *(efferences)* containing neuronal information, and flowing from the sensory areas of the cerebral cortex to the sensory organs, was capable of influencing the transmission of the stimuli themselves. Thus, the sensibility of the inner ear with respect to acoustic stimuli could also be influenced by the activity of the visual cortex. On a daily basis, one can experience that sounds and music can be ineffectively perceived during the simultaneous presentation of intensive visual information. The direct influence of visual stimuli upon the physiological activity of the inner ear, however, could not yet be validated by experiments (Hoffmann 2007). Interconnections between seeing and hearing do not appear to occur on the level of the sensory organs.

SOUND

AND VIBRATION

Even the perceptions of sound and vibration can mutually influence one another. In particular, this applies to low frequencies for which the sense of hearing is not very sensitized. Corresponding to figure 1.46 (in section 1.3.1), the hearing threshold with respect to low frequencies increases – whereas the ability to hear steadily declines. Beneath approximately 20 Hz, even acoustic processes involving great energy can no longer be heard *(infrasonic)*. However, as mentioned above, such sounds can be perceived by receptors within the abdominal region. It is likely that this occurs by virtue of the same sensory cells which also register vibrations. Infrasonic sound of a low frequency, as well as *whole-body vibrations,* can lead to a reduction of the sense of well-being and can even ultimately result in a condition of pronounced discomfort. In this sense, non-audible acoustic contributions can influence the perception of audible signals in the realm of low frequencies – or, at the least, they strengthen the negative evaluation of that which was heard (Howarth 1990). The same applies to cases in which sounds and vibrations are simultaneously exerting their own respective influences. Infrasonic sounds and vibrations play a major role, for example, during work being carried out by pneumatic hammers. In automobiles, the acoustic impression of the entire sound is partially influenced by the typical vibrations of the seats, but also by the dynamic forces of the driving which are additionally acting upon the body. In such cases, the evaluation of the sound can lead to an underestimation of the entire effect, solely on the basis of the sensibility of the sense of hearing – such as the A-weighting with a presentation of a sound level in dB(A). Nevertheless, the perception of music can also be positively influenced by the vibrations of a listener's seats. With an additional transformation of the lower frequencies of the musical signal into vibrations of the seats, the musical experience is regarded as being enriched. However, this only applies to frequency regions beneath 100 Hz – higher frequencies of vibration are generally not considered to be positive with regard to music being played (Merchel 2008).

Vibrations of very low frequencies can be, with sufficient deflection, visually perceived as well. Additionally, they influence body movements as well as the execution of mechanical activities involved in operational tasks (see e.g., Nakamura 1991). Even these secondary effects can alter the perception of vibrations. Generally speaking, the perceptual qualities of sounds and vibrations, however, can be consciously distinguished from one another. In this case, again, the answer to the question as to whether the results of perceptual experiments demonstrate a mutual influencing of the stimuli, accordingly, is considerably dependent upon the scope and the definition of the tasks.

156

2.1
CONNECTION
OF MODALITIES
WITHIN THE
PERCEPTUAL
SYSTEM
↓
2.1.3
ELEMENTARY
CONNECTIONS

2.2.1

ANALOGY RELATIONSHIPS

2.2
FINDING
SIMILARITIES –
CROSS-MODAL
ANALOGIES
↓
2.2.1
ANALOGY
RELATIONSHIPS

———

157

An important task of the perceptual system consists of correlating the various sensory stimuli with one another and assigning them, by means of common characteristics, to certain objects. Only then, it is possible to construct multi-sensory perceptual objects to which the different stimulating qualities bind themselves. The diverse attributes of an object, such as color, form, surface texture, weight, size, hardness, temperature, orientation within a given space, among many others, are indeed based on very different physical and chemical phenomena. Therefore, the processing of the stimulus requires different, i.e. specific receptors and diverse processing steps within the neuronal system. At the end of this complex processing, however, a closed, easily "comprehensible" perceptual object, to which the individual properties are sensibly attributed, must appear. For this purpose, the necessary coupling of the properties is achieved by a neuronal analysis of correlations, revealing the analogy relationships existing between the attributes.

THE TERM ANALOGY REFERS TO THE ABILITY OF THE PERCEPTUAL SYSTEM TO RECOGNIZE CORRELATIONS AND TO EVALUATE THEM FOR THE PURPOSE OF IDENTIFYING OBJECTS AND ENVIRONMENTS.

FIGURE 2.14
Analogy relationship of the design of an automobile and
natural forms in advertisement. Ford KA, 1999.

Accordingly, the conformity of a location of the perception of color with the location of the perception of form allows us to conclude that both can be attributed to an appropriately colored, appropriately shaped object. Furthermore, beyond the identification of objects, it is also possible to create relationships between objects. Figure 2.14 illustrates the relationship between the contours of an automobile and the elements of a landscape and encompasses, in particular, the shape of the trees. Its curved form is, in this case, the direct consequence of the high velocity of the wind, and it expressly indicates the dynamic nature of the vehicle. Additionally, with the assistance of the form analogy, the automobile and the natural landscape are associatively connected to one another. The utilization of analogy relationships to create associative or symbolic contents will be presented, with further examples, in section 3.2.2 (see also Haverkamp 2006a).

FIGURE 2.15
A piece of soap, a wave, a bubble?
Stefano Giovannoni, Big Bubbles, soap dish
designed for Alessi, 1999.

158

2.2
FINDING
SIMILARITIES –
CROSS-MODAL
ANALOGIES
↓
2.2.1
ANALOGY
RELATIONSHIPS

In the field of industrial design, analogies between the appearance of a product and its functions are of great significance. A design appropriately aligned with the functions of the product increases the possibilities of said product to demonstrate such functions, thus enhancing its ease of operation.

As a simple example within a sensory modality, figure 2.15 illustrates the utilization of visual analogies between a dish and the object for which it is intended. The soap dish was developed by Stefano Giovannoni, who had also made a name for himself in the field of automobile design. In its form, it exhibits aspects reminiscent of a piece of soap, a deformed bubble, or a wave resulting from a drop landing upon the surface of the water. In this case, even the color is indicative of the often-observed color of the element water itself, although it is known that this is, as a general rule, not a property of the element, but the result of light reflections. Owing to the selected analogy of form and color, the function of the soap dish is clearly determined and can be easily recognized by potential users. The inscription "soap" as the label is thus superfluous from a functional standpoint. Thereby, however, one should note that the majority of the analogies chosen here is not solely based upon the soap, but also upon characteristics such – as suds and water drops – which arise in the course of usage. In view of that, the object further appeals to the experience of the observer and thus also to learned, associative connections, which will be discussed in further detail in chapter 2.3.

For an optimal design aimed at all senses, the correlations of object properties are significant even beyond the sensory boundaries. Thus, the aforementioned definition can be expanded upon:

THE TERM CROSS-MODAL ANALOGY
REFERS TO THE ABILITY OF THE PERCEPTUAL
SYSTEM TO RECOGNIZE CORRELATION
AND TO EVALUATE OBJECTS AND ENVIRONMENTS
BEYOND THE SENSORY BOUNDARIES.

In this manner, an acoustic blinking signal will be attributed to a blinking lamp and to the blinking lights themselves, if visual and auditory signals simultaneously appear. ● Even the sound of the automobile engine reveals the conformity of the expectations with respect to the function, as long as it alters itself dependent upon the operation of the gas pedal and the acceleration of the vehicle. Given that cross-modal analogies make reference to elementary properties, they also facilitate the interconnection of unknown sensory impressions. A sound that is new to the listener, for example, can also be attributed to a certain function – or an operational element can be attributed to an unconventional form. Owing to the fact that a fixed attribution of perceptual qualities to the stimuli, and to the physical or chemical properties which give rise to stimuli, often exists, the perception of individual properties – which serve as the fundament of the analogy relationships – can be described with quantitative values. In this regard, *Psychophysics* provides the appropriate methods.

   In the observation of perceptual phenomena, it is evident that the following principles are significant with respect to cross-modal connections via *analogies:*

→   *One-to-many relation:* The activation of a sensory channel in the primary sensory field often causes the activation of further channels of other senses. In this manner, many attributes in secondary sensory channels can be allotted to a primary channel. The connection, however, is not permanently fixed, but it is more or less effective from case to case. Figure 2.16 demonstrates the difference with respect to *one-to-one* relations, being typical of many technical, strictly causal systems. Most of the previous approaches towards the observation of multisensory perceptual processes had this form of causality as a prerequisite, but they did not lead to satisfying theories, given the fact that the sheer diversity of the phenomena tends to contradict such simple, one-dimensional models.

→   As a general rule, the connections are one-sided, i.e. effective in one direction *(unidirectional),* and they can, however, also appear – in contrast to cases of genuine synesthesia – to be two-sided, *bidirectional.* Contrary to many technical systems, there is not necessarily a reciprocal relationship between the input and output quantities. For example, a similar attribution in reverse direction, such as from the visual to the auditory, does not necessarily result from the connection of the tone pitch with visual brightness.

→   The connections often exhibit *asymmetry.* The form of the connection is dependent upon the direction of the change – to greater or lesser values of the respective attribute. Thus, in perceptual experiments, the increase of the

2.2
FINDING
SIMILARITIES –
CROSS-MODAL
ANALOGIES
↓
2.2.1
ANALOGY
RELATIONSHIPS

159

tone pitch was, as a matter of preference, connected to the movement of an object away from the listener, whereas the reduction of pitch corresponded to a movement towards the left side (Eitan 2004, see section 2.2.4, table 2.3).

→ Cross-modal connections reveal relative allocations, caused by the dependency upon the context. That enables the quantitative attribution via behavioral scales (section 3.2.1). An absolute reference, however, does not exist.

→ This kind of analogy relationship can be partially determined by object identifications (concrete association) and symbolism. In this manner, accelerated acoustic repetitions with a simultaneous decrease in the tone frequency can be connected to a decrease of spatial height, by virtue of the association of a ball bouncing downhill (Eitan 2004).

→ Analogy relations also allow concrete associations (iconic connections) to be created. As discussed above, the connection of the auditory and the visual blinking signal occurs as a result of the temporally analog behavior *(synchrony)*. If this analogy relationship is established within the perceptual system, the perception of the sound alone is sufficient, thus permitting the function to be associatively recognized. Additionally, the sound of an automobile engine is associated with the robust behavior of the powertrain and with the solid construction of the components, as long as it behaves analogous to the movement of the vehicle. The possibility of creating new, associative connections through the use of analogy relationships is of great significance with respect to multisensory design, therefore, it is not necessary to make reference to associative connections already familiar to the customer as discussed in chapter 2.3. As an example, the sound of an electrical vehicular drive can be unfamiliar, but with high probability will be accepted by the customer if the sound behaves precisely analog to the vehicle operation. Thus, analogy relationships are also utilized in commercial advertising, as further analyzed in section 3.2.2. The idea of using formal analogies in order to create an associative correlation, however, is not new. Already in 1929, the filmmaker and cinematic theoretician Hans Richter alluded to the significance of the association of ideas in artistic films. These can be created or supported by analogy relationships. The *association of ideas* "is increasingly necessary when the relation of the forms, correspondingly, increasingly makes reference to the relations of the contents." (Richter 1929).

160

2.2
FINDING
SIMILARITIES –
CROSS-MODAL
ANALOGIES
↓
2.2.1
ANALOGY
RELATIONSHIPS

IN THE IMPLEMENTATION OF PERCEPTUAL EXPERIMENTS, THE POSSIBILITY OF DIFFERENT PREFERENCES BEING EXHIBITED BY THE TEST SUBJECTS MUST BE ADEQUATELY CONSIDERED.

The term *analogy* shall herein be limited to events which are directly perceivable. As a matter of contrast, for example, the descriptions *white noise* and *pink noise* are based upon a physical allocation of the spectral distribution of sound waves and light waves which is physically established, although not directly perceivable. It involves a *mathematic-physical connection* as discussed in chapter 2.6.

Experiments aimed at evaluating cross-modal connections exhibit important differences, when compared to examinations of causal contexts. For example, in the measuring of perceptual thresholds, homogenous groups of persons spread the results of the experiments around an average value. Usually the spread corresponds to a *normal (Gaussian) distribution.* The tendency towards demonstrating different preferences in the sense of a *one-to-many connection,* however, leads to frequency distributions with several maxima. For each preference, however, a normal distribution manifests itself in most cases. Thierry Lageat and Brieuc de Larrard examined the sound heard in opening a cigarette lighter. The object of the experiment was a *flip-open lighter,* a cigarette lighter which automatically lights the flame upon the opening of the protective cap. More specifically, they examined the acoustic properties which would tend to support the perception of the object as being "luxurious." Thereby, it became obvious that two groups of people had their own respective understanding of an appropriate sound: the first group preferred a dull, uniform sound with a low tone pitch; the second group, on the other hand, exhibited a preference for a clear, resonant clicking sound (Lageat, 2003).

2.2
FINDING
SIMILARITIES –
CROSS-MODAL
ANALOGIES
↓
2.2.1
ANALOGY
RELATIONSHIPS
———
161

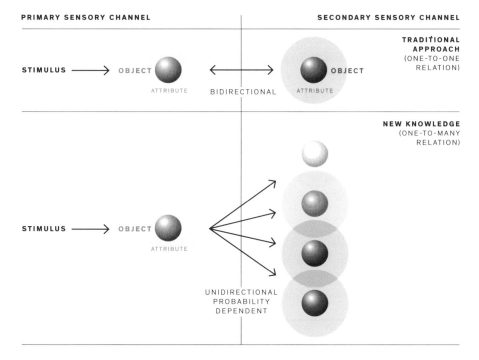

FIGURE 2.16
One-to-one and one-to-many relation. In the case of an auditory-
visual connection, the primary sensory field orients itself
with respect to the auditory perception, whereas the secondary sensory field,
on the other hand, orients itself with respect to the visual perception.

An unexamined presumption of a permanent relation existing between two individual parameters should not be made. Only when all possible preferences are known, can the stratification of the collective of test subjects, namely the division into several homogenous groups, be performed.

TEMPORAL ANALOGY

The temporal connection of perceptual events of different sensory modalities often occurs according to the *principle of common fate* (section 1.3.8) Thereby, the correlation of the temporal alteration of individual properties of perceived objects is evaluated within the perceptual system. Elementary relations, such as the simultaneousness *(synchrony)* of stimuli often suffice for the establishment of multisensory relations. Accordingly, within the design process, an acoustic blinking signal can be arbitrarily chosen with respect to its acoustic qualities, without it being necessary to make reference to a customary pattern, such as a typical relay sound. As long as there is a synchronic manner of behavior with respect to the optical signal, the connection will obligatorily be established.

IN THE ASSIGNMENT OF AUDITORY AND VISUAL SIGNALS IN THE CONTEXT OF MULTISENSORY INTEGRATION, THE QUESTION AS TO WHETHER THE PERCEPTUAL EVENTS ARE SENSED AS BEING SIMULTANEOUS OR WHETHER A TEMPORAL OFFSET EXISTS IS CRUCIAL.

162

2.2
FINDING
SIMILARITIES –
CROSS-MODAL
ANALOGIES
↓
2.2.2
TEMPORAL
ANALOGY

Generally speaking, it must be recognized that the perceptual resolution of temporal processes in the auditory domain is larger than it is in the visual domain. This could be founded upon the assumption that the processing of auditory information occurs more quickly within the brain.

The threshold values of delay, of great importance to synchrony, were examined by Armin Kohlrausch and Steven van de Par (Kohlrausch 2000; 2002; 2005). Figure 2.17 illustrates the result. For this purpose, the perception of simple audio and video signals with different delays has been evaluated. With respect to the time axis, the results exhibit a characteristic asymmetry. The differential threshold for asynchronous signals amounts to -30 ms with a delayed video signal. With a delayed audio signal, on the other hand, it amounts to +120 ms (or +90 ms, according to the results of other experiments). A possible explanation for the asymmetry is based upon the fact that the sound of a source, as compared to light, reaches the ear on a delayed basis in the case of the perception of natural processes – due to the different velocity of wave propagation. A source distance of 10 m already causes a delay of 30 ms. As a matter of comparison, values for the distance to a source of sound – such as to a speaker – are listed in figure 2.17, corresponding to the indicated delay values *(audio delay)*. The threshold values for the perception of synchrony are dependent upon the form of the signals utilized. Vocal signals result in considerably greater values, which means that greater temporal differences between auditory and visual stimuli are tolerated.

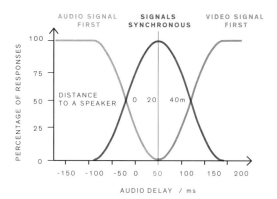

AUDIO SIGNAL FIRST   SIGNALS SYNCHRONOUS   VIDEO SIGNAL FIRST

PERCENTAGE OF RESPONSES

DISTANCE TO A SPEAKER   0   20   40m

AUDIO DELAY / ms

FIGURE 2.17
Auditory-visual synchrony. The decisional pattern of test subjects as the result of perceptual experiments.

2.2
FINDING
SIMILARITIES —
CROSS-MODAL
ANALOGIES
↓
2.2.2
TEMPOARAL
ANALOGY

___

163

The result of the experiment pertaining to synchrony can also be summarized in the following manner (Kohlrausch 2005):

→   There is a range of approximately 150 ms during which delays between auditory and visual stimuli can not be perceived.

→   A characteristic asymmetry exists, which leads to a shifting of the range of synchronous perception out of the zero position.

→   The asymmetry can also be regarded as a symmetric phenomenon around a *point of subjective similarity,* which involves a delay of 40-50 ms with respect to the audio signal.

These results were confirmed in the course of the examination of the influence of the synchrony upon the McGurk Effect (section 3.2.1), as a general tendency (van Wassenhove 2007). As a matter of principle, the perceptual system tends to connect auditory and visual signals which simultaneously reach the person observing and hearing them. This also applies to the presentation of sources of visual and auditory stimuli in artificial environments, although their signals would not simultaneously occur in reality (Arnold 2005). Due to the identification of an object with the assistance of concrete associative (iconic) connections, it is, nevertheless, also possible to allocate signals to a source regarded as being considerably asynchronous, for example, as caused by great differences of signal delay. In this manner, lightning perceived in the distance can be correlated to the thunder heard some seconds later. This does not occur on the basis of cross-modal analogy, however, and it requires that the connection of sensations of the different modalities is anchored by learning processes. Simultaneously perceived stimuli are also connected with one another, on the other hand, when the source is unknown or when artificial signals are involved.

As a consequence of the capability to correlate even asynchronous signals to one another, in principle, differences arise between the *just noticeable delay* and the *threshold of acceptance* (Kohlrausch 2002).

For driver information systems in an automobile (*Infotainment,* fig. 2.18), e.g., *navigation systems,* it is sensible to relay as much auditory information as possible, in order not to distract the vision of the driver with respect to the traffic situation. The auditory transmission of navigational commands as employed in the form of the *voice output,* however, does not necessarily represent the optimal method of vocal communication. For example, it is known that seeing the movement of the lips of the speaking person can significantly enhance the speech comprehension, particularly when the environmental sounds complicate the process of hearing. Therefore the voice output of a human-computer interface can be significantly improved if an artificial face, an *embodied conversational agent,* is shown on screen. Experimental results indicate that in a passive scenario without interactive input of the user, the quality of the output of such *talking heads* can well be described as a linear combination of auditory and visual aspects (Weiss 2010). Similarly to mimics, gestures improve the speech comprehension and help to more clearly recognize characteristics of the speech melody (Krahmer 2007). Generally speaking, the importance of visual information increases with the loss of hearing (Hoffmann 2007). Where possible, applications which allow – in contrast to the operating environment within an automobile – the additional visual support of the voice output should be utilized. Notably, systems for computer-assisted voice outputs often enable only a limited comprehensibility, given that the inflexible programmed pronunciation and a considerably simplified intonation diminish the naturalness of speech. In many cases, it makes sense to additionally equip voice output systems with visual simulations of lip movement and the imitation of speakers (see e.g., Weiss 2005).

164

2.2
FINDING
SIMILARITIES –
CROSS-MODAL
ANALOGIES
↓
2.2.2
TEMPORAL
ANALOGY

FIGURE 2.18
Instrument cluster (right-hand side) and the infotainment area (left-hand side)
in a family car with right-hand drive. Ford Mondeo, 2007.

In a similar fashion, *gestures* can also improve the speech recognition by virtue of technical systems, namely *voice entry.* This can be realized, for example, when one points with the finger to objects which are presented on a monitor parallel to the voice entry. In order to provide interactive shopping capabilities, such a system was examined. It reconstructed the shopping environment, including the salesperson, in a virtual manner *(Virtual Shop)*. Thereby, the simulation of the *facial expression* of the virtual salesperson was combined with the evaluation of gestures of the actual shopper. This lead to a considerably improved communication, as compared to systems merely functioning with simple voice input and output (Sánchez Martínez 2005).

Thus, in the course of verbal communication, the expression of happiness, for example, is coded in the auditory as well as in the visual signal, and it can be extracted from both modalities (Auberg 2003). However, both sensory channels mutually support one another – indeed, even in the case of clear visual information, speech rhythm *(prosody)* notably facilitates the interpretation. Accordingly, the multisensory information even enables the distinction between spontaneous happiness and the simulated expression given by *mechanical laughter.*

2.2
FINDING
SIMILARITIES –
CROSS-MODAL
ANALOGIES
↓
2.2.2
TEMPOARAL
ANALOGY

165

IN THE INTERPRETATION OF THE EXPRESSION AND THE EMOTIONAL CONTENTS OF VERBAL COMMUNICATION, HEARING ANDSEEING CONTRIBUTE EQUALLY – CORRESPONDING TO THE USUAL INTER-ACTION OF SPEECH, FACIAL EXPRESSION, AND GESTURE.

Nevertheless, the visual impression can also modify auditory properties. If a fearful voice is presented with a picture of a happy facial expression, the voice tends to sound happier than otherwise (Vroomen 2000).

Even the evaluation of the quality of transmission of audio-visual media is influenced by cross-modal connection. John G. Beerends and Franciscus E. de Caluwe examined the influence of the quality of the images presented in video advertising upon the perceived audio quality (cited by Kohlrausch 2002). If the image quality is high, the audio signal is also regarded as being of high value – and vice versa, as compared to the presentation of the audio signal without an image. According to this experiment, however, the audio quality exhibited a less significant influence upon the perceived quality of the image, as compared to the reverse situation. As a matter of contrast, other experiments involving speech signals indicate a considerable influence in both directions and thus serve as evidence of cross-modal connection (Kohlrausch 2002). Recent studies clearly demonstrate that auditory and visual quality are integrated to form a single audio-visual rating. The type of scenario – a human-to-human or a human-machine interface – shows impact on the subjective assessment of quality and on possible effects of dominance, i.e. whether one modality plays the main role for integration of quality aspects. Moreover, the impression of quality differs in cases of interactive communication between the user and the system (Möller 2010).

Hence, it can be inferred that the audio quality in the case of driver information of a purely auditory nature is particularly important with respect to the comprehension of such information. This applies especially to the evaluation of speech synthesis. Where possible, the voice output should accordingly be supported by visual, mimicking information. For the design and the realization of such systems, one has to distinguish the quality of the signal transmission itself from the multisensory quality of the transmitted content (Haverkamp 2010a).

SYNCHRONY
IN THE AUDITORY DOMAIN

To complement the context illustrated in figure 2.17, the problematic of the grouping of different acoustic signals, which are necessary for the building of clear, auditory perceptual objects, shall be briefly expanded upon.

The *echo threshold* determines the delay in which an *acoustic reflection* is perceived as being separate from the *direct sound*. If the level of the direct sound and the reflection are equal, the threshold value is at approximately 20 ms for impulses and at 30 ms for speech. In the case of long delays, the direct sound and the reflection are audible as separate events – and an echo arises only then. The echo threshold, however, is also influenced by further parameters, such as the duration of the impulse and the direction of the incidence (Blauert 1997, figs. 3.12, 3.14, and 3.15). Beneath the echo threshold, namely in the case of shorter delays between the direct sound and the reflection, both perceptual events merge with one another, thus building an auditory object. In this case, the temporally delayed reflection merely influences the timbre and the loudness. With respect to the perception of direction, the *law of the first wave front* applies. The directional perception of the sound is then exclusively determined by the direction of incidence of the direct sound.

Transient response times of acoustic musical instruments occupy the range between 20 and 200 ms – this duration is needed to achieve a stable tone. With the smooth onset of string instruments, however, nearly 500 ms can be reached. During the interaction of several musicians, the listener can tolerate a temporal offset of a maximum of 50 ms between the employment of the individual instruments (Meyer 1995; 2009).

166

2.2
FINDING
SIMILARITIES –
CROSS-MODAL
ANALOGIES
↓
2.2.2
TEMPORAL
ANALOGY

AS A CONSEQUENCE OF THE AFOREMENTIONED NUMERICAL VALUES OF ECHO THRESHOLDS, A SINGLE AUDITORY OBJECT CAN ONLY THEN BE HEARD WHEN THE DELAY BETWEEN DIFFERENT SOUND COMPONENTS IS LESS THAN 20 ms.

In sound design, measures must be undertaken to ensure that the complete sound radiation of a functional process or a signal source is perceived as a self-contained auditory object. In practice, however, the implementation of a physical function can often involve various partial processes. Accordingly, even a simple light switch can radiate diverse sounds in a temporally offset manner.

Figure 2.19 illustrates the acoustic behavior *(clicking)* of a switch for an electrically operated parking brake. With the assistance of the measurement result, four – mechanically determined – phases, each having a different frequency behavior, may be distinguished from one another. By virtue of constructive measures, the time delay between the single events must be held to a minimum for the purpose of enabling a subjective merging of the sound components. In this case only one auditory object is perceivable after the spectral properties of the various acoustic portions merge with one another to form a composite sound. ●

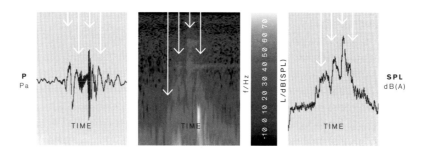

2.2
FINDING
SIMILARITIES –
CROSS-MODAL
ANALOGIES
↓
2.2.2
TEMPOARAL
ANALOGY

FIGURE 2.19
The temporal behavior of a switch for an electric parking brake.
The acoustic events are illustrated by arrows.
Left: sound pressure; middle: spectrum of the sound level;
right: sound pressure level.

A functional design will be perceived as robust only if it results in a function, which is clearly distinguished from other processes, ultimately being represented by a similarly distinct, self-contained perceptual object.

In the aforementioned example, the function of the switch consists exclusively of *activation* and *deactivation.* The brake functions *clamp* and *release* correspond to these functions. Clear visual, tactile, and auditory perceptual objects must correspond to them, otherwise the impression of reduced quality arises. For example, if further acoustic events should follow the clicking sound of the switching, it unintentionally yields the impression that the switch "clatters." Or if the user feels and sees a portion of the shift paddle moving in an asynchronous manner with respect to the tilting movement, it is regarded as "living an independent life" and thus as being non-robust. Simultaneously perceived stimuli of different sensory channels play a significant role in the building of multisensory perceptual objects. Michel Chion speaks of *synchrese,* a process by which the *synchrony* serves as the actuator of the *synthesis* of perceptual objects (Chion 1994).

ANALOGY
OF RHYTHM

A transfer of the temporal analogy from individual perceptual events to groups of signals leads to an *analogy of rhythm.* Thereby, the rhythm of a sequence of visual signals – e.g., in movies and in dance – and also the static visual structure – e.g., a pattern with recurring characteristics – can be correlated to a musical rhythm. It was ascertained rather early that auditory rhythms can influence the perception of visual rhythms. If that which is heard supports the visual rhythm, this serves to enhance the precision of that which is seen. Auditory signals which do not correspond to that which is simultaneously being seen, however, can considerably distort a visually perceived movement (Zietz 1927). If a rapidly changing image on a screen is presented to test subjects, the surprising superimposition of a sound can lead to the image being perceived as brighter or as extended in time. In the latter case, given that the image appears to be "frozen," the effect is referred to as the *freezing phenomenon* (Vroomen 2004).

Conversely, the perception of auditory structures is also influenced by simultaneous presentation of moving visual patterns. Thereby, the rhythmic sequence of the images plays a greater role than the statement of the contents (Hurte 1982). Rhythmic structures are omnipresent in everyday life. In particular, the modern mass production of goods is based upon periodically recurring intervals of time, such as the work cycle in the production of piecework and on the assembly line. Spatial rhythms correspond to them, and these spatial rhythms arise in the visual domain more or less by virtue of the systematic placing of a large amount of pieces during the storage process. The temporal structure of the work cycle transforms itself into a spatial structure of the goods being produced, e.g., the parked vehicles waiting to transport the designated goods – a rhythm of spatial character which is subsequently continued in public parking lots, in parking garages, while waiting for the traffic signal to change at the corner, and in traffic jams. The requirements of modern mass societies also lead to architectual structures in which various rhythms may be found. This applies to entrances with groups of pillars, subway stations, or factory halls, as well as to the vertical and horizontal repetition of the rectangles of expanded window areas. Figure 2.20 illustrates such an example found in the mining industry.

Visual rhythmic structures may also be found in historical buildings, for example, such as halls with pillars, and quite fundamentally as the arrangement of stones in walls or in the periodic wooden structure of half-timbered houses. Furthermore, even decorative elements often consist of recurring elements, as illustrated in figure 2.21 in the depiction of Islamic art. In this case, it involves a circular arrangement which leads to an unending rhythm.

As already mentioned, the *work cycle* of mechanical processes is a source of auditory rhythms. The application of periodic structures enters into the consciousness, however, more likely as a result of listening to music. Thereby, the normal listener prefers, as a general rule, simple rhythms of a reasonably limited length. *Aleatoric music,* i.e. music generated by chance, and complex or free rhythms, on the other hand, tend to be rejected by the broad public. Rhythmic light effects, nevertheless, support the impact of the music. The rhythm is perceived by the body and provokes the appropriate periodic movements of the body related to dancing.

Complicated rhythms initially exacerbate the intuitive motor implementation. However, even the superposition of different periodicities may lead to the apparent blurring of the temporal structure, which is then perceived as being random. An example of the superposition of many different structures with diverse periodicities was provided by the Hungarian composer György Ligeti. His *Poéme Symphonique* is based upon the sound of 100 mechanical

168

2.2
FINDING
SIMILARITIES –
CROSS-MODAL
ANALOGIES
↓
2.2.2
TEMPORAL
ANALOGY

2.2
FINDING
SIMILARITIES –
CROSS-MODAL
ANALOGIES
↓
2.2.2
TEMPOARAL
ANALOGY

169

FIGURE 2.20
A visually rhythmic structure.
Strut structure for mining coal with a roll loader.
Mining Museum (Bergbaumuseum) Bochum.

FIGURE 2.21
Islamic art especially expresses itself by virtue of the
rhythmically ornamental structures.
Dome in the harem of the Topkapi Palace, Istanbul.

metronomes, each functioning with respect to a different time scale and each having been wound up to a distinctly diverging measure. Having been started in a nearly simultaneous manner, the contributions – the *ticking* – of the individual metronomes vanish piece by piece. In the course of the different steps of the complex rhythm, the complete sound transforms from the amorphous noise to the transient quality of the individual pulses. Figure 2.22 demonstrates this effect by using 16 (instead of 100) line groups with a different line distance and a correspondingly different group length. The superposition of the groups creates a structure which evolves from a static agglomeration on the left-hand side to increasingly simplified rhythms on the right-hand side. In everyday life, comparable structures can be found, e.g., the sounds of printers or of the hard drives of computers. ●

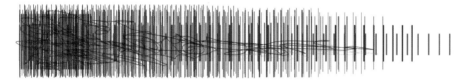

FIGURE 2.22
A depiction of the rhythmic superposition of the
metronome beats in György Ligeti's Poéme Symphonique.
Graphic illustration by the author.

(14)

170

2.2
FINDING
SIMILARITIES –
CROSS-MODAL
ANALOGIES
↓
2.2.2
TEMPORAL
ANALOGY

FIGURE 2.23
Two-dimensional line rhythms of modern
window fronts superpose one another in mirror images.
A high-rise building in Brussels.

Even textures can be pronouncedly rhythmic. In this regard, fabrics exhibit parallel and rectangular patterns. Greater structures are composed by stones, by tiles for walls or floors, or by window fronts (fig. 2.23), as well as by wooden structures, profiled metals, artificial materials, or paper. In the appendix of this book, the influence of tactile and visual structuring upon the perception can be experienced by virtue of self-testing.

Rhythmic structures are systematically employed in order to equip operating elements with surfaces facilitating a good grip and an ease of handling. In this manner, important elements of the tactile design are created according to the aspects discussed in section 2.2.7. The processing of periodic stimuli occurs in an efficient manner, for not all individual elements are analyzed in and of themselves. Instead, they are summarized and handled as a group. Accordingly, rhythmic structures require less attention than an unexpectedly occurring individual event. Due to its very good predictability, rhythmic music is often perceived as having a relaxing pattern, into which the listener may comfortably "immerse" him or herself. Moreover, in the perceptual process, periodic structures can be more easily drowned out than unsystematic individual events, as indicated by the picket-fence effect discussed in chapter 1.3.8.

With respect to the topic of synchrony, it was already mentioned that sound components can then be perceived as asynchronous when the time differential between them amounts to more than 20 to 50 ms. Accordingly, periodic auditory structures are then perceived as rhythmic if they exhibit fluctuations with a periodicity of more than 50 ms, according to fluctuation frequencies of less than 20 Hz. If the temporal distance of periodic structures is decreased to lower durations, the impression of temporal change diminishes. Instead, a constant signal is perceived. Nevertheless, the periodic fluctuation ultimately leads to an alteration of the sound quality, particularly resulting in an additional roughness.

2.2
FINDING
SIMILARITIES –
CROSS-MODAL
ANALOGIES
↓
2.2.2
TEMPOARAL
ANALOGY

171

WITH AN INCREASE IN THE FREQUENCY OF SIGNAL FLUCTUATIONS, A TRANSITION FROM TEMPORAL TO SPECTRAL QUALITIES TRANSPIRES – THE THRESHOLD AMOUNTS TO 20 Hz.

For the purposes of psychoacoustic descriptions, one may utilize either the *fluctuation strength* or the *roughness,* each being described in the excursus pertaining to psychoacoustic parameters within the course of section 1.3.1. Children love to get hold of sticks with which they create rhythmic noises as they walk along a fence or a grating. The movement gives rise to a rhythmically acoustic event synchronous to the touching of the spatial structure. This corresponds to the transformation from a spatial into a temporal – in this case, an auditory – structure. If the movement is accelerated, the aforementioned transition is from a temporal into a spectral quality.

THE DIMENSIONS OF PERCEPTION, AS DISCUSSED IN CHAPTER 1.3, SPECTRAL, TEMPORAL, AND SPATIAL, ARE OFTEN VERY CLOSELY RELATED TO ONE ANOTHER IN SITUATIONS OF EVERYDAY LIFE.

The same also applies to the visual and tactile domain. If one observes a spinning gyro which has colored surfaces or forms, these structures merge with one another during rapid evolutions – the gyro appears to stand still and to exhibit a homogenous color. Even the touching of the periodic textures of surfaces in the case of minimal velocities leads to a tactile perception of the rhythmic structure. If the velocity with which the fingers are led across the surface is increased, the impression of the temporal fluctuation of the sense of touching is diminished, whereas the impression of a static surface quality is enhanced. Using the enclosed sheets provided in the appendix of this book, one may test and see for him or herself.

2.2.3
INTERSENSORY ATTRIBUTES

There is apparently a great number of general properties with which perceptual events of each modality can be characterized. Attributes with which a characterization of perception is possible in every sensory channel are described by Hans Werner as intersensory attributes [Intersensorielle Eigenschaften]. Explicitly, he mentions the attributes: *intensity, brightness, volume, density,* and *roughness* (Werner 1966).

FIGURE 2.24
**Given that the air current is not visible,
the subjective evaluation of the quality of the ventilation can only
occur by virtue of skin perception or auditorily.**

Thus, a sound can be characterized by, for example, intensity (loudness), brightness (brilliance), volume (sonority), density, and roughness. Similarly, a perceptual event of a visual nature can be described by the equivalent attributes intensity, brightness, volume (illumination of the room), density (saturation), and roughness (graininess, flickering). Therefore, it is possible to carry out the evaluation of a sound by virtue of a comparison with visual characteristics and, where applicable, also with the inclusion of other modalities. Furthermore, the increasingly significant interconnection of all senses for product design also profits from the findings of elementary, cross-sensory characteristics, even if the number of perceptual properties which are independent of one another – *dimensions* of the perceptual quality – is not conclusively known at the present time.

For the quality of automobile ventilation – which partially takes place through visible openings corresponding to those in figure 2.24 – auditory aspects are of great significance. ● Figure 2.25 illustrates the utilization of intersensory attributes in accordance with Werner with respect to the sound quality of ventilating noises. The auditory features are listed on the left-hand side. They can be attributed to the perceived spectral, temporal, and spatial characteristics. With the exception of the brightness, which supports the impression of fresh air, and the roughness, which can be regarded as the particle contents of the air, the characterizations are directly pertinent, even with respect to the air quality. In this case, a great roughness of the sound, possibly involving impulses such as snapping or crackling, is not desired, for this would contain associative indications of unclean air. Precisely the reverse is true with respect to the sound of a vacuum cleaner, for example, for the auditory participation of particles being drawn into the hose of the machine by suction would be quite positively evaluated (Bodden 2001).

15

172

2.2
FINDING
SIMILARITIES –
CROSS-MODAL
ANALOGIES
↓
2.2.3
INTERSENSORY
ATTRIBUTES

SOUND	AIR QUALITY
INTENSITY	INTENSITY
BRIGHTNESS	FRESHNESS
VOLUME	VOLUME
DENSITY	DENSITY
ROUGHNESS	IMPURITY

FIGURE 2.25
The application of the intersensory attributes according
to Werner to the properties of the sound
of a ventilator and their functional correlations.

2.2
FINDING
SIMILARITIES –
CROSS-MODAL
ANALOGIES
↓
2.2.3
INTERSENSORY
ATTRIBUTES

173

The common etymologic roots of the German words *Hall* (reverberation) and *hell* (bright) already make reference to the nexus of auditory and visual brightness. As early as the 1920s, Erich Moritz von Hornbostel provided the characteristics indicated in Table 2.1 as cross-modal correlations of the attribute *brightness* (Hornbostel 1927).

	BRIGHT	DARK
TOUCH VIBRATION	SMOOTH	ROUGH
PRESSURE	HARD	SOFT
TOUCH	SHARP	DULL
POWER	LIGHT	HEAVY
TEMPERATURE	COLD	WARM
PAIN	PENETRATING	MUFFLED
ORGAN SENSATION	HUNGER	FULL FEELING

TABLE 2.1
Cross-modal correlations of the perceptual property of brightness.

Other, early experiments indicated that an allocation for gustatory and olfactory attributes is also easily possible. The fact that brightness can be attributed to a scent can occasionally cause, even today, reactions full of astonishment. In addition to the brightness, even the roughness was identified rather early as an intersensory attribute (Schiller 1932).

In the 1950s and 1960s, Stanley Smith Stevens carried out various experiments with respect to the interconnection of cross-sensory properties (Stevens 1956; 1961a–b; 1966a–d; 1968). Figure 2.26 provides an example of the allocation of tactile, visual, proprioceptive, and auditory stimuli pertaining to the sound pressure level of a sinusoidal tone (Stevens 1966d). In the example indicated, the test subjects had the task of adjusting the reference stimuli to such an extent that the intensity of sensation of the stimuli corresponded to that caused by the designated tone. This is possible for a slight electrical impulse on the skin as well as for the number, redness, roughness, and hardness of objects, and even for many other attributes. The parameters which are highlighted in red in the depiction – handgrip pressure, vibration, length, and brightness – are particularly important with regard to multisensory design. In the case of each parameter investigated, there proved to be a nearly exponential relation which, with a doubled logarithmic presentation as in figure 2.26, led to straight lines. Consequently, such a *cross-modality matching* offers the possibility of connecting perceptions of different sensory channels by virtue of simple mathematical functions, as sought in the concept of psychophysics. The appropriate scales thereto shall be introduced in section 3.2.1. Meticulous scaling is also necessary in the allocation of perceptual properties to numerical series, such as by the application of touch tones in the case of cell phones, whose tone pitch, for example, can be sensibly related to the magnitude of the digit which is selected in the course of dialing.

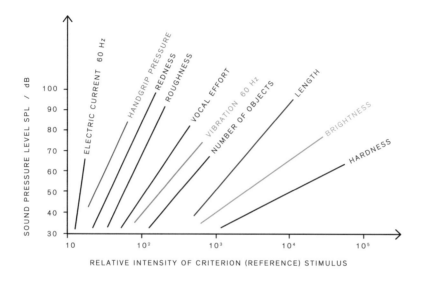

FIGURE 2.26
An example of the connection of cross-sensory properties via ratio scales (Stevens 1966d).

174

2.2
FINDING
SIMILARITIES –
CROSS-MODAL
ANALOGIES
↓
2.2.3
INTERSENSORY
ATTRIBUTES

MULTISENSORY DESIGN HAS THE OBJECTIVE OF EFFECTIVELY CORRELATING THE PERCEPTUAL QUANTITIES WHICH ARE ATTRIBUTABLE TO A PROCESS TO ONE ANOTHER, AND IN SUCH A MANNER THAT ALLOWS THE RESPECTIVE DEFINITION OF TASKS TO PROPERLY TAKE PLACE.

EXCURSUS: PSYCHOPHYSICS AND THE MATHEMATICS OF STIMULUS AND SENSATION

EXCURSUS:
PSYCHOPHYSICS
AND THE
MATHEMATICS
OF STIMULUS
AND SENSATION

175

In the latter part of the nineteenth century, it was considered necessary to mathematically describe the dependency of the phenomena of perception from the physical quantities giving rise to such phenomena. This is based upon the assumption that causal system properties, which are constant in their characteristics, are thereby significant and thus capable of being measured and of being expressed by mathematical equations, just as the laws of classic physics. Psychophysics were founded by Gustav Theodor Fechner and expanded upon by researchers such as Gottlob Friedrich Lipps, Ernst Heinrich Weber, and others (Fechner 1866, Lipps 1903). In the 1960s, within the domain of psychoacoustics, audition was particularly examined – important German research centers came into being in Munich (Zwicker 1982) and Bochum (Blauert 1997).

An essential nexus between the physical intensity of the stimulus I and the strength of the sensation P (as a parameter of resulting perception) was established by Fechner, in expanding upon the approach by Weber:

2
$$P = c \ln (I/I^0)$$

This *psychophysical function* is applied for describing the relationship between sensation and stimulation. It is determined by a physical reference quantity I_0, the application of the natural logarithm ln and a constant c, which has to be evaluated for every stimulus quantity in perceptual experiments. Known as the *Weber-Fechner Law,* this equation shaped several decades of perceptual research and led to specialized guidelines for experiments, which are concentrated on individual stimulus quantities and elementary perceptual qualities.

According to equation 2, the strength of the sensation is, as a general rule, a function of the natural logarithm of the intensity of the stimulus. In this case, the term *intensity* refers to the quantity, i.e. the amplitude of the stimulus, and not a physical energy. Io is a reference quantity which complies with the observation that the intensity of a stimulus influences the perception as a relative quantity – and not as an absolute quantity. This is substantiated by the adaptability of the perceptual system. If one plots the strength of the perception over the intensity of the stimulus and utilizes a logarithmic scale for the latter quantity, a straight line is accordingly the result. For this formulation, it is presumed that a constant (c), which defines the gradient of the straight line, exists for every kind of sensation.

The *Weber-Fechner Law* accordingly provides an approach for examining the context of the subjective strength of sensory impressions with respect to the objective intensity of physical stimuli. Analogous to equation 2, the sound pressure level L_p was also defined as a logarithmic relation existing between the sound pressure p and the value of the level:

3 $\qquad L^p = 20 \log (p/p_0)$

The sound level in Decibel [dB] is a measurement quantity which is well-established in the discipline of acoustics. It is often provided with a frequency evaluation which considers the frequency-dependent sensibility of the ear in accordance with figure 1.46, although in a notably simplified form, and which is designated as [dB(A)]. The definition of the acoustic level consistent with equation 2, however, originated in a time period in which the Weber-Fechner Law was regarded as being of absolute significance. In the present day, it is known that this involves merely an approximate approach to the matter.

The assumption of the logarithmic context between the stimulus and the sensation represents merely an idealization, and it can lead to proper descriptions only within certain ranges of the intensity scale.

Stanley Smith Stevens thus recommended the following description:

4 $\qquad P = k \, I^n$

The strength of the sensation P is thus a function of the intensity of the stimulus I, raised to the power of n. Additionally, according to this rule known as *Stevens' Power Law*, a constant k is to be applied. If one were to present such a function in a double-logarithmic measure, namely with a vertical and respectively a horizontal logarithmic axis, it would similarly result in straight lines. Moreover, the reference functions depicted in figure 2.26 also yield straight lines, given that the sound pressure level corresponding to equation 3 represents a logarithmic quantity. For the exponent n<1 the function of equation 4 describes the Weber-Fechner Law in an approximate manner. The exponent n is characteristic of the specific stimulus quantity. Accordingly, the literature pertaining to n, for example, specifies the following values (Lindsay 1977):

SENSATION OF BRIGHTNESS	0.3
SMELL OF COFFEE	0.55
TASTE OF ARTIFICIAL SWEETENER	0.8
TASTE OF SALT	1.3
COLDNESS (ON THE ARM)	1.6
THICKNESS OF WOODEN BLOCKS AS DETERMINED BY THE FINGERS	1.3
WEIGHT OF FREIGHT TO BE HOISTED	1.5
HAND PRESSURE	1.7
LENGTH OF A LINE	1.0

176

EXCURSUS:
PSYCHOPHYSICS
AND THE
MATHEMATICS
OF STIMULUS
AND SENSATION

As a general rule – although certainly not always – the task consists of a harmonious coordination of the properties crucial to perception. An example of the *harmonization* of the properties is the coordination of the visually perceived position of a rotary switch for the ventilation of the car with the intensity and the quality of the ventilation, which would, in the ideal situation, also be expressed in the intensity and the quality of the sound of the ventilation. The change in the loudness would, in optimal designing, be regarded as exactly corresponding to the angle of the rotary switch. Possible alterations in the tone pitch should also occur in a proportional manner. If numbered steps are employed, the graduating of the increments of the sound properties should precisely accommodate the numbering on the scale of the operating element, which is normally a ratio scale. For the visual appearance of rotary switches, it is accordingly self-evident to correlate the same distances along the scales of numbers with the same rotary angles.

Additional applications of the cross-modal scaling include, for example, the creation of an acoustic signal to assist the driver during the parking of an automobile, with such signal responding exactly in proportion to the distance of the vehicle to the obstacles. A similar task is to inform the driver as to the functioning of the electric parking brake (EPB) via a proportional visual signal which appears in addition to the audible sound.

Connections between auditory parameters and other modalities were already examined in the first half of the twentieth century, particularly by Albert Wellek (1931b; 1963). Owing to the fact that he discovered a broad prevalence of these cross-modal connections, he characterized them as *original synesthesiae [Ursynästhesien],* which he presumed to be solidly anchored in the human perception.

Before addressing individual aspects in a more detailed manner, table 2.2 shall initially present Wellek's list of the six original synesthesiae:

2.2
FINDING
SIMILARITIES –
CROSS-MODAL
ANALOGIES
↓
2.2.3
INTERSENSORY
ATTRIBUTES

177

NO.	VERBAL DESCRIPTION	AUDITORY PHENOMENON TONE PROPERTIES
1	THIN – THICK	HIGH – LOW
	SHARP (POINTED) – DULL (HEAVY)	HIGH – LOW
2	QUICK, MOVEABLE (LIGHT) – SLOW, AWKWARD (HEAVY)	HIGH – LOW
3	HIGH – DEEP (SPATIALLY)	HIGH – LOW
	UP – DOWN (RISING – FALLING)	HIGHER - LOWER
4	CLEAR – UNCLEAR	HIGH – LOW
	GLARING (ILLUMINATED), SATURATED – PALE (GREY), DULL	STRONG – WEAK
5	BRIGHT (WHITE) – DARK (BLACK)	HIGH – LOW
	WARM – COLD (EVEN REGARDING VISUAL COLORS)	HIGH – LOW
6	MULTICOLORED (VIVID) – SOLID (UNIFORM)	SONOROUS – MONOTONOUS

TABLE 2.2
Original synesthesia according to Wellek

The third original synesthesia additionally encompasses the visual analogy of tone sequences and lines, the presentation of the tone duration above the horizontals, and the presentation of musical trills – the quick alternations between two neighboring tones – as wave lines. At this point, the various possibilities of interconnecting the visual properties with the tone pitch are already evident.

Recent studies confirm that a cross-modality matching of tone pitch and color results in a systematic increase of color brightness (lightness) with tone pitch (McCabe 2010). This applies for pure tones as well as for piano tones. The mapping, however, is more pronounced when the sound contains harmonics, as in the case of piano tones. Therefore, the timbre itself shows a clear influence on auditory-visual correlations.

SOUND
AND COLOR

At the latest, since the experiments of Louis-Bertrand Castel during the middle of the eighteenth century, the classification of sound and color has been the subject of various research studies and artistic experiments (summarized by Jewanski 1999). It is also obvious, however, that there is no conclusive, "nearby" solution which would exclusively orient itself with respect to the color tone and also be accepted by a majority of persons. Indeed, test subjects usually tend to classify colors on the basis of the color brightness – or saturation.

2.2
FINDING
SIMILARITIES –
CROSS-MODAL
ANALOGIES
↓
2.2.3
INTERSENSORY
ATTRIBUTES

**IN ALLOCATING COLORS TO OTHER
PERCEPTUAL PROPERTIES,
SUCH AS THE TONE COLOR, THE TONE PITCH,
OR THE LOUDNESS OF TONES,
THE APPLICATION OF COLOR SCALES
WITH CONTINUALLY INCREASING
BRIGHTNESS (LIGHTNESS) IS PARTICULARLY
APPROPRIATE.**

This is based upon the finding that typical colors exhibit a characteristic brightness, for example, which appears low in the case of blue, but with higher values in the case of yellow or white. An appropriate color scale leads approximately

BLACK (DEEP TONES)	RED (MIDDLE TONE RANGE)	YELLOW (HIGH TONES)

from black to white via blue, red, orange, and yellow. Accordingly, the coding via is widely recommended for musical painting within the scope of early education of children (e.g., by Zitzlsperger 1976). Applications for the visualization of auditory phenomena shall be discussed in further detail in section 3.4.1. Additionally, chapter 2.6 addresses efforts to create analogies between colors and tones for the purpose of enriching the hearing of music and defining artistic concepts. Figure 2.27 provides an example of the application of the brightness analogy in the domain of musical theater:

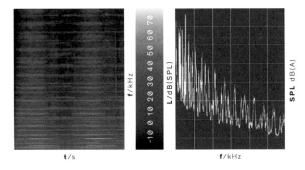

FIGURE 2.27
Connecting the visual with the auditory by virtue
of the brightness analogy. The "Grail" theme in the prelude
to the opera Lohengrin by Richard Wagner, extract.
Left: Spectrum of sound pressure level SPL versus time t.
Right: Averaged spectrum of sound pressure
level SPL versus frequency f.

2.2
FINDING
SIMILARITIES –
CROSS-MODAL
ANALOGIES
↓
2.2.3
INTERSENSORY
ATTRIBUTES

179

The "Grail" theme in the prelude to the opera *Lohengrin* by Richard Wagner
is supposed to express the intellectuality and the supernatural power of the
grail. ● This is a fabulous cup which God uses in order to greatly strengthen a
community of knights who have sworn, like monks, to relinquish all worldly
pleasures. The grail is presented as an object expressing supernatural power by
bright radiation of light – and this also corresponds to the stage directions in
the musical drama *Parsifal,* in which Wagner revisits the theme of the storyline.
The brightness of the grail is musically expressed by the high tone pitches as
well as by the brightness of the acoustic timbre heard in the flageolet technique of the violins. Figure 2.27 illustrates the various overtones with which
the brightness is expressed.

Within multisensory environments, the perceived brightness of light influences other modalities. Even the perception of sounds is more strongly influenced by the brightness, and by the color saturation of the simultaneously
offered visual stimuli, as by the color tone itself. Unpleasant or frightening
sounds exert a diminished influence when accompanied by brightness and
saturation (Cox 2007).

SOUND
AND FORM

Similarly, researchers sought to discover possible systematic relations existing
between sound qualities and visual forms. Even in this regard, no self-evident
solutions can be found which would appear to many people in an intuitive manner and which could be, for example, applied to the designing of audio-visual
art. Figure 2.28 illustrates forms which serve as the basis of an audio-visual
composition by Adriano Abbado (1988). They were designed as an analogy between acoustic color *(timbre)* and form or the structure of the surface *(shape
surface).* They correspond to sharp (left-hand side) and soft (right-hand side)
sounds and are synchronously presented with them. Abbado's audio-visual art
is particularly interesting for the search for systematic connections between

hearing and seeing, for he values precisely structured analogies between the objects of both sensory modalities (Woolman 2000). Thereby, he considers processes which are indeed applied by the perceptual system. The similarity of forms and of the onomatopoeic expression plays an important role in chapter 2.3.

The correlation of form and of surface structure *(texture)* is also of great significance to designing the interiors of automobiles, given that all operating elements – such as the *steering wheel, the gear shift, the direction-indicator control, the ventilation control,* etc. – are tactilely perceived as well. The various approaches in this regard shall be additionally addressed by the discussion pertaining to *tactile design* in section 2.2.7.

LOW AND LOUD TONES ARE OFTEN ATTRIBUTED TO LARGE FORMS AND DARK COLORS. FURTHERMORE, THIS IS SIMILARLY ACHIEVED BY A SMALL NUMBER OF OVERTONES AND LENGTHY FADE-OUT TIMES.

Conversely, high tone pitches, minimal loudness, numerous overtones, and a short fade-out all contribute to assignments being made to small and bright forms. Thereby, the influence exerted by the auditory experience of the listener with respect to small or large tone generators, which appropriately sound deep/dull or high/bright, can certainly not be ignored. For example, it is well known from everyday experience that a big bell generates a low tone, while a small one is characterized by a high pitch. chapter 2.3 directs attention to connections which are constructed by virtue of the identification of the source of the stimuli.

A special case of the analogies between visual forms and tone properties exists in the correspondence of architecture and music. Already in the Middle Ages, the proportions of houses deliberately corresponded to musical proportions – such as the frequency relations of tone intervals. At this point, we shall merely peripherally make reference to the related, rather expansive field. For Johann Wolfgang Goethe, architecture was "crystallized music." A rather capricious approach to the relationship of musical motifs to the forms of houses was undertaken by Arne Hošek (1931). As an example of modern elaborations upon the theme, one must mention the work of Markus Dermietzel (2003) with respect to the feasibility of musical compositions as blueprints for architecture.

180

2.2
FINDING
SIMILARITIES –
CROSS-MODAL
ANALOGIES
↓
2.2.3
INTERSENSORY
ATTRIBUTES

 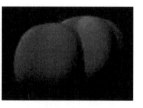

SHARP TONE   SOFT TONE

FIGURE 2.28
Analogies of sound timbre to the form and the surface
of objects as the basic principle of a multimedia composition.
Adriano Abbado, Dynamics, 1988 (Compare to fig. 2.71).

Musical notation is an important, traditional application of the analogy between tone pitch and visual form. In the presently established notation of European culture, the tone pitch corresponds to the spatial arrangement of notes along the vertical axis, whereas time corresponds to movement along the horizontal axis (fig. 2.29).

The transformation of time corresponds to the direction of writing from the left to the right. Efforts to translate auditory perceptual events into the visual sphere are often based upon this scheme. Figure 2.30 demonstrates that even children – without prior knowledge of the notational system – are capable of intuitively illustrating auditory events in a manner corresponding to this analogy.

Moreover, even genuine synesthesia typically exhibit this relation – in this case, the description *Notational Synesthesia* [Notations-Synästhesie] is also employed (Behne 2002). Indeed, according to narrations of children who have gone blind, the perception of the sound of animals can lead to visual appearances which exhibit – in addition to the genuine synesthetic colors – the analogy of tone pitch and spatial height as well (Voss 1930). The colors in figure 2.31 are not explainable by associations with visual properties of the identified animals, and they thus make reference to the synesthetic phenomena in accordance with chapter 2.5. The two pitches of the cuckoo's call were perceived in different colors – corresponding to a color synesthesia which is determined by the tone pitch. The progression of the curves presented as well as the colored spots of the cuckoo's call demonstrate, nevertheless, a correlation with respect to the tone pitch of the creature's call.

2.2
FINDING
SIMILARITIES –
CROSS-MODAL
ANALOGIES
↓
2.2.3
INTERSENSORY
ATTRIBUTES

181

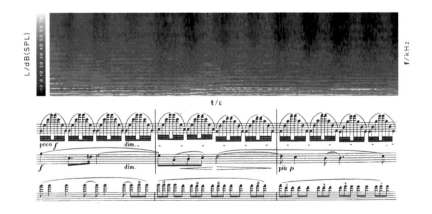

FIGURE 2.29
Visual analogies to tone pitch and time in the notation system
and as result of physical sound analysis.
Richard Wagner, Prelude to the musical drama Parsifal, measures 11 to 13.
Above: spectral presentation versus time; below: Excerpt of
the musical score sheet for the first violins and the first flutes.

Tü-Tü

FIGURE 2.30
An analogy of pitch to visual height (vertical deflection).
Illustration of a five-year-old child depicting the signal of a German ambulance,
which consists of two alternating tones of different pitches.

In the presentation of acoustic measurement results and sound recordings, one particular form of presentation has been established, whereas the spectral amplitude, as a third dimension, has been scaled in color or in gray increments. This style of depiction has been employed within this chapter in figures 2.19 (figure in center), 2.27, and 2.29. The application of analogies between tone pitches and spatial height as well as the utilization of elementary color scales will be examined once again in chapter 3.4. Even in the musical scoring of animation films, the analogy between tone pitch and spatial height remains very popular. This, however, is not a new invention, as indicated by the term *Mickey Mousing* (Flückiger 2002), which refers to the use of simple tones and sounds to support visual movement. Thereby, the analogy of tone pitch and visual height is very commonly used.

17

182

2.2
FINDING
SIMILARITIES –
CROSS-MODAL
ANALOGIES
↓
2.2.3
INTERSENSORY
ATTRIBUTES

HORSE   ROOSTER   CAT   CUCKOO

FIGURE 2.31
The analogy between tone pitch and visual height
(vertical deflection) in the perception of animal voices. Drawn after accounts
of people who have gone blind (Voss 1930).

The historical development of the notation system is indicative of a transition from the original presentation of musical movement to a presentation of static tone pitches and durations (Wellek 1931b). The following section 2.2.4 is dedicated to the multisensory implementation of sensations of movement.

SOUND, SMELL, AND TASTE

In the music to the second act of the musical drama *The Mastersingers of Nuremberg [Die Meistersinger von Nürnberg]*, Richard Wagner employed a broad timbre in order to present the scent of lilac. ●

An analogy to the perception of scents is thereby present, inasmuch as this sound is neither spectral nor temporal nor spatially differentiated in a particular manner. It involves the muffled sound of string instruments of minimal loudness, but with a broad harmonic spectrum. By virtue of the spatial distribution of the string instruments within the orchestra pit, the acoustic source is not concentrated, but rather widely dispersed. This corresponds to the fact that the source of a smell emanating from within the vicinity can only be very approximately localized. Given that the tone lets neither a melody nor a harmonic progression be recognized, it is also constructed in a temporally constant manner. Accordingly, the impression of a subtle, omnipresent sensation, which is overwhelming and directly able to touch emotions, arises in a temporal, spectral, and spatial context. The sound surface functions as the background of a melody intoned by wind instruments, characterized by tone repetitions. Similar tone repetitions employed by Wagner may also be heard in the third act of the opera *Lohengrin,* expressing the scents of a summer evening.

Even sound and taste are increasingly associated with one another. This is particularly important in radio and television, particularly when it involves trying to convey the taste of foodstuffs and drinks. Indeed, in the meantime, efforts to characterize the taste of fruit aromas or wines by virtue of short musical phrases serving as commercial jingles or sound logos have been successful (Bronner 2009). As an example, the sensations caused by the taste and the smell of citrus aroma have been comprehensibly transformed into the auditory modality ("Sound of Citrus," Hirt 2009).

2.2
FINDING
SIMILARITIES –
CROSS-MODAL
ANALOGIES
↓
2.2.3
INTERSENSORY
ATTRIBUTES

TASTE
AND FORM

To date, experiments addressing the relationship between taste and visual form have only been sporadically documented – as a rule, associative connections consistent with chapter 2.3 are more prevalent. Efforts towards a classification of forms with respect to taste sensations led to the following preferences (Riccò 2002):

SWEET	ROUND LINES AND CIRCULAR SHAPES
ACID & SALAD	FRAGMENTED LINES AND ANGULAR SHAPES
BITTER	IRREGULAR LINES AND SHAPES

An intersensory attribute which receives much attention in the case of foodstuffs is the *lightness* – in contrast to the heaviness, which can be understood as a combination of the attributes *volume* and *density*. Originally, the goal consisted merely of giving the customer *light* – meaning easily digestible – products. In the meantime, a relation by analogy has been constructed between meals which are *hard* to digest, the feeling of *heaviness* in the stomach, and the *excess of body weight.* Accordingly, a successful product should not only be *light,* it must have a *light taste,* for this perception allays the fears of the customer with regard to the negative consequences of the consumption in terms of his or her health. Thus, it is thoroughly consequential to incorporate this property directly into the name of the product, such as in the case of the pudding Wölkchen ("little cloud") of the brand DR. OETKER. Thereby, the product image is enhanced by the associative connections to the celestially resounding terminology for the sky as a metaphor for paradise, ultimately utilizing the strongly positive aspects of the related symbolism in a sensible manner.

ANALOGY OF MOTION AND KINETIC DESIGN

Initially, the movement of objects is visually perceived as the translocation of their position within the given space. If moved objects are touched, such movement is also tactilely ascertainable. Movements of the extremities are analyzed by the body's own receptors for proprioception, whereas the shifting of the entire body within the room is detected by the sense of balance by virtue of acceleration or deceleration. Owing to the capability of spatial hearing, the ear can detect the movement of acoustic sources within the room – the precision of localization is, however, considerably less than the acuity of vision. Even via the analysis of auditory characteristics – such as timbre, dynamic, and fluctuation – it is possible to deduce the fundamental processes of movement simply on the basis of sounds. A piece of chalk which is dragged across the chalkboard simultaneously causes a screeching sound that contains information as to the movement. ● This also applies to the sound of running water, the rustling of flying birds and of the leaves from trees, the shuffling of footsteps, and to various technical sounds. ● The rotating sound of a mechanical coffee grinder contains this information, just as much as the sound and the vibration of the drill of a dentist (fig. 2.32) and all other appliances driven by rotating motors. Correspondingly, the sounds of motor vehicles not only include portions of rotating components from the engines, transmissions, wheels, steering, and servomotors, but also portions of straight movement such as wind noise, the opening or closing of the side windows, the altering of the position of the seats, and of many other aspects.

18

19

184

2.2
FINDING
SIMILARITIES –
CROSS-MODAL
ANALOGIES
↓
2.2.4
ANALOGY OF
MOTION
AND KINETIC
DESIGN

A MULTISENSORY ANALOGY TO PROCESSES OF MOVEMENT IS PARTICULARLY IMPORTANT WITH RESPECT TO THE DESIGN OF VEHICLES, ALLOWING THE DYNAMIC PROPERTIES OF THE PRODUCT TO BE OPTIMIZED.

In shaping and designing the visual appearance, one thus endeavors to realize an impressive *kinetic design*. The representation of the parameters of movement by virtue of the auditory characteristics is of similar importance. This applies to the sound of the entire automobile as well as to all components, which convey information as to the proper functioning to the driver acoustically, and whose properties can be correlated to the parameters of the movement.

The representation of dynamic processes in still images began with the Italian Futurists in the early twentieth century. Pioneering elements of this methodology may be found in the movement studies conducted by the French physiologist Étienne-Jules Marey towards the end of the nineteenth century. Presentations such as figure 2.33 served as the basis of artistic and design-technical experiments pertaining to the transformation of processes of movement into visual elements. The forms used communicated dynamic expressiveness, indeed, in spite of their graphically-conditioned static nature. The Futurists were interested in such forms that conveyed the perceptual experience of movement in a particularly impressive manner, as well as in multisensory interactions. This is already expressed in figures 1.5 and 2.12. Giacomo Balla's painting *Velocity of an Automobile + Light + Sound* in figure 2.34 connects dynamic forms with auditory stimuli and the visual aspects of the illumination of the vehicle. It becomes obvious that attributes of movement actually do express themselves in an effective manner. Thus, similar forms are appropriate, even today, for conveying mobility and performance. Thereby, one must consider that visual elements of automotive design that existed in the former age of Futurism are less appropriate for indicating speed and agility by today's standards. Indeed, the designs of the first automobiles oriented themselves with respect to the primary characteristics of horse-drawn carriages.

2.2
FINDING
SIMILARITIES –
CROSS-MODAL
ANALOGIES
↓
2.2.4
ANALOGY OF
MOTION
AND KINETIC
DESIGN

185

FIGURE 2.32
Visual analogy involving rotational movement,
vibration, and pain: dental drilling. The work of a child in an art class
of Walther Behm in the 1920s (Anschütz 1931).

Other examples of the implementation of dynamic properties in Futurism may be found in respective exhibition catalogues (e.g., Nobis 2001). A criterion for the dynamic of the course of a line is its tendency towards unexpected twists and turns. If one follows a line with the eyes, it becomes clear that prognoses pertaining to the expected further course may be deduced from the already viewed piece in every moment. Lines which are more likely to contradict this estimation, for example, with unexpected or radical changes of course, can be regarded as being dynamic, or they behave – theatrically articulated – in a particularly *dramatic* fashion. As a matter of contrast, curves which are relatively easy to predict serve to convey an impression of tranquility and harmony, but they can also indicate, under certain circumstances, the weakness of the stimulation or even boredom. Sharp angles and surprising alternations between curved lines and corners, on the other hand, convey dynamic stimuli and are accordingly appropriate for expressing the corresponding properties of the

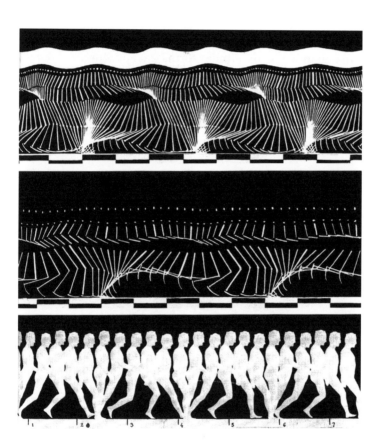

186

2.2
FINDING
SIMILARITIES −
CROSS-MODAL
ANALOGIES
↓
2.2.4
ANALOGY OF
MOTION
AND KINETIC
DESIGN

FIGURE 2.33
The findings of an earlier research project with respect to the course
of movements depict the origin of dynamic forms as the
transformation of processes of movement into visual elements.
Étienne-Jules Marey, Study of Movement, 1886.

2.2
FINDING
SIMILARITIES –
CROSS-MODAL
ANALOGIES
↓
2.2.4
ANALOGY OF
MOTION
AND KINETIC
DESIGN

187

FIGURE 2.34
Dynamic forms. Giacomo Balla, Velocity of an
Automobile + Light + Sound, 1913.
© 2011, ProLitteris, Zurich; in comparison with
the characteristics of modern automobiles.

product. One of the methods employed by the Futurists to create dramatic lines consisted in retaining the contour of a moving object seen at different times. This method results in drawings which are comparable to multiple-exposure photography that graphically documents movement. If one connects the lines which correspond to the different points in time of the process of movement, a characteristic combination consisting of lines and sharp angles arises, as illustrated in figure 2.34. Such courses of the lines, in the case of industrial products like automobiles, support the impression of dynamic mobility and of agility as desired by the customer. This is systematically employed in the concept of *kinetic design.*

FIGURE 2.35 (OPPOSITE PAGE)
An illusion of movement which is evoked by a band of static lines.
Example by the author. The abstract paintings of the artist Bridget Riley
are based upon this method.

In extreme cases, groups of lines can also directly lead to illusions of movement. Thus, bands of lines which are heavily concentrated can evoke the impression of real movement. During observation of the depiction in figure 2.35, the lines tend to blur in a manner of characteristic countermotion. Although this phenomenon is physiologically caused by the inability of the eyes to find fixed points to focus upon, this is an example of the significance of high-contrast lines for the designing of dynamic structures. Nevertheless, the pronouncedly great concentration of the depicted lines can cause perception of an ambiguity of the structure. Indeed, they suggest an unsystematic temporal behavior – the contours become blurred as soon as the observer attempts to locate them with his or her eyes. Furthermore, the aforementioned comments pertaining to shifting figures in section 1.3.9 also apply in this case. Due to the prevailing ambiguity of the structure, such effects can only in very specific applications serve as the reasonable components of robust design. As a play with illusions, nonetheless, they are quite appropriate for raising attention in a notable manner.

In automobiles, information pertaining to its movements is conveyed to the driver and to the passengers as well via different sensory channels. People in a steadily moving vehicle experience the passenger compartment as a motionless construction around which the world is moving (fig. 2.36). The acceleration, the application of the brakes, and steering actions cause forces, however, which are evaluated by the sense of balance and by the mechano-receptors within the body and thus lead to a perception of movement. With constant velocity, however, the movement can only visually be perceived, given that no accelerating forces are involved. Fast movements lead to a blurring of the object contours. Additionally, in the case of high velocity, objects outside of vehicle can be precisely perceived only if they are at a great distance in front of – and behind – the automobile. Thus, one speaks in this regard of the *tunnel effect* of the visual perception, which results in the *tunnel view* of the driver. Due to the very high velocity of jet aircraft, this effect is particularly prevalent among jet pilots and is often the cause of accidents.

Additionally, sounds contribute to the perception of movement. In particular, the sound of the motor includes information about the acceleration in the traction mode as well as delays in the coasting mode (overrun condition) of

188

2.2
FINDING
SIMILARITIES –
CROSS-MODAL
ANALOGIES
↓
2.2.4
ANALOGY OF
MOTION
AND KINETIC
DESIGN

the power train. The sounds of the tires correlate with the velocity of the vehicle via the wheel speed, but they are, nevertheless, influenced by the interaction occurring between the wheels and the surface texture of the pavement. Wind noise appears while driving at a high speed – caused by air turbulence in the front and at the rear of the automobile and particularly affiliated with random noise of a high frequency. The areas of the sideward sealing of the forward windshield and of the side-view mirrors are notably of a critical nature with regard to the generation of such wind noise. When traveling at high speeds, the driver and his or her passengers tend to accept these sounds. Audible oscillations – *fluctuations* – of the acoustic properties, however, must be avoided, for they do not behave in a manner directly corresponding to the velocity of the vehicle. Instead, these fluctuations convey a non-robust impression of the driving characteristics and additionally hint at the deficient sealing of the side windows. Furthermore, the concentration of the driver is diminished, for his or her attention is accordingly diverted away from the sensory information meaningful with respect to the proper functioning. ● ●

2.2
FINDING
SIMILARITIES –
CROSS-MODAL
ANALOGIES
↓
2.2.4
ANALOGY OF
MOTION
AND KINETIC
DESIGN

FIGURE 2.36
In a moving vehicle, the impression of movement
is of particular importance,
and many senses contribute to this perception.

MOVEMENT AS A PROPERTY OF LANGUAGE AND MUSIC

The perception of movement by virtue of auditory characteristics plays an important role not only in the case of technical processes; in the interpretation of speech and music, qualities which are suggestive of dynamic processes are intuitively involved as well.

Indeed, even in the perception of music, analogies between the movement in the spectral and temporal dimension and the spatial movement of objects play a major role. The generally prevalent capability to make this type of connection manifests itself in dancing and in conducting. In the construction of motifs in opera music, analogies to theatrical gestures are similarly of great importance. Gustav Becking made efforts to transliterate the musical rhythm utilizing *accompanying movements* [Mitbewegungen] of the body – similar to the movements of the orchestral conductor. He stated that various stylistic characteristics can be derived from those movements, as being typical of the composer (Becking 1928). The goal, nevertheless, did not consist of correlating the body movements and the music with respect to one another; instead, it was aimed at describing the movement which is perceived as a characteristic feature of music. With similar intentions, the linguist Eduard Sievers recommended the employment of body movement for his empirical method *Schallanalyse,* which he developed in order to optimize text declamation and interpretation of lyrics (Sievers 1924, Ipsen 1928).

However, he understood Schallanalyse – contrary to the contemporary understanding of the word as "sound analysis" – not as physical analysis, but rather as an investigation of the optimal intonation for a given text regarding movement conceptions on the basis of articulation and emphasis. For this purpose, he developed a method for the experimental investigation of characteristic forms of movement which could be depicted as curved lines. Figure 2.37 illustrates an example of these forms of movement, as they were ascertained by Sievers for the first stanza of a poem by Heinrich Heine. Each of the forms described by Sievers as a *measure-filling curve* [Taktfüllkurve] corresponds to a line of the poem. The depicted curves are not presented over a lineal axis of time, but instead are illustrated as being curved backwards into themselves, for they correspond to the movements of a baton in the hand of a conductor. Therefore, the time itself moves along the line. In addition to the measure-filling curves, which follow the intonation in the sense of an analogy of movement, Sievers also employed line figures which symbolically represent the kind of tension of the body during the declamation of a text.

2.2
FINDING
SIMILARITIES –
CROSS-MODAL
ANALOGIES
↓
2.2.4
ANALOGY OF
MOTION
AND KINETIC
DESIGN

191

22

DYNAMIC CHARACTERISTICS ARE NOT ONLY PERCEIVED IN COMPLEX MUSICAL PHRASES – E.G., SUCH AS MELODIES – BUT ALSO IN INDIVIDUAL TONES AND SOUNDS.

Alexander Truslit utilized analogies of movement for the purpose of musical analysis as well as for supporting interpretation, and he deduced from these efforts basic principles, with which he accentuated movement as a decisive basis – and, indeed, even as the origin – of the music (Truslit 1938). He even used line figures in order to visualize the movement being sensed for the purpose of depicting rising and falling, acceleration and deceleration.

Figure 2.38 provides a typical example of the use of a curve of movement in the interpretation of piano music. According to Truslit, one to four fundamental forms of movement can be allocated to every musical phrase, which determines the type and quality of the musical performance. The assignment of sensations to certain forms of movement, however, is not necessarily perceived by all persons in an equal manner. Nevertheless, the recommended fundamental forms arouse great interest even today (Repp 1993, Shove 1995, Haverkamp 2009b) and are, furthermore, the subject of computer-based music analyses and syntheses with respect to their appropriateness as a common basis.

Starless and cold is the night,

The sea yawns;

And outstretched flat on his paunch over the sea

Lies the uncouth North-wind.

Secretly, with a groaning, stifled voice,

Like a peevish, crabbed man in a freak of good humor,

He babbles to the ocean,

And recounts many a mad tale,

Stories of murderous giants,

And from time to time, with re-echoing laughter, he howls forth

The conjuration-songs of the Edda,

With Runic proverbs,

So mysteriously arrogant, so magically powerful,

That the while children of the sea,

High in the air upspring and rejoice,

Intoxicated with insolence.

2.2
FINDING
SIMILARITIES –
CROSS-MODAL
ANALOGIES
↓
2.2.4
ANALOGY OF
MOTION
AND KINETIC
DESIGN

FIGURE 2.37
Heinrich Heine, "Night on the Shore," 1st stanza.
Translation by Emma Lazarus (1881)
The forms of movement (measure-filling curves) are added,
as evaluated by means of Schallanalyse (Sievers 1924).

Only Henry Timmermann, however, continued Truslit's works in a direct manner (Timmermann 1940). With respect to the visualization of movements, the basic forms are discussed in chapter 3.4.

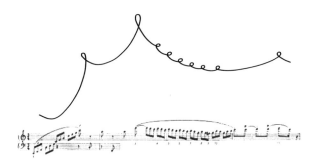

2.2
FINDING
SIMILARITIES –
CROSS-MODAL
ANALOGIES
↓
2.2.4
ANALOGY OF
MOTION
AND KINETIC
DESIGN

———

193

FIGURE 2.38
The movement curve of a musical theme
according to Truslit (1938).
Ludwig van Beethoven, Bagatelle, Op. 33, No. 5.

Manfred Clynes developed a method to objectively describe the effect of music on body activity (Clynes 1989). Instead of motion curves, however, he used curves of finger pressure applied upon a sensor configuration.

Clynes presumed a direct influence of emotions upon body tension, which reproducibly is reflected by the pressure measured in vertical and horizontal (fore and aft) direction. The pressure curves therefore present basic emotional conditions rather than arbitrary activity. For experimental determination of the characteristic curves, Clynes developed a measurement equipment named the *Sentograph*. His research work once again has demonstrated that a close connection between auditory perception and body movement exists (see chapter 3.5).

The jazz characterization of a bass run from equal quarter notes or eighth notes as a *walking bass* correlates quite consistently with this concept. Furthermore, an exposition concerning the connection of music and movement may also be found in the realm of abstract music films. In plausible, trend-setting manner, it is evident in the films of Oskar Fischinger (1930, Moritz 1993; 2004, DF1993). Partially, in a form primarily prepared for purposes of entertainment, it is also noticeable in the first part of Walt Disney's film *Fantasia* (Disney 1940, see also Culhane 1983).

Results of experiments by Zohar Eitan and Roni Granot (Eitan 2004) demonstrate that there is not only *one* possibility of building analogies between specific sensory features. Nevertheless, the number of types of cross-sensory connections which are preferred by test subjects is quite limited. The test subjects were instructed to steer a figure along a monitor screen, and during this time, different acoustic signals with systematic variations were presented. The figure was supposed to be moved analogous to the alteration of the musical parameters. Table 2.3 illustrates the results of the experiments. The chosen, preferred solutions are indicated in boldface lettering.

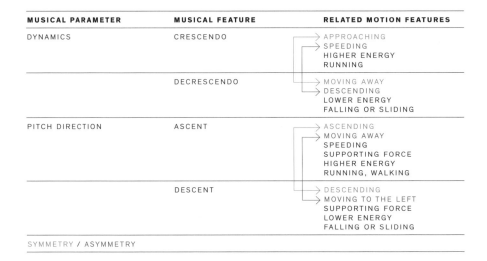

MUSICAL PARAMETER	MUSICAL FEATURE	RELATED MOTION FEATURES
DYNAMICS	CRESCENDO	APPROACHING SPEEDING HIGHER ENERGY RUNNING
	DECRESCENDO	MOVING AWAY DESCENDING LOWER ENERGY FALLING OR SLIDING
PITCH DIRECTION	ASCENT	ASCENDING MOVING AWAY SPEEDING SUPPORTING FORCE HIGHER ENERGY RUNNING, WALKING
	DESCENT	DESCENDING MOVING TO THE LEFT SUPPORTING FORCE LOWER ENERGY FALLING OR SLIDING
SYMMETRY / ASYMMETRY		

TABLE 2.3:
Results of experiments pertaining to the correlation
of the musical parameters *dynamics* and *direction
of pitch alteration* with concepts of movement (Eitan 2004).
Crescendo: increasing loudness;
decrescendo: decreasing loudness.

In this case, both symmetric and asymmetric classifications are indicated. In the case of the symmetric classification, for example, a conception of movement upwards (ascending) corresponds to the increase of tone pitch, whereas – symmetrically – a downwards movement (descending) corresponds to the decrease of tone pitch. Other test subjects, however, attribute another type of movement to the same musical parameter, namely a movement away from the subject or – asymmetrically – a movement to the left side. The results indicate that there are *obvious* connections which tend to be preferred by test subjects. As can be expected, following the discussion in section 2.2.1, however, different possibilities of allocation *(one-to-many relations)* do exist.

194

2.2
FINDING
SIMILARITIES –
CROSS-MODAL
ANALOGIES
↓
2.2.4
ANALOGY OF
MOTION
AND KINETIC
DESIGN

KINETIC DESIGN

As already suggested, the dynamics of processes can be expressed by virtue of optical and acoustic basic forms. According to the concept of synesthetic design, it is important to design the driving qualities of the automobile as significant functional aspects which are capable of being experienced and appreciated in the visual and the auditory appearances. The vehicle shall look and sound the way it also operates. Thus, the driving dynamics are also outwardly communicated, regardless of whether the automobile is driven at a constant rate or standing in a stationary position. Even prior to the test drive, the potential customers shall receive an impression of the dynamic properties of the product. The goal of kinetic design thus consists of arousing emotions, which approach the level and intensity of emotions experienced during a ride as much as possible, by virtue of the visual appearance. In this sense, the visual design attributes chosen shall correspond to the driving qualities as well as to the acoustic behavior of the vehicle during driving operations. Thereby, the kinetic design must determine the outer construction and shaping of the automobile in a consequent fashion, as demonstrated by figure 2.39.

FIGURE 2.39
Kinetic design. The FORD Iosis concept study, as presented at the IAA
(International Automobile Exhibition) in Frankfurt, 2005.

2.2
FINDING
SIMILARITIES –
CROSS-MODAL
ANALOGIES
↓
2.2.4
ANALOGY OF
MOTION
AND KINETIC
DESIGN

———

195

To the same extent, however, the immediately surrounding environment of the driver within the interior of the automobile must also be considered. Optically, the design is characterized by protruding edges with a dramatic shape, the combination of straight as well as curved lines and sharp angles. By virtue of shadowing and coloring, additional contrasts come into being, and these are, in particular, sensibly supported by the texture of the surfaces in the interior decoration.

FIGURE 2.40
The operating environment inside the automobile
is presented as being a visual, auditory, and tactile landscape existing
within an outer landscape which is being traversed.

The designing of the acoustic behavior of the vehicle must be similarly rich in contrast. It shall effectively convey the quick and decisive reaction of all aggregates to the driver. Concrete associations (iconic references) to the pronouncedly *technical* sounds, as discussed in chapter 2.3, can strengthen the dynamic appearance and accordingly advance the expression of an innovative design. Notably, innovation can be communicated with sounds which actually do not originate within the realm of recent automobile construction, e.g., reflecting instead those sounds – such as *turbine sounds* – which are quite positively associated with the highly technological world of aerospace construction. Similarly, *future sounds* – such as signals designed for driver-information systems – are also appropriate for influencing the brand image in this direction.

2.2.5
SPATIAL ANALOGIES AND SOUNDSCAPES

The spatial distribution of structures can be determined in a visual, auditory, or tactile manner. The perception within one modality, however, is influenced by other senses. For example, the visibility of sound sources modifies the perception of environmental sounds (Abe 2006). Even in the case of an isolated perception by virtue of only one modality, objects which are spatially arranged are detected. The possibilities of the localization and of the spatial resolution of perceived structures do differ, however, according to the respective sensory channel. It is the task of design to particularly feature the essential objects. This must allow the specific correlation of perceptual objects of the participating modalities with one another with respect to their spatial properties, or at least facilitate the existence of systematically planned relationships among them. Even systematic divergences can be part of a design concept.

**THE HUMAN PERCEPTUAL SYSTEM
IS NOT CAPABLE OF FOLLOWING AND
COGNITIVELY EVALUATING
A VARIETY OF SIGNALS SIMULTANEOUSLY
WITH THE SAME DEGREE OF ATTENTION
AND CONCENTRATION.
THEREFORE THE DESIGN PROCESS MUST
PROVIDE FOR THE CLEAR SELECTION
AND THE HIERARCHICAL ORGANIZATION
OF SIGNALS.**

196

2.2
FINDING
SIMILARITIES –
CROSS-MODAL
ANALOGIES
↓
2.2.5
SPATIAL
ANALOGIES
AND
SOUNDSCAPES

This applies both to auditory and to visual signals, as well as to stimuli of other sensory channels. Thereby, in the case of the human-machine interface inside a vehicle, one must differentiate between significant signals, which appropriately demand the attention of the driver, and those which should not disturb or diminish the concentration of the driver. Sounds of lesser significance shall thus blend into a uniform background from which the more important signals clearly distinguish themselves. An appropriate choice of the sound qualities makes this goal achievable. In the ideal situation, for example, a background sound exhibits minimal loudness within a broad spectral range and contains no abrupt, unpredictable oscillations. In the course of a constant driving speed, the respective sounds of the motor, the wind, and the tires should not actually merit attention. A signal which shall arouse the attention of the driver, on the other hand, is typically of a narrow-band nature and has a specific tonality. Moreover, it should be raised in loudness and draw attention to itself due to its unexpected intrusion. This corresponds to the relations between separated figures in the *foreground* and in the *background,* as experienced in visual perception, previously mentioned in section 1.3.9. A figure can be brought into the foreground as a result of the purposeful accentuation of its visual properties, or it can be "hidden" by virtue of increased similarities with respect to the background. Also in the auditory case, in addition to the aforementioned signal parameters, spatial hearing can contribute to the increased clarity of the figure. Background sounds should be designed to achieve a broad spatial distribution, whereas more important signals should exhibit a considerably more defined direction due to the very significance of their contents. Currently, measurement technology is increasingly employing techniques which do not evaluate absolute values of sound parameters, but which instead analyze them by virtue of a *relative approach* while making a conscious reference to the background (Sottek 2005).

Murray Schafer brought attention to the necessity of ranking sounds in the acoustic environment (Schaffer 1977). Even in that case, important signals appear in front of the background. In drawing an analogy to *landmarks,* the orientation points across the landscape, Schafer describes such signals as *soundmarks.* The German term *Orientierungslaut* (orientation sound) appropriately corresponds to this designation. In this case, the spatial distribution and the hierarchical graduation of the elements play essential roles. The entire acoustic environment is comparable to a landscape and is thus referred to as *soundscape.* In the German language, the description *Klanglandschaft* (literally "sound landscape") is applicable. Figure 2.41 illustrates the deduction of the soundscape from the analogy of the landscape. ●

The landscape analogy can also be applied to smaller structures within the automobile, such as the control console or the instrument panel on the dashboard. In this regard, even the spatial distribution of elements which can be reached with the hands can be considered as the *tactile landscape* or *touchscape* (fig. 2.42). Visual signals and background illumination merge to form a *lightscape.* In advertising, the distribution of design-oriented details which speak to the feelings of the (potential) users of the product is occasionally referred to as *emotionscape.* Furthermore, this term refers to the psychic, *internal landscape* of the customer, thus representing an essential element of his or her decision to purchase the product. Thereby, the emotions build the foreground to the background sensations, such as moods, and they reflect the mental state of the *body landscape* (see chapter 3.5).

The possibilities of evaluating soundscapes by virtue of cross-modal contexts have been addressed before by the author (Haverkamp 2004b; 2007d). Thereby, the perception is influenced by visual circumstances as well as by the spatial distribution of acoustic sources (Gustavino 2005). The pleasantness of soundscapes with positive meaning, such as a street market or a park, is not appropriately represented by assessment of only the auditory modality, e.g., by means of sound measurements (Defréville 2007). Accordingly, different artists are working towards achieving the *spatialization* of tone objects (e.g., such as Leitner 1998). The influence of soundscapes, particularly the *annoyance* and the disturbing influences arising, can be effectively analyzed only after the precise spatial structure of soundscapes has been considered (Schulte-Fortkamp 2000). ●

2.2
FINDING
SIMILARITIES –
CROSS-MODAL
ANALOGIES
↓
2.2.5
SPATIAL
ANALOGIES
AND
SOUNDSCAPES

———

197

THE SPATIAL ANALOGY IS AN IMPORTANT CRITERION IN OPTIMIZING MULTISENSORY INTERFACES WITHIN THE HUMAN-MACHINE SYSTEM – INDEED, ON BOTH SIDES, NAMELY THE TECHNICAL AND THE HUMAN.

Accordingly, it is sensible to consequently exploit all possibilities of spatial analogies in order to create a multisensory design. Moreover, visual and auditory signals should be spatially assigned to one another. Today, the technical possibilities of stereo and *surround-sound technologies,* as well as *wave field synthesis* allow the perception of sound from precisely the same direction in which an optical signal is visible, even if the acoustic sources are located somewhere else (compare chapter 3.6). Warning signals are more effective in capturing attention if more than one modality is involved and stimuli are presented from the same direction. This fact has been verified in case of audio-tactile cues which led to reduced braking reaction latencies of the driver (Spence 2008b).

In housing spaces, the furnishing is naturally an elementary component of the residential landscape. In this regard, visual, and tactile aspects are conveyed. Additionally, music and background sounds can enrich the atmosphere as a useful form of *ambient noise* or serve as an inviting *sound garden* enhancing the possibilities of relaxing. Already at the beginning of the twentieth century, the composer Eric Satie experimented explicitly with music aimed at achieving a form of acoustic furnishing – which he concretely referred to as *Musique d'ameublement* (Föllmer 1999, 205). The background character of such music is emphasized by the broad distribution of acoustic sources in the sense of a surrounding *wallpaper of sound* (vividly described as *Klangtapete* in German.) As already mentioned, it is not necessary that an acoustic source is located in every place in which the origin of the sound is localized by hearing – indeed, the acoustic sources could also be of a virtual nature. In salesrooms, the background music serves to create a pleasant atmosphere and to thus stimulate the purchase of the products being offered for sale. In this regard, the music includes functional elements for the purposes of, on the one hand, remaining in the background, and simultaneously, on the other hand, with the objective of achieving the desired emotional and motivational effect. The concept of the distributed accommodation of salesrooms and office spaces by virtue of a centrally installed system which plays music may be traced back to George Owen Squire, for he let this idea be patented in the 1920s. Indeed, he created the brand name *Muzak* for these purposes. This word is a thoughtful contraction of the terms *music* and *Kodak,* in order to express the combination of emotional meaning and of the casualness reminiscent of snapshots with a handheld camera. In today's world, the term *Muzak* actually refers to commercial background music of all sorts. Furthermore, the term *functional music* applies to music especially composed for the purpose of achieving a particular objective. With the development of *Ambient Music* in the 1970s, the music aimed at reaching an atmospheric mood while exhibiting ambitions of an artistic or even of an esoteric nature. An all-encompassing wallpaper of sound serves in an inviting fashion and cultivates relaxation, but it does not arouse attention

24

198

2.2
FINDING
SIMILARITIES –
CROSS-MODAL
ANALOGIES
↓
2.2.5
SPATIAL
ANALOGIES
AND
SOUNDSCAPES

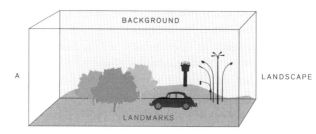

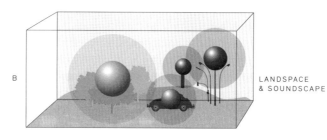

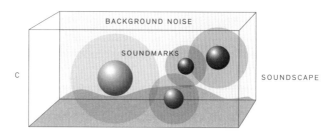

2.2
FINDING
SIMILARITIES –
CROSS-MODAL
ANALOGIES
↓
2.2.5
SPATIAL
ANALOGIES
AND
SOUNDSCAPES

199

FIGURE 2.41
The derivation of the soundscape from the analogy to the landscape.
A visual environment is defined by background properties
and significant elements of the foreground (A).
Similarly, a soundscape consists of background noise and
distinctly separate, individual acoustic sources.
The illustrations B and C demonstrate the transition from the
landscape to the soundscape.

FIGURE 2.42
Touchscape and lightscape in the operating environment of an automobile.
Both serve to build a three-dimensional structure,
which is sensibly supplemented by a differentiated soundscape.
Ford Verve concept study, 2007.

in an excessive manner. In this respect, Brian Eno, one of the principal representatives of *Ambient Music,* published a composition with the title *Music for Airports* which – in addition to elements of functional music – also exhibited influences of American Minimal Music (Eno 1978). With similar intentions, but using sound samples instead of classical instruments, Piers Headley composed *Music for Toilets* (Headley 1993). Eno demands that ambient music shall neither exclusively serve as a background, nor inescapably grasp the attention of the listeners: "Ambient music must be able to accommodate many levels of listening attention without enforcing one in particular; it must be as ignorable as it is interesting" (Eno 1978).

References with respect to the translation of the landscape analogy to the structure of psychic sensations – such as the *landscape of the soul* – shall be made here only in a peripheral manner. A consideration of the *inner landscape* of the customer with its graduation in contents of more or less significance in front of the background of a highly complex perception of the reality of life, however, is inevitable for the definition of successful products. Mungen discusses the playful interactions between the soundscape, the real, and the inner landscapes (Mungen 2004).

Methods of analyzing the perceptibility of complex spatial structures are particularly provided by *scene analysis.* This encompasses a determination of perceptual objects and events. As already suggested, a translation from the visual to the tactile and auditory modality is thoroughly possible (Bregman 1999).

2.2
FINDING
SIMILARITIES –
CROSS-MODAL
ANALOGIES
↓
2.2.5
SPATIAL
ANALOGIES
AND
SOUNDSCAPES

FUNCTIONAL
ANALOGY

The basis of the projection of technical functions onto perceptual objects is, on the one hand, the correlation of operational processes and their effects, but also, on the other hand, the systematic dependency of the technical actions on the signals which they initiate. The generation of such projections is also known as *mapping*. For a mathematical analysis, linear functions which demonstrate a connection between cause and effect are necessary. In this manner, the functional aspects of perceptual objects, such as the prediction of processes as well as the expectation of their effect, can be connected to technical functions.

2.2
FINDING
SIMILARITIES –
CROSS-MODAL
ANALOGIES
↓
2.2.6
FUNCTIONAL
ANALOGY

201

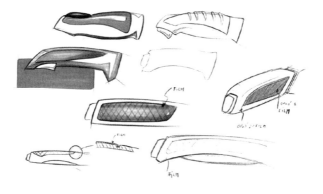

FIGURE 2.43
The bonding of ergonomic forms, of surfaces which are easy
to grasp and handle and of a tactile appearance,
can be realized by various design solutions. Blueprints for a parking
brake lever. FICOSA International, Barcelona, 2006.

THE INTERFACE BETWEEN HUMANS AND MACHINES IS BASED UPON FUNCTIONAL ANALOGIES WHICH ARE, IN IDEAL SITUATIONS, SIMULTANEOUSLY CONVEYED VIA DIFFERENT SENSES.

Every operating element must be optimized in this direction (fig. 2.43). A concept of designing, particularly represented in the case of the Bauhaus style, is expressed as follows: "The form follows the function." Initially, however, this principle applied exclusively to the visual form.

For a functional design which addresses all senses, all multisensory correlations of this fundamental principle must be extrapolated. Nevertheless, even without the utilization of a systematic overall concept, there are various examples with respect to individual modalities:

Sound: Suction-oriented vacuum cleaner sound. In this case, the sound is indicative of the desired suction performance and of the effectiveness of the device in the cleaning process. Additionally, the auditory reception of small particles is positively evaluated (Bodden 2001).

Visual appearance: Steering wheel. In addition to purely ergonomic aspects, the form of the steering wheel makes reference to the execution of ideal curving movements which it in turn enables. As figure 2.44 illustrates, the steering of early automobiles was often carried out along a level parallel to the street surface. This is, with regard to the movement of the vehicle along a horizontal plane, the sensible and intuitive but certainly not the most ergonomical solution. The Benz *Veloziped,* dating from the era when the automobile was in its infancy, already has a visible steering wheel at its disposal. The steering, nonetheless, occurred via a lever containing a pointer which approximately indicated the direction being steered.

FIGURE 2.44
The steering wheel (*Lenkstock* or literally "steering stick" in the original German) of the Benz patented motor vehicle Veloziped entitled "Velo," which was the first automobile in mass production worldwide, 1895. Schlossmuseum Jever.

202

2.2
FINDING
SIMILARITIES –
CROSS-MODAL
ANALOGIES
↓
2.2.6
FUNCTIONAL
ANALOGY

Haptic: The "handy" handle. As discussed in the next chapter, it is not only necessary to achieve a great ease of handling of the operating elements, even the visual appearance must correspond to this as much as possible.

FIGURE 2.45
The Braun shaver Sixtant SM3, 1961 – simple, functional, as if it were made out of a single piece, masculine.

Body feeling: "Sporty" acceleration of an automobile. Aspects of automobile dynamics are also conveyed by receptors within the body. The sensory information is not as specific as in the case of hearing and seeing – nevertheless, it directly influences body perception and emotions.

Smell: "Clean"-smelling cleaning agent. In the advertising industry, great efforts are undertaken to present the smell of detergents as an attribute of cleanliness itself. This is consistent with the tendency to declare an unclean visual appearance as being per se unhygienic. Often, however, dirt rims in the bathroom are not dangerous at all, whereas bacteria and viruses as carriers of possible dangers remain invisible even on a clean-looking surface.

Taste: "Refreshing"-tasting drink. The sensation of *refreshment* that is caused by a drink is not necessarily a question of the taste. In the framework of multisensory marketing, however, elements affecting the sense of taste must also be appropriately considered. As will be discussed in chapter 3.2 with respect to the subject of *refreshments,* visual elements play even here an essential role.

2.2
FINDING
SIMILARITIES –
CROSS-MODAL
ANALOGIES
↓
2.2.6
FUNCTIONAL
ANALOGY

203

Even sounds which arise in the processing of materials represent functional sounds and are appropriate for providing feedback as to the correctness of a function. Thus, for example, users expect their shavers to give them information as to the removal of their beard hairs. According to information of BRAUN GMBH, a major manufacturer of electric shaving devices, men don't accept quiet shavers – indeed, the device must confirm one's own feeling of manliness by virtue of very audible cutting sounds. In this regard, the "masculine" color scheme – *black* and *shiny metallic* – of the shaver depicted in figure 2.45 is worth noting. The "crackling" sound heard during the cutting is also helpful, notably in the search for areas of the skin which were not yet shaved as desired. As a matter of contrast, the sound of a *Ladyshave* should be muffled, allowing the soft removal of the hairs to be articulated and conveyed. Consequently, a loud "crackling" sound in this regard is not desired by women (Zips 2004). ●

AS A GENERAL RULE,
THE QUALITY OF PROCESSING SOUNDS
DELIVERS IMPORTANT INFORMATION
– THIS ALSO APPLIES
TO CLEANING PROCESSES.
●

As already suggested in section 1.2.2, the mechanical parking brake *(hand brake)* is a good example of the solid connection of sensory modalities for the purpose of conveying information about the functioning of an operational element. When the lever is pulled, the brake system exerts an increasing counterforce which is registered by the muscle receptors in the arm (proprioception). Accordingly, a direct correlation to the growing pressure of the brake pad upon the disc surface – and thus of the brake force itself – is delivered. Simultaneously, information as to the position of the brake lever is proprioceptively and occasionally visually conveyed. The flawless operability requires that the force of the hand-arm system can be applied upon the lever in a frition-locked though comfortable manner. For this purpose, an ergonomic design of the lever is necessary, some examples of which are illustrated by figure 2.43. In this case, the *tactile design* – which is discussed below – also becomes obvious, as the ease of handling is articulated in a visual manner. Via the mechanoreceptors of the skin along the surface of the hand and fingers, the solid contact between the hand and the lever during the operational activity is indicated. Additionally, the operation involves sounds: upon being raised, the lever moves the ratchets along the cogs of the detent, which guards against the unintentional release of the brake following the end of the operational activity ● This is accompanied by an audible clicking sound and by vibrational impulses which can be felt. As a result, the information pertaining to the functioning is conveyed via four sensory channels, each of which must be present, in order to design the desired high degree of reliability in a perceivable fashion (see fig. 1.16). If the mechanical system is replaced by an electrically actuated system (EPB), merely one switch is necessary to initiate the entire electrical operating process. The operational sound must then be designed to reflect the function in a purely auditory manner. ● Particularly, the sound should articulate a movement in the braking system which corresponds to a reliable function and which allows the clamping and the releasing functions to be clearly distinguished from one another. The analogy to processes of movement mentioned in section 2.2.4 is thus of great interest to designers of operational sounds.

(27)

(28)

(29)

204

2.2
FINDING
SIMILARITIES –
CROSS-MODAL
ANALOGIES
↓
2.2.6
FUNCTIONAL
ANALOGY

THE THREE-PHASES CONCEPT CONSISTS OF THE PHASE OF ACTIVATING THE SOUND (ON-SET OR ATTACK), THE BODY AS THE MAIN PHASE, AND THE FADING OUT (DECAY) OF THE SOUND.

To an increasing extent, other operational processes as well are carried out with the assistance of electromechanical actuation. In modern vehicles, the positions of the side windows, the side mirrors, the seats and their backrests, as well as of many other components can be electrically adjusted. As a general rule, an operating process may be divided into three different phases: *activation, operation,* and *deactivation.* In order to evaluate the overall operating process, it makes sense to also divide the sound process into three corresponding phases, as illustrated by figure 2.46.

In utilizing the electric window regulator as an example, the following aspect is demonstrated: during the attack phase, the drive motor is initiated, and it accelerates to reach the necessary speed in order to raise or lower the window pane. ● This is related to an increase of the frequency components of the *rotational sound,* which in turn are dependent upon the rotational speed. In general, the activation phase is very short, merely long enough to allow an impulse to be auditorily perceived. During the main phase, the rotational velocity and the rotational sound remain constant, in the ideal situation, and the window pane thus moves with a constant velocity in an upward or downward direction. Variations in the motor torque or the rotational speed would be perceived as fluctuations of the rotational sound, or as changes of the tone pitch, respectively, and they could accordingly be regarded by customers as signs of deficiencies in the robustness. Upon conclusion of the process, the driving motor is deactivated, the rotational speed falls quickly back down to a static condition, and the frequency components of the rotational sound respond by behaving analogously. The shorter the time period for the attack and decay phases, the greater the impulsiveness of the sound at the beginning and at the end of the operational activity. This suggests the precise initiation of the expected action and the equally precise conclusion of the process, but it can also result in a high impulsiveness which could annoy or even frighten the driver. Nevertheless, if both phases are temporally extended, however, this can give rise to the impression that the operation is neither responsive nor precise, or it may be regarded as reflecting a weakly dimensioned driving motor. In particular, the chosen example has one thing in common with many electromechanical operating systems, namely that a constant velocity of the process is related to the constant rotational speed and the tone pitch (the black line in fig. 2.46). In the case of a silent process, however, a functional sound can be electronically generated, where desired. In this case, it would also be possible to choose a sound in such a manner that allows the tone pitch to increase with the rising level of the window (red line in fig. 2.46). This would correspond to the analogy of tone frequency and spatial height as discussed in section 2.2.3.

2.2
FINDING
SIMILARITIES –
CROSS-MODAL
ANALOGIES
↓
2.2.6
FUNCTIONAL
ANALOGY

205

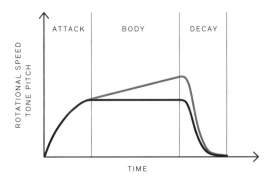

FIGURE 2.46
The Three-Phases Concept for optimizing the temporal behavior of functional sounds.

The sound researcher and composer Murray Schafer demonstrated that nearly every sound process can be described by three different phases (Schafer 1977). Figure 2.47, for example, depicts the analysis of the ringing of a telephone and the sound of a passing motorcycle. As characteristic parameters of the sound process, duration as well as frequency/mass, fluctuation/graininess, and dynamics are all considered. The diagrams also indicate some of the symbols Schafer recommends for a practical, local analysis of sounds. Such diagrams were utilized to graphically document sound environments – so-called *sound diaries*. In the example on the right-hand side, the change of the tone pitch of the motor sound as a result of the Doppler Effect may be easily recognized. The symbols for the dynamics are inspired by those in music theory.

Among further examples of the use of the Three-Phases Concept is the evaluation of the sound of an electric seat adjuster or of an electric coffee grinder. ● ● Multiple phase models are also appropriate for describing the unfolding of perceptions involving smell and taste. An example is the differentiated temporal unfolding of the taste of wine or the gradual shaping and expansion of scent components in the case of perfume.

Furthermore, even in the touching of objects such as handles, three different phases can be distinguished from one another, affecting not merely the motor skills, but also the perception as well. Initially, there is the first contact with the object. Only afterward, the complete clasping of the object follows. The phase can include further, complex touching processes. In sampling and gripping, the fingertips and the surfaces of the hands provide information as to the temperature, the texture, and the mechanical properties of the surface of the object. Moreover, geometric parameters and spatial arrangements of objects are detected. In the final phase, the contact ends as the object is released. This can involve further perceptual qualities, such as aftereffects (see section 1.3.4). Subsequent to release following the application of a great grabbing force, the diminishing of the tactile perception normally requires a number of seconds.

30

31

206

2.2
FINDING
SIMILARITIES –
CROSS-MODAL
ANALOGIES
↓
2.2.6
FUNCTIONAL
ANALOGY

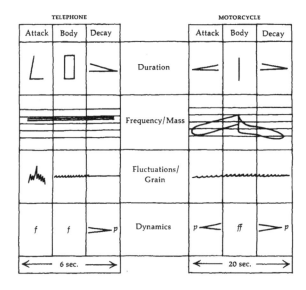

FIGURE 2.47
An example of three phases of sound in the case of the
ringing of a telephone (on the left) and of a passing motorcycle
(on the right). The temporal behavior of each sound
is characterized by duration as well as frequency/mass, fluctuation/
graininess, and dynamics (Schafer 1977).

In general, in the observation of the temporal correlation of sensations between different modalities, the coordination of the phases with respect to one another must be taken into account. Exact consideration and alignment of the phase structure would enable, for example, a description of the unfolding of the taste of a drink by virtue of a simultaneously developing sound.

TACTILE DESIGN

2.2
FINDING
SIMILARITIES –
CROSS-MODAL
ANALOGIES
↓
2.2.7
TACTILE
DESIGN

———

207

The visual impression of operating elements, for example, in the interior compartment of vehicles, must correspond harmoniously to the tactile properties. Thus, upon being touched, the tactile impression of materials should be quite consistent with the expectations arising as a result of the visual appearance. The elements operated by the driver with his or her hands and feet – such as the steering wheel, the direction-indication control, the pedals, the electric switches, and others – can only be effectively operated when feedback, regarding the functioning of the elements, is conveyed by the receptors of the tendons and muscles participating in the operating process (proprioception). Experiments with the first prototypes of the power-assisted steering *(PAS or servo steering)* have demonstrated that it is nearly impossible to safely steer a vehicle when the deflection of the steering wheel that is being operated does not lead to a proportional counterforce. The driver necessarily needs such force feedback to intuitively evaluate the position of the steering wheel and thus of the wheels themselves. Accordingly, in the case of electrical systems, such as *steer-by-wire* or *brake-by-wire,* an artificial force regeneration must be created.

EVEN IN THAT INSTANCE,
THE FOLLOWING PRINCIPLE APPLIES:
IN ORDER TO ACHIEVE THE OPTIMAL MULTISENSORY
DESIGN OF OPERATING ELEMENTS,
THE PERCEPTION IN EVERY MODALITY
MUST BE CLEAR AND WITHOUT CONTRADICTION,
THUS EXHIBITING AN OBJECT QUALITY
WHICH PRECISELY CORRESPONDS TO THE
EXPECTED FUNCTION.

FIGURE 2.48
The tactile design of the switch of a windshield wiper,
with a surface that is easy to handle and a dial with nubs for the
interval switch. Having a switch which is easy to grasp
and to handle does not suffice – the operating safety and reliability
must be visually accentuated as well. Ford Focus, 2004.

This is particularly important in the case of processes pertinent to the safety of the driver, for the execution of such an operating process must be felt by the driver as being reliable. Indeed, he or she can be certain only when experiencing that feeling of safety.

It is self-evident that operating elements must be able to be utilized in a handy manner, in order to avoid slipping or at least an unintended gliding of the hands and feet of the operator. Thereby, a significant role is played by the tactile perception of this handiness. That means that the surface must also feel *handy*. This aspect should already be visually recognizable (fig. 2.48). Additionally important is the controllability of the activated movement of the operating element. This also requires tactile feedback received upon reaching the position of the desired adjustment, for example, by virtue of vibration upon locking. Nevertheless, the feeling of safety should also come into being already upon the visual recognition of the design, indeed, even before the customer has had a chance to test the operating safety of the object. If acoustic signals are combined with the operation and the function, the following synesthetic relations exists:

VISUAL HANDINESS ⟷ THE FEELING OF THE HANDINESS OF THE SURFACE ⟷

THE CONTROLLABILITY OF THE MOVEMENT ⟷ THE EXECUTION OF THE DESIRED MOVEMENT ⟷

REACHING THE DESIRED POSITION ⟷ THE ACOUSTIC FEEDBACK
(REGARDING THE MOVEMENT AND THE POSITION OF THE OPERATING ELEMENTS) ⟷

THE INITIATION OF THE DESIRED FUNCTION ⟷ THE ACOUSTIC FEEDBACK REGARDING THE FUNCTION.

208

2.2
FINDING
SIMILARITIES –
CROSS-MODAL
ANALOGIES
↓
2.2.7
TACTILE
DESIGN

FIGURE 2.49
Even textile materials allow the connection of durability, handiness, and an appearance which expresses both properties. Strap for shutters.

FIGURE 2.50
Tactile design of the switch of a hair dryer. Braun, Creation 1600.

With respect to functionality and tactile appearance, the shutter strap depicted in figure 2.49 is nothing less than a classic of tactile design. On the one hand, it must be recognizable as a textile material, however, on the other hand, it must display a resistance to tearing and exhibit a robustness not generally associated with fabric. A relatively great force is necessary to raise the shutter. Therefore, the strap must be appropriately designed in a manner facilitating the ease of handling. In lowering the shutter, nevertheless, it must be possible to allow the strap to glide through the hands with minimal friction and without resulting in injuries due to the generation of warmth. The rough web structure of the strap indicates the necessary handiness. Shiny components, however, symbolize the application of special artificial materials which in turn symbolize robustness and a high tearing strength. The example indicates that even the designing of simple operating elements profits from a successful alignment of visual, tactile, and functional aspects.

The same applies to the switch of a hair dryer depicted in figure 2.50: the operating element must be capable of comfortably being shifted along the axis of the handle, in order to allow the choice of various operating levels. Given that the switch is integrated into the handle, it must also be capable of providing reliable, solid grip during the operation of the device. Due to the structuring of the switch elements, both requirements are combined with each other, for the act of encompassing the handle and the switch with the hand enables the solid, secure leading of the hair dryer and simultaneously prevents the unintended shifting of the operating level. In the profiling of the switch element, reference shall also be made visually to both requirements. Even though it is integrated into the handle by virtue of its form, the switch distinguishes itself from the handle in a subtle, discrete manner and appears as an independent perceptual object, indeed, as the functional design requires.

A focus on tactile features of objects was first established for design education at the Bauhaus. With reference to Filippo Tommaso Marinetti's *Tactilisme,* a proposed art style based on tactile sensations, László Moholy-Nagy instructed his students to assemble plates with a variety of materials suitable to gain haptic experience (Moholy-Nagy 1929). A current enhancement of this principle is provided by *Sensotact,* an evaluation kit for assessment of surface properties of materials used for automotive design (Sensotact 2010). This *reference framework* for touch sensations was initially developed by the design group at Renault. It consists of sets of small samples with specifically scaled properties. During the evaluation process, however, the tactile sensations are separated from the visual and the auditory perception.

2.2
FINDING
SIMILARITIES –
CROSS-MODAL
ANALOGIES
↓
2.2.7
TACTILE
DESIGN

209

2.3
RECOGNIZING FAMILIAR FEATURES – ICONIC CONNECTION

2.3.1
ASSOCIATIVE CONNECTIONS

Even by virtue of the identification of known elements, which are perceived in various modalities, a connection of multisensory perceptual objects is possible. A necessary precondition for the connection is that the sensory impressions involved were previously perceived in conjunction.

ASSOCIATIVE CONNECTIONS ARE DEDUCED FROM PERCEPTUAL EXPERIENCES VIA LEARNING PROCESSES.

In order to guarantee a clear distinction from the other strategies, cross-modal connections as presented in chapter 2.1, exclusively the *concrete, objective (real) association* will be analyzed herein. This encompasses the allocation of different sensory stimuli to their origin, the source of the stimulation, which is either the subject's own body, an object, or a life form within the outer environment of the individual.

THE PROBABILITY OF THE CORRECT IDENTIFICATION OF AN OBJECT INCREASES WITH THE NUMBER OF PERCEIVED FEATURES.

Therefore, the perception via several sensory channels increases the certainty of the recognition (see e.g., Molholm 2004). An associatively perceived stimulus creates a reference, an *index* regarding an already known object.

In this manner, a connection of visual perception may also be made to auditory stimuli along associative paths, as a concrete association. Therefore, in order to distinguish these from genuine synesthetic phenomena, Wilhelm Voss uses the term *thing perception* [Dingwahrnehmung]; Barbara Flückiger applies the term *first-order semantics* (Flückiger 2002). The word *concrete* used herein makes reference to the identification of known elements of the

210

2.3
RECOGNIZING
FAMILIAR
FEATURES –
ICONIC
CONNECTION
↓
2.3.1
ASSOCIATIVE
CONNECTIONS

2.3
RECOGNIZING
FAMILIAR
FEATURES –
ICONIC
CONNECTION
↓
2.3.1
ASSOCIATIVE
CONNECTIONS

211

perception, and reference is made in a similar fashion by virtue of terms such as *Musique Concrète* (Schaeffer 1967) or *Concrete Poetry.* In the first case, sounds of daily perception evolve into music, whereas the latter example involves the artistic processing of speech sounds and elements of the alphabet. In this case, nevertheless, the purely concrete perception, that means the identification of known elements or – articulated differently – the *iconic contents* of the perception, shall be in the foreground.

The influence of sounds which cause discomfort, such as the scratching of fingernails along a chalkboard or the buzzing of the drill of a dentist, is intensified when the respective situation corresponding to said sounds is additionally visually perceived (Cox 2007). As in daily life, the sounds in a movie which result from materials being touched or rubbed against each other can also make iconic reference to the material properties (addressed in *Materializing Sound Indices,* Chion 1994). ● ● ● ● ● ● The influence of a color sensation on the auditory perception of a sound is modified in case that not only an abstract color but a colored depiction of a known object is presented (Menzel 2009). The spread of attention from a visual image to a simultaneously presented auditory stimulus depends on the congruence of visual and auditory information, i.e. whether both are known to fit to each other (Fiebelkorn 2010). This requires identification of the sources of stimuli.

It is often reported that associations of landscapes or rooms, such as vaults or columned halls, occur during the listening to music. Thereby, "linguistic paintings," namely the so-called *onomatopoetic* elements of the music, serve as important initiators. Subsequent to the results of his surveys involving persons who went blind, Voss gives examples in which the sound of a snare drum causes the association of rolling balls, whereas the sound of a horse and carriage, on the other hand, causes the visual appearance of a pavement-like structure (see fig. 3.36; Voss 1930). The futurist Romolo Romani connects the association of the sound of water to a visual entity via wave-like structures, similar to the forms caused by a raindrop striking the surface of water (fig. 2.51). Naturally, even this process leads to the origin of sounds. Similarly, the sensations of brightness, color, and form caused by an instrumental sound are often determined, at least in part, by the optical properties of the respective musical instruments. Instrumental forms may be found, for example, in the paintings of Charles Blanc-Gatti (1934, fig. 2.52) and also in Walt Disney's film *Fantasia* as elements of the visualization of music (Culhane 1983).

Associative connections are based not only upon the identification of individual objects, but they also have their foundation in the recognition of complex environments and their atmospheres. In this regard, a question generally arises with respect to the auditory references in concrete, non-abstract paintings. Even in this case, it is necessary that the soundscapes, to which reference is made, are known and were already experienced in the form presented (Bockhoff 2007).

A common definition of a *principle of association* states that an interconnection of elements of different modalities always arises when these elements have been frequently perceived together, or when they show similarities in characteristic features (Arnheimer 1969). The nature of the emerging associations is, therefore, dependent upon the perceptual images stored in the memory.

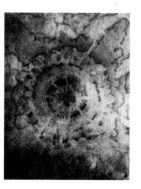

FIGURE 2.51
An associative visualization of the "murmuring" of water.
Romolo Romani, Il murmure dell'aqua, 1908–10.

FIGURE 2.52
Form elements of the acoustic source in musical painting.
Charles Blanc-Gatti, Organ, 1930.

212

2.3
RECOGNIZING
FAMILIAR
FEATURES –
ICONIC
CONNECTION
↓
2.3.1
ASSOCIATIVE
CONNECTIONS

For various reasons, the assumption of simple laws of association, as described above, however, must be drawn into question. Given that the memory plays an essential role in associative connections, it is very difficult to verify a distinct reference between the underlying stimuli and the elements of the association. Furthermore, in the case of audio-visual connection, the triggering acoustic attributes and the visual elements coupled thereto are variable, meaning that they are not to be regarded as precisely definable fragments of the perception as a whole. Moreover, elements of the perceptions of different modalities mutually influence one another and build new structures which are, nevertheless, anchored in the memory. Therefore, associations can not be thoroughly explained by simple models, such as the "classical" model.

Experiments pertaining to the connection of visual and auditory properties demonstrated that the test subjects immediately connected the sounds presented to them with mental or internal images, events, or memories (Riccò 2002).

The application of associative forms and structures is an important element of product designing, even when they are limited to the visual realm. Accordingly, in designing a new product, reference can be made to forms which were already elements of successful products, thus having impressed the memories of potential customers with appropriately good evaluations.

2.3
RECOGNIZING
FAMILIAR
FEATURES –
ICONIC
CONNECTION
↓
2.3.1
ASSOCIATIVE
CONNECTIONS

213

THE USEFUL APPLICATION
OF ESTABLISHED FORMS IN A NEW DESIGN
REQUIRES, HOWEVER, THAT
THE PERCEPTION AND EXPERIENCE
OF THE CUSTOMER
ARE KNOWN AND CONNECTED TO PRECISELY
THOSE EMOTIONS WHICH ALREADY
RESULTED IN THE SUCCESSFUL MARKETING.

Even in the case of new designs, design attributes of products already proven to be successful are often applied. Thus, digital cameras typically exhibit – by means of purposeful *retro design* – the previously successful features of analog cameras. The concentrated reference made to proven, established elements of design, by virtue of so-called *me-too products,* leads to efforts to profit from the market value of successful designs. Thereby, characteristics of other products, which are already successful in the market, are systematically applied. In such instances, the associative connection of design elements plays a decisive role.

Associative references are then of particular importance when the designing of components of the corporate design makes reference to the product itself. A typical example is the *Wienermobile* of Oscar Mayer, the American manufacturer of sausage products. The very first of these vehicles was built in 1936. It is designed in the shape of a hot dog. Accordingly, this advertising and sales stand assumes the shape of the product itself. Thereby, the associations of the product appearance, the corporate symbol, and the salesroom merge with one another. Normally, such components appear more separated from one another: The corporate logo is mounted upon the salesroom, and *nearby* the product is further exhibited as an image, a light object, or a sculpture. In the case of the Wiener mobile,

FIGURE 2.53
Wienermobile. A mobile advertising medium for hot dogs and
other sausage products of the company Oscar Mayer.
An original vehicle from 1952, Henry Ford Museum, Dearborn.

214

2.3
RECOGNIZING
FAMILIAR
FEATURES –
ICONIC
CONNECTION
↓
2.3.1
ASSOCIATIVE
CONNECTIONS

the merging also effectuates a fusion of the corporate identity and the product identity with one another.

The company Oscar Mayer was indeed also striving to expand the corporate design in a multisensory manner. As a result, the advertising song "The Oscar Mayer Jingle" was composed as early as 1963 and – according to the company – soon achieved great popularity. At the same time, children's flutes shaped in the form of sausages were distributed, indeed, using the Wienermobile. This constitutes a very good example of multisensory references made in marketing, for the sense of taste, the visual appearance and *audio branding* are directly and purposefully connected to one another. Indeed, the flute is raised to the mouth in a manner similar to the sausage – a further associative aspect. This also illustrates a sense of humor. Thus, the company profits from an additional surge of sympathy and is accordingly able to *bind* young children to the product, as desired, often for a lifetime.

Traditionally, associative references to groceries are often found in the designs of objects of utility in everyday use. As one example, among many others, figure 2.54 illustrates a terrine designed and shaped in the form of a brown hare. The animal ducks down in the typical pose in a grassy trough. It is authentically presented. The body of the brown hare serves as the cover of the product. Even the color design is very close to reality. Innumerable similar products have been produced since ancient times, mostly as components of dinnerware.

FIGURE 2.54
A terrine in the form of a brown hare.
Museum of Applied Art, Cologne.

2.3
RECOGNIZING
FAMILIAR
FEATURES –
ICONIC
CONNECTION
↓
2.3.1
ASSOCIATIVE
CONNECTIONS

FIGURE 2.55
A CD player with a "CD design." The circular form
and the centrically arranged metal plate with its text logo make
reference to the form of the medium which is
to be played by the product. Philips EXP2540, 2007.

Figure 2.55 illustrates an example from the high-tech entertainment industry, namely a CD player whose appearance makes reference to the form of the medium. This symmetrical look is not simply motivated by functional aspects; indeed, inside the housing, the location of the CD drive deviates from the axis of symmetry.

In order to initiate associative connections within the perceptual system, however, it is not absolutely necessary to create objects with completely authentic details. Simple analogies pertaining to the form often suffice to establish a reference to the known perceptual object, thus facilitating the identification of the respective objects. Children, in particular, use these facts for the purpose of effectuating allocations between objects, creating object classes and also identifying objects, even when only very elementary aspects coincide with memorized basic patterns. Accordingly, the construction of elementary analogies consistent with chapter 2.2 is an essential prerequisite for creating perceptual patterns which serve to recognize objects. Nonetheless, the reverse also applies: The recognition of objects requires initially the analysis of analogy relationships. For example, this applies to the Braun Phonosuper SK4 "Snow White's Coffin," whose name makes reference to the plexiglass hood (see also fig. 1.22).

Figure 2.56 illustrates the model of a portable radio which a three-year-old child assembled, using small interlocking plastic bricks. It exhibits the typical elements of the object represented: stereo loudspeakers, antenna (left), and power cable with wall socket (right). This demonstrates that children are capable of recognizing the essential elements which must be available for the identification of special objects, and that they can purposefully employ this capability in design. In a similar manner, all people are capable of identifying the depicted object only if they have already seen such an object.

FIGURE 2.56
Even small children are capable of finding form analogies and
employing them creatively for building iconic content.
A portable radio made of interlocking, miniature plastic bricks,
assembled by a three-year-old child.

Even in the designing of technical operating elements, it is sensible to utilize known patterns which are familiar to and used by the customer in other areas of daily life. In this manner, a central *infotainment system* was developed for the *Ford Mondeo,* of the model year 2008, whose operating console included characteristic elements associated with mobile phones. In particular, two operating elements were integrated into the steering wheel, with which the menu of the on-board computer as well as the entertainment system can be operated. Thereby, a *rocker switch* is used, allowing the driver to navigate up or down as well as to the left or to the right. A button located in the middle allows the verification of the respective commands being entered. In employing this principle, which is commonly used in mobile phones as well as in remote control systems, for example, for televisions or DVD players, the manufacturer must make certain that the overwhelming majority of customers using this system in the automobile model can operate it quite intuitively, thus making long learning periods unnecessary. Thereby, the risk of operating errors is minimized. Indeed, in everyday use, rocker switches with four, eight, or even sixteen dial positions are typical.

Tactile associations can be employed, for example, with the utilization of leather for gloves on the steering wheel as well as on other elements such as the gearshift handle and the handbrake lever. As is generally known, clothing tends to be perceived as being part of the body (Merleau-Ponty 1966). Given the use of materials which are recognized as the components of clothing, the human-machine interface can be equipped with "flowing" transition. The automobile thus gains a degree of corporeity – similar to clothing being perceived as a part of the body – and the body is accordingly regarded as an organic component of the human-machine system. This fact is independent of the specific design of operating elements. There is an essential difference, nevertheless, depending upon whether the driver regards him or herself as being merely an externally positioned operator of a machine or, on the other hand, as an integral part of a system that is – even in his or her own perception – precisely designed to accommodate the individual requirements and to allow a merging of the system and its operator. This situation is comparable to a musician who, while playing a music instrument, sees him or herself only as an operator

216

2.3
RECOGNIZING
FAMILIAR
FEATURES –
ICONIC
CONNECTION
↓
2.3.1
ASSOCIATIVE
CONNECTIONS

of the apparatus being played – thus being incapable of mastering the instrument. Only when he or she experiences the instrument as being a part of his or her own body, similar to the voice, an expressive interpretation is enabled, allowing the essential characteristic of passionate, emotional contents to be directly conveyed to the listeners.

Often, similar forms occur due to the similarity of the function. Such a functionally determined form analogy *(isomorphy)* exists, for example, between a hand-held drill and a hand-held firearm. Primarily, this form similarity arises as a result of the functions, in the case of both devices, of accurately positioning the axial direction of the drill or of the barrel as well as of shoring up and supporting the force and counterforce along this axial direction.

2.3
RECOGNIZING
FAMILIAR
FEATURES –
ICONIC
CONNECTION
↓
2.3.1
ASSOCIATIVE
CONNECTIONS

217

FIGURE 2.57
BOSCH Prio Multi-sander: a DIY home repair
product that resembles a steam iron.

A further example of a functionally determined form analogy is provided by the multi-sander depicted in figure 2.57, which is similar to the form of a steam iron. The motivation behind this design is, in both cases, the requirement of processing filigree, detailed structures in a precise manner. Accordingly, it must be possible to lead the device into small, sharp angles. In addition to the actual function, the object exhibits, when analyzed on a purely visual basis, an ease of operating typically associated with the ironing of clothing. The handle, being situated in the middle of the product, facilitates the even, smooth and consistent distribution of the force along the entire surface of the material which is to be treated. An iron must be operable in a similar fashion, allowing a uniform spreading of the force with minimal pressure being applied by the user. Generally speaking, the employment of concepts for the designing of technical components of other functionalities can significantly improve the acceptance of the product by customers. Even the operating console for small automobiles, as depicted in figure 2.58, orients itself consciously with respect to the design elements of cellphones. In this manner, despite innovative designs, the familiarity of the customer is a prerequisite. In particular, this also facilitates the learning of the operating process, thus enhancing the functionality in the human-machine interface.

Associative elements also play an essential role in the auditory representation of technical functions, in addition to the cross-modal analogies as discussed chapter 2.2.

FIGURE 2.58
The association of technical components of other functionalities.
Even this operating console exhibits aspects used
in the design of cellphones. This improves the customer
acceptance and facilitates learning how to operate the product.
Ford Verve concept car, 2007.

Time and again, auditory and visual characteristics impress themselves together into the memory. As a rule, for example, the windshield wiper is located in the field of vision during its operation. The related sound of its driving system and the possible friction sounds of the wiping blades along the windshield are thus commonly anchored, along with the visual perception, in the memory. Among the characteristic noises is also the impulsive sound, heard as the wiper blades change their direction. Thus, the process is exactly sequenced in the perception, and it can easily be recognized once again due to its periodicity. On the other hand, it is possible to recognize a potentially dangerous situation by virtue of a sudden interruption of a sound process – for example, when the sound of the engine of the automobile abruptly begins to unevenly "stammer" – or when it completely stops. Even the flying sound of a mosquito disturbs us the most when it suddenly stops – serving as an indication that the insect has landed and is about to sting.

218

2.3
RECOGNIZING
FAMILIAR
FEATURES –
ICONIC
CONNECTION
↓
2.3.1
ASSOCIATIVE
CONNECTIONS

IF THE SEQUENCE OF A PROCESS IS KNOWN,
THE SOUND WHICH IS RELATED
TO INDIVIDUAL PHASES IMPRESSES ITSELF
INTO THE MEMORY OF THE LISTENER.
IN THIS MANNER, THE FUNCTIONAL
SEQUENCE IS CODED IN THE SOUND WHICH
IS STORED IN THE MEMORY.

While iconic connection refers to objects in the memory, it is based on the learning and experience of the subject. It therefore depends on the living environment and the cultural background of an individual. Thus, frequent use of motorcycle horns can cause different types of annoyances to people who either identify this noise with a well-known culture or who are not accustomed to experience it, as a cross-cultural study with Vietnamese and Japanese listeners has shown (Phan 2009).

Among the important characteristics in the exterior visual design of automobiles is the front end. Together with the radiator grill and the headlights, this constitutes the "face" of the vehicle. With respect to customer acceptance, it is necessary to appropriately consider the related aspect of personification. Indeed, emotions can be released which could affect the image of the product, either in a positive or a negative manner. The overall character can express aggression, friendliness, determination, or robustness. In particular, the *radiator grille* is an essential component of the brand identity – it can, for example, be in the form of a crest, a kidney, an oval, or a temple.

Additional body-oriented associations in the designing of automobiles are articulated in "muscular," "athletic," "slim," and "friendly" forms. In addition to the *face,* one speaks of the *shoulders* and *body* of the product. Indeed, the Bauhaus teacher László Moholy-Nagy, who viewed the doctrine of strict forms in design skeptically, urged using the exemplary, function of the human body: "According to his perspective, the knowledge of some certain canon is considerably less important than the availability of a truly human equilibrium (...) for the human biological structure is the actual source of every organic expression" (Düchting 1996, 60). Extended to a synesthetic, multisensory design, this view also applies to the other sensory channels, in particular to the tactile and auditory modality. Thus, as further described below, even onomatopoetic and linguistic aspects play an important role in the perceptual effects of sound.

2.3
RECOGNIZING
FAMILIAR
FEATURES –
ICONIC
CONNECTION
↓
2.3.1
ASSOCIATIVE
CONNECTIONS

219

ASSOCIATIVE
FORMS OF THE LIVING
LANDSCAPE

If one takes the term *living landscape* literally, even in the case of interior design, one is inclined to illustrate it with associative references to natural landscapes. Whereas concrete allusions were frowned upon by true functionalism, like they were presented in the Bauhaus doctrine, they nevertheless re-emerged repeatedly during Pop Art and postmodernism. Associative elements are also appropriate for fundamentally determining an atmosphere or ironically alienating it. In this manner, Guido Droco and Franco Mello designed a clothes hanger entitled Cactus for Gulfram/Cirié-Turin in the form of a column cactus. In this case, the intended humor consisted of integrating an element of a landscape regarded as being hostile to life into a comfortable ambience – the *living desert* as an odd counter principle to the comfortable *living landscape.* The allusion of the Cactus is, nevertheless, purely visual, and it deliberately falls short of a completely authentic representation of the thorns – for this would render the product useless with respect to its function, and it would very likely discourage guests from utilizing it. Accordingly, the surface merely consists of a polyurethane foam structure containing nubs, which in turn gives rise to sweeping associations.

On the other hand, if it involves an analogy pertaining to the urban atmosphere of a city landscape, architectural forms are appropriate. In this regard, figure 2.59 illustrates a piece of furniture as a building – namely the cabinet Frankfurter F1 by the designers and architects Norbert Berghof, Michael Landes, and Wolfgang Rang. Similar to a cathedral or a contemporary high-rise building with two towers, it surmounts the living landscape and shines full of highly valuable elements, such as golden surfaces.

FIGURE 2.59
Allusions in a design of the postmodern era.
A piece of furniture as a building.
Norbert Berghof, Michael Landes, and Wolfgang Rang,
cabinet Frankfurter F1,
designed for Draenert, 1985–86.

Architectural forms may also be found in dinnerware, such as in the case of the dinnerware set Tea & Coffee Piazza, designed in 1983 by Charles A. Jencks for ALESSI. In this case, allusions are made to antiquated architectural forms. As mentioned before, such references were frowned upon in modernist design, but they reappeared in the designs of postmodernism, for example, in the widespread use of salt and pepper shakers as well as sugar shakers in restaurants, as depicted in figure 2.60.

220

2.3
RECOGNIZING
FAMILIAR
FEATURES –
ICONIC
CONNECTION
↓
2.3.1
ASSOCIATIVE
CONNECTIONS

FIGURE 2.60
Salt and pepper shakers and a sugar shaker,
each in the form of a column.

The influence of concrete associations upon the perception and interpretation of objects is also expressed by Claes Oldenburg's sculpture *Dropped Cone,* as illustrated in figure 2.61. In this instance, the designer plays with the two basic objects, namely the *roof of a building* and an *ice cream cone,* which associatively hardly appear to correspond to one another. In the case of the dropped ice cream cone, however, an attractive contrast arises by virtue of the – now very appropriate – form analogy to the roof of a building and, also worthy of mention, to the forms of the tower roofs of the nearby Cologne Cathedral as well.

Thereby, the artist Oldenburg emphasizes the architectural character of the sculpture, which extends beyond the purely associative realm. Indeed, as an association, the object fits well into the metropolitan atmosphere of a shopping promenade, a route along which ice cream is regularly sold – and occasionally finds its way onto the pavement. Oldenburg advocates art of a true-to-life, multisensory nature: "I am for an art," he claimed in 1961, "that takes its form from the lines of life itself, that twists and extends and accumulates and spits and drips, and is heavy and coarse and blunt and sweet and stupid as life itself." (Oldenburg 1961)

2.3
RECOGNIZING
FAMILIAR
FEATURES –
ICONIC
CONNECTION
↓
2.3.1
ASSOCIATIVE
CONNECTIONS

221

FIGURE 2.61
An associative play with the forms of the roof of a
building and an ice cream cone. Claes Oldenburg, Dropped Cone,
Neumarkt, Cologne, 2001.

ANIMAL FORMS

In many cases, official product names or nicknames are established by associations with forms prevalent in the animal world. An internationally known example is the Volkswagen VW Beetle [Käfer] with the obvious analogy to the armored shell of a ladybug beetle. Even the New Beetle exhibits associations to the ladybug as well as to the previous automobile model of the same name. Given the essential technical modifications, nevertheless, the newer product diverges considerably from the legendary Beetle.

The designation of the motor scooter Vespa by the designer Corradino d'Ascanio for PIAGGIO is also based upon analogies to animal forms. The myth of the product was established at the beginning of the 1950s. The designation Vespa [Wasp] refers to the rear of the vehicle, with its drop-shaped motor covering forming a sharp point towards the stern. These elements are reminiscent of the back portion of the body of a wasp. Furthermore, the designation additionally conveys a vivid impression of the dynamic properties of the vehicle, such as agility and swift mobility.

Animals often appear as *heraldic creatures* within the framework of brand symbolism. This will be more closely analyzed in chapter 2.4. An example of the utilization of animal forms in design may also be seen in the terrine depicted in figure 2.54.

FIGURE 2.62
Visibly cold. The ultrasonic humidifier
Solac H200 G2 Mr. Pin.

Particularly interesting is an example in which the visual design corresponds to the sensation of feeling coldness. Thereby, the coldness of the steam of an ultrasonic humidifier shall be associatively conveyed. As a matter of experience, one knows that steam is normally hot. If one touches steam – e.g., steam emanating from a water boiler – the danger of a scalding injury is very real. Even humidifiers often work with water steam resulting from the heating of water. Nevertheless, humidifiers can also be equipped with an atomizer which functions according to the ultrasonic principle. Thereby, an ultrasonic transmitter sets the water into motion and accordingly creates a cloud of very minute, cold drops of water, an *aerosol*. This aerosol can not be visually distinguished from hot water steam. Thus associatively, due to its purely optical properties, it appears to be hot. In order to avoid this effect, the ultrasonic humidifier *Solac H200 G2 Mr. Pin* was designed in the form of a penguin which sprays the aerosol through its beak (fig. 2.62). In this manner, the association of hot steam can indeed be avoided. Instead, the – true – impression of cold steam arises by virtue of the association with breathing air which, in the case of inhaling and exhaling in cold temperatures, condenses in front of the mouth, or here the beak. White and clear blue, the typical colors of the Antarctic, additionally support the associative field. This is a good example of the modification of the product appearance through the conscious integration of functionally appropriate associations. In this manner, misinterpretations can be avoided.

TECHNICAL AND FUTURISTIC FORMS

Time and again, the design of functional products is aimed at demonstrating the level of the technology involved. This objective is supported by a purposefully technical design. Figure 2.63 illustrates the example of an FM radio receiver of the 1950s. The design facilitates the emergence of the underlying

222

2.3
RECOGNIZING
FAMILIAR
FEATURES –
ICONIC
CONNECTION
↓
2.3.1
ASSOCIATIVE
CONNECTIONS

principle of modules, highlighting the casing made of bakelite, a perforated plate, rotary knobs, and a superimposed frequency scale. In this manner, the commitment of the manufacturer to technology as the primary principle of the design is effectively articulated.

2.3
RECOGNIZING
FAMILIAR
FEATURES –
ICONIC
CONNECTION
↓
2.3.1
ASSOCIATIVE
CONNECTIONS

223

FIGURE 2.63
The accentuated technical design of an FM radio.
Kleinsuper SK1, Braun GmbH, 1955–58.

The decade of the 1970s was accompanied by a growing interest in playfully enriching the functional form with associative and symbolic aspects, even though these measures did not necessarily result in reference being made to a function of the respective object. As an example, Nivico produced a television for JVC in the form of an astronaut's helmet. In this manner, the product was presented as being technically most advanced – an appropriately successful reference to the space craze prevalent at the time. Considering that the enthusiasm subsequently faded, and given the relative stagnation in manned space expeditions today, this reference is barely understandable now – although it applied quite perfectly within the framework of pop design and its often ironic allusions at the time of its origin. In this regard, one may consider a comparison of the technical forms in the ambience of the first landing on the moon (in 1969) and in the formal idiom of a science-fiction film such as Stanley Kubrick's *2001: A Space Odyssey* (which had premiered in 1968). The science-fiction genre also plays an essential role in the design of futuristic sounds. Even this aspect is featured in an exemplary manner in Kubrick's film, a cinematic masterpiece which is regarded by experts – thoroughly justified – as being among those films having the best sound design.

FIGURE 2.64
The futuristic connection of an air intake and the
headlight of an automobile, as featured in the GM Firebird II, 1956.
Henry Ford Museum, Dearborn.

Futuristic designs played significant roles in the construction of automobiles, notably in the 1950s and the 1960s, as efforts were undertaken to reflect the rapid development of new possibilities and designs of the aviation and aerospace technologies within the framework of motor vehicles for the roads. Figure 2.64 depicts the front end of the concept car *Firebird II,* whose design is obviously oriented with respect to the form of jet airplanes. The body of the automobile, being tantamount to the fuselage of an aircraft, is exclusively made of titanium. This vehicle was presented during special auto show, – called by the manufacturer GENERAL MOTORS *Motorama* – although it never went into mass production.

AERODYNAMIC FORMS

During the second half of the twentieth century, analogous to the technology of the aviation and aerospace industries, a considerable amount of attention was paid to diminishing the air resistance of road and rail vehicles. Aerodynamic forms as elements of visual design soon advanced to being the epitome of dynamic driving qualities. As a result of this enthusiastically pursued orientation, streamlined elements could even be discovered in places where aerodynamic characteristics were not necessarily required in a functional sense. In this respect, figure 2.65 illustrates corresponding forms with regard to the dynamic designing of the interior of an automobile. Behind the windshield, nonetheless, the streamlined characteristics play no role which would necessitate this contouring. For the ventilation of the interior room, this designing is actually insignificant. Accordingly, aerodynamic forms are not required by any reasons of functionality within this particular area. Nevertheless, these very forms contribute considerably to the dynamic look of the automobile in its overall appearance, for it aesthetically continues the exterior contouring within the interior of the automobile.

224

2.3
RECOGNIZING
FAMILIAR
FEATURES –
ICONIC
CONNECTION
↓
2.3.1
ASSOCIATIVE
CONNECTIONS

FIGURE 2.65
Aerodynamic forms as elements of the visual design contribute,
as depicted in this example, to the dynamic overall appearance of the vehicle,
in light of the fact that they combine the outer contouring
with the structuring of the interior of the automobile. Ford Mondeo, 2005.

This corresponds to the concept of *streamlining,* which applies a streamlined contouring in design in a broad manner, encompassing all types of products. The term was originally mentioned by Raymond Loewy, who consistently implemented this design principle (Fiell 2006). An early example of streamlined design is the passenger car Tatra 87, which was designed by Hans Ledwinka and manufactured since 1938 by Tatra, Kopřivnice, Czechoslovakia. It was characterized by an aerodynamic shape with an eye-catching dorsal fin. In the 1950s and 1960s, aerodynamic design was extraordinarily popular, for example, in the case of automobiles and the cross-country Greyhound buses in the United States – in a somewhat moderate form, this may also be seen in the bus depicted in figure 2.66.

FIGURE 2.66
The streamlined design of an express bus in 1952,
which the Nordwestdeutscher Fahrzeugbau
constructed for Ford. Already in the year 1951, a streamlined bus
was presented as the "aircraft of the road,"
significantly reflecting the forms utilized in the construction of airplanes.
Even this vehicle was manufactured for mass production.

2.3
RECOGNIZING
FAMILIAR
FEATURES –
ICONIC
CONNECTION
↓
2.3.1
ASSOCIATIVE
CONNECTIONS

225

Such a design was also popularly employed in the manufacturing of products which did not even need to rely upon aerodynamic characteristics at all, for example, such as bread slicing machines, vacuum cleaners, and refrigerators. *Streamlined design* enjoyed a significant popularity notably in the United States, and is viewed around the world as a typical Americanism in design. A particularly well-known application of this principle is illustrated in figure 2.67, which depicts the famous meat slicer designed by Egmont Arens in 1941.

FIGURE 2.67
Streamlined design in an object utilized
in the processing of foodstuffs. Egmont Arens,
Streamliner Meat Slicer (Model 410), 1941.

Focusing on vehicle requirements for minimum air resistance led to, nevertheless, a considerable confinement of the scope of aesthetic design. If all automobiles on the market approached the ideal form of aerodynamic design, for example, this would result in a limited ability of the respective brands to visually distinguish themselves from one another, and it would simultaneously allow boundaries and constraints of a physical nature to dominate over designing freedoms with respect to shapes and contours. Not without good reasons, this was criticized by automobile designers (Kieselbach 1998).

As a result of the aspects addressed in this section, one may ultimately deduce that the connection between the sensory channels occurs, in the case of a concrete association, by virtue of an identification of perceptual objects, which are, as explained before, models of physical objects. A characteristic feature of this type of connection is the answering of the question: "What is it?" – this is in contrast to the symbolic connection in accordance with chapter 2.4, which namely answers the question: "What does it mean?" Nevertheless, both of these questions require that the objects and their meanings are known, in light of the fact that associative as well as semantic connections are similarly based upon previous learning processes. Accordingly, unknown sensory perceptions, such as synthetic sounds, for example, can not be associatively connected.

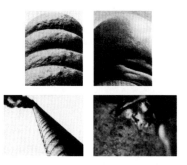

FIGURE 2.68
**An example of the distinction between an analogy (above)
and a concrete association (below)
by comparing two pictures (Richter 1929).**

226

2.3
RECOGNIZING
FAMILIAR
FEATURES –
ICONIC
CONNECTION
↓
2.3.1
ASSOCIATIVE
CONNECTIONS

In summary, multisensory connections via *iconic references (concrete association)* are characterized by the following properties:

AN IMPORTANT BASIC FUNCTION OF PERCEPTION
CONNECTION VIA THE IDENTIFICATION OF OBJECT PROPERTIES
CAPABILITY OF **ALL** PEOPLE
DETERMINED BY THE PERCEPTUAL EXPERIENCE, I.E. LEARNED
DEPENDANT UPON THE CONTEXT
IN THE CASE OF SIMILAR EXPERIENCE AND A SIMILAR CONTEXT, THEY PRODUCE SIMILAR RESULTS

Hans Richter provides an appropriate example of a distinction between an analogy and a concrete association in the visual realm (Richter 1929). Figure 2.68 offers an analogy (above) and an associative relationship (below) between the image on the right and that appearing on the left. The analogy of the bulging form arises directly as a result of a comparison of the two forms – the recognition of the objects is, therefore, not necessary. Furthermore, the analogy relationship is not influenced by the fact that bread and bald heads have absolutely nothing to do with one another. The smokestack emitting a black, billowing cloud and the sweating laborer, on the other hand, are associatively identified by the observer as being elements of the same field, namely industrial labor. This requires, nevertheless, that the smokestack as well as the laborer can each be separately identified. Additionally, their common environment must also be known. Hence, that enables the associative classification. Accordingly, similarities of individual elements of both images are not necessary – in contrast to the aforementioned analogy depicted above.

2.3
RECOGNIZING
FAMILIAR
FEATURES –
ICONIC
CONNECTION
↓
2.3.1
ASSOCIATIVE
CONNECTIONS

227

FIGURE 2.69
The light refraction of the rainbow is the origin
of associative color scales.

In efforts made to combine tone scales and color scales with one another, the rainbow spectrum is often chosen. As a result, the frequencies of tones and colors are transferred into one another. Given that the sequence of colors in a rainbow, as illustrated in figure 2.69, is known on the basis of perceptual experience, such a connection exhibits intuitive plausibility. On the other hand, it contradicts the tendency of test subjects, as discussed in chapter 2.2, to arbitrarily sort color hues corresponding to the characteristic degrees of brightness. The color scaling of auditory properties according to objective criteria will be more closely discussed in chapter 2.6.

2.3.2
ONOMATOPOEIA

For the connection of auditory stimuli to multisensory perceptual objects, ono-matopoetic phenomena are of great importance. The term *onomatopoeia* comes from the Greek words *ónoma* – meaning *name* – and *poíesis* - the term used for *doing, creating*. It refers to the linguistic imitation of sounds. Analogous to this aspect, the onomatopoeia can effectuate associations to objects, to animated creatures and to atmospheres, making use, thereby, of musical means in the course of the imitation. Furthermore, it also plays a significant role with re-spect to the linguistic description of sounds. In this regard, in the field of au-tomobile acoustics, transcriptions are used which convey the characteristic properties of the sound by virtue of tonal imitations. Table 2.4 provides some example of such verbalizations and of the classification of the acoustic source with respect to the automobile systems and components. ● ● ● ● ● ● ● ● ● ● Onomatopoetic descriptions are also suitable for evaluation of the auditory impression caused by environmental sounds (Takada 2006).

SOUND	VEHICLE SYSTEM COMPONENT	SOUND	VEHICLE SYSTEM COMPONENT
BUZZING	EXHAUST SYSTEM	SINGING	TIRES
RATTLING	GEARBOX (DIESEL MOTOR)	MOANING	BRAKES
DRONING	WHEEL SUSPENSIONS	TICKING	SPEEDOMETER CABLE
BELLING	EXHAUST SYSTEM	KNOCKING	DIESEL MOTOR
HOWLING	GEARBOX, SERVO PUMP	WHINING	DRIVESHAFT
RUMBLING	CHASSIS	WHISTLING	TURBO CHARGER, GEARBOX
RINGING	VALVES	HUMMING	WHEEL, WHEEL HUB
SCRAPING	BRAKES	QUACKING	PISTONS
GROANING	BRAKES	HISSING	AIRSTREAM
SLOSHING	GAS TANK FILLING	SQUEALING	BRAKES, TIRES
CRACKLING	INSTRUMENT PANEL	CHIRPING	BRAKES

FREQUENCY RANGE: LOW MIDDLE HIGH

TABLE 2.4
Examples of the descriptions of automobile sounds with the
assistance of onomatopoeia. The frequency range
is coded with colors of increasing brightness. Additionally, typical examples
of the critical components of vehicle acoustics are given.

In comic strips, onomatopoetic terms became style-forming elements. Further-more, in their structure comics exhibit parallels to films. Images which are se-quenced in strips demonstrate with clarity the temporal flow of the story. Addi-tionally, expressive images support the tension and the drama of the story with dynamic elements. In contrast to the situation in film, where sound can be add-ed, onomatopoeia substitutes for acoustic elements in comic strips. As a result, auditory elements are introduced into the story. In order to actually hear the sounds, it is necessary to articulate the onomatopoetic word fragments out loud.

38
47
228

2.3
RECOGNIZING
FAMILIAR
FEATURES –
ICONIC
CONNECTION
↓
2.3.2
ONOMATOPOEIA

2.3
RECOGNIZING
FAMILIAR
FEATURES –
ICONIC
CONNECTION
↓
2.3.2
ONOMATOPOEIA

229

BROOOOM
BRUMM
CRRRRRRR
DROOR
HHRRNNNNNN

AUTOMOBILE RACE SOUND

HUSCH
MUFF
RR..
ROAA
ROOOAM

TABLE 2.5-1
The onomatopoetic description of vehicle sounds
in comic-strip form (Havlik 1981).

AZZ
BASH
BAZZ
BEEP
BIAT
BIEP
BINK
BOOD
BORT
CCHCCHCHCHCCH
CHEEZ
CHORTLE
CHUG
CRAM
CRANK
CRINCK
DAKITY
DEEDIT
DING
DUMP
FEEK
FING
FRAD
FRASH
FRAT
FREEP
FROD
FWAM
FWIT

GIBIT
GIDGE
GRIND
GROND
GRUMP
HARG
HOB
HONK
HOOMP
KNASH
KONK
LEEB
LUMP
LURCH
LURP
MARF
MASH
NEEP
NIT

STREET TRAFFIC SOUND

OOP
OOT
ORK
PHUND
PILP
PLEEB
PLINK
POOMP
POONT
PRADDLE
PRAT
PUNT
RATAKLANG
(-TAKLANG)
RATTLE
RAZZ
REND
RILL

RIV
RZZZ
SCHREECH
SCREECH
SKUMP
SLAM
SMASH
SPEEL
SQUACK
SQUAK
SQUANK
SQUEE
SQUIK
TACKITY
TANGLE
THRASH
TICH
TOOT
TWEE
TWEEDLE
TWEET
VROM
WHEEZ
WINK
WHIZ
WONKWOOMP
WOOPS
WUPPLE
RRROOOAAAOO
ROAP
ROAR
ROAW
ROP
ROR
RRTT
RWOAN
... etc.

230

2.3
RECOGNIZING
FAMILIAR
FEATURES –
ICONIC
CONNECTION
↓
2.3.2
ONOMATOPOEIA

TABLE 2.5-1
The onomatopoetic description of traffic noises
in comic-strip form (Havlik 1981).

2.3
RECOGNIZING
FAMILIAR
FEATURES –
ICONIC
CONNECTION
↓
2.3.2
ONOMATOPOEIA

231

FIGURE 2.70
An onomatopoetic presentation of
traffic noises in the frame of a comic strip.
Fred Schrier, Bubble Blowers, 1974.

Nevertheless, the auditory contents may also be in essence comprehended merely by virtue of "silent" reading, given that the sounds manifest themselves as events of the imagination. Therefore, even this phenomenon is the result of an extremely complex manner of processing information which provides for the retransformation of the written language portions into elementary perceptual objects. Thereby, it is interesting to note that this form of presenting sounds is regarded as being thoroughly elementary and simple, in contrast to the sheer complexity of the processing itself. Figure 2.70 illustrates the visualization of traffic noises – indeed, even without reading all of the onomatopoetic expressions depicted, the chaos of the penetrating sounds received manifests itself intuitively.

At the beginning of the 1980s, the onomatopoeic dictionary *Lexikon der Onomatopöien* made an effort to compile the sound-imitating contained in comics within the course of an encyclopedia (Havlik 1981). It contains exactly 2,222 keywords – referred to as *Onpos* – which were featured in representative comic books of the time, primarily as circulated within the German-speaking world. Table 2.5 (pp. 229 – 30) consists of a selection of such terms that reflect the sounds heard in traffic and caused by automobiles.

Words used to describe animal sounds are almost always based upon the acoustic imitation of characteristic sound properties. Table 2.6 provides some examples of these.

48

232

2.3
RECOGNIZING
FAMILIAR
FEATURES –
ICONIC
CONNECTION
↓
2.3.2
ONOMATOPOEIA

OSCINE BIRD	CHEEPING, TWITTERING
DUCK	QUACKING
PIGEON	COOING
GOOSE	CACKLING
ROOSTER	CROWING
CHICKEN	CLUCKING
CROW	CROWING
CAT	MEOWING, PURRING, HISSING
DOG	BARKING, YELPING, WHINING, GROWLING
HORSE	NEIGHING
PIG	GRUNTING
COW	MOOING
SHEEP	BAAING
GOAT	BLEATING
MOUSE	CHEEPING
FROG	CROAKING
SNAKE	HISSING
BEE	BUZZING

TABLE 2.6
**Examples of the onomatopoetic description
of animal sounds.**

●

It is often the case that the onomatopoetic descriptions even directly determine the names of the animals, such as, for example, *cuckoo, chiffchaff, owl,* and *crow*. The fact that this is an elementary method of constructing words is demonstrably verified by the tendency of children to initially construct an onomatopoetic name for an animal – e.g., "the bow-wow" – prior to learning and employing the actual name – "the dog." Accordingly, the onomatopoetic method is also an appropriate method for adults in the conceptualization and formation of words for unknown sounds. As a phenomenon of prelinguistic communication, it supports the building of linguistic signs. In comic strips, the language itself appears in the form of speech bubbles, and the predecessors of these may be found in banners appearing in medieval paintings. Even this represents a means of referring to an auditory event within the framework of an illustration (Clausberg 2007).

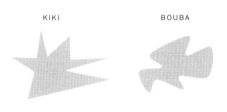

KIKI BOUBA

FIGURE 2.71
The results of an experiment which was aimed
at allocating words of spoken language with respect to visual forms
(Ramachandran 2005).

2.3
RECOGNIZING
FAMILIAR
FEATURES –
ICONIC
CONNECTION
↓
2.3.2
ONOMATOPOEIA

233

An experiment which was directed by Wolfgang Köhler as early as 1929, and later repeated by Vilayanur S. Ramachandran and Edward Hubbard in recent times, provides valuable information pertaining to the relationship between the perception of sounds and the visual realm (Köhler 1929, Ramachandran 2005). Test subjects were given a circular form and a sharply jagged form as depicted in figure 2.71. These forms were supposed to be allocated to two different words. Köhler used "takete" and "baluma" (later "maluma"). Hence, the test subjects were supposed to find out which word can be matched with which form. The results were indicative of an extraordinarily clear tendency to refer to the sharp, jagged form as "takete" and to designate the circular form to "baluma." Ramachandran and Hubbard utilized similar forms as well as the descriptions "KIKI" and "BOUBA" – documenting an equally clear orientation in the very same direction. They interpret this result in the context of a relationship, respectively, between the form of rounded lips in the articulation of "ou" and the sharp angle of the tongue in the pronunciation of "ki." This assumption points to a clear iconic connection. Furthermore, even the forms of the respective letters of the alphabet correspond to the character of the correlated from. In this regard, especially if written in the upper case, the term "BOUBA" contains letters only of circular forms, which are closed in 80 percent of the letters. On the other hand, the letters of the word "KIKI" written in a sans serif script, currently one of the more common typographical forms, comprise a total of more than ten angles between straight forms, of which various angles are pointed. Thereby, the fact that many – perhaps *all* – people who hear spoken words visualize the texts of such words on the screens of their "inner monitors" could be of significance. The question as to whether such a visualization of letters is conclusive in determining the result of the experiment, however, is actually of secondary importance. At any rate, it is clear that auditory aspects of the language can indeed influence the images of the written letters of the alphabet. Already as early as 1881, in the course of characterizing perceptual phenomena of a synesthetic nature, Eugen Bleuler and Karl Lehmann ascertained that visual appearances – so-called *photisms* – with sharply limited, pointed forms could frequently be evoked by high tones (Bleuler 1881). It is, however, not clear whether this relation is based on iconic features or if it merely must be seen as an elementary cross-modal analogy, as described in section 2.2.3 (compare fig. 2.28).

In addition to the echoing of general sounds, the onomatopoeia also encompasses the imitation of tones with musical means. Indeed, various examples of this were already provided by the vocal music of the Renaissance. In Carlo Gesualdo's madrigal *Arde il mio cor …* (My heart burns), the blazing of the flames may be heard, seen, and felt in an impressive manner, as the vocal lines of the polyphonic composition are raised with a surprising small delay between the voices. Moreover, in baroque music, the aesthetics of the expression always played a determining role, in essence, also being based upon tonal imitations. Various examples of the imitation of natural phenomena (such as storms, the force of water, fires, and earthquakes) and animal sounds and noises (e.g., birds, frogs, cats, flies) can be found in the baroque musical compositions of Georg Philipp Telemann, Johann Sebastian Bach, Antonio Vivaldi, and others, as well as in nineteenth-century program music. The most popular example generally known is Vivaldi's cycle of violin concertos, *The Four Seasons*. An analogy of movement and expressive dynamics are also often used, for example, as employed in Johann Heinrich Schmelzer's *Balletto à 4 Fechtschule* (The Fencing School), a work in which the music accentuates a battle of dynamically swirling swords. Similar elements may be identified in Heinrich Ignaz Franz Biber's musical battle scene *Battalia,* particularly in the movement "Die Schlacht" (The Battle), in which noises like the imitation of gun shots and the rumbling of cannons are introduced into the story in a notably noisy manner.

Given that musical works of a theatrical nature are presented in a multisensory fashion, as a matter of principle, it is not surprising that opera music is characteristically punctuated by onomatopoetic elements. Only two examples among many are named herein. Richard Wagner composed the conflagration of blazing flames for the music of his *Feuerzauber* (Magic Fire) scene of the musical drama *Die Walküre* (The Valkyrie). ● In the rapid tone sequences of the string instruments, the flickering of an abundance of flames manifests itself in an impressive fashion. The high tempo of the music results in the violinists not being able to play in an absolutely synchronous manner – accordingly, a sound ambience arises, reflecting the darting flames and bearing great auditory similarity to the noise of hissing flames. Figure 2.72 illustrates a further example: the onomatopoetic background of the scene "Einzug der Götter in Walhalla" (Entrance of the Gods into Valhalla) in the finale of the musical drama *Das Rheingold* (The Rhine Gold), which is set in an open mountain landscape following a thunderstorm; the landscape of a broad structure is visible in the tonal analysis, corresponding to the sound ambience that is presented. ● Furthermore, a successful imitation may also be found in the wind sounds

49

50

234

2.3
RECOGNIZING
FAMILIAR
FEATURES –
ICONIC
CONNECTION
↓
2.3.2
ONOMATOPOEIA

in *Der fliegende Holländer* (The Flying Dutchman). Already at the beginning of the overture, an auditory storm arises, which approaches noise music and thus appears to anticipate twentieth-century film sound. ●

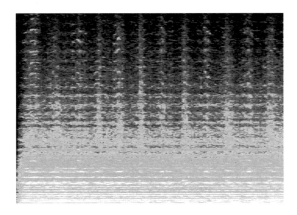

FIGURE 2.72
A musical carpet or a landscape? An analysis
of the musical background of the scene
"Einzug der Götter in Walhalla" in the finale of the musical
drama Das Rheingold, arising as a result of the quick tonal
sequence of the violinists. Vertical axis: frequency;
horizontal axis: time; color scale: sound pressure level.

2.3
RECOGNIZING
FAMILIAR
FEATURES –
ICONIC
CONNECTION
↓
2.3.2
ONOMATOPOEIA

235

Further onomatopoetic approaches in music involve the imitation of language, for example, such as the "woe motif" [Wehe Motiv] of *Der Ring des Nibelungen* (The Ring of the Nibelung) which echoes the sound of the word "We-he." In the composition *Different Trains,* the American composer of Minimal Music, Steve Reich, applies linguistic fragments with which he forms musical themes.

Indeed, the imitation of human sounds serves to increase the emotionality of the expression, as the instrumental tone approaches the tone of the voice, which in turn plays an essential role in singing. In this respect, in the era of the Renaissance, musical instruments such as the viola da gamba, the cornetto, and the recorder were well-respected, owing to the similarity of their sounds to the tone of the human voice. In Biber's *Battalia,* string instruments assumed the task of imitating the "Lamento der verwundten Musquetirer" (Lament of the wounded Musketeers) as well as the bawling sounds of intoxicated soldiers who – just as in real life – simultaneously begin to sing different songs, indeed, in different keys which do not harmonize with one another. In rock music, techniques to imitate screeching or squealing sounds *(guitar screaming)* are often employed. Similar effects may be achieved by virtue of the saxophone using extremely high tones *(high notes),* via polyphonic tones *(multiphonics),* or simply singing along during the playing of the instrument. Such effects comprise indispensable elements in rock, soul, and funk.

Furthermore, auditory icons can also arise as a result of the imitation of spoken language. In this sense, the jingle of DEUTSCHE TELEKOM is based upon the imitation of these very words: "Deut-tsche Te-le-kom" (see chapter 3.2).

EXCURSUS: THE CARNIVAL OF ANIMALS

Le Carnaval des Animaux is a composition of Camille Saint-Saëns which appeared in 1886. As a form of *program music* with a concrete background, it is a good example of the application of making reference to multisensory objects. In some of its movements, the composition presents the onomatopoetic animal sound of the lion ("Introduction et Marche royal du Lion," Introduction and Royal March of the Lion), the donkey ("Personnages à longues Oreilles," Personalities with long Ears), and of the cuckoo ("Le Coucou au Fond de Bois," The Cuckoo in the Depths of the Forest).

The confused running, clamoring, and clucking chickens and roosters (Poules et Coqs) are introduced by virtue of analogies of movement and rhythm. The movement analogy is also the leading principle of the *Hémoines* as the wild, fleeing animals, whose dynamics are expressively represented by the very quick runs of two pianos, as mandated by the musical score. Even the turtles ("Tortues") make a valuable contribution with respect to the realization of movement analogies. Additionally, Saint-Saëns makes use of associative references, as he presents the very swift "Can-Can" by Jacques Offenbach in an extremely decelerated, dragging tempo. In a similar manner, in the movement "L'Elephant," he combines Danse des Sylphes (The Elephant Dance), composed by Hector Berlioz, ironically with the less agile nature of the elephant.

Furthermore, the atmospheric picture of the "Le Coucou au Fond de Bois" is a most appropriate, onomatopoetic description of the ambience of a natural soundscape. In the midst of a rather diffuse background sound, the meaningful call of the cuckoo is soon distinctly heard.

It is obviously quite inviting to characterize the lead performer in the scene of the "Kangourus" (Kangaroos) by virtue of movement analogies. They offer to the listener jumps which slowly begin, become appreciably accelerated, and ultimately return to a slow tempo. In the *Aquarium* scene, physical movements are presented as well, although in a somewhat more leisurely fashion. Rising air bubbles are acoustically depicted by employing sequences of bell tones of great clarity – indeed, this method is frequently utilized in onomatopoetic music for the purpose of articulating the presence of silvery, gleaming objects. The birds in the "Volière" are presented in a comparatively lively manner, for their sounds are imitated by flutes in a tonally appropriate fashion.

The "Le Cygne" (Swan) scene is characterized by a solemn, although worthy melody which acoustically depicts not only the quiet gliding of the elegant creatures along the surface of the water, but displays their sheer majesty as well. The cycle is rounded off by two humorous pieces: on the one hand, pianists do that which they tend to do their whole lives through – playing their way through exercises in technique up and down the musical scales; on the other hand, fossils let their bones do the playing.

The finale leads the protagonists of the cycle back together once again.

PICTOGRAM
AND AUDITORY
ICON

2.3
RECOGNIZING
FAMILIAR
FEATURES –
ICONIC
CONNECTION
↓
2.3.3
PICTOGRAM
AND AUDITORY
ICON

———

237

It is known that objects and situations with simple lines or elementary forms can easily be described. Jeffrey Metzner demonstrated this aspect in his drawings in which events pertaining to world history, film scenes, and well-known works of art are once again alluded to by virtue of strokes – and stick-figures (Metzner 2007). Visual *icons,* the so-called *pictograms,* are based upon this principle. Increasingly, they are replacing signs that contain written data, accordingly conveying information which does not demand the comprehension of a specific language. In the globalized world, with its growing number of international facilities and institutions, this measure is of extraordinary significance. Indeed, no airport in the world could display signs with texts in every single spoken language of the passengers – and with the exception of the visual language of the pictograms, there is no common language which could be understood by all persons worldwide. Visual icons can contain hints regarding simple objects as well as short sequences of images. Figure 2.73 illustrates examples of the proper means of handling a candle. The logo of an industrial development department as presented in figure 2.74 demonstrates that iconic references may be merged with semantic content: within the figure, the department name "Chassis" (Chassis engineering) partly substitutes this subsystem of a vehicle.

FIGURE 2.73

Icons visible on the packing of a designer candle.

FIGURE 2.74
**Departmental logo with associative characteristics as
well as semantic aspects in the form of a text.
Chassis engineering department of the Ford Motor Company, Cologne.**

As early as ancient and medieval times, graphic presentations of myths as well as biblical events played an essential role. In epochs in which, by and large, most people were unable to read and write, icons were used to convey essential content. Even in twentieth-century art, elementary ciphers and graphic systems figured very prominently in prevailing discussions and controversies. On the one hand, developers of a concrete art form – such as, for example, Kazimir Malevich – undertook efforts to extract simple, meaningful forms from the context of visual symbols. On the other hand, stick-figures appeared as expressions of situations and mental states in daily life, such as, for example, by A. R. Penck. In all cases, it involved the deduction of generally comprehensible image worlds, driven by the "yearning for a universal language" (Ackermann 2007).

Pictograms are also suitable for communicating emotional content. *Emoticons* use the expressivity of mimics by depicting a simplified face. A famous example is the *smiley*

which is popular with a large variety of modifications, at times extended to all other emotional expressions. It therefore is appropriate for product assessment studies to define subjective scales, e.g., spanning from good

via neutral

238

2.3
RECOGNIZING
FAMILIAR
FEATURES –
ICONIC
CONNECTION
↓
2.3.3
PICTOGRAM
AND AUDITORY
ICON

to bad assessment

(see chapter 2.4). A variety of emoticons composed from text characters is widely used during Internet communication. Those pictograms appear with an inclination of 90°. In most cases they are placed at the end of a sentence.

:-)

In the course of interactive computer applications, icons also play an essential role. Together with a completely new technology, a variety of associative image elements was developed, each of which, in the meantime, can be easily comprehended around the world.

**IN GENERATING PICTOGRAMS,
IT IS PARTICULARLY IMPORTANT THAT THEY
CONSIST OF A MINIMAL NUMBER
OF ELEMENTS WHICH MAY BE UNDERSTOOD AS
SELF-CONTAINED PERCEPTUAL OBJECTS.**

Ambiguities and presentations tending to result in misunderstandings should be avoided, given that they complicate the comprehension.

For the purpose of the multisensory designing of informational systems and corporate identities, visual icons can be supplemented by auditory equivalents. For such *auditory icons* or *earcons,* it is important that they are based upon known sounds, tones, or musical fragments. For that purpose, auditory icons are usually extracted from everyday sounds. In contrast, earcons are compiled from synthetic elements. The comprehension of those signals is complicated, given that in the case of abstract or unknown sounds, the meaning can not simply be derived from a familiar context. These are symbols as described in chapter 2.4, and they thus require an explicit learning in order to be comprehended. In comparison to visual icons, auditory icons normally consist of less perceptual objects. If visual and auditory icons are applied together, the sounds utilized should exhibit a direct reference to the visual elements.

An important task in the recognition of auditory icons is the identification of sound patterns which are known to the group of possible receivers. In this respect, signals for railroad traffic make a purposeful reference to sounds which have been known in this environment for a long time. Warning signals which inform as to the closing of the doors of the trains, can meaningful exhibit characteristic properties of the traditional sound of the conductor's whistle. This is the case, for example, in the commuter trains of the linked transportation system of the Rhine-Ruhr metropolitan area in Germany. Auditory icons are also used in the case of computer applications. In contrast to the variety of visual signs, which are meanwhile well-established, the auditory icons are more often intended for the accommodation of individual needs *(customization).* It primarily involves signals with warning functions or those aimed at raising the attention of the user – e.g., with the information: "You have new e-mail in your inbox!"

Besides simple and short auditory icons, trials are made to transfer more complex information by use of non-verbal auditory information. Hermann et al. proposed a combination of various auditory icons with earcons to provide an impression of the weather forecast, including various parameters like temperature, humidity, cloudiness, wind, precipitation, and others (Hermann, 2003). The soundscapes created by this method last approximately twelve seconds and are intended to provide the forecast for a whole day.

2.3
RECOGNIZING
FAMILIAR
FEATURES –
ICONIC
CONNECTION
↓
2.3.3
PICTOGRAM
AND AUDITORY
ICON

239

2.3.4
ASSOCIATIONS
TO SMELL
AND TASTE

The sensory organs for taste and smell serve, in particular, in the identification of objects – but they are also supposed to assist differentiating edible from rotten foodstuffs as well as helping to avoid poisonous fluids and gases. As discussed in section 1.3.3, there is a direct connection between the olfactory organ and the associative fields within the brain. Scents can be described by identification of their origin, the source of stimulation, for example, as something smells like lemons, roses, or ammonium chloride. Color hues also influence the perceptual threshold of smells (Maga 1974). Due to these reasons, colors tend to be of considerable significance in the sales of groceries and foodstuffs.

FIGURE 2.75
**Typical colors which convey associations of a sweet and fruity taste.
Lollipops in a confectionery shop in Brussels.**

240

2.3
RECOGNIZING
FAMILIAR
FEATURES –
ICONIC
CONNECTION
↓
2.3.4
ASSOCIATIONS
TO SMELL
AND TASTE

Although systems of allocating colors to sounds, smells, or flavors are subject to individual preferences, certain color systems have been established in the packaging and advertising of groceries. Figure 2.75 illustrates color combinations which are often selected in the case of confectionery items, particularly in the case of sweet and fruity taste components. Thereby, it observably involves iconic color associations which make reference to the colors of fruits, such as, for example, the following:

YELLOW – LEMON | **ORANGE – ORANGE** | **RED–STRAWBERRY** | **PINK – RASPBERRY** | **GREEN – APPLE**

Foodstuffs which do not exhibit the familiar "species-characteristic" colors can initiate a feeling of disgust and are thus often turned down. Modern food colorants make it possible to color groceries as desired, indeed without influencing the taste of the items and without harming the health of the consumers. Nevertheless, strange food colorants, which are literally regarded as being "foreign," hardly have a chance of acceptance among customers. In this regard, a luminously blue layered cake will certainly find few friends. And meat which exhibits a gray color – without this being detrimental to the quality – will be considerably less accepted than that which has a pale pink color, even when this occurs as a result of adding a dye agent. On the other hand, in Central Europe meat and sausage should not appear to be too red, for this would give rise to associations with blood and would accordingly discourage potential consumers or scare them away. In the case of chocolates, brown color tones naturally play an important role. As a general rule, darker chocolate has a greater tendency towards a bitter taste. This distinction is implemented in the packaging by virtue of color coding. In the case of packaging for chocolate biscuits, certain providers employ blue for sweet and red for bittersweet types of chocolate. However, this allocation is not based upon color associations with regard to components of the respective products – thus, they must be learned by the customers.

2.3
RECOGNIZING
FAMILIAR
FEATURES –
ICONIC
CONNECTION
↓
2.3.4
ASSOCIATIONS
TO SMELL
AND TASTE

241

DUE TO THE PARTICULARLY ASSOCIATIVE
PREDISPOSITION OF THE SENSES
OF TASTE AND SMELL, THE RELATED COLORS
TEND TO MAKE REFERENCE TO,
AS A GENERAL RULE, THE COLORS OF
THEIR SOURCES OF STIMULATION.

The perfume designer Karl-Heinz Bork employed a color circle, as illustrated in figure 2.76, for scents (Luckner 2002). In the middle, four primary categories of smell are presented: *light, heavy, green,* and *floral notes.* Light and heavy are cross-sensory analogies, whereas green and floral notes associatively make reference to freshly cut green plants and flowery scents. The colors of the circle of scents themselves are mostly associatively chosen, such as, for example, *green smell* – green, *citrus* – yellow, *leather* – brown, *woody* – brown, etc.

An experiment on the allocation of colors to taste sensations provided results shown in figure 2.76-2. Further experiments conducted at the Politecnico di Milano indicated an extensive amount of conformity with respect to this result.

2.3
RECOGNIZING
FAMILIAR
FEATURES –
ICONIC
CONNECTION
↓
2.3.4
ASSOCIATIONS
TO SMELL
AND TASTE

FIGURE 2.76-1
A circle of scents representing the allocation
of characteristic smells to colors.

2.3
RECOGNIZING
FAMILIAR
FEATURES –
ICONIC
CONNECTION
↓
2.3.4
ASSOCIATIONS
TO SMELL
AND TASTE

———

243

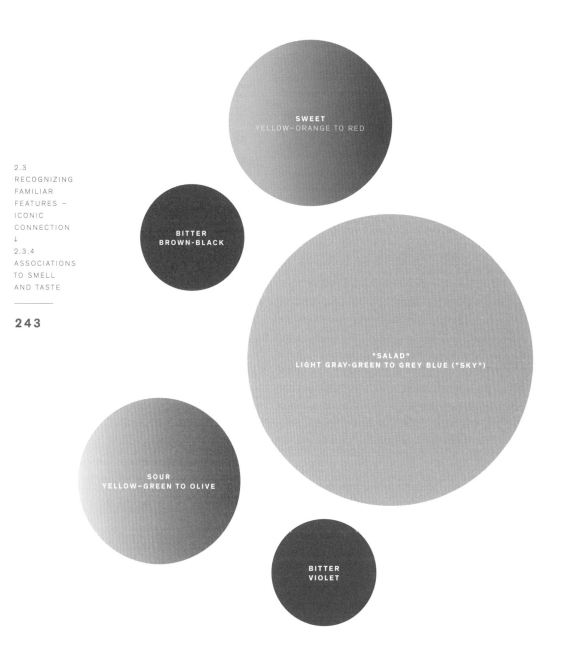

SWEET
YELLOW–ORANGE TO RED

BITTER
BROWN-BLACK

"SALAD"
LIGHT GRAY-GREEN TO GREY BLUE ("SKY")

SOUR
YELLOW–GREEN TO OLIVE

BITTER
VIOLET

FIGURE 2.76-2
An experiment pertaining to the allocation of colors to taste sensations
(Favre & November 1979, cited by Riccò 2002)

FIGURE 2.77
Foodstuff design in a manner that is "foreign"
with regard to the particular product being sold, thus exhibiting a "fun factor".
A birthday cake in the form of a soccer field for a child.

Colors which do not correspond to the familiar context of foodstuffs are popularly employed, nevertheless, in order to convey humor and irony with respect to the perceptual conflict (chapter 3.1) which is inevitably evoked. In this very manner, a cake which is designed with reference to a certain motto, for example, can provide for an additional degree of amusement during the birthday party of a young child. Thereby, the cake can be designed with a bright green glaze as its frosting, corresponding to the scene of a soccer game. The gummy bears depicted in figure 2.77, affixed to the playing field by virtue of a sugary mass, comprise a further alienation of the reality and offer an entertaining alternative to the popularly employed, brightly colored chocolate beans, whose colors are similarly designed without a direct reference to the taste. In this case, the entirety of the brightly colored candies serves as a general analogy to the sweetness of the taste and to the enthusiasm of the consumption. In this manner, associations and analogies – which do not correspond to the nature of the foodstuffs – can shape a product precisely because of the intentional provocation of perceptual conflicts in an interesting manner, thus giving it an added emotional value.

The smell of material can also influence the tactile perception. In this regard, test subjects perceived textiles as being more soft during the perception of a lemon fragrance simultaneous to the touching of those textiles – in comparison to an animal-like scent (Demattè 2006). Even this can be interpreted as the consequence of learned associations, given that soft tissues and wiping cloths are associated with cleansing substances which often contain a lemon fragrance. In contrast to that, an animal-like scent is associated with sturdy leather.

244

2.3
RECOGNIZING
FAMILIAR
FEATURES –
ICONIC
CONNECTION
↓
2.3.4
ASSOCIATIONS
TO SMELL
AND TASTE

Perceptual objects can only be generated by the perceptual system when the corresponding stimuli are distinguished from those which are interpreted as not corresponding. In other words:

**THERE CAN BE NO PERCEPTION
OF OBJECTS WITHOUT
A CONSIDERATION OF THE CONTEXT.**

2.3
RECOGNIZING
FAMILIAR
FEATURES –
ICONIC
CONNECTION
↓
2.3.5
THE CONTEXT

───────

245

This principle corresponds to the finding that a figure can manifest itself only on the basis of the "otherness" of its background. For that reason, in the designing of objects, the context – namely the environment of the expected use – must absolutely be considered, for this aspect inevitably helps to determine the perception and the evaluation as well.

For the perception of a sound, the multisensory background is essential. Here are two examples:

1. The acoustic volume of music presented via stereo equipment is adjusted in such a manner that it exhibits a pleasant value, with the room's lights on. Suddenly, the light is turned off. The music, at the same volume level, is now regarded as being too loud.

2. The residents of a house along a busy street perceive the resulting sound level as being too loud. This is so, in particular, when they sit on the terrace from which they may view the street. In order to reduce the sound level, they plant a hedgerow – now, the street may no longer be seen. From this point on, they speak of a considerable improvement of the acoustic situation in terms of it being less unpleasant. Acoustic measurements of the situation prior to and after the hedge, however, reveal a negligible difference. Due to physical reasons, this is explainable, given that the sound expands in a nearly unimpeded manner, owing to the fact that it is diffracted around the leaves of the hedge plants. Optically, the disturbing acoustic source, however, is no longer in the field of vision, and the hedge conveys, thereby, a feeling of safety. In this case, the influence of the visual stimuli upon the auditory perception contributes to the evaluation of the overall situation in a considerable manner.

Even in the perception within one modality, the environment of an object is a determining factor in the perception of the properties of that object. Indeed, numerous *optical illusions* are based upon this principle. Actually, a more appropriate description would be *visual illusions*, given the fact that the deception does not result from the optical physics but is rooted in the visual system of perception instead. Figure 2.78 demonstrates the influence of the background structure upon the perceived size of objects. Even though the three circles which are depicted are of exactly the same size, the objects located in the upper portion of the illustration are perceived as being larger than those in the lower portion. This illusion is caused by the structural perspective hinted at by the three lines. The thus designated background suggests that the circles

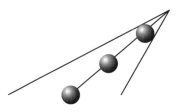

FIGURE 2.78
The influence of the background structures upon
the perceived size of objects. In this case,
three circles, with all of them being of exactly the same size,
are presented in front of three lines

FIGURE 2.79
The influence of the brightness of the environment upon
the perception of the brightness of an object.
In this situation, circular areas of exactly the same brightness,
are depicted against a background whose brightness
increases in moving from left to right.

246

2.3
RECOGNIZING
FAMILIAR
FEATURES –
ICONIC
CONNECTION
↓
2.3.5
THE CONTEXT

FIGURE 2.80
The influence of the color tone of the environment
upon the color tone of the perception of the object. In this instance,
circular areas with exactly the same color and exactly
the same brightness are presented against backgrounds
of different colors.

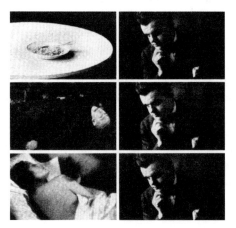

FIGURE 2.81
An example of the influence of the context upon the perception
of a scene and the evaluation of the facial expression.
The example provided by Hans Richter employs film scenes
(Richter 1929).

are arranged as spheres in a fashion leading from the bottom to the top in a spatially increasing distance with respect to the reference point of the observer.

Similarly, the perception of the brightness is also dependent upon the background. Figure 2.79 illustrates the brightness of a gray circle in comparison to the various degrees of brightness of the background. Even though the brightness of the circular surface is of exactly the same value in each of the squares, the object in front of the darkest of the backgrounds is perceived as being significantly brighter than those having brighter backgrounds. If the difference of the brightness of the foreground and backgrounds is less than the differential threshold (the just noticeable difference, JND), the object does not appear to distinguish itself from the background at all – it becomes invisible. As a result, the perceptual situation is altered in a fundamental manner: the number and the form of the perceptual objects are no longer comparable to the remaining cases, given that the number of perceptual objects declines in the case of the blending of the foreground and the background, now being perceived as another overall form, i.e. a simple square.

Differences in color are also suitable for distinguishing an object from its background. This is clearly demonstrated by figure 2.80. Even though the color of the circle area in each of the depicted squares is actually exactly the same, it appears to vary depending upon the context: on the left-hand side, it tends to be orange, whereas it seems to have a blue-like color on the right-hand side. If the color difference between the foreground and the background is less than the differential threshold, the object no longer distinguishes itself from its environment. The alteration of the perceptual situation with respect to the number and the form of the perceptual objects is then comparable to figure 2.79.

Moreover, even the facial expression of a person can be interpreted differently in differing situations. Figure 2.81 illustrates an example provided by Hans Richter (Richter 1929). The three photographs on the right are identical. According to the depiction on the left, however, the actually constant facial expression can be interpreted in various manners. In a similar manner, the atmosphere of an environment can influence the perception of individual elements, objects, or forms of behavior. As already suggested, even the subjective evaluation of the acoustic situation of a residential area can be influenced by the multisensory context, particularly by visual aspects (Gidlöf-Gunnarsson 2007). Therefore, products should always be designed with reference to the preferred environment of their utilization, and they should, furthermore, be arranged with respect to the expectations of the customer regarding the context. Thereby, the various perceptual experiences of different generations can also lead to different preferences. According to information of the sound designer of the baked goods manufacturer Bahlsen (Hanover), older people tend to prefer "soft, crispy crumble cakes," whereas younger people exhibit a preference for the "short, clear crunch" (Zips 2004). In this instance, the context within the system which causes the sound, i.e. the body, must also be taken into consideration. The act of biting into a biscuit is influenced by anatomical factors: it sounds different, indeed, according to the size of the head of the person who is consuming the biscuit, and it is also influenced by the size of the set of teeth as well as by the habits in chewing.

2.3
RECOGNIZING
FAMILIAR
FEATURES –
ICONIC
CONNECTION
↓
2.3.5
THE CONTEXT

247

2.4
UNDERSTANDING THE MEANING – SYMBOLS AND METAPHORS

2.4.1
SYMBOLIC CONNECTIONS

Multisensory connections can also arise with reference being made to the symbolic contents of the perceived attributes. Thereby, as compared to iconic connections, it involves *semantics of a higher order* (Flückiger 2002).

IN CONTRAST TO THE ICONIC RECOGNITION OF THE SOURCE OF SENSORY STIMULI – SUCH AS, FOR EXAMPLE, AN ACOUSTIC SOURCE – COMPREHENSION OF THE SYMBOLIC CONTENTS IMPLIES THE KNOWLEDGE OF THE MEANING.

248

2.4
UNDERSTANDING
THE MEANING –
SYMBOLS AND
METAPHORS
↓
2.4.1
SYMBOLIC
CONNECTIONS

Thereby, the *symbol* must be distinguished from the *icon* which contains associative information, corresponding to chapter 2.3. The term *symbol* applies to an abstract sign or signal whose meaning can not be identified by virtue of associative characteristics or with respect to the context. Moreover, it is encrypted with a *code* which must initially be learned. A symbol can be created in every sensory modality. Graphic characters and acoustic signals are just as symbolic as words or spoken language or the Braille alphabet, which is tactilely deciphered. The meaning of the symbol may first be understood after the deciphering of its code. Languages and alphabets are significant *semantic systems* which are of considerable importance in the lives of all people. In human-machine systems, inscriptions continue to be of great significance, even though efforts are undertaken, in an ever-increasing fashion, to replace them by virtue of the universal code of the icons. Inevitably, nevertheless, the driver of a car needs to understand the voice output of navigation systems just as well as the text of the operating instructions.

The ubiquitously present nature of languages and alphabet systems motivates designers of articles of daily use to involve elements even in an ironic fashion in the design. As an example, figure 2.82 illustrates a glass table, whose stand is wound in an s-form, and its title is "In the beginning was the word." As a result, reference is made to the double meaning of the dinner table as a table with an "S" as an element of humor and reflection. Additionally, the name of the product suggests that the letter *S* could mean "es," the phonetically similar German word for the personal pronoun "it." More important is the fact that the German term for a dining table, "Ess-tisch," is pronounced similar to "S-Tisch." The stand of the table offers the possibility of illumination similar to that of neon lights – accordingly, architectural and gastronomic aspects could resonate along during the perception of this object. Furthermore, the bible quotation illustrates the inversion of the creative sequence in the application of symbols: The alphabetic letter is not set upon the object in order to grant an additional meaning or purpose – to the contrary, it serves as the basis and the fundamental form upon which the object acquires its very shape.

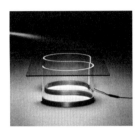

2.4
UNDERSTANDING
THE MEANING –
SYMBOLS AND
METAPHORS
↓
2.4.1
SYMBOLIC
CONNECTIONS

249

FIGURE 2.82
"In the beginning was the word" [Am Anfang war das Wort]:
A dinner table. An "S" which is illuminated on its edges serves
to support the tabletop. A Plexiglas object on a stainless steel socket
with an integrated light box and a glass plate. Designed by
Walter Giers for Draenert.

In creating a symbol, it is advisable to make use of cross-modal analogies or iconic content for the purpose of simplifying the learning process. In this regard, the symbols of the Chinese and older Japanese are principally based upon abstractions of the visual appearance of objects. Traffic signs often comprise a combination of abstract symbols (e.g., a triangle), color symbolism (red), and an icon (cow). As figure 2.83 demonstrates, even the indicating instruments in a motor vehicle also involve icons as associative elements, in order to improve the readability and the comprehension. Often, symbols assume an independent existence, however, given that they are initially learned by virtue of associations, although they are later comprehended without knowledge of their references. In particular, this must be considered with respect to the symbolic value of colors and their role in multisensory contexts.

Whereas a symbol is often based on iconic content, the definition of a symbol "as such" sometimes tends to confuse. Semantic content, on the one hand, is communicated via abstract signs or signals. On the other hand, semantic content exists in terms of further aspects added to an iconic object. Those symbolic aspects considerably exceed the simple iconic reference, which is based on identification of objects to belong to the same category. For example, the pictogram of a flag can – as an icon – point at the real object, a flag installed upon a hill, or it can include a wide range of semantics regarding national identity, institutions, politics, or history. The occasional overlap of semantic content with iconic and analogous features points to the fact that the perceptual system tends towards the integration of all perceived aspects.

FIGURE 2.83
The configuration of indicators (cluster) in an automobile is based
upon very different symbolic and associative signs.

In operatic music and film, the symbolic contents of sounds and musical motifs enable the supporting and the interpretation of the story in a nonverbal manner. Therefore, the appropriate codes must either be known to the viewers ahead of time or be capable of being learned by them within a short period of time. As a general rule, this requires that the public has knowledge of the meaning of sounds from everyday life. Nevertheless, by virtue of the purposefully intended coincidence of sounds with certain pictures and elements of the story, it is also possible to "boost" these auditory objects with symbolic contents. This process is known as *priming*. In the course of repetitions, such acoustic objects can then serve as important conveyers of the meaning of the story. A simple code becomes a *key code,* in this case, a *key sound.*

   A warning sound must be designed in such a manner that allows it to be easily heard and draw attention to itself even in a noisy environment. If the properties for the designing of the sound are defined, the connection between these parameters and the meaning to be conveyed must be learned. The same applies to optical components which are allocated to the acoustic signal. Figure 2.84 shows an example of warning devices for industrial application which provide visual and auditory signals (WERMA 2009).

250

2.4
UNDERSTANDING
THE MEANING –
SYMBOLS AND
METAPHORS
↓
2.4.1
SYMBOLIC
CONNECTIONS

VISUAL SIGNAL	RED	GREAT DANGER / DANGEROUS CONDITION
	YELLOW	CAUTION / CRITICAL CONDITION IMMINENT
	GREEN	NORMAL CONDITION
	BLUE	CONDITION REQUIRES DEFINITE ACTION
	WHITE/CLEAR	NO SPECIAL (COMMON) MEANING
AUDITORY SIGNAL	SEQUENCE OF TONES WITH VARIOUS ALTERNATING FREQUENCIES	GREAT DANGER ACT URGENTLY!
	SEQUENCE OF TONES WITH TWO ALTERNATING FREQUENCIES	GREAT DANGER ACT URGENTLY!
	TONE WITH ALTERNATING REDUCTION OR INCREASE OF FREQUENCY	DANGER ACT URGENTLY!
	INTERMITTENT, PERIODIC TONE	DANGER REACT URGENTLY!
	CONTINUOUS TONE	SAFE CONDITION

FIGURE 2.84
Meaning of visual and auditory signals used for
industrial warning devices (example).

The meaning of the specific signals from both senses and therefore the cross-sensory connection of both modalities needs to be learned individually. The recipient has only limited possibilities to derive the meaning from past experience. Therefore an appropriate learning process is essential to allow quick responses during situations which require immediate actions.

In a similar manner, a person hearing the siren of an ambulance must know and understand how to quickly and properly respond with respect to the approaching rescue vehicle. Additionally, in exactly this regard, he must also know of the distinction between the symbolism of a *blue light* and a *yellow light,* in order to properly connect it to the sound of the siren. Naturally, this assignment can also occur in a purely associative manner, for example, if the driver experiences and recognizes the correlation between both signals within the immediate vicinity. In complex daily situations, however, often only one of the signals, i.e. the visual or the auditory one, will be noticed. Figure 2.85 illustrates the acoustic analysis of the siren of a rescue vehicle of the type which is utilized in Spain, among other places. The signal is designed in such a fashion that enables it to be heard and to draw attention to itself even within a very noisy environment. Thereby, the signal consists of a sinusoidal tone whose tone pitch initially rises from 300 Hz to 700 Hz on a continual basis. Subsequently, the frequency is periodically shifted up and down between 500 Hz and 1200 Hz, this taking place with a period duration of 3 Hz, corresponding to 3 times per second. The conspicuousness of the sinusoidal tone is increased by virtue of the strong degree of periodic frequency shifting. Sinusoidal tones often occur in the environment – the frequency shifting, however, causes a distinctively unmistakable sound which is, precisely because of this reason, very appropriate with respect to the reception of a special meaning. ●

In order to understand the effect of advertising melodies *(jingles)* and of signals which raise attention *(e.g., chimes),* it is worth making an effort to consider musical symbolism in its traditional as well as contemporary functions. This is done in section 2.4.5. More detailed information pertaining to the evaluation of auditory events can be found in Schick (1984) and – more recently – in Augoyard (2006).

2.4
UNDERSTANDING
THE MEANING –
SYMBOLS AND
METAPHORS
↓
2.4.1
SYMBOLIC
CONNECTIONS

251

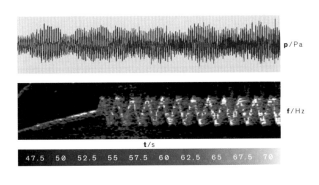

FIGURE 2.85
An acoustic analysis of the signal of a Spanish ambulance.
Above: the time function of the sound pressure;
below: the frequency spectrum over the time; color scale:
sound pressure level (SPL) in [dB].

In the designing of logos, and thus ultimately in the identification of products and brands, visual and auditory symbols are indispensable. Thereby, it is important to speak directly to the customer, to place him or her in a positive mood, and to present the image which distinguishes the manufacturer and the product. For this purpose, *personifications* are particularly important and most suitable for reaching a broad range of (potential) customers. The "Mainz Leprechaun" of the German television network ZDF *(Zweites Deutsches Fernsehen)* based in Mainz, depicted in figure 2.86, fulfills these very criteria in a multisensory sense. As a cartoon figure, he can sing, talk, dance, and maneuver himself through various daily situations. In this fashion, he has been successfully furthering the identification with the brand for decades, whereas the logo itself has undergone many modifications during the same period of time.

In summary, multisensory connections by virtue of *symbolism* are characterized by the following properties:

AN IMPORTANT BASIC FUNCTION OF INTERPRETATION OF PERCEPTUAL DATA
CONNECTION DUE TO THE SIMILARITY OF THE MEANING
CAPABILITY OF **ALL** PEOPLE
DETERMINED BY THE LEARNED CODE THAT TRANSFERS MEANING
DEPENDANT UPON THE CONTEXT
IN THE CASE OF SIMILAR EXPERIENCE AND A SIMILAR CONTEXT, THEY PRODUCE SIMILAR RESULTS

53

FIGURE 2.86
The "Mainz Leprechaun" as the symbol of the German television network ZDF
(Zweites Deutsches Fernsehen). The illustration shows him as a promotional gift
in celebrating the 30th anniversary of ZDF. Mainz, 1991.

252

2.4
UNDERSTANDING
THE MEANING –
SYMBOLS AND
METAPHORS
↓
2.4.1
SYMBOLIC
CONNECTIONS

Incomprehensible language is *iconic,* given that it is understood as the vocal utterance of a person. On the other hand, it is not semantic, owing to the fact that no code exists which would allow the meaning to be deciphered. Similarly, the ringing sound of a bell can be understood, on the one hand, as being simply the result of material vibrations, or it can be regarded, on the other hand, as an acoustic signal with an additional significance. ● In the course of an excursus, some of the general features of semantic processes – the field of *semiotics* – will initially be addressed.

Regardless of whether in politics, religion, legends, or tales, symbols play an important role. Indeed, in a certain sense, even traffic signs and warning signals are political symbols, given that they are expressions of legal regulations. In the historical realm, clan symbols, royal emblems, and heraldic animals have always been of great significance. Accordingly, *heraldry* advanced relatively early to being a science. Colors and emblems, of parties subsequently assumed this function – heraldry continues to live, however, in the form of national flags, coats of arms, and emblems of political organizations. The significance of historical symbols is detailed in special lexica, for example, in Biedermann (2001).

EXCURSUS: BASIC PRINCIPLES OF SIGNIFICATION (SEMIOTICS)

EXCURSUS:
BASIC
PRINCIPLES
OF SIGNIFICATION
(SEMIOTICS)

253

Semiotics, the *theory of the effects and the functions of signs,* provide a theoretical approach to understanding the effect and function of symbols. Significant research studies in building the theory were undertaken by, among others, Umberto Eco (1978), and an application with respect to the sound design of products may be found in Jekosch (2005).

In semiotics, a symbol *(sign)* is understood as a mental unit which is processed as a "representative" of an object. Symbols encompass, for example, traffic signs and light signals (traffic lights), national flags, acoustic signals, numeric codes, letters of the alphabet, or elements of spoken language. As elements of communication, symbols are constantly carriers of information. The *recipient,* namely the person receiving the information, however, requires background information in order to decipher the symbol – he or she must be capable of learning the meaning. Thereby, the term *meaning* refers to a relationship between a *perceptual object* and a *concept.* In this respect, a printed letter of the alphabet is not merely a coincidentally placed, arbitrary pattern of strokes, it contains a significance which can be comprehended within the context of yet other symbols, a context that conclusively determines which locations may be occupied by which patterns of strokes forming the letters.

In semiotics, a distinction is made between three elementary forms of symbols:

SYMBOL: As a freely selectable figure, with regard to its respective object, a symbol must be learned prior to it being applied within the framework of a communication. In a multisensory context, this form of a character is the basis of the symbolic connection which is addressed in this chapter.

ICON: This is a figure whose relationship to an object arises by virtue of its similarity with respect to said object. If this includes an identification of the object, it is a concrete association consistent with the discussion in chapter 2.3. In contrary, a *similarity* by virtue of analogy relationships is conveyed corresponding to chapter 2.2.

INDEX: This is a sign that points to another meaningful element, figuratively comparable to a directional sign. In linguistics, a pronoun ("this") is an index, for it is meaningless without the reference to a specific noun. Thus, an index refers to a figure whose relationship to another object is based upon causality or context parameters. In the approach presented herein, the relationship with respect to causality is a process of analogy construction. The reference to the context, however, concerns not only the analogy, but also the association and the symbolism as well. Accordingly, herein the index is not required to form a separate category of its own.

The meaning arises as a result of conformity between the data of the perception and the data of learning and of experience. This process is known as *semiosis.* It is presented in figure 2.87 by virtue of the *semiotic triangle.* In this case, as in all processes of perception, a dynamic process of constructing and verifying hypotheses serves as the foundation of deciphering the meaning, and it involves the interpreting systems organizing itself. Thereby, it is based upon *schemata* as rules governing the processing of the data pertaining to the perception and of the experience. A scheme can be *genuine (archetypical).* In such a situation, it is highly specialized and not capable of being modified. Among such examples, with respect to auditory perception, are the crying of a baby and natural warning signals, but also the screeching sounds of chalk along a chalkboard and the squeaking noise encountered in touching Styrofoam. Nevertheless, most schemas are based upon selectable conventions – and these can consciously be modified. Auditory examples of such include language and artificial warning signals.

INTERPRETANT
MEANING

3

1   **2**

REPRESENTAMEN   OBJECT
CARRIER OF   OBJECT OF
THE SYMBOL   EARLIER
PERCEPTUAL   EXPERIENCE
OBJECT

FIGURE 2.87
A semiotic triangle
adapted from Jekosch (2002).

SEMANTICS
MEANING, CONTENTS

SYNTACTICS   PRAGMATICS
REGULARITY, FORM   SENSE, GOAL, FUNCTION

FIGURE 2.88
The division of semiotics
into the three sub-areas, syntactics,
semantics, and pragmatics,
adapted from Siegle (2005).

The semiotics are, furthermore, divided into three sub-areas which illuminate the signification in different directions:

SYNTACTICS: These pertain to the relationship between symbols, such as, for example, letters of the alphabet in a word.

SEMANTICS: This field addresses the relationship between symbols and meanings, such as words and terms.

PRAGMATICS: This field addresses the relationship between symbols and functions, users or situations.

Syntactics lead to rules according to which the symbols must be arranged – these rules are known as *syntax*. The relationship between syntactics, semantics, and pragmatics can also be presented in the form of a triangle corresponding to figure 2.88 – this depiction, however, should not be confused with the semiotic triangle illustrated in figure 2.87.

In product design, it makes sense to regard form and function as matters of semiotics. In accordance with the case of auditory events observed by Jekosch (2005), the following features can generally apply to each of the modalities involved:

SYNTACTIC FORM	SYNTACTIC FUNCTION
CONFIGURATIVE ORDER	ACCENTUATION
STRUCTURE AND RHYTHM	ALLOCATION TO FOREGROUND AND BACKGROUND
SYMMETRY OR ASYMMETRY	

SEMANTIC FORM	SEMANTIC FUNCTION
SIMPLIFICATION	PRODUCT: SYMPTOM, E.G., ILLUSTRATION, TEXTURE
ALIENATION	USER: SIGNAL, E.G., ATTENTION
EXAGGERATION	IMAGE: SYMBOL, E.G., PRODUCT OR BRAND IDENTITY
UNDERDETERMINATION	
IRONIZATION	

PRAGMATIC FORM	PRAGMATIC FUNCTION
CLARITY	FUNCTIONALITY
APPEARANCE	RATIONALITY AND AESTHETICS
USABILITY	DESIRABILITY
ERGONOMICS	

Although it originally referred to visual designing, this schema can be expanded to encompass all sensory channels which are addressed by virtue of a given design.

254

EXCURSUS:
BASIC
PRINCIPLES OF
SIGNIFICATION
(SEMIOTICS)

The symbolism of colors will be more closely discussed in section 2.4.2. Generally speaking, the following applies:

Intensive colors are particularly suitable for assuming a special significance, given that they easily arouse attention and have an emotional impact.

Auditory correlations, such as national anthems and signals, often exist with respect to political emblems of a visual nature. In the military realm, a classic example is the "Grossen Zapfenstreich" (Ceremonial Taps), which was established in the Prussian army in the nineteenth-century. Thereby, the music, which is precisely specified, includes signals of flutes, trumpets, and drums which are hardly utilized in the daily routine of current military services, and they are, moreover, familiar neither to the great majority of the listeners in general nor to most of the military persons hearing them. In this regard, many musical symbols exist which are capable of being understood merely within the context of the epoch in which – and for which – they were created. Section 2.4.5 addresses this aspect in further detail.

2.4
UNDERSTANDING
THE MEANING –
SYMBOLS AND
METAPHORS

↓

2.4.1
SYMBOLIC
CONNECTIONS

255

FIGURE 2.89
The Frog King as a watering pot.
The design makes reference to the symbolic elements
of the fairy tales of the Grimm Brothers.

Symbolic and iconic elements of objects can correspond to one another. Often, however, the meaning is not comprehensible by virtue of a concrete association. Therefore, the interconnecting of the frog, the crown, the water, and the garden in the case of the Frog King watering pot illustrated in figure 2.89 does not function in an iconic fashion, given the fact that it contains perceptual objects which do not correspond to one another. Frogs do not wear crowns, they seldom sit in one's garden, and they don't tend to spit water out of their mouths. On a symbolic level, however, the connection does indeed function: the Frog King leaps out of the fairy tale and embodies the idyll in a successfully popular manner. As a result, he enriches the desired romanticism of having one's own garden or balcony. Furthermore, this strong symbolism even glosses over the expression of the artificial material from which the object is made, which is normally regarded as being unromantic. By virtue of this combination with that type of material, however, the idyll is ironically treated in the sense of Pop Art. Indeed, the Pop Art character further intensifies the artificial character of the green color with positive results. Customers who don't regard this as being jazzy enough, nonetheless, can purchase the object in even jazzier, louder colors.

Owing to the symbolic contents which it embodies, the Frog King has become something of a *heraldic animal* of the garden idyll. Even in the present-day era, heraldic animals may be found in emblems of national authority. In an associative manner, they demonstrate power, strength, or cleverness. Nevertheless, they are popular even today in their application in the commercial sector, within the framework of brand identities and corporate logos. In this respect, the legendary Frog King appears as the symbol of the shoe polish brand Erdal. Thereby, he combines the important function of the shoe cream, namely that of repelling water, with a majestic brand sensation. Although it was initially presented in green and quite naturally detailed, corresponding to the image on the left side of figure 2.90, the logo has undergone modifications in various steps since its premiere in 1903. It is supposed to be striking in its pose, styled and tending forwards, spreading optimism and, in the presentation, optimally capable of being displayed even in small size. Section 2.4.4 is dedicated to examining the meaning of animal emblems for brands and products.

FIGURE 2.90
The evolution of the Frog King logo of the Erdal shoe polish manufacturer from 1903 (on the far left) via 1919 and 1962, extending to the current logo (on the far right), which has been employed since 1972. Together, they comprise an example of deducing icons from associative references. Werner & Mertz GmbH.

The *allegory* is a special form of symbolism which illustrates a term in personified form, for example, as an individual person or as a group. Figure 2.91 provides an allegory of music, as painted by Gustav Klimt. A woman, serving as an embodiment of the music itself, is shown playing an ancient lyre. She is surrounded by other, ancient symbols, such as sphinxes. Up until the end of the nineteenth-century, in addition to simple graphical presentations of musical instruments and musicians, visual allegories provided practically the only possibility of making reference to the auditory sphere, particularly to music itself, by virtue of images (see e.g., Sauerlandt 1922, Seipel 2000, and Gottdang 2004). In the beginning, the allegoric figure was placed in the center of the illustration and surrounded by other figures, symbols, and musical instruments. However, in contrast to older presentations, the presentation by Klimt is enhanced and expanded by a further aspect: the figure appears to be moved towards the edge on the left-hand side of the image. Floral structures of the Jugendstil lavishly decorate the background. Ultimately, it is not the figure alone which embodies the music – moreover, all elements of the image, for which she makes way, contribute to this embodiment of the music. In particular, one may recognize an approach to the direct presentation of musical structures in the ornamental botanical figures, which are not precisely detailed, but rather depicted in an implied form along the edge of the abstraction. In the course of the twentieth century, within the framework of abstract art, this approach was consequently pursued.

Additionally, even people, notably artists, musicians, and athletes, can each achieve a brand identity by virtue of the stylization of their respective characteristics, regardless of whether it involves a bowler hat or a twirled moustache – Kreutz (2003) provides further examples. Thus, politicians, religious leaders, artists, or entertainers can easily be identified and are able to express their individual way of being. For example, simple, recognizable attributes are allocated to the Dalai Lama, Andy Warhol, Salvador Dali, Michael Jackson, and Jimi Hendrix, among many others.

256

2.4
UNDERSTANDING
THE MEANING –
SYMBOLS AND
METAPHORS
↓
2.4.1
SYMBOLIC
CONNECTIONS

2.4
UNDERSTANDING
THE MEANING –
SYMBOLS AND
METAPHORS
↓
2.4.1
SYMBOLIC
CONNECTIONS

257

FIGURE 2.91
Gustav Klimt, Die Musik (The Music), 1895.
The allegoric presentation of music as a woman
who is playing a lyre.

Occasionally, the symbolic meaning of elementary forms will also be discussed with reference to personal sensitivities and moods. In this regard, A.J. Kastl and I.L. Child presented the findings of their experiments in 1968 with respect to the emotional meanings of typographical fonts and their respective characteristics (cited by Siegle 2005), indicated as follows:

FONT STYLE	MOOD
round (Antiqua)	LIVELY, SCINTILLATING, DREAMY, TRANQUIL, HIGH SOARING
broken (Fraktur)	DIGNIFIED, TRADITIONAL
boldface	SAD, DIGNIFIED, DRAMATIC
serif	FACTUAL, SOPHISTICATED
sans serif	COOL, SOBER
handwriting	ELEGANT, CEREMONIAL

Useful applications of the multisensory connection by virtue of the meaning, particularly between the visual and the auditory modality, result from the symbolic contents of the color tone; this aspect shall be addressed in greater detail in the following chapters.

2.4.2
COLOR SYMBOLISM

258

2.4
UNDERSTANDING
THE MEANING –
SYMBOLS AND
METAPHORS
↓
2.4.1
SYMBOLIC
CONNECTIONS
↓
2.4.2
COLOR
SYMBOLISM

In the allocation of colors to the perceived characteristics of other sensory modalities, but also to other visual attributes as well, such as the form, it is necessary to consider the symbolic value of the color. Colors speak directly to emotions and thus serve to enrich the daily perception – "colors are coming to life." In this regard, a publishing company presents its production line of non-fiction books with the motto: "The colors of science." Generally speaking, the cognitive and emotional value of the color, just as every form of symbolism, depends upon the cultural environment. Therefore, it is subject to great divergences with respect to the nations and the epochs involved (Gage 1993, 1999; with regard to the principles of color designing, see also Gekeler 2005). In different cultures – such as, for example, in Japan – the color white is regarded as the color of mourning, whereas couples traditionally married in black in Europe during earlier centuries. Already during early times, the coloring of buildings offered a complex symbolic content. Information specifically concerning the coloring of Romanesque and Gothic cathedrals can be found in Lanthony (2000) and Leclercq (2000), whereas Charnay (2000) provides respective information regarding Chinese architecture. Traditional systems pertaining to the meaning of colors arose within the framework of heraldry as well as in the context of politics and religion, but also in the realm of magic and alchemy. The following table provides an initial view of the meaning of colors, mainly focused on European and North American culture:

2.4
UNDERSTANDING
THE MEANING –
SYMBOLS AND
METAPHORS
↓
2.4.2
COLOR
SYMBOLISM

259

YELLOW

SUN, ENERGY, POWER, WARMTH:
"STROM IST GELB"
(GERMAN ADVERTISING SLOGAN:
"ELECTRICITY IS YELLOW")

TRAFFIC LIGHT, WARNING BLINKER:
"ATTENTION!"

MEDIEVAL TIMES: ANGER,
JEALOUSY, ENVY

BLUE

COLDNESS,
TRANQUILITY,
MELANCHOLY:
"THE BLUES"

SIGNAL LIGHT:
"(EMERGENCY)
BLUE LIGHTS"

VIOLET

TRADITIONAL
(CHRISTIANITY):
PENITENCE,
PASSION

GREEN

NATURE, HEALTH,
ENVIRONMENTAL PROTECTION,
VACATION: "GRÜNER PUNKT"
(GERMAN SIGNET FOR PACKAGE
RECYCLING:
"GREEN POINT")

TRAFFIC LIGHT, SIGNAL LIGHT,
CORRECT FUNCTION: "GO!"

"GREEN AREA"

MEDIEVAL TIMES: ENVY

TRADITIONAL
(CHRISTIANITY): HOPE

WHITE

CLARITY, INNOCENCE:
"WEISSE WESTE" (GER.:
WHITE VEST, MEANING
A CLEAN RECORD)

RED

FORBIDDEN, DANGER, HEAT:
"IN THE RED," "RED AREA"

TRAFFIC LIGHT, REAR LIGHT,
BRAKE LIGHT: "STOP!"

TRADITIONAL: LOVE, EROTICISM:
"RED LIGHT DISTRICT"

HOWEVER, ALSO:
"BLOOD, VICTIM, BATTLE"

BLACK

NIGHT, DEATH, MISFORTUNE,
HOPELESSNESS: "BLACK DAY"

HOWEVER, ALSO: CERTAINTY:
"BLACK NUMBERS,"
"BLACK ON WHITE
(PRINTED LETTERS
ON PAPER)"

At present, in the audiovisual context, allocations made on the basis of color symbolism play a significant role in providing warning systems with acoustic support. Drivers of sports cars rely upon the combination of the visual appearance – namely the flat, low-lying aerodynamic form – with the sporty sound of the motor. Thereby, the combination with a characteristic color, such as "Ferrari Red," is often of great importance. In this regard, systematic experiments indicate that the perceived loudness of sports cars is also influenced by their color. Parallel to a "sporty, passing-by sound" being generated in the laboratory, an image of an automobile body whose color was either red, blue, bright green, or dark green was projected. Although the acoustic signal was constant among all colors, the red and the dark green automobiles were regarded as being 16.6 to 11.7 percent louder than the blue or the bright green automobiles (Menzel 2007). Red and dark green were quite conspicuously interpreted as being typical colors of sports cars and thus supported the building of particular "sporty" perceptual objects. Similar experiments were carried out with respect to the influence of the color of trains upon their auditory perception (Patsouras 2003). Furthermore, in this manner, the results for the color of a computer printer were determined, indeed, using German as well as Japanese test subjects (Menzel 2008). It has been proven that the loudness rating is not influenced by individual color preferences (Menzel 2010). A case study regarding the harmony of color and sound quality of vacuum cleaners showed that the sharpness of the product sound is a key parameter for the impression of harmony between both modalities. As main parameters which characterize the color interaction with the sound perception, lightness, chroma, and hue angle in the polar CIE color space have been identified (Yanagisawa 2010). Experiments regarding the combination of visual, auditory, and somatosensory sensations showed that, beside an influence on the perceived loudness, the hue of colored light can also modify the pain threshold for thermal stimuli (Landgrebe 2008).

260

2.4
UNDERSTANDING
THE MEANING –
SYMBOLS AND
METAPHORS
↓
2.4.2
COLOR
SYMBOLISM

FIGURE 2.92
**Color symbolism in the sporty design of an automobile.
Ford Fiesta Champ, 2007.**

In the given context, the color of a product provides information pertaining to the product's properties, and it also reflects the lifestyle of the customer. Figure 2.92 illustrates the color design of the Ford Fiesta Champ as a sporty niche product, which conveys associations to car racing. The characteristically checkered pattern of the flag depicted on the roof is suggestive of the victorious arrival of a car beneath the waving flag at the finish line. In the advertisement, this impression is additionally fortified by virtue of the flag itself, as represented above in the image. The color yellow symbolizes power, strength, dynamics, and energy. The influence upon the perception of the environment, as desired by the customer, enters into the picture via the coloring of the floor in the same color tone: the aesthetic appearance of the car "rubs off."

Without a doubt, color designing must be based upon research studies addressing the significance of colors, valid at the time of the product offer. In this regard, Eva Heller conducted a research study pertaining to the perception of colors in the German-speaking world at the end of the twentieth-century. She surveyed 2,000 women and men between the ages of fourteen and ninety-seven (Heller 2000). Table 2.7 provides an overview of the respective color interpretations in the sequence of the frequency of their mentioning. The list addresses only the color tones which were named most frequently with respect to each term. In order to improve the overview, the assessments *positive, neutral,* and *negative* were added to this presentation.

Only a few colors appear to receive a relatively clear evaluation: blue, green, white, pink, and silver exhibit merely a few or no negative aspects at all. On the other hand, only brown and gray are accompanied by predominantly negative connotations. Particularly, gray is deemed as representing indifference and coldness, characteristics which define the *gray,* emotionally neutralized daily routine. In Michael Ende's story *Momo,* "gray men" steal time (Ende 1973). On the other hand, red, yellow, orange, purple, black, and gold are pronouncedly polarizing – indeed, they tend to unite various positive and negative aspects. Accordingly, in the application of these colors, the exact context must be thoroughly considered. In this regard, for example, the color red in the context of a bull fight leaves quite a different impression than it does in the case of a traffic signal, "red figures" in the closing portion of a financial statement, or in a bouquet of red roses. Black as a color can be evil or elegant. Beauty and bragging lie close together in the case of gold. Moreover, the polarizing colors red, yellow, and orange are also interesting with regard to their great signal effects. See also the warning signals in figure 2.84, where red and yellow lights indicate great danger or at least a critical condition.

In light of the fact that the test subjects in Heller's research project chose no distinctive, singular color for each of the terms, but different colors, some of the results should be analyzed in detail. The frequency of the indications, as expressed on a percentage basis, provides each term with a *color field* which serves to paraphrase the obvious connections. Often, iconic relations play a considerable role in such cases. The choice of colors for the cross-modal analogy to sensations pertaining to temperatures, as illustrated in figure 2.93, indicates the *cool* hues, for example, which ideally correlate to water, ice, and snow. *Warmth,* on the other hand, is based upon the colors of embers and fire. The determinant opposing pair is represented by blue and red, two colors which are typically regarded as cold and hot, respectively.

Figure 2.94 illustrates the choice of colors for the coupled terms the calming/the exciting as well as the natural/the artificial. These terms are of great importance to the designing of products. The similarity of the color choice for

2.4
UNDERSTANDING
THE MEANING –
SYMBOLS AND
METAPHORS

↓

2.4.2
COLOR
SYMBOLISM

261

COLOR	POSITIVE	NEUTRAL	NEGATIVE
BLUE	LOYALTY TRUST SPORTINESS INDEPENDENCE RECOVERY CLEVERNESS SCIENCE HARMONY FRIENDSHIP SYMPATHY FANTASY	DISTANCE COOLNESS MASCULINITY THE GREAT	DESIRE PASSIVITY
RED	LOVE PASSION EROTICISM THE SEDUCTIVE POWER ATTRACTIVENESS HAPPINESS DYNAMICS	SEXUALITY WARMTH NEARNESS THE EXTROVERTED	AGGRESSIVENESS THE FORBIDDEN HATRED THE IMMORAL
YELLOW	THE AMUSING OPTIMISM FRIENDLINESS		ENVY JEALOUSLY FRUGALITY UNTRUTHFULNESS
GREEN	HOPE THE NATURAL THE CALMING THE HEALTHY SAFETY YOUTH THE REFRESHING THE PLEASANT		THE POISONOUS THE UNTRUTH
WHITE	OBJECTIVITY TRUTH THE IDEAL RELIGIOUSNESS	THE LIGHT THE QUIET THE NEW	
GREY	MODESTY		BOREDOM THE DECENT UNFRIENDLINESS COLD-HEARTEDNESS UNCERTAINTY
BLACK	MAGIC SECRECY POWER ELEGANCE	THE HEAVY THE HARD THE SQUARED THE CONSERVATIVE THE INTROVERTED	THE EVIL BRUTALITY INFIDELITY EGOISM
PURPLE	THE FLIPPED OUT THE EXTRAVAGANT THE INDIVIDUAL THE FANCY		VAIN THE ARTIFICIAL
PINK	TENDERNESS SENSIBILITY CHARM POLITENESS	THE FEMININE THE SMALL THE SWEET THE MILD	THE CHEAP
ORANGE	THE AROMATIC PLEASURE SOCIABILITY ENJOYMENT		THE NON-OBJECTIVE INTRUSIVENESS
BROWN	COMFORTABLENESS	AUTUMN BITTERNESS	LAZINESS THE OLD-FASHIONED THE UNEROTIC THE NARROW-MINDED STUPIDITY THE UGLY THE UNENJOYABLE
SILVER	RAPIDITY THE MODERN		
GOLD	LUXURY FESTIVITY HAPPINESS BEAUTY		SHOWING-OFF PRIDE

262

2.4
UNDERSTANDING
THE MEANING –
SYMBOLS AND
METAPHORS
↓
2.4.2
COLOR
SYMBOLISM

TABLE 2.7
**Color interpretations in the German-speaking world
according to Heller (2000).**

2.4
UNDERSTANDING
THE MEANING –
SYMBOLS AND
METAPHORS
↓
2.4.2
COLOR
SYMBOLISM

263

COOLNESS   WARMTH

THE CALMING   THE EXCITING

THE NATURAL   THE ARTIFICIAL

FIGURE 2.93 (1–2) AND 2.94 (3–6)
**Choice of colors for the coupled terms coolness/warmth,
the calming/the exciting, and the natural/the artificial.
The diagram presents the preferred colors with regard to the
respective term (Heller 2000).**

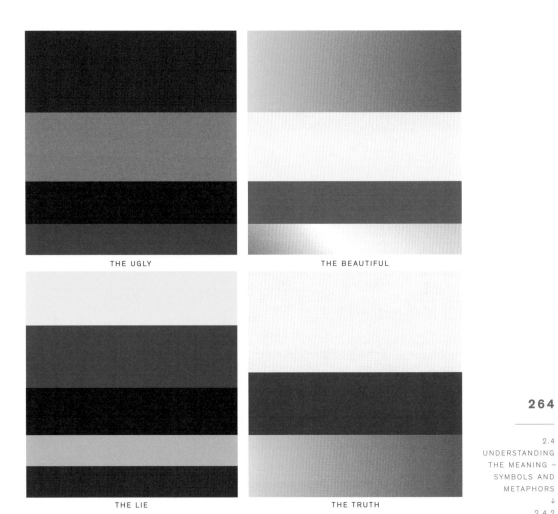

THE UGLY

THE BEAUTIFUL

THE LIE

THE TRUTH

FIGURE 2.95
Choice of colors for the coupled terms the ugly/the beautiful
and the lie/the truth (Heller 2000).

264

2.4
UNDERSTANDING
THE MEANING –
SYMBOLS AND
METAPHORS
↓
2.4.2
COLOR
SYMBOLISM

the *calming* and the *natural* is particularly worth noting. First and foremost, it involves the color green. Even the blueness of the water and brown play roles as well. White is important as a traditional symbol of *purity*. The resemblance of the *excitement* with respect to the *warmth* in figure 2.93 demonstrates the importance of the yellow and red tones to the attention and the emotional participation *(involvement)* of the customer. Nevertheless, even purple is regarded as being quite exciting. The *artificial* is articulated by various middle shades such as pink, purple, and orange as well as by virtue of the gold and gray tones. The overall impression of this color combination gives rise to a sense of artificiality. However, it must be pointed out that the mentioning of the color by the test subjects occurred on a singular basis – whereas the test subjects were not questioned regarding the individual *combinations* of color tones within the course of Heller's research project.

2.4
UNDERSTANDING
THE MEANING –
SYMBOLS AND
METAPHORS

↓

2.4.2
COLOR
SYMBOLISM

265

The choice of colors for the coupled bipolar terms the ugly/the beautiful and the lie/the truth is also interesting (fig. 2.95). Brown, black, and purple are common features of the *ugly* and the *lie*. White and gold find themselves being allocated to *beauty* as well as to *truth*. For the lie, moreover, yellow and green were supplemented by other colors, and these additional colors had already been characterized by their negative connotations in medieval times, for example, as words indicative of rage, jealousy, frugality, and poison. This is one of the few cases in which green exhibits negative aspects – the frequency of the respective mentioning, however, was small. The old meaning was apparently not completely replaced by the currently prevalent, positive associations of the healthy, the natural, the calming, and the relaxing. Moreover, yellow and red exhibit a tendency towards polarization, with yellow being a considerably negative attribute of the *lie* this time. Red is also a clear aspect of *beauty*. The cultural context is important as well: the color of death is black in Europe, whereas it is white in Japan – a greater contrast is not imaginable. The current meanings of the colors yellow and green shall be examined more closely in the following examples.

Joseph Beuys reflected the meaning of the color yellow by virtue of his object *Capri Battery* from 1985 (fig. 2.96). A yellow light bulb is connected in a conspicuous manner to a lemon, giving rise to the impression that the energy for the illumination is coming from the lemon itself. In this fashion, the energy is *fed* to the light bulb by a sun-ripened foodstuff instead of a battery. Indeed, the yellow sun allows the lemon to grow, ripen, and develop a yellow color. Nevertheless, the bulb appears as an artificial sun. Thereby, the presentation alludes to the fact that, as a basic rule, all energy forms available on earth ultimately originate in the sun, even including wind and water power, oil, gas, and coal. Furthermore, the sun is also the source of life for plants, by virtue of photosynthesis, and animals and humans receive their energy from plants and herbivores from which they nourish themselves. Undoubtedly, this touches upon a variety of philosophical questions: What is artificial, what is natural? What is externally fed, what exists in and of itself? That object exhibits an additional attraction in the form of the pear-shaped light and the apparent similarity in nature between such a light bulb and the lemon. Similar to a battery, the lemon also contains acid, and indeed it can provide a small electrical voltage during physical experiments. Although it makes a direct reference to the island of Capri, the title of the object additionally refers to the German brand of fruit juice *Capri Sun*, a sun which can be purchased by consumers in grocery stores and supermarkets.

FIGURE 2.96
Yellow = sun = energy? Joseph Beuys, Capri-Battery,
1985. © 2011, ProLitteris, Zurich.

In the course of advertising, efforts are undertaken to connect fixed, symbolic meanings and the visual appearance of products and corporate logos with one another. Thereby, the color plays an essential role.

266

2.4
UNDERSTANDING
THE MEANING –
SYMBOLS AND
METAPHORS
↓
2.4.2
COLOR
SYMBOLISM

FIGURE 2.97
Even after the color symbolism of the green dot was anchored
in the ecological consciousness of the public,
the symbolism also functions when the logo appears on
packages involving other colors.

In order to brand itself more effectively into the memory of the consumer and to achieve an additional intuitive plausibility, the color *coding* of products is often supported by iconic elements. Yellow and green, for example, are also the symbolic colors of the *dual systems* of waste utilization employed in recycling. This industry-funded system was initiated in Germany by DSD GmbH and is gaining recognition throughout Europe. Corresponding to figure 2.94, the color green is regarded by the overwhelming majority of the population as being an expression of naturalness and calming. Yellow, on the other hand, functions as a strong signal color, being utilized to distinguish the *yellow sack* and the *yellow garbage* can from the black garbage can for residual waste. However, the negative aspects of the color yellow, as presented in table 2.7, are relegated into the background. The *green dot*, as the license logo of the dual system and as a symbol of ecologically friendly means of disposal, is supported by associations with green leaves and those involving the established field of meaning, as represented by nature, health, purity, vacation, quietness, etc. Thus, the coding is so well-anchored, in this regard, that it retains the meaning, even if the symbol appears on packages without always being green – as indicated by figure 2.97, which consists of randomly chosen cutouts of packaging. Figure 2.98 illustrates the significance of the colors yellow, green, and orange within the framework of the brand symbolism of the dual system. In this case, the color green lends plausibility – indeed, regardless of the question as to whether the recycling system is environmentally sensible or not.

2.4
UNDERSTANDING
THE MEANING –
SYMBOLS AND
METAPHORS
↓
2.4.2
COLOR
SYMBOLISM

267

FIGURE 2.98
Yellow and green, as symbolic colors of the dual system,
contrast with the orange color of the garbage removal services.
In the course of the pilot project "Yellow Bin plus"
[Gelbe Tonne plus], towards the expansion of the recycling program,
a yellow bin measuring twelve meters tall was erected.
In this regard, all vehicles were provided with appropriate advertising media.

In an ecologically oriented design, the color green, owing to the aforementioned reasons, plays a similarly important role. Such concepts in designing are, for example, based upon the utilization of materials which save resources or upon the processes of recycling. Accordingly, they are also referred to as *green design*, such as by Fiell (2005b).

Colors are often essential components of brands. Therefore, it is possible to legally protect the intellectual property rights of a company with respect to individual color tones – such as the *magenta* color of the German telecommunications enterprise DEUTSCHE TELEKOM (Fig. 3.31) – or even with regard to color combinations.

Symbols can transport a very solid meaning and thus lead to a strong identification of the recipient with the product. Nevertheless, short-term, drastic devaluations are also possible, and these could accordingly result in new, similarly stable meanings replacing the previous ones.

EXCURSUS:
COLORS
AND JAZZ

Even in popular music and in jazz, color references play a significant role. Some examples of the titles of jazz pieces verify this:

PAINTED RHYTHM – STAN KENTON – 1945

BLACK BEAUTY – DUKE ELLINGTON – 1928

SONG WITH ORANGE – CHARLES MINGUS – 1959

GREEN HAZE & BLUE HAZE – MILES DAVIS – 1955

DEEP PURPLE – COMPOSED BY PETER DEROSE, LYRICS BY MITCHELL PARISH – 1933, 1938

STUDY IN BROWN – BUNNY BERIGAN – 1937

BLUE AND BROWN – CLIFFORD BROWN – 1953

OPUS IN BEIGE – STAN KENTON, COMPOSED BY GENE ROLAND – 1956

BLUE INTERLUDE – ARTIE SHAW – 1938

RED ARROW – RED RODNEY AND IRA SULLIVAN – 1957

YELLOW TANGO – DICK TWARDZIG – 1955

PASTEL BLUE – ARTIE SHAW, COMPOSED BY CHARLIE SHAVERS - 1939

MOOD INDIGO – DUKE ELLINGTON – 1930

TONE PAINTING, I, II AND III – DODO MARMAROSA – 1947

Furthermore, one of the most popular songs performed by the Rolling Stones has "Brown Sugar" as its title.

The musical history of jazz reflects the problematic nature of North American racism in the nineteenth and twentieth centuries, notably in its efforts to establish the European musical culture of the light-skinned immigrants as the "leading culture" of the society of the Unites States. This orientation was in marked contrast to the rhythmically dominated musical taste of the descendants of African slaves. On the sociopolitical level, the contrasting of skin colors served and continues to serve as a central subject of contention – with *black, brown,* and *colored* on the one side and *white* on the other. In the music itself, in fundamental terms, this conflict corresponds to the tensions existing between a rhythmically, bodily perceived style of music on the one

Ronny Red, Out of the Blue,
1959 (Blue Note Records)

hand and, on the other hand, the comparatively academic, intellectually refined form of music, with the essence of its tonal articulation being represented by melody as well as by relatively complicated harmonics, as advanced and cherished by European immigrants and their descendants. In this respect, the explicit reference made to color, as is evident in the aforementioned musical titles, may indeed be regarded as an expression of emotional profundity as well as a political metaphor and an affirmation of the particular position.

Within the framework of the *Blues*, a music form which is perceived as folksy and down-to-earth, the color blue plays a central role. In the case of the Blues, the intensive, actually melancholically colored character of the music corresponds to the preferred subject matter of life crises, poverty, unemployment, and sexual frustration. The "Blues Feeling" – in which melancholic sensations are felt – thus makes reference to negative experiences in life, particularly involving feelings of rejection. Accordingly, that is tantamount to "having the Blues," although this description also applies to the ability to musically express such emotions in a convincing fashion. In the German language, as a matter of comparison, this notion corresponds more or less to the condition of having a "blue Monday" [einen "blauen Montag" haben], a once popular description which has become somewhat less prevalent in the course of time. Even the "blue letter" [der "blaue Brief"], an historical term describing a private or even an official letter of rejection in Germany, is worthy of mention in this context, although the name, in its original usage, simply made reference to the traditional color of the envelope without specifically intending to evoke associations with regard to melancholy music. With the term "pink slip," the English language also refers to a color. In regard to the aforementioned meaning of the color blue, nevertheless, it would indeed be interesting to explore the question as to why blue was chosen as the color of the envelope containing the bad or sad news, in contrast to the colors of envelopes containing comparatively good news. At any rate, the origin of the term *Blues* is unclear – one theory suggests

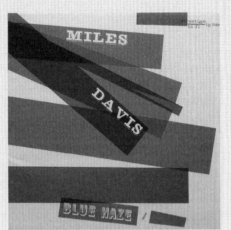

Miles Davis, Blue Haze, 1956
(PRLP 7054)

that it is a synthesis of the word "Blue Devils." The feeling of a continuous melancholy state is, nonetheless, quite appropriate as a description of the entire Blues style. Among other means, it is achieved by virtue of special tones within the tone scale – the *blue notes* – and the special coloring of the chords – the *blue chords*. Further information may be found in Behrend

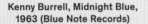

Kenny Burrell, Midnight Blue,
1963 (Blue Note Records)

Lou Levy Quartet, Jazz In Four Colors,
1956 (RCA Victor)

(1999) and Bohländer (1990).

2.4.3
SYNESTHETIC METAPHORS

Metaphors connect words involving different areas of experience with one another and enable the graphic interpretation of terms by joining diverse fields of meaning. As a consequence, the "foot of the mountain" describes the wide, expansive bedrock of the mountain which resembles a foot. The similarity exists, however, only in a certain regard, and this is visually comprehensible within the framework of a comparison of analogies. In a strictly logical sense, of course, this description is naturally false, given that a mountain can neither walk nor exhibit a true foot with toes.

THE GENERALLY WIDESPREAD ABILITY OF A LISTENER OR A READER TO IMMEDIATELY COMPREHEND A SUCCESSFUL METAPHOR MAKES IT AN IMPORTANT INSTRUMENT FOR THE SPECIFICATION OF TERMS, AS MEANINGS ARE CONNECTED TO ONE ANOTHER, ALTHOUGH THEY ARE ORIGINALLY NOT RELATED TO ONE ANOTHER.

270

2.4
UNDERSTANDING
THE MEANING –
SYMBOLS AND
METAPHORS
↓
2.4.3
SYNESTHETIC
METAPHORS

The comparison of the semantic fields of terms facilitates the creation of new terms. It is precisely the communication and conveyance of terms which appear to be quite distant from one another that ultimately leads to an enrichment of linguistic expression. Due to this reason, combinations of words originating within different sensory modalities are particularly interesting. Combinations which can be intuitively comprehended are, for example, a bright sound, penetrating pain, screaming red, a flat-tasting wine, a soft tone, and a permeating odor. Metaphors which unite different senses in accordance with this principle are referred to as synesthetic metaphors.

In nineteenth-century literature, synesthetic paraphrases play an important role (Schrader 1969, Engelen 1966). This particularly applies to lyric poetry (O'Malley 1964, Wanner-Meyer 1998). Indeed, retrospectively, various authors are regarded as having exhibited genuine synesthetic perceptual capabilities, as described in chapter 2.5. Among them are G. Keller, E.T.A. Hoffmann, C. Baudelaire, A. Rimbaud and J.K. Huysmans (Mahling 1927). As a general rule, however, this phenomenon can not be posthumously verified, although it is often discussed (Harrison 2001). The intermingling of different modalities, nevertheless, corresponds to the artistic concept which was advanced in the Romantic period and which ultimately led to the idea of the "overall artistic work." This concept is effectively described by the German term *Gesamtkunstwerk* and comprises in its essence a "synthesis of the arts." Further material in this regard may be found in Günther (1994) and in the catalogue of the art exhibition *Der Hang zum Gesamtkunstwerk,* literally "The Tendency towards a Synthesis of the Arts" (GK 1983). Normally, however, synesthetic paraphrases are, in their function as metaphors, generally understandable and do not require the reader to possess synesthetic perceptual abilities of his or her own. Due to this reason, cross-modal verbalizations can also be of great importance in the evaluation of sounds. Moreover, they are generally appropriate for evaluative experiments undertaken on the basis of *semantic differentials.* These benchmarking standards, as advanced by Charles E. Osgood, comprise a rating scale designed to measure the connotative meaning of objects. More specifically, they are constituted by *bipolar pairs of adjectives* which represent the two extremes of the respective dimension that is being surveyed (see also Excursus). Utilizing this method, a survey of test subjects as to which coupled terms would most appropriately describe the gearbox rattling in the transmission of an automobile led to the results indicated in table 2.8. Thereby, in addition to references made to human sensitivities and emotions, five onomatopoetically as well as four tactilely, four spatially, and seven visually synesthetic word pairings have been found, among them are *bright/dark, clear/obscure, dim/brilliant,* and *sharp/dull.* The set of bipolar pairs of adjectives was originally drafted in German. It is also reasonable to apply synesthetic metaphors in the course of acoustic experiments. In this manner, those elementary perceptual analogies, which would otherwise not enter into the consciousness, even though they are essential to the establishment and interpretation of perceptual objects, could nevertheless be factored into the equation. Again, of particular importance in this respect are bipolar pairs of adjectives which encompass more than merely two modalities on the basis of intersensory attributes, according to the discussion in section 2.2.3, such as *fine-grained/coarse-grained, thin/thick,* and *bright/dark.*

Furthermore, the semantic differential is also an important instrument for the evaluation of smell and taste sensations. In this respect, the guidelines for determining and evaluating the disturbing influence of immissions (odors) upon the sense of smell – which are known in German as Geruchsimmission-srichtlinie ("GIRL") – provide a polarity profile for the subjective evaluation of the odors caused by industrial and agricultural facilities. Thereby, some twenty-nine word pairs comprised by bipolar adjectives are used. In addition to *powerful/weak* and *pleasant/unpleasant,* such distinctively synesthetic pairs such as *heavy/lightweight, dark/bright, cold/warm, quiet/loud,* and *soft/hard* are also taken into consideration (GIRL 2004).

2.4
UNDERSTANDING
THE MEANING –
SYMBOLS AND
METAPHORS
↓
2.4.3
SYNESTHETIC
METAPHORS

271

OLD	NEW	SICK	HEALTHY
PERSISTENT	RESERVED	ARTIFICIAL	NATURAL
OBVIOUS	INCONSPICUOUS	ANNOYING	PLEASANT
PLEASANT	UNPLEASANT	LOUD	QUIET
AGGRESSIVE	PEACEFUL	SLOW	RAPID
FRIGHTENING	FAMILIAR	LIGHT	HEAVY
THREATENING	RELAXED	VIGOROUS	RESERVED
CALMING	STIRRING	LOOSE	TENSE
SIGNIFICANT	INSIGNIFICANT	DIM	BRILLIANT
CHEAP	EXPENSIVE	POWERFUL	WEAK
KNOWN	UNKNOWN	MASCULINE	FEMININE
DULL	TINGLING	METALLIC	WOODEN
THIN	DENSE	MODULATED	UNMODULATED
CLEAR	BLURRY	INFERIOR	SUPERIOR
ANGULAR	ROUND	TIRED	ALERT
EXTROVERTED	INTROVERTED	NERVOUS	QUIET
FINE-GRAINED	COARSE-GRAINED	POTENT	IMPOTENT
FAR	NEAR	ROUGH	SMOOTH
FAT	SKINNY	REGULAR	IRREGULAR
FLAT	THICK	SHARP	DULL
DAMPED	UNDAMPED	POINTED	DULL
CONSTANT	IRREGULAR	STATIONARY	TRANSIENT
UGLY	PRETTY	DISTURBING	PLEASANT
HARMONIOUS	INHARMONIOUS	BAD	GOOD
QUICKLY	LEISURELY	STIFF	LAX
HARD	SOFT	STRICT	TENDER
BRIGHT	DARK	TYPICAL	ATYPICAL
FIERCE	GENTLE	COMFORTING	DISCOMFORTING
BRIGHT	GRIM	RELIABLE	UNRELIABLE
BROKEN	INTACT	FAMILIAR	STRANGE
CLEAR	DIM	FULL	EMPTY
POWERFUL	WEAK	WARM	COLD

272

2.4
UNDERSTANDING
THE MEANING –
SYMBOLS AND
METAPHORS
↓
2.4.3
SYNESTHETIC
METAPHORS

TABLE 2.8
Verbalization of automobile sounds – coupled terms for the semantic differential.
These coupled terms were complied within the framework
of a "brainstorming" aimed at describing the gearbox rattling of diesel motors.

EXCURSUS:
SEMANTIC
DIFFERENTIAL AND
POLARITY PROFILE

EXCURSUS:
SEMANTIC
DIFFERENTIAL
AND
POLARITY
PROFILE

273

In order to evaluate the nature and extent of different properties in perceptual experiments, the constituting of paired terms which correspond to contrasting evaluations is highly recommended. In this manner, a *hedonistic* testing procedure which is based on the principles of *semantic differentials* comes into being. Table 2.8 indicates examples of appropriate paired terms for the evaluation of a sound. The test subjects are required to indicate the characteristics between the coupled terms either in steps, for example, by virtue of numbered scales or continually.

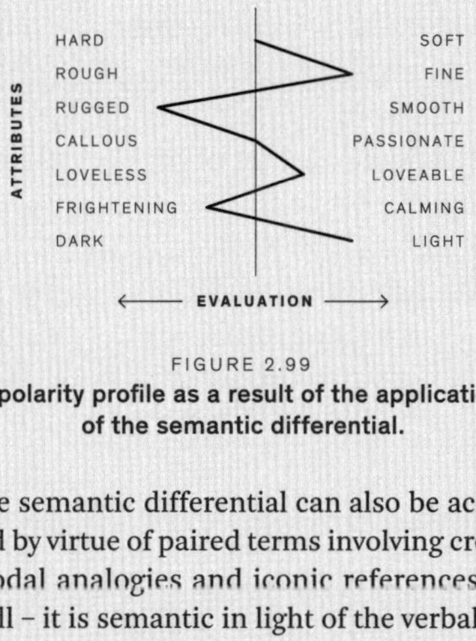

FIGURE 2.99
A polarity profile as a result of the application of the semantic differential.

The semantic differential can also be achieved by virtue of paired terms involving cross-modal analogies and iconic references as well – it is semantic in light of the verbalizations which are applied within it. The results of the application of the semantic differential can be presented as a *polarity profile (profile of meaning)*, as shown in figure 2.99, in order to provide an overview of the complete results of the evaluative experiment. There is a result line (profile) for every test person. For a larger collective of test subjects, the results must be summarized for each of the paired terms. Additionally, the *significance* has to be appropriately considered as a measure of the static meaningfulness of the observed tendencies. This is the likelihood with which the result

of the experiment indicates true differences in the perception, as applicable to larger groups of subjects. Due to statistic reasons, it is important to provide the *median* of the evaluation of each coupled term given by all of the respondents. More specifically, this represents the value in the middle of all of the evaluations. Accordingly, the opinions of 50 percent of the test subjects are located above this value, whereas those opinions of the other 50 percent of the respondents are located below this value. The presentation of the median value for every bipolar adjective pair again provides for a result line which corresponds to the example depicted, while simultaneously considering the overall group of test subjects.

In developing semantic differentials for a perceptual experiment, it is initially important to accept all coupled bipolar adjectives which have a certain likelihood of being significant. With the assistance of statistical analysis, the subsequent step seeks to extract the parameters crucial to the evaluation. This occurs with the help of a *Principal Component Analysis* (PCA). As a general rule, it is capable of reducing the overall impression of a design or a situation to a few *dimensions*. These dimensions appear as parameters which are independent of one another and simultaneously incapable of influencing the other. In a mathematical sense, the PCA comprises an *orthogonal linear transformation* of the data into a new reference system which only contains the essential aspects. The dimensions in this regard serve to generate a system of coordinates from axes which scale parameters that are independent of one another – this corresponds to the mathematical concept of orthogonality. Therewith, the axes represent the particularly important aspects. In the case of perceptual experiments, these are the properties which are of decisive importance to building perceptual objects and to their qualities.

THE APPLICATION OF
METAPHORS IN EVALUATING WINES

Wine is evidently most appropriate for being regarded as a drink with an ideal value. This leads to a price margin ranging from a few euros, dollars, or pounds per bottle for a simple table wine to several thousand euros, dollars, or pounds for a wine of exquisite origin. Accordingly, the qualitative evaluation requires a differentiated terminology as well as a, so to speak, well-ripened connoisseurship capable of predicting the likely development of the wine even within the course of several decades – for an exclusive wine it can indeed require so much time in order to fully unfold with respect to reaching its *depth* and earning its multifarious properties. Undoubtedly, even in the evaluation of wines, metaphors are employed which freely correlate to other modalities and to general mental states. Thereby, references are commonly made to cross-modal properties, *(dull, full)*, and associations made to known fruit aromas and scents can be just as frequently identified. In individual cases, comparisons are also made with respect to musical tones (Prossinger 2007). The wine glossary depicted in table 2.9 (Johnson 1986) reveals, furthermore, that the vocabulary of the wine connoisseur is also based upon cross-modal analogies, associations, and anthropomorphizing (i.e. humanizing) metaphors to a significant degree.

In principle, the act of consuming wine in a pleasant, relishing manner is a multisensory experience. Thereby, the sense of smell, in particular, plays a significant role in the differentiation of the taste sensation. Visual circumstances, such as the color of the wine, for example, support the pleasure of consumption just as much as the feeling of the drink as sensed by the lips and tongue as well as by the palate. Accordingly, the designing of highly valuable wine glasses effectuates, in addition to the optical presentation, the consolidation of the perception of the smell and of the perception of the taste (fig. 2.100). Furthermore, music is frequently very purposefully employed in contemporary times – just as it was during the Baroque era – in order to enhance the culinary experience. In this regard, reference is made herein to the *Tafelmusik* (literally "Table Music") of the German composer Georg Philipp Telemann, which appeared in print in 1733.

Given the complexity of the task, the design and production of wines can indeed be regarded as an applied art and as a work of art itself (Prossinger 2007).

274

2.4
UNDERSTANDING
THE MEANING –
SYMBOLS AND
METAPHORS
↓
2.4.3
SYNESTHETIC
METAPHORS

FIGURE 2.100:
Glasses for wine and sekt (German for "sparkling wine")
offer a combination of visual and tactile attractions with taste and smell.
Sommelier glasses, designed by Claus Josef Riedel for the
Tyrolean Glassworks, Kufstein, 1972. Museum of Applied Art, Cologne.

DRY: OPPOSITE OF SWEET

ELEGANT: LIKE A WOMAN – ELUSIVELY PLEASANT, GOOD, GROOMED, NOT EXACTLY FULL

FAT OR OILY: A HIGH CONCENTRATION OF EXTRACT AND GLYCERIN

FIERY: STRONG, RIPE AND FULL-BODIED

FINAL NOTE: THE SUSTAINED AFTERTASTE OF GOOD WINES

FINESSE: EPITOME OF FINENESS

FIZZY: FRESH, PLEASANTLY RICH IN CARBONIC ACID

FLAT OR **THIN:** NO PARTICULAR SMELL OR TASTE CHARACTERISTICS

FRESH OR **LIVELY:** HEALTHY YOUNG WINE WITH AN APPROPRIATE
CONCENTRATION OF ACID AND CARBONIC ACID

FRUITY: CHARACTERIZED BY THE AROMA AND THE ACIDITY OF GRAPES,
SOMETIMES REMINDING ONE OF OTHER FRUITS AS WELL

FULL-BODIED: RICH IN EXTRACT AND GLYCERIN

FULL-FLAVORED: RICH IN EXTRACT AND IN ALCOHOL WITH A LENGTHY FINAL NOTE

GENTLE: LIGHT, HARMONIC, WITHOUT DISTINCTIVE CHARACTERISTICS

GREAT: ALL PROPERTIES IN A STATE OF PERFECTION

HARD: MUCH ACIDITY, INHARMONIC

HARSH: A HIGH TANNIN CONCENTRATION, ASTRINGENT

HEAVY: HIGH ALCOHOL AND EXTRACT CONTENT

MASSIVE: RICH IN ALCOHOL AND FULL-BODIED

MILD: LOW IN ACID, BUT APPEALING AND RIPE

MOUTHY: APPEALING, INVITING TO DRINK

NERVED: POWERFUL AND FINE – LIKE A GOOD HORSE

NOBLE: A PERFECT CONSONANCE OF RACE, BODY, AND RIPENESS

OLD, FIRN OR **TIRED:** TOO OLD, EXHAUSTED, WITHOUT FRESHNESS

PALATABLE: LIGHT, APPEALING

PLUMP: INHARMONIC, HEAVY, AND WITHOUT A FINE ART

POOR: HAS TOO LITTLE BODY

POWERFUL: ALL QUALITIES, PARTICULARLY REGARDING THE
ALCOHOL CONTENT, SIGNIFICANTLY DEVELOPED

RACY: ELEGANT, APPEALING ACIDITY OF A FRESH, FINE ART

RIPE: READY, FULLY DEVELOPED

ROUND: HARMONIC, FULL-BODIED

SHARP: TASTE FOLLOWING SUBSEQUENT FERMENTATION IN THE BOTTLE

SOLID: WINE WITH AN APPROPRIATE ACIDITY

STALE OR **FAINT:** ACID DEFICIENCY

STRONG: CONTAINING ALCOHOL IN A SUFFICIENT AMOUNT

STRENGTHY: RICH IN ALCOHOL

SWEET: PLEASANT, LESS EXPRESSIVE

VELVETY: IN RED WINES – A BALANCED INTERACTION OF ALCOHOL AND BODY

YOUNG: A NOT THOROUGHLY RIPENED WINE

2.4
UNDERSTANDING
THE MEANING –
SYMBOLS AND
METAPHORS
↓
2.4.3
SYNESTHETIC
METAPHORS

275

TABLE 2.9
**Paraphrases use in the evaluative description of wine,
as indicated by Johnson (1986).
For elucidative purposes, synesthetic metaphors are
distinguished by the text colors as analogies,
taste associations, or anthropomorphizing descriptions.**

2.4.4
SYMBOLISM IN BRAND DESIGN

In seeking to establish the desired symbolism, the designing of logos can also make recourse to associative properties. For the purpose of building a multi-sensory brand-oriented symbolism, furthermore, auditory components are also increasingly utilized (Roth 2005, Kilian 2009, Kastner 2008).

> **GENERALLY SPEAKING, VISUALLY DISTINCTIVE FEATURES OF A BRAND OR OF AN INSTITUTION ARE REFERRED TO AS SIGNETS. AS A PICTOGRAM, THE GRAPHIC COULD SUCCESSFULLY APPEAR WITHOUT LETTERS OR NUMBERS. AS A MATTER OF CONTRAST, HOWEVER, A LOGO ALWAYS INCLUDES LETTERS OR NUMBERS.**

As a *logogram*, a logo can encompass entire words. However, *letters of the alphabet*, such as abbreviations, as well as numbers and combinations of both are more frequent. Additional graphic elements can be of an abstract nature, but they are nevertheless capable of conveying contents, given elementary analogy relationships. As an alternative to associative, iconic contents, recourse may also be mad to established symbolism, such as historic crests, heraldic animals, or colors with a specific meaning.

Accordingly, analogous to the aforementioned definition of visual signs, even a pictographic auditory signal having no linguistic reference is a signet. *Sound logos*, on the other hand, are based upon linguistic elements, such as words or individual sounds – or even upon linguistic characteristics, such as accentuation or intonation. In this regard, a sound logo is exhibited by the jingle of the German telecommunications corporation DEUTSCHE TELEKOM, which imitates the accentuation and the linguistic rhythm of the corporate name itself. The same applies to the sound logo of the INTEL Corporation, thus referring to the slogan "Intel inside." Moreover, musical phrases can even assume linguistic-oriented characteristics, thus transporting contents as well. Therefore, being able to understand musical symbolism is indispensable to designing signals. This will be discussed in the next section. Occasionally, special codings are also employed to generate sound logos. As an example, the title of the radio program *Zeitzeichen* (German for "Sign of the Times"), produced by WDR (West German Broadcasting) in Cologne, is conveyed using Morse signals. Similarly, the trailer introducing the weather segment of the televised German daily news program *Tagesschau* employed the standardized radio code QAM (weather report) for a number of years in Morse code as well. However, utilizing a codification of this type makes sense only when those persons hearing it without understanding the Morse code in and of itself – and that certainly

276

2.4
UNDERSTANDING
THE MEANING –
SYMBOLS AND
METAPHORS
↓
2.4.4
SYMBOLISM IN
BRAND DESIGN

covers the majority of them – are at least able to extract associative meaning. In this case, the Morse signals serve as the auditory features involved in the flow of the news and symbolize the purposeful conveyance of information to the listeners and viewers. Since the 1970s, a general tendency towards abbreviating the auditory features has been identified: Whereas entire melodies ("The Oscar Mayer Jingle," see section 2.3.1) or complete orchestra phrases ("Eurovision Hymn") were originally preferred, fragments with a length of merely a few seconds are common in the present day.

Symbols which represent brands can be legally protected as intellectual property by virtue of their listing in the trademark register. Such symbols are appropriately designated as *word mark, picture mark, word-picture mark, color mark,* or *sound mark.* The registration in the trademark register requires naturally the ability to graphically present the mark. The mark which is to be protected must be, as a practical matter, clear, distinctive, self-contained, easily

2.4
UNDERSTANDING
THE MEANING –
SYMBOLS AND
METAPHORS
↓
2.4.4
SYMBOLISM IN
BRAND DESIGN

——————

277

accessible and understandable, as well as capable of being permanently and objectively presented. On the other hand, however, the possibility of protecting marks which are difficult to present is limited, even if they are capable of easily being visually recognized along with other marks, such as *smell marks, movement marks,* or *taste marks.* Nevertheless, it is possible to legally protect touch marks, such as the word *Underberg* in Braille as developed for the blind – as well as *hologram marks* as a visual special case. In contrast to the majority of these special cases, auditory brand symbols have acquired a permanent place in corporate design as *sound marks,* either as the melodic presentation of a slogan (e.g., "I'm Lovin' It," "Haribo macht Kinder froh," literally "Haribo makes children happy," the catchphrase of the German candy maker Haribo) or as an independent motif. Diverse examples in this regard include the sound icons of: DEUTSCHE TELEKOM, INTEL, MASTERCARD, ALLIANZ, RICOLA, MARS, SCHNEEKOPPE, UNDERBERG, SPARKASSE, BAUSPARKASSE, SCHWÄBISCH HALL, JÄGERMEISTER, MCDONALD'S, and LUFTHANSA. Interestingly, the motorcycle manufacturer HARLEY DAVIDSON undertook efforts to legally protect the archetypical sound of its motor as a sound mark – as of the year 2000, however, it ultimately refrained from pursuing this goal, owing to objection proceedings which had extended over a number of years. ● Further examples of this type may be found in Bronner (2009b).

The visual logos of automobile trademarks can be analyzed and classified according to their intuitive features, as depicted in figure 2.101. Automobile trademarks are represented by pure text-oriented logos only to a limited extent. Additionally, many contain visual basic forms, exhibiting analogies to essential properties of the respective products, also as indicated in figure 2.101. Among them are dramatic forms and dynamic streamlining, each making reference to the dynamic driving properties, such as the *D* in the DAIHATSU streamlining design. Furthermore, technical structures strengthen the character of the product in an associative manner, such as the teeth of the cogged wheels in the case of VW or the four rings of the AUDI logo ("wheels," originally symbolizing the four companies AUDI, DKW, HORCH, and WANDERER which merged to form the Auto Union, predecessor of the AUDI AG). With its font style, the FORD logo openly values tradition – it was developed as early as 1903 by the plant engineer CHILDE HAROLD WILLS, as the FORD MOTOR COMPANY was founded.

Elements of classical symbolism, such as heraldic animals, are prevalent as well. In this respect, the Porsche logo bears direct reference to the flag of the German federal state of Baden-Wuerttemberg and to the municipal crest of the city of Stuttgart, the historical corporate base of PORSCHE. In a similar fashion, the symbol of the ALFA ROMEO contains the red cross of the municipal crest of Milan as well as a viper, an archetypal symbol dating back to the twelfth century, which is depicted as engulfing a person – that is the heraldic animal of the dynastic House of Visconti, known for its gruesome rule in Milan. This is a prime example of a form of symbolism which is accepted only due to its longstanding tradition, for it would otherwise find no acceptance, for example, if it were to be seen in a purely associative manner. The bull in the crest of LAMBORGHINI, on the other hand, is not a traditional family symbol – instead, it is based upon the personal astrological sign of the founder, Ferrucio Lamborghini.

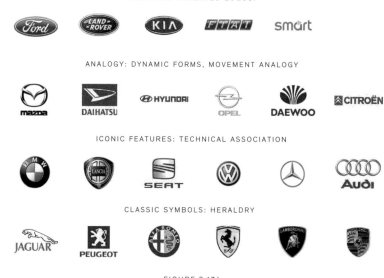

PURE TEXT-ORIENTED LOGOS:

ANALOGY: DYNAMIC FORMS, MOVEMENT ANALOGY

ICONIC FEATURES: TECHNICAL ASSOCIATION

CLASSIC SYMBOLS: HERALDRY

FIGURE 2.101
**Classification of the logos and signets
of auto trademarks.**

278

2.4
UNDERSTANDING
THE MEANING –
SYMBOLS AND
METAPHORS
↓
2.4.4
SYMBOLISM IN
BRAND DESIGN

Whereas heraldic animals support the basic character of an automobile in an associative manner as well, they are particularly suitable as brand symbols. Due to this reason, as a general rule, powerful or dynamic animals, such as horses, bulls, or feline predators are routinely depicted in the respective advertisements. Indeed, the names and the features of such animals are willingly and very purposefully employed with respect to automobile types, for example, Puma and Mustang, among others (fig. 2.102). Therefore, it is quite understandable that the manufacturers of sporty automobiles also value the onomatopoetic imitation of the roaring or bellowing sounds of lions or bulls, a preference which is conspicuously demonstrated by LAMBORGHINI, for example, in the *Autostadt*, the museum and adventure park located in the German automobile-manufacturing city of Wolfsburg. There, the Lamborghini car is presented in a setting like a bull's stable and introduced like a wrestler – its sound plays a major role during the show.

Moreover, adroitly chosen iconic references may also be of assistance in minimizing acceptance problems. In this regard, the first European small diesel tractor with 6 PS, as developed in 1928 by the FENDT company, was purposefully designated by the manufacturer as the *Dieselroß* ("Diesel horse"). With this reference to the conventional manner of working, the farmer was animated and encouraged to finally enter into the world of mechanized agriculture. Indeed, in a literally very graphic fashion, an emblem was mounted on the front of the tractor, near the corporate name, depicting a horse pulling a plow (fig. 2.103).

FIGURE 2.102
Signet of the Ford Mustang, 2005.

2.4
UNDERSTANDING
THE MEANING –
SYMBOLS AND
METAPHORS
↓
2.4.4
SYMBOLISM IN
BRAND DESIGN

279

FIGURE 2.103
Nameplate of the Fendt Dieselroß tractor.

If an established brand symbol is involved, the value of a product, as perceived by the customer, can considerably be enhanced and evenly robustly strengthened. Accordingly, symbols comprise a formidable advertising instrument in appealing to the affections of the customer. Nevertheless, as a rule, a conscious modification of the symbols can be an undertaking of great complexity, given that symbols are anchored in the course of learning processes which can require several years. On the other hand, due to external circumstances, the valuation of symbols can dramatically change within a short period of time. In such a case, strongly positive contents can switch over to the other extreme. This can occur as a result of modified social preferences which the manufacturer is thoroughly incapable of influencing. An example of a symbol which has been increasingly negatively evaluated within the past several decades is the symbol depicting an atom, as represented in figure 2.104. In the sixties, this symbol was revered as the epitome of high technology, as demonstrated on the smokestack of the atomically powered ship *Otto Hahn*. In the meantime, however, the risks of nuclear energy occupy a place in the social and environmental consciousness of the public. Indeed, that was one of the reasons why the ship was decommissioned and ultimately scrapped. Thus, the use of the atom symbol for goods of mass production would not necessarily be advisable.

A comparable principle applies to the silhouette of nuclear power plants. Furthermore, as an additional example, even the simple, functional form of satellite antennas has been seen in an increasingly negative fashion, given that these objects are broadly interpreted as characteristic of socially conflictive neighborhoods. In both of these cases, very elementary, originally value-free basic forms have assumed negative meanings within the course of time, and these new, adverse connotations, owing to the special power of symbolism, can neither be ignored nor avoided any longer.

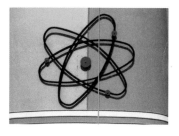

FIGURE 2.104
As a consequence of the modification of sociopolitical values, symbols can experience a drastic alteration of their significance. This also applies to the symbol as illustrated on the smokestack of the atomically powered German vessel Otto Hahn.

280

2.4
UNDERSTANDING
THE MEANING –
SYMBOLS AND
METAPHORS
↓
2.4.4
SYMBOLISM IN
BRAND DESIGN
↓
2.4.5
MUSICAL
SYMBOLISM

2.4.5
MUSICAL SYMBOLISM

In designing acoustic signals of significance, it is important to comprehend the properties of the semantic contents which are to be conveyed in an auditory manner. At this point, therefore, it is advisable to explore the symbolic contents of musical compositions. Musical symbolism is based on the centuries-old tradition practiced in the accompaniment of cultic proceedings and political ceremonies as well as in the realm of concert and theater. A fundamental theory of musical semiotics, for example, was advanced by Eero Tarasti (1994; 2002).

The symbolism of *national anthems* comprises an important political function, which exists within the framework of other symbols supportive of or representing the interests of the state, such as national flags, crests, and uniforms. In this regard, a close connection arises between auditory and visual symbolism, indeed, already as a result of the fact that both of them are simultaneously employed during official events. Occasionally, national symbolism may also be seen in the designing of articles of everyday use, as demonstrated by figure 2.105. The omnipresent use of national symbolism is, in the United States in particular, a typical feature characteristic of the self-conception of the national identity. The anchoring of the symbolism in the emotions of the citizen, in the case of such a hymn for example, is more important than the concrete, textual contents of the anthem itself. In the national anthem of the United States, "The Star-Spangled Banner," the name of the flag appears directly within the text and indeed in the title of the anthem, although the name of the nation itself is not mentioned at all. The text is based upon verses dating back to the nineteenth century, and they provided retrospectively the foundation of a composition and soon assumed national character. Similar to the German national hymn, entitled "Das Deutschlandlied" with verses written in 1841 by August Heinrich Hoffmann von Fallersleben (the musical composition by Joseph Haydn dates back to 1797), the U.S. anthem contains text passages which are no longer used today. In particular, the opening word and the refrain of the first stanza of the German anthem, describing the land in spatial, geopolitical dimensions which no longer represent the current situation, became the symbol of the inhuman, chauvinistic militarism of the National Socialists. In the U.S. anthem, verses expressing defiance towards and the will to combat the British Empire may easily be found, given the fact that the text by the amateur poet Francis Scott Key had been written in 1814, during the War of 1812, as the newly founded United States of America, fighting to maintain their independence from the former motherland, defeated the British in Chesapeake Bay.

2.4
UNDERSTANDING
THE MEANING –
SYMBOLS AND
METAPHORS
↓
2.4.5
MUSICAL
SYMBOLISM

281

FIGURE 2.105
The application of national symbolism in designing a telephone.
The object is a reproduction of an historical telephone in the candlestick style.
The décor (Bicentennial Design) demonstrates consumer
enthusiasm at the time of the 200th anniversary of the United States.
Bell Systems Design Line, 1975.

Generally speaking, national symbolism has the objective of binding the citizens by virtue of a common ideal, thus representing the national identity in and of itself. This characteristic of *uniting* the people is also conspicuously evident in the text of the German hymn: "Unity and justice and freedom ..." [Einigkeit und Recht und Freiheit ...]. Moreover, the U.S. national anthem underwent a most interesting revaluation, owing to the interpretation played by the rock guitarist Jimi Hendrix at the Woodstock Festival in 1969. In a refined manner, Hendrix employed onomatopoetic methods which made clear references to the Vietnam War, thus articulating his sentiments and the public at large in its overwhelming opposition to the war and to the governing administration. In this respect, the American national anthem was modified to serve as a hymn against the actions of the administration. Accordingly, the music *united* the protest movement against the war. The symbolism merely changed its political camp, but not its role offering unity and identification.

CHARPENTIER AND
EUROVISION

An interesting example of the transmission and modification of musical symbolism is the theme music for programs of *Eurovision*. This is an institution of the European Broadcasting Union (EBU) for implementing international media projects, notably with respect to exchanges involving television and radio programs. The EBU network is comprised of some seventy-four television and radio stations in Europe, North Africa, and the Middle East. In 1954, as a jingle for the Eurovision projects was sought, in order to accompany the visual logo as depicted in figure 2.106, it was intended to avoid using compositions which were at least partially protected by copyright laws. As a result, the prelude from *Te Deum* by the French composer Marc-Antoine Charpentier, who had composed it shortly after 1690, was chosen. ● The designated version was played by the Chorale des Jeunesses Musicales des France and the Orchestre de Chambre des Concerts Pasdeloup under the direction of Louis Martini. Due to the catchy nature of this theme music as the "Eurovision hymn," it soon developed into a permanent component of the broadcast and television projects of Eurovision. Today, as a result, the motif is directly associated with the large-scale productions of programs with primarily popular contents, and it is evidently not regarded as contradicting the orientation of the musical contributions made to the *Eurovision Song Contest*, although the songs of the competition are a true contrast.

2.4
UNDERSTANDING
THE MEANING –
SYMBOLS AND
METAPHORS
↓
2.4.5
MUSICAL
SYMBOLISM

FIGURE 2.106
**Logo of Eurovision from the 1950s,
as used by the BBC.**

At the time of its origin, the composition *Te Deum* was naturally created in quite a different context, well before the age of modern mass media. A clear form of symbolism which is purposefully structured is already discernible by virtue of the theme and its instrumentation. More specifically, *Te Deum* is a solemn hymn played during the coronation of kings and emperors. Dotted rhythms in the theme signify the royal gestures which were simultaneously applied in references made to God.

The composition is quite possibly related to the victory of the French army in the Battle of Steinkerque (1692). Indeed, that is likely the reason why the theme of the overture of *Te Deum* begins with a drum roll – and soon involves trumpets resounding in a triumphant manner. Accordingly, the most important instruments of military music merge with one another already within the first measures, thus very plausibly suggesting the pompously orchestrated public appearance of a king. Owing to the combination of the elements *church, king,* and *victory*, the musical symbolism is quite unmistakably defined. In the course of time, nevertheless, this original meaning has made way for the present-day reference to large-scale, iridescent media events. The original prelude consisting of a timpani solo with its martial gestures was not utilized by *Eurovision*. Moreover, even the rhythmic detail comprised by the dotted eighth notes, which makes reference to the king in the French Baroque music, was primarily replaced by straight eight hnotes. Given the heightened pitch of modern orchestras in comparison to the atmosphere of the older version, the current pitch corresponds to D sharp minor instead of D major. Nevertheless, the musical gestures are still understood with respect to their initial ambience as characterized by pompous royal appearances and ceremonial activities. Furthermore, references are also made by the original visual logo of *Eurovision*, which symbolizes the interaction of European broadcasters and is simultaneously reminiscent of floodlights or chandeliers – although this is achieved by a great number of optical symbols which are actually rather atypical with regard to more contemporary standards. The impression harmonizes with the majestically shining character of the sounds of trumpets and string instruments and the *bright* musical key D major, which Charpentier himself described as "happy and very martial" [joyeux et très guerrier], according to Hitchcock (2003). Today, Charpentier's theme is legally protected as a sound mark of the European Broadcasting Union.

2.4
UNDERSTANDING
THE MEANING –
SYMBOLS AND
METAPHORS
↓
2.4.5
MUSICAL
SYMBOLISM

WAGNER
AND THE LEITMOTIF

Supporting the plot of a theatrical piece by virtue of handing over the narrative function to the music itself is an essential element of *Gestalt* in Wagner's musical dramas. Even today, the methodology of supporting the meaning by the allocation of leitmotifs is widely used for cinematic sounds and music as well as for advertisement and audio branding. As *key codes* and *key sounds*, leitmotifs assume a significant function. A specific problem of the introduction of newly composed motifs is the fact that the composer can assume that his or her public possesses the necessary knowledge as to the leitmotifs being employed only in the fewest of cases. Wagner utilized cross-modal analogies and onomatopoetic methods to a quite notable extent in order to consolidate and strengthen the codes pertinent to the plot. In this manner, vividly demonstrated natural motifs serve as the very foundation of the leitmotif-based universe in *Der Ring des Nibelungen* ("The Ring of the Nibelung"). Normally, analogies involving theatrical gestures play a significant role in building motifs in opera music (Dahlhaus 1971). figure 2.107 illustrates the principle of the "loading" of musical motifs of significance in an interaction with onomatopoetic aspects, cross-modal analogies, and the narrative context which is constructed by virtue of the text foundation and the sequence of the theatrical plot.

Figure 2.108 depicts a practical example of the utilization of leitmotifs by Wagner, as they were presented to opera enthusiasts in a textbook (Burghold 1910). In the book, the scenery and the lyrics of the songs are indicated. The outer side of an additional foldout table illustrates the repertory of leitmotifs which are correlated to the text. The motifs are denominated for the purpose of increasing the legibility. In the audio example, the "Gralstrauer" and the "Parsifal Motif" (nos. 11 and 20 in fig. 2.108) can be heard. ● Initially, the leitmotifs significant to the next scenes are presented in the orchestral introduction. During the vocal passages, they support the meaning by resounding at the appropriate point, and they are correlated to the songs as well as to one another. Incidentally, the listing of important motifs and their designations was not initiated by Wagner. Instead, it was later developed to assist music listeners.

Due to the considerable support of the dramatic development by virtue of succinct leitmotifs in Wagner's music, the technique of musical accompaniment as a means of conveying meanings was adopted by sound films and extensively used. In particular, the music in Hollywood films of the 1940s and 1950s is widely based upon this principle (Adorno 1974). Thereby, considerably fewer leitmotifs are utilized as in the case of Wagner – nevertheless, these are just as precisely applied to elements of the story. The function of leitmotifs, however, is not limited to music in the classical sense. Moreover, even the smallest sound fragments can assume and fulfill this function, as long as they make reference to the cinematic context. In this regard, sounds in film serve as more than mere accessories which decorate the plot they also support the story line, the dramaturgy, and the emotional content. The relationship of a sound to the situation being presented can also be ironized or alienated. A noteworthy example is provided by the excellent sound comedy of Jacques Tati in *Les Vacances de Monsieur Hulot* ("Mr. Hulot's Holiday") of 1953. In this work, relatively few isolated sounds are placed into the service of comedy. In this manner, a squeaking swing door contrasted with the involuntarily leisurely atmosphere of the vacation house. Furthermore, on the grounds of the cemetery, the tube of an antiquated automobile tire recently fallen in the bushes and soon covered by leaves is mistaken for a wreath for a burial which had just taken place (!). Not knowing of its true origin, someone hangs the tube on a gravestone, but the tube soon becomes deflated, accompanied by hissing and whistling, thus symbolizing, as a caricature, the pure futility of all of the efforts undertaken to resist the perishable nature of the incident, or at least to beautify it.

In a fashion similar to that utilized in films, auditory elements of commercials can be used to allow additional meaning according to the intended marketing strategy to be effectively conveyed. Generally speaking, the effectiveness of sound logos and jingles as key sounds is based upon the leitmotif technique.

**JINGLES
ARE THE LEITMOTIFS OF A
SOCIETY CHARACTERIZED BY
MEDIA PROCESSES.**

56

284

2.4
UNDERSTANDING
THE MEANING –
SYMBOLS AND
METAPHORS
↓
2.4.5
MUSICAL
SYMBOLISM

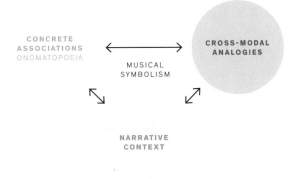

2.4
UNDERSTANDING
THE MEANING –
SYMBOLS AND
METAPHORS
↓
2.4.5
MUSICAL
SYMBOLISM

285

FIGURE 2.107
**The building of musical symbolism with the leitmotif
technique of Richard Wagner.**

FIGURE 2.108
**The leitmotif technique as the link of music and theatrical scenery.
Richard Wagner, Parsifal. Lyrics with denominations of the leitmotifs
and the notations on the foldout table of
Julius Burghold, ca. 1910.**

EXPLORING INDIVIDUAL PERCEPTION – GENUINE SYNESTHESIA

2.5.1
GENUINE SYNESTHESIA

As already indicated in chapter 2.1, the term *synesthesia* paraphrases, in its narrower sense, phenomena which are characterized by the additional appearance of a sensory impression during the stimulation of another sense (Cytowic 2002; 2009, Emrich 2001, Dittmar 2009, Sidler 2006a). Initially, the first studies encompassed all possible forms of cross-modal connection. It was soon clear, however, that there are special phenomena involved in the connections between the sensory modalities, which are prevalent among relatively few people. Today, these phenomena are described as *genuine synesthesiae*.

In this manner, in the case of tone-color synesthesia, which may also be defined as *color hearing*, auditory stimuli can lead to visual perceptions. Figure 2.109 provides some examples of colored visual structures which were initiated by the sounds of the voices of different persons. Such phenomena are individual. However, they demonstrate considerable constancy with regard to the respective persons being examined. This means, in effect, that phenomena of the sort depicted in figure 2.109 can reappear in a practically unchanged manner, if the initiating stimuli should once again return. Current research studies involving connections between the senses concern themselves, in particular, with such phenomena, given that the researchers hope to arrive at essential findings pertaining to the fundamental neuronal processes by virtue of comparisons made to the perception of non-synesthetes. Moreover, progress in the development of imaging processes in brain research – such as in the case of *functional magnetic resonance tomography* (fMRT) – now enables parallel activity between different cerebral areas to be identified and presented (see, among others, Robertson 2005). Additionally, by virtue of deductions made with respect to brain potentials *(electroencephalography,* EEG*),* it is possible to obtain information regarding the chronological sequence of the activation. Indeed, the combination of both methods leads to valuable knowledge regarding the interaction of areas which process the information of different senses. As a result, this facilitates the freeing of synesthetic perception from the aura of speculation. Nevertheless, from the patterns of neuronal activity, it is not

286

2.5
EXPLORING
INDIVIDUAL
PERCEPTION
– GENUINE
SYNESTHESIA
↓
2.5.1
GENUINE
SYNESTHESIA

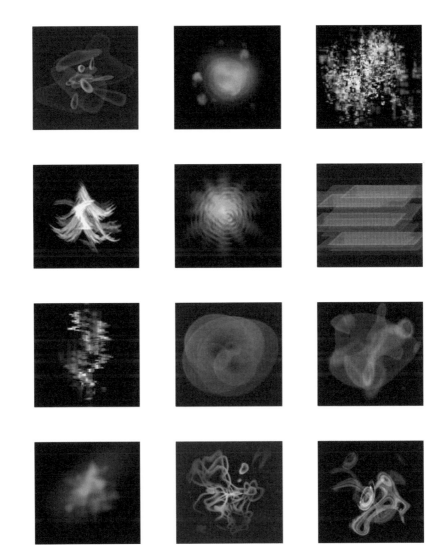

2.5
EXPLORING
INDIVIDUAL
PERCEPTION
– GENUINE
SYNESTHESIA
↓
2.5.1
GENUINE
SYNESTHESIA

287

FIGURE 2.109
Visual synesthetic patterns in the perception
of the synesthete Alexandra Dittmar –
initiated by the sounds of the voices of twelve people.

possible to make conclusions regarding the induced contents in the conscious-ness – this is inhibited by the *qualia problem*, as already discussed in section 1.3.6. Accordingly, research on synesthesia can not afford to forgo descriptions or il-lustrative presentations of subjective phenomena. On the other hand, the tests which are conducted in perceptual psychology allow the reliability of the data to be examined, thus fortifying the credibility of the descriptions.

In light of the intensified research undertaken in recent years, significant findings which would facilitate a greater comprehension of general perceptual processes can also be expected sooner or later. In particular, the relationship of the affecting stimulus to the neuronal activity which it initiates, and to the subjective perceptual quality involved, is an indispensably crucial compo-nent of design approaches that consciously incorporate perceptual processes. Therefore, the phenomenology of genuine synesthesiae shall be explored in detail at this point.

Initially, the genuine – i.e. the natural, inherent – synesthesiae shall be defined by virtue of their characteristic properties.

I

SYNESTHESIAE ARE RARE

Due to the relatively few survey sample sizes, even today the frequency of syn-esthetically predisposed people within the overall population can not be deter-mined with precision. The literature of the last fifteen years indicates an increase of the estimated number of synesthetes with regard to the overall population. The details vary dramatically from 1:100,000 – i.e. that there is one synesthete per 100,000 people (Cytowic 1997, 33) – down to 1:22 (Sagiv 2006). An overview of the estimate may be found in Dittmar (2007). Women comprise the vast ma-jority of subjects with genuine synesthesia. Nevertheless, the percentages of women and men with respect to one another are the subject of intense debate – in this regard, proportions ranging from 2:1 to 6:1 are assumed (Dittmar 2007, 27). It is worth noting, nonetheless, that most of the synesthesia researchers are men, and they themselves in most cases are not synesthetes, whereas the participants in the synesthesia conventions and meetings of synesthetes are primarily women. More often than not, synesthesiae appear within the frame-work of replacement functions, for example, after a person has gone blind (Voss 1930, Harrison 2001, Collignon 2009). This underlines the distinct neuronal plasticity of the brain which enables it to compensate for visual deprivation.

288

2.5
EXPLORING
INDIVIDUAL
PERCEPTION
– GENUINE
SYNESTHESIA
↓
2.5.1
GENUINE
SYNESTHESIA

II

SYNESTHESIAE ARE INTRA-INDIVIDUALLY CONSTANT AND THEREFORE INDEPENDENT OF THE CONTEXT

Genuine synesthesiae exhibit an extreme degree of constancy throughout their entire lifetime. They can only slightly be influenced by the respective percep-tual context, if at all. This also means that the perceptual appearances are sol-idly coupled with certain primary stimuli and inevitably emerge together with these stimuli. The constancy of coupling distinguishes phenomena of *genuine synesthesia* from those caused by iconic connection *(concrete association),* which are significantly influenced by contextual parameters. People with synesthetic perceptions do not have, as a general rule, exceptionally developed talents for learning associations (Gray 2006).

The descriptions of synesthetic phenomena from different epochs exhibit similarities with respect to one another (e.g., compare Bleuler 1881 to Mahling 1927, Cytowic 2002, Emrich 2001, and Dittmar 2007). The constancy of the phenomena was verified already in the early days of synesthetic research: "The secondary sensations are hardly subject to more influence by psychic processes than the primary sensations; moreover, they are unalterable" (Bleuler 1881).

2.5
EXPLORING
INDIVIDUAL
PERCEPTION
– GENUINE
SYNESTHESIA
↓
2.5.1
GENUINE
SYNESTHESIA

289

III
SYNESTHESIAE ARE
INTER-INDIVIDUALLY DIFFERENT

Fundamentally, there are no two synesthetes with exactly the same phenomena. Even if the allocation of similar sensory characteristics may be identified among two different persons, such as tone pitch and colors, the color tones are, nevertheless, different from one another.

IV
SYNESTHESIAE EXIST AS EVENTS OF
PERCEPTION OR IMAGINATION

This is not surprising, if one assumes, consistent with the contemporary state of knowledge (e.g., Damasio 2006), that even conceptual images are based upon activity of the primary areas of the brain, areas which in turn correspond to the activity upon the arrival of stimuli via the sensory organs. Consequently, synesthetic experiences are *either* connected to sensory stimuli *or* exist as memories of sensory stimuli.

V
SYNESTHESIAE ARE ALWAYS SPECIFIC
AS SECONDARY SENSATIONS

Synesthetes know with great precision exactly which secondary sensation is allocated to which modality. Accordingly, it is directly clear, for example, that the primary stimulus is an auditory stimulus, whereas the secondary perception is of a visual nature. This means that synesthesia is not connected to a *mixture* of the senses and can thus not be explained with such an argument. Only those secondary modalities which are also primarily existent can be activated during synesthetic perception. In this regard, people who have gone blind as a result of damage to the eyes, for example, tend to have a higher percentage of visual synesthesiae than people without visual disability, given the fact that they have a developed optical center at their disposal (Voss 1930). Persons who are born blind, however, have neither a primary visual perception nor secondary sensations of a visual nature. Secondary sensations are always just as specific as primary sensations. Therefore, synesthetes often have difficulty describing their secondary sensations in a precisely graphic fashion or in choosing the perceived color tone among the colors represented within a presented scale of colors. Indeed, in such experiments, the respondents often criticize themselves for not being able to find the exactly corresponding color tone, even though they have access to a very large number of colors.

VI

SYNESTHESIAE ALWAYS FUNCTION
ONLY IN ONE DIRECTION

The effect of synesthesiae as directed connections *(unidirectional)* differs considerably from cross-modal analogies or concrete associations, which are, in principle, effective in both directions *(bidirectional)*. As indicated in section 2.2.1, however, even bi-directional connection can show asymmetries, i.e. the preferred connection of an auditory tone with a color can exhibit a diverging preference in the opposite direction. In contrast, phenomena of genuine synesthesia are mostly characterized by a complete lack of connection in the inverse direction. Synesthetes often mention the initiation of visual perceptions by virtue of auditory stimuli. Figure 2.110 illustrates examples of visual form perception by virtue of photographs which were chosen owing to their great similarity to the perception. Even if a person, notably in an unusual case, has additional visual-auditory connections at his or her disposal, the result of the reverse connection is not identical by means of comparison. If a sinusoidal tone of a certain tone pitch leads to the perception of a golden circle, for example, the result of the visual perception of such a circle is, as a general rule, not an audio tone of the same pitch. Instead, it is a completely different sound.

290

2.5
EXPLORING
INDIVIDUAL
PERCEPTION –
GENUINE
SYNESTHESIA
↓
2.5.1
GENUINE
SYNESTHESIA

 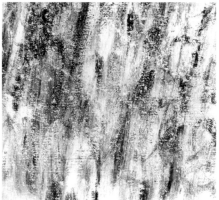

FIGURE 2.110
**The photographs depicted correspond to synesthetic perceptions
of the synesthete Matthias Waldeck. On the left: "clicking sounds";
on the right: "the rubbing of hands."**

SYNESTHESIAE CAN ALSO APPEAR BETWEEN
PROPERTIES OF A MODALITY

This is particularly so in cases involving the visual modality, for example, in the subjective color accompaniment of letters of the alphabet. Parallels in other modalities have not been reported up until now, however, they were also not systematically sought. This would mean, more or less, that the color tone of a musical instrument would change according to the melody being played. Possibly, a special role is played by the visual system, given that colored as well as colorless images are processed. The visual color perception is – in contrast to the perception of tone colors – an optional function, and in its absence, all other properties such as form, size, movement, etc. are perceivable without limitation.

2.5
EXPLORING
INDIVIDUAL
PERCEPTION
– GENUINE
SYNESTHESIA
↓
2.5.1
GENUINE
SYNESTHESIA

———

291

VIII
SYNESTHESIAE CAN ALSO INVOLVE
SEMANTIC REFERENCES

This applies, for example, to number forms, namely to subjective forms of numerical series, months, days, or seasons of the year, as well as to general secondary sensations which are connected to the *meaning* of primary stimuli. In this case, a word which is heard leads to different perceptions, depending upon whether it is comprehended or not. Synesthetic perception which is influenced by meanings is also referred to as *cognitive synesthesia*. In contrary, if the secondary perception is only dependent upon the stimulus itself, this is described as *sensory synesthesiae*.

IX
SYNESTHETIC PERCEPTION OCCURS PARALLEL
TO THE PRIMARY PERCEPTION

Genuine synesthetic phenomena are always of a secondary nature. They supplement the primary perceptions typical of the sensory modalities and do not influence them. In this sense, a subject with auditory-visual synesthesia hears an acoustic event and simultaneously sees the color which is caused by said event. Up until this point, secondary perceptions without a primary proportion have not been described. That means, according to the current state of knowledge, there are no color hearers who are able to visually sense an acoustically initiated perception without being able to hear something during the process.

X
SYNESTHESIAE ARE OFTEN CONNECTED
TO DISTINCTIVE EMOTIONS

This observation led to theses asserting that synesthetic connections generally occur by virtue of the limbic system, the system also involved in the processing of emotions. Richard Cytowic initially advanced this theory (Cytowic 1989), however, he rescinded it somewhat later (Cytowic 2002) – and even Hinderk

Emrich seized on this idea (Emrich 2001). The allocation of certain secondary perceptions to emotional evaluations, however, appears to be inter-individually different, thus explaining why no general rules exist even in this regard. Bleuler already commented: "Unpleasant primary sensations can give rise to pleasant secondary sensations and vice versa" (Bleuler 1881). Nevertheless, a generally recognized finding today is the notion that emotions can serve to initiate synesthetic perceptions among certain people. In this respect, Emrich coined the term *emotional synesthesia*. Parallel to the presence of extreme feelings, the synesthetic appearances can also be of a very distinctive nature. The music painter Walter Behm reports of such a situation, as he learned of the fatal fall of a friend during a hike in the mountains. The shock caused the complete coloring of Behm's entire visual field in a purple tone (Ahlenstiel 1962). The phenomena of the emotional synesthesia appear to be quite incapable of being reproduced, however, and they are accordingly elusive with regard to systematic examinations. This could be based upon the fact that emotions are generally subject to constant modifications (Dittmar 2007, 40). As a consequence, the primary stimulus of this form of synesthesia would not be measurable, thus making it incapable of being precisely determined in the course of experiments, as compared to cases involving physical experiments.

—

It can be assumed that the predisposition for synesthetic perception is hereditary (Harrison 1997). Indeed, evidence of this was documented relatively early in this field of research, e.g., by Bleuler (1881).

Experiments in genuine synesthesia must rely upon the surveying of people. In the present day, the Internet provides ideal opportunities for such undertakings: appropriate web-based surveys are contemporarily conducted by Sean Day (2001; 2005; 2007), the team surrounding David Eagleman (2008; 2009), Hinderk Emrich and his colleagues (2001), and other researchers. Furthermore, the first systematic surveys were already conducted towards the end of the nineteenth century by Eugen Bleuler and Karl Lehmann (Bleuler 1881), Édouard Claparède (Flournoy 1892; 1893), and Gustav Theodor Fechner (1876). Summaries of the early results may already be found in Suarez de Mendoza (1890), later Bleuler (1913), Wellek (1931a), and Mahling (1927).

By virtue of his scientific research, Richard Cytowic succeeded in renewing the discussion regarding synesthesiae towards the end of the twentieth century, after the subject – as a result of the ascent of *behaviorism* in perceptual psychology – had been regarded as scientifically insignificant for more than a half century (Cytowic 1993). He provides five principal characteristics of genuine synesthesiae (Cytowic 2002):

292

2.5
EXPLORING
INDIVIDUAL
PERCEPTION
– GENUINE
SYNESTHESIA
↓
2.5.1
GENUINE
SYNESTHESIA

INVOLUNTARY BUT ELICITED: UNINTENTIONAL (SPONTANEOUS) AND CAUSED BY STIMULI
SPATIALLY EXTENDED: PROJECTED
PERCEPTS ARE CONSISTENT AND DISCRETE: CONTINUAL WITH A MINIMAL INTRA-INDIVIDUAL VARIANCE
MEMORABLE: EASILY REMEMBERED
EMOTIONAL: ACCOMPANIED BY FEELINGS OF VALIDITY

This list is indeed in accord with essential points of the aforementioned definition. The observed projection of synesthetic phenomena is based upon reports
according to which the perceptual events always appeared outside of the head
of the respective synesthete. However, this is not necessarily so in the case of
each synesthete. Moreover, perception always appears as a projection, even if it
involves perceptions within the body itself. Given that perceptions even in the
case of non-synesthetes are often connected to strong emotions – for example,
involving intense colors or listening to music – emotionality can not be, in and
of itself, a characteristic property of genuine synesthesia.

2.5
EXPLORING
INDIVIDUAL
PERCEPTION
– GENUINE
SYNESTHESIA
↓
2.5.1
GENUINE
SYNESTHESIA

293

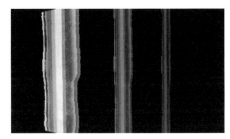

THE CLATTERING OF A DOOR
IN THE WIND

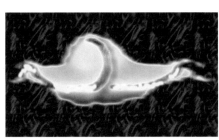

THE SOUND OF A PASSING AUTOMOBILE,
AS PERCEIVED FROM WITHIN A HOUSE.

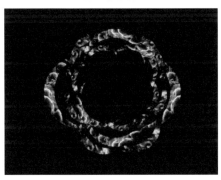

THE SOUND OF AN ELECTRIC LAWNMOWER
DURING IDLE RUNNING.

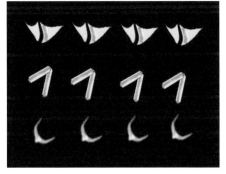

THE TICKING OF THREE DIFFERENT CLOCKS.
FROM TOP TO BOTTOM:
PENDULUM WALL CLOCK,
ELECTROMECHANICAL ALARM CLOCK,
WRISTWATCH.

FIGURE 2.111
Visual synesthesia as initiated by listening to sounds.
Graphic illustrations of the synesthete Eckhard Freuwört, 2007.

Figure 2.111 illustrates visual patterns of a synesthete which he observed while
listening to different types of sounds (see also Freuwört 2004).

Statistics pertaining to the most commonly experienced types of genuine synesthesia were initiated by Sean Day, who also published the results on
the Internet (Day 2007; see also Day 2006). Table 2.10 reflects the status of his
survey in January of 2007. The results are based on the reports provided by 871
persons, all having been surveyed via the Internet.

In the list of the twenty-two most common connections, as presented here,
only phenomena which were mentioned more than 1 percent of all nominations
have been registered. All in all, forty-eight different types of synesthesiae were

mentioned. In the case of a single individual, genuine synesthesia can exhibit different forms of connection between the senses – accordingly, multiple mentioning occurs frequently. The color markings designate the participating sensory channels. As a matter of principle, every perceptual quality of each modality can assume the role of a primary or a secondary perception. However, most occurrences are within the visual and auditory areas:

THE PRIMARY PERCEPTION OF THE 22 MOST COMMON CONNECTIONS EXHIBITS 45 PERCENT VISUAL AND 28 PERCENT AUDITORY STIMULI.

THE SECONDARY, SYNESTHETIC PERCEPTION IS DOMINATED BY THE VISUAL MODALITY BY AS MUCH AS 98 PERCENT.

The connection between hearing and seeing is accordingly very frequent among the connections of different sensory channels and shall thus be handled first.

294

2.5
EXPLORING
INDIVIDUAL
PERCEPTION
– GENUINE
SYNESTHESIA
↓
2.5.1
GENUINE
SYNESTHESIA

ALLOCATION	PRIMARY PERCEPTION	SECONDARY PERCEPTION	PERCENTAGE OF MENTIONING
GRAPHEME → COLOR	VISUAL	VISUAL	64.9%
TIME UNIT → COLOR	SYMBOLIC	VISUAL	23.1%
MUSICAL SOUND → COLOR	AUDITORY	VISUAL	19.5%
GENERIC SOUND → COLOR	AUDITORY	VISUAL	14.9%
PHONEME → COLOR	AUDITORY	VISUAL	9.2%
MUSIC NOTE → COLOR	VISUAL	VISUAL	9.0%
ODOR → COLOR	OLFACTORY	VISUAL	6.8%
TASTE → COLOR	GUSTATORY	VISUAL	6.3%
SOUND → TASTE	AUDITORY	GUSTATORY	6.1%
PAIN → COLOR	SOMATIC	VISUAL	5.5%
PERSONALITY → COLOR (AURA)	VISUAL	VISUAL	5.4%
TOUCHING → COLOR	TACTILE	VISUAL	4.0%
SOUND → TOUCH	AUDITORY	TACTILE	3,9%
VISION → TASTE	VISUAL	GUSTATORY	2,8%
VISION → SOUND	VISUAL	AUDITORY	2.6%
TEMPERATURE → COLOR	SOMATIC	VISUAL	2.5%
ORGASM → COLOR	SOMATIC	VISUAL	2.1%
EMOTION → COLOR	SOMATIC	VISUAL	1.6%
SOUND → SMELL	AUDITORY	OLFACTORY	1.6%
VISION → TOUCH	VISUAL	TACTILE	1.5%
TOUCHING → TASTE	TACTILE	GUSTATORY	1.1%
VISION → SMELL	VISUAL	OLFACTORY	1.1%

TABLE 2.10
Statistics of the most commonly reported types of genuine synesthesia.
Results of an Internet survey of 871 synesthetes (Day 2007).

HEARING COLORS – SEEING ACOUSTIC TONES

The hearing of colors is one of the forms of "involuntary parallel sensations," which were often mentioned in the literature prior to 1980. Thereby, it is understood as being the sensation of colors as experienced during the hearing of acoustic tones and sounds. It involves *subjective color-sound relationships.* Corresponding to the aforementioned characteristics, these phenomena appear involuntarily among synesthetes. Every one of those persons exhibits an individual scheme of allocation which remains constant and independent of the context of the perception throughout his or her entire life. In French, this phenomenon is described as *audition colorée,* in English as *color hearing.* In this regard, Anschütz recommended using the term *analytic synopsis* [Analytische Synopsie] (Anschütz 1927c, see also Haverkamp 2006c). Since Bleuler and Lehmann, the visual appearances have been referred to as photism (Bleuler 1881).

In addition to the synesthetes, in the narrow sense of the word, most people are capable of spontaneously allocating colors to an auditory event by virtue of analogy relationships corresponding to those discussed in chapter 2.2. However, this connection is not absolute. Instead, it experiences modifications depending upon the perceptual situation, namely the context. Moreover, in functioning as a *Tertium Comparationis,* literally the third part of the comparison, it normally avails itself of further visual benchmarks, such as brightness or saturation. In order to establish a verbal distinction of both phenomena, Klaus-Ernst Behne speaks of *synesthesia sensu Cytowic* in contrast to the *cross-modal analogy* (Behne 1992 and 2002). In the meantime, nevertheless, the term *genuine synesthesia,* as applied here, is widely used.

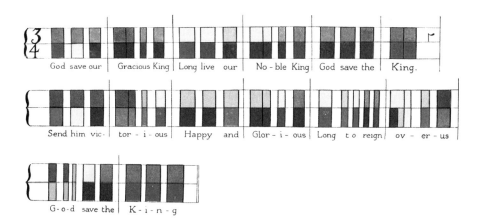

FIGURE 2.112
One of the earliest color illustrations of the synesthetic allocation of color tones to music (Lind 1994).

Figure 2.112 depicts one of the oldest examples of presenting auditory perception in color, as illustrated by the architect E. G. Lind. In this regard, Lind used color pairs. However, it is not known if the color pairs solely correspond to the tone pitches in a movement with two voices, or if the acoustic tones of the vocal portion exert an influence upon the color tone. A similar presentation, although with individual color tones, is provided by Lind with respect to the speech of a lawyer: "Brilliant ending of lawyer Spoke Stith's address to the jury" (Lind 1894). Even though Lind sought to develop systematic allocations between tone pitch and color hue, his visualizations exhibit a considerable degree of individuality, as is typical of genuine synesthesia.

The absolute connection of color perceptions with a certain tone or sound attribute, in the case of a color hearer, is comparable to the capabilities of perceiving a perfect pitch in the absolute allocation of a *tone pitch* to the perceived tone frequencies. As previously discussed in chapter 2.2, the *tone pitch* can be regarded as a visual-spatial attribute within the framework of cross-modal analogies. As in the case of hearing colors, the connection in the case of the perfect pitch is also absolute, independent of the context and remains existent through the lifetime of the person affected.

2.5
EXPLORING
INDIVIDUAL
PERCEPTION
– GENUINE
SYNESTHESIA
↓
2.5.2
HEARING
COLORS –
SEEING
ACOUSTIC
TONES

FIGURE 2.113
Visual perception in hearing birdcalls, according to the descriptions
of the blind musician Paul Dörken (Anschütz 1936).

Every synesthete exhibits his or her own personal scheme of allocating primary and secondary sensations, and this scheme does not only make reference to different colors, it also relates to other partial aspects of the perception. As a result, color perceptions arise among some persons as a consequence of certain tone pitches and among others due to certain timbres, intervals, temporal structures, or other auditory attributes. Even birdcalls are capable of creating the initiating stimuli (fig. 2.113). Anschütz examined the color allocation to musical pitches in the case of the blind musician Paul Dörken, who also had absolute pitch (Anschütz 1927b):

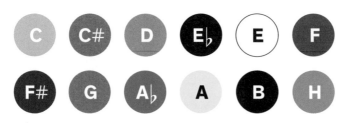

The complete absence of systematic concepts is actually characteristic of genuine synesthetic color scales. Most typically, this distinguishes them from scales which refer to mathematical/physical connections (chapter 2.6). As demonstrated by many illustrations within this book, a distinct perception of forms can arise in the case of acoustically induced color perceptions. These *photisms* can appear as stationary or non-stationary two-dimensional or three-dimensional objects. Even in this case, there is a permanent though highly complex relationship between the stimulus parameters and the secondary perception. Some of these cases are already rather extensively documented in the color-tone research literature, often with pictures which were created by the respondents themselves, and then critically reviewed (Anschütz 1927 a–d; 1928; 1929; 1930; 1931; 1936 a, b). The forms of purely genuine synesthetic perceptions are fundamentally abstract and exhibit no characteristics of iconic connection. Nevertheless, there are mixed forms in which the influences of cross-modal analogies are considerable.

2.5
EXPLORING
INDIVIDUAL
PERCEPTION
– GENUINE
SYNESTHESIA
↓
2.5.2
HEARING
COLORS –
SEEING
ACOUSTIC
TONES

297

FIGURE 2.114
Synesthetic form perception, stimulated by sound,
according to pictures of Hugo Meier-Thur (Anschütz 1927c; d).
Above: "roughly resounding automobile horn";
below: "small motorcycle."

Figure 2.114 exhibits monochromatic visual appearances which were caused, respectively, by an automobile horn and the rattling of a motorcycle. Further examples of form perceptions which were initiated by technical equipment are quintessentially illustrated in figure 2.115. The subdued colors in the picture on the left-hand side are traced by the painter Heinrich Hein back to the minimal loudness of the motor vehicle at a distance of approximately one hundred meters. The gray-green blots correlate with the rattling of the motor, whereas the stripes rising from below, on the left-hand side, correspond to the rolling sound. The picture of the motor sound of a fishing boat, according to Hein's information, can be traced back to a four-cycle engine with a loud, banging ignition, whereas the "bangs" break away as light brown shreds from an otherwise closed mass. The color of this mass is regarded as being precisely suitable for the tone color of the motor's sound; the strong brightness of the background corresponds to the great acoustic volume. This is the typical visualization of a bang, which may analogously be found in figure 2.4 (chapter 2.1). In a very detailed fashion, the image on the right-hand side corresponds to the impulse sounds of a mechanical alarm clock, as Hein describes with great precision (Hein 1927, 156–57). Thereby, in the course of time, the perceptual image shifts downward, while each eye-like figure develops from the right to the left. The figure arises through the impact of the balance, whereas the red, heart-shaped figure to the right of it corresponds to the respective impact of the crown-wheel. Moreover, the three synesthetic appearances as described exhibit no movement. Even these are examples of experiments in which acoustic stimuli were verbally described – recordings of sounds used in those early experiments, however, do not exist. Furthermore, it must be recognized that these sounds, due to reasons of technological development, are comparable to those of today only in a quite limited fashion.

 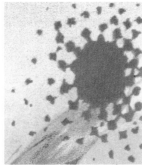 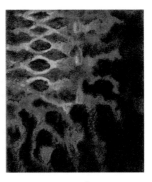

FIGURE 2.115
Synesthetic form of perception, stimulated by sound, according
to pictures by Heinrich Hein (1927). Left: the sound of a "quietly moving" car;
middle: engine sound of a fishing boat; right: sounds of an alarm clock.

The graphic illustrations of figure 2.116 also emphasize, by virtue of the images initiated by music, the concept which Anschütz defined as *complex synopsis* (Komplexe Synopsie): the perception of visual structures with forms, colors, and movement, as they were described and sketched by the synesthete and painter Max Gehlsen (Anschütz 1927c; see also Haverkamp 2006c).

298

2.5
EXPLORING
INDIVIDUAL
PERCEPTION –
GENUINE
SYNESTHESIA
↓
2.5.2
HEARING
COLORS –
SEEING
ACOUSTIC
TONES

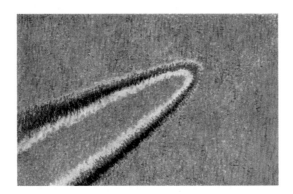

FIGURE 2.116-1
From the musical drama Tristan and Isolde by Richard Wagner.
Visual perception arising while listening to music,
drawing by Max Gehlsen, 1927.

The figure is perceived as the listener hears the musical drama *Tristan and Isolde* by Richard Wagner, and it is correlated to the "day motif" which appears at the beginning of the second act. It should be taken into account that in this opera the day is regarded as a metaphor for the practical constraints on life imposed by reason – in contrast to the night as a domain of emotional freedom and self-determination. Accordingly, the orchestra plays the day motif in a relatively loud manner and with bright acoustic tones. The melody line is reminiscent of a flashing bolt of lightning. This evidently leads to the perception of a blue ribbon with a bright, luminous background, a motif which thus resembles a *phosphene* (see below and chapter 3.3).

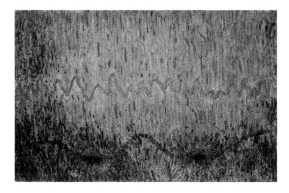

FIGURE 2.116-2
Music from a musical box, the Indian Intermezzo "Aisha" by John Lindsay.
Visual perception arising while listening to music,
drawing by Max Gehlsen, 1927.

2.5
EXPLORING
INDIVIDUAL
PERCEPTION
– GENUINE
SYNESTHESIA
↓
2.5.2
HEARING
COLORS –
SEEING
ACOUSTIC
TONES

299

This image is described as the perception arising while listening to the intermezzo from "Aisha" by Sullivan, as played by a "large, polyphonic musical box." However, the information pertaining to the composer is obviously false. More likely, it involves the *Indian Intermezzo* – "Aisha" by the composer John Lindsay, a piece which was also available on a cylinder for the Edison Amberola 50 phonograph. The bass line appears as a continuous band in the lower portion of the visualization. The bright red line in the middle consists of small beads and moves through the visual field from the right. The beads correspond to the melody arising from the tones of the musical box.

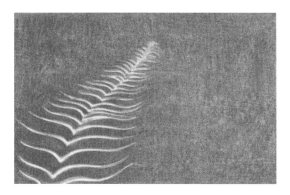

FIGURE 2.116-3
"The Call of the Valkyries" from the musical drama Die Walküre
(The Valkyrie) by Richard Wagner.
Visual perception arising while listening to music,
drawing by Max Gehlsen, 1927.

This image represents the visual perception arising when hearing the beginning of the third act of the musical drama *Die Walküre* (The Valkyrie) by Richard Wagner, as the female singers interpret the "Call of the Valkyries" [Walkürenruf] Initially, the progression of the tone pitch of the motif leads to one of the curved forms. In the course of the music, this figure is multiplied. Although the presentation leaves a perspective-oriented impression, the visual appearance is described, nonetheless, as two-dimensional. Thereby, it is clear that not every visual-synesthetic appearance is perceived as being three-dimensional – indeed, even movement is not always being demonstrated.

FIGURE 2.116-4
From the overture to the opera Der Freischütz
(The Marksman) by Carl-Maria von Weber.
Visual perception arising while listening to music,
drawing by Max Gehlsen, 1927.

300

2.5
EXPLORING
INDIVIDUAL
PERCEPTION
– GENUINE
SYNESTHESIA
↓
2.5.2
HEARING
COLORS
– SEEING
ACOUSTIC
TONES

This image arises as the listener is hearing a passage from the overture to the opera *Der Freischütz* (The Marksman) by Carl-Maria von Weber. The appearance commences with the use of the musical key C minor, and the orange figures start moving into the center of the picture from the right-hand side. At this point in time, the double bow appears above and below these figures – thereby, it corresponds to the overall impression of the passage and emphasizes the developing suspense.

There are often reports mentioning the existence of permanent connections between certain attributes of the photisms and specific attributes of the initiating acoustic stimuli. In this respect, for example, August Petersen describes the permanent connection of the perception of bright, fan-shaped images with the hearing of music from stringed instruments (Petersen 1931). Even this example demonstrates that synesthetic perception is often closely related to neuronal processes of pattern recognition.

The forms described by synesthetes exhibit great similarities with respect to those forms which are perceived in a half-sleep state directly before or after sleeping. In this regard, one speaks of a *hypnagogic* or a *hypnopompic condition*. These appearances were first described by the physiologist Johannes Müller (1826; see also Ebbecke 1951, Czycholl 2003). Moreover, there are also similarities with regard to perceptions during drug-induced hallucinations and subsequent to pathological alterations within the brain (Cytowic 2002, Siegel 1992).

The synesthetic form perceptions provide information relevant to the fundamental forms of perception implemented in the visual system, which are necessary in the construction of complex, visual images. However, they generally do not enter in the consciousness themselves. In those cases in which these basic forms are perceived as luminous structures, they are referred to as *phosphenes*. Eichmeier and Höfer have determined the frequency of these *endogenous image patterns* in the case of electric stimulation of the visual nerve and have also demonstrated their parallelisms with the existence of elementary ornaments of Stone Age ceramics as well as in the drawings of children (Eichmeier 1974, see chapter 3.3).

Although these cases involve isolated incidents as examined within the framework of genuine synesthesia, the perceptual phenomena as described are of great significance and comprise a notable contribution towards understanding the connection of the auditory modality with the visual sensory channel, in particular. Accordingly, these phenomena are essential to the designing of the form which accommodates the acoustic properties of an object.

Relatively early, the literature contemplated and even accepted, in principal, the possibility of an auditory perception which can be visually stimulated. Initially, however, there were only relatively few descriptions of this form of synesthesia. More recently, however, there has been a considerable rise in such reports, as the interview in the film *Synaesthesia* by Jörg Adolph and Stefan Landorf indicates (Adolph 1997). Colored light, for example, evokes tones of different frequencies or timbres; while reading, sound sequences appear. These phenomena are also described as *phonisms*.

2.5
EXPLORING
INDIVIDUAL
PERCEPTION
– GENUINE
SYNESTHESIA
↓
2.5.2
HEARING
COLORS –
SEEING
ACOUSTIC
TONES

301

2.5.3
SMELL, TASTE, AND EVERYTHING ELSE

As table 2.10 indicates, even the senses of smell and taste can sometimes serve as initiators of visual synesthesiae. In this regard, 13.1 percent of the synesthetes in the survey reported visual phenomena as a consequence of such stimuli. In addition to the known, direct transmission of the stimuli to associative regions of the brain, these research results are also evidence of the fact that both senses are connected to the primary fields of vision. Furthermore, it is known that a generally close connection exists between the sensory areas for smell and taste, which leads to a mutually fortifying influence. Accordingly, the sense of smell also plays a great role in the tasting of meals, without it being perceived as existing separately from the sense of taste. Some authors, such as Zietz (1962), deduce that a distinctive, generally prevalent synesthetic connection exists. However, thus far, this has not been systematically investigated on a large scale – possibly due to the fact that this is thoroughly self-evident in daily life. Consequently, this connection does not appear in table 2.10 as a variant form of synesthesia.

COLOR-TONE RESEARCH IN GERMANY DURING THE 1920S AND 1930S

→ EXCURSUS: "FARBE-TON FORSCHUNG"

Between 1925 and 1936, Georg Anschütz initiated various activities in synesthetic research with Hamburg University as the focal point. The efforts resulted in four congresses on *color-tone research* in the years 1927, 1930, 1933, and 1936. Numerous documents in this regard may be found in three volumes with the title *Farbe-Ton Forschungen 1–3* and in various publications. These publications provided the first comprehensive compilation of color visualizations of synesthetic phenomena (Anschütz 1927b; 1927c; 193; 1936a, Hein 1927). Furthermore, an accompanying exhibition to the first congress encompassed approximately 2,000 images and documents – this scope was even exceeded by the second congress (Anschütz 1931, page 407).

The first two congresses were extensively documented (Grundner 1930, Anschütz 1931). Figure 2.117 shows the poster announcing the second convention. In addition to achieving the all-embracing description and analysis of synesthetic phenomena, efforts were undertaken to effectively consolidate psychological research (Anschütz 1927–1936b), musical psychology (Wellek 1931b; c; e), education (among others Rainer 1925, Voss 1930) and multi-media art (e.g., Pešánek 1931) with one another.

Within the framework of the color-tone research, detailed studies of bibliographical sources were examined and hundreds of publications were evaluated (Mahling 1927, Argelander 1927, Wellek 1931a). The social upheavals and presumably the pressure exerted by the national socialistic regime as well, however, led to a retreat from the thematic focus of genuine synesthesia. Instead, common topics and applications moved increasingly to the forefront, in particular, the development of sound movies. Consequently, less specific connections via analogies, associations, and symbolism played an ever-increasing role. Significantly, the subjects of the third

congress in 1933 were: "Sound Movies, New Stages, New Music" as well as "Peak Performances of German and Foreign Film: Film as the Art of our Times." Accordingly, the color-tone research experienced the fate shared by many artists who had been actively involved in synesthetics in the 1920s, but, for various reasons, ultimately were forced to work in the realm of commercial movies. As a result, the color light musicians Alexander László and Adrian Klein, who later changed his name to Adrian Cornwell-Clyne, were very successful in the United States – László as a film composer and Klein as a specialist in color film technology. With the second volume of the color-tone research studies (Anschütz 1936a) and the fourth not completely documented congress, the research was concluded. A summary of the types of synesthetic phenomena documented up until that point may be found in Anschütz (1936b).

At the beginning of the 1930s, the color-tone research had already achieved a scientific level which was not exceeded until new methods of brain research were employed towards the end of the twentieth century. The publications authored by Anschütz contain very detailed descriptions and analyses of visual synesthetic phenomena, including precise information about the acoustic recording used in the experiment and an exact reference to the number of musical measures. In acknowledging this contribution, it should be noted that such extensively documented presentations are quite rare indeed, even in the context of contemporary scientific literature.

302

COLOR-TONE
RESEARCH IN
GERMANY
DURING THE
1920S AND
1930S
↓
EXCURSUS:
"FARBE-TON
FORSCHUNG"

COLOR-TONE
RESEARCH
IN GERMANY
DURING
THE 1920S
AND 1930S
↓
EXCURSUS:
"FARBE-TON
FORSCHUNG"

———————

303

FIGURE 2.117:
Poster of the second congress for color-tone research
in Hamburg, 1930, designed by Rudolph Gahlbeck. Museum für Kunst
und Gewerbe (Museum for Art and Design) Hamburg.

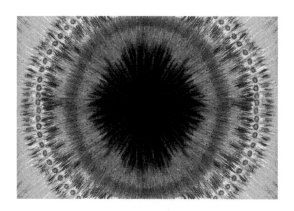

FIGURE 2.118
Multiple synesthesiae: the smell of heliotrope blossoms gives rise
to the visual image as depicted by Eduard Reimpell.
Reconstructed by mirroring of the original illustration which
shows only a quarter of the circle (Anschütz 1929).

Secondary perceptions as the result of genuine synesthesia can build stimuli of their own which couple to further modalities. That gives rise to *multiple synesthesiae*. Figure 2.118 depicts a visual object which arose upon smelling the scent of a flower and was subsequently documented graphically. A ring of light points encompasses the object externally and stimulates, furthermore, auditory sensations. The sound which arose in the perception as a result of this chain of stimuli was described as a "mixture of rain and music sounds" (Anschütz 1929).

304

2.5
EXPLORING
INDIVIDUAL
PERCEPTION –
GENUINE
SYNESTHESIA
↓
2.5.3
SMELL,
TASTE, AND
EVERYTHING
ELSE

FIGURE 2.119
Pain synesthesia: the work of schoolchildren
in the art class of Walter Behm, 1920s (Anschütz 1931).
Left: "slap in the face";
right: "bite on the tongue."

More often than not, tactile stimuli, temperature, and pain similarly lead to visual phenomena. In situations in which they contain colors as well as concrete forms, these forms often resemble those perceived in the case of impulsive, loud, and unpleasant sounds. Figure 2.119 shows the work of schoolchildren in response to suddenly appearing pain sensations, such as a bite on the tongue or a slap in the face.

SUBJECTIVE
COLOR-FORM
RELATIONS

2.5
EXPLORING
INDIVIDUAL
PERCEPTION
– GENUINE
SYNESTHESIA
↓
2.5.4
SUBJECTIVE
COLOR-FORM
RELATIONS

305

There are often reports of people seeing letters of the alphabet in color, even if they appear in black and white. This phenomenon is officially referred to as *chromatic-graphemic synesthesia* – or is simply called *word-color synesthesia*. To-day, it is regarded as the most frequent kind of synesthesia – illustrated in table 2.10 with 64.9 percent of the responses (compare Emrich 2001). Figure 2.120 illustrates some examples.

Even the perception of colors following spoken words, particularly vowels, is common among color hearers. Time and again, there are reports indicating that the genuine synesthetic seeing of single characters in color furthermore leads to color perceptions in the cognitive processing of words and numbers and indeed also entire texts. Such phenomena are even observed without there hav-ing been an acoustic stimulus. Table 2.11 depicts an early example that matches today's studies with respect to the phenomena observed, thus demonstrating that genuine synesthesia is independent of the context of a particular era.

TABLE 2.11
Vowel photisms as reported by three sisters
according to the Swedish alphabet, by Klinckowström, 1891,
cited by Mahling (1927).

The classical definition of synesthesia as the connection between *different* senses is not satisfied in the case of chromatic-graphemic synesthesia, given that the allocation of the visual features form and color occurs within a single modality. A classification as a phenomenon connatural to genuine synesthesia is meaningful, however, in light of the fact that the connection exhibits gen-erally similar characteristics. Most color hearers also mention, in addition to photisms generated by auditory stimuli, the perception of colored numbers and letters. In older literature, the perception of colored figures is thus pre-dominantly traced back to the sound of spoken language. Even the connection of visual appearances with phonemes (sounds) is not a seldom occurrence among synesthetes (see table 2.10). More recent research studies demonstrate, however, that the visual appearance of the figure serves as a direct stimulus in the majority of the cases (e.g., Day 2006). The permanent connection of colors with respect to numbers and letters is an indication of the close relationship of synesthetic appearances with processes of the recognition of patterns. In this regard, it is apparent that neuronal processes are involved which are similar to those involved in the connection of different modalities. Presentations of the spatial distribution of brain activity have shown that the different properties of visual perception – color, form, movement – can be processed in separate, not necessarily neighboring areas (Zeki 1993).

With a view on the design of text, it can be concluded that an arbitrary assignment of colors to letters of the alphabet is generally problematic. This applies, in particular, in situations involving frequently changing allocations, such as in the case of cell phone displays. It is likely that even the decision of the customer with regard to a certain product is already influenced by elementary connections similar to genuine synesthesiae, although they proceed – in contrast – unconsciously.

306

2.5
EXPLORING
INDIVIDUAL
PERCEPTION –
GENUINE
SYNESTHESIA
↓
2.5.4
SUBJECTIVE
COLOR-FORM
RELATIONS

FIGURE 2.120
Chromatic-graphemic synesthesia.
Top: color perception of Braille (script for the blind)
according to reports by four persons who had lost
their eyesight (Voss 1930).
Bottom: color perception of letters and numbers
as reported by three test subjects (2003).

MOVEMENT OF SYNESTHETIC IMAGES

2.5
EXPLORING
INDIVIDUAL
PERCEPTION
– GENUINE
SYNESTHESIA
↓
2.5.5
MOVEMENT
OF SYNESTHETIC
IMAGES

307

People exhibiting a predisposition to visual synesthesiae also often report the perception of moving images caused by the stimuli of other sensory channels. In this manner, the visual secondary perception can include bubbles which are slowly sinking (Anschütz 1927, 105), balls which roll across the "inner monitor" (Ruth 1898), "rotating, swirling sparks" (Anschütz 1927, 106), or any other phenomenon of movement.

In describing the visual appearances he experienced while listening to Richard Wagner's *Feuerzauber* (Magic Fire Music), during the third act of *Die Walküre* (The Valkyrie), the painter Max Gehlsen notes: "With the words 'Whosoever fears the tip of my spear …' (…) a spiraling figure develops (…) which fills out the entire visual field. The figure is constantly moving, as if it were continually developing anew from the core. (…) In the twirling, countless sparks are spraying, as if it involved a grindstone." (Anschütz 1927c, 106)

A quarter of a century earlier, Christoph Ruths had also mentioned his visual perception of sparks and fire when listening to the same musical piece: "As the magic fire begins and the triangle resounds, the gleaming sparks and the red-hot flames lunge forth from the rocks in a phantom-like manner." (Ruths 1898, 51) With respect to this composition, Gehlsen also noted a field of violet wedges moving upward and of sinking bubbles (compare fig. 3.34). The bubbles exhibited differing speeds and these appeared to be correlated to overlaying musical structures. In the case of the bubbles, he observed a relationship between the visual forms and the tones of the harps (Anschütz 1927c, 106).

FIGURE 2.121
Temporal alteration of a synesthetic image, stimulated by
listening to the German folk song: "Es steht
ein Baum im Odenwald …"(There Stands a Tree in the Odenwald).
Illustration by Heinrich Hein (1927).

Often, continual alterations to stationary images are also experienced. Figure 2.121 documents efforts to emphasize this change by virtue of a series of paintings. The images arise while listening to a German folk song of the 1930s. Heinrich Hein, the painter who illustrated this series, noted that the entire duration of the changing perceptual images amounted to approximately seventeen seconds: "Given that even the slightest alteration of the rhythm, tone pitch, and emphasis modifies the character of the piece, a completely constant picture can not be expected if the instantaneous expression of the piece is truly reflected." (Anschütz 1927c, 171)

Today, interactive tools are available which are capable of presenting moving synesthetic images as computer animations in a considerably improved manner; for example, as proved by Markus Dermietzel with his *Synaesthetic Sound Synthesis* project for elementary tones (Dermietzel 2003).

Similarly, Matthias Waldeck discusses the relation between perceived musical movement and the movement of synesthetic perceptual images: if the music is accelerated, this could lead to a rotation of visual appearances (Behne 2002, 37).

The composer José López Montes makes direct reference to the relationship between music and the sensation of movement: "In music, I have a dynamic synesthesia. The relations between music and movement appear to be automatic to me ..." (Sidler 2006a, 100)

Natalia Sidler describes her visual perception while listening to the piano piece "Oiseaux tristes", the second part of Maurice Ravel's *Miroirs:* "Small, amoeba-like forms, moving with various degrees of vitality, build an interwoven, inscrutable mesh, supplemented by silver gleaming droplets in differing tones of green and blue, which wobble and leap across a surface resembling toad skin. The entire image continually rotates along its own axis, considerably more slowly than the music." (Sidler 2006a, 102–3)

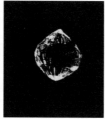

308

2.5
EXPLORING
INDIVIDUAL
PERCEPTION –
GENUINE
SYNESTHESIA
↓
2.5.5
MOVEMENT OF
SYNESTHETIC
IMAGES

FIGURE 2.122
Visual pattern, as stimulated by the vertical movement
of the right arm in the darkness. The results of self-experimentation
by Georg Schliebe (1932).

In some cases, a relation exists between the stimulated visual appearances and movements of the body. Within the course of self-experimentation involving movements of the upper extremities in complete darkness, the Gestalt psychologist Georg Schliebe observed bright traces caused by changes in the position of his hands (Schliebe 1932). The form of the traces was influenced by the span of the movement, as figure 2.122 demonstrably indicates. The movement of hands and arms left behind these traces, indeed, in a manner resembling the line left behind by chalk moved along a chalkboard. Additionally, Schliebe mentioned a strong emotional involvement felt during the experiment.

In this case, the visual patterns corresponded likewise to the perception of movement and emotion. The distinctive interaction of perceptual movement in the auditory and visual areas, on the one hand, and the genuine synesthetic experience, on the other, is also demonstrated by rare cases in which the seeing of movement causes the perception of sound. Among others, the photographer Marcia Smilack reports: "I do not hear sound if I look at static colors or shapes, it is the movement that elicits the response. On the other hand, I do hear the sounds when I look at my images after I take them and they are no longer the actual experience (...); I suspect that is because my images capture movement and re-elicit the feeling of the movement when I see the pictures" (Smilack in correspondence with the author in 2006).

2.5
EXPLORING
INDIVIDUAL
PERCEPTION
– GENUINE
SYNESTHESIA
↓
2.5.5
MOVEMENT
OF SYNESTHETIC
IMAGES

309

FIGURE 2.123
The movement of water as well as the distortion
of mirror images it causes can lead to the perception of auditory events.
Adagio, photo by Marcia Smilack, 2004.

Figure 2.123 shows an example of reflections along the water surface as the stimulus of auditory synesthesia. Thereby, the photographer describes the very seldom occurring case of bi-directional synesthesia: "One night, as I was sorting through my Venice photographs with Ravel playing in the background, I suddenly noticed that the image I was looking at *sounded*, at that moment, exactly like the music *looked*" (Smilack 2008).

2.5.6
VISUALIZATION
OF MEANING

Frequently, it is reported that series of numbers such as dates or the time of day form groups and appear in color before the "inner eye." The color seeing of temporal units thus appears in the second position in Table 2.10. *Number forms* were already described towards the end of the nineteenth century, among others by Galton (1883), Flournoy (1893), and Lemaitre (1901). Number forms are of a two- or three-dimensional nature and often additionally exhibit color or texture. Similarly, sequences of words which are related to one another can appear to form groups and create further visual characteristics. Figure 2.124 provides an example of the systematization experiments conducted by Théodore Flournoy.

Figure 2.125 illustrates the ring-shaped representation of the months of the year and of the days of the week with additional color perceptions (Duffy 2001). The ring shape corresponds to the cyclical returning of the terms. In explaining these perceptual phenomena, the assumption of connections between the primary sensory areas is not sufficient, given that not the form, but the *meaning* of the numbers and letters is of decisive importance to the visualization. Thus, such semantic forms constantly exhibit a sequence of numbers and terms corresponding to their meaning. However, this can also involve a subjective meaning, for example, if the year of one's own birth protrudes from the row of preceding years. In contrast to sensorial synesthesia, the appearances described here are defined as *cognitive synesthesia*, given that higher centers of neuronal processing react with respect to primary areas, in this case the visual cortex. Thereby, synesthetic perceptions are coupled with processes of deciphering meaning (see also Posner 2002). Among many people hearing spoken language, the script simultaneously appears as a visual phenomenon. This involuntary visualization can be regarded either as a form of genuine synesthesia or as a form of iconic connection.

Furthermore, the visualization of the *aura*, as discussed in esotericism, can be assigned to synesthesiae. Auras are colored, luminous appearances which seem to, in the perception of some subjects, surround other people. Synesthetically analyzed, these involve color perceptions derived from the form of the silhouette of the person being viewed. Often, however, the personality and the charisma of the person, and the sympathy or antipathy towards the subject being perceived, play a certain role in the peculiarity of auras. Accordingly, this phenomenon corresponds either to a cognitive or an emotional synesthesia.

310

2.5
EXPLORING
INDIVIDUAL
PERCEPTION –
GENUINE
SYNESTHESIA
↓
2.5.6
VISUALIZATION
OF MEANING

2.5
EXPLORING
INDIVIDUAL
PERCEPTION
– GENUINE
SYNESTHESIA
↓
2.5.6
VISUALIZATION
OF MEANING

311

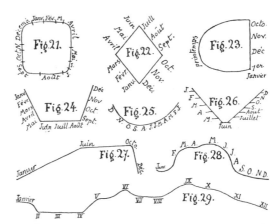

FIGURE 2.124
Examples of diagrams of a year illustrated by
different test subjects (Flournoy 1893).

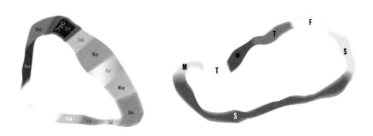

FIGURE 2.125
Perceived forms of temporal units. Illustrated by Carol Steen.
Left: the months of the year according
to the synesthete Patricia Duffy.
Right: the days of the week according to the
synesthete Michael Torke.

WHY SYNESTHESIA? FUNCTION AND SIGNIFICANCE

In contrast to the connection of sensory modalities via analogies, iconic features, and meanings, the purpose of synesthetic connections is not directly clear. In this regard, three theses are specifically discussed:

1. Elementary connections between the senses are existent among the majority of people, although such connections do not sink into the consciousness. In this respect, synesthesiae would serve as the expression of generally available processes. The capability of synesthetic perception would limit itself to an expanded consciousness for internal processes or to sensing subjective appearances with exceptional plasticity and authenticity.

2. Synesthetic perception is a "new sense" which permits the connections of sensory information and sensations beyond the traditional borders and thus enriches the perception (van Campen 2008). In this respect, synesthesia is occasionally interpreted as an indication of the higher development of brain functions (Freuwört 2003). Nevertheless, it must be noted that the higher development of neuronal functions in general tends to reflect an increase in the flexibility and thus a retreat from permanent connections, such as genuine synesthesia. Moreover, this is also indicated by the evolutionary development of living beings. Animals tend to be more specialized than persons: fish swim better, birds fly better, and land animals run faster than humans. Owing to the higher development of the human brain, however, people can help themselves with great flexibility, e.g., learning to swim and learning to build and operate airplanes and automobiles.

3. Synesthetic phenomena may also be understood as the results of the construction of perceptual hypotheses to compensate for sketchy sensory data. The frequency of occurrence of the synesthetic perception of colors of characters points in this direction. Normally, every natural object of the outer world exhibits a color. Nevertheless, letters and numbers are artificial objects which are defined by form and meaning, but not by color. This permits the assumption that colors are hypothetically generated during the learning of the alphabet and numbers which then remain as permanent components of the symbol perception, given that they are not corrected by any external color information. This would also explain the very high percentage of visual synesthesiae, in the sense of a replacement function, among persons who have gone blind. In this regard, persons who have gone blind mention, even shortly after the loss of eye function, that they experience a considerably high percentage of visual perceptions which are induced in an auditory or in a tactile fashion. In 1893, Frederick Starr reported a frequency of visual-synesthetic perceptions of approximately 50 percent within a group of test subjects who had gone blind (cited by Harrison 2001). Persons who are blind upon birth, however, apparently know of no differentiated visual perceptions and no color perception.

312

2.5
EXPLORING
INDIVIDUAL
PERCEPTION –
GENUINE
SYNESTHESIA
↓
2.5.7
WHY
SYNESTHESIA?
FUNCTION
AND
SIGNIFICANCE

Examples of tactile perception initiated in an auditory manner in the case of people who have gone blind are discussed at length by Voss (1930).

In addition, early hypotheses regarding the origin of synesthetic perceptions are examined by Mahling (1927) and Argelander (1929). Although various approaches have been proposed (e.g., by Hubbard 2007), a comprehensive theory of synesthesia still seems to be a distant prospect with respect to the many questions which remain unanswered (Marks 2009). Today, synesthetic research also serves to explain the connections of the brain functions necessary to allow every person to recognize, understand, and effectively manipulate objects in the external world as well as the internal world of the body.

Generally, the diversity of synesthetic perceptions demonstrates that direct connections between nearly all cerebral areas are possible. In particular, permanent connections between primary areas could exist, e.g., between fields which are responsible for individual properties of perceptions involving hearing, seeing, and smelling. In this case, the perception of a sound can cause additional color perceptions; further examples, such as movement or spatiality (fig. 2.126), can also play a role. In this respect, permanent connections between higher areas involved in deciphering meaning and primary areas are possible. Numeric sequences would then be able to form specific groups. Furthermore, couplings of areas which participate in the origin of feelings are often connected to primary sensory areas such as the auditory cortex or the visual cortex. Emotions can thus assume colors.

2.5
EXPLORING
INDIVIDUAL
PERCEPTION
– GENUINE
SYNESTHESIA
↓
2.5.7
WHY
SYNESTHESIA?
FUNCTION
AND
SIGNIFICANCE

313

ALTOGETHER, BEYOND ALL
INDIVIDUAL DIFFERENCES, SYNESTHESIAE
DEMONSTRATE THAT EVERY
PHENOMENON OF PERCEPTION
IS INFLUENCED BY VARIOUS FUNCTIONAL
UNITS OF THE BRAIN, REGARDLESS
OF WHETHER THE PARTICIPATING BRAIN
AREAS ARE ADJACENT.

The functional proximity of different areas of the brain, which does not need to be a spatial proximity, certainly influences all perceptual processes and the generation of multisensory objects of perception. Only in this manner, indeed, can processes of sensory integration, recognition of objects, and interpretation of meaning interconnect with great rapidity.

FIGURE 2.126
The sculpture depicts a visual, three-dimensional pattern
stimulated by the beat of a drum heard while listening to music.
Carol Steen, Triangle, Steel, Bronze, and Silver, 1997.

2.6
CONSCIOUSLY CONSTRUCTING – MATHEMATICAL AND PHYSICAL CONNECTIONS

2.6.1
ALGORITHMS AND CONCEPTS

Within a process of design, the conscious construction of connections between the modalities includes the connection of properties by virtue of a scheme of allocation, more specifically, an algorithm. In a simplified manner, figure 2.127 illustrates the principle of the systematic transformation of a set of parameters $x_1 \dots x_n$ into a set of features $y_1 \dots y_n$ of another sensory channel. Today's *media players* as well as the "classic" systems of color-light music function in this manner. The scheme can make reference to physical parameters, such as the frequencies or wavelengths of sound and light, thus providing for *physical connections*. However, it can also be configured in a completely free manner. In order to achieve surprising results, random processes can be applied – with regard to music, one speaks of *aleatoric processes*.

FIGURE 2.127
A scheme of consciously constructed connections
between the modalities. By virtue of mathematical functions,
namely algorithms, a parameter set of a sensory
channel is transformed into features of another modality.

Approaches involving the conveyance of auditory structures into the visual area with the assistance of objective (e.g., mathematical) concepts, are driven by the wish to establish the existence of generally valid connections which result in clear correlations.

Usually, visualizations of media players are based on parameters $x_1 \dots x_n$ extracted after sampling the time function of sound (as shown in fig. 1.37) or from a spectral representation (see fig. 1.39). Sampling transforms the continuous signal into a series of discrete values where each represents the magnitude at a specific point in time. The spectrum is calculated by an algorithm

314

2.6
CONSCIOUSLY
CONSTRUCTING –
MATHEMATICAL
AND
PHYSICAL
CONNECTIONS
↓
2.6.1
ALGORITHMS
AND
CONCEPTS

providing a digital version of the so-called *Fast Fourier Transformation* (FFT). The resulting spectrum is also given by a series of discrete numbers. Both series, including temporal or spectral data, are appropriate to provide input for a visualization. Thus, for example, a parameter x_i can be an instantaneous magnitude or a peak value of a spectral line, which as parameter y_i controls the position or the brightness of a visual structure presented on the screen.

CONSCIOUSLY DESIGNED CONNECTIONS BETWEEN DIFFERENT MODALITIES ARE COMPREHENSIBLE ONLY WHEN THE ALLOCATIONS BETWEEN THE SENSORY FEATURES REFER TO ELEMENTS OF ANALOGY, ICONIC FEATURES, OR SYMBOLISM.

2.6
CONSCIOUSLY
CONSTRUCTING –
MATHEMATICAL
AND
PHYSICAL
CONNECTIONS
↓
2.6.1
ALGORITHMS
AND
CONCEPTS

315

Observing the methodology of the Swiss painter Robert Strübing, Thomas Lehner speaks of an *art converter* [Kunstkonverter] which transforms music into paintings, and vice versa (Lehner 1973). Such a consciously constructed scheme, however, is not necessarily comprehensible to observers or listeners. As indicated in this chapter, even simple allocations can lead to results which intuitively allow no reference to be made between the related modalities.

CHARACTERISTICS OF THE PERCEPTION OF VISUAL AND AUDITORY SIGNALS

Given that the physical analysis of auditory and visual stimuli exhibits certain commonalities, particularly the wave character as the basis of the transmission of energy to the sensory organs, it makes sense to examine sensory performance with respect to possible analogies:

	AUDITORY	VISUAL
FREQUENCY RANGE:	16–16,000 Hz	390–790 THz
WAVE LENGTH:	20–0.02 m	780–380 nm
NUMBER OF OCTAVES:	10	< 1
SPATIAL RESOLUTION:	LOW	HIGH
SPECTRAL RESOLUTION:	HIGH	LOW

The minimal relative width of the frequency area of visible light constitutes an essential difference: it is smaller than an octave and corresponds approximately to the interval of a major seventh, whereas the frequency range of the audible sound encompasses approximately ten octaves.

In terms of perceptual psychology, there is a great difference in the manner in which frequency information is evaluated in each of the respective modalities. A complex sound spectrum can lead to the simultaneous perception of several basic tones and of the timbres which are allocated to these tones; and it can, moreover, exhibit further products of the interaction of individual spectral proportions. As a result, music arising from a combination of different acoustic sources, namely the various music instruments, has a special attraction. On the other hand, the visual perception of random spectra leads to the perception of a single color. The perception of a certain color can be caused by very different combinations of individual spectral lines – the color perception encompasses, thus, in contrast to the perception of the tone color, an elementary ambiguity.

This deficiency, nevertheless, is compensated by a considerably more exact spatial perception, as compared to the auditory area. The summarizing of every light spectrum which exerts influence upon one point of the retina as one color tone explains why acoustic signals – e.g., such as music – can not be exactly transformed into equivalent visual structures, although this objective was pursued by the *color-light music*.

Even the visual configuration is often subject to mathematical concepts. This is so, in particular, when logical structures and a purposeful functionality without ornamental accessories are to be articulated. In this regard, Max Bill describes a characteristic feature of "good design": "The enveloping lines of the objects or of the individual parts appear to be or are actually constructed according to a mathematical basis." (Erni 1983, 5)

Beside other applications, consciously configured color analogies are utilized in technical acoustics for the purpose of describing the spectral properties of test sounds. A sound which contains all audible frequencies in a uniform manner is described as *white noise*. ● This term is chosen in analogy to the fact that light which encompasses all frequencies of the visible spectrum in equal intensity is perceived as white. Accordingly, the description of the sound as white is not the result of an intuitive process, but rather the consequence of a mentally reflective comparison of signal properties. In many cases, a test sound in which the lower frequencies were additionally raised is required instead of white noise, in order to optimize electroacoustic equipment. In the case of visible light, this corresponds to an increase in the red portion, thus changing white light into pink. According to the aforementioned analogy, the respective test sound is also described as *pink noise*. ● Therefore, even this description has its origin in the physical analogy of light and sound. Both terms were thus constructed very consciously according to physical knowledge. In the meaning of this analogy, *silence* is black, given that this color tone corresponds to the absence of a luminous stimulus (Schafer 1967).

Therein, the fundamental difference to symbolic allocations is demonstrated: in regions where English, French, and German are spoken, silence is regarded as golden. This is indicative of the ideal value. Physical analogies are undoubtedly logical, yet they are not intuitively comprehensible. In individual cases, synesthetic perception can lead to results similar to those of physical analogies – this is, however, in consideration of the great variability of such perceptual phenomena, more likely than not the result of a coincidence than of physical laws.

57

58

316

2.6
CONSCIOUSLY
CONSTRUCTING –
MATHEMATICAL
AND
PHYSICAL
CONNECTIONS
↓
2.6.1
ALGORITHMS
AND
CONCEPTS

COLORING OF SOUND OCCURS DUE TO SPECTRAL DISTORTIONS CAUSED BY SPECIFIC PROPERTIES OF TRANSMISSION SYSTEMS.

As a result, loudspeakers can color the sound of the music being radiated, or this occurs intentionally by means of frequency filters. Even the special resonance properties of rooms cause the coloring of sounds – an effect which can be purposefully utilized in the configuration of movie soundtracks. The coloring contains information as to the size of the room and its configuration, or it indicates whether sounds are involved which can be heard outside. In music, tone colors can be sensibly influenced by the choice of sound sources, e. g., a string ensemble can be supplemented by woodwind instruments.

PHYSICAL ANALOGY

2.6
CONSCIOUSLY
CONSTRUCTING –
MATHEMATICAL
AND
PHYSICAL
CONNECTIONS
↓
2.6.1
ALGORITHMS
AND
CONCEPTS

317

Physical processes are based upon alterations of different quantities which may be allocated to various senses as stimuli. In this manner, the expansion of acoustic waves is related to periodic movements of the molecules within the medium utilized by the waves for their expansion. The movement of the air molecules which leads to auditory perception is not visually perceivable, owing to the minimal size of the particles and the minimal deflection of their oscillation. Upon the excitation of low frequencies along sheet metal or membranes, however, slow movements with large displacement can arise, and these can be perceived by the naked eye, such as along the membrane of a bass speaker. All wave processes are based upon the movements of particles or changes in electromagnetic fields. The movement can only be perceived, however, when the alterations of the physical quantities occur in a slow manner.

**THE BOUNDARIES OF THE SPECIFIC
SENSORY PERCEPTION OF HUMAN BEINGS
DO NOT CORRESPOND EXACTLY
TO THE DEMARCATIONS OF PHYSICAL
PHENOMENA AND MEASUREMENT PARAMETERS.
DEPENDING UPON CERTAIN CONSTRAINTS,
SIMILAR PHYSICAL PROCESSES ARE
CAPABLE OF ACTIVATING DIFFERENT SENSORY
CHANNELS.**

Accordingly, light within the visible frequency range will be visually perceived, whereas light with a larger wavelength in the infrared range will be perceived as thermal radiation, but without being seen. Sound is received by the ear as the oscillation of the air molecules, whereas the thermal movement of the molecules is sensed as warmth. Very slow, periodic oscillations of the air within the range of a few Hertz are not audible, but they can also be detected as infrasonic sounds by the mechanoreceptors within the body. Slow movements of the body will either be perceived by the vestibular system or, as oscillations, by the body receptors. Thus, whole-body oscillations can, according to the frequency, lead to seasickness or be perceived as the relative movement of organs. In the case of high frequencies, the oscillation energy does not propagate to the receptors of the inner body. Instead, they merely result in the tactile stimulation of the skin receptors. Therefore, it is evident that the allocation of stimuli to specific sensory areas indicates a special neuronal behavior of the creation of perceptual models, and this correlates to physical processes only in a limited manner.

The purpose of the perceptual system does not consist of exactly reproducing the nomological, natural laws of the human environment. Moreover, a thoroughly individual model of reality is created, and this model has the primary goal of creating perceptual qualities, thus allowing orientation to be conveyed and enabling actions and responses.

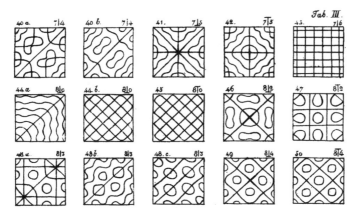

FIGURE 2.128
Different Chladni tone figures of a rectangular plate (Chladni 1817, table III).

2.6
CONSCIOUSLY
CONSTRUCTING –
MATHEMATICAL
AND
PHYSICAL
CONNECTIONS
↓
2.6.1
ALGORITHMS
AND
CONCEPTS

The application of algorithms to create structures which can be perceived via the sensory channels also addresses the question as to the subjective effect of mathematical relationships. With a view to the visual evaluation of structures, for example, the meaning of the *Golden Ratio* with regard to the perception of proportions has been discussed many times. It describes the case in which the ratio of two distances to one another corresponds to the ratio of the larger distance to the sum of both distances. This is the case with a ratio of 0.618. The Golden Ratio was employed in art and architecture for the purpose of creating proportions on a mathematical base. It is unclear, however, whether such a configuration gains attraction based upon innate perceptual preferences, or whether the objective analysis is the first to allow an added value to be recognized (Lidwell 2004, 96). The same problem is presented in the application of mathematical principles for the creation of rhythmic structures – a topic which is greatly discussed in music research.

For the comprehension of sound and oscillation processes, today, visualizations of the movement of structures are customary. Hence, the parallelism of auditory and visual phenomena in the physical process is revealed. The experimental acoustician Ernst Florens Friedrich Chladni observed, already towards the end of the eighteenth century, that fine sand on a vibrating plate groups itself in conspicuous patterns. Figure 2.128 shows examples of the *Chladni tone figures* from one of the two original publications (Chladni 1787; 1817). The black lines indicate locations of small oscillation magnitude in which the sand grains remain, as they are displaced from the white areas by virtue of the strong surface movements emerging there. In the comparatively higher oscil-

EXCURSUS: STANDING WAVES

Mechanical waves can expand along structures which are capable of oscillating. Thereby, such structures will be mechanically deformed, e.g., bent or compressed. Even a tightened string periodically changes its form. A mechanical wave is based upon periodic deflections of molecules around a rest position with a frequency which corresponds to the number of oscillation periods per second. The actual wave arises as a result of neighboring molecules being pulled along. In this manner, oscillation energy extends itself across the structure. If two waves encounter one another in a location of the structure, the deflections, oscillation speeds, and oscillation accelerations sum together. The waves, however, do not mutually disturb one another as they expand. In case of unimpeded wave propagation, there are no stationary patterns; one also speaks of *running waves*. At certain frequencies, indeed only when waves are reflected at obstacles, stationary patterns can expand corresponding to the figures 2.128, 2.129, and 2.130. These *standing waves* are caused by the fact that in certain locations, at any time, an addition of the physical quantities of the arriving and reflected waves occurs – *antinodes* thus come into being. In other locations, however, a wave cancellation takes place – nodal lines are developed there. At every resonance frequency, a characteristic pattern of antinodes and nodes is developed.

The frequency and pattern depend upon material properties and geometry, particularly upon the position of reflecting areas. Generally, reflections originate in every location in which the properties of the structure undergo changes for the expansion of the waves. The ability of the structure itself to oscillate is independent of the external excitation. With the assistance of *modal analysis*, a mathematical model is developed – on the basis of measurements – which reflects resonance condition and patterns,

the so-called eigenforms of the structure. In absolute terms, a prediction of the oscillation properties is only possible when the structure, its geometry, and the defining material properties can be recreated as a computer model *(CAE Models, Finite Elements Analysis)*. Waves can develop even within fluids and gases. In air-filled cavities with reflecting surfaces, therefore, standing waves can also arise. The characteristic airborne sound resonances in pipes are used in the case of wind instruments, for example, in order to create tones of a defined pitch. The longer the pipe, the deeper the tone which fulfills the resonance requirement.

955 Hz   2399 Hz

2984 Hz   8414 Hz

10869 Hz   11388 Hz

FIGURE 2.129
Oscillation forms of a brake disk at different resonance frequencies.

lation forms – at higher frequencies – presented, fine-structured albeit uniform patterns arise. The characteristic structures are only obvious at certain frequencies. The higher the excitation frequency, the more complex and fine the pattern. Today, it is known that the patterns are the result of resonance phenomena and are caused by the *standing waves* which arise at certain frequencies.

Today, by virtue of various methods of laser metrology, excellent means are available for making even the smallest of structural movements visible. Predominantly, *laser holography* or *laser interferometry* are utilized. Figure 2.219 illustrates the oscillation patterns along a brake disk with respect to a selection of critical resonance frequencies. At these frequencies, the waves stimulated on the structure overlap to form stationary patterns. The patterns presented exhibit the *deformation*, i.e. the *deflection* of the structure at a certain time in the oscillation process. Thereby, diverse colors represent the differing values of the deflection.

Figure 2.130 indicates different possibilities of presenting the process of oscillation of the brake disk and the caliper. In this example, the point in time of maximum deflection has been analyzed. The oscillation was measured by virtue of a laser procedure, *electronic speckle pattern interferometry* (ESPI). In principal, both two- and three-dimensional presentations are appropriate. Additionally, it is helpful to compile profiles of oscillations along characteristic lines. Below on the right, the result for the red and blue line is depicted, which are shown in the image at the lower left.

320

2.6
CONSCIOUSLY
CONSTRUCTING
– MATHEMATICAL
AND
PHYSICAL
CONNECTIONS
↓
2.6.1
ALGORITHMS
AND
CONCEPTS

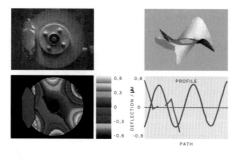

FIGURE 2.130
Different possibilities of visualizing the oscillation form of a brake disk.
Above: photo of the experimental structure and three-dimensional presentation of an oscillation form; below: presentation of the deflection with color coding and profiles of the deflection oriented in radial (red) and circumferential (blue) direction.

Colors support the clarity and the interpretability of visualizations. Figure 2.131 shows examples of possible color scales to demonstrate the oscillation behavior of a mechanical structure. The specimen, thereby, was stimulated by an electromechanical *shaker*. At any rate the depiction indicates the deformation of the material at a certain point in time within the course of the oscillation process. Thereby, the deformation is presented in a drastically exaggerated manner. In addition to the three-dimensional presentation, the application of color codes serves for purposes of clarification. Scales of increasing brightness are particularly important for presenting the quantities whose algebraic signs do not change, such as energy quantities with exclusively positive values. In such a case, the color tone is not significant and is chosen primarily due to aesthetic

2.6
CONSCIOUSLY
CONSTRUCTING –
MATHEMATICAL
AND
PHYSICAL
CONNECTIONS
↓
2.6.1
ALGORITHMS
AND
CONCEPTS

321

considerations. However, given that the oscillation presented in the image is associated with the periodic deflection of the structure in both directions – i.e. certain surfaces are deformed upwards, whereas others are simultaneously deformed downwards – a *plus-minus* scale is more appropriate. The color coding in red and green illustrates the deflection from an idle position, which appears as a darker area in the presentation. The symbolic connotation of the colors red and green as a positive or negative evaluation can, nevertheless, be regarded as disturbing in some cases of application and can even lead to erroneous interpretations. An *isophonic scale* as a presentation of areas of equal, radiated sound pressure can also be applied to the deflection of mechanical structures, as already indicated by figures 2.129 and 2.130. This presentation is popular among users of laser holography and has the advantage that areas of equal deflection can be exactly followed, owing to the lines between the zones of different colors. Thereby, the meaning and the sequence of the colors are secondary. Beside symbolic content, the color scales may also include iconic references, e.g., by use of characteristic color tones of winter, spring, autumn, rainbow, or even hellfire. In choosing color scales, it is generally advisable to consider cross-modal analogy, iconic features, and symbolism, if possible, if the software offers different color scales for the evaluation. The choice, nevertheless, should always be made consciously, but with reference to intuitive plausibility. Further examples of applications from the field of acoustics can be found in Haverkamp (2000 and 2004c).

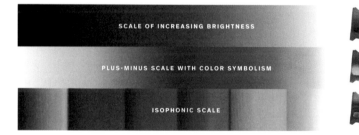

FIGURE 2.131
Examples of the use of color scales to visualize
the oscillation of a vehicle body component.

Starting with the Chladni tone figures (fig. 2.128), the physician and natural scientist Hans Jenny developed and photographically documented a phenomenology of the structures and the dynamics of waves and oscillations. Jenny described the creation of aesthetic forms by virtue of the excitation of oscillations of mechanical structures as *cymatics* (Jenny 1967). Similar to Chladni, he experimented initially with sand which he spread along oscillating metal plates. Additional experiments with fluids, such as glycerin or mercury, and with lycopodium powder constantly led to new two- and three-dimensional patterns. Moreover, he constructed a *tonoscope* which enabled sounds spoken into a microphone to be directly transformed into oscillation images. Additionally, he used these methods in the dynamic visualization of music. It was demonstrated that periodic and short-term acoustic processes bring forth elementary visual forms and structures which are – although they are caused by physical processes – often characterized by unexpected artistic or aesthetic attractions.

2.6.2
OBJECTIVE
COLOR-SOUND
RELATIONS

The desire to document systematic relations between colors and sounds is very old. Thus, it is interesting to examine this field with respect to possible conclusions, particularly in connecting visual and auditory perception. Until the beginning of the twentieth century, the allocation of colors to elements of music was merely the subject of theoretical analyses. Today, lighting, film, and computers offer various possibilities of realization. Whereas performances of classical repertories tend to forego using the support of colored light – primarily due to reasons of tradition – with the exception of opera and ballet, pop and jazz performances without lightshows are nearly unthinkable. Simultaneously, the video clip provides broad possibilities of visualization – ranging from the presentation of moving abstract forms to the interpretation of the music in specific scenes and storylines. Thereby, nonetheless, uncommitted approaches are preferred, instead of seeking to establish a theoretical foundation of the multimedia production and to systematically assigning colors and forms to certain elements of the music.

322

2.6
CONSCIOUSLY
CONSTRUCTING
– MATHEMATICAL
AND
PHYSICAL
CONNECTIONS
↓
2.6.2
OBJECTIVE
COLOR-SOUND
RELATIONS

    With respect to the performance of musical compositions and the philosophical interpretation of music, there were early efforts to connect tones, intervals, or sounds with colors (Jewanski 2007). Indeed, from Greek antiquity up until the beginning of the eighteenth century, the notion of a color-sound relationship was widely accepted. In different times and in different countries, however, diverging assignations were made (Jewanski 1999). Often, with reference to the magical number seven, there was the presumption of a seven-stage scale. Aristotle already proposed a scale according to color brightness ranging from black via blue, green, purple, red, and yellow to white, which was preferred into the seventeenth century. This color scale made reference to seven consonant musical *intervals* – thus, not to *tones*, but to distances between the tones. Given the number seven, a reference could easily be made to cosmological systems of thinking, for example with regard to the number of planets within the solar system in terms of the harmony of the spheres. With the discovery of Uranus in 1781, this connection became invalid. The theory of color-sound relationships acquired a special significance in the eighteenth century by virtue of Louis-Bertrand Castel, who developed a system of allocation in which every color corresponds to a chromatic tone, instead of intervals being counterparts to colors:

This system of allocation was retained in all twelve octaves, while the deeper tones are characterized by minimal brightness and the higher tones, logically, by greater brightness. Castel became a well-known personality by virtue of his conception and – most likely – initial performance with a musical instrument designated as a *clavecin oculaire*, which presented the corresponding color upon the striking of a musical tone. In the eighteenth century, Castel's efforts caused a heated discussion as to the significance of allocating colors to sounds. At the beginning of the nineteenth century, in the course of scientific development, physical analogies came into consideration. With regard to the wave character of light and sound, for example, efforts were made to extrapolate the musical octave scheme into the frequency area of visible light in order to allow the calculation of analogous colors for the tones of an octave. In this respect, in 1801, Thomas Young designated the color yellow-green for the key of C (Jewanski 1999). Of course, the result of the calculation is dependent upon the presumed tone frequency. As a contemporary reference value, the classification a = 440 Hz is used as standard pitch. In the eighteenth century, however, a = 415 Hz was the norm. Even lower reference values such as the *French chamber pitch* with a = 400 Hz were applied.

2.6
CONSCIOUSLY
CONSTRUCTING –
MATHEMATICAL
AND
PHYSICAL
CONNECTIONS
↓
2.6.2
OBJECTIVE
COLOR-SOUND
RELATIONS

323

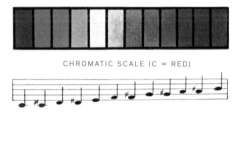

CHROMATIC SCALE (C = RED)

ADAPTION OF THE COLOR SCALE
TO THE WHOLE GAMUT

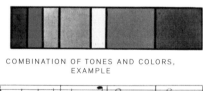

COMBINATION OF TONES AND COLORS,
EXAMPLE

FIGURE 2.132
Recommendations of various color scales for the visualization
of music (top and middle). The bottom example demonstrates the presumption
that a color chord is produced by virtue of an additive color mixing.
Whereas the consonance of several auditory tones grants the hearing impression
an additional quality, the color impression here degrades into a muted
brown tone (Rimington 1911).

In the course of scientific and industrial development, there was increased interest in visualizing music, particularly at the beginning of the twentieth century (Kienscherf 1996, see also Haverkamp 2003). This is further documented by the large number of patents for technical processes by the first half of the century alone (Betancourt 2004). Leading representatives of the development of artistic concepts and practical applications were, for example, Alexander Wallace Rimington, Adrian Klein, Alexander László, Mary Elizabeth Hallock-Greenewalt, Mary Ellen Bute, Thomas Wilfrcd, and Oskar Fischinger.

Figure 2.132 illustrates examples of the systematic allocation of the painter and color-light musician Alexander Wallace Rimington (1911). Colors were allocated to the tones of an octave corresponding to the sequence of the light frequencies (top) or distributed along the entire scope of tones (middle). ● ● The problem with the numerical allocation of tone and light frequencies consists of the fact that the audible tone scope encompasses approximately ten octaves, whereas the range of visible light comprises less than one octave – i.e. the highest visible light frequency is smaller than the doubled value of the lowest visible frequency.

An additional problem regarding the allocation of colors to pitches of individual tones is obvious in the bottom image of figure 2.132: polyphonic chords lead to a *fading* or an *obscuration* of the allocated color tone – depending upon whether an additive or a subtractive color mixing is applied, i.e. whether colored light is mixed or pigments are combined with one another. ● Whereas the auditory quality increases in the case of polyphonic tones, the chromaticity as a visual quality diminishes due to the color mixing.

Therefore, Alexander László correlated color *harmonies* with musical *intervals* which are created by means of permutation of a scale with eight steps (László 1925). Corresponding to figure 2.133, these eight colors were chosen from a twenty-four-part color wheel by Wilhelm Ostwald (1920). The colors were arranged along two circular cardboard discs which were integrated into one another in such a fashion that, upon rotating the inner disc with respect to the outer disc, different color harmonies arose from each of two color tones. Every position of the sequence corresponds to a musical interval thus represented by eight color groups of one's choice. With all possible angles of rotation, eight permutations are possible, three of which are illustrated in figure 2.133. ● ● ● ● Three rows of color pairs behave as mirror images of one another. Accordingly, they show the same combinations, although the colors above and below are inverted. This is the case with the musical interval *third*, for example, for which two scales come into being, according to the direction of rotation, and these are described by László as *U-Terz* (Lower third) and *O-Terz* (Upper third). Analogous to musical perception, prime and octave lead to pairs of the same color. The fifth corresponds to a symmetrical row which contains every color pair twice. In this respect, a very simple process of allocation leads to connections which can not easily be comprehended by the observer of a color-light musical performance. Retrospectively, due to the ambiguity of the classification, it is extremely difficult to clearly designate the interval to which the color pair refers, even with an exact analysis. Detailed presentations and analyses of László's work may be found in Selwood (1985; 2006) and Jewanski (1997; 2000; 2006a; 2006b).

59
60
61
62
63
64
65

324

2.6
CONSCIOUSLY
CONSTRUCTING
– MATHEMATICAL
AND
PHYSICAL
CONNECTIONS
↓
2.6.2
OBJECTIVE
COLOR-SOUND
RELATIONS

2.6
CONSCIOUSLY
CONSTRUCTING –
MATHEMATICAL
AND
PHYSICAL
CONNECTIONS
↓
2.6.2
OBJECTIVE
COLOR-SOUND
RELATIONS

325

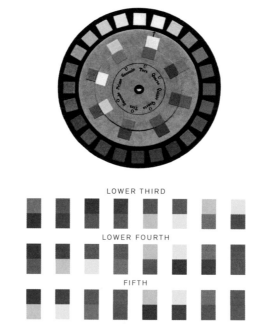

FIGURE 2.133
The method developed by Alexander László for constructing color
harmonies analogous to music with the assistance
of a color wheel. Three results of the classification are presented.
The octave leads to pairs of equal color tones.

There are numerous further examples of audio-visual connections as designed for the arts and music (see e.g., Riccò 2008; 2009). The Russian symbolist Alexander Scriabin integrated a light voice described as *Luce*, which gives the light of colored spotlights in the form of notes, in his symphonic composition *Prometheus, Le Poème du feu*, Op. 60 (Eberlein 1985). Arnold Schönberg adopted color instructions in his "drama with music," *Die glückliche Hand* (The Lucky Hand), Op. 18. Between 1909 and 1914, the painter Wassily Kandinsky developed theatrical musical pieces in which the color plays the primary role in the program: *Black and White, Green Sound, The Yellow Sound, Purple*. Furthermore, Bauhaus experiments in the 1920s – particularly those of Kurt Schwerdtfeger and Ludwig Hirschfeld-Mack – revolved around audio-visual forms (Hapkemeyer 2000). *Kinetic Art (Kinetism)* enriches the tension between seeing and hearing (Pešánek 1931, Malina 1974), the same applies to approaches made by light art (Weibel 2006). The technical possibilities of artistic configuration have been significantly expanded by virtue of lasers, cybernetics, electronics, and computers (Claus 1985). A new dimension was reached with the vast possibilities of interactivity, thus blurring the traditional border between the active, formative artist and the inactive, simply perceiving recipient.

While the technical realization of multimedia applications was increasingly made possible, the readiness to determine systematic assignments between tones, sounds and colors, however, has declined over the course of the twentieth century. Systematic concepts have made way for greater creative freedom and emotionality.

At the Zurich School of Music, Drama and Dance (HMT), under the direction of Natalia Sidler, a color piano was developed for the contemporary performance of color-light music (fig. 2.134, Sidler 2006b). The instrument has a variety of sound-generating objects, such as cymbals, metal plates, and singing bowls. By virtue of an interface, a process computer can be integrated, allowing the projection of color surfaces to be controlled. The programming, however, is not fixed, but flexible, permitting it to be involved in the audio-visual composition. The keyboard has color markings whose brightness increases with the tone pitch of the sound generator.

Contemporary approaches to combine auditory and visual elements are also pursued at the Institute for Music and Acoustics at the Center for Art and Media Karlsruhe (ZKM). Its director, Ludger Brömmer, regards the visual approach as a good means of explaining auditory forms. He views images as an expansion of musical expression, similar to an additional instrument. Visual design is comparable to composing music.

FIGURE 2.134
Color piano of the project Color-Light Music (2002)
at the Zurich School of Music, Drama and Dance (HMT).
Photographs by Dennis Savini.

2.6
CONSCIOUSLY
CONSTRUCTING
– MATHEMATICAL
AND
PHYSICAL
CONNECTIONS
↓
2.6.2
OBJECTIVE
COLOR-SOUND
RELATIONS

An important principle of the artistic multimedia composition is the *destruction* of perceptual objects – a method developed by Pierre Schaeffer within the framework of his *Musique Concrète* based on everyday sounds (Schaeffer 1967). This consists of dissembling the composition into elementary units he called *grains*, which are then subsequently recombined to form a new *granular synthesis*. Accordingly, on the basis of *sampled* materials – i.e. materials take from the acoustic environment – something new arises, spatially, temporally, and spectrally defined: a *sound sculpture*. Furthermore, a reference to mathematical algorithms is favored. For example, a systematic transformation of visual, *fractal* structures in the hearing space is desired (Grossmann 2005). For the connection of visual and auditory attributes in product design, however, one must acknowledge that an artistically "truthful" or at least optimal allocation within the area of color-light music has not yet been established. Indeed, for the allocation of colors and sounds, the *intuitive* connections on the basis of cross-modal analogies, iconic features, and common symbolic allocations are at the forefront. Those intuitive strategies become even more significant if interactive input is allowed to purposefully influence a performance. As an example, music visualizations by Johannes Deutsch are manipulated by the activity of the live performing orchestra itself. Again, intuitive features play a major role to provide comprehensibility of the interaction between the presented auditory and visual events (Deutsch 2007, see also chapter 3.4.2).

CUMULATION OF SENSORY CONTRIBUTIONS

SEGREGATION OR INTEGRATION

3.1
CUMULATION
OF THE
SENSORY
CONTRIBUTIONS
↓
3.1.1
SEGREGATION
OR INTEGRATION

329

With the presentation of different strategies of connection between the senses, part 2 made an effort to convey an overview of the variety of capabilities of cross-sensory connection.

THE PARALLEL PROCESSING OF DIFFERENT STRATEGIES CONNECTING THE MODALITIES IS AN IMPORTANT FEATURE OF THE PERCEPTUAL SYSTEM. FOR PRODUCT DESIGN, THIS PROVIDES A POTENTIAL OF REFERRING TO MULTISENSORY CONNECTIONS AS WELL AS TO INCREASE AWARENESS OF POSSIBLE CONTRADICTIONS AND ERRORS IN THE CONFIGURATION.

Prior to more closely examining of the formation of multisensory perceptual objects – beyond the sensory boundaries and via different strategies – the simultaneousness of the connections shall once again be reflected on. As a starting point, appropriate examples are taken from images of visual synesthetic phenomena.

Thereafter, the model of cross-sensory interaction will be extended to include cumulation of the contributions of the various connection strategies. Often, different processes overlap one another. In this regard, figure 3.1 presents the spatial distribution of visual synesthetic phenomena as depicted by the synesthete Matthias Waldeck. In addition to colors and forms, even texts of spoken language appeared in spatial distribution: "When I hear words, I also see them on my inner monitor, from the direction in which they are spoken. If additional disturbing sounds come into play, it is possible that I can't read the word and thus can't understand it. As long as I can't read it, I can't react to what was said. That is quite annoying in the case of larger events, given that the words often overlap one another and I thus see merely a mixture of letters." (Waldeck 2008).

FIGURE 3.1
Conversational situation in a street café.
Presentation of the synesthete Matthias Waldeck
in describing his own perception.

The detailed explanation of the visual phenomena presented
in figure 3.1 is: "That is how such a situation would *appear* to me:
- The yellow lines and red points are music.
- The black strip to the right is a slamming door.
- The points below to the left represent high-heeled shoes.
- The yellow spot to the right is a car horn.
- A gray-white spot above the high-heeled shoes represents a crackling sound.
- The red form to the left shall depict the shattering of a falling glass.
- Various voices overlap one another." (Waldeck 2008)

Frequently, synesthetic images also contain a connection to cross-modal analogies. Figure 3.2 shows a visual appearance which was caused by the sound of a mechanical coffee grinder. ● The overall process corresponds to the winding movement, which is reflected in the cyclical course of the sound. The crunching of the coffee beans is depicted by explosion-like structures similar to figure 2.4. It is possible that, in addition to the rotational movement represented in the sound, the knowledge as to the use of the grinder with gyrating arm movements was of significance.

    The recurrent connection of phenomena of genuine synesthesia, cross-modal analogy, and iconic references has come to be the subject of various discussions in research on synesthesia. In order to verbally distinguish special synesthetic phenomena from common ways of coupling, among others, the paired terms *authentic* or *non-authentic audition colorée* [echte oder unechte audition colorée] (Bos 1929) and *synesthesia* or *pseudo-synesthesia* (Baron-Cohen 1997) were applied. Evaluative terms such as these, however, hardly serve to clarify the situation. Although genuine synesthesiae are often perceived as being considerably more impressive or more real than cross-modal analogies, both phenomena are completely authentic and thus do not justify the assessment as *pseudo*-appearances. Indeed, such terms do not advance the objectivity of the discussion.

66

330

3.1
CUMULATION
OF THE
SENSORY
CONTRIBUTIONS
↓
3.1.1
SEGREGATION
OR INTEGRATION

3.1
CUMULATION
OF THE
SENSORY
CONTRIBUTIONS
↓
3.1.1
SEGREGATION
OR INTEGRATION

331

FIGURE 3.2
An example of the combination of a movement analogy
and associative elements in the case of a visual
perception caused by the sound of a mechanical coffee grinder.
Graphic by Hugo Meier-Thur (Anschütz 1927c).

The parallelism of different strategies of connection is particularly evident in the presentation of the synesthete Alexandra Dittmar in figure 3.3. The graphic conveys the impression of visual appearances while listening to music. On the left-hand side, it shows iconic elements of the sound sources in the form of musicians and instruments. To the right, visual phenomena of genuine synesthesia, which were caused by instrumental sounds, are presented. In contrast to the iconic elements, the synesthetic forms show their typical abstract appearance. From top to bottom, they are related to the following instruments: trumpets and transverse flutes, violins and violas, bassoons and trumpets. In the middle, a merging of pear and apple can be seen, which symbolizes the fusion of the senses, and is a consciously chosen visual metaphor. The visual phenomena arose while listening to the Andante of the Symphony No. 38 in D major, K. 504 *(The Prague Symphony)*, by Wolfgang Amadeus Mozart.

FIGURE 3.3
Visual synesthetic appearances arising while listening to
symphonic music. Alexandra Dittmar, Birpfel, 2003.

Alexandra Dittmar commented as to her image in the following manner: "'*Birpfel*' [an appropriate translation may by "Pearpple"] implies quite simply that I simultaneously have non-synesthetic and synesthetic experiences such as pear and apple in one [Birne und Apfel in einem] and can also enjoy a concert in both respects."

As a rule, presentations of synesthetic images can not be interpreted without the self-reporting of their producers. These may also contain common iconic elements or be based on conscious constructions. Nevertheless, image elements are identifiable, given the congruence with respect to objects of the outer world – or portions of thereof. Accordingly, they can be distinguished from the abstract results of genuine synesthesia. Therefore, even drawings and paintings which present phenomena of audio-visual connections can then – by third persons – be designated as *iconic,* if concrete objects are recognized beyond a doubt. In this regard, the allocation by this cross-sensory strategy exhibits a *systematic approach to an associative comparison.* Sensory stimuli can thus directly comprise the initiator of an iconic connection. On the other hand, abstract forms originating in genuine synesthetic perception can additionally be connected to memorized concrete objects. This results in a secondary, iconic representation. August Petersen provides an example in which a synesthetic perception in the form of a phosphene-like feather structure similar to the bow of a ship leads to the visualization of a ship (Petersen 1931).

Synesthetic images often exhibit a mixture of genuine synesthetic phenomena with iconic references. An analysis of the pictures published in the field of color-sound research (described in chapter 2.5.2) demonstrates that the portion of iconic elements among painters without genuine synesthetic predispositions – e.g., among participants in classes for young children – is considerably greater than it is among synesthetics, in comparison (Haverkamp 2003b).

In explaining synesthesiae, efforts are also made to generally trace genuine synesthetic perception back to associative, iconic processes. Accordingly, color perceptions in the case of letters of the alphabet could have also been caused by color coding in school books or by the use of colored writing utensils in the classroom. Many people assign colors to the days of the week, for example, in the manner they are accustomed to seeing them in TV program guides. Already at the beginning of the twentieth century, Richard Wallaschek undertook efforts towards a systematic interpretation of synesthetic perception as pure associative processes (Wallaschek 1905; 1930). However, the considerable constancy of genuine synesthetic appearances over time speaks against a general explanation of synesthesiae by virtue of associative, i.e. iconic, processes. Associations are, nevertheless, connected to the performance of memory and are subject to an appropriately strong variability. Moreover, they can become unclear or even forgotten over the course of time, and their reconstruction can require very different durations of neuronal processing. In the nineteenth century, the concept of color coding for the purpose of facilitating learning was not common, even though similar synesthetic phenomena had been observed. Furthermore, there is considerable evidence supporting the theory that iconic and genuine synesthetic connections between the senses are based upon very different cognitive mechanisms.

With respect to the frequent mixing of different processes of cross-sensory assignment, a question arises as to the manner in which the perceptual system consolidates the varying strategies of connection in order to create distinct, multisensory objects of perception. Without intending to hypothetically anticipate the results of brain research at this point, the model presented in figure 2.1 shall be expanded in order to discuss the necessary processes.

3.1
CUMULATION
OF THE
SENSORY
CONTRIBUTIONS
↓
3.1.1
SEGREGATION
OR INTEGRATION

Initially, it is clear that individual perceptual properties in every modality must be integrated: in hearing, the perception of individual tones with a specific tone pitch and tone color arises from individual overtone spectra; in seeing, spatially adjacent surfaces of the same color and texture are allocated to one identical object.

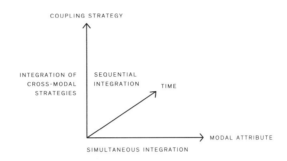

3.1
CUMULATION
OF THE
SENSORY
CONTRIBUTIONS
↓
3.1.1
SEGREGATION
OR INTEGRATION

333

FIGURE 3.4
Three dimensions of perceptual integration.
The cumulation of the results of multisensory analyses in the
perceptual system requires the integration via all
of the perceived attributes of objects (simultaneous integration) as well
as the consideration of temporal changes (sequential integration).
Given that different strategies of connection between the
sensory channels can be effective at the same time, even the results of
these processes must be combined to yield an overall result
(integration of cross-modal strategies).

THE CONTEMPORANEOUS SUMMARIZING
OF PERCEPTUAL PROPERTIES
IS ALSO REFERRED TO AS SIMULTANEOUS
INTEGRATION (BREGMAN 1999).
THE CUMULATION OF PROPERTIES IS,
NEVERTHELESS, POSSIBLE ONLY SUBSEQUENT
TO THE CONCURRENT DISTINCTION
FROM PROPERTIES OF
OTHER OBJECTS – SEGREGATION.

Accordingly, in the highly complex sound of an orchestra, different instruments can be distinguished from one another by virtue of the tone pitch and the acoustic quality. Additionally, the specific qualities of tone mixtures, such as, for example, the identification of the respective characteristics of the chord sound, factor into the equation as well. The high complexity of human auditory processing is evident when one attempts to analytically deduce appropriate distinctions from the frequency spectrum of such a sound (e.g., fig. 2.27).

A FURTHER ESSENTIAL TASK OF
INTEGRATION CONSISTS OF ALLOCATING
TEMPORALLY DEPENDENT
PROCESSES (SEQUENTIAL INTEGRATION).

Thus, tones which are played subsequent to one another on musical instruments do not appear as an unrelated sequence – to the contrary, the perceptual system aims at consolidating these to form sensible units. As a result, the perception of melodies arises which are temporally limited and which distinguish themselves from the simultaneously presented, musical context. The same occurs if different sound processes are consolidated to form a functional unit. In the visual realm, similar physical objects, which are viewed in a rapid sequence in different locations, are often supplemented by a quality of movement, allowing perception of an identical object that moves within the space. The sequential integration is often based upon processes of configuration which are similar to the *Principle of Common Fate* (section 1.3.8), which is also of considerable significance in the multisensory context.

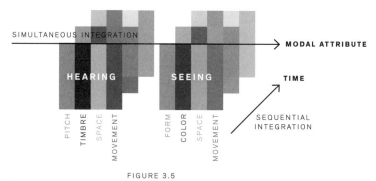

FIGURE 3.5
Simultaneous and sequential integration consider the attributes
of a sensory channel as well as the connection between the modalities,
such as, for example, between hearing (left) and seeing (right).

334

3.1
CUMULATION
OF THE
SENSORY
CONTRIBUTIONS
↓
3.1.1
SEGREGATION
OR INTEGRATION

If one examines the possibilities of connecting different modalities, as described in part 2, and considers the necessity of simultaneous and sequential integration, a question arises as to the determination of clearly defined perceptual objects. Due to the parallelism of processing, the different strategies do not necessarily lead to a concordant result free of contradiction. Instead, the different results of the comparison on the level of analogies, iconic features, and meanings must be united in a self-contained perceptual object. Additionally, according to the circumstances, the results of thinking processes and special synesthetic phenomena are to be taken into consideration. Thus, in the terminology of Gestalt psychology, the perceptual system has the task of building a *Good Gestalt* which unites all perceptual qualities of an object without contradiction and which considers all cross-modal strategies.

This initially requires an integration of all strategies of cross-sensory connection. If this does not occur without contradiction, a perceptual conflict arises. Overall, the building of perceptual objects occurs by virtue of the consideration of the three dimensions presented in figure 3.4. Simultaneous and sequential processes of integration are already effective within one modality, as the above-mentioned example of listening to music easily indicates. Simultaneous chords and sequential melodies arise as a result of individual acoustic stimuli. With the addition of further modalities corresponding to figure 3.5, similar processes are necessary, which are now effective even beyond the sensory boundaries.

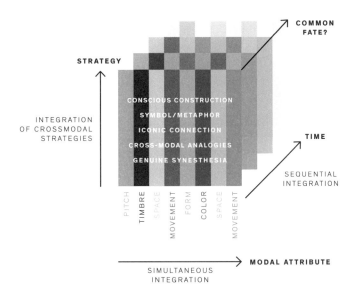

3.1
CUMULATION
OF THE
SENSORY
CONTRIBUTIONS
↓
3.1.1
SEGREGATION
OR INTEGRATION

FIGURE 3.6
A comprehensive model of multisensory connection, in consideration
of the three dimensions of integration.

A THIRD COMPONENT, THE INTEGRATION OF THE RESULTS OF ALL CROSS-MODAL STRATEGIES, SHALL SUPPLEMENT THE DESCRIBED PROCESSES OF SIMULTANEOUS AND SEQUENTIAL INTEGRATION.

The complete picture is achieved due to the consideration of possible strategies of connection between the modalities. With a view to the already presented model of the five primary strategies with its variety of the thereby summarized processes – which have been discussed in their essential features in part 2 – the scheme is expanded corresponding to figure 3.6. The color markings indicate that genuine synesthetic phenomena and cross-modal analogies are, as a general rule, based upon individual perceptual properties in respect to sensations. The same usually applies to consciously constructed connections. The case of connection of perceived auditory and visual movement via the *Principle of Common Fate* is depicted in the image in an exemplary manner. Iconic and symbolic connections make reference to, on the other hand, groups of sensory qualities whose stimulating sources are identified and whose meanings can be deciphered.

The overall result of the cross-sensory connection within the perceptual system, however, is not simply the sum of the individual contributions of sensory properties and strategies of connection. On the contrary, it is a holistic construction (see section 2.1.2) which is based upon mutual influence and the transformation of individual sensory stimuli (see also Anceschi 2000, with reference to Chion 1994). As a result, new perceptual qualities arise which none of the participating channels can generate for itself.

3.1.2
PERCEPTUAL CONFLICTS

Given the complexity of the parallel processing of information within the brain, it is conceivable that the processed data can contain contradictory information. In this case, a perceptual conflict arises. In contrast to technical methods of data processing, which are primarily based upon systematic and causal principles such as Boolean algebra, the human brain is capable of creating clear – or at least ostensibly clear – perceptual objects, even despite obvious contradictions of the sensory information. That is the basic requirement of decisive action, essentially the basis for being able to act at all in unknown situations. Without particular measures taken in advance, a technical, strictly logic-based system is incapable of resolving contradictions. A computer program is, in this case, not reactive, for it "hangs" or "crashes."

In processing sensory information, three forms of perceptual conflicts are important:

I.	CONTRADICTORY DATA ARE PROVIDED VIA DIFFERENT SENSORY CHANNELS.
II.	CONTRADICTORY RESULTS ARISE FROM DIFFERENT STRATEGIES OF THE CONNECTION BETWEEN THE SENSORY CHANNELS.
III.	CONTRADICTIONS EXIST BETWEEN PERCEIVED AND MEMORIZED PATTERNS.

3.1
CUMULATION
OF THE
SENSORY
CONTRIBUTIONS
↓
3.1.2
PERCEPTUAL
CONFLICTS

These three forms of perceptual conflicts shall be discussed as follows:

CONTRADICTORY DATA VIA DIFFERENT SENSORY CHANNELS

If conflicting data arrive via different sensory channels, the information must be appropriately adjusted in order to enable perceptual objects free of contradiction to arise. One also speaks of a *cue conflict*. In the output of multisensory information via technical systems, e.g., via human-machine interfaces, conflicting data must generally be avoided, given that they would otherwise decelerate the perceptual process and increase the risk of errors during their utilization (Molholm 2004). On the other hand, in the configuration of product attributes, perceptual conflicts are occasionally – in advertising often – provoked, in order to make the products more interesting or to increase the attention of potential customers. Figure 3.7 illustrates the products of a manufacturer of confectionery, items whose visual appearance is intentionally falsified. It involves chocolate candies which are configured as olives and presented in a wooden basket with an appropriate spoon and olive foliage. The perceptual conflict effectuates an additional experience by virtue of contrasting the expected taste of olives with the true taste of chocolates.

FIGURE 3.7
Olives au Chocolate: chocolate candies which are
arranged as sweet olives and presented in the appropriate context.
Created by La Cure Gourmande, Belgium.

3.1
CUMULATION
OF THE
SENSORY
CONTRIBUTIONS
↓
3.1.2
PERCEPTUAL
CONFLICTS

337

IF CONFLICTING STIMULI
ARRIVE VIA DIFFERENT CHANNELS,
THE CONFLICT ARISING WITHIN
THE PERCEPTUAL SYSTEM
IS RESOLVED EITHER BY THE DOMINANCE
OF A MODALITY (MASKING)
OR A RECIPROCAL MODIFICATION
OF BOTH SENSORY DATA
(MERGING), WHICH LEADS TO A NEW,
CONFLICT-FREE RESULT.

Dominance encompasses a complete suppression *(inhibition)* of the weaker stimuli. Merging, on the other hand, is based on the building of compromises. That requires an interference between different sensory channels (Anceschi 2000). The dominance of a specific modality is also related to the focus of attention, which itself can be triggered by stimuli which have been presented immediately before (Lukas 2009).

IN CASES IN WHICH THE PERCEPTUAL
CONFLICT CAN BE RESOLVED
NEITHER BY DOMINANCE NOR BY MERGING,
IT WILL BE EXPERIENCED
AS A COGNITIVE DISSONANCE,
WHICH IS ACCOMPANIED BY NEGATIVE
EMOTIONS OR BODILY REACTIONS –
SUCH AS NAUSEA.

There are approaches which interpret seasickness as the result of a perceptual conflict between seeing and vestibular perception of movement.

When the fingers move across a rough surface, a sound which influences the tactile perception is often audible. Parallel to the coarseness being felt, the sound exhibits characteristic modulations. If auditory signals whose properties do not exactly correspond to the momentary tactile sensation are artificially created within the course of an experiment, this can effectuate a modification of the tactile perception. This applies, in particular, to changes in the auditory parameters *modulation frequency* and *loudness* (Altinsoy 2007). Accordingly, the tactile perception orients itself with respect to the auditory perception. The perceptual conflict is thus overplayed by the dominance of hearing. Furthermore, it is also known that the visual impression of the surface influences the touch sensation. With respect to the perception of textures, therefore, one may presume the existence of a hierarchical order preferring seeing to hearing and to the touch sensation. The great significance of the visual in perceiving surfaces is the basis of *tactile design,* as discussed in section 2.2.7.

Frequently, the spatial perception is characterized by visual dominance. Therefore, in many cases the visual stimuli define the perceived spatial distribution rather than the auditory (Bertelson 1981, Pick 1969, Lukas 2010), tactile (Gibson 1933), or proprioceptive modality (Pick 1969). As a consequence, ventriloquists use the influence of synchronous effects in order to mislead the public regarding the true source of the sound. This phenomenon is known as the *ventriloquism effect.* A ventriloquist speaks without obvious movement of the lips, while simultaneously producing exaggerated movements of the puppet's mouth. Given the movement synchronous to the speaking, the mouth appears to be the unequivocal source of the sound. In this manner, the auditory information for the localization of the acoustic source is faded out in favor of the visual information (Alais 2004, Vroomen 2004).

If stimuli from other modalities appear in parallel to visual stimuli, the visual dominance can cause failure to respond to those other modalities. In this case, at least the speed of responding to the visual stimulus is increased in comparison to the other modalities presented (Lukas 2010). Visual dominance is also experienced when film images which influence the sense of balance suggest the movement of the observer. A so-called *pseudo-kinetosis* comes into being, for example, when cinematic presentation shows a roller-coaster ride and thus creates a sensation of dizziness. Given that such phenomena occur in driving simulators, one speaks of a *simulator syndrome* (Anceschi 2000). The meaning of the visual is also indicated in comparing the subjective heaviness of two objects of different sizes. If the weight of both objects is similar, the smaller object is normally perceived as being heavier.

Auditory dominance often arises, on the other hand, when the number of auditory and the number of visual objects diverge from one another in the case of perceived synchronous processes. In this manner, an individual visual impulse in the form of a flash of lightning can appear, in the case of the simultaneous presentation of a sequence of acoustic impulses, as a sequence of several flashes (Shams 2002). This effect may be explained by early cross-modal interactions between the auditory and the visual cortex (Mishra 2007).

If the divergences of the sensory information lie within the thresholds of the just noticeable difference, no conflict situation arises, even if the physical or chemical stimuli themselves contain contradictions. In this regard, it is possible to synchronize movie actors authentically, even though an exact concurrence of the sounds of the words and the movements of the lips is hardly achieved at all. In this case, nevertheless, the perceived mimicry can influence the sensed sound quality of the words. For example, if the syllable *ba*

3.1
CUMULATION
OF THE
SENSORY
CONTRIBUTIONS
↓
3.1.2
PERCEPTUAL
CONFLICTS

is acoustically presented while the film depicts the lip movements for the syllable *ga,* neither of the two syllables will be perceived. Instead, the syllable *da* is perceived as a result of merging. This phenomenon is named the *McGurk effect* after its discoverer (McGurk 1976). The effect of the merging of auditory and visual contents, however, only occurs when the image and the sound are perceived as being primarily synchronous: the sound may not appear more than 30 ms before the image, whereas a delay of the sound can be tolerated up to 170 ms (van Wassenhove 2007, compare the somewhat diverging result of Kohlrausch in section 2.2.2).

CONFLICTING RESULTS
OF THE CONNECTION BETWEEN
SENSORY CHANNELS

3.1
CUMULATION
OF THE
SENSORY
CONTRIBUTIONS
↓
3.1.2
PERCEPTUAL
CONFLICTS

———

339

Different strategies of connection between the modalities can lead to different results. The perceptual conflicts which are thereby created are a clear indication of the fact that different forms of processing are executed simultaneously.

By virtue of the deciphering of color words – such as *red, green, gold* – such conflicts can be demonstrated. Figure 3.8 illustrates such an example. The legibility of color words can be improved by virtue of an appropriate marking in the corresponding color (left). A perceptual conflict arises, on the other hand, when the associative markings are interchanged (right). This substantially diminishes the legibility of the words. In order to properly comprehend the words, the perceptual system must expend much greater efforts. This phenomenon is utilized in the *Stroop test* – named after the psychologist John Ridley Stroop – in analyzing processes of language recognition (Stroop 1935). The perceptual conflict considerably increases the amount of time necessary to read the color words. Accordingly, test subjects generally require more time in order to comprehend an appropriately "falsely" marked text (Rich 2005).

Furthermore, cross-modal Stroop effects have been discovered between various senses, e.g., audition and vision (Hanauer 2003), vision and olfaction (Pauli 1999), or smell and taste (White 2007).

A Stroop test is also employed to understand the informational processing among people with *chromatic-graphemic synesthesia* (see section 2.5.4). Given that among these people a certain color is inalterably allocated to every letter of the alphabet in the perception, color markings also influence the speed of reading. If the markings correspond exactly to the colors as perceived by the synesthetes, the reading can be processed considerably quicker as otherwise, for example, if the colors were consequently interchanged. Indeed, it could even result in a double perceptual conflict if the markings of the color words neither associatively correspond to the meaning of the word nor make reference to the connection within the framework of the word-color synesthesia. The perceptual conflict between the genuine synesthetic and the semantic level with colored letter or words is also known as the *alien color effect (ACE),* as mentioned in Dittmar (2009).

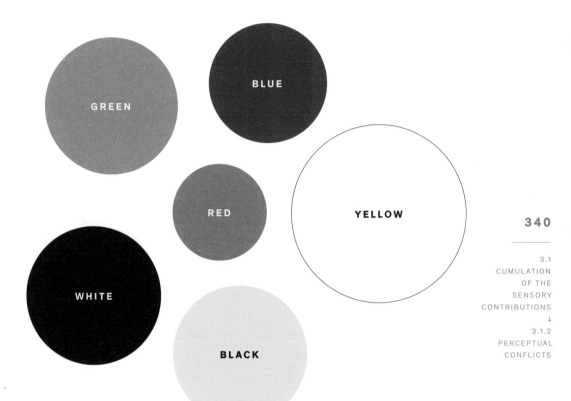

3.1
CUMULATION
OF THE
SENSORY
CONTRIBUTIONS
↓
3.1.2
PERCEPTUAL
CONFLICTS

FIGURE 3.8
**Perceptual conflict by virtue of the color
designation of color names.**

Among the synesthetes affected, the color recognition itself is complicated, in addition to the reading. Neurological research demonstrates that the perceptual conflict which is initiated causes the activation of additional brain areas which presumably contribute to the resolution of the conflict.

FIGURE 3.9
Demonstration of the disturbing influence of a visual synesthetic form, caused by a sound, on language appearing as a text on the "inner monitor." Fragment, photograph by Matthias Waldeck.

3.1
CUMULATION
OF THE
SENSORY
CONTRIBUTIONS
↓
3.1.2
PERCEPTUAL
CONFLICTS

341

Among synesthetes who visualize spoken language as text and even perceive sounds as visual objects, both aspects can influence one another in a disturbing fashion. In this regard, Matthias Waldeck reports of the overlaying of visual forms onto the text heard. This effect complicates the language comprehension. Figure 3.9 demonstrates this by comparison to an image of a damaged sign. Waldeck comments in this regard: "The photo depicts a typical situation for me. I see all spoken words on my inner monitor. If a disturbing sound which is too strong comes into play, it is superimposed onto the letters and a word fragment, as indicated in the photo, comes into being. That can result in the word not being legible, thus denying me the chance to understand it." (Waldeck 2008).

PERCEPTUAL CONFLICTS PLAY A SIGNIFICANT ROLE IN ADVERTISING, AIMED AT RAISING THE ATTENTION AND STIMULATING THE CONCENTRATION OF THE OBSERVER.

Figure 3.10 illustrates an example in which color symbolism and the perceived color obviously contradict one another. This commercial postcard, advertising the service of the cleaning of mattresses, is intended to draw attention to itself by virtue of the *red card* in green. The meaning of the color red from soccer, representing the red card which is a strict symbol of dismissal from the playing field, contradicts in a maximal manner to the accepting function of green, which is seen as positively strengthening actions. Neither the red card nor the color green can be regarded as making a direct reference to the advertising company. However, both fulfill the goal of animating the customer to seek a resolution of the perceptual conflict and to thus turn the card over, allowing the name and address of the company to be seen. In terms of color symbolism, the use of red as a sign of dismissal is here applied to unhygienic mattresses, whereas green represents healthy sleep.

FIGURE 3.10
The use of a perceptual conflict to increase the attention
of the observer in advertising.
The advertising postcard of a company specializing
in cleaning mattresses.

Perceptual conflicts are also referred to as *mental interference effects.* In addition to the aforementioned *Stroop interference,* the *Garner interference* is of importance. This encompasses the influence on recognition of a pattern by virtue of the temporal modification of adjacent structures (Lidwell 2003).

CONTRADICTIONS BETWEEN PERCEIVED AND STORED PATTERNS

342

3.1
CUMULATION
OF THE
SENSORY
CONTRIBUTIONS
↓
3.1.2
PERCEPTUAL
CONFLICTS

In the most seldom of cases, the perceptual objects stored in the memory and the currently received sensory information coincide exactly with one another – even if it involves articles of daily usage which were already very frequently perceived. On the other hand, objects with unusual perceptual characteristics are, at first, not recognizable and can not be allocated to groups of known objects with respect to function and properties. Thereto, an unknown object must first be analyzed, in order to either generate a new perceptual object or to appropriately accommodate or expand existing contents in the memory. Within certain boundaries, instead of the contents in memory, even the currently distributed sensory information can also be adapted.

IN THE CONFIGURATION OF NEW PRODUCTS,
THIS MEANS THAT THE MORE
A PRODUCT CAN BE ALLOCATED TO A KNOWN
CATEGORY OF OBJECTS, E.G., THE
CATEGORY "SPORTS CAR," THE MORE
KNOWN PERCEPTUAL FEATURES IT EXHIBITS.

On the other hand, an object which offers only known elements to the perception often appears uninteresting due to this very reason – for it does not awaken the attention of the customer. Unknown elements of the configuration increase the stimulation, but they run the risk of alienation. In this case, the expectation of the customer with respect to the product and its placing among similar objects must be precisely considered. A traditionally configured product must exhibit known elements which can be associatively allocated. A future-oriented product is, by way of contrast, more likely to be characterized by new, innovative features. However, even such a product must allow a clear classification to be made – e.g., an automobile for the road should be identifiable as such, in order to win acceptance. In this regard, new and previously not perceived elements of design can have their limitations.

With respect to learning, the *proactive interference* with its limitation of the learning process by virtue of memory contents is distinguished from the *retroactive interference,* in which the learning limits the already available memories (Lidwell 2003). In the first case, it is difficult to remember a name when similar names are stored. In the second case, the learning of a word leads to the forgetting of a similar word.

3.1
CUMULATION
OF THE
SENSORY
CONTRIBUTIONS
↓
3.1.2
PERCEPTUAL
CONFLICTS

343

FIGURE 3.11
The perception contradicts stored patterns.
Meret Oppenheim, Object (fur-covered cup), 1936.
© 2011, ProLitteris, Zurich.

Figure 3.11 illustrates an example of playing with the expectations with respect to a given object. A common perceptual conflict arises during the consumption of foodstuffs if the feeling upon chewing and swallowing contradicts the expectations caused by the taste. For example, a furry sensation experienced by the tongue can diminish the pleasure. On the other hand fur was popular for a long time as a material for clothing, given its pleasant, soft, and warming nature and the positive tactile sensations which it can stimulate. The fur-covered *Object* by the artist Meret Oppenheim plays with these contradictions: no one would drink from a furry cup and use such a spoon. The direct, already visually stimulated sensation of the perceptual conflict, however, increases the attractiveness of this object. In conclusion, the following should be noted with respect to perceptual conflicts:

THE PERCEPTUAL SYSTEM TENDS TO COMPENSATE FOR THE INCOMPLETENESS AND THE DIVERGENCES OF SENSORY IMPRESSIONS. THIS IS BASED UPON THE FUNDAMENTAL PROPOSITION THAT THE PERCEIVABLE OBJECTS THEMSELVES ARE COMPLETE AND FREE OF CONTRADICTION. AN IMPORTANT ASPECT IN THE DESIGN OF OBJECTS IS THE KNOWLEDGE OF THE BOUNDARIES, THE POINTS AT WHICH DEVIATIONS CAN BE COMPENSATED FOR, OR AT LEAST TOLERATED, WITHOUT A NEGATIVE EVALUATION.

THE CHOICE OF CUSTOMER-EFFECTIVE STRATEGIES

After the parallelism of different strategies of connection of the sensory modalities has been identified, along with the processes which they enable in the perceptual system, the question arises as to which of the numerous possibilities should serve as the foundation for the design of objects and human-machine interfaces on an individual basis. Actually, not all mechanisms of connection need to be considered – moreover, it is important to choose a few, particularly important objects for a planned product and to select the appropriate perceptual properties. Indeed, that is the basis of the optimization of the product. Nevertheless, it is advisable to consider, where possible, the intuitive strategies of the cross-modal analogy, the iconic reference, and the symbolism, each with at least one property. Such combinations unite the strength of established symbolism with the directness of associative connections and the flexibility of analogy relationships. Figure 3.12 illustrates an example of the associative and symbolic connection of objects in print advertising of the 1950s. At the time, the car radio was routinely stylized as a new, indispensable component of the vehicle. For this purpose, symbolic and iconic elements are utilized in the graphics. The latter are based upon, nonetheless, form analogies between floodlights and rotary knobs as well as between the radiator grill and the frequency scale. In addition to gestures and mimicry, symbolic elements such as notes, blossoms, and a heart promise the added value of driving and riding in a car with a radio. The corporate logo contains elements of a radio tower and thus makes reference to the manufacturer instead of the broadcaster as the suggested primary source of positive feelings. The fact that the female driver enjoys the music with her eyes closed hints at the – possibly intended – humor of the era, as the driving skills of a woman were often called into question by men.

Generally, one may assume a hierarchy of the three intuitive strategies in the design process. The diagram presented in figure 3.13 serves as a simplified model.

344

3.2
THE CHOICE
OF CUSTOMER-
EFFECTIVE
STRATEGIES

SYMBOLISM BUILDS UPON ICONIC REFERENCES, WHICH IN TURN ARE BASED UPON ANALOGY RELATIONSHIPS.

Only when the symbolism is firmly anchored within the customer group, indeed to the extent that an alteration of the meaning does not come into consideration during the lifecycle of the product, it is able to be utilized without the support of other strategies. It is nevertheless more certain and assuring to strengthen the established symbolism by virtue of iconic properties. Even the generation of new symbolic contents, e.g., upon which the *Green Dot* builds the associatively shaped color symbolism, can occur in this manner (see section 2.4.2). Iconic elements can be generated by analogies, as demonstrated

3.2
THE CHOICE
OF CUSTOMER-
EFFECTIVE
STRATEGIES

345

FIGURE 3.12
The associative connection of the car radio
with the car itself. Advertising for Blaupunkt
car radios, end of the 1950s.

by the form analogies of figure 3.12. The configuration of new iconic and symbolic connections according to the triangular model must, therefore, occur from below in an upwardly direction. Analogy relationships enable maximal flexibility – thus, new connections can be quickly branded into the memory. Symbolism exhibits the greatest strength *(power)* of the connection, given that it enables the best possible attention and emotional participation *(involvement)* of the individual perceiving it. However, it requires a learning process and is endangered by *reassessments (shiftings)*. Furthermore, it must be noted that the neuronal operation of symbolic content requires the longest processing time.

FIGURE 3.13

PROCESSING TIME — FLEXIBILITY — STRENGTH OF THE CONNECTION

SYMBOLISM
SEMANTIC RELATIONS

ICONIC REFERENCES
OBJECT IDENTIFICATION

CROSS-MODAL ANALOGY
CORRELATION
OF BASIC FEATURES

DIRECTION OF DESIGN

The role of analogies, iconic references, and
symbolism in the design process.

346

3.2
THE CHOICE
OF CUSTOMER-
EFFECTIVE
STRATEGIES

**IT IS THUS NECESSARY TO ESTABLISH
SYMBOLIC CONTENTS BY VIRTUE
OF A FOUNDATION CONSISTING OF ICONIC
FEATURES AND ANALOGIES.**

FIGURE 3.14
Combination of symbolism, iconic references,
and analogies in the configuration of traffic signs.
Left: form analogy crossing;
middle: icon, skidding automobile as a concrete association;
right: icon, gradient combined with numbers.

Even the researcher of artificial intelligence, Douglas R. Hofstadter, in observing parallelism between mathematical form analogy *(isomorphy)* on the one hand and perception on the other, arrives at the conclusion that the discovery of analogous structures represents a decisive step towards creating meanings. An essential characteristic of the isomorphy is the possibility of depicting a complex structure onto another one, indeed in such a fashion that every part corresponds to a part of the other structure. This means that the related parts play a similar role in their respective structure. With regard to cognitive processes, the discovery of an isomorphy between two known structures amounts to a significant development in knowledge. Such discoveries of isomorphisms are those which create meaning in the human brain (Hofstadter 1979).

Traffic signs offer a good example of the combination of symbolic and iconic references with analogies. These signs create functional categories with simple fundamental forms – like circle, triangle, square, and arrow – and symbolic colors. In the case of the warning signs presented in figure 3.14, the abstract basic form *triangle* is combined with the highly symbolic color *red*. In this manner, the general symbol for the functional category "attention" is created. In order to increase the concrete nature of the warning, further elements are added: the *crossing* is symbolized by virtue of a form analogy. Nevertheless, the actual meaning – the instruction to apply the "right-before-left rule" – is not automatically evident. Moreover, it requires explicit learning. The icon of the *skidding automobile,* as employed in the middle, however, is an iconic reference with considerable clarity. The icon for *climbing,* as seen on the right, is also rather comprehensible, but it is not clear as to whether it involves a street with an ascent or with a descent. Here, at any rate, one follows the convention that a movement towards the right symbolizes the direction of travel – corresponding to the widely used direction of writing and to the typical presentation of time axes. Nonetheless, the proper interpretation of the numbers as a percentage value requires prior knowledge of its definition. However, it is not possible for most people to exactly allocate the indicated value precisely to an incline. As a rule, the given value is assessed either as "relatively large" or "relatively small."

3.2
THE CHOICE
OF CUSTOMER-
EFFECTIVE
STRATEGIES
↓
3.2.1
ASSISTANCE
IN DECISION-
MAKING

347

3.2.1
ASSISTANCE IN DECISION-MAKING

The systematic configuration of the multisensory aspects of products has the initial task of considering all different strategies of connection with the various partial processes in their totality, whereas the second step consists of selecting the decisive parameters and applying a purposeful optimization. In this respect, it is advisable to first compile a comprehensive matrix indicating all possibilities. Indeed, it is appropriate not only to list the *features* suitable for connections in every sensory modality oneself, but also to directly indicate the *possibility of connection* in the fields of the matrix.

The following example is illustrated by figure 3.15. In the upper left field of the matrix one can indicate whether it is possible, by virtue of the product configuration, to create a visual-auditory connection via cross-sensory analogies and using the intersensory attribute *intensity.* The color markings indicate which connections are to be numerically identified with the appropriate scales – this is generally possible with cross-sensory analogies – and designate where the configuration must be based upon qualitative correlations with an iconic or a symbolic context. The excursus regarding the scaling theory will provide more detailed information. In the design concept, it must also be determined whether the features are to be placed in the foreground or the background. This influences the connections between the sensory channels, for the allocation to the foreground or to the background shall be maintained beyond the modalities. For different classifications, such as the emotional analogy and connections between the basic forms, a fundamental methodology has not yet been developed.

It must be emphasized that a matrix of the form as presented in figure 3.15 should not contribute to unnecessarily increasing the complexity of the design process. Nevertheless, it is advisable to initially consider all features and strategies of connection in their totality in order to find reasonable simplifications. As a rule, the overall picture can be reduced to a few features upon which the synesthetic design can be based.

The essential connections between the modalities must be determined in individual cases by virtue of perceptual experiments. Prior to the experiment, the group of test subjects must be stratified according to the composition of the target group. This means dividing the overall group of possible customers into homogenous subgroups with similar expectations and patterns of decision. For the selection of the features preferred by the customers, schemata corresponding to figure 3.16-2 are of value. In the case depicted therein, visual elements can be correlated to the acoustic signal presented, by virtue of analogy relationships (top), iconic features (middle), or symbols (bottom). In this respect, the subjectively sensed, most appropriate connection is to be chosen. In a similar fashion, even different auditory signals can be allocated to a depicted visual structure, or tactile and olfactory aspects can be applied.

348

3.2
THE CHOICE
OF CUSTOMER-
EFFECTIVE
STRATEGIES
↓
3.2.1
ASSISTANCE IN
DECISION-MAKING

THE CHOICE OF THE SIMILAR OR THE DISSIMILAR CONFIGURATION OF THE CONNECTIONS OF ALL FEATURES BETWEEN THE MODALITIES IS ULTIMATELY A QUESTION OF THE CONCEPT WHICH SERVES AS THE FOUNDATION.

In researching associative connections, the *Stroop test* as described in chapter 3.1 is also appropriate. Thereby, the test subjects are required to spontaneously allocate terms to certain categories. Thus, it is not difficult to allocate first names to the categories *masculine* and *feminine.* If different categories are considered one after another – such as *household* or *career* – it can be verified as to whether associative interactions exists between the categories. In the example mentioned, it is possible to demonstrate the existence of gender-specific allocations. In a similar manner, even contexts in the allocation of different modalities can be examined.

The procedure of the systematic reference to connections between the modalities in the configuration process, as recommended herein, however, should not be understood as the compulsion to align all features in a similar fashion. Thus, it is not mandatory to correlate the inter-sensorial properties at all. An optimal, consensual adjustment would include, for example, that the visual and tactile roughness of a product correspond to one another and that the roughness of a functional sound is accordingly adjusted with appropriate precision. Figure 3.17 illustrates the basic possibilities of concept building.

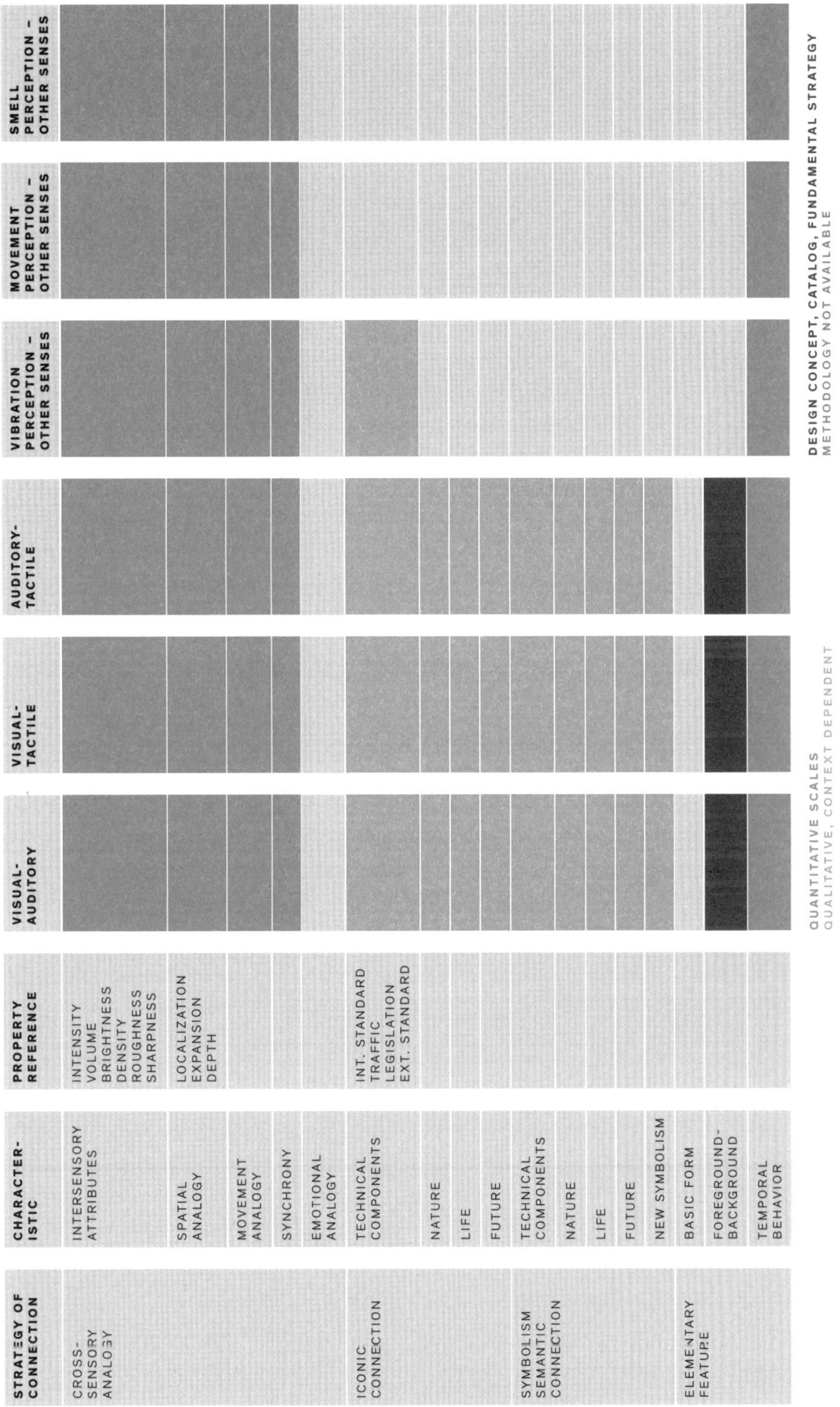

3.2
THE CHOICE
OF CUSTOMER-
EFFECTIVE
STRATEGIES
↓
3.2.1
ASSISTANCE
IN DECISION-
MAKING

349

FIGURE 3.15
Example of a decisional matrix for evaluating
and selecting the object properties which are essential to the
multisensory appearance of a product.

FIGURE 3.16-1
Schemes of selection for the allocation of sounds to visual
elements on the level of cross-modal analogy.
In the example, a noise signal is presented simultaneously to a set of symbols.

68

69

.352

3.2
THE CHOICE
OF CUSTOMER-
EFFECTIVE
STRATEGIES
↓
3.2.1
ASSISTANCE
IN DECISION-
MAKING

FIGURE 3.16-2
Schemes of selection for the allocation of sounds to visual
elements on the level of iconic features (green/top) and symbolism (blue/bottom).
In the example, the sound of an insect or the sound logo of the
Eurovision are presented simultaneously to a set of symbols (top to bottom).

The polarity profiles (see fig. 2.99) presented therein demonstrate the possible audio-visual strategies in the realm of movies. These strategies are characterized as *paraphrasing, counterpointing,* and *polarizing.* A consensual (left) or a contradicting (middle) characteristic can be aimed at. For example, a dramatic picture sequence can be supported by dramatic music or, on the other hand, it can be contrasted by intentionally quiet auditory elements. However, it is also possible to shift the primary emphasis of the expression via *polarization* only onto the visual or auditory configuration (to the right). In this case, uneventful, low-level optics would be contrasted with a lively film soundtrack. The classification and designation corresponds to the *ideally typical film music profiles* according to Hansjörg Pauli (1976, cited by Behne 1994). A consensual optimizing of the features creates a great degree of *coherence* and *harmony.* An oppositional optimization supports, by way of contrast, the *suspense* and binds the *awareness,* but can also give rise to the impression of an erroneous or non-systematic configuration – up to and including a perceptual conflict. As previously discussed in chapter 3.1, perceptual conflicts can also be a component of a conscious configuration.

With regard to sounds and music in films, one has to distinguish between *diegetic sounds,* which have their origin in the film world, like sounds produced during the film story, and *extradiegetic sounds,* which originate from an external source, like the film music. In principle, this differentiation also applies for sounds used in web applications and computer games. While external sounds in this case can address information for user interaction or – in the opposite direction – can be influenced by user input, the term *transdiegetic sounds* is sensibly used to describe the crossing of this border (Jørgensen 2007).

All in all, the complexity of the sensory stimuli should not be too great: for the auditory-visual harmonization, it is advisable to contrast complex music with simple images. However, if the music is structured in a simple manner, the visual stimuli could be more complex (Hurte 1982). Where possible, the mental overload or confusion of the recipient of sensory stimuli should be avoided.

3.2
THE CHOICE
OF CUSTOMER-
EFFECTIVE
STRATEGIES
↓
3.2.1
ASSISTANCE
IN DECISION-
MAKING

353

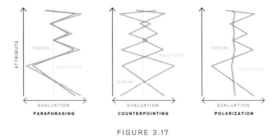

FIGURE 3.17
Audio-visual strategies in film, demonstrated by the application
of polarity profiles. The characterization corresponds to the ideally typical music
profiles according to Pauli.

After the features of all modalities essential to the synesthetic design have been determined and critically chosen, a configuration concept must be selected, according to which these can purposefully make reference to one another. The profiles depicted in figure 3.17 can serve as an orientation. Increments as desired are possible between the extremes. At any rate, however, the intentional choice and the mental consideration with respect to the configuration process are important.

EXCURSUS: REGARDING THE SCALING THEORY

For multisensory design, it is important to correlate elements of perception of one modality with those of another sense. Such elements are, for example, perceptual objects or their properties. For assessment of perceived features and quality, ranking scales are frequently used. Often the numbering ranges from 1 to 10, with 10 being the best rating. Those scales map the *mean opinion score* (MOS), which, in the field of automotive engineering, is named the *vehicle evaluation rating* (VER). In principle, elements can be characterized solely by virtue of their qualitative features – in this case, it involves *attributive data*. On the other hand, if it is possible to quantitatively describe elements with numeric values, *variable data* are available.

Two forms of attributive scales will be distinguished form one another:

NOMINAL SCALE
In this case, the elements can be named. These are equal, however, i.e. coordinate. Therefore, it is not possible to bring them into a sensibly ordered sequence.

Examples:
→ Use of numbers within Sudoku games
→ Apples, pears, bananas, oranges
→ Taste: bitter, sweet, salty
→ Braking sounds: squeaking, groaning, howling
→ Movement to the right, to the left, or straight ahead
→ Traffic light: Stop! Attention! Drive!

The perception of a color tone also suffices merely for a nominal scale, for there is generally no specific color sequence motivated in terms of perceptual psychology, if further parameters such as brightness are excluded. A physically sensible arrangement of colors corresponding to the light frequency or to the light wavelength exhibits no direct reference to the perception. The situation is different, however, with respect to the brightness or the saturation: in perceptual experiments, both values could be described by ratio scales (see below).

ORDINAL SCALE (RANKING SCALE)
In addition to naming the elements within the framework of a nominal scale, the ordinal scales allow the sequencing of the elements without the allocation, however, of numerical values.

Examples
→ According to size: lime, lemon, orange, grapefruit
→ Trade Class: A, B, or C
→ Temperature sensation: cold, warm, hot
→ Brake noise: squeaking at 2.4 or 6 kHz
→ Test result: passed, failed
→ Quality evaluation: product rejected, borderline, satisfactory, good, very good, outstanding
→ School grades: 1, 2, 3, 4, ... or A, B, C, D, ...

Value figures appear here as well, however, they make no numerical reference to one another. As a rule, the sense of hearing will categorize a squeaking of different frequencies purely qualitative as low, middle, or high. Only the musically schooled ear or a listener capable of the absolute pitch perception will perceive 4 kHz as being "twice as high" as 2 kHz. Even if numbers are used, the scale of school grades tends to be regarded as qualitative. The qualitative difference between 3 and 4 does not have to exactly correspond to that between 1 and 2, and 4 is not "twice as bad" as 2. In contrast to the attributive features, the allocation of elements occurs with variable data - which are identified by numerical values - via *metric scales:*

INTERVAL SCALE

This numerical scale behaves in an "interval-proper" manner. Equal distances between numbers correspond, therefore, to equal changes in the properties of the described elements. For example, a change in a certain numerical value at every point along the scale indicates an equal change in the quality which is described by the scale. Therefore, that certain numerical value corresponds to a certain change in a feature. This property of the interval scale is known as *additivity.*

Examples
→ Sound pressure level in dB (see section 2.2.3): the addition of a level value corresponds to the multiplication of the sound pressure with a certain factor, regardless of the range of the scale level on which the values may be found. Even at 0 dB, an acoustic event is existent. A doubling of the level, however, causes a greater increase than only a doubling of the loudness.
→ Temperature scale in °C: This scale is characterized by the fact that an increase from 10 to 20°C corresponds to an increase from 30 to 40°C. Nevertheless, the temperature 40°C is not perceived to be twice as warm as 20°C.

RATIO SCALE

According to the ratio scale, not only constant intervals correspond to constant changes in the properties. Moreover, the numerical values can be placed directly into the relationship. A numerical value of 100 thus corresponds, by way of comparison, to the value 50 exactly as a doubling of the observed parameter. This is possible, if the scale exhibits a defined zero point which corresponds to a zero point of the property described.

Examples
→ Temperature scale in Kelvin
→ Psychophysical quantities such as loudness in [sone] or brightness

The temperature scale in Kelvin exhibits a clearly defined zero point which physically corresponds to the complete absence of warmth and the complete immobility of molecules. The zero point of the Celsius scale, however, arbitrarily makes reference to the freezing of water – and, thereby, a random motion (Brownian motion) of the molecules takes place. Nearly all psycho-physical values arise as a result of efforts to derive ratio scales for describing the relation of perception and stimulus. In the loudness scale in *sone*, for example, 4 sone are twice as loud as 2 sone; 0 sone are not yet perceivable. In a similar manner, the value 0 of brightness equals complete darkness.

EXAMPLES OF APPLICATION

Hereafter, some examples of product design will be presented, allowing the intertwining of the strategies of connection and the deployment of inter-sensorial properties to be demonstrated. The presentation of these examples does not mean that the products have been configured in the sense of a systematic approach, as such an approach is described in this book. In individual aspects, however, a synesthetic design is already achieved among different products. The examples are intended to animate the reader to conduct his or her own analyses.

It is also important to indicate the cross-sensory strategies which enable the manufacturer to influence the customer's evaluation of the multisensory overall appearance of a product. With the assistance of analogy relationships, it is accordingly possible to fundamentally alter even strongly fixed associative fields of products. Furthermore, it is possible to connect the sound, the visual appearance, and the attributes of other senses in such a manner that the result is accepted by the customer as an obvious unity. Thus, a sporty automobile concept must no longer limit itself to customary associations, such as making reference to the sound behavior of classic racing cars – moreover, the acoustic configuration can achieve plausibility by virtue of analogies to attributes of other modalities as well as expectation with regard to the functionality. If analogies are consciously and systematically applied, a greater creative freedom and the improved acceptance of innovative approaches can be gained. Additionally, the market capability of the product can be predicted with greater certainty and can thus be optimized.

356

3.2
THE CHOICE
OF CUSTOMER-
EFFECTIVE
STRATEGIES
↓
3.2.2
EXAMPLES OF
APPLICATION

WRITING

The handling of a ballpoint pen is supported by the perception via various sensory channels. The patenting of the ballpoint pen occurred in 1938. Initially, it was used by the British and American air forces, given its operability even amidst pressure fluctuations in the environment without running out – as compared to a fountain pen. Following World War II, the ballpoint pen achieved great popularity in the civilian sector as well. Currently, several million pieces are sold every day. In Germany in the 1950s, this item was among – along with chewing gum and Coca-Cola – the most popular products which were adopted from the United States. In addition to their purely functional features, such as reliability and the longer usage of the refill, the widespread popularity of the product as a promotional gift results in high sales figures. Figure 3.18 illustrates some examples for its utilization as a promotional gift in the engineering realm.

The principal component of the ballpoint pen is the pipe-shaped refill (reservoir) filled with a viscous ink paste. At the tip, a small metal sphere is enveloped in a chamber, and this sphere rolls along the sheet of paper and releases, thereby, a defined amount of ink. Ball point pens are primarily furnished with a push button, enabling the refill cartridge to be extended and to be retrieved after usage, guaranteeing that the writing tip is thus protected and also incapable of causing any unintended staining. The refill cartridge is locked in both positions. Feedback as to the proper extension and retrieval of the refill cartridge occurs tactilely, auditorily, and visually. In extending the cartridge, the thumb moves against the increasing reactive force of the spring. Simultaneously, the grinding of the mechanics on the casing is audible and can be felt. The response of the locking is indicated by a click sound which can also be sensed by a vibrating impulse. ● Now, the operational force on the push button must be reduced, in order to allow the locking mechanism to move into place and lock. Thereby, once again, a considerable impulse is audible and capable of being felt. The extension and the retrieval of the cartridge back into the resting position require the expenditure and the dissolution of a force – this leads to, in turn, a second impulse stimulation. Thus, the extension and the retrieval accordingly involve four audibly noticeable impulses – a fact which is unpleasantly conspicuous, for example, when participants in a discussion nervously activate the mechanism. Actually, this can be avoided with a rotating mechanism which, as a general rule, does not exhibit a particularly auditory signal effect. Furthermore, an additional advantage of the push-button mechanism is the possibility to activate it with a single hand. This necessitates merely a change in the position of the hand. The robust and reliable operation of the mechanism is conveyed via cross-modal analogies of the tactile with the auditory, notably by virtue of the simultaneously audible and perceivable impulses. Nevertheless, some ballpoint pens exhibit audible movements of the push button of its own which are not systematically related to the operational process. The roughness of the grinding of the push-button mechanism and the sound quality of the clicks additionally convey associative information regarding the overall quality of the product.

3.2
THE CHOICE
OF CUSTOMER-
EFFECTIVE
STRATEGIES
↓
3.2.2
EXAMPLES OF
APPLICATION

357

FIGURE 3.18
Ballpoint pens are popular promotional gifts –
not only in engineering.

The movement of the push-button can also be visually observed. In the case of some ballpoint pens, the writing position and the resting position can be distinguished from one another by virtue of the location of the button. Given the tactile and auditory feedback pertaining to the operational process, however, the visual components are of secondary significance.

The functional meaning of sounds heard during the writing process itself is often underestimated. ● ● ● ● ● ● Different functional principles of pens lead to characteristic properties. In the case of the ballpoint pen, the writing sound provides important information as to the hardness of the surface which is being written upon. This may not be too soft (quiet sound), but it should also be neither too smooth (no sound or altered sound quality) nor too rough (dropouts in the sound). In these cases, an evenly flowing rolling of the ballpoint and thus the transport of the ink can not be guaranteed. Hence, the proper function during writing is also conveyed by the rolling sound of the ballpoint. Even then, in spite of the perfect functioning, undesired side noise can be generated, contributing to a reduction of the quality attraction.

SAFETY

As already discussed, using the example of the parking brake of automobiles, in the case of operational elements crucial to the safety of a function, feedback as to the proper nature of the operational process is of considerable significance. Thereby, it is advisable to convey this feedback simultaneously by virtue of various modalities. In this regard, the company HOPPE offers window catches which are equipped with a special lock designed to deny the opening of the window from the outside via the closing leverage. The safety function, i.e. the locking of this special mechanism, is conveyed by an auditory signal, namely by a clicking sound. ● figure 3.19 illustrates this locking mechanism in a graphic of the manufacturer. The auditory configuration of the locking mechanism employs a combination of the strategies *cross-modal analogy* and *iconic connection.* The click sound is heard at certain rotational angles and it is reminiscent of the sound of the closing of a safe. These sound properties were consciously chosen in order to grant the feeling of a considerable degree of security. Thus, the clear audibility of each click was given priority in the designing phase.

79

358

3.2
THE CHOICE
OF CUSTOMER-
EFFECTIVE
STRATEGIES
↓
3.2.2
EXAMPLES OF
APPLICATION

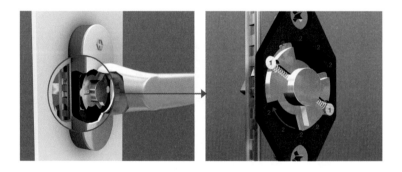

FIGURE 3.19
Window catch with a mechanics to protect against
burglars and to create a sound of safety.
The pictures demonstrate the safety mechanism which also
generates the sound. Secustik System of the Hoppe AG,
introduced in 2000.

As figure 3.20 shows, the product advertising makes purposeful visual reference to the desired connection between the functional handle and the sound which is based upon the association with the security of a safe. Even the product name *Secustik* sensibly emphasizes this concept by virtue of an amalgamation of the words *secure* and *acoustics* [Akustik].

FIGURE 3.20
The combination of function and an associative sound.
Presentation in the print advertising of
the Secustik System of the Hoppe AG, 2000.

AIR

3.2
THE CHOICE
OF CUSTOMER-
EFFECTIVE
STRATEGIES
↓
3.2.2
EXAMPLES OF
APPLICATION

359

Streaming air is utilized to supply meeting and residential rooms with fresh air as well as to remove disturbing particles. The sounds which thereby arise give essential information as to the quality of the air and as to the effectiveness of the process. In the case of fresh air supply, air which is pure – indeed as fresh – as possible is desired. Significant information regarding the quality of ventilation is conveyed by virtue of the inter-sensory properties as already indicated in figure 2.25. Loudness, spatiality, and density of the sound make reference to the effectiveness of the ventilation, whereas tone color and roughness address the air quality. The roughness, in particular, is a quantity for the perceived impurity of the air. Therefore, it is necessary to minimize the roughness as much as possible. Additionally, sharpness and fluctuation must be considered: great sharpness reveals a too narrowly measured air outlet, whereas the fluctuation allows conclusions to be made as to the poor performance or the inadequate robustness of the ventilator.

In operating a vacuum cleaner, on the other hand, the impurity of the absorbed air indicates the effectiveness of the cleaning process. Therefore, the roughness – caused by the dust particles – and the impulsiveness of the sounds are actually desirable (see section 2.2.3).

The interaction of function, ergonomics, visual attraction and sound behavior shall be expounded upon in the following example:

The *Root Cyclone* vacuum cleaner developed by James Dyson demonstrates its innovative technology by virtue of a distinctly technical, future-oriented visual appearance (fig. 3.21). The transparent dust container provides a view of the core of the principle – the stripping of dust particles by virtue of centrifugal force. The configuration proudly presents its technical components, for nothing is – as compared to the "good form" of the 1950s – hidden beneath a neutral coat. Moreover, it obviously aims at acquiring sensual aspects extracted from the functional clarity. For this purpose, the color, but also the form elements as well as the large wheels appear to be quite "stylish." Essential elements seem to be influenced by a science fiction ambience. The turbine-like optics is supported by an appropriate sound. Upon being activated, a whistling sound whose tone pitch increasingly rises – corresponding to the rising rotational speed – becomes audible, and this gives rise to associations with the starting of an aircraft engine. The overall sound is light and thus abounding in high frequency components. Nevertheless, such a sound is not perceived by all people as being pleasant – indeed, it is considerably more technical than a typical suction sound, which would actually suffice in order to fulfill the function. The uncompromising commitment to innovative technology, nonetheless, is clearly articulated in a visual fashion as well as in an auditory manner. In times of founded skepticism towards an unrestrained ideology of technical progress, however, this configuration is greeted by acceptance, given that it involves a distinctly sustainable technology which no longer requires disposable components such as the dust bag.

FIGURE 3.21
**The visual attraction reflects the commitment
to innovative technology. James Dyson,
Root Cyclone vacuum cleaner DC29, 2009.**

360

3.2
THE CHOICE
OF CUSTOMER-
EFFECTIVE
STRATEGIES
↓
3.2.2
EXAMPLES OF
APPLICATION

REFRESHMENTS

Trade with drinks is flourishing, and the expectations of experiencing *freshness* are great. Newspaper reports from 2007 note that only one of two Germans occasionally drinks water from the faucet in order to quench his or her thirst. Moreover, every tenth person even refrains from using faucet water in preparing coffee and tea. Offensive commercials for mineral water attempt to increase the popularity of water in bottles. In addition to advertisements with particularly healthy, mineral components and the sensation of freshness enhanced by carbonic acid, increasing usage is also made of aromas, such as, in particular, fruit aromas. Although the drinking water from the faucet is one of the most intensively monitored forms of foodstuffs, and, though one can even inquire as to its composition and receive an answer from the provider, the subjective perceptual qualities and the related, ingeniously associated evaluations are – in an environment of health and healing consciousness – of a decisive nature for the sales.

Analogies are particular suitable for modifying the image associated with a product and for thus reaching new customer groups. Therefore, they are increasingly utilized in advertising. Firmly anchored iconic features and symbolisms can undoubtedly result in achieving stable customer groups by virtue of the fixed market position of a product; however, they complicate the accommodation of new circumstances and expansion in general. These problems can only be avoided by anchoring modified fields of association. The manifest nature of new iconic references can, nevertheless, be plausibly presented via the systematic application of analogies.

3.2
THE CHOICE
OF CUSTOMER-
EFFECTIVE
STRATEGIES
↓
3.2.2
EXAMPLES OF
APPLICATION

361

FIGURE 3.22
Drops of water and effervescent bubbles on bottles and glasses
as a sign of freshness. The pile of luminous points
corresponds to elementary, endogenous basic patterns of the
perceptual system (left and right, respectively, according to Horowitz 1970).

An essential characteristic of freshness is offered by water drops appearing on bottles and glasses, as depicted in figure 3.22. Occasionally, even the television monitor appears to become moist from within if a refreshing drink is consumed in a commercial. In this manner, the freshness of the drink is conveyed visually. The same function is fulfilled by pictures of water in natural waterfalls or in lakes surrounded by a forest. Here, a pile of luminous points as a gleaming reflection sometimes assumes the role of the water drops. Some gleaming pearls support even the symbolic contents of slogans for Krombacher Pils (Krombach Pilsner Beer) as a "Pearl of Nature." Similarly, sparkling bubbles in mineral water, wheat beer, and brisk champagne are also employed as signs of particular freshness. Returnable bottles of mineral water contain semicircular elevations which make reference to the bubble or drop motif. Thus, as figure 3.23 illustrates, this motif additionally acquires a solid, tactile component. The design of these "Pearl Bottles" was conceived in 1969 by Günter Kupetz. The pile of luminous points corresponds to elementary basic patterns of the perceptual system. The depiction on the left-hand side of figure 3.22 is influenced by the arrangement of such *endogenous* patterns compiled by Mardi Jon Horowitz (1970, see also Eichmeier 1974). The presentation in this case appears to be inverted, in order to emphasize the character of phosphenes. Bright structures along a dark background, which correspond to the elementary basic patterns of the perception, particularly raise the attention of the observer.

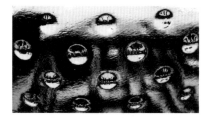

FIGURE 3.23
Tactile bubbles on the surface of a glass bottle.
Günter Kupetz, Pearl Bottle, 1969.

362

3.2
THE CHOICE
OF CUSTOMER-
EFFECTIVE
STRATEGIES
↓
3.2.2
EXAMPLES OF
APPLICATION

FIGURE 3.24
The form of the water bottle conveys
the characteristic of flowing water in building
amorphous structures. Ross Lovegrove,
Water Bottle, designed for Ty Nant, 2001.

FIGURE 3.25
Left: "Trickling Well"; right: "Splashing Well."
The work of schoolchildren in the art class of Rudolph Gahlbeck,
1920s (Anschütz 1930).

A characteristic of fluids is the building of amorphous structures with literally *flowing* transitions. Containers of liquids, on the other hand, usually exhibit clear and geometric forms which contradict the properties of the contents. Figure 3.24 indicates, however, that it is also possible to express the impermanence of a fluid by virtue of the configuration of a glass. The overall appearance is reminiscent of a melting block of ice as well as the form of streaming water flowing out of the faucet. Thus, the configuration of the bottle conveys iconic aspects of freshness and purity.

Sounds of trickling and splashing water often awaken the visual impression of a pile of bright points. This is, among others, evident in the work of schoolchildren illustrated in figure 3.25, which, in addition to pointed and star-shaped structures, also exhibits serpentine lines. Thereby, the colors blue and green, with their symbolism based on iconic features, play a similarly essential role in advertising. Further examples from television and print advertising demonstrate the application of analogy relationships, such as, for example, movement analogies and inter-sensory properties in the definition of the product appearance. In the following cases described, it involves efforts to free beer from its image as a "masculine drink" and to grant the product an erotic component. Even though beer is now just as naturally consumed by women, the product image is still characterized by associations of men drinking at the bar, bowling nights, and football broadcasts. Indeed, with such a product, an erotic element comparable to that advanced by sparkling wine or champagne can hardly be identified. Nevertheless, in exploring and developing analogy relationships in commercials, the connection of beer consumption and erotic can acquire great plausibility:

MOVEMENT: In a commercial for Bit-SUN (a derivative of Bitburg Pilsner), a movement analogy is consequently utilized. Within the framework of the plot, men playing with beer bottles correspond to the movement of female bodies: The pushing of the bottle along the bar also moves the woman towards the guest, the placing and the tilting of the bottle at the mouth mirrors the bodily contact and the movements of a dancing pair, removing the label of the bottle corresponds to undressing.

PRICKLING: The decisive analogy in the commercial for Schöfferhofer Wheat Beer is provided by virtue of the property of *prickling,* which creates a connection between wheat beer and champagne just as between drinking and erotic feelings. This analogy is further strengthened by the allusion of drinking from the navel of the woman (naturally a French woman), a classic erotic allusion which was originally related to champagne or sparkling wine. The enjoyment of wheat beer, moreover, promises *sustainability* in the analogy to erotic feelings, "for it prickles longer than one drinks."

GOLD: In a similar manner, with the slogan "For golden moments!," a commercial for Warsteiner Pilsner Beer simultaneously attempts to stage the golden-yellow, luminous drink – waiting in the sidelights – and to establish a connection between the color aspects of the product and its symbolic contents.

3.2
THE CHOICE
OF CUSTOMER-
EFFECTIVE
STRATEGIES
↓
3.2.2
EXAMPLES OF
APPLICATION

363

All elements of advertising which are intended to demonstrate the properties of the product are strongly influenced by the context. Figure 3.26 demonstrates that, for example, water drops on a glass surface can also carry negative messages. In the context of street traffic during rain, the water drop motif used so successfully as a positive aspect in advertisement for refreshment drinks, changes its meaning completely and thus suffers a negative evaluation.

FIGURE 3.26
**In this context, drops lead to
negative evaluations.**

TIME

Indeed, there is hardly a physical quantity which influences the life of modern man as much as time. Time structures daily life with great precision. Neither the mastering of the daily routine, nor the communication between people, nor the course of economic processes of all forms can apparently be enabled without the division and the scheduling with reference to the time. In particular, the work routine is affected, for trade and production mandate exact temporal planning. Exhibiting an impressive symmetry to professional life, however, even the time for recreational activities is minutely planned. Only then can the apparently too scarcely available free hours be optimally utilized. "On the pulse of the time," the recreational time tends to be configured in an adequate rhythm with respect to the occupational rhythm. People subject themselves voluntarily to the interplay of traffic lights on the streets, to schedules in sport clubs and of concert events, and with television programs, which is often determined well in advance. Production efficiency, as defined by time planning for the purpose of earning money, thus corresponds symmetrically to the efficiency of consumption, which has the objective of gaining an emotional added value in the individual lifestyle.

In observing the precisely clocked life in the industrial societies of the twentieth and twenty-first centuries, however, it should not be overlooked that human life was also subject to numerous natural, periodic processes even prior to the computation of time and temporal planning. This applies to the pulse of the heart functions as well as to other biorhythms, e.g., the interaction of sleep and wake periods, the temporally defined development steps from the embryo to the adult life, and the entirety of life. The periodical movements of celestial bodies, moreover, give rise to the periodic interaction of day and night, the position of the sun, the moon, the planets, and the stars and thus of the

364

3.2
THE CHOICE
OF CUSTOMER-
EFFECTIVE
STRATEGIES
↓
3.2.2
EXAMPLES OF
APPLICATION

annual seasons. The precise temporal planning of modern human being thus perfects the integration into the periodic processes, which is naturally already existent. Accordingly, temporal planning is a necessity and a burden from which people – at least temporarily – attempt to flee. The visual configuration of modern watches makes direct reference thereto. It reflects either the desire of the users to achieve absolute precision or to relativize the compulsion to subject themselves to the strict rhythm. Therefore, in the past and nowadays as well, watches are quite suitable as status symbols which reflect lifestyle (fig. 3.27).

Figure 3.28 illustrates a wristwatch whose elements of configuration are reduced to a functional minimum. The precision is expressed by the high-contrast geometry, sharp edges, symmetry, and technical colors. The wristwatch presented articulates a factual relationship to time. The configuration is based upon elementary basic forms which build cross-sensory analogies to temporal sensation. This is supplemented by a very visible secondhand which is even recognizable in darkness.

3.2
THE CHOICE
OF CUSTOMER-
EFFECTIVE
STRATEGIES
↓
3.2.2
EXAMPLES OF
APPLICATION

365

With regard to the visual perceptibility in configuring the dial, namely the face of the watch, it must be recognized that vertical and horizontal structures are more visible than the diagonal ones. This so-called *oblique effect* guarantees the exposed accentuation of the times 3, 6, 9, and 12 o'clock, as well as an obvious subdivision of the hours in the units of 15 minutes. Diagonal lines of various inclinations are sufficiently visible, nevertheless, if the angle between both of them is at least 30 degrees. As a result, the 12-hour display of analog watches is preferred to the 24-hour display, for the angular difference in the case of the latter amounts to merely 15 instead of 30 degrees – such watches are thus less legible (Lidwell 2004).

Among many watch models, the division into different sub-displays strengthens the impression of a reliable technical system. In this regard, moreover, the stopwatch function represents the quintessence of perfection, which is aspired with a sportive attitude. Technically interested people prefer, nevertheless, digital watches. Even the date display and the other calendar functions enhance the professional attraction and the diversity of the product, as often desired by business leaders and by customers who value such an image. The success of the manager is dependant upon the precision of his or her temporal planning just as much as the life of a diver depends upon the diver's watch.

The configuration of watches for people who wish to distance themselves from the, as they see it, hostile precision of daily temporal burdens, however, is quite different. In such cases, the number of visual signs symbolizing the minutes and the hours on the watch are often dramatically reduced to a minimum – or they are completely absent. A line suffices for the information of the hour and the approximate minute in the case of analog watches, e.g., in the position 12 o'clock. Thus, a secondhand would tend to conflict with the self-conception of such users. Instead of precise technical details, associative and emotionally meaningful elements are employed in the configuration. In this regard, displays in lively colors are more likely to reflect the general lifestyle of the user, as compared to a rigid subjugation to temporal burdens. The strict symmetry of the dial is interrupted by asymmetrical structures. With the assistance of iconic references and symbolism, these elements combine design, temporal sensation, and the emotion of being alive.

FIGURE 3.27
Ancient watch design between the poles of precision
and lifestyle – a proven status symbol.
Window of an antiques shop in Istanbul, Turkey.

366

3.2
THE CHOICE
OF CUSTOMER-
EFFECTIVE
STRATEGIES
↓
3.2.2
EXAMPLES OF
APPLICATION

FIGURE 3.28
A wristwatch with a markedly simple, functional design.
Braun AW 12, 2007.

EXCURSUS:
TIME AND LIFE

The relationship of modern man to time is characterized by ambivalence. This is particularly clear in the late-nineteenth-century painting *Der Kaktusliebhaber* (The Cactus Lover) (fig. 3.29). It depicts a magistrate who, standing between stacks of files, sentimentally gazes at the red blossom of a cactus plant.

At the top of the picture, a monstrously large clock is visible, lurking in its oversized form as a gloomy object and so defining the scene. This can be interpreted as a prophetic reference to the dominant role of time in the industrial age which becomes increasingly prevalent in the modern age of global communication. The dominating role of time, however, is contrasted here by a "small journey into tranquility." With its unusually slow growth, the cactus symbolizes the eternity to which the magistrate devotes himself. A small eternity is also necessary for a cactus to yield a blossom. Moreover, in contrast to the slow growth, as a general rule, the blossom withers away rather quickly. Cactus blossom often exhibit their mostly colorful beauty during a single day, sometimes even only during the night.

Thus, the observation of the blossom can not be postponed. Therefore, the magistrate depicted is not merely a fan of these plants in their timeless existence, but also, in particular, a connoisseur of pensive tranquility reflected by the blossoming cactus. This is also supported by the posture of the magistrate and also by the fact that the plant faces him as well. Undoubtedly, this aspect contains a touch of irony with which the painter creates a caricature of the scene: for enthusiasts of house plants know that plants on the windowsill constantly orient themselves towards the light and thus towards the window. The cactus friend, surrounded by the stacks of his unattended work, must have rotated the plant himself in order to enjoy the illusion of timelessness.

The picture described accordingly illustrates the possibilities and the dilemma associated with time as a dominant principle of everyday life, and this is precisely the point comprehended in the design of modern clocks.

FIGURE 3.29
Time as a predominant
principle and the desire for timelessness.
Carl Spitzweg, Der Kaktusliebhaber
(The Cactus Lover), ca. 1850.

SUBJECTIVE AND OBJECTIVE TIME

Time is a phenomenon which takes effect as an alteration of physical and chemical circumstances and is reflected in the perception. The subjectively perceived time exhibits a great variability. Even the interaction between hearing and seeing influences the perception of the time: thus, a musical piece is perceived as being longer when a static picture is thereby presented. On the other hand, the temporal perception is shortened if the very same musical piece is accompanied by an animated film sequence. In a comparable manner, the duration of a film sequence appears lengthened if it is observed without sound – in contrast to control experiments with musical accompaniment (Anceschi 2000).

The momentary perception of time distinguishes itself considerably from the memorizing of temporal courses in the past. The difference between subjective experience in the present on the one hand, and the overview of greater points of time in the memory on the other, is aptly described by Thomas Mann in his novel *The Magic Mountain [Der Zauberberg],* in which he additionally differentiates between an eventful and a monotonous life:

"Emptiness and monotony may stretch a moment or even an hour and make it 'boring,' but they can likewise abbreviate and dissolve large, indeed the largest units of time, until they seem nothing at all. Conversely, rich and interesting events are capable of filling time, until hours, even days, are shortened and speed past on wings; whereas on a larger scale, interest lends the passage of time breadth, solidity, and weight, so that years rich in events pass much more slowly than do paltry, bare, featherweight years that are blown before the wind and are gone." (Mann 1924, trans. John E. Woods, 1996).

368

3.2
THE CHOICE
OF CUSTOMER-
EFFECTIVE
STRATEGIES
↓
3.2.2
EXAMPLES OF
APPLICATION

MULTISENSORY LOGOS

As already discussed in chapter 2.4, in the configuration of logos and signets, it is increasingly important to involve different senses in the process (Roth 2005, Hehn 2007, Kilian 2009). Within the realm of synesthetic design, even here, a coordination of the various strategies of the perceptual system to the maximum extent possible should be the goal. Two examples of this:

FIGURE 3.30
Logo of the Milk Union Hocheifel (MUH).

The logo of the Milk Union Hocheifel in figure 3.30 combines the abbreviation of the corporate name with the icon of the manufacturer – the milk cow. The abbreviation of the corporate name contains the onomatopoetic imitation of the characteristic sound of the animal as expressed in language. Thus, the animal's sound itself becomes a sound icon. Correspondingly, the letter *m* is modified to depict a cow. Indeed, the *m* is simultaneously a text component and a visual icon. Accordingly, this represents an exact coordination of visual and auditory components of the trademark on the level of iconic references. The blue line initially supports the impression of an etiquette – a mark in the original sense of the word. The oval form may be found among many logos – e. g., the emblems for FORD and KIA. This is based on the form of sheet metal stickers which used to be screwed onto the products. In the variation of the logo as presented here, however, the color blue of the line also advances the notion of a cow on the pasture along a stream. And it may also be interpreted as a curve of movement, which once again emphasizes the melody of the animal sound. The clear reference of the mark to the milk cow itself succeeds in transferring the great sympathy felt for the animal to the product.

The logo of DEUTSCHE TELEKOM in figure 3.31 also illustrates a connection between auditory and visual elements – particularly in the original form which was used until 2007 (left). The associated jingle consists of five individual tones. ● It imitates the word melody of the corporate name: "Deut-sche-te-le-kom." Accordingly, an imitation of language by music is formed. Every dot corresponds to a tone of the same tone pitch. On the other hand, a higher tone is allocated to the T – the allocation corresponds to the conventions of a notation system, or rather to a *notational synesthesia*.

3.2
THE CHOICE
OF CUSTOMER-
EFFECTIVE
STRATEGIES
↓
3.2.2
EXAMPLES OF
APPLICATION

369

·· ╦ Deutsche Telekom   **· · · · · ·** ╦ **· ·**

FIGURE 3.31
Logos of the Deutsche Telekom.
Left: original logo with an exact reference to the sound logo;
right: short form of the logo as used since August 2007.

This represents an intentional application of cross-modal analogies in the connection of the modalities. However, the illustrated logo represents merely the basic model of the sign. By virtue of constant alteration, it is modified in order to sustain the attention of potential customers. Similarly, the melody is modified by different acoustic tone colors. For example, during a Christmas action, the sound of bells was used. Accordingly, an additional iconic reference comes into play without compromising the already present elements of connection. Thereby, the identification of the acoustic source is decisive: only by virtue of the specific sound of "jingle bells" is the broad associative spectrum of the Christmas holidays epitomized. Today, the logo appears completely in magenta as the trademark color of the DEUTSCHE TELEKOM GROUP (fig. 3.31 below). The color magenta is an example of the purposeful establishment of color symbolism. The three characteristic dots are now located on the right side of the logo – the number of dots on the left side can be varied according to the application. The primary colors magenta, gray, and black serve to distinguish different trademark labels from one another, such as T-MOBILE, T-SYSTEMS, and T-HOME (DT 2007). Thus, new forms are derived from simple basic elements. For commercial material, the corporate design additionally prescribes secondary colors which exhibit a maximal color saturation of 60 percent and convey a light, bright mood. The font TeleGrotesk is consistently used. In this example, the visual differentiation of trademark elements is overall greater than that of the sounds which are employed – variations of the sound logo are instead limited to modifications of the tone color.

3.2.3

HUMAN-
COMPUTER
INTERACTION

In the interactive utilization of computer systems, it is particularly useful to convey information via various sensory channels. The concentration of the data conveyance upon one modality quickly leads to overburdening – *overflow* – of the sensory channel. As depicted in chapter 1.3, every sensory channel has a limited channel capacity at its disposal, due to physiological reasons. If this information is exclusively conveyed in a visual manner, there is a greater risk of operational errors as a result of the overflow of the visual receptivity. If quick reactions of operators – e.g., by the pilot of a jet airplane – are required, even a short-term overflow can have drastic consequences.

**A CONVEYANCE OF DATA
VIA SEVERAL SENSORY CHANNELS
INCREASES THE CAPACITY
OF PROCESSING AND MINIMIZES
THE RISK OF ERRORS.**

370

3.2
THE CHOICE
OF CUSTOMER-
EFFECTIVE
STRATEGIES
↓
3.2.3
HUMAN
-COMPUTER
INTERACTION

Additionally, the storage capacity of the memory will be utilized in a better manner, and information gaps in a modality can be compensated for by information via other senses. In this fashion, the increased redundancy improves the certainty of the data transmission and thus the precision with which objects can be recognized and situations can be evaluated (Anceschi 2000). Even the comprehension of auditory responses can be improved with the participation of further sensory channels, such as that of the visual system, allowing the risk of erroneous interpretations to be minimized.

The purely visual configuration of computer applications is already the subject of detailed publications (see e.g., Khazaeli 2005). As already described above, however, it is advisable to configure interactive systems generally as multimedia products. As a rule, these provide the information in the form of *hypertexts,* in which no linear reading direction must be observed, allowing instead the free, sensible rambling of the reader across a network of connections. Such products are *interactively* applicable, given that they enable the user to influence or to steer the system behavior through his or her own entries. The output of such systems *triggers* the holistic perception, as it addresses multisensory representations of the environment which are arranged within the individual (Anceschi 2000). These representations were identified in section 1.3.4 as perceptual objects. In that which follows, different elements of the interactive entry and output of information will be more closely examined. It is revealed that cross-modal analogies for functional allocations of operational activity and system reaction are of deciding significance.

KEYBOARD

Feedback as to the function of the keyboard pertains to the tactile sensation of force and displacement as well as to the characteristic sound. ● An ergonomically configured key has a pressure point which is to be overcome by a defined finger force. A movement of the key, which ends on a stroke, can be perceived only afterwards. Even the path of the overall movement as well as the dynamic counterforce must be precisely defined and consistent. On a keyboard, as a rule, these parameters are equal among all keys, in order to give the impression of a robust configuration. Overcoming the pressure point initiates the activation of a function. Therefore, it is important to convey a particularly precise response as feedback. Supporting the tactile information by an impulse sound is additionally recommended. Furthermore, a consciously designed surface texture of the keys can provide tactile indications of the finger position or the function of specific keys, in either an iconic or symbolic manner. Simple salient bars often indicate the position of the index fingers of each hand. It may also be useful to identify each key tactilely with engraved symbols or characters.

3.2
THE CHOICE
OF CUSTOMER-
EFFECTIVE
STRATEGIES
↓
3.2.3
HUMAN-
COMPUTER
INTERACTION

371

MOUSE

The computer mouse is guided by the wrist, the thumb, and the ring finger – the index finger, the middle finger, and the ring finger, thereby, serve to operate the keys and the scroll wheel. The form and the surface of the mouse must facilitate the exact handling without unintentional relative movements between the mouse and the hand. The friction arising between the mouse and the pad beneath it *(mouse pad)*, nevertheless, must be minimal and consistent. The transition from the static to the dynamic friction at the beginning of the movement of the mouse should occur easily and precisely. The properties of the light reflection in the optical sensor or the roll friction of the ball mechanism also influence the operability and, in particular, the precision with which the cursor follows the mouse movement. In addition to the visual and the tactile aspects, the grinding sound which arises in moving the mouse provides important feedback as to the execution of the steering task. ●

FIGURE 3.32
Ergonomically shaped computer mouse
with scroll wheel, optical scanning, and wireless transmission.
Microsoft, 2006.

The movement of the *mouse* and the *cursor* must appear to be congruent. Disturbance variables include, on the one hand, the limited precision of the location detection of the mouse. Thereby, imprecise movements of the cursor occur without being tactilely perceptible. On the other hand, the slide resistance for the mouse movement along the pad is never entirely smooth. While perceptible, it can only be motorically compensated for in a limited manner. Furthermore, the perception of the cursor movement on the monitor can be influenced by the texture or the movement of the background (Riccò 2003).

The *scroll wheel* of the mouse serves the function of providing increments for the vertical movement of documents on the monitor. In addition to the proprioceptive information of the finger position, the feedback occurs via mechanical impulses and auditory "clicks." For the operational reliability, the precision of mechanical and acoustic pulses is just as important as the synchronization between the pulse and the incremental movement of the picture *(image jump)*. The incremental movement must occur precisely in order to exactly alternate between individual pictures. In the case of quick movement, the pulses mesh to a continual sound with great roughness – the incremental movements of the monitor contents appear as a continual movement. Thus, the position of the objects moved along the monitor is a function of the finger behavior. The displacement of the finger movement is transformed into a displacement on the screen. Even the keys of the mouse have to be characterized by precise pressure points and acoustic signals.

372

3.2
THE CHOICE
OF CUSTOMER-
EFFECTIVE
STRATEGIES
↓
3.2.3
HUMAN-
COMPUTER
INTEGRATION

STATIONARY MOUSE

The functional principle is based on a static ball *(trackball)* which is rotated with the fingers or the palm of the hand. Thereby, the spatial demands are reduced, and the operational element can also be mechanically fixed to a laptop. The steering depends on the path and the angle of the rotational movement of the ball. With respect to immovable computers, however, the stationary mouse is generally not as prevalent. In the case of laptops, the integrated operational elements such as a *touchpad* and a *trackpoint* serve as viable alternatives.

TOUCHPAD

With a touchpad, the movement of a finger across a sensory surface leads to the movement of the cursor on the monitor. Thus, the path of movement along the monitor is proportional to the path of the finger on the pad. Even in this case, the static friction must be small in order to guarantee a flowing transition from the static to the dynamic friction. The pad should not stick nor should it feel sticky as an aftereffect – this could lead to an erroneous reaction of the user. If the force required at the beginning of the finger movement, in order to overcome the static friction of the finger resting upon the pad, is considerably greater than the force necessary to continue the movement, an excessively rapid movement can occur, limiting the control of the cursor movement. This creates – just as the sticking upon the raising of the finger – a feeling of reduced control and of a non-robust system behavior.

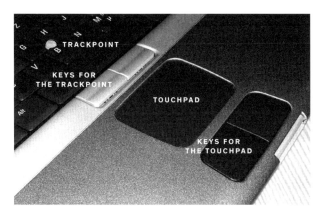

3.2
THE CHOICE
OF CUSTOMER-
EFFECTIVE
STRATEGIES
↓
3.2.3
HUMAN-
COMPUTER
INTEGRATION

373

TRACKPOINT

The distance to the neighboring key amounts to, in the case of this operating element, merely a few millimeters. In contrast to the touchpad, the static friction between the finger and the surface of the trackpoint must be considerable. Dynamic friction must be avoided in order to prevent the finger from releasing a neighboring key. Due to reasons of space, the decisive mechanical value for the feedback is not the displacement, but the force necessary to shift the trackpoint from its original position. The applied force determines the speed of the cursor – it is proprioceptively and tactilely perceived.

TOUCHSCREEN

In the case of the *touchscreen,* the finger has to be applied with a relatively large angle in order to be able to carry out the functions. That results in a high probability of static friction. A pressure point is often not available, and the feedback pertaining to the proper execution of a release process must, therefore, be artificially created in the form of optical and acoustic reactions. Tactile feedback, however, can artificially be created by application of small vibration exciters which generate sensible periodic movement of the screen surface. Such feedback can significantly improve the usability and accuracy of a touchscreen. If combined with auditory feedback, synergy effects have been demonstrated (Altinsoy 2010).

Thereby, the defined proximity of partial sub-areas with which functions are associated is important. If these surfaces are smaller than the contact surface of the fingers, a tool, such as a pen, is necessary for operating. Special pens such as the *stylus* and the *touchpen* are used for this purpose. Due to the accurate spatial alignment of elements for input and output, respectively, touchscreens gain increasing popularity as customer interfaces (e.g., cash and ticket terminals) and hand-held devices (portable media players, cellular phones).

In order to optimize spatial classifications, the application of a three-dimensional view in the monitor is appropriate. In the framework of a stereoscopic presentation, both eyes have to be supplied with different signals. This can occur by a two-color presentation – e.g., red-green – whereas the image elements of only one color can be conveyed via a color filter to each eye. For interactive purposes, the entry of spatial movement is possible as a result of movement sensors in a remote control which conveys the steering signals to the computer by virtuc of a cable or in a wireless mode. Today, many video games, e.g., those which are steered by a Wii remote control, function according to this principle. Thus, it is possible to engage in sports with realistic body movements. In order to simplify the usage, the input device was intentionally equipped with associative features of sports equipment in combination with a traditional remote control. A comparable technology is applied to simulate movements in virtual environments. For this purpose, movement sensors are affixed to the extremities and the head. Force and pressure sensors, which are integrated into special gloves, enable the user to provide input haptically.

As already mentioned, in addition to the visual monitor information, auditory feedback is also essential to the execution of steering functions – thus, the human-machine interaction is considerably improved. Thereby, along with cross-modal analogies, the iconic contents of sounds also move into the foreground. Known sounds, such as the rolling sound of a ball, are preferred by computer users as feedback as compared to abstract sounds – they also require the least learning endeavor (Rath 2008). Therefore, efforts are undertaken to limit real sounds to their minimal associative contents *(cartooning)*. In this manner, one receives generally valid sound objects which are synthetically created, but which make clear iconic reference to known processes, such as the walking of persons or the rolling of a ball (Rocchesso 2003).

374

3.2
THE CHOICE
OF CUSTOMER-
EFFECTIVE
STRATEGIES
↓
3.2.3
HUMAN-
COMPUTER
INTEGRATION

3.3
ELEMENTARY
FORMS
↓
3.3.1
BASIC FORMS
OF PERCEPTION

375

As a rule, genuine synesthesiae are connected to the perception of simple, abstract forms. In this regard, the graphics of figure 3.34 illustrate a series of bubble-like structures and cubes which appear to move in space. The perceptions were observed while listening to music.

Similar patterns can appear as *hypnagogic visions* shortly before sleeping. In addition to these phenomena, comparable forms can be found in descriptions of hallucinations and of appearances following pathological alterations of the brain. Migraine attacks can also be accompanied by luminous, ring-shaped, sharp-pointed appearances which are referred to as *fortification figures,* given that they are reminiscent of the structural designs of medieval fortresses. One also assumes that the visions of the medieval mystic Hildegard of Bingen were influenced by the visual phenomena of migraine (Sacks 1985). The consumption of drugs can also evoke visual appearances which are similar to those of genuine synesthesia. In contrast to the great consistency of synesthetic perceptions, drugs lead to phenomena of greater variability which are reproducible only to a minimal amount.

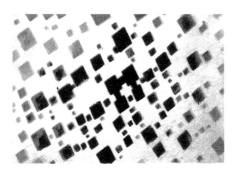 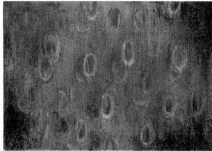

FIGURE 3.34
Basic forms in images of genuine synesthesia (Anschütz 1927).
Left: bubbles wandering from top to bottom
through the field of view while listening to Richard Wagner's "Magic Fire"
of the musical drama Die Walküre (The Valkyrie) (Max Gehlsen).
Right: static cubes distributed in a room – while listening to a traditional
folk melody based on staccato tones (Heinrich Hein).

FIGURE 3.35
Basic forms of visual perception – redundant elements
in hallucinations and visual imagery (Horowitz 1970).
For clarification of the phosphene character, the original graphic
was inverted in the brightness.

376

3.3
ELEMENTARY
FORMS
↓
3.3.1
BASIC FORMS
OF PERCEPTION

In cases in which visual basic forms appear as luminous structures, these are characterized as *phosphenes.* Horowitz provides an overview of the basic forms as presented in figure 3.35. These patterns are apparently arranged within the perceptual system and can thus be referred to as *endogenous image patterns.* The presentation is comparable to other aspects of the literature, e.g., the analysis of visual perception in a mescaline high (Klüver 1926), or in the course of the described experiments with the artificial stimulation of the optic nerve (Eichmeier 1974).

Perceptions of elementary visual forms also occur often in connection with supplementary functions, e.g., after the affected person has gone blind. Figure 3.36 illustrates an example which was caused upon hearing a drum roll (Voss 1930).

Even forms which are affiliated with esoteric viewpoints are often similar to those in reports of synesthetic perception. Typical examples are provided by the *thoughtforms* and *music forms* of theosophy (Leadbeater 1999, Hodson 1976). Here, visual forms appear upon hearing music. Esoteric and religious world views, however, are constantly the result of a combination of *perception* and *interpretation* – the latter is not the subject of this discourse. Nevertheless, the question as to which perceptual phenomena influence such views is interesting (Dann 1998). In the mass media, much attention is given to ascertaining what clairvoyants *know.* It would be more interesting, however, to ask what they *see.*

As mentioned before, Josef Eichmeier and Oskar Höfer examined the visual perception of numerous people during the electrical or magnetic stimulation of the optic nerve (Eichmeier 1974). Thereby, phosphene structures were stimulated, sketched by the test subjects, and finally allocated to a catalog of endogenous image patterns. Even pressure stimuli upon the eye lead to similar appearances. Lateral pressure upon the eyeball results in a circular or star-shaped structure appearing on the opposing side of the visual field. Furthermore, if the head is struck, the affected person can "see stars."

FIGURE 3.36
Visual perception, caused by the sound of a drum.
According to the description of a person gone blind (Voss 1930).

3.3
ELEMENTARY
FORMS
↓
3.3.1
BASIC FORMS
OF PERCEPTION

The similarity of the observed form classes of the phosphenes to the basic patterns of children's drawings and to ceramics of the Stone Age is conspicuous. Figure 3.37 compares the frequency of occurrence of phosphenes during electrical stimulation to the frequency of ornamental structures of the Upper Paleolithic in Europe (according to quantitative data in Eichmeier 1974, 54). Even though there are differences between these respective frequencies, the similarity of the observed form classes is clear. In the ornaments of the Stone Age ceramics, only one structure appears which was not observed during the electrical stimulation of the optic nerve – the meandering structure.

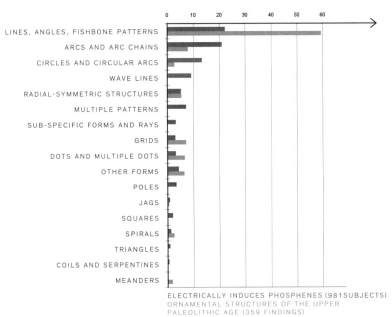

FIGURE 3.37
Frequency of occurrence of the phosphene form classes during
electrical stimulation (Eichmeier 1974) as compared to the frequency
of ornamental structures of the Upper Paleolithic in Europe
(according to Eichmeier 1974; based on data from Müller-Karpe 1966).

As mentioned before, August Petersen described the permanent coupling of the synesthetic perception of a bright, fan-shaped object to the hearing of the sounds of stringed instruments (Petersen 1931, see chapter 2.5). Similar structures were also found by Eichmeier and Höfer and allocated to the form class "lines, angles and fishbone patterns" (Eichmeier 1974).

The perception of endogenous image patterns evidently provides information pertaining to the basic forms of perception implemented into the visual system, which are required to construct complex visual pictures but which generally do not enter into the consciousness as forms themselves. Knowledge as to these building blocks is thus valuable in choosing the appropriate, elementary forms for design.

Visual forms observed during acoustically stimulated synesthesia apparently represent the forms significant to the elementary connection of auditory and visual perception. Approaches for multisensory configuration can be derived from this. Accordingly, these basic patterns should fundamentally be integrated into experiments on sound perception to connect both modalities.

FOR A SYNESTHETIC DESIGN WHICH INVOLVES ALL SENSES, IT IS IMPORTANT TO DEVELOP APPROPRIATE FORM CATALOGUES EVEN FOR OTHER SENSES AS WELL, IN PARTICULAR FOR THE AUDITORY AND TACTILE PERCEPTION.

3.3
ELEMENTARY
FORMS
↓
3.3.1
BASIC FORMS
OF PERCEPTION

Thereby, one must first answer the question as to which simple structures should already be perceived as separate, self-contained forms. These are the "atoms" from which complex objects – and thus perceptual objects – are configured. Classifications of elementary forms provide an important basis for examining connections between the modalities. This requires clarifying the second question, namely the question as to which basic forms in the perception prefer to interact with one another – and which ones do not. If this question is answered, for example, the form of a switch can be chosen which optimally harmonizes with the – possibly functionally determined – click sound. Conversely, the auditory configuration of the click can accommodate the visual and tactile appearance.

AS A PREREQUISITE, THE FORM CLASSES AND THEIR PREFERRED CONNECTION BETWEEN THE MODALITIES FOR EACH TARGET GROUP OF INTEREST SHOULD BE EXAMINED AND CONFIRMED.

Approaches for determining the appropriate catalogues of basic elements may be found in the area of olfactory cognition. Here, complex sensory stimuli are composed on the basis of elementary essences. A compilation of the essences as an instrument of the configuration of smells is also referred to as a *scent organ* [Duftorgel], reminiscent of a musical organ with a keyboard, as in Luckner (2002). In an analogy thereto, Friedrich Blutner regards elementary auditory patterns as *hearing essences* (Blutner 2002). Towards a conception of abstract music films, Oskar Fischinger made reference to the notion of the *color organ*, although the color in his films, in contrast to form and movement, actually tends to comprise a secondary element (Moritz 1993, 65).

The existence of synesthetic perceptual phenomena in which colors are allocated to visual figures such as letters of the alphabet or numbers touches upon the design problem of colors and forms. The Russian painter and art theoretician Wassily Kandinsky extensively discussed the contexts of form and color harmony (Kandinsky 1911). The considerations led to, among others, the allocation scheme presented in figure 3.38. Although the scheme initially appears arbitrary, it comprises, nevertheless, an allocation of the *angledness* of forms to color tones. Kandinsky later expanded and systematized the allocation of colors to angles (Kandinsky 1926). Additional angular degrees subsequently correspond to a scale with colors whose characteristic brightness constantly decreases:

YELLOW (30°)   ORANGE (60°)   RED (90°)   PURPLE (120°)   BLUE (150°)   BLACK (180°)

3.3
ELEMENTARY
FORMS
↓
3.3.1
BASIC FORMS
OF PERCEPTION

379

FIGURE 3.38
The three basic color tones yellow, red, and blue
distributed with respect to the three basic forms of the same surface
contents triangle, square, and circle. The allocation also
applies to the spatial forms tetrahedron, cube, and sphere.
According to a color panel of Rudolf Paris, Bauhaus (Düchting 1996).

FIGURE 3.39
Expansion of the allocation of colors and forms.
According to Eugen Batz, Bauhaus 1929/30 (Düchting 1996).

Therefore, yellow and red are allocated to the equilateral triangle and the square. The circle is blue, as the blunt angle 150° is seen as a "premonition of the curved." Figure 3.39 illustrates a free expansion of the color allocation to the triangle, the square, and the circle with an effort undertaken towards building intermediate steps. As systematic combinations can be built from colors by virtue of additive or subtractive mixtures, the deduction of combined forms is unclear. However, different approaches are conceivable; for example, the uniting of parts of every form to create new objects. This can be seen in figure 3.39, below in the middle: the deduced violet form is created by the halves of the square and the circle. Another possibility consists of the aforementioned scaling of angular degrees with colors corresponding to the color brightness.

3.3.2
ELEMENTARY DESIGN

In examining elementary basic forms of perception, a question arises as to the applicability of simple elements within the framework of synesthetic design. If efforts to create such basic forms in every sensory modality succeed, a direct allocation and optimization of design features is possible beyond the sensory boundaries. Every product design is based upon a combination of forms. These define elements which clearly distinguish themselves from one another, but which lead to, nevertheless, a coordinated, harmonic unity (fig. 3.40). The fusion of expressive forms clearly distinguished from one another thus leads to a dynamic form language (fig. 3.41).

FIGURE 3.40
Combination of forms and colors in a taillight.

FIGURE 3.41
The expression arises as a result of the combination of distinctive forms.

380

3.3
ELEMENTARY
FORMS
↓
3.3.2
ELEMENTARY
DESIGN

Gestalt concepts of modernity orient themselves, in particular, with respect to elementary forms which are initially of a visual – in New Music of an auditory nature. In the first half of the twentieth century, visual concepts were represented by the design movement De Stijl and the Bauhaus (1919–1933) and linked to approaches of functionalism. Moreover, De Stijl, in particular, combined the simple, geometric form with the primary colors yellow, blue, and red as well as with white and black. This is also evident in the paintings of Piet Mondrian.

In the 1950s, comparable form concepts were reapplied in order to combine a "purged" design, free of ornaments, with functional clarity. As various teachers of the Bauhaus had been immigrating to the US, e. g., Walter Gropius, László Moholy-Nagy, Josef Albers, and Ludwig Mies van der Rohe, significant influences of Bauhaus design took root there. The educational methods inspired teaching at various institutes, like Black Mountain College (1933–56), the Graduate School of Design at Harvard University, and the Chicago "New Bauhaus," which was directed by László Moholy-Nagy from 1937.

In Germany, the University of Applied Sciences for Design in Ulm played a major role (1953–68) in the continuation of Bauhaus concepts; for example, products of the Braun company display essential features of this design direction. In this regard, figure 3.42 shows the construction of a household appliance from clear, elementary forms. The practical, consequently functional design refrains from every form of ornamentation and thus corresponds to the rationalistic style of the postwar era in Germany. Another example is the Braun SK4 record player with a transparent cover, also known as "Snow White's Coffin" (see also fig. 1.22).

In the Burg Giebichenstein of the University for Art and Design in Halle, the Bauhaus tradition was further advanced. Towards the end of the twentieth century, the primary focus there shifted from a visual to a multisensory design (Luckner 2002).

3.3
ELEMENTARY
FORMS
↓
3.3.2
ELEMENTARY
DESIGN

381

FIGURE 3.42
Elementary forms as a basis of configuration.
Gerd Alfred Müller, KM 3 Kitchen Machine, designed for
Braun GmbH (1955–1964).

Fundamental approaches to a "basic design," which orients itself with respect to basic forms, are also pursued by the faculty for industrial design at the Politecnico di Milano (Anceschi 2002). There, as well, reference is made to approaches involving the application of visual forms in design, as developed at the Bauhaus with reference to elementary perceptual processes. The objects developed in this manner are characterized by simple, abstract geometric forms and the use of as few materials as possible. The relationship between design and processes of visual perception were examined, in particular, by the Bauhaus artists László Moholy-Nagy and Josef Albers within the course of their practical work.

As already indicated, the forms observed during the acoustically stimulated visual synesthesia provide information as to the basic elements important to an elementary connection of auditory and visual perception. Generally speaking, every visual, auditory, and tactile structure can be composed by elementary basic forms. For clarification, figure 3.43 compares the design of a headlight with a selection of endogenous image patterns – these are typical phosphene structures (Eichmeier 1974).

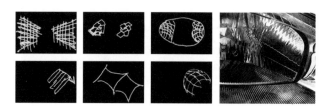

FIGURE 3.43
Design of a headlight as compared to
endogenous image patterns observed upon the electrical stimulation
of the visual system (Eichmeier 1974).

Thus, it is advisable to base a consequently synesthetic design on elementary basic forms. In addition to the already well-researched visual basic forms, the equivalent auditory and tactile basic forms are also to be determined. By means of perceptual experiments, the forms by virtue of which allocations allow themselves to be constructed between the modalities should subsequently be ascertained. Tracing the product appearance back to simple basic forms, however, does not necessarily mean a dogmatic fixation with respect to modern concepts; moreover, iconic and symbolic aspects can be purposefully superimposed. Ultimately, every configuration can be traced back to elementary components.

**ELEMENTARY FORMS,
AS THE DETERMINING BUILDING BLOCKS
OF MULTISENSORY CONFIGURATION,
MUST CONSTANTLY BE CONSIDERED IN ORDER
TO OPTIMALLY UTILIZE FUNDAMENTAL
CONNECTIONS BETWEEN THE MODALITIES.**

382

3.3
ELEMENTARY
FORMS
↓
3.3.2
ELEMENTARY
DESIGN

A functional reference can be quickly established by virtue of simple forms (fig. 3.44), which are particularly appropriate in carrying meaning. Therefore, the forms of packaging for CDs (square) and DVDs (rectangle) are associatively deduced from the forms of covers for LPs and video cassettes. Both are easily distinguishable, even though the actual product exhibits a completely identical form (circle). Among product families which generally exhibit a rectangular form, quadratic forms are more distinguishable and can directly advance to trademark status, as in the case of RITTER SPORT chocolate and of PIXI children's books in Germany. Michael Bernd Siegle describes the *circle, the cube, the triangle, the cross,* and the *arrow* as primal signs with fundamental symbolism (Siegle 2005).

An assessment with respect to meaning and function must accompany the definition of appropriate basic forms. That results in the *hierarchization* in the sense of the landscape/soundscape concept described in section 2.2.5 which consequently distinguishes between elements of the foreground and the background. Additionally, functional units must be sensibly combined. In the configuration, mechanisms of grouping in the perceptual system, as discussed at the beginning of section 1.3.7, should be considered as well. Figure 3.45 shows an example of a successful hierarchization in the operational environment of the driver of an automobile. The instrument cluster, ventilation, and radio with CD player are clearly separated from one another, and yet they form a unit, which is framed by a curved line. Careful hierarchization is also necessary with respect to the auditory environment. Without a clear incrementalization, the Gestalt formation of the perception is overburdened – an impression of uncalculated noise arises. The work of Giacomo Balla, as depicted in figure 3.46, visually illustrates this process. The juxtaposition of ambiguous figures (see section 1.3.9) creates a structure which confuses the observer as to the foreground and the background. Depending upon which image section is being observed, different figures appear in the foreground. Changes in the sampling movement of the eyes can result in a surprising alternation of forms between the foreground and the background. In this manner, the observer sees an analogy to noise.

3.3
ELEMENTARY
FORMS
↓
3.3.2
ELEMENTARY
DESIGN

383

FIGURE 3.44
Design based upon elementary basic forms. In this regard,
the functional appearance is combined with an overall aesthetic appearance.
The combination of black matte and shiny surfaces creates a
phosphene-like effect. Braun Impression KF600 Coffee Maker, 2007.

FIGURE 3.45
An example of the successful hierarchization of an operational surface.
The rounded, curved overall structure encompasses various areas for the instrument cluster,
ventilation, and entertainment. Ford KA, 2006.

FIGURE 3.46
An insufficient differentiation of individual figures with respect to
the background can be interpreted as an analogy to noise. Giacomo Balla, Forme Rumore
("Noise Forms" or "Noisy Forms"), 1917. © 2011, ProLitteris, Zurich.

3.4
VISUALIZATION OF NOISE AND MUSIC

3.4.1
ARTISTIC AND TECHNICAL VISUALIZATION

Within the framework of multimedia applications, it is interesting to create visual structures which correspond as plausibly as possible to given sounds and music passages. Furthermore, noise measurement technology has the task of presenting complex acoustic phenomena in a manner allowing the elements necessary for auditory perception to be more easily recognized. The analysis by the sense of hearing is then supplemented by a visual evaluation of the graphics deduced from the acoustic recordings. Noise often exhibits broadband, spectral, and temporally less differentiated structures, which are caused by random processes. Such sound processes correspond to images which are appropriately less differentiated in the vertical and the horizontal directions. Visual noise appears on the television screen, for example, when no signal is received. A comparable image arises upon looking in darkness: thereby, an image of light points appears which arises due to the spontaneous activity of the sensory cells themselves. The noise even overlays the retinal image of minimally illuminated objects. Comparable effects appear on the sensory chip of a digital camera in the case of insufficient light intensity.

Figure 3.47 illustrates efforts to artificially develop structures corresponding to auditory noise. It involves still images of an abstract film which is conceived as *visual music* without sound (Riccò 2007). The spectral, broadband structure of typical noise is transformed into a wide, animated structure which continually changes, without giving the eye an opportunity to focus on an individual, salient object. Consistent with section 2.2.5, these forms allow the interpretation as typical background figures. Efforts to recreate music with visual structures without auditory stimuli led to various approaches of *color-light music* (Goldschmidt 1928, Stoltenberg 1937) and abstract films (e.g., Hans Richter 1921, Viking Eggeling 1924; see also Richter 1952, DF 1989) at the beginning of the twentieth century. With the visual recreation of music in film, in particular, one was confronted with the question of the organization of time. It was soon clear that such attempts would be thoroughly incapable of completely replacing music. However, they advance the philosophical approach to formal aspects of music and visual arts – while searching for a universal language. Dieter Schnebel's *MO-NO: Music to Read* (Schnebel 1979) as well as various ef-

384

3.4
VISUALIZATION
OF NOISE
AND MUSIC
↓
3.4.1
ARTISTIC AND
TECHNICAL
VISUALIZATION

3.4
VISUALIZATION
OF NOISE
AND MUSIC
↓
3.4.1
ARTISTIC AND
TECHNICAL
VISUALIZATION

385

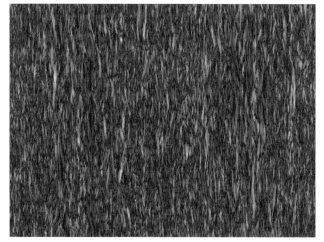

FIGURE 3.47
Sound structures of the abstract animation film
WONOKROMO by Adriano Abbado, 2004. The film is based on two
sound-like structures which are sequentially presented
and continually altered.

forts to describe music in the form of static images (Maur 1985, Fink 1987, Brougher 2005, Jewanski 2009; see also Adorno 1967) point in this direction.

In the presentation of measured or calculated sound parameters, it is also important to consider elementary perceptual analogies as much as possible, in order to enable the observer to comprehend as quickly as possible and to avoid mistakes. In terms of the scaling theory, visual features chosen for the presentation need to correspond to the scaling types of the sound attributes (see excursus in section 3.2.1). As an example, the color tones can only be applied as non-quantified, attributive data. If one does not take differences of brightness into consideration, the colors build a nominal scale and can thus be applied only as an analogy to the auditory features without ranking and without a quantitative description.

AN OPTIMAL OR A NATURAL COLOR SCALE IN TERMS OF PERCEPTUAL PSYCHOLOGY DOES NOT EXIST.

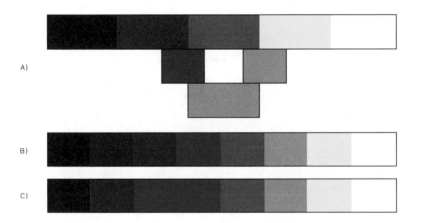

386

3.4
VISUALIZATION
OF NOISE
AND MUSIC
↓
3.4.1
ARTISTIC AND
TECHNICAL
VISUALIZATION

FIGURE 3.48
The building of color scales in consideration of brightness:
A) according to Francois d'Aguilon, 1613;
B) according to Anschütz, 1928;
C) according to Eugen Batz, Farbleiter ("Color ladder"), rotated
in this presentation by 90 degrees, Bauhaus, 1930.

The color choice is a question of individual preferences – such as color listening as a synesthetic phenomenon – as well as a question of sociocultural circumstances which make reference to associations and to the comprehension of color symbolism. Often, the color sequence of the rainbow is chosen as the color scale, which corresponds to the arrangement according to wavelengths of monochromatic light. Before Isaac Newton illustrated the relationship between wavelengths and colors by virtue of dissecting prisms (Newton 1721), however, color scales which arrange color tones according to increasing brightness were regarded as *natural.* Figure 3.48a illustrates such a color scale dating back to the seventeenth century. Thereby, violet and orange are regarded as color tones which can be deduced from the primary color scale. This scale also does not include green – it is, nevertheless, deduced from orange and violet. From antiquity into the nineteenth century, colors were more likely to be distinguished from one another by virtue of their brightness instead of their color tone itself (Roque 2002). Experiments of the 1920s, as depicted in figure 3.48b, also indicated that most persons tended to allocate colors according to their brightness (Anschütz 1928, 16). The allocations of color scales to tone pitches, vowels, times of the day, increments of distance, days of the week, and numbers also correspond to this tendency.

In contrast to the objective allocations described in section 2.6.2, this involves subjective *color-tone relations.* As compared to section 2.5.4, however, these relations are not individual, but of a common nature. A comprehensive subjective theory of color perception was already developed by Goethe (1810). However, this was initially met by opposition supporting the knowledge advanced by Isaac Newton, who oriented himself with respect to the physical properties of light (Newton 1721). As a matter of principle, both were right in their own way: physical phenomena generate stimuli by virtue of which processes of visual perception are initiated, which ultimately lead to the sensation of subjective perceptual qualities.

Contrary to the pure color tone, the brightness is seen as a rational scale, exhibiting a zero point – darkness – and a quantitative reference, thus being suitable for the visualization of corresponding acoustic attributes, such as the loudness (see also McCabe 2010).

3.4
VISUALIZATION
OF NOISE
AND MUSIC
↓
3.4.1
ARTISTIC AND
TECHNICAL
VISUALIZATION

387

GENERALLY SPEAKING,
A COLOR SCALE DESCRIBING AUDITORY
PHENOMENA IS PARTICULARLY
WELL-RECEIVED WHEN IT IS CHARACTERIZED
BY CONTINUALLY INCREASING OR
DECREASING BRIGHTNESS.

Nevertheless, the brightness or saturation for a color tone can not be randomly chosen. Moreover, there is a characteristic brightness for every color tone – e.g., great brightness for yellow and white, middle brightness for green and red, minimal brightness for blue, brown, and purple.

Therefore, a color scale with an appropriately accommodating characteristic brightness should be utilized for the description of an auditory attribute which corresponds to an ordinal, interval, or rational scale. Figure 3.49 provides an example of the presentation of the sound pressure level of an automobile in a *Campbell diagram* with a color scale ranging from black via blue, red and yellow to white. The graphic makes reference to the interior sound as measured in the passenger compartment while increasing engine speed from the idle state to the maximum. ● ● The presentation applies a brightness which continually increases with the acoustic level, thus supporting the building of a cross-modal analogy. This color scale has already been proposed by Eugen Batz of the Bauhaus (fig. 3.48c, Düchting 1996).

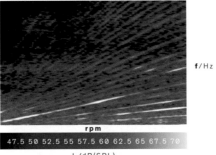

f/Hz

rpm

47.5 50 52.5 55 57.5 60 62.5 65 67.5 70

L/dB(SPL)

FIGURE 3.49
Presentation of engine noise in a Campbell diagram utilizing
a color scale with monotone increasing brightness.
Ordinate: frequency in Hz; abscissa: rotational speed rpm as revolutions n
per minute; color scale: sound pressure level in dB.

In the synesthetic context observed here, this color scale for the presentation
of automobile sounds exhibits the following advantages:
- The monotonous increase from cold to warm color tones corresponds
  to the increase of thermal, kinetic, and acoustic energy.
- The dominant primary frequencies of the engine *(engine orders)* appear
  yellow/white and symbolize the energy of the combustion process.
- The light lines of the engine orders on a darker background are similar
  to *phosphenes,* thus arousing attention and being easy to identify as
  patterns.
- The contrasting pair *red/green* with the distinctively symbolic polarity
  positive/negative is avoided. The characteristic brightness of both colors
  is almost equal; green is thus superfluous in this case.

Due to the aforementioned advantages, the described scale should be preferred
to the *rainbow scale,* given that the latter does not exhibit continually increasing brightness. Moreover, the herein depicted *Campbell diagram* accommodates the cross-modal analogy construction by virtue of the upwardly directed
frequency axis – corresponding to the increase of tone *pitch.* The rotational
speed axis presented from left to right, analogous to the direction of writing,
corresponds, furthermore, to the continual increase of dynamic properties
with the rotational speed.

The question remains as to which degree a visualization which is based
upon physical data corresponds to subjective perceptual contents. Synesthetic images often resemble the results of sound analyses. Figure 3.50 demonstrates this finding on the basis of the sound of a singing bowl (Haverkamp
2006c). ●

The visual perception arising from the juxtaposition of different tones
corresponds approximately to the graphic presented to the left. The height of
the lines behaves analogous to the tone pitch of the partial tone; simultaneously, the brightness of color and the brightness of sound are corresponding.
The time is presented as proceeding from left to right, corresponding to the
direction of writing in European culture. The graphic to the left, however, is
not constructed. Instead, it corresponds to the image which arrives upon the

388

3.4
VISUALIZATION
OF NOISE
AND MUSIC
↓
3.4.1
ARTISTIC AND
TECHNICAL
VISUALIZATION

sound being heard. The singing bowl applied comes from Nepal, although it has a construction form typical of Tibet. Due to the very thin wall, the bowl generates various partial tones upon being struck with a wooden clapper. Some partial tones are independent of one another – they are partially perceived as individual tones. They exhibit different intensities, although the temporal duration of the fading out strongly varies. Additionally, some partial tones demonstrate a distinct modulation, i.e. a rhythmic alternation of the loudness comparable to the vibrato played on a musical instrument. The sound analysis to the right demonstrates that the vibrato consists in an alternation of the sound pressure, i.e. an amplitude modulation. In the perceptual image, this effect appears as an alternation in the thickness of the line corresponding to the partial tone. Other partial tones, however, exhibit no alternation. In the case of a simple acoustic stimulus – e.g., an individual tone – and for the subordinated simple perception, Anschütz applies the term *analytic synopsis* [Analytische Synopsie] (Anschütz 1927a). The example discussed shows, however, that even an individual sound is already capable of evoking a rather complex synesthetic image.

3.4
VISUALIZATION
OF NOISE
AND MUSIC
↓
3.4.1
ARTISTIC AND
TECHNICAL
VISUALIZATION

389

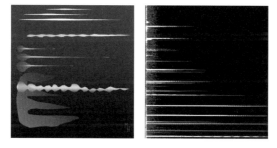

FIGURE 3.50
Visualizations of the sound of a singing bowl.
Left: subjective perceptual image. Drawing by the author according to own perception.
Right: result of a physical sound analysis.

FIGURE 3.51
Visualization of the sound of a bat, based on a physical analysis.
The temporal axis of the three-dimensional diagram
proceeds from the front to back, the frequency axis from left to right.
The colors and the heights of the curves mark the relative
strength of the frequency portions.

Given that spatial hearing is possible and that auditory perceptual objects thus generally appear to be spatially expanded, it is advisable to present such measurement results in a three-dimensional form. Figure 3.51 shows the technical visualization of the call of a bat, the *lesser horseshoe bat*. ●

For this purpose, the ultrasonic signal, which is incapable of being heard by people due to its high frequency in the range 100 to 120 kHz, was initially transformed to the audible range.

The temporal axis of the diagram proceeds from front to back, the frequency axis from left to right. The colors and the height of the individual curves mark the strength of the frequency portions. In this manner, even simple sounds present themselves as a landscape. The application of a spatial structure for an initially non-spatial sound signal is problematic, however, given that the mono recordings do not contain spatial information. Additionally, the depiction of the strength of the signal – the sound pressure level – by both color and height, signifies a further redundancy in the presentation. The scales themselves were not presented in this example. Thus, by virtue of a purely mathematical transformation of the physical measurement results, an image arises with an impressive emotional value.

The Cologne artist Klaus Osterwald also utilizes the results of acoustic analyses in the development of visual forms. He forms sculptures, transforming the temporal processes and release curves of daily sounds into three-dimensional objects of ceramics (Osterwald 2008). Further examples are presented in Daniels (2010).

3.4.2
MUSICAL NOTATION, GRAPHICS, AND FILM

390

3.4
VISUALIZATION
OF NOISE
AND MUSIC
↓
3.4.1
ARTISTIC AND
TECHNICAL
VISUALIZATION
↓
3.4.2
MUSICAL
NOTATION,
GRAPHICS,
AND FILM

An example of a generally prevalent cross-modal analogy is the connection of tone pitch and spatial height, which is of great importance to musical notation. As detailed in section 2.2.3, Wellek interpreted this perceptual relation as a *primeval synesthesia* permanently anchored in humans (Wellek 1931b; 1963).

The first chronicles of music contain merely the texts of songs. These were later supplemented by lines which originally pertained to the declamation of spoken texts as *accents,* but as *accent neumes* they subsequently symbolized the change of the tone pitch in songs. As a rule, an increase was represented by an upwardly pointing line and a decrease by a downwardly pointing line. The remains of this ancient art of musical notation may be found in the accents of some languages. In French, for example, the upwardly pointing accent (´) is characterized as *aigu,* literally *pointed,* whereas *pointed* as a reference to tone pitch is regarded as a synonym for *height.* Similarly, this applies to the accent *grave* (`), which requires lowering the voice.

From the *accent neumes*, more precise details have been developed to note tone pitch by a symbol in line notation. Thereby, line codes *(neumes)* were used to signify the movement from one musical degree to the next. With the transition of neumes to medieval *square notation,* the designation of movement disappeared, to the benefit of signs which only symbolized the individual tone pitch, however, and not the movement from one tone to the next. Figure 3.52 shows three notations, one above the other, from which two describe the movement, whereas the middle – more modern – notation, however, signifies the individual tones. The presentation of individual tones in the line system is also epitomized by modern notation systems. The difficulty of reading notes consists not only in deciphering of tone pitch, tone duration, and the dynamics. Moreover, the musical movement must be reconstructed by summarizing the individual tones to sensible units *(phrasing)*. The notation image provides only limited clues in this regard, e.g., additional symbols in the form of phrasing slurs. As a general rule, sensible phrasing must be learned.

3.4
VISUALIZATION
OF NOISE
AND MUSIC
↓
3.4.2
MUSICAL
NOTATION,
GRAPHICS,
AND FILM

391

FIGURE 3.52
Development of notation using neumes.
Gregorian chant "Pascha nostrum" supplemented by two notations
from the Carolingian period – sheet music issued by St. Pierre Solesmes
Benedictine Abbey (Graduale Triplex 1979).
L: Laon Script (Metz notation)
C: cantatorium (St. Gallen notation)

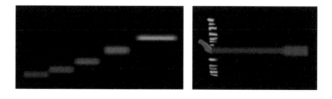

FIGURE 3.53
Subjective visualization of a tone sequence (left)
and a chord (right) of a glass harmonica.
Graphic by Matthias Waldeck, 2005.

The connection of tone frequency and spatial height is an example of how cross-modal analogies of perception can be fundamental and generally prevalent. Often, visual synesthetic images exhibit line patterns analogous to the development of musical lines or melodies in which the line height is connected to the tone frequency and the temporal development corresponds to the writing direction in the respective culture. This form of synesthesia is known as *notational synesthesia* (Behne 2002). Figure 3.53 indicates a tone sequence as well as a chord of a glass harmonica in the subjective visualization of Matthias Waldeck, to whose synesthesia Behne refers. ● ● In the depiction, a distinct similarity to the representation in the notational system can be found.

As already mentioned in section 2.2.4, sound processes and music can be characterized not only by virtue of tone pitches, color tones, and temporal sequence. Additionally, dynamic properties such as *movement* are perceived. Alexander Truslit addressed the question of the visualization of perceived movement while listening to music (Truslit 1931; 1938). His methods applied curved lines, which are seen as representations of forms of musical movements. These are similar to the trace left behind by chalk along a chalkboard, while the basic movement is also articulated in an auditory fashion. Truslit's movement curves can also be rendered by the movements of hands and arms, similar to conducting an orchestra. Thus, the movement curves are not simply directed along a straight temporal axis, e.g., monotonous from the left to the right, but contain loops and may appear to be bent towards the center of the image. The temporal development thus occurs along the movement curve. Given his work as the head of the movement-oriented Elisabeth Caland music academy in Berlin, Truslit was aware of the meaning of movement conceptions and real bodily movements in the analysis and interpretation of musical works. In developing appropriate visualizations, he initially made reference to synesthetic music images which were increasingly the subject of perceptual psychological analyses at the beginning of the twentieth century (see chapter 2.5). Truslit examined some of the images published within the framework of the color-tone research of the 1920s (Anschütz 1927c) and utilized this in deducing movement curves. These curves are not identical with the tone pitch sequence, but they vary depending upon the agogics and the dynamics of the interpretation. In the second step, therefore, musical sequences were performed in various manners and it was examined as to which measure the visualization of the musical process by different persons led to general results.

87
88
392
3.4
VISUALIZATION
OF NOISE
AND MUSIC
↓
3.4.2
MUSICAL
NOTATION,
GRAPHICS,
AND FILM

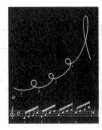

FIGURE 3.54
Truslit's experiment aimed at connecting musical movement
and visual form (Truslit 1938). Left: musical phrase and movement form
(curve) as the basis of the presentation;
middle and right: visualizations after listening to music
– without knowledge of the movement form.

According to Truslit's understanding, an optimal movement form, a *primeval movement* [Ur-Bewegung], exists for every musical form and must be discovered by the interpreters. Experiments have indicated that trained test subjects are capable of identifying the movement forms serving as the foundation of an interpretation. Figure 3.54 shows the results of such an experiment. A musician had the task of playing the tone sequence shown below on the left with the movement form sketched above on the left. ● A painter – indeed Walther Behm – and two of his students had, thereby, the task of finding a corresponding visual equivalent, without knowledge of the form serving as the basis. The results displayed in the middle and to the right tend to be comparable to the original, fundamental movement form (Truslit 1938).

All movement forms pertinent to the interpretation, according to Truslit's concept, can be traced back to three basic forms: *open movement, closed movement,* and *curved movement* (fig. 3.55b–d). ● The sheer stringing together of tones, however, is to be avoided, given that it is perceived as being unnatural and non-musical (fig. 3.55a). The configuration of the musical movement occurs via parameters of the individual tones within the melody, indeed, particularly by virtue of duration, strength or loudness, tone pitch, and tone color. The knowledge of the significance of dynamic processes in the music peaks in Truslit's *Law of Movement:* "Movement is the primeval element of music" (see also Haverkamp 2009b). The specific forms stated by Truslit may be questioned. Recent researchers, however, again have found sets of elementary forms of musical motion, which can be classified as *iconic archetypes* (Kendall 2004).

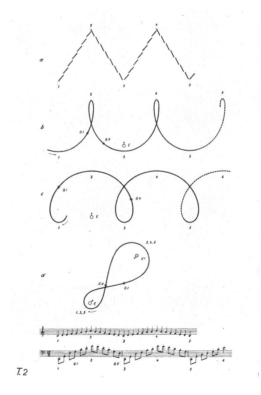

3.4
VISUALIZATION
OF NOISE
AND MUSIC
↓
3.4.2
MUSICAL
NOTATION,
GRAPHICS,
AND FILM

393

FIGURE 3.55
The four basic forms of musical movement according to Truslit.
It encompasses an "unnatural" (above)
and three "natural" forms (middle and below).
The natural forms include the open, closed, and curved form
(Truslit 1938).

The notably close similarity of the subjective impression to the visualization of measurement data, which is often observed, is demonstrated by the following example: The third piece of the Five Orchestral Pieces, Op. 16 by Arnold Schönberg (1909) – later appearing with the title *Farben* (Colors) – was characterized as *musical pointillism* due to the specific hearing impression. Thereby, reference is made to the variant form of impressionistic painting cultivated by Georges Seurat in which all image elements are based upon the combination of individual color points. At the time of Schönberg, a detailed sound analyses and the visual presentation of measurement data typical of today were, owing to technical reasons, not possible. Nevertheless, a present-day technical sound analysis and visualization reveal a *pointillistic* structure. Figure 3.56 shows the result of the analysis of this *color-tone composition*. For the sound analysis undertaken here, an algorithm designated as *Relative Approach* by HEAD acoustics was applied, emphasizing the individual audible elements as compared to the acoustic background. In indicating the relative amplitude, a color scale supporting the impressionistic overall appearance was employed.

In spite of some approaches, however, one is still a long way away from transforming musical structures into images on the basis of sound recordings which actually correspond to the hearing impression in a precise manner. Generally, in this regard, technical visualizations do not indicate chords and melodies in the grouped forms in which they are heard. An exact consideration of perceptual gestalt building processes in accordance with section 1.3.8 is necessary to more closely approach the hearing impression.

394

3.4
VISUALIZATION
OF NOISE
AND MUSIC
↓
3.4.2
MUSICAL
NOTATION,
GRAPHICS,
AND FILM

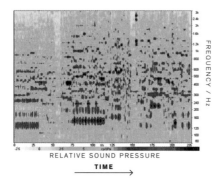

RELATIVE SOUND PRESSURE

TIME →

FIGURE 3.56
Pointillistic structure of the third piece of the
Five Orchestral Pieces, Op. 16 by Arnold Schönberg: Farben, 1909.
Result of a sound analysis with a Relative Approach
as relative sound pressure and frequency over the time.

Whereas colors are important to the visualization of sounds and music, some composers, on the other hand, consider colors as elements of the composition. As an example, the composer Olivier Messiaen, known for the use of color references in his music, also makes reference to landscape colors in Japan in the composition *Sept Haïkaï* (Seven Haikus). Accordingly, in the fifth piece "Miyajima et le Torii dans la Mer," he describes an original landscape with hills covered with deep green pine trees, a Shintô temple on the sea shore, and a typically red, symbolical temple gate, a *torii*, standing in the water. It is articulated as follows: "Imagine this play of colors: the greenness of the pines, the gold, and the white of the Shintô temple, the blue of the sea, the red of the torii. I wanted to raise this impression almost literally in my music. The composition is actually green, red, gold and white, and I've even added a few other colors thereto: purple, light purple, crimson (my favorite colors) – as I combine different tones and instrumental sounds." (Cited by Zeller 1982)

According to Messiaen's descriptions in other places, his tendency to interpret musical sounds in colors could be regarded as a characteristic of genuine synesthesia corresponding to chapter 2.5, even if the composer tends to incorporate colors into formal systems (Fink 2004). In the case of the afore-mentioned composition, he uses these color sensations for an associative landscape description. He even employs the color allocations in the sheet music. However, due to the genuine synesthetic character, i.e. the individual distinction of Messiaen's allocation of colors to sounds, it would be difficult for an experienced musician as well as for the listener to exactly follow the connection. Nevertheless, this compositional aspect represents a further enrichment of the music, whose abundance of acoustic *color* tones is available to every listener.

Efforts to intuitively implement formal aspects of music in forms and colors are also based on analogy observations. Oskar Rainer developed appropriate approaches for *"musical graphics"* at schools, with these being systematized by Hans Sündermann and Berta Ernst (Rainer 1925, Sündermann 1981, Adam 2000). His experiments did not lead to a method, however, which can be applied according to exact rules; intuitive methods in consideration of holistic approaches are nevertheless regarded as essential. Nonetheless, those advocating musical graphics assume the general validity of form analogies and of permanent allocations of colors to harmonies. The application of musical graphics is principally in the educational realm.

3.4
VISUALIZATION
OF NOISE
AND MUSIC
↓
3.4.2
MUSICAL
NOTATION,
GRAPHICS,
AND FILM

395

> **AS INDICATED BY THE WORK OF SCHOOLCHILDREN IN VARIOUS INSTANCES, THE OVERALL CHARACTER OF MUSICAL WORKS CAN BE WELL – AND IN SOME CASES REPRODUCIBLY – RENDERED BY INGENUOUS PAINTING.**

Efforts were also undertaken, on the other hand, to create compositions using musical images without knowledge of the basic work. This led to works with a basic character nearly corresponding to the original work, although it exhibited formal deviations as well. Overall, the knowledge in this area proves that certain cross-modal analogies are generally prevalent, thus facilitating connections of the auditory with the visual modality. For the connection of visual design characteristics with the auditory features of future products, a reanimation of the discussion as to the *musicality of the form* will deliver additional impulses. Figure 3.57 shows the comparison of a – subjectively perceived – musical structure to the design characteristics of an automobile.

In the second half of the twentieth century, concepts of musical graphics were once again taken into consideration in order to develop a new form of notation as a basis for the presentation of New Music. The initial goal was to overcome the conventions associated with the utilization of the *classical* notation to the benefit of free compositional methods and to integrate the graphic configuration of the sheet music as an essential component into the artistic work. The thus arising *image sheet music* – in a classical sense – served as guidelines for the interpreting musicians, but they exhibited, nevertheless, as *musical graphics* even without acoustic implementation, a purely illustrative musicality. Image sheet music often also includes approaches towards visualizing sounds, e.g., the work *Articulation* by György Ligeti (1958) with the subsequently created listening sheet music by Rainer Wehinger (1970). Further examples: Earle Brown, *December 1952;* Karlheinz Stockhausen, *Elektronische Studien II* (1956); John Cage, *Aria for Voice (Any Range)* (1960); as well as Leon Schidlowsky's *Babel* (1976) from a series of collage-like image sheet music (Schidlowsky 1979).

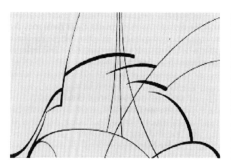

396

3.4
VISUALIZATION
OF NOISE
AND MUSIC
↓
3.4.2
MUSICAL
NOTATION,
GRAPHICS,
AND FILM

FIGURE 3.57
Musical graphics and musicality of the form.
Design characteristics of a modern automobile compared
to the visualization of a composition.
J.S. Bach, Prelude in C major from The Well-Tempered Clavier.
Visual transcript by Franz Urbach (Rainer 1925).

Given that music exhibits a changing structure in the course of time, one can undoubtedly regard visualizations in film as desirable. After abstract music films in the early era of cinema could be produced only with great effort (Moritz 1972; 1994; 2004, Selwood 1985; 2006), the computer currently provides new possibilities. In this regard, the multimedia artist Michal Levy presents step by step the construction of a high-rise building, being inspired by John Coltrane's *Giant Steps*. The construction elements are assembled in exact synchronization to the musical structure (fig. 3.58). Moreover, a metropolitan structure is built within the building (fig. 3.58, middle and bottom). Towards the end, the overall architectural structure is dissolved into building blocks again. Cross-sensory analogies provide for the precise alignment of the visual stream and the music. Additionally, image elements appear which are similar to the perception of genuine synesthesia. One may compare the picture on the bottom right with the presentation in the synesthetic image in figure 3.34 (see also Haverkamp 2010b).

3.4
VISUALIZATION
OF NOISE
AND MUSIC
↓
3.4.2
MUSICAL
NOTATION,
GRAPHICS,
AND FILM

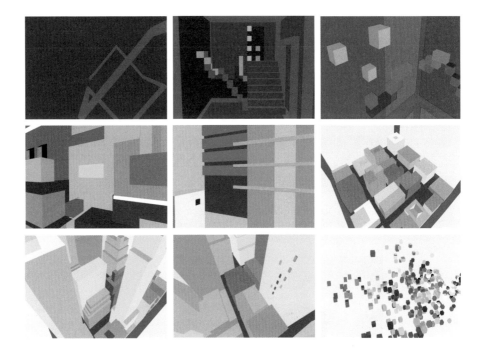

FIGURE 3.58
Presentation of the sequence (storyboard) of the animation
to John Coltrane's work Giant Steps by the multimedia artist Michal Levy –
in rows from left to right (Levy 2001).

As an advanced example, the visualization of Gustav Mahler's 2nd Symphony in C minor, *Resurrection* Symphony, by Johannes Deutsch shall be mentioned. Being designed for live performance with a symphony orchestra, it was realized in cooperation with the *Ars Electronica Futurelab* (Linz, Austria) and performed in 2006 at the Kölner Philharmonie (Deutsch 2007). The animation refers to the composition by means of a color concept which supports narrative aspects of the music (fig. 3.59). Eighteen elementary forms carry the colors and are subject to various form transformations and groupings in space (fig. 3.60). Those forms were constructed physically and have been scanned into the virtual environment (fig. 3.61). Without losing their abstract appearance, the visual elements correlate to the thematic stages of the symphony: suffering, romanticism, irony, love, doubt, and hope. The visualization, however, does not strictly follow the musical content, but unfolds a kind of parallel universe. Johannes Deutsch explains: "This work is a matter of blending together two interpretations: one expressed musically and the other visually."

In contrast to a predetermined sequence of animation, the presentation is of an interactive nature. Sounds of the musical instruments directly influence the scenery by initiating synchronous light effects, object pulsation, and movement. To complete the advanced ambition, the visualization has been realized for three-dimensional view. Further examples of the cinematic implementation of music can be found in figures 3.47 and 3.67.

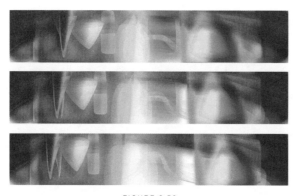

FIGURE 3.59
Johannes Deutsch, Vision Mahler, 2006.
Concept of object transformation, detail of the third movement.

FIGURE 3.60
Johannes Deutsch, Vision Mahler, 2006.
Elementary objects used as the basis of the animation,
made of papier mâché.

398

3.4
VISUALIZATION
OF NOISE
AND MUSIC
↓
3.4.2
MUSICAL
NOTATION,
GRAPHICS,
AND FILM

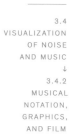

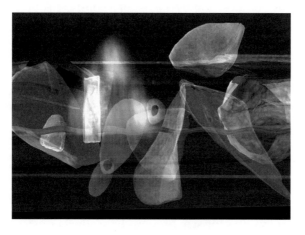

FIGURE 3.61
Johannes Deutsch and Ars Electronica Futurelab, Vision Mahler, 2006.
Screenshot no. 34 taken from the third movement.

PERCEPTION
AND EMOTION

The emotional attachment of the customer to brands can be positively influenced by attractive, multisensory design. Somatic motives such as bodily activity, enjoyment, and eroticism can also play an important role (Kastner 2008). Thus, some basic findings regarding the emotional conditions shall be outlined here.

**EMOTIONS ARE BASED UPON
AN INTERACTION OF THE PERCEPTION
OF EXTERNAL STIMULI WITH THE
PERCEPTION OF BODY REACTIONS.
THEREBY, IT INVOLVES
PHENOMENA WITH A FUNDAMENTALLY
MULTISENSORY NATURE.**

Emotions are processes which only partially enter into the consciousness. The term *feelings*, on the other hand, characterizes that which is sensed as the result of this process. Thus, feelings are the sensations stimulated by emotions. The question as to what emotions actually are was and continues to be discussed in research – intensively and controversially. However, one assumes the existence of relatively few basic families of emotions, which are supplemented by a variety of deductions and subgroups within the course of life (Goleman 1995, 331ff). Given that unconscious processes can play a major role in the distinction of emotions, one finds it often difficult to clearly comprehend their own emotions – it is even more difficult to articulate their emotions. Thus, emotions appear to be subjectively less clearly circumscribed, less *tangible* than phenomena of the perception. This should be illustrated by figure 3.62. Nevertheless, as a rule, emotions cause unambiguous motivations, which are the basis and the impulse for purposeful responses.

Paul Ekman discovered that four types of emotions can be clearly identified by virtue of the associated facial expression of people of all cultures (cited by Goleman 1995, 332). These are the core emotions fear, anger, sadness, and enjoyment. Ekman later expanded the list with love, surprise, and disgust (Ekman 1999). Each of these emotions can be clearly allocated by virtue of photographs of the corresponding facial expression, indeed, from one culture to another, even by isolated tribes such as the *Fore* in New Guinea (Ekman 2004). This speaks for the universality of core emotions. Ekman states that a person is capable of more than 10,000 different facial expressions which can be evoked by forty-three facial muscles (Ekman 2004, 14). The mimics caused by true feelings, however, can be distinguished from those of conscious simulation – i.e. an artificial smile differs from a natural smile. Both are based on processing in different cerebral regions (Damasio 2006).

Emotions are the result of data processing in the cerebral area, which is reflected via sensations of bodily conditions (feelings) within the consciousness.

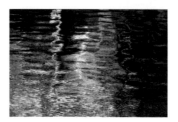

FIGURE 3.62
Emotions appear to be subjectively less tangible
than phenomena of the perception.
An Emotion, photograph by Marcia Smilack, 2004.

Typical are emotional sensations due to certain mental states which are perceived as bodily conditions and often – although not always – connected to somatic, i.e. actual, bodily reactions:

IN LOVE:	"BUTTERFLIES IN THE STOMACH"
STRESSED OUT:	"UNDER (PHYSICAL) PRESSURE"
RELIEVED:	"A LOAD OFF MY CHEST"

Damasio (2006) uses the term *feeling* exclusively to describe this specific perception of emotions. Via feelings, perceptions of external events – such as the arrival of an individual person – are connected to bodily sensations. Given that intensive bodily sensations appear to be strongly evaluated, i.e. positive or negative, a clear allocation is important. Without clarity, false values could be transported while pertaining to certain people, objects, processes, or even products. False negative evaluations can, in extreme situations, evoke superstitious apprehension ("driving a black car results in misfortune") or general fears ("participating in road traffic results in an accident"). Emotions arise obviously from the simultaneous interaction of perceptual objects of the external world – to which even areas of one's own body could belong, if the stimulus originates there – and bodily perceptions. The interaction can appear alternately via certain areas of the brain, so-called *convergence zones,* as Damasio presumes (Damasio 2006, 162). Thereby, the correlation between perception of external conditions and of the body is simultaneously accompanied by cognitive processes.

For associative connections, the emotional evaluation of the perceptual contents has grave consequences: they influence the speed with which images are formed and processed. Thus, feelings of elation are accompanied by acceleration and concentration of the associative connection, whereas e.g., sadness is characterized by cognitive modes which decelerate and dilute this activity (Damasio 2006, 164). Emotionally colored stimuli – e.g., in the auditory modality – can also significantly increase the reaction performance in a different – e.g., the visual – modality, and thus boost early sensory stages of processing. (Brosch 2008). Furthermore, the emotional content of music can influence the interpretation of visual stimuli, and thus provide a *musical priming.* Sad or happy music is therefore capable of enhancing the perceived sadness or happiness of faces (Logeswaran 2009).

Similar to the concrete contents of the perception, feelings and moods outside of the person experiencing them are not within grasp. Even here, the question of *Qualia* is important (section 1.3.6). However, emotions strongly influence actions and motivations – they are thus of great significance with respect to the decision of a customer regarding a certain product. Emotions are recognizable and classifiable by virtue of observed actions, facial expressions, and gesticulations, even though they may not be similarly perceived between individuals. Manfred Clynes developed a method to measure the motional activity caused by emotions (Clynes 1977). Test subjects had to contact a button of the measurement unit, the so-called *sentograph,* with one finger. They were asked to express various emotions, notably love, hate, grief, pleasure, awe, anger, and sexual attraction. During the test, the mechanical force applied by the finger-tip was measured in horizontal (fore-aft) and vertical (up-down) direction. Characteristic dynamic forms of reactions were found – the *sentic forms.* Figure 3.63 provides average curves derived from fifty single measurements. Although Clynes experiments have not been received without controversy, his result provides insight into bodily reactions which can be caused, or at least influenced by emotions.

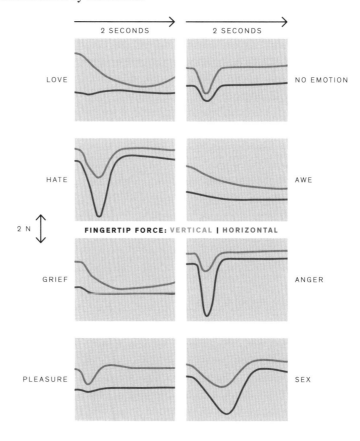

FIGURE 3.63
Conception of specific emotions causes characteristic
temporal behavior of the fingertip force. Sentic forms evaluated by Clynes.
"No emotion" provides a reference curve by means of a consciously
steered push operation (Clynes 1977).

A CHARACTERISTIC ELEMENT
OF AN EMOTION IS ITS PERCEPTION
AS A CONDITION OF THE BODY –
A FEELING.

The bodily perception thus reflects processes of cognitive brain activity – the body becomes a "theatre for the emotions." According to Damasio, there are three varieties of feelings:

I.
FEELINGS OF BASIC,
CONGENITALLY ARRANGED UNIVERSAL EMOTIONS
(PRIMARY EMOTIONS)

notably the five feelings: happiness, sadness, anger, fear, and disgust. These are caused by emotions in the sense of the psychologist William James (1920). According to this, a fundamental process exists which causes environmental stimuli of congenital and inalterable mechanisms to initiate a certain pattern of bodily reactions (Damasio 2006, 129ff). Damasio also speaks of primary emotions which are based on *pre-organized mechanisms:* they are already existent early in life, most likely of congenital nature. Thus, they already enable children to react quickly to possible dangers. Therefore, these emotions can not be of an associative nature. They are based upon elementary properties: size, wingspread (eagle), type of movement (quick, surprising, erratic), sound quality (e.g., growling or grumbling) or high, tonal sounds (squeaking, screaming), as well as certain bodily conditions (heart pains). This process requires an evaluation of the sensually processed stimulus which occurs in the limbic system. Figure 3.64 shows a basic scheme of emotional processes. Stimuli initiate bodily reactions via the *limbic system,* notably via the *amygdala,* as well as via the *hypothalamus.* Those reactions are perceived parallel to the objects which cause the stimuli.

II.
FEELINGS OF SUBTLE UNIVERSAL EMOTIONS
(SECONDARY EMOTIONS)

which in the course of life are deduced from experiences of the basic universal emotions (I). Damasio refers to these as *secondary emotions.* Although they build upon the primary emotions, they are increasingly modified as a person grows older. The feeling of the emotion enables a flexible, cognitively supported reaction to the stimulus. The neuronal apparatus of the primary emotion continues to be effective. Additionally, the stimulus is analyzed by thinking processes and activated by areas in the front portion of the brain, which also influence the limbic system.

Secondary emotions cause a "hypothetical" feeling experience caused by the conception in three stages:

1. The conscious consideration or conception of a situation leads to conceptual images in the primary areas of the cerebral cortex (see Chapter 2.1).

2. These cause the unconscious retrieval of stored, emotional reactions from experience.
3. Accordingly, bodily reactions are initiated via the limbic system, as in the case of primary emotions.

III.

BACKGROUND FEELINGS

which reflect the temporary overall condition of the body. According to Damasio, these are value-free – neither positive nor negative – hints as to the background condition of the body – he speaks of "the sense of being." "The background feeling is our image of the body landscape when it is not shaken by emotion" (Damasio 2006, 150–51). Other authors also regard *moods* as background experiences which encompass conditions of longer duration with an unclear character, but also containing evaluations (Knoblich 2003, 40). In comparison to sensations of the aforementioned categories I and II, background sensations exhibit, in addition to lesser intensity, a greater continuity – they undergo changes in a considerably slower manner. With the assistance of the background sensations, we can answer questions as to the overall condition, such as the question "How are you doing?," heard on a daily basis.

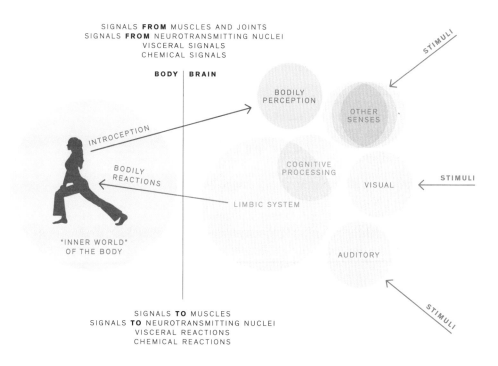

SIGNALS **FROM** MUSCLES AND JOINTS
SIGNALS **FROM** NEUROTRANSMITTING NUCLEI
VISCERAL SIGNALS
CHEMICAL SIGNALS

BODY | BRAIN

STIMULI

BODILY PERCEPTION

OTHER SENSES

INTROCEPTION

BODILY REACTIONS

COGNITIVE PROCESSING

VISUAL   STIMULI

LIMBIC SYSTEM

"INNER WORLD" OF THE BODY

AUDITORY

STIMULI

SIGNALS **TO** MUSCLES
SIGNALS **TO** NEUROTRANSMITTING NUCLEI
VISCERAL REACTIONS
CHEMICAL REACTIONS

FIGURE 3.64
Model of the construction of emotions as the interaction
of external stimuli with bodily perception. The external stimuli are often replaced
by conceptual or memory images which influence the generation
of emotions in a comparable fashion. Alternately, the emotional activation
of processes in the body is completely simulated in the brain.

In addition to the moods, the *temperaments* determine the emotional life. They can be regarded as the readiness to evoke an emotion or a mood (Goleman 1995). Emotional disturbances such as clinical depression or phobias are not taken into consideration within this book.

Initially, emotions are based upon the direct participation of functions of the entire body. The bodily reactions they cause, however, also appear to be strongly diversified even if the feelings are similar. Thus, one may presume that, in the case of the modification of primary feelings (from I to II), the body is increasingly disconnected until the original condition connected to the bodily reaction is completely simulated within the brain (Damasio 2006, 155ff). Then, the "flat feeling" in the stomach is not physically measurable, but an *emotional memory image* is generated in the head. The perception of the emotionally driven body reaction then resembles the perception of phantom pains. In this regard, for example, patients continue to have the feeling of being able to move hands and fingers following an amputation. Even these are memory images of earlier perceptions.

In contrast to emotion, *intuition* is the result of "subconscious thinking." At any rate, it is possible for intuition to be bodily perceived, for example, if someone "has the feeling" that the solution of a problem should be sought in a certain direction. As indicated below, however, there are attempts to explain intuition via *somatic markers* as a part of emotional processes.

Intuition often leads to useful results. If sufficient knowledge and experience are available, the likelihood of proper decisions being made will be greater. The input data, however, and the chain of reasoning remain in the dark. If both are consciously understood, the result of an intuitive process is often correct and understandable.

AN IMPORTANT ADVANTAGE
OF INTUITIVE THINKING
IS THE RAPIDITY WITH WHICH DECISIONS
CAN BE REACHED.

Conscious thinking based upon causal steps, however, requires considerably more time.

Given that feelings – just like perceptions due to external stimuli – contain subjective qualities, efforts to objectively, comparatively describe feelings among persons are denied by the *qualia problem*. Feelings are condition-based circumstances associated to individuals. Secondary emotions thus have a history connected to other persons and society and can only be understood by virtue of this history. "Taking emotions seriously therefore means taking individuals as subjects seriously" (Ulrich 1999). In spite of this uniqueness, there are apparently similarities as well, explaining why similar feelings can be perceived by different persons in comparable situations, who in turn initiate comparable actions. The – certainly simplified – classification of emotions in *basic families (core emotions)* presents an interesting approach which can serve as the foundation of special experiments. Within these basic families, there are various modifications which come into being. Thus, the feelings towards different friends or sexual partners are thoroughly different. Even in cases of affection or love, for example, there are personalized nuances. In a similar manner, the sensation of an emotion towards a product, such as an automobile, will vary, if minimal changes of the configuration are carried out.

Daniel Goleman presumes the existence of eight primary families of emotions. At that point, less clear than Damasio, he is apt to take the terms emotions and feelings as synonyms. As compared to Damasio, love, surprise, and shame are added to the list. In the following, the basic families as well as some deductions are given (Goleman 1995, 331–32):

- **ANGER:** fury, outrage, resentment, wrath, exasperation, indignation, vexation, acrimony, animosity, annoyance, irritability, hostility, and, perhaps at the extreme, pathological hatred and violence
- **SADNESS:** grief, sorrow, cheerlessness, gloom, melancholy, self-pity, loneliness, dejection, despair, and, when pathological, severe depression
- **FEAR:** anxiety, apprehension, nervousness, concern, consternation, misgiving, wariness, qualm, edginess, dread, fright, terror; as a psychopathology, phobia, and panic
- **ENJOYMENT:** happiness, joy, relief, contentment, bliss, delight, amusement, pride, sensual pleasure, thrill, rapture, gratification, satisfaction, euphoria, whimsy, ecstasy, and, at the far edge, mania
- **LOVE:** acceptance, friendliness, trust, kindness, affinity, devotion, adoration, infatuation, agape
- **SURPRISE:** shock, astonishment, amazement, wonder
- **DISGUST:** contempt, disdain, scorn, abhorrence, aversion, distaste, revulsion
- **SHAME:** guilt, embarrassment, chagrin, remorse, humiliation, regret, mortification, and contrition

Feelings also serve to confirm cognitive processes and memory performance. This is demonstrated by results of brain research regarding veridical versus illusory memories (Kim 2007). Memories are retrieved from two different areas of the brain. Details of a memory come from the medial temporal lobes, whereas the parietal lobe provides the feeling of having already experienced it. Déjà-vu experiences occur, on the other hand, when only the parietal lobe is active. Then, the momentary experience is regarded as a memory, without the details being available.

The perception of stimuli changing in time, such as those which occur while listening to music, is usually accompanied by corresponding alterations in moods. It is thus necessary to evaluate the time-dependency of emotion, for it does not appear appropriate to summarize feelings over long time periods. For some years, the software EMuJoy has allowed the continuous input of emotional parameters while listening to music (Nagel 2007). Thus, it can be determined whether relatively constant emotions are felt during a certain music piece or, instead, whether short term variations occur. The test subjects provide continuous input via a monitor cursor in a diagram of four quadrants, which is stretched by parameter pairs, e.g., *stimulating/soothing* and *positive/negative.* After finishing the test, the time-dependent result of every subject can be replayed synchronous to the music.

As a rule, each major perceptual content is emotionally evaluated. Damasio uses the aforementioned term *somatic markers* (Damasio 2006).

SOMATIC MARKERS ALLOW FOR EFFICIENT DECISION-MAKING ON THE BASIS OF PREVIOUS EXPERIENCE, WHICH WERE ASSOCIATED WITH FEELINGS.

Thus, an estimation of the temporal development of a situation is deduced from previous emotions allocated to a certain perception or situation, and this in turn appears as a feeling and prepares the body for the expected perceptual content. This process of "marking" also explains the direct effectiveness of intuition. It is assumed that somatic markers are based on processes related to the establishment of secondary emotions. Body reactions thus play an essential role. In addition to the knowledge stored in the memory, the emotional evaluation of conditions of the consciousness and of perceptions, accumulated via somatic markers, significantly contributes to the prognosis of future events (Damasio 1991). Accordingly, actions can be intuitively driven. It is also likely that somatic markers direct the attention to certain contents, thus producing a hierarchy and influencing the activity of the working memory.

IN SUMMARY, ACCORDING TO CURRENT KNOWLEDGE, EMOTIONS CAN BE UNDERSTOOD AS THE RESULT OF INTERACTION BETWEEN PHYSIOLOGICAL ACTIVATION AND THE COGNITIVE INTERPRETATION THEY MAKE REFERENCE TO.

This encompasses congenital processes as well as the perception of body reactions. Thereby, even thinking, conception, and memory play an essential role. This is easily comprehensible in everyday life, for feelings can be considerably influenced by a subjective viewpoint and one's own evaluation of situations and events.

For product design, accordingly, it is important to take the individual demands of the customer seriously. In marketing, a basic mood and emotionality must be sought, which raises awareness to the associative variety of multisensory concepts. The perspective of the customer is crucial, for it is they who grant the product the attention of the senses.

INDIVIDUALIZING

In the case of ring tones for cell phones, individual, specific choices are quite popular. This, however, is not due to purely functional reasons. Indeed, in order to distinguish the device from that of one's neighbor, a choice of merely a few variations would suffice. Cell phone ring tones are, nevertheless, used as an expression of the person within a certain group.

FIGURE 3.65
The emotional relationship of a customer
to his or her automobile is determined by individual factors –
as this collector's item indicates.

FIGURE 3.66
"Eat colorfully": emotional discord can be caused by objects
with conflicting features, as demonstrated by this eat-art ensemble of crochets.
Patricia Waller, Buffet, yarn, fabric, synthetic material, wood, 1999. © 2011, ProLitteris, Zurich.

This means that the individually chosen tone sequence sends signals to the public which are to be comprehended as an expression of the personality of the individual receiving the call. Given that the ownership of a cell phone, in spite of its general prevalence, tends to support a positive image, it is deemed sensible to assist this in an auditory manner as well – whereas the actual phone conversation itself remains more or less private. By virtue of the Internet, a variety of cell phone tones is available. The offer ranges from the sounds of vintage telephones to music and everyday sounds of all forms. In addition to synthetic tone sequences, complex recordings of real acoustic sources come into play as *true sounds.*

In principal, the automobile also offers the possibility of the individualization of auditory and visual signals – this is less noticed by customers than in the case of cell phones and computer interfaces. An exception is the adjustment of the national language in visual menus and in the audio response of the navigation system. The possibility of distinct individualization requires flexible systems. *Great flexibility,* however, reduces the *usability* (Lidwell 2003), given that such systems necessitate lengthy preparation and considerable effort in the configuration.

In general, the emotional relationship of a customer to an automobile is strongly influenced by individual factors. This justifies the offering of niche products, special models, and customized furnishings. Nevertheless, furnishings and price do not necessarily need to build the basis of the individuality achieved. Moreover, originality may provide an emotional added-value. This is particularly the case involving *collector's items.* In figure 3.65, an alternative viewpoint is articulated by the inscription "Patita con Pan." Literally "Foot with Bread," it metaphorically means "Man with Money" – an irony advancing the automobile to a Rolls-Royce.

The aforementioned classification of the basic families of emotions is only a first approach in analyzing the different qualities of feelings. Often, *mixed feelings* – a conflict of different qualia without a clear preference – can be observed. Even perceptual conflicts can lead thereto. Thus, figure 3.65 can induce a mixture of positive (stimulating) and negative (repulsive) feelings due to the discrepancy between associative stimulation of the taste sensation and the unusual tactile quality of the crochets. In a similar manner, impressions which cause fear can simultaneously evoke the stimulus of a creeping sensation. However, a more detailed comprehension is necessary in order to better predict the influence of feelings upon motivations and actions. Naturally, this is of decisive importance with respect to marketing.

3.6

FUTURE PERSPECTIVES OF SYNESTHETIC DESIGN

3.6.1
DESIGN WITH ALL SENSES – FOR ALL SENSES

A future product design must take the relation between sensory modalities into greater consideration than is currently the case today – in spite of positive approaches already being undertaken. For the design of products and multimedia applications, the dominance of the visual over the other senses must be abandoned to the benefit of a true multisensory design. In addition to the fundamental expansion of the horizon of the designers and constructors, this also requires an adjustment of the design process.

410

3.6
FUTURE
PERSPECTIVES
OF SYNESTHETIC
DESIGN
↓
3.6.1
DESIGN WITH
ALL SENSES –
FOR
ALL SENSES

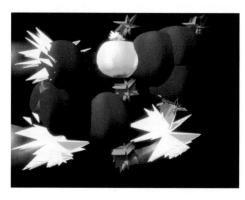

FIGURE 3.67
Soft and sharp sounds, from an audio-visual animation
by Adriano Abbado, 1988.

Synesthetic design is not merely an optional approach to be applied at the discretion of the designer. Moreover, a systematic implementation is required. As a consequence, industrial processes of product development will need reorganizational efforts in order to favor the equal treatment of visual, auditory, tactile, and body perception. Figure 3.67 illustrates this using inter-sensory properties in a three-dimensional, audio-visual context (compare figure 2.28). In processes of development, it is not sensible to give sole priority to the visual aspects, whereas the other senses are considered at a later time. To the contrary, a simultaneous and interactive configuration of all modalities meaningful to the product is required – a parallelism of development which corresponds to the parallelism of the perceptual processing of sensory information.

3.6
FUTURE
PERSPECTIVES
OF SYNESTHETIC
DESIGN
↓
3.6.1
DESIGN WITH
ALL SENSES
– FOR
ALL SENSES

411

CONCEPTS AND REQUIREMENTS MUST BE ORIENTED WITH RESPECT TO THE STRATEGIES OF CROSS-MODAL CONNECTION IN THE PERCEPTUAL SYSTEM ESSENTIAL TO PRODUCT DESIGN.

The first step of product development consists of listing all possibilities of connections between the sensory channels. In this regard, there is a variety of possibilities, as already discussed in part 2 of this book. As a rule, it suffices to have a choice among a few, appropriate strategies. In addition to this choice, the second step consists of designating the product properties in every modality in which the chosen strategy can be best implemented.

SYNESTHETIC DESIGN DOES NOT AUTOMATICALLY INVOLVE INCREASED EFFORTS IN DEVELOPING PRODUCTS. HOWEVER, IT INCREASES THE RELIABILITY WITH WHICH THE APPROPRIATE PERCEPTUAL FEATURES CAN BE INTEGRATED INTO A MULTISENSORY CONFIGURATION.

In addition to seeing, hearing, and touching, product design of the future must systematically be expanded to include the senses of smell and taste – even in fields in which these aspects were traditionally relegated to the background, such as in the automotive industry. This requires research as to the possibilities of its application.

Therefore, the designer must exercise to sense the information that refers to other modalities during stimulation of a specific sensory channel. Thereby, among others, the following questions must be answered:

- What does the visual impression of an object reveal regarding the feeling upon being touched?
- What does a sound express regarding the functionality, movement, and visual appearance which can be expected?
- Which information regarding appearance and functionality can be tactilely perceived?
- What does the touching of foodstuffs and the tactile impression in the mouth reveal about the expected taste?
- What does the visual impression of a material reveal about its smell?
- What does the smell of a foodstuff reveal about its taste?

Universities and colleges need to fulfill an important task in training future-oriented designers. In this regard, traineeship should purposefully employ the *didactic experiment* as the basis of developing pragmatic solutions.

The first didactic experiments in this respect were conducted at the Bauhaus, e.g., by László Moholy-Nagy (1929). Correlations of visual and auditory features have been investigated with students by Oskar Rainer (1925) and Wilhelm Voss (Voss 1930) – these experiments led to intensive discussions during the conferences for color-tone research (Anschütz 1931).

Recently, outstanding approaches towards the multisensory training of designers have been undertaken by the German University of Halle: in addition to projects combing visual and auditory properties, educational events covering such topics as *design olfactory* are offered. This encompassed three aspects: *smell training, composition techniques,* and *application.* The goal consisted of expanding the practical competencies of the designer with respect to olfactory characteristics of perception and the creation of atmospheres (Luckner 2002, 265). For smell training, the scent organ [Duftorgel] was employed. As already addressed, it consists of a shelf with scent samples in small bottles arranged according to olfactory properties. In analogy to the music, it is of special interest to configure sequences of smell perceptions like *scent melodies* as well as the creation of *scent harmonies.* The term *scent organ* also includes a visual analogy in consideration of the perfume bottles arranged near and over one another.

At the Politecnico di Milano, multisensory design is didactically and theoretically examined. At that university, the term *synesthetic design* was first established (Riccò 1999), although it did not include the systematic approach presented in this book.

The concept of synesthetic design as described herein is also taught by the author at the KISD (Köln International School of Design, Cologne) in the course of a scientific seminar, including practical and theoretical studies. Figure 3.68 provides an example of a practical approach to interaction design, as developed by students.

412

3.6
FUTURE
PERSPECTIVES
OF SYNESTHETIC
DESIGN
↓
3.6.1
DESIGN WITH
ALL SENSES
– FOR
ALL SENSES

IN ALL FIELDS, SYNESTHETIC DESIGN REQUIRES AN INTERACTIVE STIMULATION OF CONCEPT THINKING, CREATIVITY, AND SENSITIZED PERCEPTION.

This fundamental relation, which must initiate a continuous, recursive process, is demonstrated by figure 3.69.

FIGURE 3.68
Concept for tactile iconic elements applied to a keyboard,
as the result of a student's project
at the KISD (Köln International School of Design).
Jon McTaggert and Jacomo Rygulla, 2010.

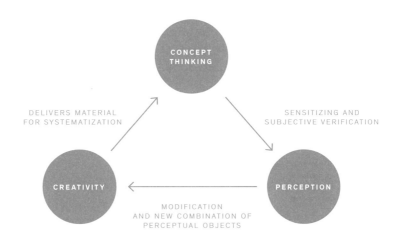

3.6
FUTURE
PERSPECTIVES
OF SYNESTHETIC
DESIGN
↓
3.6.1
DESIGN WITH
ALL SENSES
– FOR
ALL SENSES

413

FIGURE 3.69
**Schema of the development of multisensory
approaches to design.**

The synesthetic orientation of product design also requires abandoning the separation of functional engineering and design as the field of aesthetics and sensuality. Given that, for example, that which the customer expects of the product is an essential – and not an additional – element of design, it makes sense to retreat from the strict separation of the two fields from one another. The task of design consists of more than addressing the technical aspect – moreover, the sensually tangible must be organically deduced from the functional. In the future, not only the designers will be responsible for the sensorial aspects of the product, but all areas in close cooperation. An approach according to the motto: "The sensuality of an automobile is more likely to be created by the designers than by the engineers" (Engelhardt 1998), should be an approach of the past. Indeed, design should be understood as a holistic task involving perception with all senses in all areas. All organizational areas participating in product development are to be equally responsible, regardless of whether they work on engineering, construction, visual contouring, materials, sound design, marketing, or others. The cooperation of particularly different departments, however, can be challenging. Different occupational processes and thinking styles can lead to misunderstandings and uncertainties regarding the contents of the design task. Experience in film production can be quite helpful, for this generally involves an extremely distinct division of labor. The ensuring of a common agreement is the task of design management, which serves the function of interpreting between the areas and thus provides the basis of constructive communication (Kastner 2008).

In particular, the auditory environment requires a careful configuration which avoids every superfluous sound. Analogous to *landscaping,* the meticulous cultivation of the landscape similar to a market garden, *soundscaping* should be pursued as the optimizing and harmonizing of the auditory environment. Therefore, it is necessary to sensitize the experts and skilled employees involved in soundscape design. The ability to consciously configure the auditory environments demands, initially, a systematic study of one's own, subjectively characterized sound perception – Murray Schafer speaks of *ear cleaning* (Schafer 1967; 1977). In connection with the knowledge of historical sound environments – and naturally with the deployment of modern techniques of sound analysis – the optimization and cultivation of contemporary soundscapes in the sense of *acoustic ecology* (Truax 1999) can be achieved. However, this can not mean reversing the tide of historic development – back to a sound romanticism which idealizes historical soundscapes. Moreover, new aspects must arise with the integration of meaningful, traditional elements. Some aspects are thoroughly comparable; for example, the sound pressure level of historical markets is similar to that of modern, urban environments. This is also demonstrated by a soundscape comparison of the old Egyptian bazaar with shopping centers in modern parts of Istanbul (Oczevik 2007).

A trend back towards more or less natural sounds can also be identified in the configuration of auditory signals. Whereas efforts were made from the 1970s to the 1990s to employ increasingly artificial, computer-generated signals, the current tendency aims once again at purposefully utilizing natural sounds, which are referred to as *true sounds.* Auditory events should sound particularly *authentic,* i.e. associatively corresponding well to the perceived function or situation. Hence, in the case of the voice of navigation systems, naturalness is greatly valued (Zips 2004). It is therefore advisable to enrich the displayed landscape with iconic landmarks, as figure 3.70 demonstrates in an exemplary manner.

414

3.6
FUTURE
PERSPECTIVES
OF SYNESTHETIC
DESIGN
↓
3.6.1
DESIGN WITH
ALL SENSES
– FOR
ALL SENSES

FIGURE 3.70
A navigation system of the future could look like this.
The three-dimensional presentation of realistic objects on the monitor
corresponds to the transition from the analogy
of the street map to an iconic representation of the route recommended
by the system. Concept image, Blaupunkt, 2007.

The configuration of products in consideration of all senses requires not only a synesthetic concept, but also the simulation of the operation in a multisensory environment.

The typical psychophysical research methods of today are barely appropriate for examining connections between the senses. They are mostly based upon a fundamental separation of sensory stimuli and sensations of different modalities – analogous to classical physics, in which individual values and their causal influences are observed. The separation of the sensations is made possible by the ability of the perceptual system to focus upon individual senses and their specific characteristics. Ernst Terhard uses the term *analytic perception* (Terhard 1998). In contrast thereto, the *synthetic perception* allows the individual characteristics to be holistically combined to form perceptual objects. In the classical experiment, a reference between individual stimulus values (such as light intensity) and sensation (brightness) is possible by virtue of the conscious concentration of the test subjects upon single perceived features. In this manner, however, the influence of multisensory strategies of perception is considerably excluded.

3.6
FUTURE
PERSPECTIVES
OF SYNESTHETIC
DESIGN
↓
3.6.1
DESIGN WITH
ALL SENSES
– FOR
ALL SENSES

415

**THE FACT THAT PSYCHOPHYSICAL EXPERIMENTS –
REPRESENTING THE MAJORITY
OF THE CURRENT PERCEPTUAL EXAMINATIONS –
OFTEN EXHIBIT NO CLEAR INTERACTION
BETWEEN THE SENSORY MODALITIES
IS THUS A RESULT OF THE METHODOLOGY APPLIED.**

Basically, this demonstrates an important rule which is applicable to all forms of perceptual research: the experimental concept influences or even determines the result. Psychophysical experiments are based upon the trained dominance of the analytic perception and are thus appropriate with regard to discovering relationships between individual sensations and stimuli. In the future, new research methods are necessary in order to avoid focusing on individual sensory channels and characteristics, thus approaching the everyday perception in contrast to perceptual experiments on the basis of psychophysics.

A step in the direction of appropriate methods is provided by the utilization of multisensory environments in the perceptual experiment. Testing driving qualities and the operation of automobiles in driving simulators and optimizing them has already been undertaken for a long time (Tomaske 2006). It allows subjective driving impressions to be evaluated prior to the street experiment. The simulation also offers multisensory input useful for acoustic optimization. The application ranges from the presentation of additional images to a consideration of the complete environment of the driver (Heinrichs 2001). The experimental signals can be played in the standing vehicle via headphones or loudspeakers, corresponding to figure 3.71. Therefore, the application of an auditorily accurate recording and playback is essential in order to enable a spatially proper perception of the acoustic signals. The overall impression is supported by a visual, virtual environment outside the vehicle. The execution of such tests requires, in addition to complex test environments, new methods of overall evaluation (see e.g., Schulte-Fortkamp 2005).

FIGURE 3.71
Visual recordings and the real driver environment
support the sound evaluation and configuration in the laboratory,
as here at HEAD acoustics, Herzogenrath, Germany.

An advantage of the evaluation in this manner is that the test subject does not have to forcibly concentrate on driving operations – the risk of dangerous situations does not exist. However, the *aurally compensated* playback is, in the case of headphones being used, referring to the position of the head – the auditory space moves along with the movements of the head. With new approaches in loudspeaker renditions, it is possible to artificially create nearly authentic acoustic fields. Traditional methods such as stereophonic approaches, however, lead only to the perception of auditory events in a limited sector in front of one's own face. Additionally, the head should be located in a spatially closely confined area in order to effectively reproduce the effect. These disadvantages can be improved by a *surround method* (e.g., 5.1 surround), but not completely eliminated. An authentic rendition at all points in the room is first possible using *holophony (ambisonics),* which requires a large number of loudspeakers, or with *wave field synthesis,* achievable with less acoustic sources (see the overview in Blauert 2008). Using one of these methods provides a spatially authentic auditory perception which is independent of the actual position of the head (Theile 2007a; 2007b).

416

3.6
FUTURE
PERSPECTIVES
OF SYNESTHETIC
DESIGN
↓
3.6.1
DESIGN WITH
ALL SENSES
– FOR
ALL SENSES

FIGURE 3.72
Auditory playback during driving permits
the evaluation of desired sound design under real conditions.
Mobile sound simulator, HEAD acoustics.

During the real operation of an automobile as in figure 3.72, however, the inevitably available sounds disturb the playing of artificial signals. With the assistance of *active noise control (ANC),* such disturbing influences can be faded out. This method is based on the additional playing of sounds which eliminate existing acoustic waves by virtue of interference effects. Instead, artificial signals can be presented as desired. For example, replacing the real engine sound with a desired test sound is possible (Schirrmacher 2002). The procedure is also employed in order to considerably reduce the environmental sound otherwise heard while using headphones – e.g., in airplanes. The development of special, noise-reducing sound radiators is also an example of such innovative acoustics (Necati 2000).

The possibility of perceptual experiments via the Internet should also be mentioned. It offers a large number of test subjects – worldwide – the opportunity to participate. This is particularly advantageous when rare phenomena such as genuine synesthesia are involved. The possibilities of controlling the test conditions, however, are limited. Nevertheless, there are already persuasive examples in this regard. (Eagleman 2007; 2008, Cox 2007).

3.6
FUTURE
PERSPECTIVES
OF SYNESTHETIC
DESIGN
↓
3.6.1
DESIGN WITH
ALL SENSES
– FOR
ALL SENSES
↓
3.6.2
RUBUSTNESS

417

3.6.2
ROBUSTNESS

ROBUSTNESS
AS AN IMPRESSION OF QUALITY

In the future, the demands for quality and robustness among products will continue to increase. Although marketing measures influence the view of the customer with respect to the product, the quality perception as well as the multisensory appearance and the functional features of the product remain in the foreground. In order to achieve a robust impression, the number of perceptual objects in every sensorial area must correspond to the overall configuration. In the auditory case, an impression of deficient quality can arise, among others, if several sound portions which are distinguishable from one another are allocated to *one* event. Here are various examples:

→ **SECONDARY NOISE:** During driving operations, dynamic forces are exerted upon the automobile, generating low-frequency vibrations, which can also lead to the emission of sound. This *primary sound* is, due to the minimal sensibility of the ear with respect to low frequency, mostly not audible. In many cases, due to the reduction of vibrations by the flooring and the seats in the vehicle, vibrations are not felt. The impact, nevertheless, can lead to automobile components such as parts of the interior trim slapping against one another or shifting. Both can generate very audible, often disturbing sounds as *secondary noise* (Steinberg 2005). These phenomena, known as *Squeak and Rattle (S&R),* are not related to a desired function, for they create senseless perceptual objects (fig. 3.73). In addition to the disturbing influence and the distracting of the attention, they also cause a feeling of inferior quality, given that unsystematic relative movements of vehicle components – which should functionally comprise a unit – become noticeable.

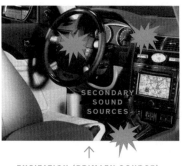

EXCITATION (PRIMARY SOURCE),
E.G. ROUGH ROAD

FIGURE 3.73
Squeak and rattle in the automobile can generate additional
sound sources without a functional context.

→ **DOOR-CLOSING SOUND:** A door being closed should shut without difficulty. A robust impression is given, thereby, when the sub-processes involved are perceived as part of a unit. Thus, an auditory object – the door-closing sound – and a visual object – the closing door – correspond to the expected function. Further auditory objects, such as the subsequent rattling of parts or the humming of a spring, could needlessly create additional auditory objects and thus minimize the impression of a precise configuration (fig. 3.74).

418

3.6
FUTURE
PERSPECTIVES
OF SYNESTHETIC
DESIGN
↓
3.6.2
ROBUSTNESS

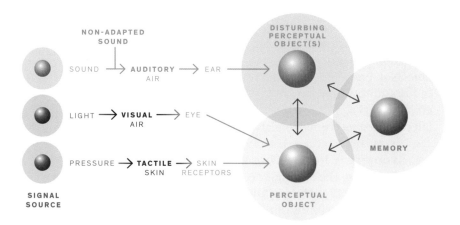

FIGURE 3.74
Sounds which are not adapted to the configuration in
other sensory channels might not be assigned to
the desired multisensory object, thus causing additional disturbing
sound objects (compare fig. 1.62).

3.6
FUTURE
PERSPECTIVES
OF SYNESTHETIC
DESIGN
↓
3.6.2
ROBUSTNESS

419

91

→ **REDUNDANT OBJECTS:** The impact of redundant perceptual objects is demonstrated in the visual realm, for example, by the difficulty of finding one's way in a hall of mirrors. It can be similarly distracting if an operational element consists of diverse parts which behave differently, without satisfying specific functions. Working with a "rickety" computer mouse also would not convey a feeling of robustness and precision. Analogously, in the field of gustatory perception, an undesired, additional taste sensation can produce a redundant or a detrimental perceptual object. A pleasant aftertaste, however, can modify perception in a positive manner, as desired by wine connoisseurs and gourmets. The same applies to integrating aromas. These subtly support, in a positive situation, the impression of products, but they can also generate perceptual objects which may be regarded as inappropriate or disturbing.

→ **ECHOES:** The disturbing influence of echoes in large rooms can be interpreted as the impact of redundant perceptual objects. Instead of a real person speaking, for example, two or three are perceived as "interrupting" one another.

→ **AFTEREFFECTS:** In a similar manner, aftereffects are to be considered. These are perceptions which appear when a function or a task is already completed (section 1.3.4). Disturbing perceptual objects which fail to convey the necessary synchronism in the representation of a function may also be described as *afterimages* or *aftertastes.* Only *one* consistent, multisensory perceptual object should correspond to a function. The influence of a sum of perceptual objects is very difficult to determine, given the holistic quality of perception as described in section 2.1.2. This even applies if the influence of every individual object is known.

A non-robust overall appearance arises if:
→ too many perceptual objects are allocated to a function
→ unsystematic or unexpected correlations of perceived properties are generated
→ negatively evaluated properties are present ●

Various methods enable the reduction of the number of redundant or disturbing perceptual objects. Initially, one must attempt to eliminate the stimulus sources of these perceptions. In cases in which it is not possible to directly deactivate redundant stimulus sources, the perceptual objects thereby created should be merged with other, useful perceptions. In the auditory field, this can occur via the auditory blending of sounds. In doing so in this manner, however, perceptual objects are significantly modified, and their properties have to be once again optimized with respect to the quality impression. A further possibility consists of concealing disturbing perceptual objects by virtue of other perceptions, for example by *masking* sounds or *camouflaging* visual objects. Blending and concealing must take the spatial perception into consideration. Figure 3.75 demonstrates the result of holistic configuration in automotive construction.

FIGURE 3.75
A product captivates and persuades by combining design,
functionality, and a qualitative impression in a coherent overall concept.
Ford Verve concept car, 2007.

420

3.6
FUTURE
PERSPECTIVES
OF SYNESTHETIC
DESIGN
↓
3.6.2
ROBUSTNESS

A HIGH QUALITATIVE IMPRESSION IS PRODUCED WHEN ALL PERCEIVABLE PROPERTIES COMBINE TO CREATE A COHERENT OVERALL CONCEPT WHICH MATCHES THE CUSTOMER'S DESIRE WITHOUT LOSING CLARITY DUE TO REDUNDANT OR DISTURBING ELEMENTS.

An example of the drastic reduction of the qualitative impression is the *defect sound.* It arises when something becomes torn, broken, fragmented, or otherwise impaired in an audibly perceptible manner. This term is also applied to sounds which associatively suggest a defect, even though the object has not suffered an irreversible alteration. At any rate, such sounds diminish the impression of robust quality. Similar phenomena affect the other modalities: the tactile sensation is affected if one feels that parts are rubbing, chafing, or jiggling against one another, an unsystematic displacement occurs, or an unequal resistance is felt. The impression of visual defects can be caused by irregularities of the surface structure, such as torn areas or evidence of corrosion. The irregular shifting of parts of functional units (components) against one another can also be interpreted as indication of an inadequately dimensioned mechanical junction. For the perception of possible defects via various senses, there are not yet enough appropriate technical terms. Thus, it makes sense to speak of *multisensory, auditory, visual,* or *tactile defect impression.*

As a rule, complex industrial products are the result of serial production. Individual goods, however, do distinguish themselves slightly from one another. Already in the initial phase of the mass manufacturing of automobiles, Henry Ford determined that no automobile is exactly identical to the other (Ford 1922). Although a strict consistency is sought with respect to all parameters which influence quality, and in spite of the high standards achieved, even today reproducibility in the mass production process remains a great challenge. The elaborate, multisensory design of a product requires that the chosen properties can be reproduced with equal quality and, furthermore, that they constantly exert an influence on the customer. Thereby, the *repeatability* of an identical constellation should be distinguished from the *reproducibility* of principal contexts.

3.6
FUTURE
PERSPECTIVES
OF SYNESTHETIC
DESIGN
↓
3.6.2
ROBUSTNESS

───────

421

For synesthetic design, the repeatability indicates as to how well the product properties in the manufacturing can be fixed with respect to all components. On the other hand, it is important that judgement studies with customer groups are repeated. This provides information as to the temporal constancy of the perception with which – for the respective product – the essential features will be experienced.

Nevertheless, the reproducibility addresses the quantity of the divergence of the judgments of different customers. It permits an assessment as to what extent specific characteristics of perception can be generalized to further groups, cultures, and social strata – and thus indicates the general validity of the chosen configuration. For this purpose, it is important to evaluate the essential subjective qualities, namely the qualia. This requires an estimation of the dependency of the perception and, in particular, of the cross-sensory connections of the context. An important role is played by short-term aspects, such as temporary differences of individual living conditions, as well as long-term changes of preferences and evaluations. With respect to the various strategies of cross-sensory connection applied by the perceptual system, repeatability and reproducibility are given as follows:

→ **GENUINE SYNESTHESIA:** Genuine synesthesiae exhibit a considerable repeatability, given that those special perceptual phenomena remain constant over a long period of time. The reproducibility of perceptual experiments, however, is relatively minimal, owing to the fact that different people experience different connections between the modalities (see chapter 2.5).

→ **CROSS-MODAL ANALOGY:** Due to the fundamental function of cross-modal analogy, significant repeatability *and* reproducibility can generally be assumed. The dependency of the connection upon different individual preferences, however, requires a meticulous examination in the perceptual experiment.

→ **ICONIC AND SYMBOLIC CONNECTIONS:** For the repeatability of associative (iconic) and symbolic connections, the stability of the memory images arranged in the consciousness and of the knowledge to decipher the meaning is essential. The reproducibility, however, requires a common basis of knowledge that is not necessarily available among different cultures.

A principal problem consists of estimating future fluctuations of perceptual preferences and short-term re-evaluations. Only after this has been done with great certainty can the most robust multisensory properties can be chosen as the basis of design.

AN EFFECTIVE DESIGN NEEDS TO ROBUSTLY WITHSTANDS FLUCTUATIONS IN THE CONTEXT.

Therefore, an internationally valid design language is needed. Basic elements of configuration must be understood as the *universal language* which media-oriented artists of modernity seek (see section 3.4.1). The artistry of design will increasingly require taking cultural and stratum-specific expectations seriously and to satisfy them.

As demonstrated in chapter 2.2, cross-modal analogies can be presumed to be generally valid beyond national borders and educational horizons. This, however, has not yet been confirmed on a detailed basis. Nevertheless, the iconic and symbolic references which are most important to the connections between the modalities differ from culture to culture, given that they are conveyed by learning in a certain environment. Although the worldwide available media for mass communication achieve a certain degree of equalization, traditional images and symbols retain their meaning as well. The effective associative fields and semantic systems, which individually influence perception within different cultures, must be very precisely known for an optimization of design. Up until this point, there have been insufficient studies that provide appropriate knowledge on an international basis. Therefore, data banks for color and sound symbolism are essentially needed, just as much as lists of tactile features of preferred materials and preferences in the smell and taste perception. The comprehensive task of collecting all relevant data can be achieved with the assistance of computer-controlled expert systems. The requirements for a synesthetic design which accepts and receives cultural particularities can only actually be met if detailed knowledge is gathered and documented.

Such data banks also facilitate the development of appropriate concepts for perceptual experiments. In particular, quicker and conclusive approaches for the division of the target groups in homogenous sub-groups can be found. Indeed, only then is it possible to receive statistically verifiable results even for highly complex perceptual processes. Initially, a *stratification,* i.e. the division of the interested persons in homogenous groups, is necessary.

GIVEN THAT THE MAJORITY OF CONNECTIONS BETWEEN THE MODALITIES ARE ALSO INFLUENCED BY PREFERENCES WHICH ARE DEPENDENT UPON THE INDIVIDUAL, THE POSSIBILITY OF VARIABLE CUSTOMER CHOICE SHOULD BE EXAMINED IN ALL ANALYSES.

422

3.6
FUTURE
PERSPECTIVES
OF SYNESTHETIC
DESIGN
↓
3.6.2
ROBUSTNESS

Otherwise, it could result in drastically erroneous interpretations. Without preferences and cultural particularities being considered, it is possible that the data are insufficient for a simple statistic, such as the normal distribution, but exhibit complex distributional functions whose causes are unclear.

In the planning of experiments, moreover, it should be taken into consideration that connections between the senses could exhibit *asymmetries* – up to and including one-sided (unidirectional) connections as a "one-way street" of neuronal data transfer (see chapter 2.2). One thinks of an experiment, for example, in which the presentation of auditory test signals leads to the choice of certain visual forms which are regarded as being "obvious." The control experiment as to the choice of sounds which best correspond to the preferred forms does not necessarily lead to the same result. In special cases, it might occur that test subjects do not even regard themselves as being capable of reaching a satisfying result of cross-sensory assignment in a control experiment – in contrast to the original experiment. There is then a one-sided connection, which is, for example, characteristic of genuine synesthesiae.

In the experiment, it is advisable to systematically vary all parameters which could influence the perception and the evaluation of the customer. Within the course of experimental planning on a statistical basis *(Design of Experiments, DOE)*, a matrix providing all influencing factors of all pertinent sensory channels can be identified. This results in *main effects* and *interactions* between the parameters examined. If the visual brightness influences the perception of a sound strongly and depending upon the form, size, softness, or smell of objects, this involves a main effect. However, if the multisensory, effect of the color tone is modified by the brightness, an interaction arises between both of these perceptual properties. The experiments must be constantly conducted with a sufficiently large choice of subjects in order to achieve statistical significance. Moreover, all customer groups should be adequately represented. In the majority of cases, the results exhibit that only relatively few attributes actually influence customer evaluation. With priority, these features must be optimized in the framework of design. Thus, time and money should be invested in a careful analysis which initially considers all possibilities of connections between the senses. Although this increases the efforts and expenditures in the early phase of product development, this procedure will ultimately lead to a reduction of the overall costs in most cases, given that it provides the basis for limiting oneself to the subsequently essential features.

Features whose influence upon perception are thoroughly distinguishable from one another are particularly valuable for design. Independent values are not correlated to one another, i.e. they are *orthogonal factors.* They function as the axes of a coordinate system. If an *orthogonal design* is found, the essential features can be employed and optimized independent of one another. An orthogonal design enables the greatest freedom of configuration. On the other hand, in the realm of a synesthetic design, the utilization of the interaction of properties, which are correlated to one another, provides the greatest possible *matching* and *coherence* of the product features between the modalities. Therefore, the features which correlate to one another must be consensually optimized.

3.6
FUTURE
PERSPECTIVES
OF SYNESTHETIC
DESIGN
↓
3.6.2
ROBUSTNESS

423

By use of a *randomized* sequence of individual tests within an experiment, sequence effects can be avoided. Thereby, a possible systematic influence of a single test on the next task will be minimized. Test subjects should also receive the chance to practice the experiment. In the ideal situation, that occurs directly before the beginning of the experiment and without the knowledge of the test subjects themselves, for example, with a smooth transition to the actual experiment.

If statistically *significant* features for the connections between the modalities are found, it is then possible to exclude other, less significant attributes.

However, it does not make sense to examine the individual perceptual features with respect to possible cross-sensory interactions already in the initial experiment, given that it is not certain which strategy of connection shall serve as a basis. The separate optimization of the perceptual properties in the modalities is not the primary goal – moreover, the likelihoods of the use of certain strategies of connection in the perceptual system must build the basis of a specific design.

Repeating an experiment should produce identical results. Thereby, the reproduction of the overall result is more important than the exact repetition of every individual test.

FIGURE 3.76
**In the future, the choice of individual parameters
will gain further significance. Selector switch for the
chassis control, Ford S-Max, 2007.**

424

3.6
FUTURE
PERSPECTIVES
OF SYNESTHETIC
DESIGN
↓
3.6.2
ROBUSTNESS

The choice of essential features on the basis of perceptual experiments, however, does not always lead to a generally valid concept of multisensory design. Nevertheless, the task of satisfying individual preferences with a universal design can be fulfilled, given that individual choice possibilities are offered, as depicted in figure 3.76 in the form of a chassis control.

In conclusion, the procedure of synesthetic product design can be summarized in the following simplified form – this similarly applies to all kinds of multisensory configurations:

→   Choice of the appropriate customer group

→   Perceptual experiment:

DIVIDING THE CUSTOMER GROUP INTO HOMOGENOUS SUB-GROUPS (STRATIFICATION)

DETERMINING THE PERCEPTUAL FEATURES ESSENTIAL TO THE CUSTOMER –
WITHIN EACH MODALITY

DETERMINING THE OPTIMAL STRATEGIES OF CROSS-SENSORY CONNECTION FOR THESE FEATURES

→   Choice of the appropriate product features with respect to
producibility and sustainability

- → Optimizing perceivable product features, with preference to those cross-sensory connections which enable robust customer acceptance, in which fluctuations of the context parameters show only a minimal influence upon the evaluation of the product
- → Verifying the impact of product features on the perceptual qualities and cross-sensory connections in the perceptual experiment
- → Prototype design and construction
- → Validating the features and the perceived quality of the product as intended for production.
- → Production release

ACCESSIBILITY

3.6
FUTURE
PERSPECTIVES
OF SYNESTHETIC
DESIGN
↓
3.6.2
ROBUSTNESS

425

Even if the best possible utilization of all modalities in the satisfaction of configuration tasks is particularly attractive, in order to achieve generally valid solutions it must be taken into consideration that not every person has the complete spectrum of sensory abilities at their disposal. In the design of public places, universal signals for traffic, websites, and articles of daily use, the needs of people with reduced perceptual abilities must be considered. Naturally, color scales will be perceived differently by people with visual deficiencies with respect to colors than those with normal optical abilities. The same applies to the comprehension of auditory icons or functional sounds in the case of the hearing-impaired or in the execution of interactive tasks in the case of those with motor skill deficiencies.

AN ACCESSIBLE DESIGN WHICH
TAKES THE PERFORMANCE DEFICIENCIES
OF SENSORY ORGANS AND
MOTOR SKILL INTO CONSIDERATION
DOES NOT NEED TO AVOID
SENSUOUS ELEMENTS.

Elements of consideration must be *compatible,* however, they should fulfill their function even if they can be perceived in a limited manner. Thus, a website needs to be capable of conveying the essential information and emotional content, even in the case of deficient sensory performance of the user. Particularly, the integration of various sensory channels improves, as a result of related redundancies, the certainty of the transmission. For example, the use of the color symbolism of *red* and *green* to designate *negative* or *positive* aspects for people with red-green sight deficiencies can not be interpreted – the problem can be avoided, however, if graphic or auditory elements convey the meaning. Figure 3.77 provides an example with respect to visual abilities.

FIGURE 3.77
Simple example for improvement of visual
perceptibility of simple signs.

For those with red-green color blindness, the arrow on the left my not be perceived. A black border strip or a different coloring help to avoid this problem. A simple black-and-white figure is also appropriate, but does not include color symbolism and emotional content which is conveyed by additional colors. If enhanced to additional sensory channels, further possibilities can be utilized to improve the communication, e.g., by

→   application of additional sound
→   exclusive use of sounds
→   customization of spoken language
→   application of universal icons
→   tactile feedback

An overloading of the sensory channels with parallel data flows can be avoided by providing the possibility of choice *(customization)*. Accordingly, the human-machine interfaces can be adjusted to the individual perceptual performance. This can be based upon individual parameters such as the form and the size of symbols or of surfaces for mouse clicks, contrast, color saturation, or color tone. Entire modalities can also be integrated or excluded. This affects, on the one hand, the engaging of auditory and tactile feedback to visual information. On the other hand, it makes sense to improve the comprehensibility of audio outputs via visual data, e.g., through the video output of sign language. In the future, a more systematic design of multisensory warning signals will benefit in capturing the attention of a driver while he or she is involved in a variety of complex tasks (Spence 2010). This especially applies to the ever-growing percentage of the elderly within the total population.

426

3.6
FUTURE
PERSPECTIVES
OF SYNESTHETIC
DESIGN
↓
3.6.2
ROBUSTNESS

SIMPLICITY

Definition of product features within each modality requires selection of those basic forms which can be positively correlated. As described in section 3.3.2, design of objects by means of simple elements provides an appropriate basis for synesthetic approaches. Basic visual elements are thus combined with those which stimulate the auditory, tactile, and further sensory channels. Whereas the most elementary forms have extensively been discussed, e.g., in the field of constructivism in the arts (Kandinsky 1911; 1926), only few approaches are focused on the auditory realm (Schaeffer 1976), and much less deal with the other senses.

In the near future, taking into account further overload of human perception, objects will more and more awake interest which consist of simple, clear, multisensory, and thus easily perceivable components. Simplicity and perfect cross-sensory alignment are core strategies of synesthetic design.

Figure 3.78 provides an example of a ventilator design which consequently relinquishes the popular iconicity of a propeller. Instead, an unhindered pass-through of fresh air is suggested. In such cases, the impression of a continuous air stream needs to be supported by a constant sound exhibiting "fresh" sound quality, as discussed in section 2.2.3. It is self-evident that the uniformity of the tactile properties of the air stream must support the other modalities.

3.6
FUTURE
PERSPECTIVES
OF SYNESTHETIC
DESIGN
↓
3.6.2
ROBUSTNESS

427

FIGURE 3.78
**Propeller-free fan. Dyson Air Multiplier,
front view, 2009.**

SUSTAINABILITY

To a rapidly increasing degree, it is necessary to ground the design of products in resource conservation. This applies to raw materials and energy as well as to all elements of the ecological system serving as the basis of human livelihood. A synesthetic design offers the possibility to concentrate product features to a pertinent minimum necessary for perception and utilization – and thus considerably reducing the waste of resources.

**A PRODUCT IS CHARACTERIZED
BY THAT WHICH REACHES
THE CUSTOMER AS A RESULT OF
MULTISENSORY PERCEPTION.**

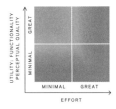

FIGURE 3.79
**The goal of configuration is an optimal perceptual quality
with minimal efforts, as this diagram depicting
effort and utility demonstrates.**

92

428

3.6
FUTURE
PERSPECTIVES
OF SYNESTHETIC
DESIGN
↓
3.6.3
SUSTAINABILITY

The goal of design is to achieve a maximum of utility with a minimum of efforts, i.e. optimal handling, functionality, and customer satisfaction. The goal is achieved if products are reduced to the elements essential to the building of multisensory perceptual objects of the desired functionality. Figure 3.79 illustrates this on the basis of the diagram of effort and utility.

The currently increasing scarcity of resources and the warming of the global climate demand radical changes in the properties of existing products and impel the search for thoroughly new concepts of design. The necessitated use of renewable energy will also usher in new perceptual properties, e.g., other visual impressions, sounds, tactile sensations, etc. ● These have to be applied harmoniously with respect to the existing contexts (see fig. 3.80).

The optimization of the perceptual quality, however, should not be used to mislead the customer into believing in functionality and material properties which do not actually exist. In this regard, the *propriety of the impression* is required, thus guaranteeing the long-term success of a product.

A sophisticated synesthetic design leads to the appearance of a product "speaking for itself." Often, packaging as the conveyer of sensory attributes is also solely employed to raise attention and positively characterize the product. In the case of a careful, attractive configuration, however, a harmoniously consistent impression of the object itself is made, which renders further advertising media redundant in many cases. It is a challenge of the future to generally avoid short-lived products and components of such products.

As a result of technical reasons, products today usually exhibit a long durability. This thus allows the opportunity to increasingly conserve material resources. The duration of the topicality of a product, however, is continually shortened by the ever-increasing rapidity of novelty launches in the market.

**PREVENTION IS BETTER
THAN RECYCLING.**

3.6
FUTURE
PERSPECTIVES
OF SYNESTHETIC
DESIGN
↓
3.6.3
SUSTAINABILITY

429

FIGURE 3.80
Contemporary sources of renewable energy
provide new perceptual qualities and affect landscapes
as well as soundscapes.

If it is possible to modify the sensory stimuli provided by an established product to the extent that it achieves a more contemporary appearance, without being completely renewed, it represents a major step towards sustainable economics, thus facilitating the conservation of resources. These possibilities are already offered by computer-aided systems whose features are essentially determined by the *software.* For example, sounds can be generated electronically. If the electronics are controlled by the software – typically the case today – it is thus possible to adapt the sound to changing taste without electronic components needing to be exchanged. This also applies to the software-controlled impression of displays for the input and output of data.

**ROBUST AND UNIVERSAL COMPUTER DEVICES
ENABLE THE MODIFICATIONS AND
INNOVATIONS OF FEATURES COMPLETELY
VIA THE SOFTWARE, WITHOUT
USING FURTHER MATERIAL RESOURCES.**

The popularity of bicycles has increased over the past twenty years. Similarly popular are the sporting forms of mobility of skateboards, roller skates, windsurfing and skiing. This demonstrates that the experience of dynamic driving sensations is not exclusively related to automotive vehicles. Thereby, the driving fun is not necessarily connected to energy consumption. In the future, the manufacturers whose products ultimately offer a maximum of perceptual quality with a minimum of energy consumption – and thus of costs – will succeed. Therefore, the fundamental properties of the perceptual system as well as the principal connections between the sensory modalities must be understood and systematically taken into consideration.

In times of an increasing overload of information, however, the objective is not to create even more stimuli via even more sensory channels. Modern humans tend to suffer more from sensual overload than from a scarcity of stimuli. Due to this reason, it is increasingly difficult to reach people with new images, compositions, aromas, and technical data. With regard to this problematic aspect, the approach of synesthetic design enables a maximum of multisensory perception to be offered with a minimum of input stimuli and information that needs to be processed. This is possible if the strategies of connection between the modalities, as discussed herein, are optimally utilized in the design process.

IT MUST BE THE GOAL OF CONTEMPORARY DESIGN TO ACHIEVE A MAXIMUM OF CONCLUSIVE PERCEPTUAL QUALITY WITH A MINIMUM OF SENSORY STIMULI.

If this book, by virtue of fundamental knowledge, concepts, and examples, contributes to conveying an impression of the path to be taken in the future, it has thus achieved its goal.

430

3.6
FUTURE
PERSPECTIVES
OF SYNESTHETIC
DESIGN
↓
3.6.3
SUSTAINABILITY

ABBADO, ADRIANO. "Perceptual Correspondences of Abstract Animation and Synthetic Sound." MS Thesis, MIT, 1988.

ABE, KOJI, KENJI OZAWA, YÔITI SUZUKI, AND TOSHIO SONE. "Comparison of the Effects of Verbal versus Visual Information about Sound Sources on the Perception of Environmental Sounds." In *Acta Acustica united with Acustica* 92 (2006): 51–60.

ACKERMANN, MARION, AND PIRKKO RATHGEBER, EDS. *Pictograms – The Loneliness of Signs.* Stuttgart: Deutscher Kunstverlag, 2007.

ADAM, KAMILLA. *Farbklänge zu Klangfarben in Bewegungsspuren. Neuorientierung in der Musikalischen Graphik Oskar Rainers.* Vienna: Österreichischer Kunst- und Kulturverlag, 2000.

ADOLPH, JÖRG, AND STEFAN LANDORF. *Synaesthesie.* Documentary film. Munich: hff, 1997.

ADORNO, THEODOR W. *Über einige Relationen zwischen Musik und Malerei.* Berlin: Verlag Gebr. Mann, 1967.

ADORNO, THEODOR W. *Versuch über Wagner.* Frankfurt am Main: Suhrkamp Verlag, 1974.

AHLENSTIEL, HEINZ, AND REINHARD KAUFMANN. *Vision und Traum. Betrachtungen über Darstellungsformen in Trugbildern.* Stuttgart: Ferdinand Enke Verlag, 1962.

ALAIS, DAVID, AND DAVID BURR. "The Ventriloquist Effect Results from Near-optimal Bimodal Integration." *Current Biology* 14 (2004), 257–62.

ALTINSOY, M. ERCAN, AND SEBASTIAN MERCHEL. "Einfluss des audiotaktilen Feedbacks auf die Qualität von Touchscreens für Digital Audio Workstations." *Proceedings of DAGA'10, Berlin.* Berlin: Deutsche Gesellschaft für Akustik DEGA, 2010, 557–58.

ALTINSOY, ERCAN. *Auditory-Tactile Interaction in Virtual Environments.* Aachen: Shaker Verlag, 2006.

ALTINSOY, ERCAN. "Einfluss von auditiven Wahrnehmungsereignissen auf die taktile Rauhigkeitswahrnehmung." *Proceedings of DAGA'07, Stuttgart.* Berlin: Deutsche Gesellschaft für Akustik DEGA, 2007, 859–60.

ANCESCHI, GIOVANNI, AND DINA RICCÒ. "Research of Communication Design: a Synesthetic Approach." *Proceedings of Design plus Research,* Politecnico di Milano, 2000.

ANSCHÜTZ, GEORG. *Kurze Einführung in die Farbe-Ton-Forschung.* Leipzig: Akademische Verlagsgesellschaft, 1927a.

ANSCHÜTZ, GEORG. "Untersuchungen zur Analyse musikalischer Photismen (Sonderfall Paul Dörken)." In *Farbe-Ton-Forschungen Vol.1,* edited by Georg Anschütz, 3–67. Leipzig: Akademische Verlagsgesellschaft, 1927b.

ANSCHÜTZ, GEORG. "Untersuchungen über komplexe musikalische Synopsie (Sonderfälle Max Gehlsen, Hugo Meier und Dr. H. Hein)." In *Farbe-Ton-Forschungen Vol.1,* edited by Georg Anschütz, 68–212. Leipzig: Akademische Verlagsgesellschaft, 1927c.

ANSCHÜTZ, GEORG, ED. *Farbe-Ton-Forschungen Vol.1.* Leipzig: Akademische Verlagsgesellschaft, 1927d.

ANSCHÜTZ, GEORG. *Farbenhören und Kunstschaffen.* Mitteilungen der Pelikan-Werke, no. 29. Hanover and Vienna: Verlag Günther Wagner, 1928.

ANSCHÜTZ, GEORG. "Das Farbe-Ton-Problem im psychischen Gesamtbereich. Sonderphänomen komplexer optischer Synästhesien ('Sichtgebilde')." *Deutsche Psychologie* 5, no. 5 (1929).

ANSCHÜTZ, GEORG. *Die Farbe als seelischer Ausdruck. Mitteilungen der Pelikan-Werke*, no. 37. Hanover and Vienna: Verlag Günther Wagner, 1930.

ANSCHÜTZ, GEORG, ED. *Farbe-Ton-Forschungen Vol.3. Bericht über den 2. Kongress für Farbe-Ton-Forschung.* Hamburg: Psychologisch-ästhetische Forschungsgesellschaft, 1931.

ANSCHÜTZ, GEORG, ED. *Farbe-Ton-Forschungen Vol. 2* (published after Vol. 3). Hamburg: Psychologisch-ästhetische Forschungsgesellschaft, 1936a.

ANSCHÜTZ, GEORG. "Zur Typologie und Theorie des 'Farbenhörens'." In *Farbe-Ton-Forschungen Vol.2*, edited by Georg Anschütz, 521–30. Hamburg: Psychologisch-ästhetische Forschungsgesellschaft, 1936b.

ARGELANDER, ANNELIES. *Das Farbenhören und der synästhetische Faktor der Wahrnehmung.* Jena: Verlag von Gustav Fischer, 1927.

ARNHEIMER, RUDOLF. *Visual Thinking.* Berkeley University of California Press, 1969.

ARNOLD, DH., A. JOHNSTON AND S. NISHIDA. "Timing Sight and Sound." *Vision Research* (2005) 1275–84.

ARNOLD, ULLI, AND WERNER SCHMIDT. *Barock in Dresden.* Leipzig: Edition Leipzig, 1986.

ASANGER, ROLAND, AND GERD WENNINGER, EDS. *Handwörterbuch Psychologie.* Weinheim: Beltz Psychologie Verlags Union, 1999.

AUBERGÉ, VÉRONIQUE, AND MARIE CATHIARD. "Can We Hear the Prosody of Smile?," *Speech Communication 40* (2003) 87–97.

AUGOYARD, FRANCOIS, AND HENRY TORGUE, EDS. *Sonic Experience: A Guide to Everyday Sounds.* Montreal: McGill-Queen's University Press, 2006.

BASBAUM, SÉRGIO ROCLAW. "Synesthesia and Culture: Synesthetic Experience and the Installation of Modernity." Proceedings of the Third International Congress "Synaesthesia: Science and Art", Granada, 2009.

BANHAM, RUSS. *The Ford Century: Ford Motor Company and the Innovations that Shaped the World.* San Diego: Tehabi Books, 2002.

BARON-COHEN, SIMON, AND JOHN E. HARRISON, EDS. *Synaesthesia: Classic and Contemporary Readings.* Oxford and Cambridge: Blackwell Publishers, 1997.

BECKING, GUSTAV. *Der musikalische Rhythmus als Erkenntnisquelle.* Augsburg: Benno Filser Verlag, 1928.

BEHNE, KLAUS-ERNST. "Am Rande der Musik: Synästhesien, Bilder, Farben." In *Musikpsychologie. Empirische Forschungen – Ästhetische Experimente,* edited by Klaus-Ernst Behne, Günther Kleine, and Helga de la Motte-Haber, 94–120. Wilhelmshaven: Noetzel Verlag, 1992.

BEHNE, KLAUS-ERNST. *Gehört-Gedacht-Gesehen. Zehn Aufsätze zum visuellen, kreativen und theoretischen Umgang mit Musik.* Regensburg: Con Brio Fachbuch, 1994.

BEHNE, KLAUS-ERNST. "Synästhesie und intermodale Analogie – Fallstudie eines Notations-Synästhetikers." In *Synästhesie. Interferenz – Transfer – Synthese der Sinne,* edited by Hans Adler, 31–41. Würzburg: Verlag Königshausen & Neumann, 2002.

BEHRENDT, JOACHIM-ERNST. *Das Jazzbuch. Von New-Orleans bis in die achtziger Jahre.* Revised and continued by Günther Huesmann. Frankfurt: Fischer Taschenbuch Verlag, ⁸1999. English edition: *The Jazz Book.* New York: Lawrence Hill & Company, 1975.

BERMAN, GRETA, AND CAROL STEEN. *Synesthesia: Art and the Mind.* Hamilton, Ont.: McMaster Museum of Art, 2008.

BERTELSON, P., AND M. RADEAU. "Cross-Modal Bias and Perceptual Fusion with Auditory-Visual Spatial Discor-dance." Perception and Psychophysics 29 (1981) 578–84.

BETANCOURT, MICHAEL, ED. *Visual Music Instruments Patents.* Volume One: 1876 to 1950. San Bernardino, CA: Borgo Press, 2004.

BIEDERMANN, HANS. *Knauers Lexikon der Symbole.* Digital Library. Berlin: Directmedia Publishing, 2001.

BLANC-GATTI, CHARLES. *Des sons et des couleurs.* Paris: Editions d'art chromophoniques, ²1934.

BLAUERT, JENS. *Spatial Hearing: The Psychophysics of Human Sound Localization.* Revised edition. Cambridge, Mass.: MIT Press, 1997.

BLAUERT, JENS. "3-D-Lautsprecher-Wiedergabemethoden." *Proceedings of DAGA'08, Dresden.* Berlin: Deutsche Gesellschaft für Akustik DEGA, 2008, 25–26.

BLAUERT, JENS, AND RAINER GUSKI. "Critique of Pure Psychoacoustics." *Proceedings of NAG/DAGA'09, Rotterdam.* Berlin: Deutsche Gesellschaft für Akustik DEGA, 2009, 1518–9.

BLEULER, EUGEN, AND KARL LEHMANN. *Zwangsmäßige Lichtempfindungen durch Schall und verwandte Erscheinungen auf dem Gebiete der anderen Sinnesempfindungen.* Leipzig: Fues's Verlag, 1881. Also available as reprint by the University of Michigan Library.

BLEULER, EUGEN. "Zur Theorie der Sekundärempfindungen." *Zeitschrift für Psychologie* 65 (1913), 1ff.

BLUTNER, FRIEDRICH E. "Produkt-Sound-Design und die Wiederentdeckung einer ganzheitlichen Akustik." In *Multisensuelles Design. Eine Anthologie,* edited by Peter Luckner, 231-257. Halle: Hochschule für Kunst und Design, 2002.

BOCKHOFF, MICHAEL. "Soundscapes in der abendländischen Malerei." *Proceedings of DAGA'07, Stuttgart.* Berlin: Deutsche Gesellschaft für Akustik DEGA, 2007, 857–58.

BODDEN, MARKUS, AND HEINRICH IGLSEDER. "Aktive Geräuschgestaltung bei Staubsaugern." *Proceedings of DAGA'01, Hamburg.* Oldenburg: Deutsche Gesellschaft für Akustik DEGA, 2001.

BOHLÄNDER, CARLO, KARL-HEINZ HOLLER, AND CHRISTIAN PFARR. *Reclams Jazzführer.* Stuttgart: Philipp Reclam jun., ⁴1990.

BÖHME, GERNOT. *Atmosphären.* Frankfurt am Main: Suhrkamp, 1995.

BÖHME, GERNOT. "Synästhesie im Rahmen einer phänomenologischen Theorie der Wahrnehmung." In *Synästhesie. Interferenz – Transfer – Synthese der Sinne,* edited by Hans Adler, 45–56. Würzburg: Verlag Königshausen & Neumann, 2002.

BOS, MARIA C. *Über echte und unechte audition colorée.* Leipzig: Verlag Johann Ambrosius Barth, 1929.

BREGMAN, ALBERT S. *Auditory Scene Analysis: The Perceptual Organization of Sound.* Cambridge, Mass.: MIT Press, ¹1990, ²1999.

BRONNER, KAI, AND RAINER HIRT. "Research on the Interaction between the Perception of Music and Flavour." Poster presented at the 9th International Multisensory Research Forum, Hamburg, 2008.

BRONNER, KAI. "Jingle all the Way? Basics of Audio Branding." In *Audio Branding: Brands, Sound and Communication,* edited by Kai Bronner and Rainer Hirt, 77–87. Baden-Baden: Nomos Verlagsgesellschaft, Edition Reinhard Fischer, 2009a.

BRONNER, KAI, AND RAINER HIRT, EDS. *Audio Branding: Brands, Sound and Communication.* Baden-Baden: Nomos Verlagsgesellschaft, Edition Reinhard Fischer, 2009b.

BROSCH, TOBIAS, DIDIER GRANDJEAN, DAVID SANDER, AND KLAUS R. SCHERER. "Cross-modal Emotional Attention: Emotional Voices Modulate Early Stages of Visual Processing." *Journal of Cognitive Neuroscience* 21, no. 9 (2008) 1670–79.

BROUGHER, KERRY, JEREMY STRICK, ARI WISEMAN, AND JUDITH ZILCZER, EDS. *Visual Music: Synaesthesia in Art and Music since 1900.* London and New York: Thames & Hudson, 2005.

BRUNER, J. S., AND L. POSTMAN. "An Approach to Social Perception." In *Current Trends in Social Psychology,* edited by W. Dennis and R. Lippitt, 71–118. Pittsburgh: Univ. Pittsburgh Press, 1951.

BURGHOLD, JULIUS, ED. RICHARD WAGNER: *Parsifal. Ein Bühnenweihfestspiel. Text mit den hauptsächlichsten Leitmotiven und Notenbeispielen.* London Verlag B. Schott's Söhne, ca. 1910.

CALVERT, GEMMA A., CHARLES SPENCE AND BARRY E. STEIN, EDS. *The Handbook of Multisensory Processing.* Cambridge, Mass.: MIT Press, 2004.

CAMPENHAUSEN, CHRISTOPH VON. *Die Sinne des Menschen. Einführung in die Psychophysik der Wahrnehmung.* Stuttgart and New York: Thieme, ²1993.

CATREIN, CHRISTOPH. *Vertauschte Sinne. Untersuchungen zur Synästhesie in der römischen Dichtung.* Munich: K.G. Saur Verlag, 2003.

CHARNAY, YVES. "Der Farbcode der chinesischen Architektur." In *Spektrum der Wissenschaft – Spezial: Farben*, 86–87. Heidelberg: Spektrum der Wissenschaft Verlagsgesellschaft, 2000.

CHLADNI, ERNST FLORENS FRIEDRICH. *Entdeckungen über die Theorie des Klanges.* Leipzig: Weidmanns Erben und Reich, 1787.

CHLADNI, ERNST FLORENS FRIEDRICH. *Neue Vorträge zur Akustik.* Leipzig: Verlag Breitkopf und Härtel, 1817.

CHION, MICHEL. *Audio-Vision: Sound on Screen.* New York: Columbia University Press, 1994.

CLAUS, JÜRGEN. *ChipppKunst: Computer-Holographie-Kybernetik-Laser.* Frankfurt and Berlin: Ullstein, 1985.

CLAUSBERG, KARL. "Aura und Ausdruck – Synästhesien der Beseelung." In *Ausdruck – Ausstrahlung – Aura. Synästhesien der Beseelung im Medienzeitalter*, edited by Karl Clausberg, Elize Bisanz, and Cornelius Weiller, 41–86. Bad Honnef: Hippocampus Verlag, 2007.

CLYNES, MANFRED. *Sentics. The Touch of the Emotion.* Dorset: Prism Press, 1989.

COLLIGNON, O., P. VOSS, M. LASSONDE, AND F. LEPORE. "Cross-modal Plasticity for the Spatial Processing of Sounds in Visually Deprived Subjects." *Exp Brain Res.* 192, no. 3 (2009) 343–8.

COLLOPY, FRED. "Color, Form, and Motion. Dimensions of a Musical Art of Light." *Leonardo* 33, no. 5 (2000) 355–60.

COX, TREVOR J. "The Effect of Visual Stimuli on the Horribleness of Awful Sounds." *Applied Acoustics* 69, no. 8 (2008) 691–703.

CULHANE, JOHN. *Walt Disney's Fantasia.* New York: Abradale Press / Harry N. Abrams, Inc., Publishers, 1983, reprint 1987.

CYTOWIC, RICHARD E. *The Man Who Tasted Shapes.* Cambridge, Mass.: MIT Press, 1993.

CYTOWIC, RICHARD E. "Synesthesia: Phenomenology and Neuropsychology." In *Synaesthesia: Classic and Contemporary Readings*, edited by Simon Baron-Cohen and John E. Harrison, 17–42. Oxford and Cambridge: Blackwell Publishers, 1997.

CYTOWIC, RICHARD E. *Synesthesia: A Union of the Senses.* New York: Springer Verlag, ¹1989.

CYTOWIC, RICHARD E. *Synesthesia: A Union of the Senses.* Cambridge, Mass.: MIT Press, ²2002.

CYTOWIC, RICHARD E., AND DAVID M. EAGLEMAN. *Wednesday is Indigo Blue: Discovering the Brain of Synesthesia.* Cambridge, Mass.: MIT Press, 2009.

CZYCHOLL, DIETMAR. *Die phantastischen Gesichtserscheinungen. Vom Sehen bei geschlossenen Augen und seiner Erforschung.* Berlin: Verlag für Wissenschaft und Bildung, 2003.

DAHLHAUS, CARL. *Richard Wagners Musikdramen.* Velber: Friedrich Verlag,1971; Stuttgart: Philipp Reclam Jun., 1996.

DAHLHAUS, CARL. *Die Idee der absoluten Musik.* Kassel: Bärenreiter Verlag, ³1994.

DAMASIO, A. R., D. TRANEL, AND H. DAMASIO. "Somatic Markers and the Guidance of Behavior: Theory and Pre-liminary Testing." In Frontal Lobe Function and Dysfunction, edited by H. S. Levin, H. M. Eisenberg, and A. L. Benton, 217–29. New York, 1991.

DAMASIO, ANTONIO R. *Descartes' Error. Emotion, Reason and the Human Brain* (1994). London: Vintage, 2006.

DANN, KEVIN T. *Bright Colors Falsely Seen: Synaesthesia and the Search for Transcendental Knowledge.* New Haven & London: Yale University Press, 1998.

DANIELS, DIETER, AND SANDRA NAUMANN. *Audiovisuology 1. See this Sound: An Interdisciplinary Compendium of*

Audiovisual Culture. Cologne: Verlag der Buchhandlung König, 2010.

DAY, SEAN A. "Trends in Synesthetically Colored Graphemes and Phonemes." *Iconicity in Language*, 2001.

DAY, SEAN A. "Some Demographic and Socio-cultural Aspects of Synesthesia." In *Synesthesia: Perspectives from Cognitive Neuroscience*, edited by Lynn C. Robertson, and Noam Sagiv, 11-33. Oxford: Oxford University Press, 2005.

DAY, SEAN A. "Was ist Synästhesie?" In *Farbe-Licht-Musik. Synästhesie und Farblichtmusik*, edited by Natalia Sidler, and Jörg Jewanski, 15-30. Bern: Peter Lang Verlag, 2006.

DAY, SEAN A. "Demographic Data." http://home.comcast.net/~sean.day, 2007.

DEFRÉVILLE, BORIS, ARNAUD CAN, AND CATHERINE LAVANDIER. "The Hedonic Side of Soundscape Perception: Let's Go for a Walk in the City of Paris!" *Proceedings of INTER-NOISE 07*. Istanbul: Turkish Acoustical Society, 2007.

DEMATTÈ, LUISA M., DANIEL SANABRIA, RACHEL SUGARMAN, AND CHARLES SPENCE. "Cross-Modal Interactions between Olfaction and Touch." *Chemical Senses* 31, no. 4 (2006) 291-300.

DERMIETZEL, MARKUS. *Musik als Entwurfsgrundlage für Architektur?* Cologne: e-book, 2003: http://www.gro.de/index.php?m-a-ebook_en (accessed March 11, 2011).

DEUTSCH, JOHANNES. *Vision Mahler*. DVD, arthaus music, 135 min., 2007.

DF1989. *Hans Richter, Malerei und Film*. Kinematograph, no. 5. Frankfurt am Main: Deutsches Filmmuseum, 1989.

DF1993. *Optische Poesie – Oskar Fischinger, Leben und Werk*. Kinematograph, no. 9. Frankfurt am Main: Deutsches Filmmuseum, 1993.

DISNEY, WALT. *Fantasia*. Animated film, 125 min., 1940.

DITTMAR, ALEXANDRA, ED. *Synaesthesia: A "Golden Thread" through Life?* Essen: Verlag Die Blaue Eule, 2009.

DT. *Corporate Design: Guideline for the Basic Elements*, Deutsche Telekom AG, 2007.

DÜCHTING, HAJO. *Farbe am Bauhaus. Synthese und Synästhesie.*

Neue Bauhausbücher. Berlin: Verlag Gebr. Mann, 1996.

DUFFY, PATRICIA LYNNE. *Blue Cats and Chartreuse Kittens: How Synesthetes Color Their World*. New York: Freeman WH & Co., 2001.

EAGLEMAN, DAVID, ARIELLE D. KAGAN, STEPHANIE S. NELSON, DEEPAK SAGARAM, AND ANAND K. SARMA. "A Standardized Test Battery for the Study of Synesthesia." *Journal of Neuroscience Methods* 159, no. 1 (2007) 139-145.

EAGLEMAN, DAVID. "The Synesthesia Battery," http://www.synesthete.org (accessed July 20, 2010).

EBBECKE, ULRICH. *Johannes Müller, der große rheinische Physiologe*. Including a reprint of Johannes Müller's treatise: *Über die phantastischen Gesichtserscheinungen*. Hanover: Verlagsbuchhandlung Schmorl & von Seefeld Nachf., 1951.

EBERLEIN, DOROTHEE. "Čiurlionis, Skrjabin und der osteuropäische Symbolismus" In *Vom Klang der Bilder: Die Musik in der Kunst des 20sten Jahrhunderts*, edited by Karin von Maur, 340-45. Munich: Prestel Verlag, 1985.

ECO, UMBERTO. *A Theory of Semiotics*. Bloomington: Indiana University Press, 1978.

EGGELING, VIKING. *Symphonie Diagonale*. Abstract experimental film, 4 min., Germany, 1924.

EHRENFELS, CHRISTIAN VON. "Über Gestaltqualitäten." In *Vierteljahresschrift für wissenschaftliche Philosophie*, 14 (1890), 249-92.

EICHMEIER, JOSEF, AND OSKAR HÖFER. *Endogene Bildmuster*. Munich: Verlag Urban & Schwarzenberg, 1974.

EITAN, ZOHAR, AND RONI E. GRANOT. "Musical Parameters and Images of Motion." *Proceedings of the Conference on Interdisciplinary Musicology*, edited by R. Parncutt et al. Graz, 2004.

EKMAN, PAUL. "Basic Emotions." In *Handbook of Cognition and Emotion*, edited by T. Dalgleish and M. Power. Sussex: John Wiley & Sons, Ltd., 1999.

EKMAN, PAUL. *Emotions Revealed: Understanding Faces and Feelings*. London: Orion Books, 2004.

EMRICH, HINDERK M., UDO SCHNEIDER, AND MARKUS ZEDLER. *Welche Farbe hat der Montag? Synästhesie: das Leben mit verknüpften Sinnen.* Leipzig: Hirzel Verlag, 2001.

ENDE, MICHAEL. *Momo.* Stuttgart: Thienemann Verlag, 1973.

ENGELBRECHT, CHRISTIANE, WOLFGANG MARX, AND BRITTA SWEERS. *Lontano – 'Aus weiter Ferne'. Zur Musiksprache und Assoziationsvielfalt György Ligetis.* Hamburg: von Bockel Verlag, 1997.

ENGELEN, BERNHARD. *Die Synästhesien in der Dichtung Eichendorffs.* Dissertation. Cologne: 1966.

ENGELHARDT, BERND. Final remarks in *The Drive to Design. Geschichte, Ausbildung und Perspektiven im Autodesign,* edited by Ralf J. F. Kieselbach. Stuttgart: avedition, 1998.

ENO, BRIAN. *Music for Airports.* LP, 1978. Reissued on CD by Virgin Records/ EMI 2004.

ERNI, PETER. *Die gute Form. Eine Aktion des Schweizerischen Werkbundes. Dokumentation und Interpretation.* Baden: LIT Verlag Lars Müller, 1983.

FECHNER, GUSTAV THEODOR. *Vorschule der Ästhetik.* Leipzig: Verlag Breitkopf und Härtel, 1876, ³1925.

FECHNER, GUSTAV THEODOR. *Elemente der Psychophysik.* Leipzig: 1860.

FICK, ADOLF. *Lehrbuch der Anatomie und Physiologie der Sinnesorgane.* Lahr: M. Schauenburg, 1864.

FIEBELKORN, IAN C., JOHN J. FOXE, AND SOPHIE MOLHOLM. "Dual Mechanisms for the Cross-sensory Spread of Attention: How Much do Learned Associations Matter?" *Cerebral Cortex* 20, no. 1 (2010), 109–20.

FIELL, CHARLOTTE, AND PETER FIELL. *Design of the 20th Century.* Cologne: Taschen Verlag, 2005a.

FIELL, CHARLOTTE, AND PETER FIELL. *Designing the 21st Century.* Cologne: Taschen Verlag, 2005b.

FIELL, CHARLOTTE, AND PETER FIELL. *Industrial Design A–Z.* Cologne: Taschen Verlag, 2006.

FILK, CHRISTIAN, MICHAEL LOMMEL, AND MIKE SANDBOTHE, EDS. *Media Synaesthetics. Konturen einer physiologischen Medienästhetik.* Cologne: Herbert von Halem Verlag, 2004.

FINK, MONIKA. *Musik nach Bildern. Programmbezogenes Komponieren im 19. und 20. Jahrhundert.* Innsbruck: Edition Helbling, 1987.

FINK, MONIKA. "Farben-Klänge und Klang-Farben im Werk von Olivier Messiaen." In *Synästhesie in der Musik – Musik in der Synästhesie,* edited by Volker Kalisch, 148–56. Essen: Verlag Die Blaue Eule, 2004.

FISCHER, ROSA-LINDE, AND STEPHAN GETZMANN. "Wahrnehmung akustischer Bewegungen und visueller Positionen – ein Fall audiovisueller Integration?" *Proceedings of DAGA'08, Dresden.* Berlin: Deutsche Gesellschaft für Akustik DEGA, 2008, 363–64.

FISCHINGER, OSKAR. *Studie Nr. 5.* Abstract musical film. Germany, 1930.

FITZEK, HERBERT, AND WILHELM SALBER. *Gestalt-Psychologie. Geschichte und Praxis.* Darmstadt: Wissenschaftliche Buchgesellschaft, 1996.

FLADE, ANTJE. "Wahrnehmung." In *Handwörterbuch Psychologie,* edited by Roland Asanger, and Gerd Wenninger. Weinheim: Beltz Psychologie Verlags Union, 1999.

FLOURNOY, THÉODORE. "Enquête sur l'Audition Colorée". In *Extrait des Archives des Sciences physiques et naturelles, troisième Période,* vol. 28, no. 11, Geneva: 1892.

FLOURNOY, THÉODORE. *Des Phénomènes de Synopsie (Audition Colorée).* Paris and Geneva: Félix Alcan, Ch. Eggimann & Cie, 1893.

FLÜCKIGER, BARBARA. *Sound Design. Die virtuelle Klangwelt des Films.* Marburg: Schüren Verlag, ²2002.

FÖLLMER, GOLO. "Klangorganisation im öffentlichen Raum." In *Klangkunst. Tönende Objekte und klingende Räume,* edited by Helga de la Motte-Haber, 193–227. Laaber: Laaber Verlag, 1999.

FORD, HENRY. *My Life and Work.* Garden City, NY: Doubleday, Page & Co., ¹1922.

FREUWÖRT, ECKHARD. *Vernetzte Sinne. Über Synästhesie und Verhalten.* Norderstedt: Books on Demand, 2004.

GAGE, JOHN. *Color and Culture: Practice and Meaning from Antiquity to Abstraction.* London and New York: Thames & Hudson, 1993.

GAGE, JOHN. *Color and Meaning: Art, Science and Symbolism.* London and New York: Thames & Hudson, 1999.

GALTON, FRANCIS. *Inquiries into Human Faculty and its Development.* London: Macmillan, 1883.

GEGENFURTNER, KARL R., SEBASTIAN WALTER, AND DORIS I. BRAUN. *Visuelle Informationsverarbeitung im Gehirn.* Tutorial Universität Gießen, 2000. http://www.allpsych. uni-giessen.de/karl/teach/aka.htm (July 18, 2010).

GEKELER, HANS. *Handbuch der Farbe. Systematik, Ästhetik, Praxis.* Cologne: DuMont, 2005.

GESCHWIND, NORMAN. "Die Großhirn- rinde." In *Gehirn und Nervensystem*, 112–21. Heidelberg: Spektrum der Wissenschaft, ⁶1985.

GETZMANN, STEPHAN, AND J. LEWALD. "Repräsentationales Momentum bei der visuellen und auditiven Bewe- gungswahrnehmung." *Proceedings of DAGA'08, Dresden.* Berlin: Deutsche Gesellschaft für Akustik DEGA, 2008, 365–66.

GIBSON, J.J. "Adaption, After-Effect, and Contrast in the Perception of Curved Lines." *Journal of Experimental Psychology* 16 (1933) 1–31.

GIDLÖF-GUNNARSSON, ANITA, EVY ÖHR- STRÖM, AND MIKAEL ÖGREN. "Noise Annoyance and Restoration in Differ- ent Courtyard Settings: Laboratory Experiments on Audio-Visual Interac- tions." *Proceedings of Inter-Noise 2007.* Istanbul: Turkish Acoustical Society, 2007.

GIRL: *Feststellung und Beurteilung von Geruchsimmissionen (Geruchsimmis- sions-Richtlinie) in der Fassung vom 29. Februar 2008 und einer Ergänzung vom 10. September 2008.* Ministerium für Umwelt, Naturschutz und Reak- torsicherheit, Bundesr. Deutschland.

GK 1983. *Der Hang zum Gesamtkunstwerk – Europäische Utopien seit 1800.* Aarau: Verlag Sauerländer, 1983.

GOETHE, JOHANN WOLFGANG VON. *Farbenlehre* [1810]. With introduction and comments by Rudolf Steiner. 5 volumes. Stuttgart: Verlag Freies Geistesleben, ⁶1997.

GOLEMAN, DANIEL. *Emotional Intelligence.* New York: Bantam Books, 1995.

GOLDSCHMIDT, RICHARD HELLMUTH. *Postulat der Farbwandelspiele.* Sitzungsberichte der Heidelberger Akademie der Wissenschaften. Heidelberg: Carl Winter Universitäts- buchhandlung, 1928.

GOLDSTEIN, E. BRUCE. *Sensation and Perception.* International student edition. Belmont, CA: Wadsworth, Cengage Learning, ⁸2009.

GOSSMANN, JOACHIM. "Towards an Audi- tory Representation of Complexity." *Proceedings of ICAD 05, International conference on Auditory Display.* Limerick: 2005.

GOTTDANG, ANDREA. *Vorbild Musik. Die Geschichte einer Idee in der Malerei im deutschsprachigen Raum 1780– 1915.* Munich: Deutscher Kunstver- lag, 2004.

GRADUALE TRIPLEX. *seu Graduale Romanum Pauli PP. VI cura recognitum & rhythmicis signis a Solesmensibus monachis ornatum Neumis Laudunensibus (Cod. 239) et Sangallen- sibus (Codicum San Gallensis 359 et Einsidlensis 121) nunc auctum.* Sablé sur Sarthe: Abbaye Saint Pierre, ¹1979.

GRAY, JEFFREY. "Synästhesie – Mit den Ohren sehen." In *Spektrum der Wis- senschaft Dossier: Gehirn und Erleben.* Stuttgart: Spektrum der Wissenschaft Verlagsgesellschaft, 2006, 22–29.

GRIFFIN, M. J. *Handbook of Human Vibration.* London: Academic Press, Harcourt Brace Jovanovich, Publishers, 1990.

GRUNDNER, ROLF. *Bericht über den ersten Kongress für Farbe-Ton-Forschung und über die Sitzungen der Psycholo- gisch-ästhetischen Forschungs- gesellschaft in Hamburg (1927–1930).* Hamburg: 1930.

GÜNTHER, HANS, ED. *Gesamtkunstwerk. Zwischen Synästhesie und Mythos.* Bielefeld: Aisthesis Verlag, 1994.

GUSTAVINO, CATHERINE, BRIAN F. G. KATZ, JEAN-DOMINIQUE POLACK, DANIEL J. LEVITIN AND DANIÈLE DUBOIS. "Ecological Validity of Soundscape Reproduction." *Acta Acustica united with Acustica,* 91 (2005) 333–41.

HABERMANN, HEINZ. *Kompendium des Industrie-Design. Grundlagen der Gestaltung.* Berlin: Springer Verlag, 2003.

HACKE, AXEL, AND MICHAEL SOWA. *Der weiße Neger Wumbaba. Kleines Handbuch des Verhörens.* Munich: Kunstmann Verlag, 2004.

HANAUER, J.P., AND P.J. BROOKS. "Developmental Change in the Cross-Modal Stroop Effect." *Percept Psychophy* 653 (2003) 359–66.

HAPKEMEYER, ANDREA, AND PETER STASNY. *Ludwig Hirschfeld-Mack: Bauhäusler und Visionär.* Ostfildern-Ruit: Hatje Cantz Verlag, 2000.

HARRISON, JOHN AND SIMON BARON-COHEN. "Synaesthesia: a Review of Psychological Theories." In *Synaesthesia: Classic and Contemporary Readings*, edited by Simon Baron-Cohen and John E. Harrison, 109–22. Oxford and Cambridge: Blackwell Publishers, 1997.

HARRISON, JOHN. *Synaesthesia: The Strangest Thing.* Oxford: Oxford University Press, 2001.

HAUSKELLER, MICHAEL. *Atmosphären erleben. Philosophische Untersuchungen zur Sinneswahrnehmung.* Berlin: Akademie Verlag, 1995.

HAVERKAMP, MICHAEL. *Laboruntersuchung zur akuten Wirkung stoßhaltiger Ganzkörper-Schwingungen auf den Menschen.* Dissertation. Fortschritts-Berichte des VDI Reihe 11, no. 129. Düsseldorf: VDI-Verlag, 1990.

HAVERKAMP, MICHAEL. "Solving Vehicle Noise Problems by Analysis of the Transmitted Sound Energy." *Proceedings of ISMA 25, Noise and Vibration Engineering.* Leuven: Katholieke Universiteit Leuven, 2000.

HAVERKAMP, MICHAEL. "Synästhetische Wahrnehmung und Geräuschdesign. Grundlagen: Verknüpfung auditiver und visueller Attribute." In *Subjektive Fahreindrücke sichtbar machen II*, edited by Klaus Becker, 114–42. Renningen-Malmsheim: expert-Verlag, 2002.

HAVERKAMP, MICHAEL. "Visualisierung auditiver Wahrnehmung – historische und neue Konzepte. Ein phänomenologischer Überblick." *Proceedings of DAGA'03, Aachen.* Oldenburg: Deutsche Gesellschaft für Akustik DEGA, 2003a, 620–621.

HAVERKAMP, MICHAEL. "Visualization of Synaesthetic Experience during the Early 20th Century – an Analytic Approach." International conference on Synaesthesia, Hannover, 2003b. On http://www.michaelhaverkamp.de (March 11, 2011).

HAVERKAMP, MICHAEL. "Synästhetische Wahrnehmung und Design. Grundlagen: Verknüpfung auditiver und visueller Attribute." In *Synästhesie in der Musik – Musik in der Synästhesie*, edited by Volker Kalisch, 110–31. Essen: Verlag Die Blaue Eule, 2004a.

HAVERKAMP, MICHAEL. "Audio-Visual Coupling and Perception of Sound-Scapes." *Proceedings of CFA/DAGA'04, Strasbourg.* Oldenburg: Deutsche Gesellschaft für Akustik DEGA, 2004b, 365–366.

HAVERKAMP, MICHAEL ET AL. "Creep Groan – Phenomenology and Remedy." *ATZ: Automobiltechnische Zeitschrift* 7/8, 2004c.

HAVERKAMP, MICHAEL. "Beurteilung und Gestaltung von Geräuschen auf Basis intermodaler Analogien." In *Subjektive Fahreindrücke sichtbar machen III*, edited by Klaus Becker, 182–204. Renningen-Malmsheim: expert-Verlag, 2006a.

HAVERKAMP, MICHAEL. "Audio-Visuelle Verknüpfungen im Wahrnehmungssystem und die Eingrenzung synästhetischer Phänomene." In *Farbe-Licht-Musik. Synästhesie und Farblichtmusik*, edited by Natalia Sidler, and Jörg Jewanski, 31–74. Bern: Peter Lang Verlag, 2006b.

HAVERKAMP, MICHAEL. "Analytische und Komplexe Synopsie." In *Farbe-*

Licht-Musik. Synästhesie und Farblicht-musik, edited by Natalia Sidler, and Jörg Jewanski, 93–99. Bern: Peter Lang Verlag, 2006c.

HAVERKAMP, MICHAEL. "Synästhetische Aspekte der Geräuschgestaltung im Automobilbau." In *Audio Branding. Entwicklung, Anwendung, Wirkung akustischer Identitäten in Werbung, Medien und Gesellschaft,* edited by Kai Bronner, and Rainer Hirt, 228–44. Munich: Reinhard Fischer Verlag, 2007a.

HAVERKAMP, MICHAEL. "Percezione Sines-tesica e Design del Rumore." *Progetto Graphico* 5, no. 10. Roma: 2007b, 162–69.

HAVERKAMP, MICHAEL. "Essentials for Description of Cross-sensory Interac-tion during Perception of a Complex Environment." *Proceedings of Inter-Noise 2007.* Istanbul: Turkish Acousti-cal Society, 2007c.

HAVERKAMP, MICHAEL. "Synesthetic Design – Building Multi-sensory Arrangements." In *Audio Branding: Brands, Sound and Communication*, edited by Kai Bronner and Rainer Hirt, 163–78. Baden-Baden: Nomos Verlagsgesellschaft, Edition Reinhard Fischer, 2009a.

HAVERKAMP, MICHAEL. "Music and Motion – Alexander Truslit and the Research on Synesthesia." In *Synästhesie der Gefühle,* edited by Jasmin Sinha, 135–60. Luxembourg: Synaisthesis Verlag, 2009b.

HAVERKAMP, MICHAEL. "Look at that Sound! – Visual Aspects of Auditory Perception." *Proceedings of the Third International Congress "Synaesthesia: Science and Art."* Granada, 2009c.

HAVERKAMP, MICHAEL. "Synesthetic Approach for Evaluation of the Cross-sensory Quality of Multimedia Applications." QOMEX 2010, Interna-tional Workshop on Quality of Multi-media Experience. Trondheim, 2010a.

HAVERKAMP, MICHAEL. "Visualizing Auditory Perception: Correlations, Concepts, Synesthesia." Proceedings of Galeyev's Readings. Prometheus-Center, Kazan, 2010b.

HAVLIK, E.J. *Lexikon der Onomatopöien.*

Die lautimitierenden Wörter im Comic. Frankfurt am Main: Verlag Dieter Fricke, 1981.

HEADLEY, PIERS. *Music for Toilets.* CD. Berlin: Tresor/Interfish Records, 1993.

HEHN, PATRICK. *Emotionale Marken-führung mit Duft.* Göttingen-Rosdorf: ForschungsForum, 2007.

HEIN, HEINRICH. "Untersuchungen über die Gesetzmäßigkeiten der Zuord-nung von Farben zu Tönen." In *Farbe-Ton-Forschungen,* vol. 1, edited by Georg Anschütz, 213–96. Leipzig: Aka-demische Verlagsgesellschaft, 1927.

HEINRICHS, RALF AND WINFRIED KREBBER. "Sound-Design Verifikation mittels Sound Simulation Vehicle." *Procee-dings of DAGA'01, Hamburg.* Olden-burg: Deutsche Gesellschaft für Akus-tik DEGA, 2001.

HELLER, EVA. *Wie Farben auf Gefühl und Verstand wirken.* Munich: Droemer Verlag, 2000.

HELMHOLTZ, HERMANN VON. *Handbuch der physiologischen Optik.* Hamburg and Leipzig: Verlag von Leopold Voss, [3]1910. English edition: *Treatise on Physiological Optics,* vol. 1–3. Optical Society of America, 1924, Reprint: Do-ver Phoenix Editions, 2005.

HELMHOLTZ, HERMANN VON. *Die Lehre von den Tonempfindungen als physio-logische Grundlage für die Theorie der Musik.* Brunswick: 1863. English edi-tion: *On the Sensations of Tone as a Physiological Basis for the Theory of Music.* Reprint of the 2nd English edition 1885: Nabu Press, 2010.

HERMANN, T., J. DREES, AND H. RITTER: "Broadcasting Auditory Weather Reports – a Pilot Project." Proc. of the International Conference on Auditory Display ICAD 03, 2003, 208–11.

HIRT, RAINER, MICHAEL HOPPE, AND MARKUS REINER. "Sound of Citrus." http://www.audity-agency.com/referenzen/sound-of-citrus/ein-fuehrung.php, 2009, (July 18, 2010).

HITCHCOCK, H. WILEY. *Charpentier: Te Deum.* CD booklet: harmonia mundi HMC901298, 2003.

HODSON, GEOFFREY. *Music Forms.* Chennai: The Theosophical Publish-ing House, [1]1976.

HOFFMANN, ECKHARD, AND STEFFEN KREIKEMEIER. "Physiological Basics of Sound Design." 2nd international VDT Symposium on Sound Design. Ludwigsburg, 2007.

HOFSTADTER, DOUGLAS R. *Gödel, Escher, Bach: an Eternal Golden Brain.* New York: Basic Books, 1979.

HOLLEIN, MAX, AND JESPER JØRGENSEN. *Frequenzen [Hz] [Medienkombination]. Audiovisuelle Räume.* Ostfildern-Ruit: Hatje Cantz Verlag, 2002.

HORNBOSTEL, ERICH MORITZ VON. "Über Geruchshelligkeit." *Pflügers Archiv* 227 (1927),517–38.

HOROWITZ, MARDI JON. *Image Formation and Cognition.* London: Butterworths, 1970.

HOŠEK, ARNE. "Elemente der Allkunst." In *Farbe-Ton-Forschungen,* vol.3, edited by Georg Anschütz, 58–79. Hamburg: Psychologisch-ästhetische Forschungsgesellschaft, 1931.

HOWARTH, H. V., AND M. J. GRIFFIN. "Subjective Response to Combined Noise and Vibration: Summation and Interaction Effects." *Journal of Sound and Vibration,* 143, no. 3 (1990) 443–54.

HUBBARD, EDWARD M., JULIA SIMNER, AND JAMIE WARD. "Anatomically Constrained Cross-Activation: A Grand Unified Theory of Synaesthesia." *Proceedings of the Second International Congress "Synaesthesia: Science and Art," Granada.* Milano: Edizioni POLI.design, 2007, 345–64.

HURTE, MICHAEL. *Musik, Bild, Bewegung. Theorie und Praxis auditiv-visueller Konvergenzen.* Bonn-Bad Godesberg: Verlag für systematische Musikwissenschaften, 1982.

IPSEN, GUNTHER, AND FRITZ KARG. *Schallanalytische Versuche. Eine Einführung in die Schallanalyse.* Heidelberg: Carl Winters Universitätsbuchhandlung, 1928.

JAMES, WILLIAM. *Psychology.* New York: H. Holt and Company, [2]1920.

JEKOSCH, UTE. "Assigning Meaning to Sound – Semiotics in the Context of Product-sound Design." In *Communication Acoustics,* edited by Jens Blauert, 193–221. Berlin and Heidelberg: Springer, 2005.

JENNY, HANS. *Kymatik – Cymatics: The Structure and Dynamics of Waves and Vibrations.* Basel: Basilius Press, 1967.

JEWANSKI, JÖRG. "Die Farblichtmusik Alexander Lászlós." *Zeitschrift für Kunstgeschichte* 1 (1997) 12–43.

JEWANSKI, JÖRG. *Ist C = Rot? Eine Kultur- und Wissenschaftsgeschichte zum Problem der wechselseitigen Beziehung zwischen Ton und Farbe. Von Aristoteles bis Goethe.* Sinzig: Studio, Verlag Schewe, 1999.

JEWANSKI, JÖRG. "Wie ein Komet am Sternenhimmel. Die Erstaufführung von Alexander Lászlós Farblichtmusik am 16. Juni 1925." In *Grenzgänge – Übergänge: Musikwissenschaft im Dialog,* edited by Antje Erben, Clemens Gresser, and Arne Stollberg, 51–82. Hamburg: von Bockel Verlag, 2000.

JEWANSKI, JÖRG. "Von der Farbe-Ton-Beziehung zur Farblichtmusik." In *Farbe-Licht-Musik. Synästhesie und Farblichtmusik,* edited by Natalia Sidler, and Jörg Jewanski, 131–209. Bern: Peter Lang Verlag, 2006a.

JEWANSKI, JÖRG. "Eine neue Kunstform – die Farblichtmusik Alexander Lászlós." In *Farbe-Licht-Musik. Synästhesie und Farblichtmusik,* edited by Natalia Sidler, and Jörg Jewanski, 211–65. Bern: Peter Lang Verlag, 2006b.

JEWANSKI, JÖRG. "Color Organs and their Connections with Synaesthesia. Three Case Studies: Castel – Rimington – László." *Proceedings of the Second International Congress "Synaesthesia: Science and Art," Granada.* Milan: Edizioni POLI.design, 2007, 527–35.

JEWANSKI, JÖRG, AND HAJO DÜCHTING. *Musik und Bildende Kunst im 20. Jahrhundert. Begegnungen – Berührungen – Beeinflussungen.* Kassel: University Press, 2009.

JØRGENSEN, KRISTINE. "On the Transdiegetic Sounds in Computer Games." *Northern Lights* 5, Intellect Ltd (2007).

JOHNSON, HUGH. *The World Atlas of Wine.* London: Mitchell Beazley, 1985. German edition: *Der Grosse Weinatlas. Die Weine und Spirituosen der Welt.* Bern: Hallwag Verlag, [19]1986.

KAHNWEILER, DANIEL-HENRY. *Juan Gris, Leben und Werk*. Paris: Gallimard, 1946.

KANDINSKY, WASSILY. *Über das Geistige in der Kunst* [1911]. Bern: Benteli Verlag, [10]1952.

KANDINSKY, WASSILY. *Punkt und Linie zu Fläche. Beitrag zur Analyse der malerischen Elemente* [1926]. Bern: Benteli Verlag, [9]1964.

KASTNER, SONJA. *Klang macht Marken. Sonic Branding als Designprozess*. Wiesbaden: Gabler Verlag, 2008.

KENDALL, ROGER A. "Music and Video Iconicity: Theory and Experimental Design." *J Physiol Anthropol Appl Human Sci* 24, no. 1 (2005) 143–49.

KHAZAELI, CYRUS DOMINIK. *Systemisches Design. Intelligente Oberflächen für Information und Interaktion*. Reinbek: Rowohlt Verlag, 2005.

KIENSCHERF, BARBARA. *Das Auge hört mit. Die Idee der Farblichtmusik und ihre Problematik*. Frankfurt am Main: Verlag Peter Lang, 1996.

KIESELBACH, RALF J. F., ED. *The Drive to Design. Geschichte, Ausbildung und Perspektiven im Autodesign*. Stuttgart: avedition, 1998.

KILIAN, KARSTEN. "Acoustics as Resonant Element of Multi-sensory Brand Communication." In *Audio Branding: Brands, Sound and Communication*, edited by Kai Bronner and Rainer Hirt, 149–61. Baden-Baden: Nomos Verlagsgesellschaft, Edition Reinhard Fischer, 2009.

KIM, HONGKEUN, AND ROBERTO CABEZA. "Trusting Our Memories: Dissociating the Neural Correlates of Confidence in Veridical versus Illusory Memories." *The Journal of Neuroscience* 27, no. 45 (2007) 12190–97.

KITAGAWA, NORIMICHI, AND SHIGERU ICHIHARA. "Hearing Visual Motion in Depth." Nature 416 (2002) 172–74.

KLEIN, ADRIAN BERNARD. *Coloured Light – an Art Medium*. Being the 3rd edition enlarged of *Colour-Music* (1926). London: The Technical Press Ltd., 1937.

KLÜVER, HEINRICH. "Mescal Visions and Eidetic Vision." *American Journal of Psychology* 37 (1926), 502–15.

KNOBLICH, HANS, ANDREAS SCHARF, AND BERND SCHUBERT. *Marketing mit Duft*. Munich: R. Oldenbourg Verlag, 2003.

KÖHLER, WOLFGANG. *Gestalt Psychology*. New York: Liveright, 1929.

KOHLRAUSCH, ARMIN, AND STEVEN VAN DE PAR. "Experimente zur Wahrnehmbarkeit von Asynchronie in audio-visuellen Stimuli." *Proceedings of DAGA 2000, Oldenburg*. Oldenburg: Deutsche Gesellschaft für Akustik DEGA, 2000.

KOHLRAUSCH, ARMIN. "Audio-Visuelle Interaktion." *Proceedings of DAGA'02, Bochum*. Oldenburg: Deutsche Gesellschaft für Akustik DEGA, 2002, 24–25.

KOHLRAUSCH, ARMIN, AND STEVEN VAN DE PAR. "Audio-Visual Interaction in the Context of Multi-Media Applications." In *Communication Acoustics*, edited by Jens Blauert, 109–138. Berlin and Heidelberg: Springer, 2005.

KOLNEDER, WALTER. *Die Kunst der Fuge*. Heinrichshofen Verlag, 1977.

KRAHMER, EMIEL, AND MARC SWERTS. "The Effect of Visual Beats on Prosodic Prominence: Acoustic Analyses, Auditory Perception and Visual Perception." *Journal of Memory and Language* 57, no. 3 (2007) 396–414.

KREUTZ, BERND. *Marken von A bis Z*. Ostfildern-Ruit: Hatje Cantz Verlag, 2003.

KUBRICK, STANLEY. *2001: A Space Odyssey*. Science fiction movie, UK, 1968.

LAGEAT, THIERRY, AND BRIEUC DE LARRARD. "Sensory Marketing: Designing Pleasurable Products." Courtaboeuf: Eurosyn, 2003.

LANDGREBE, M., K. NYUYKI, E. FRANK, T. STEFFENS, S. HAUSER, P. EICHHAMMER, G. HAJAK AND B. LANGGUTH. "Effects of Colour Exposure on Auditory and Somatosensory Perception – Hints for Crossmodal Plasticity." *Neuro Endocrinol Lett*. 29, no. 4 (2008) 518–21.

LANTHONY, PHILIPPE. "Forscher und Farbe." In *Spektrum der Wissenschaft – Spezial: Farben*, 6–9. Heidelberg: Spektrum der Wissenschaft Verlagsgesellschaft, 2000.

LÁSZLÓ, ALEXANDER. *Die Farblichtmusik*. Leipzig: Breitkopf & Härtel, 1925.

LAZARUS, EMMA. *Poems and Ballads of Heinrich Heine.* New York: R. Worthington, 1881.

LEADBEATER, CHARLES W., AND ANNIE BESANT. *Thought-Forms* [1901]. Grafing: Aquamarin Verlag, [8]1999.

LECLERCQ, BÉNÉDICTE. "Gotische Architektur in strahlendem Bunt." In *Spektrum der Wissenschaft – Spezial: Farben,* 84–85. Heidelberg: Spektrum der Wissenschaft Verlagsgesellschaft, 2000.

LEHNER, THOMAS. *Der Kunstkonverter. Die phantastische Erfindung des Basler Maler-Pianisten Robert Strübin. Über die Verwandlung von Musik in Malerei und wieder zurück.* Nuremberg: Institut für moderne Kunst, 1973.

LEITNER, BERNHARD. *Sound : Space.* Ostfildern: Hatje Cantz Verlag, 1998.

LEMAITRE, AUG(USTE). *Audition colorée et Phénomènes connexes observés chez des écoliers.* Paris and Geneva: Félix Alcan, Ch. Eggimann & Cie, 1901.

LEVY, MICHAL. *Giant Steps.* Animation film based on the music by John Coltrane, 2001. http://michalevy.com/ (accessed July 19, 2010).

LIDWELL, WILLIAM, KRISTINA HOLDEN, AND JILL BUTLER. *Universal Principles of Design.* Gloucester, Mass.: Rockport Publishers, 2003.

LIETZMANN, HANS. *Schallanalyse und Textkritik.* Tübingen: Verlag von J.C.B. Mohr (Paul Siebeck), 1922.

LIND, E.G., F.A.I.A. *The Music of Colour: Including the essay "The number seven."* Baltimore: unpublished typescript, 1894.

LINDSAY, PETER H., AND DONALD A. NORMAN. *Human Information Processing: An Introduction to Psychology.* New York: Academic Press, [2]1977.

LIPPS, GOTTLOB FRIEDRICH. *Grundriss der Psychophysik.* Leipzig: G.J. Göschen'sche Verlagshandlung, 1903.

LOGESWARAN, NIDHYA, AND JOYDEEP BHATTACHARYA. "Crossmodal Transfer of Emotion by Music." *Neuroscience Letters* 455 (2009) 129–33.

LORIN, J. ELIAS ET AL. "Dissociating Semantic and Perceptual Components of Synaesthesia: Behavioural and Functional Neuroanatomical Investigations." Cognitive Brain Research 16 (2003), 232–37.

LUCKNER, PETER, ED. *Multisensuelles Design. Eine Anthologie.* Halle an der Saale: Hochschule für Kunst und Design, 2002.

LUKAS, SARAH. *Cross-Modal Selective Attention in Switching Stimulus Modalities.* Hamburg: Verlag Dr. Kovač, 2009.

LUKAS, SARAH, ANDREA M. PHILIPP, AND IRING KOCH. "Switching Attention between Modalities: Further Evidence for Visual Dominance." *Psychological Research* 74 (2010) 255–67.

LURIA, ALEXANDER R. *The Mind of a Mnemonist.* New York: Basic Books, 1968. Original edition: *Malenkaja knishka o bolschoj pamjati,* 1968.

LURIA, ALEXANDER R. *The Working Brain: An Introduction to Neuropsychology.* London: Penguin Books, 1973.

MACH, ERNST. *Die Analyse der Empfindungen und das Verhältnis des Physischen zum Psychischen.* Jena: Fischer, [4]1903.

MAGA, J. A. "Influence of Color on Taste Thresholds." *Chemical Senses and Flavor* 1, no. 1 (1974), 115–19.

MAHLING, FRIEDRICH. "Das Problem der 'Audition colorée'". In *Farbe-Ton-Forschungen Vol. 1,* edited by Georg Anschütz, 297–432. Leipzig: Akademische Verlagsgesellschaft, 1927.

MALINA, FRANK J., ED. *Kinetic Art: Theory and Practice.* New York: Dover Publications, 1974.

MANNEBECK, HEINRICH. "Olfaktorische / olfaktometrische Meßmethoden zur Bestimmung der verschiedenen Geruchseigenschaften." *Proceedings Gerüche in der Außenluft.* Düsseldorf: VDI-Bildungswerk, 1999.

MARKS, LAWRENCE E. *The Unity of the Senses: Interrelations among the Modalities.* New York: Academic Press, 1978.

MARKS, LAWRENCE E. "Synaesthesia: Perception and Metaphor." In *Aesthetic Illusion: Theoretical and Historical Approaches,* edited by Frederick Burwick, and Walter Pape. Berlin, New York: Walter de Gruyter, 1990.

MARKS, LAWRENCE E. "Synaesthesia Across the Spectrum." Proceedings of the Third International Congress "Synaesthesia: Science and Art,"

Granada, 2009.

MARTINO, GAIL, AND LAWRENCE E. MARKS. "Synesthesia: Strong and Weak." *Current Directions in Psychological Science* 10, no. 3 (2001), 61–65.

MANN, THOMAS. *Der Zauberberg*. Berlin: S. Fischer Verlag, 1924. English edition: *The Magic Mountain*. Trans. John E. Woods. New York: Vintage, 1996.

MAUR, KARIN VON, ED. *Vom Klang der Bilder: Die Musik in der Kunst des 20. Jahrhunderts*. Munich: Prestel Verlag, 1985.

MCCABE, MATTHEW LEONARD. "Color and Sound: Synaesthesia at the Crossroads of Music and Science." Dissertation. University of Florida, 2010.

MCGURK, H., AND J. MACDONALD. "Hearing Lips and Seeing Voices." *Nature* 264 (1976) 746–48.

MENZEL, DANIEL. "Psychoakustische Untersuchungen zum Einfluss der Farbe auf die Lautheit von Sportwagen." *Proceedings of DAGA'07, Stuttgart*. Berlin: Deutsche Gesellschaft für Akustik DEGA, 2007, 855–56.

MENZEL, DANIEL, E. FACCINELLI, AND HUGO FASTL. "Untersuchung von Farbeinflüssen auf die Lautheit mit einem Einregelverfahren." *Proceedings of DAGA'08, Dresden*. Berlin: Deutsche Gesellschaft für Akustik DEGA, 2008, 383–84.

MENZEL, DANIEL, THOMAS DAUENHAUER, AND HUGO FASTL. "Crying Colours and their Influence on Loudness Judgements." *Proceedings of NAG/ DAGA'09, Rotterdam*. Berlin: Deutsche Gesellschaft für Akustik DEGA, 2009, 1528–31.

MENZEL, DANIEL, TANJA SCHULZE, AND HUGO FASTL. "Zum Einfluss der Farbpräferenz auf die Lautheitsbeurteilung." *Proceedings of DAGA'10, Berlin*. Berlin: Deutsche Gesellschaft für Akustik DEGA, 2010, 873–74.

MERCHEL, S., AND ERCAN ALTINSOY. "5.1 oder 5.2 Surround – Ist Surround taktil erweiterbar?" *Proceedings of DAGA'08, Dresden*. Berlin: Deutsche Gesellschaft für Akustik DEGA, 2008, 377–78.

MERLEAU-PONTY, MAURICE. *Phénoménologie de la Perception*. Paris: Gallimard, 1945.

METZGER, WOLFGANG. "Figural-Wahrnehmung." In *Handbuch der Psychologie*, edited by D. K. Gottschaldt et al. Vol. 1, 693–744. Göttingen: Verlag C. J. Hogrefe, 1966.

METZNER, JEFFREY. *Strich für Strich. Große Momente der Film-, Kunst- und Weltgeschichte*. Frankfurt am Main: Eichborn Verlag, 2007.

MEYER, JÜRGEN. *Akustik und musikalische Aufführungspraxis*. Frankfurt: Verlag Bochinsky, [3]1995.

MEYER, JÜRGEN. *Acoustics and the Performance of Music*. Berlin: Springer, [5]2009.

MISHRA, JYOTI, ANTIGONE MARTINEZ, TERRENCE J. SEJNOWSKI, AND STEVEN A. HILLARY. "Early Cross-modal Interactions in Auditory and Visual Cortex Underlie a Sound-induced Visual Illusion." *The Journal of Neuroscience* 27, no. 15 (2007) 4120–31.

MÖLLER, SEBASTIAN, BENJAMIN BELMUDEZ, MARIE-NEIGE GARCIA, CHRISTINE KÜHNEL, ALEXANDER RAAKE, AND BENJAMIN WEISS. "Audio-Visual Quality Integration: Comparison of Human-Human and Human-Machine Interaction Scenarios of Different Interactivity." QOMEX 2010, International Workshop on Quality of Multimedia Experience. Trondheim, 2010.

MOHOLY-NAGY, LÁSZLÓ. *Von material zu architektur*. Bauhausbücher Band 14. Köthen: druckhaus köthen, 1929. Reprint Berlin: Verlag Gebr. Mann, [2]2001.

MOLHOLM, SOPHIE, WALTER RITTER, DANIEL C. JAVITT, AND JOHN J. FOXE. "Multisensory Visual-Auditory Object Recognition in Humans: a High-density Electrical Mapping Study." *Cerebral Cortex* 14, no. 4 (2004), 452–65.

MOORE, BRIAN C. J. *An Introduction to the Psychology of Hearing*. San Diego: Academic Press, [5]2003.

MORITZ, WILLIAM, AND ELFRIEDE FISCHINGER. *Oskar Fischinger und die Filmemacher der U.S.-Westküste*.

Retrospektive und Querschnitt. Doku-mentation. Bonn: Kulturabteilung der Amerikanischen Botschaft, 1972.

MORITZ, WILLIAM. "Oskar Fischinger." In *Optische Poesie – Oskar Fischinger, Leben und Werk.* Kinematograph No. 9. Frankfurt am Main: Deutsches Film-museum, 1993.

MORITZ, WILLIAM. *Optical Poetry: The Life and Work of Oskar Fischinger.* Bloomington: Indiana University Press, 2004.

MÜLLER, JOHANNES. *Über die phantas-tischen Gesichtserscheinungen. Eine physiologische Untersuchung mit einer physiologischen Urkunde des Aristote-les über den Traum.* Koblenz: bei Jacob Hölscher, 1826.

MÜLLER-KARPE, HERMANN. *Handbuch der Vorgeschichte, Vol. 1, Altsteinzeit.* Munich: Verlag C. H. Beck, 1966.

MUNGEN, ANNO. "Landschaften des Äußeren, des Inneren. Bill Violas Visualisierung von Edgar Varèses 'Déserts'". In *Synästhesie in der Musik – Musik in der Synästhesie,* edited by Volker Kalisch, 157–68. Essen: Verlag Die Blaue Eule, 2004.

NAGEL, F., R. KOPIEZ, O. GREWE, AND E. ALTENMÜLLER. "'EMuJoy' - Software for Continuous Measurement of Perceived Emotions in Music. Basic Aspects of Data Recording and Interface Features." *Behavior Research Methods* 39, no. 2 (2007), 283–90.

NAKAMURA, HIROYUKI, AND MICHAEL HAVERKAMP. "Effects of Whole-body Vertical Shock-type Vibration on Hu-man Ability for Fine Manual Control." *Ergonomics* 34, no. 11 (1991), 1365–76.

NECATI, G.A., E.J. DOPPENBERG, AND M. ANTILA. "Noise Radiation Reduction of a Car Dash Panel." Proceedings of ISMA 25, Noise and Vibration Engineering. Leuven, 2000, 855–62.

NEWTON, ISAAC. *Opticks, or a Treatise of the Reflexions, Refractions, Inflexions and Colours of Light.* London, 1721.

NOBIS, NORBERT, ED. *Der Lärm der Strasse. Italienischer Futurismus 1909–1918.* Mailand: Edizioni Gabriele Mazzotta, 2001.

NOESSELT, TOEMME, AND JON DRIVER. "Multisensory Interplay Reveals Crossmodal Influences on 'Sensory-specific' Brain Regions, Neural Responses, and Judgments." *Neuron* 57, no. 1 (2008), 11–23.

NOWACK, W. *Die schallanalytische Methode von Eduard Sievers. Darstellung und Kritik.* Langensalza: Hermann Beyer & Söhne, 1924.

O'MALLEY, GLENN. *Shelley and Synesthesia.* Evanston: Northwestern University Press, 1964.

OTTO, FRANK, AND BERNT KÖHLER-ADAMS. *Trip.* Experimental film, Germany, 2007.

OCZEVIK, ASLI, ZERHAN YUKSEL CAN, LEDA DE GREGORIO, AND LUIGI MAFFEI. "A Study on the Adaptation of Sound-scape to Covered Spaces." *Proceedings of Internoise* 2007. Istanbul: Turkish Acoustical Society, 2007.

OLDENBURG, CLAES. *Manifesto 'I am for an Art', 1961.* http://userpages.chorus.net/burleigh/art/iam4.html (accessed August 17, 2010).

OSTERWALD, KLAUS. *Verdächtige Geräusche (Suspicious Sounds).* http://www.ludwigforum.de/Ausstellungen/archiv/2008/osterwald/index.html (accessed July 9, 2010).

OSTWALD, WILHELM. *Die Farbenfibel.* Leipzig: Verlag Unesma, 1920.

PATSOURAS, CHRISTINE. *Geräuschqualität von Fahrzeugen – Beurteilung, Gestaltung und multimodale Einflüsse.* Aachen: Shaker Verlag, 2003.

PAULI P., L.E. BOURNE JR., H. DIEKMANN, AND N. BIRBAUMER. "Cross-Modality Priming between Odors and Odor-Congruent Words." *American Journal of Psychology* 112 (1999) 175–86.

PEACOCK, KENNETH. "Instruments to Perform Color-Music: Two Centuries of Technological Experimentation." *Leonardo* 21(4) (1988) 397–406.

PEŠÁNEK, ZDENĚK. "Bildende Kunst vom Futurismus zur Farben- und Formki-netik." In *Farbe-Ton-Forschungen Vol. 3,* edited by Georg Anschütz, 193–204. Hamburg: Psychologisch-ästhetische Forschungsgesellschaft, 1931.

PETERSEN, AUGUST. "Das individuelle Bau-element in den Photismen." In *Farbe-Ton-Forschungen Vol. 3,* edited by

Georg Anschütz, 230–39. Hamburg: Psychologisch-ästhetische Forschungsgesellschaft, 1931.

PHAN, HAI ANH THI, TAKASHI YANO, HAI YEN THI PHAN, TSUYOSHI NISHIMURA, TETSUMI SATO, AND YORITAKA HASHI-MOTO. "Annoyance Caused by Road Traffic Noise with and without Horn Sounds." *Acoust. Sci. & Tech.*, The Acoustical Society of Japan 30, no. 5 (2009) 327–37.

PHILLIPS, TOM. *Music in Art: Through the Ages.* Munich and New York: Prestel Verlag, 1997.

PICK, H.L., D.H. WARREN, AND J.C. HAY. "Sensory Conflict in Judgements of Spatial Direction." *Perception & Psychophysics* 6 (1969) 203–5.

POSNER, ROLAND, ED. *Synästhesie als Zeichenprozess.* Zeitschrift für Semiotik 24, no. 1. Tübingen: Stauffenburg, 2002.

PROSSINGER, HERMANN. "In Vino Veritas – Synästhesie und Weingenuss." In *Ausdruck – Ausstrahlung – Aura. Synästhesien der Beseelung im Medienzeitalter,* edited by Karl Clausberg, Elize Bisanz, and Cornelius Weiller, 207–24. Bad Honnef: Hippocampus Verlag, 2007.

RAINER, OSKAR. *Musikalische Graphik. Studien und Versuche über die Wechselbeziehungen zwischen Ton- und Farbharmonien.* Vienna: Deutscher Verlag für Jugend und Volk, 1925.

RAMACHANDRAN, V. S., AND EDWARD M. HUBBARD. "The Emergence of the Human Mind: Some Clues from Synesthesia." In *Synesthesia: Perspectives from Cognitive Neuroscience,* edited by Lynn C. Robertson, and Noam Sagiv, 147–90. Oxford: Oxford University Press, 2005.

RATH, MATTHIAS, AND ROBERT SCHLEICHER. "On the Relevance of Auditory Feedback for Quality of Control in a Balancing Tasks." *Acta Acustica United with Acustica* 94 (2008) 12–20.

REPP, BRUNO H. "Music as Motion: a Synopsis of Alexander Truslit's (1938) 'Gestaltung und Bewegung in der Musik'". *Psychology of Music* 21 (1993) 48–72.

RICCÒ, DINA. *Sinestesie per il design. Le interazioni sensoriali nell'epoca dei multimedia.* Milan: RCS Libri S.p.A., 1999.

RICCÒ, DINA, AND SILVIA GUERINI. "Synesthetic Design: The Laboratory of Basic Design as Place of Experimentation on the Intersensory Correspondences." Poster presented at the International Multisensory Research Forum. Geneva, 2002.

RICCÒ, DINA, ANTONIO BELLISCIO, AND SILVIA GUERINI. "Design for the Synesthesia: Audio, Visual and Haptic Correspondences Experimentation." Proceedings of the First International Meeting of Science and Technology of Design. Lisboa: 2003.

RICCÒ, DINA, AND MARÍA JOSÉ DE CÓRDOBA, EDS. "MuVi. Video and Moving Image on Synesthesia and Visual Music." *Proceedings of the Second International Congress "Synaesthesia: Science and Art," Granada.* Milan: Edizioni POLI.design, 2007.

RICCÒ, DINA. *Sentire il design. Sinestesie nel progretto di communicazione.* Roma: Carocci editore, 2008.

RICCÒ, DINA. "Synesthetic Aspects in the Visual Communication of the Music: Mental Imagery and Graphic Representation." *Proceedings of the Third International Congress "Synaesthesia: Science and Art," Granada,* 2009.

RICH, ANINA N., AND JASON B. MATTINGLEY. "Can Attention Modulate Colorgraphemic Synesthesia?" In *Synesthesia: Perspectives from Cognitive Neuroscience,* edited by Lynn C. Robertson, and Noam Sagiv, 108–23. Oxford: Oxford University Press, 2005.

RICHTER, HANS. *Rhythmus 21 – Film ist Rhythmus.* Experimental Film, Germany, 1921.

RICHTER, HANS. *Filmgegner von heute – Filmfreunde von morgen* (1929). Frankfurt am Main: Fischer-Taschenbuch-Verlag, 1981.

RICHTER, HANS. "Easel-Scroll-Film." *Magazine of Art* (1952).

RIEDELSHEIMER, THOMAS. *Touch the Sound: A Journey with Evelyn Glennie.* Documentary film, 2005.

RIMINGTON, ALEXANDER WALLACE. *Colour-Music: The Art of Mobile Colour.*

London: Hutchinson & Co, 1911.

ROBERTSON, LYNN C., AND NOAM SAGIV, EDS. *Synesthesia: Perspectives from Cognitive Neuroscience.* Oxford: Oxford University Press, 2005.

ROCCHESSO, DAVIDE, AND FEDERICO FONTANA, EDS. *The Sounding Object.* Florence: Mondo Estremo, 2003. http://www.soundobject.org (accessed July 19, 2010).

ROCK, IRVIN. *Perception.* New York: Scientific American Books, 1984.

ROEDERER, JUAN G. *Physics and Psychophysics of Music.* New York: Springer Verlag, 1973.

ROQUE, GEORGES. "Licht und Farbe." In *Spektrum der Wissenschaft - Spezial: Farben,* 10–13. Heidelberg: Spektrum der Wissenschaft Verlagsgesellschaft, 2000.

ROTH, SIMONE. *Akustische Reize als Instrument der Markenkommunikation.* Wiesbaden: Deutscher Universitäts-Verlag, 2005.

RUTHS, CHRISTOPH. *Experimentaluntersuchungen über Musikphantome.* Vol. 1. Damstadt: Kommissionsverlag von H. L. Schlapp, 1898.

ROWEDDER, ANNA K. *For You – A Journey to the World of Perception.* Luxembourg: Synaisthesis Verlag, 2009.

SACKS, OLIVER. *The Man who Mistook his Wife for a Hat.* New York: Summit Books / Simon & Schuster, 1985.

SAGIV, NOAM, AND JAMIE WARD. "Cross-modal Interaction. Lessons from Synesthesia." In *Visual Perception - Fundamentals of Awareness: Multi-Sensory Integration of High-Order Perception,* edited by S. Martinez-Conde et al., 263–75. London: Elsevier, 2006.

SÁNCHEZ MARTÍNEZ, MARÍA JOSÉ. "Improving Speech Recognition by Means of Pointing Gestures." *Proceedings of DAGA'05, München.* Oldenburg: Deutsche Gesellschaft für Akustik DEGA, 2005, 549–50.

SATHIAN, K., AND R. STILLA. "Cross-modal Plasticity of Tactile Perception in Blindness." *Restor Neurol Neurosci.* 28, no. 2 (2010), 271–81.

SAUERLANDT, MAX. *Die Musik in fünf Jahrhunderten der europäischen Malerei.* Königstein and Leipzig: Karl Robert Langewiesche Verlag, 1922.

SCHNEIDER, WULF. *Sinn und Un-Sinn. Architektur und Design sinnlich erlebbar gestalten.* Leinfelden-Echterdingen: Konradin Verlag, ²1995.

SCHAEFFER, PIERRE. *La musique concrete.* Paris: Presses Universitaires de France, 1967.

SCHAEFFER, PIERRE, AND GUY REIBEL. *Solfege de l'objet sonore* [1976]. Paris: Groupe de recherches musicales. Institut national de l'audiovisuel, 2005.

SCHAFER, MURRAY. *Ear Cleaning: Notes for an Experimental Music Course.* Ontario: BMI Canada Ltd, 1967.

SCHAFER, MURRAY. *The Tuning of the World.* Toronto: McCelland and Steward, 1977.

SCHAWELKA, KARL. *Quasi una musica. Untersuchungen zum Ideal des "Musikalischen" in der Malerei ab 1800.* Munich: Mäander Verlag, 1993.

SCHICK, AUGUST, AND KLAUS P. WALCHER, EDS. *Bedeutungslehre des Schalls.* Bern: Peter Lang Verlag, 1984.

SCHIDLOWSKY, LEON. *Musikalische Graphik.* Stuttgart: Staatsgalerie Stuttgart, 1979.

SCHILLER, PETER VON. "Die Rauhigkeit als intermodale Erscheinung." *Zeitschrift für Psychologie* 127 (1932) 265–89.

SCHLIEBE, GEORG. "Über motorische Synästhesien." In *Ganzheit und Gestalt. Archiv für Psychologie* 85, edited by Friedrich Sander, 1932.

SCHIRRMACHER, ROLF. "Von der aktiven Geräuschminderung zum Active Sound Design." *Proceedings of DAGA'02, Bochum.* Oldenburg: Deutsche Gesellschaft für Akustik DEGA, 2002, 8–15.

SCHNEBEL, DIETER. *MO-NO. Music to Read.* Cologne: Verlag M. DuMont Schauberg, 1969.

SCHRADER, LUDWIG. *Sinne und Sinnesverknüpfungen.* Heidelberg: Carl Winter Universitätsverlag, 1969.

SCHULTE-FORTKAMP, BRIGITTE, AND BEAT HOHMANN. "Von Soundscapes zu Annoyance." *Proceedings of DAGA 2000, Oldenburg.* Oldenburg: Deutsche Gesellschaft für Akustik DEGA, 2000.

SCHULTE-FORTKAMP, BRIGITTE, AND KLAUS GENUIT. "Exploration of Associated Imaginations on Sound

Perception: A Subject-centered Method for Benchmarking of Vehicles." SAE technical paper 2005-01-2263. SAE international, 2005.

SEIPEL, WILFRIED, ED. *Dipingere la musica: Strumenti in posa nell'arte del Cinque e Seicento*. Milan: Skira, 2000. German edition: *Dipingere la musica – Musik in der Malerei des 16. und 17. Jahrhunderts*. Vienna: Kunsthistorisches Museum, 2001.

SELWOOD, SARA. "Farblichtmusik und abstrakter Film." In *Vom Klang der Bilder. Die Musik in der Kunst des 20sten Jahrhunderts*, edited by Karin von Maur, 414–21. Munich: Prestel Verlag, 1985.

SELWOOD, SARA. "Color Music and Abstract Film." In *Light Art from Artificial Light: Light as a Medium in 20th and 21st Century Art*, edited by Peter Weibel and Gregor Jansen, 408–23. Ostfildern: Hatje Cantz Verlag, 2006.

SENSOTACT. *A Tactile Reference Frame*. http://www.sensotact.com/pages/generalites_englpag.html (accessed April 12, 2010).

SHAMS, LADAN, YUKIYASU KAMITANI, AND SHINSUKE SHIMOJO. "What you See Is What you Hear." *Nature* 408 (2000), 788.

SHAMS, LADAN, YUKIYASU KAMITANI, AND SHINSUKE SHIMOJO. "Visual Illusion Induced by Sound." *Cognitive Brain Research* 14, no. 1 (2002), 147–52.

SHOVE, PATRICK, AND BRUNO H. REPP. "Musical Motion and Performance: Theoretical and Empirical Perspectives." In *The Practice of Performance*, edited by J. Rink. Cambridge: Cambridge University Press, 1995.

SIDLER, NATALIA, AND JÖRG JEWANSKI, EDS. *Farbe-Licht-Musik. Synästhesie und Farblichtmusik*. Bern: Peter Lang Verlag, 2006a.

SIDLER, NATALIA. "Der Farblichtflügel." In *Farbe-Licht-Musik. Synästhesie und Farblichtmusik*, edited by Natalia Sidler, and Jörg Jewanski, 427–66. Bern: Peter Lang Verlag, 2006b.

SIEGEL, RONALD K. *Fire in the Brain*. London: Penguin Books, 1992.

SIEGLE, MICHAEL BERND. *LOGO. Grundlagen der visuellen Zeichengestaltung. Eine Einführung in das Grafik-Design am Beispiel der Logo-Gestaltung*. Itzehoe: Verlag Beruf + Schule, [4]2005.

SIEVERS, EDUARD. *Ziele und Wege der Schallanalyse*. Heidelberg: Carl Winter's Universitätsbuchhandlung, 1924.

SMILACK, MARCIA. *Reflectionism*. http://www.marciasmilack.com/ (accessed July 19, 2010)

SOTTEK, ROLAND, AND KLAUS GENUIT. "Models of Signal Processing in Human Hearing." *International Journal of Electronics and Communication* 59 (2005) 157–65.

SPENCE, CHARLES, AND JON DRIVER, EDS. *Crossmodal Space and Crossmodal Attention*. Oxford: Oxford University Press, 2004.

SPENCE, CHARLES. "Audiovisual Multisensory Integration." *Acoust. Sci. & Tech.* 28, no. 2 (2007), 61–70.

SPENCE, CHARLES, AND CRISTY HO. *The Multisensory Driver (Human Factors in Road and Rail Transport)*. Farnham: Ashgate Publishing, 2008a.

SPENCE, CHARLES, AND CRISTY HO. "Multisensory Driver Interface Design: Past, Present, and Future." *Ergonomics* 51 (2008b), 65–70.

SPENCE, CHARLES. "Crossmodal Spatial Attention." *ANN. N.Y. Acad. Sci.* 1191 (2010) 182–200.

STEINBERG, KLAUS F. *Mit allen Sinnen. Das große Buch der Störgeräuschakustik*. Kleve: copyus Verlags GmbH, [2]2005.

STERNBERG, ROBERT J. *Cognitive Psychology*. Wadsworth Publishing, [5]2008.

STEVENS, STANLEY SMITH (S. S.). "The Direct Estimation of Sensory Magnitude – Loudness." *American Journal of Psychology* 69 (1956), 1–25.

STEVENS, S. S. "The Psychophysics of Sensory Function." In *Sensory Communication*, edited by W. A. Rosenblith. Cambridge, Mass.: MIT Press, 1961a.

STEVENS, S. S. "To Honor Fechner and Repeal his Law." *Science* 133 (1961b), 80–86.

STEVENS, S. S. "A Metric for the Social Consensus." *Science* 151 (1966a), 530–41.

STEVENS, S. S. "On the Operation Known as Judgment." *American Scientist* 54 (1966b), 385–401.

STEVENS, S. S. "Power-group Transformations under Glare, Masking, and Recruitment." *Journal of the Acoustical Society of America* 39 (1966c), 725–35.

STEVENS, S. S. "Matching Functions between Loudness and ten other Continua." *Perception & Psychophysics* 1(1) (1966d), 5–8.

STEVENS, S. S. "Ratio Scales of Opinion." In *Handbook of Measurement and Assessment in Behavioral Sciences,* edited by Dean K. Whitla, 171–99. Reading, Mass.: Addison-Wesley Publishing Company, 1968.

STOLTENBERG, HANS L. *Reine Farbkunst in Raum und Zeit und ihr Verhältnis zur Tonkunst. Eine Einführung in das Filmtonbuntspiel.* Berlin: Verlag Unesma. ²1937.

STROOP, JOHN RIDLEY. "Studies of Interference in Serial Verbal Reactions." *Journal of Experimental Psychology* 18 (1935), 643–62.

SUAREZ DE MENDOZA, FERDINAND. *L'Audition Colorée. Étude sur les fausses Sensations secondaires physiologiques et particulièrement sur les Pseudo-Sensations de Couleurs associées aux perceptions objectives des sons.* Paris: Octave Doin, Éditeur, 1890.

SÜNDERMANN, HANS, AND BERTA ERNST. *Klang-Farbe-Gebärde, Musikalische Graphik.* Vienna: Anton Schroll & Co, 1981.

SZEEMANN, HARALD. *Der Hang zum Gesamtkunstwerk – Europäische Utopien seit 1800.* Aarau: Verlag Sauerländer, 1983.

TAKADA, MASAYUKI, KAZUHIKO TANAKA, AND SHIN-ICHIRO IWAMIYA. "Relationships between Auditory Impressions and Onomatopoeic Features for Environmental Sounds." *Acoust. Sci. & Tech.* 27, no. 2 (2006).

TARASTI, EERO. *A Theory of Musical Semiotics.* Bloomington: Indiana University Press, 1994.

TARASTI, EERO. *Signs of Music: A Guide to Musical Semiotics.* Berlin: Mouton de Gruyter, 2002.

TATI, JACQUES. *Les vacances de Monsieur Hulot.* Comedy film, France, 1953.

TERHARD, ERNST. *Akustische Kommunikation.* Berlin: Springer Verlag, 1998.

THEILE, GÜNTHER, AND HELMUT WITTEK. "Wave Field Synthesis – a Promising Spatial Audio Rendering Concept." *Journal of the Institute of Image Information and Television Engineers* (2007a).

THEILE, GÜNTHER. "Neue Anwendung der Wellenfeldsynthese: Binaural Sky." *FKT* 10/2007 (2007b).

TIMMERMANN, HENRY. *Über den Ursprung der Musik aus der Bewegung.* Hamburg: Verlag Niemann & Moschinski, 1940.

TOMASKE, WINFRIED, AND MARTIN MEYWERK. "Möglichkeiten zur Vermittlung von subjektiven Fahreindrücken mit Fahrsimulatoren." In *Subjektive Fahreindrücke sichtbar machen II,* edited by Klaus Becker, 1–16. Renningen-Malmsheim: expert-Verlag, 2006.

TRUAX, BARRY, ED. *Handbook for Acoustic Ecology.* Vancouver: Simon Fraser University and ARC Publications, ²1999.

TRUSLIT, ALEXANDER. "Das Element der Bewegung in der Musik und in der Synopsie." In *Farbe-Ton-Forschungen Vol. 3,* edited by Georg Anschütz, 175–89. Hamburg: Psychologisch-ästhetische Forschungsgesellschaft, 1931.

TRUSLIT, ALEXANDER. *Gestaltung und Bewegung in der Musik. Ein tönendes Buch vom musikalischen Vortrag und seinem bewegungserlebten Gestalten und Hören.* Berlin-Lichterfelde: Christian Friedrich Vieweg, 1938.

TULLIO, PIETRO. *Das Ohr und die Entstehung der Sprache und Schrift.* German translation by Auguste Jellinek. Berlin: Urban und Schwarzenberg, 1929.

ULICH, DIETER. "Emotion". In *Handwörterbuch Psychologie,* edited by Roland Asanger, and Gerd Wenninger. Weinheim: Beltz Psychologie Verlags-Union, 1999.

VAN CAMPEN, CRETIEN. *The Hidden Sense: Synesthesia in Art and Science.* Leonardo Book. Cambridge, Mass.: MIT Press, 2008.

VAN WASSENHOVE, VIRGINIE, KEN W. GRANT, AND DAVID POEPPEL. "Temporal Window of Integration in Auditory-visual Speech Perception." *Neuropsychology* 45, no. 3 (2007), 598–607.

VO, QUANG-HUE, ED. *Soundengineering. Kundenbezogene Akustikentwicklung in der Fahrzeugtechnik.* Renningen-Malmsheim: expert-Verlag, 1994.

VOSS, WILHELM. "Das Farbenhören bei Erblindeten. Untersuchungen über Wesen und Art der Photismen bei blinden Synoptikern unter besonderer Berücksichtigung des Formproblems." In *Farbe-Ton-Forschungen Vol. 2,* edited by Georg Anschütz, 5–207. Hamburg: Psychologisch-Ästhetische Forschungsgesellschaft, 1936.

VROOMEN, JEAN, AND BEATRICE DE GELDER. "Sound Enhances Visual Perception: Cross-modal Effects of Auditory Organisation on Vision." *Journal of Experimental Psychology: Human Perception and Performance* 26 (2000), 1583–90.

VROOMEN, JEAN, AND BEATRICE DE GELDER. "Perceptual Effects of Cross-modal Stimulation: Ventriloquism and the Freezing Phenomenon." In *The Handbook of Multisensory Processing,* edited by Gemma A. Calvert, Charles Spence, and Barry E. Stein, 141–52. Cambridge, Mass.: MIT Press, 2004.

WALDECK, MATTHIAS. *Description of Synesthetic Phenomena.* http://www.synaesthesieforum.de/galerie/007mat/ (accessed July 20, 2010)

WALLASCHEK, RICHARD. *Psychologie und Pathologie der Vorstellung.* Leipzig: Verlag von Johann Ambrosius Barth, 1905.

WALLASCHEK, RICHARD. *Psychologische Aesthetik.* Vienna: Rikola Verlag, 1930.

WANNER MEYER, PETRA. *Quintett der Sinne. Synästhesie in der Lyrik des 19. Jahrhunderts.* Bielefeld: Aisthesis Verlag, 1998.

WARD, JAMIE, AND JULIA SIMNER. "Lexical-gustatory Synaesthesia: Linguistic and Conceptual Factors." *Cognition* 89 (2003), 237–61.

WEHINGER, RAINER. *Listening Sheet Music of György Ligeti: Artikulation.* Mainz: B. Schott's Söhne, 1970.

WEIBEL, PETER. "The Development of Light Art." In *Light Art from Artificial Light: Light as a Medium in 20th and 21st Century Art,* edited by Peter Weibel und Gregor Jansen, 86–223. Ostfildern: Hatje Cantz Verlag, 2006.

WEISS, BENJAMIN, CHRISTINE KÜHNEL, AND SEBASTIAN MÖLLER. "Audio-Visual Quality as Combination of Unimodal Qualities: Environmental Effects on Talking Heads." *Proceedings of DAGA'10, Berlin.* Berlin: Deutsche Gesellschaft für Akustik DEGA, 2010, 561–62.

WEISS, CHRISTIAN. "Audio-Visuelle Synthese mittels HMM basierter Segmentauswahl." *Proceedings of DAGA'05, München.* Oldenburg: Deutsche Gesellschaft für Akustik DEGA, 2005, 555–56.

WEISS, PETER H. ET AL. "Associating Colours with People: a Case of Chromatic-lexical Synaesthesia." *Cortex* 37 (2001), 750–53.

WELLEK, ALBERT. "Die Farbe-Ton-Forschung und ihr erster Kongress." *Zeitschrift für Musikwissenschaft* 9 (1927), 576–84.

WELLEK, ALBERT. "Der musikalische Blitz und seine Geschichte." *Zeitschrift für Musik* XCV (1928), 415.

WELLEK, ALBERT. "Zur Geschichte und Kritik der Synästhesie-Forschung." *Archiv für die gesamte Psychologie* 79 (1931a), 325–84.

WELLEK, ALBERT. "Die Entwicklung unserer Notenschrift aus der Synopsie." In *Farbe-Ton-Forschungen Vol. 3,* edited by Georg Anschütz, 143–53. Hamburg: Psychologisch-ästhetische Forschungsgesellschaft, 1931b.

WELLEK, ALBERT. "Das Laut-Sinn-Problem unter dem Gesichtspunkt der Farbe-Ton-Forschung und die Synästhesien der Sprache." In *Farbe-Ton-Forschungen Vol. 3,* edited by Georg Anschütz, 240–53. Hamburg: Psychologisch-ästhetische Forschungsgesellschaft, 1931c.

WELLEK, ALBERT. "Hamburger Tagungsberichte I.: Die Hamburger Zweite Farbe-Ton-Tagung und ein notationsgeschichtliches Ereignis (1.–5. Okt. 1930)." *Zeitschrift für Musikwissenschaft* 13 (1931d), 145–49.

WELLEK, ALBERT. *Das absolute Gehör und seine Typen.* Leipzig: Verlag von Johann Ambrosius Barth, 1938.

WELLEK, ALBERT. *Musikpsychologie und Musikästhetik. Grundriss der* systematischen Musikwissenschaft. Frankfurt am Main: Akademische Verlagsgesellschaft, 1963.

WERMA SIGNALTECHNIK: Product catalog. Rietheim-Weilheim, 2009.

WERNER, HEINZ. "Intermodale Qualitäten." In *Handbuch der Psychologie,* edited by D. K. Gottschaldt et al. Vol. 1, 278–303. Göttingen: Verlag C. J. Hogrefe, 1966.

WHEELER, RAYMOND H. *The Synaesthesia of a Blind Subject.* Eugene: University of Oregon Publications l (5), 1920.

WHITE, TERESA L., AND JOHN PRESCOTT. "Chemosensory Cross-Modal Stroop Effects: Congruent Odors Facilitate Taste Identification." *Chem. Senses* 32 (2007), 337–41.

WIDMANN, A., T. GRUBER, T. KUJALA, M. TERVANIEMI, AND E. SCHRÖGER. "Binding Symbols and Sounds: Evidence from Event-Related Oscillatory Gamma-Band Activity." *Cerebral Cortex* 17, no. 11 (2007) 2696–702.

WILBER, KEN. *Sex, Ecology, Spirituality.* Boston: Shambhala Publications, 1995.

WOOLMAN, MATT. *Sonic Graphics – Seeing Sound.* New York: Rizzoli International Publications, 2000.

YANAGISAWA, HIDEYOSHI, TAMOTSU MURAKAMI, S. NOGUCHI, KOICHI OHTOMI, AND RIKA HOSAKA. "Quantification Method of Diverse Kansei Quality for Emotional Design – Application of Product Sound Design." *ASME 2007 Design Engineering Technical Conferences and Computers and Information in Engineering Conference* (2007) CD-ROM DETC2007-34627.

YANAGISAWA, HIDEYOSHI, RYO YOSHINAGA, TAMOTSU MURAKAMI, KOICHI OHTOMI, AND RIKA HOSAKA. "Sense of Harmony between Product Sound Quality and Color Sensation: A Case Study of Vacuum Cleaner." Proceedings of Internoise 2010. Lisboa, 2010.

ZEKI, SEMIR. *A Vision of the Brain.* Oxford: Blackwell Science, 1993.

ZELLER, HANS RUDOLF. "Messiaens kritische Universalität. Versuch über neue und 'außereuropäische' Musik." In *Olivier Messiaen. Musik Konzepte. Die Reihe über Komponisten* 28, edited by Heinz-Klaus Metzger, and Rainer Riehn, 56–77. Munich: edition texte + kritik, 1982.

ZEPTER, MICHAEL CORNELIUS. "Zum Aspekt des Phantastischen in der Kleidung." *Kunst Therapie* 18 (1989), 29–41.

ZIETZ, KARL, AND HEINZ WERNER. "Über die dynamische Struktur der Bewegung." *Zeitschrift für Psychologie* 105 (1927), 226–49.

ZIETZ, KARL. "Gegenseitige Beeinflussung von Farb- und Tonerlebnissen." *Zeitschrift für Psychologie* 121 (1931).

ZIETZ, KARL. *Einführung in die allgemeine Psychologie.* Bunswick: Waisenhaus-Buchdruckerei und Verlag, 41962.

ZIPS, MARTIN. "Der Klang der Dinge. Wie Sound-Designer versuchen, Kekse und Rasierapparate begehrenswert zu machen." http://design.fh-duesseldorf.de/k_pers/l_lehrbws/harden/Der_Klang_der_Dinge.pdf (accessed July 20, 2010).

ZITZLSPERGER, HELGA. *Musik in Linien und Farben – Rhythmisch musikalische Erziehung mit dynamischen Notenbildern.* Weinheim: Beltz Verlag, 1976.

ZÖLLER, THOMAS, AND FAWZI ATTIA. "Perception Thresholds for Sinusoidal and Impulsive Vibration on the Brake Pedal." *Proceedings of DAGA'06, Braunschweig.* Berlin: Deutsche Gesellschaft für Akustik DEGA, 2006, 425–26.

ZWICKER, EBERHARD. *Psychoakustik.* Berlin: Springer-Verlag, 1982.

ZWICKER, EBERHARD, AND HUGO FASTL. *Psychoacoustics: Facts and Models.* Berlin: Springer-Verlag, 21999.

INDEX

PICTURE
CREDITS

(in alphabetic order)

ADRIANO ABBADO: 2.28, 3.47, 3.67
BLAUPUNKT GMBH, Hildesheim: 3.12, 3.70
ROBERT BOSCH GMBH, Stuttgart: 2.57
BRAUN GMBH, Kronberg: 1.20, 1.22, 1.48,
2.45, 2.63, 3.28, 3.42, 3.44
BULTHAUP GMBH & CO. KG, Bodenkirchen:
1.27
D. JAMES DEE / CAROL STEEN: 2.126
JOHANNES DEUTSCH: 3.59, 3.60
JOHANNES DEUTSCH / ARS ELECTRONICA
FUTURELAB: 3.61
DEUTSCHE TELEKOM AG, Bonn: 3.31
ALEXANDRA DITTMAR: 2.109, 3.3
DRAENERT STUDIO GMBH, Immenstaad:
2.59, 2.82
DUALES SYSTEM DEUTSCHLAND GMBH,
Cologne: 2.98
DYSON GMBH, Cologne: 3.21, 3.78
FICOSA INTERNATIONAL, Barcelona: 2.43
GERALD VON FORIS, Munich: 3.65
FORD WERKE GMBH, Cologne: 1.1, 1.6, 1.7,
1.15, 1.24, 1.26, 1.31, 2.14, 2.18, 2.36,
2.39, 2.40, 2.42, 2.58, 2.65, 2.66, 2.74,
2.83, 2.92, 2.102, 3.40, 3.41, 3.45, 3.73,
3.75, 3.76
ECKHARD FREUWÖRT: 2.111
HEAD ACOUSTICS GMBH, Herzogenrath:
3.71, 3.72
HOPPE AG, Stadtallendorf: 3.19, 3.20
MICHAL LEVY, Israel: 3.58
MILCH-UNION HOCHEIFEL EG, Pronsfeld:
3.30
MUSEUM FÜR KUNST UND GEWERBE,
Hamburg: 2.117
DENNIS SAVINI, Zurich: 2.134
MARCIA SMILACK: 1.32, 2.123, 3.62
SPRING WATER COMPANY, Amstelveen:
3.24
CAROL STEEN, New York: 2.125
JON MCTAGGERT: 3.68
MATTHIAS WALDECK: 2.6, 2.110, 3.1, 3.9,
3.53
WERNER & MERTZ GMBH, Mainz: 2.90

PROLITTERIS, Zurich:
Giacomo Balla: 2.34, 3.46
Joseph Beuys: 2.96
Roy Lichtenstein: 1.23
Meret Oppenheim: 3.11
Patricia Waller: 1.3, 3.66

All further photos, pictures and diagrams
are provided by the author.
Graphic enhancement of diagrams by
Andreas Hidber, Basel

IMPRINT

This book has originally been published in German as "Synästhetisches Design – Kreative Produktentwicklung für alle Sinne" by Hanser Verlag, Munich (ISBN 978-3-446-41272-9).

TRANSLATION FROM GERMAN
INTO ENGLISH:
Dr. Michael Dudley, Adverbismax.de

PROJECT MANAGEMENT:
Daniel Morgenthaler, Robert Steiger

LAYOUT, TYPESETTING, COVER DESIGN,
REDRAWING OF ILLUSTRATIONS:
Andreas Hidber, accent graphe, Basel

A CIP catalogue record for this book is available from the Library of Congress, Washington D.C., USA.

Bibliographic information published by the German National Library. The German National Library lists this publication in the Deutsche National-bibliografie; detailed bibliographic data are available on the Internet at http://dnb.d-nb.de.

© 2013 Birkhäuser Verlag GmbH
4055 Basel, Switzerland
Part of De Gruyter

Printed on acid-free paper produced from chlorine-free pulp. TCF ∞

Printed in Germany

ISBN 978-3-0346-0715-5

9 8 7 6 5 4 3 2 1

www.birkhauser.com

HOW TO ACCESS
THE SOUND FILES WITH
A MOBILE DEVICE

1

2

3

4

**OPEN
READER APP**

SCAN THE QR CODE
READER APP ACTIVATES CAMERA

**LET THE READER
DECODE**
(MAY TAKE SOME
SECONDS)

**LISTEN TO
SOUND
EXAMPLE**

DIRECT QR CODES

1 SOUND EXAMPLES 1-9

1

2

3

12

13

14

15

16

26

27

28

29

30

40

41

42

43

44

54

55

56

57

58

67

68

69

70

71

81

82

83

84

85

CD
CONTENTS

The enclosed CD includes ninety-two sound examples. The recording serves only to demonstrate specific facts as described in the text. Thereby, sounds presented are not necessarily examples of an exceptionally good sound design. The quality of recording varies – partly, historical recordings have been used which are only available on shellac discs (89, 90).
→ The recording level has been adjusted with respect to an optimum audibility. Thus, the sound recordings are not appropriate for comparisons of the loudness. Exceptions which are comparable with each other are:
• sounds of small ventilators (7),
• sounds created by touching surfaces (32 – 37)
• and sounds observed during writing (71 – 78).

9

2
SOUND
EXAMPLES
10-65

10

11

22

23

24

25

36

37

38

39

50

51

52

53

64

65

3
SOUND
EXAMPLES
66-92

66

77

78

79

80

91

92